Proceedings

The 20th Annual International Symposium on

COMPUTER ARCHITECTURE

May 16 –19, 1993 San Diego, California

Sponsored by

IEEE Computer Society
Technical Committee on Computer Architecture

Association for Computing Machinery
SIGARCH

Φ®

IEEE Computer Society Press
Los Alamitos, California

Washington • Brussels • Tokyo

Published by the
IEEE Computer Society Press
10662 Los Vaqueros Circle
PO Box 3014
Los Alamitos, CA 90720-1264

IEEE Computer Society Press Order Number 3810-02
IEEE Catalog Number 93CH3284-7
Library of Congress Number 85-642899
ISBN 0-8186-3810-9 (paper)
ISBN 0-8186-3811-7 (microfiche)
ISBN 0-8186-3812-5 (case)
ISSN 0884-7495
ACM Order Number 415930
ACM Library Series ISBN 0-89791-579-8 (Hardcover)
ACM SIGARCH ISSN 0163-5964

Additional copies can be ordered from:

IEEE Computer Society Press	IEEE Service Center	IEEE Computer Society	IEEE Computer Society
Customer Service Center	445 Hoes Lane	13, avenue de l'Aquilon	Ooshima Building
10662 Los Vaqueros Circle	PO Box 1331	B-1200 Brussels	2-19-1 Minami-Aoyama
PO Box 3014	Piscataway, NJ 08855-1331	BELGIUM	Minato-ku, Tokyo 107
Los Alamitos, CA 90720-1264			JAPAN

ACM Order Dept., PO Box 64145, Baltimore, MD 21264

Production Editors: Mary E. Kavanaugh and Edna Straub
Cover art: Joseph Daigle / Schenk-Daigle Studios
Printed in the United States of America by Braun-Brumfield, Inc.

 The Institute of Electrical and Electronics Engineers, Inc.

General Chair's Message

This year marks the 20th anniversary of the International Symposium on Computer Architecture (ISCA) — the flagship conference of the computer architecture community. It also marks the first time ISCA has joined forces with a number of other important conferences and workshops in what has become known as the Federated Computing Research Conference — FCRC.

The main goal of FCRC is to obtain the benefits of having the computing research community meet together as a larger group. Despite the drawbacks associated with a gathering of this magnitude, I hope this organizational framework will be a rewarding experience offering the scientific benefits resulting from greater opportunity to meet and interact with peers in other specialties. FCRC is also intended to provide much greater visibility for the field of Computer Science as a discipline.

At the same time, however, FCRC permits each of the constituent meetings to retain its traditional structure and research identity. Thus ISCA will continue to be independently administered and have sole responsibility for its own program.

I would like to thank John Hennessy, the Program Chair, and the entire Program Committee for putting together an exciting and well-balanced program. I also want to express my sincere appreciation to the members of the ISCA Organizing Committee, including Victor K. Prasanna (Tutorials), Alex Nicolau (Workshops), Pen-Chung Yew (Panels), Doug Blough (Publicity and Publications), Skevos Evripidou (Finance), and the ISCA Advisory Committee consisting of Jean-Loup Baer, Jean-Luc Gaudiot, Howard Jay Siegel, and Larry Snyder, for their guidance throughout the entire planning and development process. Many thanks go also to Debbie Hall (ACM) and Anne-Marie Kelly (IEEE Computer Society) for their continuous advice and assistance.

In addition to the technical programs organized by the constituent conferences, the beautiful city of San Diego has much to offer in terms of entertainment. Among its many attractions, the most popular are the charming Old Town, dating back to the original settlement of this area by the Spanish missionaries, beautiful Balboa Park with one of the largest zoos in the world, and Mission Bay with its world-famous Sea World. ISCA participants, as part of their registration, will be able to attend a banquet and special show at Sea World.

Welcome to ISCA '93!

Lubomir Bic
University of California, Irvine

Program Chair's Message

I am delighted to introduce this collection of papers selected for The 20th International Symposium on Computer Architecture. The papers reflect the high quality of research ongoing in the architecture field, as well as the diversity of interests.

We received a total of 208 submissions for the conference (the third largest number of submissions in our 20-year history). The quality of the submissions was simply outstanding. To review these papers, we used a combination of the program committee and external referees. Each paper was sent to at least two program committee members and to several external reviewers.

The use of electronic refereeing was an enormous success. In total, we received 926 referee reports (or 4.3 reports per paper) from the 20 program committee members and 330 external reviewers. The referees' reports totaled almost 24 MB of text! The use of electronic reviews allowed us to extract and return reviewers' comments to the authors electronically, as well as to handle reports that arrived only a day before the program committee meeting. I strongly recommend the use of electronic reviewing to all future program chairs. Special thanks go to Hank Levy who supplied the software, and to Andrew Erlichson, who modified it at Stanford and helped me learn enough PERL so that I could hack the scripts myself.

The program committee met on Friday, January 8, 1993 with 18 of the 20 members in attendance. The program committee meeting maintained the anonymity of the authors during the meeting. While this led to a few interesting conversations (e.g., this author did not cite the famous work of X — not knowing that the author was X himself), the committee felt that it could do its work without knowing the identity of the authors.

We selected 32 papers for the conference, for an acceptance rate of 15.7 percent. Of these papers, seven were assigned to program committee members who agreed to act as shepherds to help the authors improve their papers.

Many people contributed to making the task of program chair manageable. The many external referees, who returned the vast majority of the reports we requested, and the program committee, each of whom spent many hours reading papers, deserve the credit for helping select this fine program. Lubomir Bic and Doug Blough helped with arranging the program and getting the authors' kits out. Finally, my assistant, Margaret Rowland, did a great job of tracking the 209 papers, sending out hundreds of review requests, gently but firmly requesting reviews, and arranging an efficient and productive program committee meeting. Margaret has put more hours into bringing this program together than anyone else, and I couldn't have managed this job without her.

John Hennessy
Stanford University

ISCA '93 Organizing Committee

General Chair

Lubomir Bic, University of California, Irvine

Program Chair

John Hennessy, Stanford University

Advisory Committee

Jean-Loup Baer, University of Washington
Jean-Luc Gaudiot, University of Southern California
Howard J. Siegel, Purdue University
Larry Snyder, University of Washington

Symposium Committee

Douglas Blough...................... University of California, Irvine .... Publicity and Publications
Skevos Evripidou .... Southern Methodist University .... Finance
Alex Nicolau........................... University of California, Irvine .... Workshops
Victor K. Prasanna .... University of Southern California ... Tutorials
Pen-Chung Yew .... University of Illinois .... Panels

Program Committee

Forest Baskett .... Silicon Graphics Computer Systems
Anita Borg .... Digital Equipment Corporation
Joel Emer... Digital Equipment Corporation
Thomas Gross... Carnegie Mellon University
Anoop Gupta.. Stanford University
Wen-mei Hwu... University of Illinois
Manolis Katevenis.. University of Crete
Randy Katz... University of California, Berkeley
H.T. Kung... Harvard University
Kai Li .... Princeton University
Trevor Mudge... University of Michigan
Gregory Papadopoulos.. Massachusetts Institute of Technology
Bob Rau .... Hewlett-Packard Laboratories
Alan J. Smith... University of California, Berkeley
Guri Sohi .... University of Wisconsin-Madison
Norihisa Suzuki.. IBM Corporation
Patricia Teller.. New Mexico State University
Evan Tick .... University of Oregon
Uri Weiser .... Intel Israel

ISCA '93 Referees

A. Adl-Tabatabai
S. Adve
A. Agarwal
D. Alpert
R. Alpert
R. Alverson
J. Andrews
B. Ang
S. Anik
Z. Ariola
B. Athas
M. Atiquzzaman
A. Ayers
J. Babb
J.-L. Baer
N. Bagherzadeh
J. Barton
M. Beckerle
C. Beckmann
J. Bennett
B. Bershad
L. Bic
P. Biswas
D. Black
T. Blank
M. Blatt
K. Bolding
G. Borriello
P. Borrill
E. Boyd
P. Boyle
E. Brewer
M. Brorsson
J. Brustoloni
M. Butler
S. Butner
M. Carlton
A. Carnevali
R. Caspi
D. Chaiken
K. Chan
J. Chandy
M. Charney
T. Charuhas
B. Chen
P. Chen
D. Cheriton
G. Chesson
A. Chien
D. Chiou
F. Chong
P. Chow
D. Clark

R. Cohn
B. Colwell
J. Conery
D. Culler
F. Dahlgren
W. Dally
S. Damianakis
S. Darbha
A. Davis
J. Demmel
J. Dennis
L. Dennison
D. Dill
D. Ditzel
T. Dobry
P. Dowd
A. Drapeau
M. Dubois
G. Egan
B. Eitan
J. Ellis
S. Erlich
J. Fang
M. Farrens
E. Felten
R. Finlayson
A. Fisher
J. Fisher
B. Flachs
M. Flynn
T. Fossum
J. Frankel
M. Franklin
S. Freudenberger
J. Fu
R. Fujimoto
G. Gao
J. Gee
K. Gharachorloo
G. Gibson
A. Golbert
M. Golden
S. Goldschmidt
J. Goodman
H. Goosen
A. Gottlieb
M. Grammatikakis
J. Gray
J. Greenwood
R. Gupta
M. Gutman
J. Gyllenhaal
G. Haab

M. Halbherr
R. Hank
D. Harper
A. Harsat
J. Hayes
J. Heinlein
M. Heinrich
S. Hemami
D. Hessel
M. Hill
S. Hinrichs
J. Hoe
M. Holland
M. Holliday
M. Horowitz
R. Hou
J. Huck
M. Humphrey
K. Iwano
W. Jalby
D. James
S. Jha
T. Joe
C. Joerg
E. Johnson
K. Johnson
M. Johnson
R. Johnson
N. Jouppi
B. Karp
G. Karypis
V. Kathail
T. Kato
S. Keckler
J. Keen
K. Keeton
P. Keleher
R. Kessler
J. Kim
T. Kiyohara
A. Klaiber
P. Kogge
D. Kranz
H.-K. Ku
J. Kubiatowicz
B. Kumar
K. Kumon
J. Kuskin
R. Kutter
M. Lam
V. Lambert
J. Larus
J. Laudon

viii

D. Lavery
E. Lazowska
T. LeBlanc
E. Lee
D. Lenoski
D. Lin
V. Lo
R. Lomax
D. Lomet
G. Lowney
G.-Y. Lueh
B. Maggs
S. Mahlke
B. Mangione-Smith
T. Mann
E. Markatos
P. Markstein
B. Marsh
D. Mason
M. Mavronicolas
S. McFarling
T. Meng
E. Miller
M. Mittal
J. Mogul
R. Morris
T. Mowry
R. Mraz
H. Mulder
D. Nagle
W. Najjar
T. Nakatani
M. Nemirovsky
E. Neonakis
T. Ngo
L. Ni
R. Nikhil
C. Nikolaou
M. Nilsson
R. Nix
A. Nowatzyk
K. Nowka
B. Noyce
D. O'Hallaron
M. Ohara
K. Olukotun
R. Palmer, Jr.
Y. Patt
D. Patterson
H. Patterson
A. Peleg
K. Peterson
J. Pfeiffer, Jr.
T. Pinkston
J. Plank

A. Pleszkun
D. Pnevmatikatos
A. Porterfield
S. Przybylski
N. Quach
D. Quammen
U. Ramachandran
K. Ramakrishnan
G. Ramamoorthy
J. Rattner
N. Reddy
M. Reilly
J. Rexford
K. Richardson
S. Richardson
M. Rinard
A. Rogers
E. Rosen
M. Rosenblum
E. Rothberg
J. Rothman
C. Rowen
E. Rubenstein
K. Rudd
R. Saavedra
J. Salmon
A. Sameh
M. Schlansker
M. Scott
S. Scott
B. Sears
D. Serpanos
A. Shaw
S. Shimizu
K. Shin
K. Shirriff
D. Shoemaker
R. Short
D. Siewiorek
R. Simoni
J. Singh
D. Sites
K. Sitze
G. Slavenburg
B. Smith
D. Smith
J. Smith
M. Smith
L. Snyder
K. So
S. Steely
P. Steenkiste
P. Stenström
L. Stephens
J. Stoy

M. Stratakis
T. Stricker
K. Subramanian
R. Sugumar
D. Tabak
H. Takagi
M. Talluri
Y. Tamir
J.-H. Tang
G. Taylor
J. Telle
S. Tezuka
C. Thacker
S. Thakkar
R. Thekkath
S. Toledo
J. Torrellas
H. Touati
J. Tse
P.-S. Tseng
P. Tu
A. Tucker
P. Tzelnic
M. Upton
R. Valentine
P. Van Roy
P. Vatsolaki
M. Vernon
T. von Eicken
E. Waldman
T. Warfel
N. Warter
J. Webb
W.-D. Weber
J.-D. Wellman
C.-C. Weng
F. Weng
B. Wheeler
J. Wilkes
A. Wilson, Jr.
D. Windheiser
J. Winget
L. Wittie
D. Wong
D. Wood
I.-C. Wu
W. Wulf
Q. Xu
Y. Yaari
D. Yeung
C. Young
M. Zagha
X. Zhong
W. Zwaenepoel

Table of Contents

SESSION 2:

Architectural Characteristics of Scientific Applications

Architectural Requirements of Parallel Scientific Applications with Explicit Communication

R. Cypher *   A. Ho *   S. Konstantinidou *   P. Messina †

IBM Research Division*
Almaden Research Center

Caltech Concurrent Supercomputing Facilities†
California Institute of Technology

Abstract

This paper studies the behavior of scientific applications running on distributed memory parallel computers. Our goal is to quantify the floating point, memory, I/O and communication requirements of highly parallel scientific applications that perform explicit communication. In addition to quantifying these requirements for fixed problem sizes and numbers of processors, we develop analytical models for the effects of changing the problem size and the degree of parallelism for several of the applications. We use the results to evaluate trade-offs in the design of multicomputer architectures.

1 Introduction

Multicomputers that consist of hundreds or even thousands of microprocessors are currently offered by several companies including Intel, nCUBE and Thinking Machines. Such multicomputers are particularly well-suited to performing scientific calculations, both because of the large computational requirements of scientific calculations and because many scientific applications exhibit natural data parallelism. As a result, a number of scientific applications have already been created for multicomputers and many more are currently under development.

A critical issue in the design of a multicomputer architecture is a quantitative understanding of the applications that it will be supporting. In particular, the applications' requirements for floating point, memory, I/O and communication must be quantified in order to obtain a well-balanced architecture. In addition, the specific design of an I/O system or a communication system depends on the traffic patterns that the system must support.

Several studies of the architectural requirements of parallel applications that use a shared-memory model have been performed [1, 4, 13]. The characteristics of applications with explicit communication only recently have come under scrutiny. The communication characteristics of CAD applications and numeric algorithms running on a 16 node hypercube have been considered previously [7]. Given the existence of commercial multicomputers with large numbers of processors and of serious scientific applications running on them, it is now possible to see how these machines are being utilized and to use this information to guide the design of the next generation of multicomputers. In this paper we study a wide range of existing scientific applications and quantify their architectural requirements. Only complete applications, including the loading of input data and the storing of results, are studied. We examine their memory and I/O requirements, their computation vs. communication ratio, and characteristics of their message traffic. In addition we focus on three of the applications and develop analytical models for the effects of scaling the problem size and the number of processors used.

The remainder of the paper is organized as follows. In Section 2 the methodology used to gather the data is presented. Section 3 presents the applications studied. The results for fixed problem sizes and their architectural implications are discussed in Section 4. The effects of scaling are examined in Section 5. Finally, conclusions are given in Section 6.

2 Methodology

We studied eight scientific applications running on three different types of multicomputers. The applications examined represent a wide range of architectural requirements and problem domains. In order to obtain the results presented in Section 4, we created a list of application characteristics that we wished to quantify. Each application was analyzed according to the questions on this list. Two of the applications (QCD and VORTEX) were analyzed by the authors of this paper, while the remaining applications were analyzed by an author of the given application. The analytical models of the effects of scaling, which are presented in Section 5, were obtained by examining and modeling the code. Validation tests were performed to compare predictions made by the models with observed behavior given different problem sizes and numbers of processors.

3 Applications

In this section we present the applications that were studied. All of the applications studied exploit data parallelism. They all use single-program, multiple-data (SPMD) code in which every processor executes the same program. However, because each processor has its own copy of the code and because all of the machines studied operate in MIMD mode, the processors operate asynchronously unless they need to communicate.

Five of the applications run on the 512 processor Intel Touchstone Delta System located at the Caltech Concurrent Supercomputing Facilities (CCSF). Each processor in this machine has 16MB of memory, of which 12MB are available to the application programmer. One of the applications runs on a 256 processor nCUBE-1 located at the CCSF. This machine has 0.5MB of memory per processor, of which 0.4MB are available to the application programmer. The two remaining applications run on a 64 processor nCUBE-2 located at the CCSF and a 512 processor nCUBE-2 located at Sandia, respectively. Each of these machines has 4MB of memory per node, 3.8MB of which are available to the application programmer. The processors in the Delta system are connected in a two-dimensional mesh, while the processors in the nCUBE computers are connected as a binary hypercube. The type of computer and number of processors used by each application, as well as the language used and the size of the code, are listed in Table 1.

Global Climate Simulation. This application, which we call CLIMATE, uses a general circulation model of the earth's atmosphere to perform long range (100 year to 1000 year) studies of climate change. The application operates in two domains, namely a physical domain and a spectral domain. The physical domain is a 32 x 64 x 18 grid which is partitioned among the processors so that the vertical dimension (of length 18) is local to each processor. The spectral domain is a 22 x 22 upper triangular matrix of spectral co-

APPL	LANG	SCL	MTYPE	PRC
CLIMATE	Fortran	80K	Delta	256
SEMI	Fortran	50K	Delta	512
MOLECULE	Fortran	1K	nCUBE 2	512
RENDER	C	2K	Delta	32
EXFLOW	C & Fortran	12K	Delta	512
QCD	C	2K	nCUBE 1	256
VORTEX	Fortran	1K	nCUBE 2	64
REACT	C & Fortran	42K	Delta	512

Table 1: Applications Summary: Columns give application (APPL), language used (LANG), number of lines of source code (SCL), type of machine used (MTYPE), and number of processors used (PRC).

efficients, each of which is a complex number. This matrix is represented as a 1-dimensional vector which is partitioned evenly between the processors. The primary cause of communication is the transformation between the two domains, which requires the use of FFT operations and the calculation of global sums. Because the results of the climate studies have not yet been published, we are unable to give the names and affiliations of the application's authors.

3-D Semiconductor Device Simulation. This application, SEMI, is a 3-D semiconductor device simulator that utilizes a parallelized 3-D Poisson solver [3, 5]. The simulation domain is approximated by an irregular 3-D grid which is decomposed into contiguous blocks that are allocated to the processors. An iterative method is employed to solve a system of equations. Each iteration requires a matrix vector multiply, two inner products and the solution of a lower tridiagonal system. Two patterns of communication are employed, namely an irregular 3-D mesh and a binary tree. The data were provided by Ke-Chih Wu at Stanford University.

Molecular Dynamics Simulation. Molecular dynamics simulations can be used to compute properties such as diffusion rates and viscosities for liquids and polymers and to calculate conformational properties of organic molecules such as proteins. The application studied here, MOLECULE, assumes that each atom interacts only with other atoms that are within a fixed cut-off distance [12]. The application assigns the N atoms to the P processors, with each processor receiving N/P atoms. In each time step, the states of all of the atoms are sent to all of the processors using a hypercube pattern of communication. Each processor uses the fixed cut-off distance to select which of the N atoms interact with its assigned N/P atoms and updates the states of its atoms. The experiment simulated 32,000 atoms and 10,000 time steps. The data were provided by Steve Plimpton at Sandia National Laboratories.

3-D Perspective Rendering. In order to obtain a 3-dimensional perspective view of a planet's surface, it is necessary to integrate satellite image data with surface elevation data. The application RENDER [9] integrates a 6000 x 6000 pixel 24-bit color image with 16-bits of elevation data per pixel to obtain 480 x 640 pixel 24-bit output images. The run considered here produces 30 frames of output, which corresponds to approximately 1 second of animation.

The input image is decomposed along a single dimension, with each processor storing a contiguous set of complete rows of pixels. Rows near decomposition boundaries are stored twice in order to reduce the communication requirements. Each processor first projects its local portion of the input image onto a focal plane. These separate focal planes are then combined, using a recursive-doubling procedure, to obtain an output image from which the hidden surfaces have been removed. The resulting image is then sent to disk and the process is repeated with a different viewpoint to obtain the next output image. The data were provided by Peggy Li at the Jet Propulsion Laboratory.

3-D Fluid Flow Using Adaptive Grids. The application EXFLOW [14] uses adaptive grids to simulate 3-D fluid flow around a fixed body. EXFLOW begins with a grid of 160 tetrahedra which is distributed among the processors, refined to a working resolution of 1000 tetrahedra, and load-balanced. Then the application performs 12 stages of calculating the steady-state flow, adaptively refining the grid based on the calculated steady-state solution, and load-balancing the refined grid. The pattern of communication used in the calculation of the steady-state flow is data-dependent and is dynamic through the course of the application. The adaptive refinement and load-balancing performs a hypercube pattern of communication in order to obtain global values and a ring pattern of communication in order to redistribute the refined grid. The run studied here creates a grid with 693,000 tetrahedra by the final stage, the surface of which is then sent to disk. The data were provided by Roy Williams at the Caltech Concurrent Supercomputing Facilities.

Quantum Chromodynamics. Quantum chromodynamics (QCD) is the theory of quarks and gluons and how they interact to form particles such as protons and neutrons. The QCD application [11, 6, 2, 10] studied here operates on a 4-dimensional periodic lattice (torus). The QCD code performs numerous stages of simulation, where each stage loops through the lattice edges and updates them. Each such update requires 12 multiplies of 3 x 3 complex matrices as well as the generation of a suitable random number. The generation and testing of the random numbers can take different amounts of time for different links, thus leading to the possibility of a load imbalance. After updating the links, a projection is applied to assure that the 3 x 3 matrices have legal values. The run of the QCD code studied here uses a 16 x 16 x 16 x 16 lattice which is partitioned into 4 x 4 x 4 x 4 sublattices. The simulation is run for 100 stages, at which point the resulting matrices are written to disk.

2-D Fluid Flow Using the Vortex Method. The application VORTEX [8] models the evolution of vortices in a 2-dimensional fluid. All vortices have an effect on all other vortices, so each stage of the simulation calculates $\Theta(N^2)$ interactions among the N vortices. The vortices are evenly distributed to the processors. Each stage of the simulation creates two copies of each vortex, one of which remains stationary and one of which is shifted to other processors. The shifts are performed along a ring which includes all of the processors, and multiple vortices are shifted together in order to reduce the communication latency overhead. Whenever a shifted copy of a vortex V enters a new processor, the interaction of V with all of the stationary vortices at that processor are calculated. When the shifted copy of the vortex returns to its original processor, the stationary copy is updated. After each stage, the processors communicate in a binary tree with the root reporting the progress of the algorithm to the host computer. The run of VORTEX studied here simulates 100 stages of the evolution of 4096 vortices and then reports the final positions of all of them to the host.

Quantum Chemical Reaction Dynamics. Quantum chemical reaction dynamics simulations predict the behavior of chemical reactions based on first principles. The quantum chemical reaction application studied here, REACT [15, 16, 17], simulates a collision between a hydrogen atom and a hydrogen molecule.

The application consists of four major phases. In the first phase, a set of 2K eigenvalues and eigenvectors is calculated for each of 200 10K x 10K tridiagonal matrices. Although the calculations for the 200 matrices are logically independent, each calculation requires more memory than is present in a single processor. As a result, the eigenpairs for each matrix are calculated in a data parallel manner, using all of the processors. The calculated eigenpairs are then partitioned evenly among the processors. In the second

APPL	DATA	DATA/PROC	CODE/PROC	OS/PROC	% USED
CLIMATE	1750MB	7168KB	4096KB	4096KB	94
SEMI	1000MB	2048KB	NA	4096KB	NA
MOLECULE	1000MB	2048KB	200KB	200KB	60
RENDER	280MB	8960KB	260KB	4096KB	81
EXFLOW	732MB	1464KB	720KB	4096KB	38
QCD	17MB	70KB	98KB	100KB	52
VORTEX	0MB	3KB	492KB	200KB	17
REACT	536MB	1072KB	432KB	4096KB	34
AVE	665MB	2854KB	900KB	4096KB	54
MAX	1750MB	8960KB	4096KB	4096KB	94

Table 2: Memory Requirements: Columns give application, total memory used for data, memory used for data per processor, memory used for code per processor, memory used for operating system per processor, and percent of memory present that is used for data, code and operating system.

phase, each set of eigenpairs is used to calculate a set of 2K x 2K dense symmetric matrices, called propagation matrices. These calculations are strictly local, and the calculated propagation matrices are sent to disk. The third phase reads the propagation matrices from disk and performs the logarithmic derivative propagation algorithm on them. Each application of this algorithm performs 3 matrix inversions (using Gauss-Jordan elimination) and 1 matrix multiply, all of which are implemented in a data parallel manner. The resulting matrices are then sent to disk. Finally, in the fourth phase these matrices are read from disk and an asymptotic analysis is performed for each of them. These calculations are strictly local.

This experiment uses 1000 channels, 10 energy levels, 50 total angular momentum quantum numbers, and 6 symmetries. The data were provided by M. Wu at the Caltech Concurrent Supercomputing Facilities.

4 Results and Architectural Implications

The data from the applications are presented in Tables 2 through 10. In this section we summarize the data presented in these tables and consider their architectural implications. The accuracy of the data in Tables 2 through 10 varies. The data for SEMI are rough approximations based on an analysis of the code and are accurate to within a power of 10. The data for CLIMATE and RENDER are approximations based on instrumentation and analysis of the code and are accurate to within 20%. The data for MOLECULE, EXFLOW and REACT are primarily from instrumentation and are accurate to within a few percent. The data for QCD and VORTEX are from a complete analysis of the code and are exact (except for rounding in the presentation of the data).

Many of the tables that present I/O and communication data give values in terms of a quantity per Mflop (or Gflop) performed in the entire machine. These rates are expressed in terms of floating point operations performed, rather than in terms of CPU or wall clock time, in order to make the results less dependent on the particular machine being used.

4.1 Memory

Table 2 shows the memory requirements of the applications. Total memory required for data varies from 193KB to 1.75GB and averages 665MB. Memory per processor required for code averages 900KB and reaches 4MB. For many of the applications, a substantial fraction of the memory used is devoted to storing multiple copies of the program and of the operating system. While only two of the applications used 80% or more of the available memory, this does not imply that more memory per node would be wasted. For example REACT uses only 34% of the memory, but this is only because intermediate results are stored on disk. If more memory were available, REACT could be restructured to store these results in memory, thus reducing the I/O requirements and significantly improving performance. In addition, many of the applications studied could utilize larger memories to solve larger problems.

4.2 Processing

Processing requirements of the applications are listed in Table 3. The single most notable common characteristic of the applications studied is that they are all floating point intensive. Clearly, for this type of workload any investment in improving the performance of floating point operations would seem justifiable. On the other hand, an improvement in the speed of computation (processor cycle time and/or number

APPL	FL. OPS.	FL. OPS/P	PREC.
CLIMATE	2970G	12200M	32
SEMI	10000G	20000M	64
MOLECULE	1000G	2000M	32
RENDER	24G	768M	32
EXFLOW	3994G	7987M	32
QCD	119G	474M	32
VORTEX	42G	677M	32
REACT	27648G	55296M	64

Table 3: Processing Requirements: Columns give application, total number of floating point operations performed, floating point operations performed per processor, and number of bits used to represent floating point numbers.

of floating point units) would increase the percentage of time spent communicating, unless the communication performance were improved simultaneously. For some applications the efficiency could be maintained by increasing the granularity of the computation, thus causing fewer messages to be sent per floating point operation performed. This of course implies more data per processor, thus requiring larger memory per processor. These scaling issues are examined in more detail in Section 5.

Most of the applications use single-precision (32-bit) arithmetic, but two of them require double-precision (64-bit) arithmetic. An author of SEMI has stated that quadruple-precision (128-bit) arithmetic would be helpful, as the rounding error introduced by using double-precision arithmetic causes numerical instability that limits the size of problem that can be solved. The extremely large amounts of memory present in current and next generation parallel machines argues for larger integer representations. More specifically, if 32-bit integers are used the address space is limited to 4G words. The need for such large integers could be increased if communication primitives which allow direct reading and writing of a remote processor's memory are supported.

4.3 I/O

Table 4 shows the I/O requirements of the applications studied. Only SEMI and REACT perform significant amounts of I/O to store and access intermediate results. The volume of I/O performed per Mflop varies from nearly 0B to 8858B and averages 1207B. The applications can be divided into two classes based on when they perform I/O operations. Applications in the first class (namely CLIMATE, SEMI, RENDER and REACT) perform I/O operations regularly throughout the run, while applications in the sec-

ond class (namely MOLECULE, EXFLOW, QCD and VORTEX) perform I/O operations only at the beginning and end of the run. Applications in the first class perform far more I/O, averaging 2400B per Mflop as compared with only 14B per Mflop for the applications in the second class. As a result, an I/O load of 2400B per Mflop is probably a reasonable assumption for scientific applications which perform I/O regularly throughout the run. In fact, given that the I/O requirements considered here do not include the loading of the programs into the processors and given the bursty nature of I/O requests, a significantly larger I/O bandwidth may be useful. Finally, some applications could be restructured to take advantage of improved I/O performance. For example, REACT currently performs duplicate floating point operations in order to limit the amount of I/O performed.

4.4 Communication

Tables 5 through 7 give information about the number of messages sent between processors and their lengths[1]. The volume of communication per Mflop performed varies from 5KB to 1956KB and averages 329KB. The number of messages sent per Mflop performed varies from 0.2 to 810 and averages 201.4. It is likely that the applications studied were developed with the communication capabilities of the current generation of parallel machines in mind. As a result, it seems likely that future applications will have even larger communication loads than those studied. In addition, the communication demands tend to come in bursts, further increasing the need for high bandwidth in the communication network.

One of the most surprising results of our study was the variation in message lengths. QCD sends only 72B messages, RENDER sends only 76KB and longer messages, and applications such as CLIMATE, MOLECULE, EXFLOW and REACT send messages with widely varying lengths. The average message size varies from 72B for QCD to 512000B for RENDER. The mean, over all applications, of the average message size is 72637B. However, a more meaningful average message size is obtained by examining the messages sent when an equal number of floating point operations is performed by each of the eight applications. Given such a mix of the applications, an average of 329KB are sent per Mflop performed and an average of 201.4 messages are sent per Mflop performed, yielding an average message size of 1673B. Table 7 shows a

---

[1] The data presented in the first three columns of Tables 6 and 7 for CLIMATE are for 0-9B, 10-99B, and 100-1023B, respectively.

APPL	INPUT	OUTPUT	VOLUME	VOL/MFLOP	DISK	TAPE
CLIMATE	1MB	1500MB	1500MB	517B	10MB	1500MB
SEMI	10MB	100MB	1000MB	100B	1000MB	0MB
MOLECULE	0MB	0MB	0MB	0B	0MB	0MB
RENDER	180MB	28MB	208MB	8858B	208MB	0MB
EXFLOW	0MB	1MB	1MB	0B	1MB	0MB
QCD	0MB	6MB	6MB	52B	6MB	0MB
VORTEX	0MB	0MB	0MB	3B	0MB	0MB
REACT	0MB	160MB	3400MB	126B	1600MB	0MB
AVE	24MB	224MB	764MB	1207B	353MB	187MB
MAX	180MB	1500MB	3400MB	8858B	1600MB	1500MB

Table 4: I/O Requirements: Columns give application, size of input data, size of output data, total volume of I/O messages (both absolute and per Mflop performed in the entire machine), total disk space used, and total amount of tape used.

APPL	VOLUME	VOL/MFLOP	COUNT	COUNT/MFLOP	AVE SIZE
CLIMATE	965GB	325KB	1956M	660.0	505B
SEMI	120GB	12KB	15M	1.5	8192B
MOLECULE	1956GB	1956KB	44M	44.0	45568B
RENDER	2GB	98KB	0M	0.2	512000B
EXFLOW	562GB	144KB	256M	65.6	2248B
QCD	7GB	57KB	94M	810.0	72B
VORTEX	1GB	35KB	1M	29.4	1245B
REACT	132GB	5KB	12M	0.4	11264B
AVE	468GB	329KB	297M	201.4	72637B
MAX	1956GB	1956KB	1956M	810.0	512000B

Table 5: Communication Requirements: Columns give application, total volume of messages between processors (both absolute and per Mflop performed in the entire machine), total number of messages between processors (both absolute and per Mflop performed in the entire machine), and average message size.

APPL	1-16	16-128	128-1K	1K-8K	8K-64K	64K-512K	512K-4M
CLIMATE	58.0	2.3	24.7	15.0	0.0	0.0	0.0
SEMI	0.0	0.0	0.0	0.0	100.0	0.0	0.0
MOLECULE	0.0	0.0	11.1	33.3	33.3	22.2	0.0
RENDER	0.0	0.0	0.0	0.0	0.0	59.9	40.1
EXFLOW	2.0	43.3	41.8	12.8	0.0	0.0	0.2
QCD	0.0	100.0	0.0	0.0	0.0	0.0	0.0
VORTEX	0.0	0.0	0.0	100.0	0.0	0.0	0.0
REACT	0.0	2.1	28.0	15.0	55.0	0.0	0.0

Table 6: Message Sizes: Entries give percent of messages sent by application with lengths in given range. Range $X - Y$ includes messages with X or more bytes and fewer than Y bytes.

APPL	1-16	16-128	128-1K	1K-8K	8K-64K	64K-512K	512K-4M
CLIMATE	392192	15360	166192	101376	0	0	0
SEMI	0	0	0	0	1536	0	0
MOLECULE	0	0	5006	15019	15019	10012	0
RENDER	0	0	0	0	0	121	81
EXFLOW	1252	27794	26793	8188	0	0	108
QCD	0	810	0	0	0	0	0
VORTEX	911	0	9	29147	0	0	0
REACT	0	10	127	68	250	0	0
AVE	49294	5497	24766	19225	2100	1267	24
MAX	392192	27794	166192	101376	15019	10012	108

Table 7: Message Rates by Size: Entries give number of messages sent by application with lengths in given range, per Gflop performed in entire machine. Range $X - Y$ includes messages with X or more bytes and fewer than Y bytes.

more detailed breakdown of the message lengths when an equal number of floating point operations is performed by each application. As can be seen from that table, the median message length is in the range 16B through 127B (and is probably near 32B), which is much smaller than the mean of 1673B. In fact, over 48% of the messages sent are shorter than 16B. Furthermore, the data presented here represent only the messages sent by the application. If the operating system sends acknowledgments for messages received and issues requests and grants for buffer space, the fraction of messages which are less than 16B may be even larger. On the other hand, a more detailed analysis shows that with this same mix of applications, over 80% of the data communicated is sent in messages which are 8KB or longer.

The implication of the message size data is clear: communication networks should be able to perform well with either very short or very long messages as well as with a mixture of very short and very long messages. Numerous studies of routing on communication networks for massively parallel computers have indicated that traffic consisting of small messages requires different network optimizations and protocols than traffic consisting of very large messages. As an example circuit-switching performs well if the messages are very long whereas packet-switching or virtual cut-through routing is advantageous with smaller messages. Unfortunately, the variety in message sizes observed indicates that no one communication network design can be optimal for all applications.

A programming technique that affects message sizes is the practice of *bundling* small messages. When multiple small messages are being sent from the same source processor to the same destination processor, it is common to bundle them into a single larger message. This is done in order to reduce the effect of the software overhead associated with sending each message. Thus, as the software overhead of communication is reduced, it is expected that message sizes will decrease.

In most of the applications examined the communication pattern is known at compilation time and remains fixed throughout the run. This allows for optimization in the placement of processes onto processors as well as optimization of the communication protocols (such as the creation of virtual circuits with dedicated buffers between pairs of processors that communicate frequently). Only SEMI and EXFLOW have communication patterns that depend on the input data and only EXFLOW changes its communication patterns throughout the run. As sophisticated algorith-

APPL	TREE	HC	TORUS (dim)
CLIMATE	Yes	Yes	No
SEMI	Yes	No	No
MOLECULE	Yes	Yes	No
RENDER	No	Yes	No
EXFLOW	No	Yes	Yes (1)
QCD	No	No	Yes (4)
VORTEX	Yes	No	Yes (1)
REACT	Yes	No	Yes (2)

Table 8: Communication Patterns: Columns give application, if a binary tree pattern of communication is used, if a hypercube pattern of communication is used, and if a torus pattern of communication is used (and the dimension of the torus pattern).

mic techniques such as adaptive grids and adaptive load balancing become more common, it is likely that more applications will have dynamic communication patterns. Furthermore, load balancing can destroy the regularity of the communication structure as the entities that are communicating may move between processors.

The communication patterns used by the examined application set are shown in Table 8. At least half of the applications studied use tree, hypercube, and torus patterns of communication, respectively. Of the applications with a torus pattern of communication, two communicate in a 1-dimensional torus (a ring), one communicates in a 2-dimensional torus, and one communicates in a 4-dimensional torus. None of the applications studied uses a regular mesh pattern of communication without "wraparound" messages between opposite boundaries.

One interesting observation is that the hypercube pattern of communication does not necessarily imply the need for a communication network with a large bisection bandwidth. Two of the applications, MOLECULE and RENDER, communicate in a hypercube pattern where messages along each dimension i are of length $x2^i$ for some constant x. When P processors communicate in this manner, they send a total of approximately xP^2 bytes, of which only xP bytes cross dimension 0, so only a fraction of $1/P$ of the data crosses the bisector.

We were surprised by how infrequently broadcasts and barrier synchronizations are performed (see Table 9). None of the applications performed even a single subset broadcast or subset barrier per Gflop. The number of global broadcasts and global barrier synchronizations were at most 33 per Gflop and 10 per Gflop, respectively. As a result, special hardware support for these operations was not justified for the

APPL	BROADCAST		BARRIER	
	GLOB	SUBST	GLOB	SUBST
CLIMATE	33	0	0	0
SEMI	10	0	4	0
MOLECULE	0	0	10	0
RENDER	0	0	0	0
EXFLOW	0	0	0	0
QCD	0	0	0	0
VORTEX	0	0	2	0
REACT	0	0	0	0
AVE	5	0	2	0
MAX	33	0	10	0

Table 9: Collective Communication: The first column gives the application. The remaining columns give the numbers of global broadcasts, subset broadcasts, global barriers, and subset barriers, per Gflop performed in entire machine.

APPL	SEND			RECEIVE	
	IMM	CP	BLK	IMM	BLK
CLIMATE	0	50	50	50	50
SEMI	NA	NA	NA	NA	NA
MOLECULE	0	100	0	0	100
RENDER	0	100	0	0	100
EXFLOW	0	100	0	0	100
QCD	0	0	100	0	100
VORTEX	0	0	100	0	100
REACT	0	0	100	0	100

Table 10: Send and Receive Types: Columns give application, percentages of sends that are immediate sends, copy sends, and blocking sends, and percentages of receives that are immediate receives and blocking receives.

set of applications studied. However, hardware support for global broadcasts could be useful in loading the programs in the processors. Other forms of collective communication such as global reductions were observed in the applications studied, but they were not quantified in our study.

Finally, Table 10 shows the types of send and receive operations used. These operations are classified by how quickly they return after being called. An *immediate send* returns even before the message being sent has been copied out of the sender's memory space. As a result, the sender must verify that the message has been copied into system space before overwriting the message (systems with immediate sends provide a special test operation for this purpose). A *copy send* returns once the message has been copied into system storage, but it does not guarantee that a matching receive has been issued. A *blocking send* does not return until the receiver has issued a matching receive. An

immediate receive returns even before the requested message has been sent (and as a result a test must be performed to detect arrival). A *blocking receive* does not return until the desired message has arrived and been stored in the receiver's memory. Blocking sends and receives can simplify programming and debugging by guaranteeing synchronization between the sender and receiver, while immediate (and copy) sends and receives can reduce communication overhead by overlapping communication and computation. As can be seen from Table 10, copy sends are relatively common, but immediate sends and receives are not. Perhaps improvements in compiler technology will lead to the automatic generation of immediate sends and receives (and their corresponding test operations), thus making them more common in the future.

4.5 Summary

The most surprising result of this study was the diversity of the characteristics of the examined applications. The only features that were shared by all of the applications were their use of the SPMD model and their extensive use of floating point operations.

The memory requirements of the applications and the amounts of I/O and communication per Mflop give useful clues to the creation of a well-balanced parallel architecture. However, as application developers have encountered limitations in the current generation of parallel computers, they have adapted their algorithms to overcome the limitations. It is therefore likely that the applications could be restructured to obtain better performance if the architectural limitations were removed. For example, QCD stores floating point numbers as short integers, thus saving memory[2] but increasing the floating point requirements (as a result of switching between representations). Other applications (such as REACT) encounter I/O bandwidth limits, so users choose to recalculate rather than store and retrieve data. In such applications the ratio of I/O operations to floating point operations would increase if the I/O bandwidth increased. Increased I/O bandwidth may also increase the use of check-pointing and may allow for real-time graphics.

The running times of the applications studied are shown in Table 11. These data are of course highly dependent on the characteristics of the machines on which they were implemented. It should be noted that the values given in the last column include the time for synchronizing between communicating processors,

---

[2]QCD does not use all of the memory available on the nCUBE-1, but it was designed for an earlier generation machine which had less memory per processor.

APPL	TIME	PROC	I/O	COMM
CLIMATE	292 min	25	3	72
SEMI	108 min	58	38	4
MOLECULE	59 min	35	0	65
RENDER	3 min	65	15	20
EXFLOW	216 min	76	4	20
QCD	133 min	77	9	14
VORTEX	24 min	90	0	10
REACT	132 min	83	10	7

Table 11: Running Time: Columns give application, running time, percent of running time spent processing, percent of running time spent performing I/O, and percent of running time spent performing communication or synchronization.

and as a result include the effects of load imbalances.

5 Effects of Scaling

The results presented in the previous section were for a fixed size problem on a fixed size parallel machine. In this section we investigate the effects of scaling the size of the problem being solved and/or the number of processors being used. We focus on five quantities, namely total memory required for data, total number of floating point operations performed, total volume of I/O messages, total volume of messages between processors, and total number of messages between processors. Formulas for each of these five quantities as a function of problem size and number of processors were derived for the applications QCD, VORTEX and REACT. Different runs of these applications were performed to validate the accuracy of the formulas. The remainder of this section presents the formulas that were obtained and examines the effects of scaling with fixed problem sizes and with fixed grain sizes.

5.1 Parameterized Requirements

Formulas for the architectural requirements of QCD, VORTEX and REACT are shown in Table 12. Formulas for data memory, I/O volume and communication volume are in bytes.

QCD operates on a 4-dimensional torus which is partitioned evenly among the P processors, with each processor holding a $D_1 \times D_2 \times D_3 \times D_4$ sublattice. The lattice is updated S times. The dependent parameter V is defined as $V = D_1 D_2 D_3 D_4$ and the dependent parameter L is defined as $L = D_1 D_2 D_3 + D_1 D_2 D_4 + D_1 D_3 D_4 + D_2 D_3 D_4$. In the run considered in the previous section, $P = 256$, $D_1 = D_2 = D_3 = D_4 = 4$, $S = 100$, $V = 256$ and $L = 256$. The formulas

QCD Architectural Requirements	
Data Memory	$(240V + 72D_1 D_2 D_3 + 5077)P$
Fl. Ops.	$19427SVP$
I/O Volume	$96VP$
Com. Volume	$1080SLP$
Com. Count	$15SLP$

VORTEX Architectural Requirements	
Data Memory	$48N + 8P$
Fl. Ops.	$(27S + 9)N^2 + (51S + 9)N + 17P$
I/O Volume	$32N$
Com. Volume	$(60S + 20)NP + 16N\log P + (12S+4)P^2$ $+(4S + 6)P\log P + 20(P - 1)$
Com. Count	$(3S + 1)P^2 + SP\log P + 16(P - 1)$

REACT Architectural Requirements	
Data Memory	$(64S + 151)N^2 + 2NP$
Fl. Ops.	$1200S(N^3 + 10N^2)$ $+PJN^3(S + 320E)/4096$
I/O Volume	$340EN^2$
Com. Volume	$400SN^2 + PEJN^2/2$
Com. Count	$JSP(E + 50)(N/750 + 1/N)$

Table 12: Architectural Requirements of QCD, VORTEX and REACT.

for QCD are exact, except that the number of floating point operations is based on the assumption that the expected number of calls to the Monte Carlo routine (called Trial) required to obtain a success is 3.35 (which was the observed expected value).

VORTEX distributes N vortices evenly among P processors and simulates their behavior for S time steps. In the run considered in the previous section, $P = 64$, $N = 4096$ and $S = 100$. The formulas for VORTEX are exact.

REACT uses P processors to calculate the reaction cross section for a system with N channels, J total angular momentum quantum numbers, E total energies, and S symmetries. In the run considered in the previous section, $P = 512$, $N = 1000$, $J = 50$, $E = 10$ and $S = 6$. The formulas for REACT were created and validated by Mark Wu at Caltech. They are approximations that were found to be accurate to within 6% when the parameters are varied by a factor of 10 or less.

5.2 Scaling with Fixed Problem Size

We will first consider the effect of increasing the number of processors used while solving the same size problem. This analysis will show which features of the applications limit the use of increased parallelism to obtain faster solutions. The results are presented

APPLICATION	CHARACTERISTICS	NUMBER OF PROCESSORS						
		P	2P	4P	8P	16P	32P	64P
QCD	Data Memory	1.00	1.07	1.21	1.50	2.14	3.28	5.56
	Fl. Ops.	1.00	1.00	1.00	1.00	1.00	1.00	1.00
	I/O Volume	1.00	1.00	1.00	1.00	1.00	1.00	1.00
	Com. Volume	1.00	1.25	1.50	1.75	2.00	2.50	3.00
	Com. Count	1.00	1.25	1.50	1.75	2.00	2.50	3.00
VORTEX	Data Memory	1.00	1.00	1.01	1.02	1.04	1.08	1.16
	Fl. Ops.	1.00	1.00	1.00	1.00	1.00	1.00	1.00
	I/O Volume	1.00	1.00	1.00	1.00	1.00	1.00	1.00
	Com. Volume	1.00	2.01	4.04	8.17	16.74	35.08	76.55
	Com. Count	1.00	3.95	15.67	62.39	248.89	994.07	3973.00
REACT	Data Memory	1.00	1.00	1.01	1.01	1.03	1.06	1.12
	Fl. Ops.	1.00	1.73	3.20	6.14	12.01	23.75	47.22
	I/O Volume	1.00	1.00	1.00	1.00	1.00	1.00	1.00
	Com. Volume	1.00	1.98	3.94	7.87	15.72	31.43	62.84
	Com. Count	1.00	2.00	4.00	8.00	16.00	32.00	64.00

Table 13: Scaling of QCD, VORTEX and REACT applications with Fixed Problem Size: Entries give architectural requirements using 256 (P) through 16384 ($64P$) processors. All entries are normalized.

in Table 13. All entries are normalized so that the requirements for P processors equal 1. QCD scales quite efficiently, with the floating point operations and I/O performed being constant and the remaining quantities increasing by a factor of 5.56 or less. The increase in the memory required is due to arrays which are duplicated in all of the processors. The increase in interprocessor communication is due to the increase in the 4-dimensional "surface-to-volume" ratio of the sublattices stored in each processor. The message sizes remain constant. One inefficiency of scaling which is not evident from Table 13 is an increase in the variability in processing times due to the smaller number of Monte Carlo trials performed per processor.

As VORTEX is implemented with more processors, communication becomes a bottleneck (Table 13). The floating point operations and I/O are constant and the memory requirements increase by only a factor of 1.16. However, the volume of interprocessor communication increases by a factor of 76.55 and the number of messages between processors increases by a factor of 3973. The volume of communication increases approximately linearly with the number of processors because a copy of each vortex is sent to every other processor during each time step. The number of messages increases approximately quadratically with the number of processors because the processors communicate in the form of a ring. In each time step data are shifted around this ring. Because each shift involves P messages, and because P shifts are required, a total of P^2 messages are sent. Also, note that as the number of processors increases the messages become shorter, thus making the communication latency an increasingly important issue.

In REACT, the memory and I/O requirements are largely independent of the number of processors being used. However, the number of floating point operations performed increases almost linearly with the number of processors! This surprising behavior (which nearly matches the behavior of a sequential application which is executed P times on P processors) is due to the repeated calculations which are performed in order to limit I/O operations. Even when 512 processors are used, approximately 74% of the floating point operations performed are logically unnecessary and are performed solely to reduce I/O. As the number of processors used increases, this fraction approaches 100% and a different algorithm would have to be used. Finally, note that the message sizes are almost independent of the number of processors.

In summary, load imbalances and communication overhead limit the scaling of QCD, communication overhead (latency in particular) limits the scaling of VORTEX, and repeated floating point operations limit the scaling of REACT. In general, different applications experience different limitations when scaling with a fixed problem size. Thus, as the number of processors in massively parallel machines increases some of the applications will be able to efficiently use only a subset of the processors. This observation argues for parallel machines that are partitionable to smaller sets of nodes and that can efficiently handle the communication and I/O traffic of multiple problems executing simultaneously. Finally, it should be noted that the percentage of memory devoted to storing a copy of the program and operating system in each processor

APPLICATION	CHARACTERISTICS	NUMBER OF PROCESSORS						
		P	2P	4P	8P	16P	32P	64P
QCD	Data Memory	1.00	2.00	4.00	8.00	16.00	32.00	64.00
	Fl. Ops.	1.00	2.00	4.00	8.00	16.00	32.00	64.00
	I/O Volume	1.00	2.00	4.00	8.00	16.00	32.00	64.00
	Com. Volume	1.00	2.00	4.00	8.00	16.00	32.00	64.00
	Com. Count	1.00	2.00	4.00	8.00	16.00	32.00	64.00
VORTEX	Data Memory	1.00	2.00	4.00	8.00	16.00	32.00	64.00
	Fl. Ops.	1.00	4.00	16.00	63.98	255.89	1023.55	4094.18
	I/O Volume	1.00	2.00	4.00	8.00	16.00	32.00	64.00
	Com. Volume	1.00	4.00	16.00	63.98	255.92	1023.66	4094.62
	Com. Count	1.00	3.95	15.67	62.39	248.89	994.07	3973.00
REACT	Data Memory	1.00	2.00	4.01	8.03	16.09	32.29	64.86
	Fl. Ops.	1.00	4.90	25.59	138.79	768.21	4297.89	24177.50
	I/O Volume	1.00	2.00	4.00	8.00	16.00	32.00	64.00
	Com. Volume	1.00	3.96	15.78	62.95	251.58	1005.79	4021.79
	Com. Count	1.00	2.83	8.00	22.61	63.96	180.89	511.62

Table 14: Scaling QCD, VORTEX and REACT with Fixed Grain Size: Entries give architectural requirements using 256 (P) through 16384 ($64P$) processors. All entries are normalized.

increases with this type of scaling.

5.3 Scaling with Fixed Grain Size

We will now consider the effect of increasing the number of processors used while simultaneously increasing the size of the problem that is being solved. In particular we will assume that the problem size increases so that each processor devotes the same amount of memory to data storage, regardless of the number of processors used. Our goal is to see if all five of the quantities studied here grow at an equal rate when this type of scaling is performed. The results are shown in Table 14. All entries are normalized so that the requirements for P processors equal 1.

In QCD, the effect of scaling was considered while maintaining the same size sublattice per processor. The parameter S was kept fixed at 100. As can be seen from the table, all of the quantities grow at exactly the same rate when the grain size is fixed.

In VORTEX the effect of scaling was considered by maintaining a constant N/P ratio and keeping S fixed at 100. While the memory and I/O requirements grow linearly with P, the remaining quantities grow approximately quadratically with P. As a result, the I/O and memory requirements become less important, while the floating point and communication requirements become increasingly important (and the number of messages per floating point operation remains fixed).

In considering the effect of scaling REACT with a fixed grain size, parameters J, E and S were kept fixed and the ratio N^2/P was held constant. The ratio N^2/P was selected because it gives a good approximation of the memory requirements per processor. The memory and I/O requirements scale proportionally to P, the number of messages between processors grows proportionally to $P^{1.5}$, the volume of communication between processors grows proportionally to P^2, and the number of floating point operations grows proportionally to $P^{2.5}$. As a result, the communication and I/O requirements become smaller relative to the amount of floating point processing. However, as was discussed in the subsection on scaling with a fixed problem size, an increasingly large fraction of the floating point operations are duplicates which are logically unnecessary.

In summary, the effects of scaling with a fixed grain size are very dependent on the application. Some applications (such as QCD) which are based on local interactions between the data have fixed architectural requirements per processor when the grain size is fixed. Other applications have global interactions, so the amount of memory, processing, I/O and communication required per processor is determined by the size of the overall problem being solved as well as the grain size.

6 Conclusions

In this paper we have studied the behavior of parallel scientific applications that perform explicit communication. We quantified the architectural requirements of these applications in terms of memory, processing and I/O. We also studied their communication patterns and traffic characteristics and we modeled the effects of scaling. The applications that we studied are necessarily affected by characteristics of the parallel machines for which they were designed. For example, the memory per processor and number of processors available limit the size of the problem which is being solved. However, by examining a wide range of applications and by considering the effects of scaling the problem size and the number of processors used, we feel that important insights into the architectural requirements of future scientific applications may be obtained.

The strongest conclusion of our study is that the applications we examined vary widely in their characteristics. For example, the number of messages sent per Mflop performed varies by a factor of over 4000 and the average message size varies by a factor of over 7000. Over 48% of the messages sent are shorter than 16 bytes but over 80% of the communicated data is sent in messages which are 8KB or longer. As a result it appears that future multicomputer architectures will have to be extremely flexible, supporting multiple users and widely varying applications, even if they are used solely for scientific applications.

Acknowledgments

We would like to thank Ke-Chih Wu, Steve Plimpton, Peggy Li, Roy Williams and Mark Wu for providing data about their applications. We would also like to thank Mark Wu for developing and validating the models for the effects of scaling his application. In addition, we would like to thank Dragutin Petkovic for his support and Heidi Lorenz-Wirzba for her help with the computing environment. Finally, we would like to thank Narasimha Reddy for many helpful discussions.

References

[1] A. Agarwal and A. Gupta. Memory-reference characteristics of multiprocessor applications under MACH. In *Proc. 1988 ACM SIGMETRICS Conf. on Measurement and Modeling of Computer Systems*, pp. 215–225.

[2] C. Baillie and D. Walker. Lattice QCD – as a large scale scientific computation. Technical Report C^3P-641, California Institute of Technology, 1988.

[3] R. Lucas, K. Wu and R. Dutton. A parallel 3-D Poisson solver on a hypercube multiprocessor. In *Proc. IEEE Intl. Conf. on Computer-Aided Design*, pp. 442–445, 1987.

[4] F. Darema-Rogers, G. Pfister and K. So. Memory access patterns of parallel scientific programs. In *Proc. 1987 ACM SIGMETRICS Conf. on Measurement and Modeling of Computer Systems*, pp. 46–57.

[5] K. Wu, G. Chin and R. Dutton. A STRIDE towards practical 3-D device simulation – numerical and visualization considerations. *IEEE Trans. on Computer-Aided Design*, vol. 10, no. 9, pp. 1132–1140, 1991.

[6] J. Flower. *Lattice Gauge Theory on a Parallel Computer*. PhD thesis, California Institute of Technology, 1987.

[7] J.-M. Hsu and P. Banerjee. Performance measurement and trace driven simulation of parallel CAD and numeric applications on a hypercube multicomputer. In *Proc. 17th Annual Intl. Symp. on Computer Architecture*, pp. 260–269, 1990.

[8] A. Leonard. Vortex methods for flow simulation. *J. Computational Physics*, 37, 289 (1980).

[9] P. Li and D. Curkendall. Parallel 3-D perspective rendering. In *Proc. First Intel Delta Applications Workshop*, Technical Report CCSF-14-92, California Institute of Technology, pp. 52–58, 1992.

[10] P. Messina, C. Baillie, E. Felten, P. Hipes, R. Williams, A. Alagar, A. Kamrath, R. Leary, W. Pfeiffer, J. Rogers and D. Walker. Benchmarking advanced architecture computers. *Concurrency: Practice and Experience*, vol. 2(3), pp. 195–255, Sept. 1990.

[11] S. Otto. *Monte Carlo Methods in Lattice Gauge Theories*. PhD thesis, California Institute of Technology, 1983.

[12] S. Plimpton and G. Heffelfinger. Scalable parallel molecular dynamics on MIMD supercomputers. In *Proc. Scalable High Performance Computing Conf.*, pp. 246–251, Apr. 1992.

[13] A. Reddy and P. Banerjee. A study of I/O behavior of perfect benchmarks on a multiprocessor. In *Proc. 17th Annual Intl. Symp. on Computer Architecture*, pp. 312–321, 1990.

[14] R. Williams. Performance of dynamic load balancing algorithms for unstructured mesh calculations. *Concurrency*, vol. 3, pp. 457–481 (1991).

[15] M. Wu, S. Cuccaro, P. Hipes and A. Kuppermann. Quantum mechanical reactive scattering using a high-performance distributed-memory parallel computer. *Chem. Phys. Lett.*, 168, 429–440 (1990).

[16] M. Wu, A. Kuppermann and B. Lepetit. Theoretical calculation experimentally observable consequences of the geometric phase on chemical reaction cross sections. *Chem. Phys. Lett.*, 186, 319–328 (1991).

[17] M. Wu and A. Kuppermann. Prediction of the effect of the geometric phase on product rotational state distributions and integral cross sections. *Chem. Phys. Lett.*, (1992) in press.

Working Sets, Cache Sizes, and Node Granularity Issues for Large-Scale Multiprocessors

Edward Rothberg

Intel Supercomputer Systems Division
14924 N.W. Greenbrier Parkway
Beaverton, OR 97006

Jaswinder Pal Singh and Anoop Gupta

Computer Systems Laboratory
Stanford University
Stanford, CA 94305

Abstract

The distribution of resources among processors, memory and caches is a crucial question faced by designers of large-scale parallel machines. If a machine is to solve problems with a certain data set size, should it be built with a large number of processors each with a small amount of memory, or a smaller number of processors each with a large amount of memory? How much cache memory should be provided per processor for cost-effectiveness? And how do these decisions change as larger problems are run on larger machines?

In this paper, we explore the above questions based on the characteristics of five important classes of large-scale parallel scientific applications. We first show that all the applications have a hierarchy of well-defined per-processor working sets, whose size, performance impact and scaling characteristics can help determine how large different levels of a multiprocessor's cache hierarchy should be. Then, we use these working sets together with certain other important characteristics of the applications—such as communication to computation ratios, concurrency, and load balancing behavior—to reflect upon the broader question of the granularity of processing nodes in high-performance multiprocessors.

We find that very small caches whose sizes do not increase with the problem or machine size are adequate for all but two of the application classes. Even in the two exceptions, the working sets scale quite slowly with problem size, and the cache sizes needed for problems that will be run in the foreseeable future are small. We also find that relatively fine-grained machines, with large numbers of processors and quite small amounts of memory per processor, are appropriate for all the applications.

1 Introduction

As larger multiprocessors are built, determining the appropriate distribution of resources among processors, cache and main memory becomes increasingly challenging for a designer. Small-scale, bus-based, shared-memory multiprocessors usually provide relatively large per-processor caches (several hundred Kbytes to a few Mbytes) and tens of Mbytes of physical memory per processor. These decisions make sense for small-scale machines. For example, with a small number of processors, the memory per processor must be large in order for the machine to have enough total memory to perform interesting computations. And large caches make sense for several reasons: (i) multiprogramming and the need to accommodate several applications

simultaneously, (ii) the use of a shared bus interconnect and the need to reduce traffic on it, and (iii) the fact that there are only a few caches and a large amount of main memory, so that caches cost only a small fraction of the machine.

On large-scale parallel machines, many of these reasons for large caches and main memories per processor no longer necessarily hold. The desirable amounts of main memory and cache per processor are therefore not obvious. These desirable ratios are also very difficult to determine owing to the wide range of issues involved, including application characteristics, machine usage patterns, hardware cost and performance estimates, and even determining the appropriate metrics to optimize.

In this paper, we focus on one crucial input into the above design decisions: the characteristics of applications that are likely to run on high-performance multiprocessors. By studying relevant application characteristics such as memory usage, working set sizes, communication to computation ratios, concurrency and load balancing, and by examining how these characteristics scale to larger problems and machine sizes, we reflect upon the appropriate amounts of memory and cache per processor for five important classes of scientific applications. These classes are: direct equation solvers, iterative equation solvers, spectral transform methods (represented here by a Fast Fourier Transform), hierarchical N-body methods, and volume visualization (volume rendering) methods.

We divide our treatment of every application into two parts. First, we examine the working sets of the applications, which help in determining how large the levels in the machine's cache hierarchy should be to keep performance losses due to capacity misses low. We find that all the applications have a well-defined *hierarchy of working sets*, such that a cache that is large enough to hold a given working set can yield dramatic performance benefits over a cache that is slightly smaller than that working set. We also find that the working sets of all the applications are bimodally distributed, consisting of a few small working sets and one large one that usually comprises a processor's entire partition of the data set. In most cases, the working set that is critical to good performance is one of the smaller ones. In three of the applications (direct solvers, iterative solvers, and the FFT), this important working set—and hence the cache size needed for good performance—is very small and does not scale with problem or machine size. Even in the other two applications (N-body and volume rendering), the working set is quite small and scales very slowly with problem size, so that small caches will suffice for the foreseeable future. There is one application (the iterative solver) in which a large working set also has an important performance impact; however, accommodating this working set requires the cache to be essentially as large as the local data set per processor, which is not a realistic design point for the near future.

In the second part of our treatment of an application, we use the information about working set sizes as well as other relevant application characteristics to reflect upon desirable grain sizes for machines. The grain size (or granularity) of a machine can be loosely defined as the amount of main memory and cache per processor on the machine. Using several approximations and simplifying assumptions, we find that all but one of our applications can effectively use large numbers of processors with small amounts of main memory and cache each. The argument for fine-grained machines from an applications perspective is further strengthened when time constraints are incorporated in the scaling model. However, there are reasons why one might not want to actually build machines with small amounts of memory per processor in the near term, and we discuss some of these.

The paper is organized as follows. In the next section, we describe the methodology and framework we use to study the applications. Sections 3 through 7 discuss the individual applications. In Section 8, we discuss our results and some caveats to the argument for fine-grained machines. Finally, Section 9 summarizes the main conclusions of the paper.

2 Methodology and Framework

In this section, we describe the common framework we use to present the results for each application. Sections 2.1 through 2.3 exactly mirror the structure of the computation description, working set size and grain size discussions in each individual application section, and also describe the methodology we use to obtain our results. Section 2.4 states some additional simplifying assumptions that we make.

2.1 Description of Computation

Our discussion of each application begins with a description of the most important steps of the computation. To make our investigations concrete, we also describe a *prototypical problem*. Our prototypical problem for every application is one whose data set is 1 Gbyte and is distributed at 1 Mbyte per node on a 1024 node machine. This is intended to represent a fine-grained machine configuration.

2.2 Working Set Hierarchy

The second subsection for each application identifies the important application working sets. To determine the sizes of these working sets, we simulate a cache-coherent, shared-address-space multiprocessor architecture, with each processor having a single level of cache and an equal fraction of the total main memory. For a given problem size and number of processors, we simulate different cache sizes and look for knees in the resulting performance (or miss rate) versus cache size curve.

To exclude the effects of *conflict* misses, which are influenced by a host of low-level artifacts, we use fully associative caches with an LRU replacement policy. To the extent that conflict misses are important, working set sizes measured this way are aggressive estimates of desirable cache size, and real caches—with low degrees of associativity—will need to be somewhat larger. For the first three applications we consider, the difference between a cache with limited associativity and a fully associative cache is not significant, since the cache conflict problem can easily be avoided. We comment on the use of direct-mapped caches for the other two applications in their respective sections. Finally, to exclude *cold-start* misses where appropriate, we omit the first few time-steps or iterations in those applications that

are in reality expected to proceed over many time-steps or iterations. Thus, what we measure are misses due to *inherent communication* and finite cache *capacity*.

The first three applications we consider are well-understood and highly predictable computational kernels. In these cases (direct solvers, iterative solvers, and the FFT), we determine the working set sizes analytically, and use simulation to confirm our estimates for some examples. Since these applications are highly floating-point intensive, the metric we use to describe cache miss rates is number of double-word read misses per double-precision floating-point operation. The other two applications, Barnes-Hut and volume rendering, are full-scale applications that are not as regular, analytically describable, or floating point dominated. In these cases, we use simulation to look for knees in the read miss rate (read misses divided by number of read references) rather than misses per FLOP. We focus on read misses since these are likely to have a much greater impact on performance than write misses, the latencies of which can be easily hidden in these programs.

Scaling: Having determined the working set sizes for the prototypical problem, we then look at how these sizes scale with various application parameters and numbers of processors. We assume for this discussion that machines are made larger by adding processors, each processor bringing with it an amount of cache and memory equal to the cache and memory per processor on the original machine. We first examine how the working sets scale with individual parameters, and then look at how they scale under certain accepted models of scaling problems to run on larger machines. The two scaling models we consider are memory-constrained (MC) and time-constrained (TC) scaling. Given a larger machine, the MC scaling model assumes that a user will scale the problem to fill the available main memory on the machine, regardless of the effect this has on execution time. The TC scaling model, on the other hand, assumes that the user will increase the problem size so that the new problem takes as much time to solve on the new machine as the old problem took on the old machine. For more information about these scaling models, see [9].

2.3 Grain Size

Having understood the working sets, we then examine other application characteristics that affect the desirable granularity of processing nodes. In particular, we study the implications of interprocessor communication costs, load balance, and problem concurrency for node granularity. We begin by looking at the impact of these issues for the prototypical problem, and then we study how this changes with the problem and machine size.

Communication Costs: To determine the relative cost of interprocessor communication for each application, we first calculate a computation to communication ratio for the prototypical problem. To provide some feeling for what ratios we would consider sustainable, let us consider relevant parameters on existing and likely future parallel machines. One example is the Intel Paragon machine. Each node in this machine will have four 50-MFLOPS processors, yielding 200 MFLOPS per node. The machine uses a 2-D mesh interconnect with 200-Mbyte-per-second channels. Let us first consider nearest-neighbor communication. In this case, the bandwidth in the Paragon is limited by that of the node-to-router link, which is 200 Mbytes/sec peak. The sustainable ratio, in FLOPs per double-word, is therefore $\frac{200}{200/8} = 8$. For more random communication, sustainable communication volume is determined by the bisection width of the network. For a 32x32 (1024) node Paragon, the number of network links across a bisector is 64. Assuming that half of all random messages cross this bisector, each processor can generate only 64/512, or one-eighth as much traffic as in the nearest-neighbor case, yielding a sustainable ratio of 64 FLOPs/word. Similarly, the sustainable ratios on the Thinking Machines CM-5 are about 50 FLOPs per word for nearest-neighbor communication and about 100 for general communication (assuming 128MFLOPS vector nodes, 20Mbyte/sec nearest-neighbor communication bandwidth and 5Mbyte/sec general bandwidth).

As technology progresses, we should see both faster floating point processors and faster communication chips. For this paper, we simply assume that computation to communication ratios of 1-15 FLOPs/word are extremely difficult to sustain, 15-75 are sustainable but not easy, and above 75 are quite easy to sustain. (Of course, all the analytical and experimental data we provide remain valid even if the reader makes different assumptions about sustainability than we do.)

Load Balance and Concurrency: Two other potential sources of difficulty in obtaining high parallel performance are load imbalances and deficiencies in available problem concurrency. We comment on the expected impact of these for the prototypical problem.

Desirable Grain Size: We then attempt to determine what would constitute a desirable processor grain size for the prototypical problem. Our goal is not to make fine distinctions in grain size, but rather only very coarse ones. That is, we are not trying to determine whether the appropriate grain size is 1 Mbyte or 2 Mbyte of main memory per processor, but rather whether it is on the order of 1 Mbyte, 10 Mbytes or 100 Mbytes. To estimate a desirable grain size, we examine the expected parallel performance—based on communication cost, load balance, and concurrency considerations—for two variations of the prototypical problem with very different granularities. The first is a 1 Gbyte problem on 64 processors, resulting in 16 Mbytes of data per processor. The second is the same problem on 16 thousand processors, resulting in 64 Kbytes of data per processor.

Scaling: Finally, we consider how this desirable grain size changes as the problem is scaled.

2.4 Other Assumptions

We make a few additional simplifying assumptions in our analysis. We assume that the processor is based on commodity processor technology and thus is a given; its performance does not change when the number of processors is changed. We also assume that since the machine supports a shared address space, it is optimized for small data exchanges between processors and thus provides inexpensive interprocessor synchronization. Finally, we ignore the impact of contention in various parts of the machine as well as that of locality in the network topology, with the exception of our coarse notion of local versus random communication patterns discussed earlier in this subsection.

3 Direct Methods for Solving Linear Systems

The first application we consider is the LU factorization of large, dense matrices. This important and widely used computation factors a matrix A into the form $A = LU$, where L is lower-triangular and U is upper-triangular. The most common source of large dense LU problems is radar cross-section problems, where people currently solve problems that require several hours on today's largest parallel machines.

While we specifically examine dense LU factorization in this section, our analysis actually applies to a wider set of applications. Applications with very similar structure include dense

QR factorization, dense Cholesky factorization, dense eigenvalue methods, and in many respects sparse Cholesky factorization.

3.1 Description of Computation

Dense LU factorization can be performed extremely efficiently if the dense $n \times n$ matrix A is divided into an $N \times N$ array of $B \times B$ blocks, $(n = NB)$ [11]. The following pseudo-code, expressed in terms of these blocks, shows the most important steps in the computation.

```
1.  for K = 0 to N do
2.      factor block A_KK
3.      compute values for all blocks
            in column K and row K
4.      for J = K + 1 to N do
5.          for I = K + 1 to N do
6.              A_IJ ← A_IJ − A_IK A_KJ
```

The dominant computation here is Step 6, which is simply a dense matrix multiplication.

The parallel computation corresponding to a single K iteration in the above pseudo-code is shown symbolically in Figure 1. Two details have been shown to be crucial for reducing interpro-

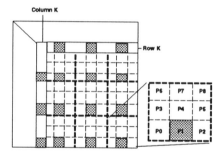

Figure 1: Dense block LU factorization.

cessor communication volumes and thus obtaining high performance. First, the blocks of the matrix are assigned to processors using a 2-D scatter decomposition [2]. That is, the processors are thought of as a $P \times Q$ grid, and block (I, J) in the matrix is assigned to processor $(I \bmod P, J \bmod Q)$. A simple 3×3 processor example is shown in Figure 1. Second, the matrix multiplication in Step 6 above is performed by the processor that owns block $A_{I,J}$. Within one K iteration, a processor thus uses blocks in the appropriate rows of column K (those blocks owned by a processor in the same row of the processor grid) and the appropriate columns of row K to update blocks it owns. The shaded blocks in Figure 1 are the blocks that processor P1 uses in one K iteration.

Three factors must be traded off in choosing an appropriate block size B. Larger blocks lead to lower cache miss rates. However, larger blocks also increase the fraction of the computation performed in the less parallel portion of the computation (Steps 2 and 3 in the earlier pseudo-code), and can also cause load balancing problems. Relatively small block sizes ($B = 8$ or $B = 16$) can be shown to strike a good balance between these factors.

3.2 Working Set Hierarchy

Our prototypical 1 Gbyte data set on 1024 processors corresponds to a roughly $10,000 \times 10,000$ LU factorization problem.

Since people are currently solving $50,000 \times 50,000$ dense systems arising from radar cross-section applications on 128 processor machines, our choice of a smaller problem on a larger machine is actually somewhat aggressive.

The structure of *LU* factorization is sufficiently simple that we can derive working set sizes analytically. Figure 2 shows analytical cache miss rates for an $n = 10,000$ matrix, using block sizes of $B = 4$, 16, and 64, and $P = 1024$ processors. The graph shows double-word cache misses as a fraction of double-precision floating-point operations. The important levels

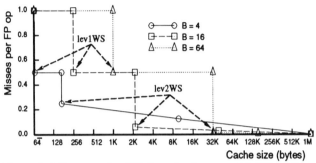

Figure 2: Miss rates for *LU* factorization, $n = 10,000$, $PE = 1024$.

of the working set hierarchy are as follows. The level 1 working set (lev1WS) consists of two columns of a block, and is roughly 260 bytes for $B = 16$. Once two columns fit, one column can be reused, roughly halving the overall miss rate. The second working set (lev2WS) consists of an entire $B \times B$ block, and is roughly 2200 bytes for $B = 16$. When this working set fits in the cache, the miss rate drops to roughly $1/B$. The other block sizes ($B = 4$ and $B = 64$) naturally lead to different level 1 and level 2 working sets sizes and miss rates.

Clearly, the cache sizes required to hold the lev2WS are much smaller than the caches people are building on parallel machines today, even for relatively large block sizes ($B = 16$ or 32). The resulting miss rates are small enough to yield high performance. Almost all the misses would be serviced from a processor's local memory, provided the matrix blocks are placed in the local memories of their owner processors. Also, the misses are predictable enough to be easily prefetched.

The next working set (lev3WS) includes all blocks in row/column K that affect blocks owned by a particular processor (e.g., the shaded blocks in row/column K of Figure 1). The size of lev3WS is $2NB^2/\sqrt{P} = 2nB/\sqrt{P}$ (roughly 80 Kbytes for $B = 16$). If the lev3WS fits in cache, then the miss rate is further reduced by a factor of 2 to $1/2B$. However, the miss rate is small enough even before the lev3WS is reached, so that the lev3WS is of only minor importance to performance.

The final working set (lev4WS) is the set of all blocks belonging to a processor. If the cache accommodates the lev4WS (of size n^2/p), the miss rate is equal to the communication miss rate.

Scaling: When considering problem or machine size scaling, we note that the most important working set, the lev2WS, depends only on the block size B. It is independent of n and P. In other words, a small amount of cache is sufficient for any problem or machine size.

3.3 Grain Size

Communication Costs: *LU* factorization of an $n \times n$ matrix performs roughly $2n^3/3$ floating-point operations. Every block

in the matrix is communicated to a row or column of $\sqrt{P}$ processors, yielding an overall communication volume of $n^2\sqrt{P}$. The computation to communication ratio is thus $2n/(3\sqrt{P})$, and depends only the grain size (n^2/P). For our prototypical problem, with its 1 Mbyte grain size, this yields a ratio of roughly 200 floating-point operations per floating-point word of communication—a relatively low bandwidth requirement. Also, most of these interprocessor communication costs can be hidden from the processors (using software prefetching, for example).

Load Balance and Concurrency: Another important issue that affects parallel performance is the load balance and available concurrency of the computation. For our $10,000$ by $10,000$ prototypical dense *LU* example with $B = 16$, each of the 1024 processors is assigned roughly 380 blocks from the matrix. This is a large enough number of blocks for dense *LU* factorization that load balancing and concurrency issues do not detract significantly from achieved parallel performance either.

Desirable Grain Size: Clearly, a 1024-processor machine with 1 Mbyte of data per processor would produce good processor utilization. Let us consider whether the grain size can reasonably be reduced to solve the same 1 Gbyte problem. Consider solving the problem on a 16K processor machine with 64 Kbytes of memory per processor. The computation to communication ratio would decrease by a factor of four to 50 operations per communicated datum, more difficult but still quite possible to sustain. The larger effect comes from load imbalance. With $B = 16$, each processor would now be assigned 25 blocks, which would reduce processor performance somewhat. This load balance problem could be improved by reducing the block size, but at a cost of increased cache miss rates. In either case, the higher computation to communication ratio, combined with the performance loss due to either poorer load balance or higher cache miss rates, would reduce per-processor performance. Thus, while a 1 Mbyte grain size is easy to sustain for a 1 Gbyte problem, a 64 Kbyte grain size is not so easy.

Scaling: Let us now see how the desirable grain size changes as larger problems are run. Keeping the grain size fixed at 1 Mbyte per processor allows us to factor a 20,000 by 20,000 matrix on 4096 processors. Compared with the prototypical problem, this problem would require the same amount of cache memory, would produce the same computation to communication ratio, and would generate a very similar computational load balance (since each processor still handles 380 blocks ($B = 16$)). We therefore conclude that the desirable grain size is independent of the problem size.

Keeping the grain size fixed while increasing the number of processors results in memory-constrained (MC) scaling. Since the amount of computation (which scales as n^3) grows much faster than the data set size (which scales as n^2), the parallel execution time grows quite quickly under MC scaling, which may therefore be an unacceptable scaling model for this application. If, on the other hand, a time-constrained scaling model were used, the per-processor data set would shrink with increasing P (of course, the performance of the individual processors would decrease as well). Constraints on execution time therefore provide another argument for finer-grained processing nodes on large-scale machines.

3.4 Summary

To summarize, we have found that dense *LU* factorization places very modest demands on a parallel machine. A small cache is sufficient to reduce the cache miss rate to nearly negligible levels, even for large problems on large machines. Similarly, a small amount of per-processor memory (1 Mbyte or less) is sufficient to yield good performance, regardless of n and P.

4 Iterative Methods for Solving Linear Systems

The next class of computations we consider are iterative methods for solving linear systems of equations (or for finding eigenvalues of large sparse matrices). Iterative methods, which begin with a guess at the solution and iteratively attempt to improve this guess, are finding increasing use in solving large systems of equations in parallel. At the heart of these iterative methods is a sparse matrix-vector multiply, typically accompanied by some combination of vector additions and dot products. While we specifically consider the conjugate gradient (CG) method for solving sparse linear systems of equations here, the results should be similar for a range of other iterative methods.

4.1 Description of Computation

Each iteration of the CG method performs a single sparse matrix-vector multiply, 3 vector additions, and 2 dot products. The matrix-vector multiply is the dominant computation. This operation is most easily described by considering the sparse matrix A as a graph $G = (V, E)$, with a vertex $v \in V$ corresponding to each row/column in A and a weighted edge $i, j \in E$ corresponding to each non-zero $A_{i,j}$. The sparse matrix-vector multiply $b \leftarrow Ax$ is performed by associating an x value with each vertex in the graph, and iterating over all vertices. For every vertex i, the value of b_i is computed by summing the products of the weights of the edges (i, j) incident to i with the x values at the adjacent j vertices.

The CG computation is parallelized by partitioning the vertices in the graph representation of the matrix among processors. Consider the case where the graph representation of the sparse matrix is a simple 2-D grid (Figure 3). The example grid is partitioned among 4 processors in the figure. At each CG iteration,

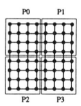

Figure 3: A 2-D grid partitioned among 4 processors.

a processor iterates over the points assigned to it, computing new values for b at its vertices. Interprocessor communication is necessary when a processor handles a vertex that is adjacent to a vertex belonging to another processor (the vertices on the boundaries between processor partitions in Figure 3), since the value at the other end of that edge was presumably changed in the previous iteration.

Our prototypical 1 Gbyte problem on 1024 processors corresponds to a roughly 4000×4000 2-D grid. An important trend in problem domains that use iterative methods is toward 3 dimensional problems. In this case, the prototypical problem corresponds to a $225 \times 225 \times 225$ 3-D regular grid.

4.2 Working Set Hierarchy

A processor sweeps through the entire set of nodes assigned to it in every iteration, touching the data corresponding to every edge incident to these nodes. Thus, unless this entire data set fits in the cache, the computation provides few opportunities to reuse data.

The working set hierarchies for our 2-D and 3-D grid examples on 1024 processors are shown in Figure 4. For the 2-D problem, the lev1WS consists of the x values from three adjacent sub-rows of points assigned to a processor. This lev1WS is quite small, consisting of roughly 5 Kbytes of data in the prototypical 2-D problem. While the impact of this 5 Kbyte working set on miss rate is significant, the miss rate remains high even after this working set fits in the cache. The lev2WS consists

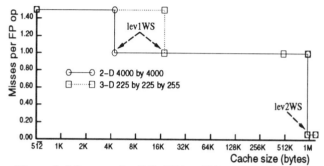

Figure 4: Miss rates for CG, 4000×4000 grid, $P = 1024$.

of the entire set of data owned by a processor. At this point, the miss rate drops to the communication miss rate. However, it is generally unreasonable to expect this set of entries to fit in cache.

For the 3-D grid computation, the working sets are quite similar. The major difference is in the lev1WS, which now consists of 2-D cross-sections from the 3-D region assigned to each processor, and thus represents a larger data set than the 1-D sub-rows from the 2-D grid. In the prototypical problem, the lev1WS grows from 5K to 18K. Note that these numbers are still smaller than the first-level caches found in nearly all modern processors.

Scaling: If we expect the per-processor data set to be larger than the processor cache, then the only working set that can fit in the cache is the lev1WS. Since each processor receives an $n/\sqrt{P} \times n/\sqrt{P}$ portion of the $n \times n$ 2-D grid, the size of the lev1WS is proportional to $n/\sqrt{P}$. The size of this working set therefore remains quite moderate. A problem that requires 16 Mbytes of storage per processor, for example, would have lev1WS sizes of 18 Kbytes and 90 Kbytes for 2-D and 3-D grids, respectively. Furthermore, the size of lev1WS can actually be kept constant through the use of blocking techniques.

The fact that fitting the lev2WS (a processor's entire partition of the grid) in the cache has a substantial impact on the performance of CG brings up an interesting design issue. Particularly under time-constrained scaling, the data set per processor may not be very large on large-scale machines, so that it may make sense to build larger caches and fit the lev2WS in the cache. This amounts to fitting the entire data set in cache memory, so that there is no need for DRAM memory. While this may be an interesting design point for very large-scale machines, we restrict ourselves here to a more conservative model where the per-processor data set is much larger than the cache.

4.3 Grain Size

Communication Costs: The total amount of computation in one CG iteration on an $n \times n$ 2-D grid is roughly $10n^2$ operations. Each processor owns a $n/\sqrt{P} \times n/\sqrt{P}$ grid of points. The $4n/\sqrt{P}$ points along the perimeter must be communicated to neighboring processors in every iteration. The computation to communication ratio is thus $5n/(2\sqrt{P})$, and once again depends only on the grain size. For the 1 Mbyte grain size of our prototypical problem, the ratio would be roughly 300 FLOPs per word. This high ratio, combined with the fact that the communication latencies can be easily hidden due to the very regular structure of the computation, make a 1 Mbyte per processor grain size quite appropriate for CG on 2-D grid problems.

For a 3-D grid problem, each processor would own a 3-D subgrid that is $n/\sqrt[3]{P}$ on a side. The processor would have to communicate the values on the 6 2-D faces of its subgrid to other processors. The computation to communication ratio would be $7n/(3\sqrt[3]{P})$, yielding a ratio of roughly 50 for the prototypical problem. This ratio is not as easily sustained as the ratio for 2-D problems, but it is still feasible.

Load Balance and Concurrency: The regularity of a grid computation makes load balancing quite simple. The only limitation on concurrency is the global sum that accompanies the two dot product operations. Given our assumptions about the costs of interprocessor communication and processor synchronization, the cost of the fully parallel portion should dwarf the cost of the less parallel global sum in the prototypical problem. Thus, the problem exposes sufficient concurrency for 1024 processors.

We should note that many important problems (e.g., unstructured problems that model complex physical structures) will not be nearly as regular as the 2-D and 3-D grids considered here. This reduced regularity will require more sophisticated strategies for partitioning the problem among a set of processors. This will have three important effects. First, the computational load balance among the processors will certainly not be as good. Second, the computation to communication ratio for problems with the same data set size will most likely be significantly higher. Finally, the partitioning step itself will represent a computational overhead whose cost increases with the number of processors. This partitioning step will generally possess limited parallelism, so the presence of more processors would not necessarily reduce its cost.

We conclude from the above discussion that a 1024 processor machine with 1 Mbyte of memory per processor would be quite appropriate for regular 2-D problems. The appropriate grain size for irregular problems or 3-D problems may be somewhat larger.

Desirable Grain Size: Let us see if we can use a 16K-processor machine with only 16 Kbytes or memory each to solve a 1 Gbyte problem. The computation to communication ratios increase to roughly 75 and 20 for 2-D and 3-D grids, respectively. Thus, the desirable grain size is somewhere between 1 Mbyte an 16 Kbytes for the prototypical CG problem as well.

Scaling: Now consider how the appropriate grain size would change with a scaled problem. The important thing to note here is that the computation to communication ratio for both 2-D and 3-D grid problems depends only on the volume of data on one processor, and is independent of the number of processors. Thus, if a grain size of 1 Mbyte per processor produces sustainable communication volumes on P processors, then it would also produce sustainable volumes on $2P$ processors, given a problem that is twice as large. The one other issue that might be relevant when considering scaling is the cost of the global sum operation in the dot products. While this cost clearly increases with P, the rate of increase ($O(\log P)$) is sufficiently slow that, under our machine model, this cost would not be a significant performance drain for practical P.

4.4 Summary

We therefore conclude that the conjugate gradient method requires a somewhat larger grain size than dense LU factorization.

The desirable grain is still quite small, however. A 1 Mbyte per processor data set size appears reasonable.

5 Transform Methods (FFT)

The next computation we consider is the 1D complex fast Fourier transform (FFT). Our analysis in this section also applies to the complex 2D and 3D FFT. These computations form the computational core of a wide variety of applications from the fields of image and signal processing as well as climate modeling.

5.1 Description of Computation

The structure of the FFT computation is captured by the familiar butterfly network. For an $N = 2^M$ point FFT, the computation proceeds in M stages, where in stage s, pairs of data points at a distance of 2^s interact with each other to produce the points at stage $s + 1$.

In a straightforward parallel implementation, each processor handles a contiguous set of points. During the first $\log N - \log P$ stages of the butterfly, processors work locally with no interprocessor communication. In each of the remaining $\log P$ stages, all N points are exchanged between processors,

Unfortunately, the simple, so-called radix-2 FFT computation described above, makes very poor use of the memory system. It sweeps through all N points in one stage of the butterfly before moving on the next stage, thus making little use of the processor cache. In the last $\log P$ stages of the butterfly, the processors perform only a single computation step on each communicated point, thus producing a very low computation to communication ratio. Both the cache usage and the computation to communication ratio can be improved dramatically by increasing the *radix* of the computation (see [1] and [12]). Increasing the radix is equivalent to 'unrolling' the butterfly, performing multiple butterfly stages in a single pass through the data. A radix-8 FFT, for example, would combine three butterfly stages into a single stage, where each step in this new stage performs operations on 8 points simultaneously. A radix-r FFT would combine $\log r$ butterfly stages into a single stage, operating on r points simultaneously.

An efficient parallel FFT is therefore structured as follows. To minimize interprocessor communication, the overall computation is performed with as large a radix as possible. This turns out to be radix-D, where D is the number of points assigned to each processor (i.e., $D = N/P$). Thus, the $\log N$ stages of the butterfly are grouped into sets of $\log D$ stages. At each radix-D stage, a processor receives D points from other processors, performs $\log D$ stages of the butterfly on these points, and sends the resulting D data points to the processors that use them in the next stage.

To make good use of the processor cache, the radix-D stages are further subdivided into smaller internal groups. For example, a processor might perform the $\log D$ stages in the radix-D computation three-at-a-time, essentially performing a radix-8 computation within the radix-D computation. We call this smaller radix the internal radix. This further sub-division produces a smaller processor working set than would be present if all $\log D$ stages were performed in a single sweep. We use this more efficient parallel FFT in the results we present below.

5.2 Working Set Hierarchy

The prototypical 1 Gbyte problem corresponds to a 64 million point complex FFT on 1024 processors, yielding 64K points per processor.

Working set hierarchies for radix-2, radix-8, and radix-32 FFT computations on this data set are shown in Figure 5.

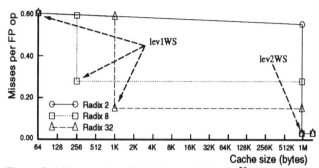

Figure 5: Miss rates for 1D FFT, $n = 64M = 2^{26}$, $PE = 1024$.

The first and most important working set (lev1WS) contains the set of data items needed to perform a single step of a stage sweep. If the internal radix is 2, the lev1WS simply consists of the two data points that are at distance 2^s from each other. The miss rate is 0.6 misses per op when the lev1WS with radix 2 fits in the cache. For internal radices of 8 and 32, lev1WS consists of the relevant 8 or 32 data points, and brings the miss rates to roughly 0.25 and 0.15 misses per operation, respectively. These misses can be easily prefetched. Thus, a small cache is sufficient to significantly reduce the miss rate for parallel FFT.

The only other working set in a parallel FFT (lev2WS) is simply the entire data set assigned to a processor.

Scaling: The size of the important, level 1 working set depends only on the internal radix. The choice of internal radix is independent of the problem size and the machine size, and a small radix suffices to keep the capacity miss rate small. Consequently, a small cache (a few Kbytes) is sufficient for any problem size or machine size. The lev2WS depends on N and P, but is not expected to fit in a cache.

5.3 Grain Size

Communication Costs: The computation to communication ratio is most easily estimated by considering the operations that a processor performs in a single stage of the radix-D computation ($D = N/P$). Within a single stage, a processor performs $5D \log D$ operations, and then communicates all $2D$ double-words computed in that stage to other processors. Thus, the overall computation to communication ratio $\frac{5}{2} \log D = \frac{5}{2} \log \frac{N}{P}$, and depends only the grain size $\frac{N}{P}$.

This ratio is unfortunately inexact due to quantization effects. Consider our prototypical problem, with 1024 processors and 64K points per processor. The resulting radix-64K FFT groups the butterfly into sets of $\log 64K$ or 16 stages. The difficulty is that the whole problem only requires $\log 64M = 26$ stages. The second stage would therefore perform only 10 stages of computation for one communication stage, less than the 16 stages assumed by the model.

The actual computation to communication ratio can be determined by noting that the whole computation performs $5N \log N$ operations, and it communicates the $2N$ words of data twice between processors. For our prototypical problem, $N = 64M$, yielding a ratio of 33. While this ratio would be sustainable if the communications were between neighbor processors, unfortunately it can be shown that communication in the FFT exhibits little locality for most processor interconnection topologies. The exception is a hypercube topology, which is becoming less and less common in large-scale parallel machines. The ratio of 33 operations per word would thus be difficult to sustain.

Load Balance and Concurrency: A very simple distribution of the FFT computation is quite adequate for load balancing. Furthermore, there is more than enough available concurrency to keep a very large number of processors busy (ignoring processor stalls due to communication).

Desirable Grain Size: We have seen that a 1 Mbyte data set per processor produces a computation to communication ratio that is difficult to sustain. A finer-grain machine would clearly exacerbate the problem. Let us therefore examine how this ratio would change if the same problem were solved on a coarser-grain machine. On a machine with one-sixteenth as many processors ($P = 64$), we find that the computation to communication ratio surprisingly does *not* change. This is an artifact of the quantization of levels discussed earlier: there are still two communication stages in the computation.

Let us now consider just how coarse the machine grain must be to produce a sustainable computation to communication ratio. If we even use the optimistic expression for computation to communication ratio of $\frac{5}{2} \log \frac{N}{P}$ derived earlier, a ratio of R requires the number of data points per processor to be $N/P = 2^{\frac{2}{5}R}$. The exponential growth rate of per-processor memory required to improve computation to communication ratios has been previously noted in [4]. The consequences of this growth rate are quite severe. Increasing the computation to communication ratio from 33 to a more easily sustained ratio of 60, for example, would require the per-processor data set to be increased to roughly 270 Mbytes. A ratio of 100, which may be required by some machines for good performance, would require approximately 18 Terabytes of data per processor. It is clearly unrealistic to try to significantly increase the computation to communication ratio by increasing the node grain size.

Scaling: Since the main factor limiting performance, the computation to communication ratio, depends only on grain size, the "desirable" grain size is essentially independent of the problem size or number of processors. MC scaling therefore produces comparable processor utilization on larger machines.

5.4 Summary

The FFT is a difficult computation for large scale parallel machines. While the FFT is easily blocked for a cache to provide high per-processor performance, the communication volume inherent in the computation is sufficiently high that communication costs will certainly dominate the execution time. While one might conclude that the solution to this high communication volume is to increase the processor grain size, unfortunately the grain size increase that would be required to significantly reduce communication volumes is unrealistically large.

6 Hierarchical N-Body Methods

The classical N-body problem is to simulate the evolution of a system of bodies (e.g. stars in a galaxy) under the forces exerted on each body by the whole system. Typical domains of application include astrophysics, electrostatics and plasma physics, among others. As in many other computational domains, hierarchical solution methods have recently attracted a lot of attention for N-body problems, since they construct efficient algorithms by taking advantage of fundamental insights into the nature of physical processes. The two most prominent hierarchical N-body methods are the Barnes-Hut and Fast Multipole methods. We shall use a three-dimensional galactic Barnes-Hut simulation as our example in this paper [10].

6.1 Description of Computation

The computation in N-body problems proceeds over a number of time-steps. Every time-step computes the forces experienced by all bodies, and uses these forces to update the positions and velocities of the bodies. The force-computation is by far the most time-consuming phase in a time-step, and we focus on it in our analysis (although our measurements include the whole application).

The main data structure used by the Barnes-Hut method is an octree which represents the computational domain. The root of the octree is a cubical space that contains all particles in the system. Internal cells of this tree represent recursively subdivided space cells, and the leaves represent individual bodies. The tree is traversed once per body to compute the net force acting on that body. The force-calculation starts at the root of the tree and conducts the following test recursively for every cell it visits. If the center of mass of the cell is far enough away from the body, the entire subtree under that cell is approximated by a single particle at the center of mass. Otherwise, the cell must be "opened" and each of its subcells visited. A cell is determined to be far enough away if the relationship $\frac{l}{d} < \theta$ is satisfied, where l is the length of a side of the cell, d is the distance of the body from the center of mass of the cell, and θ is a user-defined accuracy parameter (θ is usually between 0.5 and 1.2). In this way, a body traverses deeper down those parts of the tree which represent space that is physically close to it, and groups distant bodies at a hierarchy of length scales. For large problems, higher order moments than the center of mass (for example, quadrupole moments) are used to increase force-computation accuracy without making θ too fine. We assume the use of quadrupole moments in our discussion.

6.2 Working Set Hierarchy

There are three important levels of the working set hierarchy in these methods. These are shown in Figure 6 for a small problem simulating 1024 particles on 4 processors. We start with a smaller problem in this application than the prototypical problem used for other applications because the working sets here are measured through simulation rather than analysis, and because it is impossible to simulate the prototypical problem on our multiprocessor simulator. The small problem, however, exposes all the important characteristics and constant factors, and the scaling trends that we discuss below have been verified by simulating some larger problems and machines.

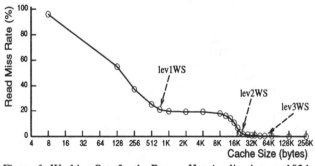

Figure 6: Working Sets for the Barnes-Hut Application: n=1024, theta=1.0, p=4, quadpole moments.

The lev1WS in this application is the amount of temporary storage used to compute an interaction between a particle and another particle/cell. It is only about 0.7 Kbytes in size. Having a cache large enough to hold the lev1WS reduces the miss rate from 100% with no cache to about 20% in most cases we have simulated. While this is a large reduction, the miss rate is still not low enough for effective performance since most of these misses are to nonlocal data, and are not predictable enough to be easily prefetched.

The lev2WS is the most important working set in the application. It comprises the amount of from the tree needed to compute the force on a single particle. These data include particle positions as well as cell positions and moments. If the partitioning of particles among processors is done appropriately, most of these data will be reused in computing the forces on successive particles. Caches large enough to hold this working set take the miss rate quite close to the inherent communication miss rate obtained with infinite caches (0.2% for this problem). For this small problem, the size of the lev2WS is 20 Kbytes.

Beyond the lev2WS, the miss rate decays much more slowly until the cache size reaches the lev3WS. The size of the lev3WS is roughly the maximum of (i) the amount of data in a processors partition and (ii) the amount of data that a processor needs to compute the forces on all the particles in its partition. Thus, the lev3WS size decreases with increasing number of processors and increases with increasing force computation accuracy (decreasing θ). However, since the lev3WS marks the culmination of a slow decrease in miss rate, and since the capacity miss rate is already very small after the lev2WS is reached, the lev3WS is not important to performance and we do not consider it further.

Scaling: A realistic problem that people run today is one with 64K particles and $\theta=1.0$. When run for 512 time-steps, this problem takes about three days on a single processor of an SGI 4D/240. We use this problem, running on 64 processors, as the starting point for our discussion of scaling. The lev1WS and lev2WS sizes for this problem are 0.7 Kbytes and 32 Kbytes, respectively.

The total data set size increases linearly with the number of particles, and is about 230 bytes per particle when quadrupole moments are used. It is independent of θ and essentially independent of the number of processors.

The lev1WS stays at 0.7 Kbytes independent of the number of particles, the number of processors, and θ. It changes slightly only with the order of moments used, and hence with the nature of an individual interactions.

The size of the important lev2WS is proportional to the number of interactions computed per particle, which is of order $\frac{1}{\theta^2} \log n$ [3]. The lev2WS therefore scales very slowly with the number of particles n, more quickly with the accuracy parameter θ, and is independent of the number of processors p. The constant of proportionality in the above size expression is about 6 Kbytes. How the lev2WS scales with larger problems therefore depends on how n and θ are scaled, as we examine below.

Under memory-constrained (MC) scaling, n would increase linearly with p. If no other parameters are scaled, the size of the lev2WS grows very slowly, going from 32 Kbytes with 64K particles to 40 Kbytes with a million particles (about the largest number of particles that people run on the largest parallel machines today) and to only 60 Kbytes with a billion particles (inconceivable today). Scaling only n, however, is naive. In practice, all of n, θ and the time-step resolution Δt are likely to be scaled simultaneously, in order to scale their contributions to the overall simulation error at the same rate [9]. This leads to the following rule: If n is scaled by a factor of s, Δt must be scaled by a factor of $\frac{1}{\sqrt{s}}$ and θ by a factor of $\frac{1}{\sqrt[3]{s}}$ when quadrupole moments are used. A caveat is that θ is likely to be decreased at this rate only up to a certain extent ($\theta=0.5$ or so), at which point higher order moments such as octopole moments would be used to increase force computation accuracy without reducing θ much.

The lev2WS grows faster with MC scaling under this realistic parameter scaling rule, since θ—the dominant contributor to the working set size—is also scaled. Even under this model, a billion particle problem (θ=0.6, octopole moments) would have a lev2WS of under 300 Kbytes. However, MC scaling of this sort causes the execution time to grow rapidly, so that MC scaling is in fact unrealistic in practice for this application.

Time-constrained scaling, while asymptotically limited in the amount the problem can be scaled, is more realistic in practice. In this case, the contributions of changing Δt and θ to the execution time don't allow n to scale linearly with p. In fact, n scales slower than $\sqrt{k}$, where k is the factor by which p is scaled. θ therefore scales more like $\frac{1}{\sqrt[6]{k}}$. The result is that both the data set size and the lev2WS (proportional to $\frac{1}{\theta^2} log\, n$) still increase in size, but much more slowly than under memory-constrained scaling. For example, starting from our 64K particle problem on 64 processors (θ=1.0), a 1K processor machine under TC scaling would run 256K particles (θ=0.84) rather than the 1 million (θ=0.71) under MC scaling. The lev2WS size in this case is only 25 Kbytes. A million processor machine would run not a billion particles but rather only about 32 million (θ=0.6, octopole moments), and the lev2WS size would be about 140 Kbytes.

The bottom line is that although the important working set for this application is not trivial for large problems, it is still well under 100 Kbytes for the largest problems people can run today, and is likely to stay reasonably small even for problems whose solution is beyond the realm of possibilities today.

6.3 Grain Size

Communication Costs: Modeling the amount of communication in the Barnes-Hut method accurately is very difficult. Using some curve fitting from [7] and some of our own, we find that the communication per processor required to compute forces in a time-step scales as $\frac{n^{1/3}\theta^3}{p^{1/3}}log^{4/3}p$, and that the communication to computation ratio is therefore $\theta\frac{p^{2/3}}{n^{2/3}}\frac{log^{4/3}p}{log\, n}$. Every unit of computation (a particle-particle or particle-cell interaction) is equivalent to about 80 instructions when quadrupole moments are used, and every unit of communication in the above expression is 3 double words of data.

Our prototypical problem for grain size discussions, which uses 1 Mbyte of main memory per processor on a 1024 processor machine (1 Gbyte total), solves a problem with about 4.5 million particles (a very large but feasible computation by today's standards). Let us assume that $\theta = 1.0$. Every processor is responsible for about 4500 particles, and the communication to computation ratio is very small, less than 1 double word per 10,000 processor busy cycles. Since the access patterns of this application are not predictable, communication latencies might not be hidden as effectively as in the regular computations we have discussed so far. However, the communication to computation ratio is very small, and communication does not become a bottleneck until the number of particles per processor becomes very small.

Load Balance and Concurrency: The concurrency in the application scales as the number of particles n, and load imbalance is also not a significant factor until the number of particles per processor (n/p) becomes very small. Given that n is typically large (4.5 million in the prototypical problem), this also means that very large numbers of processors can be used effectively.

Desirable Grain Size: The important per-processor growth rates for this application in terms of n, θ, Δt and p are as fol-

lows. The data set size scales as $\frac{n}{p}$, the computation as $\frac{1}{\theta^2}\frac{n\, log\, n}{p\Delta t}$, the working set as $\frac{1}{\theta^2}\, log\, n$, the concurrency as n, the communication as $\frac{n^{1/3}\theta^3}{p^{1/3}\Delta t}log^{4/3}p$, and the communication to computation ratio as $\theta\frac{p^{2/3}}{n^{2/3}}\frac{log^{4/3}p}{log\, n}$.

Clearly, we would get very good speedups on our 1 Gbyte problem on a coarser-grained machine than 1 Mbyte per processor, such as the 64-processor machine with 16 Mbytes of memory per processor. However, solving a 1 Gbyte problem on 64 processors would take a very long time. Let us see what happens when we go to the finer-grained machine instead, solving the same 1 Gbyte problem with 16K processors and 64 Kbytes of memory per processor. Every processor now has about 280 particles. The communication to computation ratio increases to about 1 double word per 1000 instructions, but is clearly very small still. However, particularly given the large number of processors, load balancing may become a problem at this point. The result is that the grain size can probably be pushed to a few hundred kilobytes per processor for a 1 Gbyte problem without compromising parallel performance much.

Scaling: Finally, let us see how the desirable grain size scales with problem size. A memory-constrained scaling model, in which the processor grain size remains constant, provides high processor utilization for this application. The number of particles per processor remains the same, so load balancing is not affected, and the communication to computation ratio either increases extremely slowly (if the accuracy is not scaled as well) or stays constant (if accuracy is scaled) [8]. The cache size needed per processor grows, but is still relatively small, as we have seen. However, such memory-constrained scaling to keep the grain size constant causes the execution time to increase very rapidly. If the goal is to run a problem in the same amount of time, n does not grow nearly as quickly as p. The grain size needed therefore decreases, as does the efficiency of a node (since both communication and synchronization increase relative to computation, and the load balance gets worse).

6.4 Summary

Our results show that fine-grained machines, with well under 1 Mbyte of memory and a couple of hundred kilobytes of cache, can be very effective for this application. A couple of issues, however, may inhibit going to a very fine grain. First, for large problems, the amount of fully associative cache needed will be as large as or larger than the local memory per node. The use of realistic—set-associative or direct-mapped—caches would further increase the required cache size, resulting in an expensive design point that may not be appropriate for other kinds of computations. Preliminary results with direct-mapped caches for small problems show that the knees in the miss rate versus cache size curves are not as well-defined as with fully associative caches, and that the direct-mapped cache size required to hold the important working set is about three times as large as the corresponding fully associative cache size. Set-associative caches and data restructuring might reduce this factor of three. While we have not simulated large problems with direct-mapped caches, there is little reason to believe that the factor increase in required cache size will be much different as the problem scales.

The second issue is that although the force-calculation phase can be parallelized very efficiently on large numbers of processors, some other phases—such as building the octree and computing the moments of cells—do not yield quite as good speedups due to larger amounts of synchronization and contention that they encounter. These phases consume a small fraction of the execution time on moderately parallel machines (at least up to 512 processors for large problems), but may become significant for very fine-grained machines with very large numbers of processors.

7 Volume Rendering

Our next application is from the field of scientific visualization. Volume visualization techniques are of key importance in the analysis and understanding of multidimensional sampled data. This application, which renders volumes using optimized ray tracing techniques, uses a parallel version of the fastest known sequential algorithm for volume rendering [6].

7.1 Description of Computation

The volume to be rendered is represented by a cube of voxels (or volume elements). The outermost loop of the computation is over a series of frames or images. Successive frames correspond to changing angles between the viewer and the volume being rendered. For each frame, rays are cast from the viewing position into the volume data through every pixel in the image plane corresponding to that frame. The voxel data are resampled at evenly spaced locations along each ray by trilinearly interpolating the values of surrounding voxels. Rays are not reflected at all, but pass straight through the volume unless they encounter too much opacity and are terminated early. Finally, ray samples are composited to produce an image or frame. The goal of the application is to render individual frames in real time (30 frames/second), so that an interactive user can view the volume from arbitrarily changing positions efficiently.

7.2 Working Set Hierarchy

There are three important levels of the working set hierarchy in this application. Data reuse is afforded across sample points along a ray (lev1WS), across successive rays (lev2WS), and perhaps across successive frames (lev3WS). These working sets are shown in Figure 7 for a 256x256x113 voxel data set of a human head. While smaller than our prototypical 1 Gbyte problem (the data set is about 30 Mbytes) for reasons of simulation feasibility, this data set is a very realistic real-time challenge for today's parallel machines.

The voxel data in this application are read-only. An octree data structure is used to find the first interesting (non-transparent) voxel in a ray's path efficiently, as well as to determine whether the neighboring voxels around a sample point are interesting. The lev1WS consists of the voxel and octree data that are reused across neighboring sample points along a ray. This working set is very small: about 0.4 Kbytes. A cache that accommodates it reduces the read miss rate to about 15%, which is still too large to be acceptable, particularly since the misses are potentially to nonlocal data and the access patterns are not regular enough to be easily prefetched.

The lev2WS is the most important working set. It measures the fraction of the data used in computing a ray that is typically reused by the next ray. This reuse owes itself to the partitioning scheme, which assigns every processor a contiguous rectangular subblock of pixels in the image plane. Successive rays cast by a processor therefore pass through adjacent pixels and tend to reference many of the same voxels in the volume. The lev2WS is about 16 Kbytes for this data set, and a cache that accommodates this working set reduces the read miss rate to about 2%.

After the lev2WS is reached, the miss rate diminishes more slowly until the lev3WS is reached. The size of the lev3WS depends on how quickly the angle between the viewing position and the data set is changed between successive frames. If the change is gradual, as in our simulations, a given processor references many of the same voxels in successive frames; otherwise,

the overlap may be negligible. Thus, the lev3WS size can vary from the voxels referenced by a processor in one frame to almost the entire voxel data set. For our data set and simulations, the lev3WS is about 700 Kbytes, and a cache that accommodates it brings the miss rate down to the communication miss rate of 0.1%. The lev3WS is therefore large, but is not very important to performance and we do not consider it further.

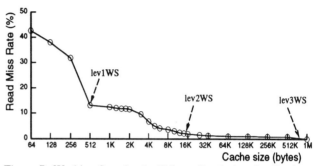

Figure 7: Working Sets for the Volume Rendering Application: 256x256x113 head, p=4.

Scaling: With n voxels along a single dimension, the data set for the volume rendering application is roughly $4n^3$ bytes. The two important parameters that might be scaled in this application are n and the number of processors p. The lev1WS size is independent of either of these. The lev2WS is also independent of p, but grows proportionally to n, corresponding to the number of voxels sampled along a ray. The size of the lev2WS is roughly $(4000 + 110*n)$ bytes. Note that n here is only the cube root of the data set size.

Since the execution time grows at the same rate as the data set size (n^3), time-constrained scaling is essentially the same as memory-constrained for this application. Thus, the important working set grows as only the cube root of the number of processors under either scaling model, with a very small constant factor of only 110 bytes. Even for a very large, 1024x1024x1024 problem, far from renderable in real time on even the largest machines today, the lev2WS is only 116 Kbytes large. For a while, also, the push in using larger machines is going to be to render relatively small data sets in real time, rather than to render bigger data sets. Finally, as data sets get larger, the octree will probably be used to skip transparent voxels along a ray even after the first nonempty voxel is found, which may reduce the size of the lev2WS. Thus, the important working set of this application is likely to remain relatively small (under 100 Kbytes or so) for a while to come.

7.3 Grain Size

Communication Costs: The most important and heavily referenced data structure, the voxel data set, is accessed in a read-only fashion. Thus, if the entire voxel data set were replicated in the local memory of every processing node, there would be essentially no communication during rendering (except the small amount of communication generated by the ray-stealing performed to ensure load balancing toward the end of the rendering phase [6]). However, such replication would imply either unreasonable amounts of local memory per processor or that large data sets cannot be run. In our shared address space implementation, the data set is not replicated at all in main memory but only to some extent in the caches. Because of this, communication is generated when accessing voxel data, since voxel data get replaced in the caches.

If the cache provided is significantly smaller than the lev3WS, as is very likely, we can assume that almost all of the voxel data that a processor accesses during a frame are not in its cache at the beginning of that frame. Since the viewing angle changes, the most reasonable data distribution across local memories is an interleaved or random one to minimize contention. Thus, the first accesses to voxel data in a frame have no more than a random chance of being satisfied in local memory, and are likely to generate communication. Two bytes of data are read per voxel, so that the total volume of communication in a frame is somewhat larger than $2n^3$ bytes (since processors overlap to some extent in the voxels they access). Since a frame involves more than $300n^3$ instructions, the computation to communication ratio is very large, close to 600 instructions per word of communicated data, independent of n or p (see the limitations of this analysis below). If caches yield reuse across frames, the computation to communication ratio will be even larger.

Our prototypical problem amounts to a 600x600x600 voxel problem on a 1024-processor machine, with every processor being responsible for about 1000 rays. Since the computation to communication ratio is independent of n or p, it is 600 instructions per word in this case as well.

Load Balance and Concurrency: After a processor has processed its statically assigned rays, it steals rays from other processors if it is idle. Stealing introduces additional synchronization and communication, and is the main source of performance loss if the number of rays stolen by a processor is large compared to the number initially assigned to it. In the prototypical problem, every processor is assigned 1000 rays, so that the amount of stealing is not significant.

Desirable Grain Size: The important per-processor growth rates for this application in terms of n and p are as follows. The data set size scales as $\frac{n^3}{p}$, the computation as $\frac{n^3}{p}$, the important working set as n, the communication as $\frac{n^3}{p}$, and the communication to computation ratio stays roughly fixed. The concurrency in the application is equal to the number of rays, which grows as n^2: There is one ray per pixel, and there are n^2 pixels in the 2-d image plane projected from the data set.

Running the 600x600x600 voxel data set on a coarser-grained machine than 1 Mbytes per processor (e.g. 64 processors with 16 Mbytes per processor) is obviously not a problem from the viewpoint of processor efficiency. However, a 64 processor machine would clearly not be able to render this data set in real time. Let us see what happens when we solve the same 600x600x600 voxel problem on a finer-grained machine, with 16K processors and 64 Kbytes of memory per processor. The communication to computation ratio (ignoring task stealing) is still about 600 instructions per word. However, every processor now processes roughly $\frac{(600\sqrt{3})^2}{16384}$ or 66 rays, likely to be too few for good load balancing without excessive stealing. As in Barnes-Hut, a grain size of a few hundred kilobytes is therefore likely to be adequate for good parallel performance on the 1 Gbyte data set.

Scaling: Finally, we examine how the desirable grain size changes as larger problems are run. If the data set size is increased by a factor of k, keeping the memory per processor or grain size fixed (and therefore scaling p by a factor of k) will cause every processor to process a smaller number of rays (decreasing by a factor of $k^{1/3}$, since the size of a ray grows by a factor of $k^{1/3}$). This is not a problem until the number of rays per processor becomes very small, in which case increased synchronization and communication due to task stealing detract from performance. To maintain the same number of rays per processor and hence roughly the same processor efficiency, the amount of memory per processor (the grain size) must increase

by a factor of $k^{1/3}$ when the data set size is increased by k (the working set size per processor also grows as $k^{1/3}$). That is, the number of processors increases by a factor of $k^{2/3}$ rather than k. However, the execution time grows as $k^{1/3}$ as well in this case, which is not desirable from the viewpoint of real-time rendering.

Fortunately, the number of rays needed per processor to retain high processor efficiencies is small. And we mentioned earlier that the data set sizes are not likely to get too much larger in the near future, since the goal today is still to get moderately sized data sets rendered in real time. Thus, the memory needed per processor for this application is small and likely to remain so for some time to come.

7.4 Summary

Our general conclusion is that fine-grained machines (under 1 Mbyte of memory per processor) are likely to perform very well on this application.

8 Discussion

We begin our discussion by bringing together the results for the various applications. Table 1 shows the growth rates for the most important application characteristics, including data set sizes, total operations performed on these data, available concurrency, communication volumes, and the sizes of the most important working sets. Table 2 then shows the implications of these data, including the sizes of the important working sets for our prototypical 1 Gbyte, 1024 processor problem, expressed as a function of total data size (DS), and the desirable amounts of per-processor memory. Table 2 also shows growth rates for both as the problem is scaled. (We note that for the FFT the 'desirable' grain size of 1 Mbyte is not really all that desirable, but that enormous increases would be required to improve the situation.)

Our results show that reasonably fine-grained parallel machines, with memory of 1 Mbyte per processor or less, can be effective for the application classes studied here. However, we now briefly discuss some pragmatic reasons, both hardware and software, why coarser-grained machines are likely to continue being built in the near term.

On the hardware side, one reason is the fact that memory chips have large capacity but currently provide very narrow interfaces (1–8 bits wide). Thus, building the high-bandwidth memory systems that are needed by high-performance processors requires the use of multiple memory chips in parallel, resulting in substantial amounts of total memory per node. Another reason is that the distributed-address-space programming model that is common in today's large-scale parallel machines severely limits the ability of a processor to efficiently access memory that is not local to it. Such a model also makes fine-grained parallel computation less attractive because of the large fixed costs associated with exchanging data between processors. A final hardware reason is the relative costs of processors and memory. It makes little sense, for example, to place $50 worth of memory on a $1000 node. A machine with 4 times as much memory would not cost significantly more and would be much more versatile. Many of these reasons may disappear, however, due to continually improving technology and integration levels. Within a decade, we are likely to see chips with more than 100 million transistors each [5]. This will allow processors, caches, and memory to reside on the same chip. Decisions about how to partition the transistors on a chip among processor, cache, and memory will then involve entirely different tradeoffs. The data presented in this paper show that fine-grain machines should be seriously considered, since applications can use them effectively.

Table 1: Important application growth rates.

Application	Data	Ops	Concurrency	Communication	Important Working Set
LU	n^2	n^3	n^2	$n^2\sqrt{P}$	const.
CG	n^2	n^2	n^2	$n\sqrt{P}$	const.
FFT	n	$n\log n$	n	$n\log P$	const.
Barnes-Hut	n	$\frac{1}{\theta^2}n\,log\,n$	n	$n^{1/3}\theta^3 p^{2/3}log^{4/3}p$	$\frac{1}{\theta^2}\log n$
Volume Rendering	n^3	n^3	n^2	n^3	n

Table 2: Summary of important application parameters (DS is total data set size).

Application	Cache		Memory	
	Growth Rate	Size for 1G prob on 1K P	Growth Rate	Desirable grain size
LU	const.	8K	const.	$< 1M$
CG	const.	5K	const.	1M
FFT	const.	4K	const.	1M
Barnes-Hut	$\log DS$	45K	const.	$< 1M$
Volume Rendering	$\sqrt[3]{DS}$	70K	$\sqrt[3]{DS}$	$< 1M$

On the software side, reasons for coarser grain nodes include support for a sophisticated node operating system, support for multiprogramming, and the flexibility to run applications with limited parallelism more effectively. However, these capabilities are not necessarily as important on large-scale machines as they are on small ones.

In summary, the grain size issue is a complex one. In this paper, we have taken an applications-oriented view; the other issues must also be taken into account to reach more definitive conclusions about how to actually build large-scale parallel machines. We are currently exploring these other tradeoffs. Overall, it may turn out that designs that split the cost equally between processors and memory will be the most competitive, in that they will be within a small constant factor of the optimal design for any given application.

9 Concluding Remarks

We have presented an application-driven study of issues relevant to determining the appropriate distribution of resources among processors, cache, and main memory for large-scale multiprocessors. We first showed that all of the application classes we studied have a hierarchy of working sets, each of whose size, performance impact and scaling properties we identified. Our conclusion is that relatively small (in some cases trivially small) caches suffice for all the applications. One reason for this is the bimodality in the working sets of applications: The working sets are either very small, so that small caches suffice, or too large to be expected to fit in caches. Fortunately, the small working sets have the most impact on performance.

Next, we examined certain other important characteristics of the computations—communication, computation, data requirements, concurrency, and load balancing behavior—to reflect upon desirable grain sizes for machines to support these computations effectively. We found that relatively fine-grained machines, with large numbers of processors and small amounts of cache and memory per processor, are appropriate for all of the applications.

References

[1] David H. Bailey. FFTs in External or Hierarchical Memories. *Journal of Supercomputing*, 4:23–25, 1990.

[2] Geoffrey Fox et al. *Solving Problems on Concurrent Processors, Volume I: General Techniques and Regular Problems*. Prentice Hall, 1988.

[3] Lars Hernquist. Hierarchical N-body methods. *Computer Physics Communications*, 48:107–115, 1988.

[4] H.T. Kung. Memory requirements for balanced computer architectures. In *Proceedings of the 13th Annual International Symposium on Computer Architecture*, 1986.

[5] Gordon Moore. VLSI: Some fundamental challenges. *IEEE Spectrum*, pages 30–37, April 1979.

[6] Jason Nieh and Marc Levoy. Volume rendering on scalable shared-memory MIMD architectures. In *Proceedings of the Boston Workshop on Volume Visualization*, October 1992.

[7] John K. Salmon. *Parallel Hierarchical N-body Methods*. PhD thesis, California Institute of Technology, December 1990.

[8] Jaswinder Pal Singh, John L. Hennessy, and Anoop Gupta. Implications of hierarchical N-body techniques for multiprocessor architecture. Technical Report CSL-TR-92-506, Stanford University, 1992.

[9] Jaswinder Pal Singh, John L. Hennessy, and Anoop Gupta. Scaling parallel programs for multiprocessors: Methodology and examples. *IEEE Computer*, 26(7), July 1993. To appear. Also Stanford Univeristy Tech. Report no. CSL-TR-92-541, 1992.

[10] Jaswinder Pal Singh, Chris Holt, Takashi Totsuka, Anoop Gupta, and John L. Hennessy. Load balancing and data locality in hierarchical N-body methods. *Journal of Parallel and Distributed Computing*. To appear. Prelim. version available as Stanford Univeristy Tech. Report no. CSL-TR-92-505, Jan. 1992.

[11] R. van de Geijn. Massively parallel LINPACK benchmark on the Intel Touchstone Delta and iPSC/860 systems. Technical Report CS-91-28, University of Texas at Austin, August 1991.

[12] Charles van Loan. *Computational Frameworks for the Fast Fourier Transform*. SIAM, 1992.

SESSION 3:

TLBs and
Memory
Management

Design Tradeoffs for Software-Managed TLBs

David Nagle, Richard Uhlig, Tim Stanley,
Stuart Sechrest, Trevor Mudge & Richard Brown

Department of Electrical Engineering and Computer Science
University of Michigan
e-mail: uhlig@eecs.umich.edu, bassoon@eecs.umich.edu

Abstract

An increasing number of architectures provide virtual memory support through software-managed TLBs. However, software management can impose considerable penalties, which are highly dependent on the operating system's structure and its use of virtual memory. This work explores software-managed TLB design tradeoffs and their interaction with a range of operating systems including monolithic and microkernel designs. Through hardware monitoring and simulation, we explore TLB performance for benchmarks running on a MIPS R2000-based workstation running Ultrix, OSF/1, and three versions of Mach 3.0.

Results: New operating systems are changing the relative frequency of different types of TLB misses, some of which may not be efficiently handled by current architectures. For the same application binaries, total TLB service time varies by as much as an order of magnitude under different operating systems. Reducing the handling cost for kernel TLB misses reduces total TLB service time up to 40%. For TLBs between 32 and 128 slots, each doubling of the TLB size reduces total TLB service time up to 50%.

Keywords: Translation Lookaside Buffer (TLB), Simulation, Hardware Monitoring, Operating Systems.

1 Introduction

Many computers support virtual memory by providing hardware-managed translation lookaside buffers (TLBs). However, some computer architectures, including the MIPS RISC [1] and the DEC Alpha [2], have shifted TLB management responsibility into the operating system. These software-managed TLBs can simplify hardware design and provide greater flexibility in page table structure, but typically have slower refill times than hardware-managed TLBs [3].

At the same time, operating systems such as Mach 3.0 [4] are moving functionality into user processes and making greater use of virtual memory for mapping data structures held within the kernel. These and related operating system trends place greater stress upon the TLB by increasing miss rates and, hence, decreasing overall system performance.

This work was supported by Defense Advanced Research Projects Agency under DARPA/ARO Contract Number DAAL03-90-C-0028 and a National Science Foundation Graduate Fellowship.

This paper explores these issues by examining design tradeoffs for software-managed TLBs and their impact, in conjunction with various operating systems, on overall system performance. To examine issues which cannot be adequately modeled with simulation, we have developed a system analysis tool called Monster, which enables us to monitor actual systems. We have also developed a novel TLB simulator called Tapeworm, which is compiled directly into the operating system so that it can intercept all of the actual TLB misses caused by both user process and OS kernel memory references. The information that Tapeworm extracts from the running system is used to obtain TLB miss counts and to simulate different TLB configurations.

The remainder of this paper is organized as follows: Section 2 examines previous TLB and OS research related to this work. Section 3 describes our analysis tools, Monster and Tapeworm. The MIPS R2000 TLB structure and its performance under Ultrix, OSF/1 and Mach 3.0 is examined in Section 4. Experiments, analysis and hardware-based performance improvements are presented in Section 5. Section 6 summarizes our conclusions.

2 Related Work

By caching page table entries, TLBs greatly speed up virtual-to-physical address translations. However, memory references that require mappings not in the TLB result in misses that must be serviced either by hardware or by software. In their 1985 study, Clark and Emer examined the cost of hardware TLB management by monitoring a VAX-11/780. For their workloads, 5% to 8% of a user program's run time was spent handling TLB misses [5].

More recent papers have investigated the TLB's impact on user program performance. Chen, Borg and Jouppi [6], using traces generated from the SPEC benchmarks, determined that the amount of physical memory mapped by the TLB is strongly linked to the TLB miss rate. For a reasonable range of page sizes, the amount of the address space that could be mapped was more important than the page size chosen. Talluri et al. [7] have shown that although older TLBs (as in the VAX-11/780) mapped large regions of memory, TLBs in newer architectures like the MIPS do not. They showed that increasing the page size from 4 KBytes to 32 KBytes decreases the TLB's contribution to CPI by a factor of at least 3[1].

---

1. The TLB contribution is as high as 1.7 cycles per instruction for some benchmarks.

Operating system references also have a strong impact on TLB miss rates. Clark and Emer's measurements showed that although only 18% of all memory references were made by the operating system, these references resulted in 70% of all TLB misses. Several recent papers [8-10] have pointed out that changes in the structure of operating systems are altering the utilization of the TLB. For example, Anderson et al. [8] compared an old-style monolithic operating system (Mach 2.5) and a newer microkernel operating system (Mach 3.0), and found a 600% increase in TLB misses requiring a full kernel entry. Kernel TLB misses were far and away the most frequently invoked system primitive for the Mach 3.0 kernel.

This work distinguishes itself from previous work through its focus on software-managed TLBs and its examination of the impact of changing operating system technology on TLB design. Unlike hardware-managed TLB misses, which have a relatively small refill penalty, the design trade-offs for software-managed TLBs are rather complex. Our measurements show that the cost of handling a single TLB miss on a DECstation 3100 running Mach 3.0 can vary from 20 to more than 400 cycles. Because of this wide variance in service times, it is important to analyze the frequency of various types of TLB misses, their cost and the reasons behind them. The particular mix of TLB miss types is highly dependent on the implementation of the operating system. We therefore focus on the operating system in our analysis and discussion.

3 Analysis Tools and Experimental Environment

To monitor and analyze TLB behavior for benchmark programs running on a variety of operating systems, we have developed a hardware monitoring system called Monster and a TLB simulator called Tapeworm. The remainder of this section describes these tools and the experimental environment in which they are used.

3.1 System Monitoring with Monster

The Monster monitoring system enables comprehensive analyses of the interaction between operating systems and architectures. Monster is comprised of a monitored DECstation 3100[1], an attached logic analyzer and a controlling workstation. Monster's capabilities are described more completely in [11].

In this study, we used Monster to obtain the TLB miss handling costs by instrumenting each OS kernel with marker instructions that denoted the entry and exit points of various code segments (e.g. kernel entry, TLB miss handler, kernel exit). The instrumented kernel was then monitored with the logic analyzer whose state machine detected and dumped the marker instructions and a nanosecond-resolution timestamp into the logic analyzer's trace buffer. Once filled, the trace buffer was post-processed to obtain a histogram of time spent in the different invocations of the TLB miss handlers. This technique allowed us to time code paths with far greater accuracy than can be obtained using a system clock with its coarser resolution or, as is often done, by repeating a code fragment N times and then dividing the total time spent by N.

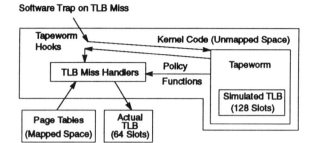

Figure 1: Tapeworm

The Tapeworm TLB simulator is built into the operating system and is invoked whenever there is a real TLB miss. The simulator uses the real TLB misses to simulate its own TLB configuration(s). Because the simulator resides in the operating system, Tapeworm captures the dynamic nature of the system and avoids the problems associated with simulators driven by static traces.

3.2 TLB Simulation with Tapeworm

Many previous TLB studies have used trace-driven simulation to explore design trade-offs [5-7, 12]. However, there are a number of difficulties with trace-driven TLB simulation. First, it is difficult to obtain accurate traces. Code annotation tools like pixie [13] or AE [14] generate user-level address traces for a single task. However, more complex tools are required in order to obtain realistic system-wide address traces that account for multiprocess workloads and the operating system itself [5, 15]. Second, trace-driven simulation can consume considerable processing and storage resources. Some researchers have overcome the storage resource problem by consuming traces on-the-fly [6, 15]. This technique requires that system operation be suspended for extended periods of time while the trace is processed, thus introducing distortion at regular intervals. Third, trace-driven simulation assumes that address traces are invariant to changes in the structural parameters or management policies[2] of a simulated TLB. While this may be true for cache simulation (where misses are serviced by hardware state machines), it is not true for software-managed TLBs where a miss (or absence thereof) directly changes the stream of instruction and data addresses flowing through the processor. Because the code that services a TLB miss can itself induce a TLB miss, the interaction between a change in TLB structure and the resulting system address trace can be quite complex.

We have overcome these problems by compiling our TLB simulator, Tapeworm, directly into the OSF/1 and Mach 3.0 operating system kernels. Tapeworm relies on the fact that all TLB misses in an R2000-based DECstation 3100 are handled by software. We modified the operating systems' TLB miss handlers to call the Tapeworm code via procedural "hooks" after every miss. This mechanism passes the relevant information about all user and kernel TLB misses directly to the Tapeworm simulator. Tapeworm uses this information to maintain its own data structures and to simulate other possible TLB configurations.

---

1. The DECstation 3100 contains an R2000 microprocessor (16.67 MHz) and 16 Megabytes of memory.

2. Structural parameters include the page size, the number of TLB slots and the partition of TLB slots into pools reserved for different purposes. Management policies include the placement policy (direct mapped, 2-way set-associative, fully-associative, etc.) and the replacement policy (FIFO, LRU, random, etc.).

Benchmark	Description
compress	Uncompresses and compresses a 7.7 Megabyte video clip.
IOzone	A sequential file I/O benchmark that writes and then reads a 10 Megabyte file. Written by Bill Norcott.
jpeg_play	The xloadimage program written by Jim Frost. Displays four JPEG images.
mab	John Ousterhout's Modified Andrew Benchmark [9].
mpeg_play	mpeg_play V2.0 from the Berkeley Plateau Research Group. Displays 610 frames from a compressed video file [23].
ousterhout	John Ousterhout's benchmark suite from [9].
video_play	A modified version of mpeg_play that displays 610 frames from an uncompressed video file.

Operating System	Description
Ultrix	Version 3.1 from Digital Equipment Corporation.
OSF/1	OSF/1 1.0 is the Open Software Foundation's version of Mach 2.5.
Mach 3.0	Carnegie Mellon University's version mk77 of the kernel and uk38 of the UNIX server.
Mach3+AFSin	Same as Mach 3.0, but with the AFS cache manager (CM) running in the UNIX server.
Mach3+AFSout	Same as Mach 3.0, but with the AFS cache manager running as a separate task outside of the UNIX server. Not all of the CM functionality has been moved into this server task.

Table 1: Benchmarks and Operating Systems

Benchmarks were compiled with the Ultrix C compiler version 2.1 (level 2 optimization). Inputs were tuned so that each benchmark takes approximately the same amount of time to run (100-200 seconds under Mach 3.0). All measurements cited are the average of three runs.

A simulated TLB can be either larger or smaller than the actual TLB. Tapeworm ensures that the actual TLB only holds entries available in the simulated TLB. For example, to simulate a TLB with 128 slots using only 64 actual TLB slots (Figure 1), Tapeworm maintains an array of 128 virtual-to-physical address mappings and checks each memory reference that misses the actual TLB to determine if it would have also missed the larger, simulated one. Thus, Tapeworm maintains a strict inclusion property between the actual and simulated TLBs. Tapeworm controls the actual TLB management policies by supplying placement and replacement functions called by the operating system miss handlers. It can simulate TLBs with fewer entries than the actual TLB by providing a placement function that never utilizes certain slots in the actual TLB. Tapeworm uses this same technique to restrict the associativity of the actual TLB[1]. By combining these policy functions with adherence to the inclusion property, Tapeworm can

---

1. The actual R2000 TLB is fully-associative, but varying degrees of associativity can be emulated by using certain bits of a mapping's virtual page number to restrict the slot (or set of slots) into which the mapping may be placed.

Operating System	Run Time (sec)	Total Number of TLB Misses	Total TLB Service Time (sec)*	Ratio to Ultrix TLB Service Time
Ultrix 3.1	583	9,177,401	11.82	1.0
OSF/1	892	11,691,398	51.85	4.39
Mach 3.0	975	24,349,121	80.01	6.77
Mach3+AFSin	1,371	33,933,413	106.56	9.02
Mach3+AFSout	1,517	36,649,834	134.71	11.40

Table 2: Total TLB Misses Across the Benchmarks

The total run time and number of TLB misses incurred by the seven benchmark programs. Although the same application binaries were run on each of the operating systems, there is a substantial difference in the number of TLB misses and their corresponding service times.

* Time time based on measured median time to service TLB miss.

---

simulate the performance of a wide range of different-sized TLBs with different degrees of associativity and a variety of placement and replacement policies.

The Tapeworm design avoids many of the problems with trace-driven TLB simulation cited above. Because Tapeworm is driven by procedure calls within the OS kernel, it does not require address traces at all; the various difficulties with extracting, storing and processing large address traces are completely avoided. Because Tapeworm is invoked by the machine's actual TLB miss handling code, it considers the impact of all TLB misses whether they are caused by user-level tasks or the kernel itself. The Tapeworm code and data structures are placed in unmapped memory and therefore do not distort simulation results by causing additional TLB misses. Finally, because Tapeworm changes the structural parameters and management policies of the actual TLB, the behavior of the system itself changes automatically, thus avoiding the distortion inherent in fixed traces.

3.3 Experimental Environment

All experiments were performed on an R2000-based DECstation 3100 (16.7 MHz) running three different base operating systems (Table 1): Ultrix, OSF/1, Mach 3.0. Each of these systems includes a standard UNIX file system (UFS) [16]. Two additional versions of Mach 3.0 include the Andrew file system (AFS) cache manager [17]. One version places the AFS cache manager in the Mach Unix Server while the other migrates the AFS cache manager into a separate server task.

To obtain measurements, all of the operating systems were instrumented with counters and markers. For TLB simulation, Tapeworm was imbedded in the OSF/1 and Mach 3.0 kernels. Because the standard TLB handlers for OSF/1 and Mach 3.0 implement somewhat different management policies, we modified OSF/1 to implement the same policies as Mach 3.0.

Throughout the paper we use the benchmarks listed in Table 1. The same benchmark binaries were used on all of the operating systems. Each measurement cited in this paper is the average of three trials.

4 OS Impact on Software-Managed TLBs

Operating system references have a strong influence on TLB performance. Yet, few studies have examined these effects, with most confined to a single operating system [3, 5]. However, differences between operating systems can be substantial. To illustrate this point, we ran our benchmark suite on each of the operating systems listed in Table 1. The results (Table 2) show that although the same application binaries were run on each system, there is significant variance in the number of TLB misses and total TLB service time. Some of these increases are due to differences in the functionality between operating systems (i.e. UFS vs. AFS). Other increases are due to the structure of the operating systems. For example, the monolithic Ultrix spends only 11.82 seconds handling TLB misses while the microkernel-based Mach 3.0 spends 80.01 seconds.

Notice that while the total number of TLB misses increases 4 fold (from 9,177,401 to 36,639,834 for AFSout), the total time spent servicing TLB misses increases 11.4 times. This is due to the fact that software-managed TLB misses fall into different categories, each with its own associated cost. For this reason, it is important to understand page table structure, its relationship to TLB miss handling and the frequencies and costs of different types of misses.

4.1 Page Tables and Translation Hardware

OSF/1 and Mach 3.0 both implement a linear page table structure (Figure 2). Each task has its own level 1 (L1) page table, which is maintained by machine-independent pmap code [18]. Because the user page tables can require several megabytes of space, they are themselves stored in the virtual address space. This is supported through level 2 (L2 or kernel) page tables, which also map other kernel data. Because kernel data is relatively large and sparse, the L2 page tables are also mapped. This gives rise to a 3-level page table hierarchy and four different page table entry (PTE) types.

The R2000 processor contains a 64-slot, fully-associative TLB, which is used to cache recently-used PTEs. When the R2000 translates a virtual address to a physical address, the relevant PTE must be held by the TLB. If the PTE is absent, the hardware invokes a trap to a software TLB miss handling routine that finds and inserts the missing PTE into the TLB. The R2000 supports two different types of TLB miss vectors. The first, called the user TLB (uTLB) vector, is used to trap on missing translations for L1U pages. This vector is justified by the fact TLB misses on L1U PTEs are typically the most frequent [3]. All other TLB miss types (such as those caused by references to kernel pages, invalid pages or read-only pages) and all other interrupts and exceptions trap to a second vector, called the generic exception vector.

TLB Miss Type	Ultrix	OSF/1	Mach 3.0
L1U	16	20	20
L1K	333	355	294
L2	494	511	407
L3	———	354	286
Modify	375	436	499
Invalid	336	277	267

Table 3: Costs for Different TLB Miss Types

This table shows the number of machine cycles (at 60 ns/cycle) required to service different types of TLB misses. To determine these costs, Monster was used to collect a 128K-entry histogram of timings for each type of miss. We separate TLB miss types into the six categories described below. Note that Ultrix does not have L3 misses because it implements a 2-level page table.

L1U	TLB miss on a level 1 user PTE.
L1K	TLB miss on a level 1 kernel PTE.
L2	TLB miss on level 2 PTE. This can only occur after a miss on a level 1 user PTE.
L3	TLB miss on a level 3 PTE. Can occur after either a level 2 miss or a level 1 kernel miss.
Modify	A page protection violation.
Invalid	An access to an page marked as invalid (page fault).

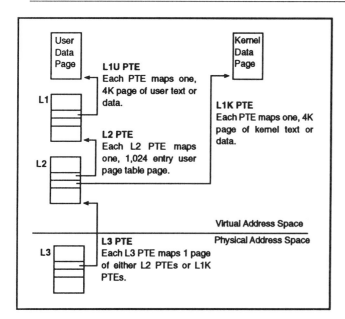

Figure 2: Page Table Structure in OSF/1 and Mach 3.0

The Mach page tables form a 3-level structure with the first two levels residing in virtual (mapped) space. The top of the page table structure holds the user pages which are mapped by level 1 user (L1U) PTEs. These L1U PTEs are stored in the L1 page table with each task having its own set of L1 page tables.

Mapping the L1 page tables are the level 2 (L2) PTEs. They are stored in the L2 page tables which hold both L2 PTEs and level 1 kernel (L1K) PTEs. In turn, the L2 pages are mapped by the level 3 (L3) PTEs stored in the L3 page table. At boot time, the L3 page table is fixed in unmapped physical memory. This serves as an anchor to the page table hierarchy because references to the L3 page table do not go through the TLB.

The MIPS R2000 architecture has a fixed 4 KByte page size. Each PTE requires 4 bytes of storage. Therefore, a single L1 page table page can hold 1,024 L1U PTEs, or 4 Megabytes of virtual address space. Likewise, the L2 page tables can directly map either 4 Megabytes of kernel data or indirectly map 4 GBytes of L1U data.

OS	Mapped Kernel Data Structs.	Service Migration	Service Decomp.	Add. OS Services
Ultrix	Few	None	None	X Server
OSF/1	Many	None	None	X Server
Mach 3.0	Some	Some	Some	X Server
Mach3+AFSin	Some	Some	Some	X Server & AFS CM
Mach3+AFSout	Some	Some	Many	X Server & AFS CM

Table 4: Characteristics of the OS's Studied

For the purposes of this study, we define TLB miss types (Table 3) to correspond to the page table structure implemented by OSF/1 and Mach 3.0. In addition to L1U TLB misses, we define five subcategories of kernel TLB misses (L1K, L2, L3, modify and invalid). Table 3 also shows our measurements of the time required to handle the different types of TLB misses. The wide differential in costs is primarily due to the two different miss vectors and the way that the OS uses them. L1U PTEs can be retrieved within 16 cycles because they are serviced by a highly-tuned handler inserted at the uTLB vector. However, all other miss types require from about 300 to over 400 cycles because they are serviced by the generic handler residing at the generic exception vector.

The R2000 TLB hardware supports partitioning of the TLB into two sets of slots. The lower partition is intended for PTEs with high retrieval costs, while the upper partition is intended to hold more frequently-used PTEs that can be re-fetched quickly (e.g. L1U) or infrequently-referenced PTEs (e.g L3). The TLB hardware also supports random replacement of PTEs in the upper partition through a hardware index register that returns random numbers in the range 8 to 63. This effectively fixes the TLB partition at 8, so that the lower partition consists of slots 0 through 7, while the upper partition consists of slots 8 through 63.

4.2 OS Influence on TLB Performance

In the operating systems studied, there are three basic factors which account for the variation in the number of TLB misses and their associated costs (Table 4 & Figure 3). The central issues are (1) the use of mapped memory by the kernel (both for page tables and other kernel data structures), (2) the placement of functionality within the kernel, within a user-level server process (service migration) or divided among several server processes (OS decomposition) and (3) the range of functionality provided by the system (additional OS services). The rest of Section 4 uses our data to examine the relationship between these OS characteristics and TLB performance.

4.2.1 Mapping Kernel Data Structures

Mapping kernel data structures adds a new category of TLB misses: L1K misses. In the MIPS R2000 architecture, an increase in the number of L1K misses can have a substantial impact on TLB performance because each L1K miss requires several hundred cycles to service[1].

Ultrix places most of its data structures in a small, fixed portion of unmapped memory that is reserved by the OS at boot time. However, to maintain flexibility, Ultrix can draw upon the much larger virtual space if it exhausts this fixed-size unmapped memory. Table 5 shows that few L1K misses occur under Ultrix.

In contrast, OSF/1 and Mach 3.0[2] place most of their kernel data structures in mapped virtual space, forcing them to rely heavily on the TLB. Both OSF/1 and Mach 3.0 mix the L1K PTEs and L1U PTEs in the TLB's 56 upper slots. This contention produces a large number of L1K misses. Further, handling an L1K miss can result in an L3 miss[3]. In our measurements, OSF/1 and Mach 3.0 both incur more than 1.5 million L1K misses. OSF/1 must spend 62% of its TLB handling time servicing these misses while Mach 3.0 spends 37% of its TLB handling time servicing L1K misses.

4.2.2 Service Migration

In a traditional operating system kernel such as Ultrix or OSF/1 (Figure 3), all OS services reside within the kernel, with only the kernel's data structures mapped into the virtual space. Many of these services, however, can be moved into separate server tasks, increasing the modularity and extensibility of the operating system [8]. For this reason, numerous microkernel-based operating systems have been developed in recent years (e.g. Chorus [19], Mach 3.0 [4], V [20]).

By migrating these services into separate user-level tasks, operating systems like Mach 3.0 fundamentally change the behavior of the system for two reasons. First, moving OS services into user space requires both their program text and data structures to be mapped. Therefore, they must share the TLB with user tasks, possibly conflicting with the user tasks' TLB footprints. Comparing the number of L1U misses in OSF/1 and Mach 3.0, we see a 2.2 fold increase from 9.8 million to 21.5 million. This is directly due to moving OS services into mapped user space. The second change comes from moving OS data structures from mapped kernel space to mapped user space. In user space, the data structures are mapped by L1U PTEs which are handled by the fast uTLB handler (20 cycles for Mach 3.0). In contrast, the same data structures in kernel space are mapped by L1K PTEs which are serviced by the general exception (294 cycles for Mach 3.0).

4.2.3 Operating System Decomposition

Moving OS functionality into a monolithic UNIX server does not achieve the full potential of a microkernel-based operating system. Operating system functionality can be further decomposed into individual server tasks. The resulting system is more flexible and can provide a higher degree of fault tolerance.

Unfortunately, experience with fully decomposed systems has shown severe performance problems. Anderson et al. [8] compared the performance of a monolithic Mach 2.5 and a microkernel Mach 3.0 operating system with a substantial portion of the file system functionality running as a separate AFS cache manager task. Their results demonstrate a significant performance gap

---

1. From 294 to 355 cycles, depending on the operating system (Table 3).
2. Like Ultrix, Mach 3.0 reserves a portion of unmapped space for dynamic allocation of data structures. However, it appears that Mach 3.0 quickly uses this unmapped space and must begin to allocate mapped memory. Once Mach 3.0 has allocated mapped space, it does not distinguish between mapped and unmapped space despite their differing costs.
3. L1K PTEs are stored in the mapped, L2 page tables (Figure 2).

System	Total Run Time (sec)	L1U	L1K	L2	L3	Invalid	Modify	Total
Ultrix	583	9,021,420	135,847	3,828	————	16,191	115	9,177,401
OSF/1	892	9,817,502	1,509,973	34,972	207,163	79,299	42,490	11,691,398
Mach3	975	21,466,165	1,682,722	352,713	556,264	165,849	125,409	24,349,121
Mach3+AFSin	1,371	30,123,212	2,493,283	330,803	690,441	168,429	127,245	33,933,413
Mach3+AFSOut	1,517	31,611,047	2,712,979	1,042,527	987,648	168,128	127,505	36,649,834

Table 5: Number of TLB Misses

System	Total TLB Service Time (sec)	L1U	L1K	L2	L3	Invalid	Modify	% of Total Run Time
Ultrix	11.82	8.66	2.71	0.11	————	0.33	0.00	2.03%
OSF/1	51.85	11.78	32.16	1.07	4.40	1.32	1.11	5.81%
Mach3	80.01	25.76	29.68	8.61	9.55	2.66	3.75	8.21%
Mach3+AFSin	106.56	36.15	43.98	8.08	11.85	2.70	3.81	7.77%
Mach3+AFSOut	134.71	37.93	47.86	25.46	16.95	2.69	3.82	8.88%

Table 6: Time Spent Handling TLB Misses

These tables show the number of TLB misses and amount of time spent handling TLB misses for each of the operating systems studied. In Ultrix, most of the TLB misses and TLB miss time is spent servicing L1U TLB misses. However, for OSF/1 and various versions of Mach 3.0, L1K and L2 misses can overshadow the L1U miss time. The increase in Modify misses is due to OSF/1 and Mach 3.0's use of protection to implement copy-on-write memory sharing.

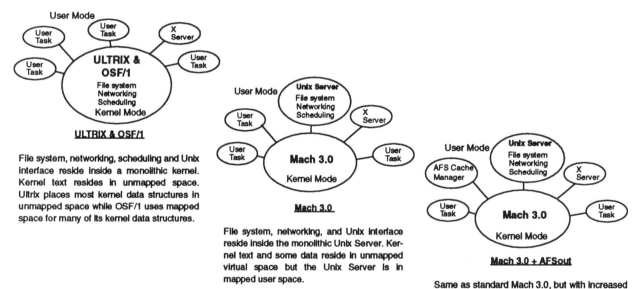

ULTRIX & OSF/1

File system, networking, scheduling and Unix interface reside inside a monolithic kernel. Kernel text resides in unmapped space. Ultrix places most kernel data structures in unmapped space while OSF/1 uses mapped space for many of its kernel data structures.

Mach 3.0

File system, networking, and Unix interface reside inside the monolithic Unix Server. Kernel text and some data reside in unmapped virtual space but the Unix Server is in mapped user space.

Mach 3.0 + AFSout

Same as standard Mach 3.0, but with increased functionality provided by a server task. The AFS Cache Manager is either inside the Unix Server or in its own, user-level server (as pictured above).

Figure 3: Monolithic and Microkernel Operating Systems

A comparison of the monolithic Ultrix and OSF/1 and the microkernel Mach 3.0. In Ultrix and OSF/1, all OS services reside inside the kernel. In Mach 3.0, these services have been moved into the UNIX server. Therefore, most of Mach 3.0's functionality resides in mapped virtual space. Mach3+AFS is a modified version of Mach 3.0 with the AFS Cache Manager residing in either the Unix Server (AFSin) or as a separate user-level server (AFSout).

between the two systems with Mach 2.5 running 36% faster than Mach 3.0, despite the fact that only a single additional server task is used. Later versions of Mach 3.0 have overcome this performance gap by integrating the AFS cache manager into the UNIX Server.

We compared our benchmarks running on the Mach3+AFSin system, against the same benchmarks running on the Mach3+AFSout system. The only structural difference between the systems is the location of the AFS cache manager. The results (Table 5) show a substantial increase in the number of both L2 and L3 misses. Many of the L3 misses are due to missing mappings needed to service L2 misses.

The L2 PTEs compete for the R2000's 8 lower TLB slots. Yet, the number of slots required is proportional to the number of tasks concurrently providing an OS service. As a result, adding just a single, tightly-coupled service task overloads the TLB's ability to map L2 page tables. Thrashing results. This increase in L2 misses will grow ever more costly as systems continue to decompose services into separate tasks.

4.2.4 Additional OS Functionality

In addition to OS decomposition and migration, many systems provide supplemental services (e.g. X, AFS, NFS, Quicktime). Each of these services, when interacting with an application, can change the operating system behavior and how it interacts with the TLB hardware.

For example, adding a distributed file service (in the form of an AFS cache manager) to the Mach 3.0 Unix server adds 10.39 seconds to the L1U TLB miss handling time (Table 6). This is due solely to the increased functionality residing in the Unix server. However, L1K misses also increase, adding 14.3 seconds. These misses are due to the additional management the Mach 3.0 kernel must provide for the AFS cache manager. Increased functionality will have an important impact on how architectures support operating systems and to what degree operating systems can increase and decompose functionality.

5 Improving TLB Performance

In this section, we examine hardware-based techniques for improving TLB performance under the operating systems analyzed in the previous section. However, before suggesting changes, it is helpful to consider the motivations behind the design of the R2000 TLB.

The MIPS R2000 TLB design is based on two principal assumptions [3]. First, L1U misses are assumed to be the most frequent (> 95%) of all TLB miss types. Second, all OS text and most of the OS data structures (with the exception of user page tables) are assumed to be unmapped. The R2000 TLB design reflects these assumptions by providing two types of TLB miss vectors: the fast uTLB vector and the much slower general exception vector (described in Section 4.1). These assumption are also reflected in the partitioning of the 64 TLB slots into two disjoint sets of 8 lower slots and 56 upper slots (also described previously). The 8 lower slots are intended to accommodate a traditional UNIX task (which requires at least three L2 PTEs) and UNIX kernel (2 PTEs for kernel data), with three L2 PTEs left for additional data segments [3].

Our measurements (Table 5) demonstrate that these design choices make sense for a traditional UNIX operating system such as Ultrix. For Ultrix, L1U misses constitute 98.3% of all misses. The remaining miss types impose only a small penalty. However,

Type of PTE Miss	Counts	Previous Total Cost from Table 6 (sec)	New Total Cost (sec)	Time Saved (sec)
Mach3+AFSin				
L1U	30,123,212	36.15	36.15	0.00
L2	330,803	8.08	0.79	7.29
L1K	2,493,283	43.98	2.99	40.99
L3	690,441	11.85	11.85	0.00
Modify	127,245	3.81	3.81	0.00
Invalid	168,429	2.70	2.70	0.00
Total	33,933,413	106.56	58.29	48.28

Table 7: Recomputed Cost of TLB Misses Given Additional Miss Vectors (Mach 3.0)

Supplying a separate interrupt vector for L2 misses and allowing the uTLB handler to service L1K misses reduces their cost to 40 and 20 cycles, respectively. Their contribution to TLB miss time drops from 8.08 and 43.98 seconds down to 0.79 and 2.99 seconds, respectively.

these assumptions break down for the OSF/1- and Mach 3.0-based systems. In these systems, the non-L1U misses account for the majority of time spent handling TLB misses. Handling these misses substantially increases the cost of software-TLB management (Table 6).

The rest of this section proposes and explores four hardware-based improvements for software-managed TLBs. First, the cost of certain types of TLB misses can be reduced by modifying the TLB vector scheme. Second, the number of L2 misses can be reduced by increasing the number of lower slots[1]. Third, the frequency of most types of TLB misses can be reduced if more total TLB slots are added to the architecture. Finally, we examine the tradeoffs between TLB size and associativity.

Throughout these experiments, software policy issues do not change from those originally implemented in Mach 3.0. The PTE replacement policy is FIFO for the lower slots and Random for the upper slots. The PTE placement policy stores L2 PTEs in the lower slots and all other PTEs in the upper slots. The effectiveness of these and other software-based techniques are examined in a related work [21].

5.1 Additional TLB Miss Vectors

The data in Table 5 show a significant increase in L1K misses for OSF/1 and Mach 3.0 when compared against Ultrix. This increase is due to both system's reliance on dynamic allocation of kernel mapped memory. The R2000's TLB performance suffers, however, because L1K misses must be handled by the costly generic exception vector which requires 294 cycles (Mach 3.0).

To regain the lost TLB performance, the architecture could vector all L1K misses through the uTLB handler, as is done in the newer R4000 processor. Based on our timing and analysis of the

---

1. The newer MIPS R2000 processor [1] implements both of these changes.

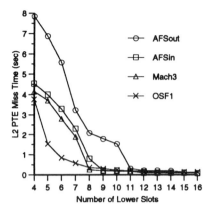

Figure 4: L2 PTE Miss Cost vs. Number of Lower Slots

The total L2 miss time for the mab benchmark under different operating systems. As the TLB reserves more lower slots for L2 PTEs, the total time spent servicing L2 misses becomes negligible.

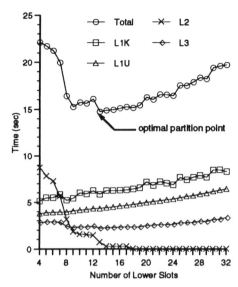

Figure 5: Total Cost of TLB Misses vs. Number of Lower TLB Slots

The total cost of TLB miss servicing is plotted against the L1U, L1K, L2 and L3 components of this total time. The number of lower TLB slots varies from 4 to 32, while the total number of TLB entries remains constant at 64.

The benchmark is video_play running under Mach 3.0.

TLB handlers, we estimate that vectoring the L1K misses through the uTLB handler would reduce the cost of L1K misses from 294 cycles (for Mach 3.0) to approximately 20 cycles.

An additional refinement would be to dedicate a separate TLB miss vector for L2 misses. We estimate the L2 miss service time would decrease from 407 cycles (Mach 3.0) to under 40 cycles.

Table 7 shows the same data for Mach3+AFSin as Table 5, but recomputed with the new cost estimates resulting from the refinements above. The result of combining these two modifications is that total TLB miss service time drops from 106.56 seconds down to 58.29 seconds. L1K service time drops 93% and L2 miss service time drops 90%. More importantly, the L1K and L2 misses no longer contribute substantially to overall TLB service time. This minor design modification enables the TLB to much more effectively support a microkernel-style operating system with multiple servers in separate address spaces.

Multiple TLB miss vectors provide additional benefits. In the generic trap handler, dozens of load and store instructions are used to save and restore a task's context. Many of these loads and stores cause cache misses which require the processor to stall. As processor speeds continue to outstrip memory access times, the CPI in this save/restore region will grow, increasing the number of wasted cycles and making non-uTLB misses much more expensive. TLB-specific miss handlers should not suffer the same performance problems because they contain only a single data reference to load the missed PTE from the memory-resident page tables.

5.2 Lower Slots & Partitioning the TLB

The MIPS R2000 TLB fixes the partition between the 8 lower slots and the 56 upper slots. This partitioning is appropriate for an operating system like Ultrix [3]. However, as OS designs migrate and decompose functionality into separate user-space tasks, 8 lower slots becomes insufficient. This is because, in a decomposed system, the OS services that reside in different user-level tasks compete by displacing each other's L2 PTE mappings from the TLB.

To better understand this effect, we measured how L2 miss rates vary depending on the number of lower TLB slots available. Tapeworm was used to vary the number of lower TLB slots from 4 to 16 while keeping the total number of TLB slots fixed at 64.

OSF/1 and all three versions of Mach 3.0 ran the mab benchmark over the range of configurations and the total number of L2 misses was recorded (Figure 4).

For each operating system, two distinct regions can be identified. The left region shows a steep decline which levels off near zero seconds. This shows a significant performance improvement for every extra lower TLB slot made available to the system, up to a certain point. For example, simply moving from 4 to 5 lower slots decreases OSF/1 L2 miss handling time by almost 50%. After 6 lower slots, the improvement slows because the TLB can hold most of the L2 PTEs required by OSF/1[1].

In contrast, the Mach 3.0 system continues to show significant improvement up to 8 lower slots. The additional 3 slots needed to bring Mach 3.0's performance in line with OSF/1 are due to the migration of OS services from the kernel to the UNIX Server in user space. In Mach 3.0, whenever a task makes a system call to the UNIX server, the task and the UNIX server must share the TLB's lower slots. In other words, the UNIX server's three L2 PTE's (text segment, data segment, stack segment) increases the lower slot requirement, for the system as a whole, to 8.

Mach3+AFSin's behavior is similar to Mach 3.0 because the additional AFS cache manager functionality is mapped by the UNIX server's L2 PTEs. However, when the AFS cache manager is decomposed into a separate user-level server, the TLB must hold three additional L2 PTEs (11 total). Figure 4 shows how Mach3+AFSout continues to improve until all 11 L2 PTEs can simultaneously reside in the TLB.

---

1. Two for kernel data structures and one each for a task's text, data and stack segments.

34

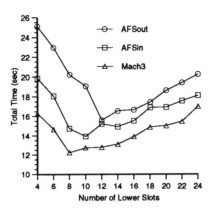

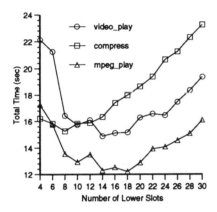

Figure 6: Optimal Partition Points for Various Operating Systems and Benchmarks

As more lower slots are allocated, fewer upper slots are available for the L1U, L1K and L3 PTEs. This yields an optimal partition point which varies with the operating system and benchmark.

The upper graph shows the average of 3 runs of the ousterhout benchmark run under 3 different operating systems. The lower graph shows the average of 3 runs for 3 different benchmarks run under Mach 3.0.

Unfortunately, increasing the size of the lower partition at the expense of the upper partition has the side-effect of increasing the number of L1U, L1K and L3 misses as shown in Figure 5. Coupling the decreasing L2 misses with the increasing L1U, L1K and L3 misses yields an optimal partition point shown in Figure 5.

This partition point, however, is only optimal for the particular operating system. Different operating systems with varying degrees of service migration have different optimal partition points. For example, the upper graph in Figure 6 shows an optimal partition point of 8 for Mach 3.0, 10 for Mach3+AFSin and 12 for Mach3+AFSout, when running the Ousterhout benchmark.

Applications also influence the optimal partition point. The lower graph in Figure 6 shows the results for various applications running under Mach 3.0. compress has an optimal partition point of 8. However, video_play requires 14 slots and mpeg_play requires 18 slots. Some of the additional slots are used to hold the X Server's L2 PTEs. This underscores the importance of understanding both the decomposition of the system and how applications interact with the various OS services because both determine the use of TLB slots.

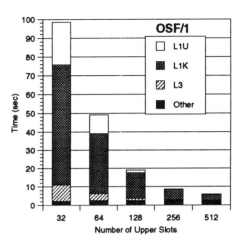

Figure 7: TLB Service Time vs. Number of Upper TLB Slots

The total cost of TLB miss servicing for all seven benchmarks run under OSF/1. The number of upper slots was varied from 8 to 512, while the number of lower slots was fixed at 16 for all configurations.

5.3 Increasing TLB Size

In this section we examine the benefits of building TLBs with additional upper slots. The trade-offs here can be more complex because the upper slots are used to hold three different types of mappings (L1U, L1K and L3 PTEs) whereas the lower slots only hold L2 PTEs.

To better understand the requirements for upper slots, we used Tapeworm to simulate TLB configurations ranging from 32 to 512 upper slots. Each of these TLB configurations was fully-associative and had 16 lower slots to minimize L2 misses.

Figure 7 shows TLB performance for all seven benchmarks under OSF/1. For smaller TLBs, the most significant component is L1K misses; L1U and L3 misses account for less than 35% of the total TLB miss handling time. The prominence of L1K misses is due to the large number of mapped data structures in the OSF/1 kernel. However, as outlined in Section 5.1, modifying the hardware trap mechanism to allow the uTLB handler to service L1K misses reduces the L1K service time to an estimated 20 cycles. Therefore, we recomputed the total time using the lower cost L1K miss service time (20 cycles) for the OSF/1, Mach 3.0 and Mach3+AFSout systems (Figure 8).

With the cost of L1K misses reduced, TLB miss handling time is dominated by L1U misses. In each system, there is a noticeable improvement in TLB service time as TLB sizes increase from 32 to 128 slots. For example, moving from 64 to 128 slots decreases Mach 3.0 TLB handling time by over 50%.

After 128 slots, invalid and modify misses dominate (listed as "other" in the figures). Because the invalid and modify misses are constant with respect to TLB size, any further increases in TLB size will have a negligible effect on overall TLB performance. This suggests that a 128- or 256-entry TLB may be sufficient to support both monolithic operating systems like Ultrix and OSF/1 and microkernel operating systems like Mach 3.0. Of course, even larger TLBs may be needed to support large applications such as CAD programs. However, this study is limited to TLB support for operating systems running a modest workload. The reader is referred to [6] for a detailed discussion of TLB support for large applications.

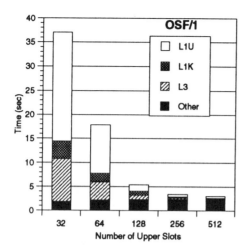

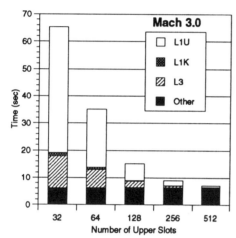

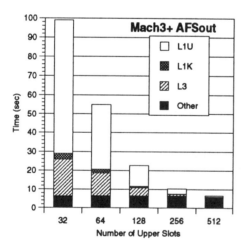

Figure 8: Modified TLB Service Time vs. Number of Upper TLB Slots

The total cost of TLB miss servicing (for all seven benchmarks) assuming L1K misses can be handled by the uTLB handler in 20 cycles and L2 misses are handled in 40 cycles. The top graph is for OSF/1, the middle for Mach 3.0 and the bottom for Mach3+AFSout. Note that the scale varies for each graph.

Other is the sum of the invalid, modify and L2 miss costs.

Processor	Associativity	Number of Instruction Slots	Number of Data Slots
DEC Alpha 21064	full	8+4	32
IBM RS/6000	2-way	32	128
TI Viking	full	64 unified	——
MIPS R2000	full	64 unified	——
MIPS R4000	full	48 unified	——
HP 9000 Series 700	full	96+4	96+4
Intel 486	4-way	32 unified	——

Table 8: Number of TLB Slots for Current Processors

Note that page sizes vary from 4K to 16 Meg and are variable in many processors. The MIPS R4000 actually has 48 double slots. Two PTEs can reside in one double slot if their virtual mappings are to consecutive pages in the virtual address space. [7]

5.4 TLB Associativity

Large, fully-associative TLBs (128^+ entries) are difficult to build[1] and can consume a significant amount of chip area. To achieve high TLB performance, computer architects could implement larger TLBs with lesser degrees of associativity. The following section explores the effectiveness of TLBs with varying degrees of associativity.

Many current-generation processors implement fully-associative TLBs with sizes ranging from 32 entries to 100^+ entries (Table 8). However, technology limitations may force designers to begin building larger TLBs which are not fully-associative. To explore the performance impact of limiting TLB associativity, we used Tapeworm to simulate TLBs with varying degrees of associativity.

The top two graphs in Figure 9 show the total TLB miss handling time for the mpeg_play benchmark under Mach3+AFSout and the video_play benchmark under Mach 3.0. Throughout the range of TLB sizes, increasing associativity reduces the total TLB handling time. These figures illustrate the general "rule-of-thumb" that doubling the size of a caching structure will yield about the same performance as doubling the degree of associativity [24].

Some benchmarks, however, can perform badly for TLBs with a small degree of set associativity. For example, the bottom graph in Figure 9 shows the total TLB miss handling time for the compress benchmark under OSF/1. For a 2-way set-associative TLB, compress displays pathological behavior. Even a 512-entry, 2-way set-associative TLB is outperformed by a much smaller 32-entry, 4-way set-associative TLB.

These three graphs show that reducing associativity to enable the construction of larger TLBs is an effective technique for reducing TLB misses.

---

1. Current-mode sensing avoids some of the problems associated with large CMOS CAMs [22].

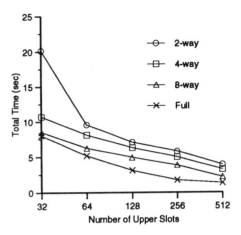

mpeg_play **under Mach3+AFSout**

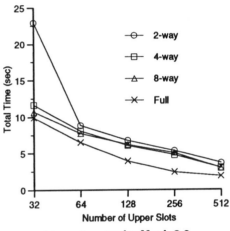

video_play **under Mach 3.0**

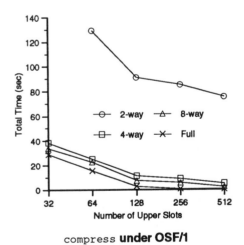

compress **under OSF/1**

Figure 9: Total TLB Service Time for TLBs of Different Sizes and Associativities

6   Summary

This paper demonstrates to architects and operating system designers the importance of understanding the interactions between TLBs and operating systems. Software-management of TLBs magnifies the importance of this understanding, because of the large variation in TLB miss service times that can exist.

TLB behavior depends upon the kernel's use of virtual memory to map its own data structures, including the page tables themselves. TLB behavior is also dependent upon the division of service functionality between the kernel and separate user tasks. Currently popular microkernel approaches rely on server tasks, but can fall prey to performance difficulties. Running on a machine with a software-managed TLB like that of the MIPS R2000, current microkernel systems perform poorly with only a modest degree of service decomposition into separate server tasks.

We have presented measurements of actual systems on a current machine, together with simulations of architectural problems, and have related the results to the differences between operating systems. We have outlined four architectural solutions to the problems experienced by microkernel-based systems: changes in the vectoring of TLB misses, flexible partitioning of the TLB, providing larger TLBs and changing the degree of associativity to enable construction of larger TLBs. The first two can be implemented at little cost, as is done in the R4000.

References

[1] Kane, G. and J. Heinrich, *MIPS RISC Architecture*. 1992, Prentice-Hall, Inc.

[2] Digital, *Alpha Architecture Handbook*. 1992, USA: Digital Equipment Corporation.

[3] DeMoney, M., J. Moore, and J. Mashey. *Operating system support on a RISC*. in *COMPCON*. 1986.

[4] Accetta, M., *et al. Mach: A new kernel foundation for UNIX development*. in *Summer 1986 USENIX Conference*. 1986. USENIX.

[5] Clark, D.W. and J.S. Emer, *Performance of the VAX-11/780 translation buffer: Simulation and measurement*. ACM Transactions on Computer Systems, 1985. 3(1): p. 31-62.

[6] Chen, J.B., A. Borg, and N.P. Jouppi. *A simulation based study of TLB performance*. in *The 19th Annual International Symposium on Computer Architecture*. 1992. Gold Coast, Australia: IEEE.

[7] Talluri, M., *et al. Tradeoffs in supporting two page sizes*. in *The 19th Annual International Symposium on Computer Architecture*. 1992. Gold Coast, Australia: IEEE.

[8] Anderson, T.E., *et al. The interaction of architecture and operating system design*. in *Fourth International Conference on Architectural Support for Programming Languages and Operating Systems*. 1991. Santa Clara, California: ACM.

[9] Ousterhout, J., *Why aren't operating systems getting faster as fast as hardware?* WRL Technical Note, 1989. (TN-11).

[10] Welch, B. *The file system belongs in the kernel*. in *USENIX Mach Symposium Proceedings*. 1991. Monterey, California: USENIX.

[11]   Nagle, D., R. Uhlig, and T. Mudge, *Monster: A tool for analyzing the interaction between operating systems and computer architectures*. 1992, The University of Michigan.

[12]   Alexander, C.A., W.M. Keshlear, and F. Briggs, *Translation buffer performance in a UNIX environment*. Computer Architecture News, 1985. 13(5): p. 2-14.

[13]   MIPS Computer Systems, I., *RISCompiler Languages Programmer's Guide*. 1988, MIPS.

[14]   Larus, J.R., *Abstract Execution: A technique for efficiently tracing programs*. 1990, University of Wisconsin-Madison.

[15]   Agarwal, A., J. Hennessy, and M. Horowitz, *Cache performance of operating system and multiprogramming workloads*. ACM Transactions on Computer Systems, 1988. 6(Number 4): p. 393-431.

[16]   McKusick, M.K., et al., *A fast file system for UNIX*. ACM Transactions on Computer Systems, 1984. 2(3): p. 181-197.

[17]   Satyanarayanan, M., *Scalable, secure, and highly available distributed file access*. IEEE Computer, 1990. 23(5): p. 9-21.

[18]   Rashid, R., et al., *Machine-independent virtual memory management for paged uniprocessor and multiprocessor architectures*. IEEE Transactions on Computers, 1988. 37(8): p. 896-908.

[19]   Dean, R.W. and F. Armand. *Data movement in kernelized systems*. in *Micro-kernels and Other Kernel Architectures*. 1991. Seattle, Washington: USENIX.

[20]   Cheriton, D.R., *The V kernel: A software base for distributed systems*. IEEE Software, 1984. 1(2): p. 19-42.

[21]   Uhlig, R., et al., *Software TLB management in OSF/1 and Mach 3.0*. 1993, University of Michigan.

[22]   Heald, R.A. and J.C. Holst. *6ns cycle 256 kb cache memory and memory management unit*. in *IEEE International Solid-State Circuits Conference*. 1993. San Francisco, CA: IEEE.

[23]   Patel, K., B.C. Smith, and L.A. Rowe, *Performance of a software MPEG video decoder*. 1992, University of California, Berkeley.

[24]   Patterson, D. and Hennessy, J., *Computer architecture A quantitative approach*. 1990. Morgan Kaufmann Publishers, Inc.San Mateo, California.

Architectural Support for Translation Table Management in Large Address Space Machines

by

Jerry Huck
Hewlett Packard
19410 Homestead Ave.
Cupertino, CA 95014

Jim Hays
EcoSystems Software, Inc.
10055 Miller Ave., Suite 201
Cupertino, CA 95014

Abstract

Virtual memory page translation tables provide mappings from virtual to physical addresses. When the hardware controlled Translation Lookaside Buffers (TLBs) do not contain a translation, these tables provide the translation. Approaches to the structure and management of these tables vary from full hardware implementations to complete software based algorithms.

The size of the virtual address space used by processes is rapidly growing beyond 32 bits of address. As the utilized address space increases, new problems and issues surface. Traditional methods for managing the page translation tables are inappropriate for large address space architectures.

The Hashed Page Table (HPT), described here, provides a very fast and space efficient translation table that reduces overhead by splitting TLB management responsibilities between hardware and software. Measurements demonstrate its applicability to a diverse range of operating systems and workloads and, in particular, to large virtual address space machines. In simulations of over 4 billion instructions, improvements of 5 to 10% were observed.

1. Introduction

Virtual memory, *VM*, is a fundamental abstraction of storage used by computer systems to support concurrent execution of processes. Processes can be protected from other processes execution and processes can view storage in a simplified, uniform manner.

Virtual memory defines a mapping function from one address space to some other address space. Traditionally, that mapping is a single translation from a virtual address, local to the process, to a physical address that directly accesses storage. These mappings are termed *translations*. The instruction set provides management instructions to enable and disable the translations, change translations, and control the protection model that is often associated with the translation mechanism.

Virtual memory translation is often specified by the architecture in terms of a memory-based table with the expectation that some intermediate storage element will hold a subset of these translations. The translation lookaside buffer (TLB) is the most common structure used to hold this subset. The processor interrogates the TLB with a virtual address and searches for the corresponding translation. If found, the hardware uses the translation to validate the access and locate the data. Many approaches to the design of TLBs have been implemented and measurements taken of their behavior [Clar85][Tayl90].

If the TLB does not contain the translation (an event known as a *TLB miss*), then typically some type of memory based table, the *page table*, is accessed and the translation is entered into the TLB.

Besides the translation, the page table entry usually holds protection information that controls access (read/write/execute) and status bits. The status bits might record if the page has been recently referenced (reference bit) and if the page has been written (dirty bit). The operating system may store additional information in the page table not needed by the TLB, status bits, or links to other software tables.

Overall performance of a computer system is dependent on TLB access and management overhead. Measurements of large scale applications, databases, networking, and operation systems behavior indicate that a significant number of the CPU cycles can be consumed in TLB management. Later sections will better quantify the costs; large scale data-base intensive applications incur 5-18% overheads. Extreme cases show greater than 40% TLB overhead.

The page table structure of any VM system attempts to optimize three different characteristics:

1. Minimize the time to service a TLB miss.

2. Minimize the physical memory space to maintain the translations for the currently mapped pages.

3. Maximize the flexibility for software to support a variety of VM mechanisms and capabilities.

Computer systems support the page table structure using hardware, or hardware with some assistance by software, or entirely by software. Hardware approaches seek the highest performance while software only mechanisms retain the flexibility to easily adapt the page table structures to changing requirements.

No practical organization optimizes this set of characteristics for all types of workloads. Organizations effective for one workload may be a poor match for another. Different operating systems make different demands on the translation mechanisms.

The trends in computing point to changes in the utilization of the address space. Object-oriented systems, mapped files, shared objects, and distributed computing all increase the size of the address space used by a process, encourage more sharing and decrease the locality of the resulting virtual memory address stream. The translation structure's performance is influenced by these changes. Later measurements quantify the very different behavior of simple program and more complex operating system execution.

Independent of the particular organization, all page tables are simply a data structure that is primarily designed for efficient retrieval of a translation using the virtual address as a search key. Searching is a large field and well researched field.

0884-7495/93 $3.00 © 1993 IEEE

Many data structures and search techniques are possible. Choosing a high performance implementation is difficult. The addition of just a single extra memory reference may be very costly. Each clock cycle of the TLB miss handler must be carefully considered and measured. For example, some page structures use a hash table for searching. Theory suggests that hash tables should be a prime number in size. Practice dictates that these tables are all powers of 2 in size.

The following section describes the two common page table structures and analyzes their characteristics. This is followed by the proposed alternative. The final section quantifies the performance of these structures over a range of workloads and operating systems.

2. Existing Virtual Memory Architectures

Two styles of page table organization dominate virtual memory architectures today: *forward-mapped* and *inverted*. Forward-mapped page tables are the most common structure used for 32-bit or less virtual memory architectures. Inverted, or alternatively *reverse-mapped*, page tables - IPTs - have been typically used by large address space architectures.

2.1 Forward-mapped page tables

Forward-mapped or alternatively *multi-level* page tables generally use bits out of the virtual address to index a hierarchy of tables. The final level of the hierarchy, the leaf, contains a validity indicator, the physical page number, and any status or protection bits. For a particular virtual address, there is one single location that holds the translation. Most architectures with this structure allow portions of the hierarchy to be unallocated by using validity bits in the higher levels. Some architectures provide a short circuit approach that promotes leaf pages to a higher place in the hierarchy when the address space is sparsely used. Figure 1 shows an example table illustrating this mechanism. The root pointer is used to start the search. Each index merges bits from the entry with more of the virtual address bits. The complete physical address is formed with the page offset bits in the virtual address and physical page number in the leaf page.

The forward-mapped table is generally a per-process table. Some control register holds a pointer to the first level of the table. The amount of storage being used for the page tables is a function of the amount of allocated virtual memory. Portions of the table need not be resident if none of its entries are mapped.

The page table itself can be referenced virtually or physically. If physically referenced, then some table manager controls the amount of physical memory being used.

As an example, to map 32-bits of address space with 4Kbyte pages, a system might allocate 1024 entries in the root table. Each root table entry in turn points to leaf pages each containing 1024 entries.

Since these per process page tables map the same virtual address values, the virtual address is often augmented in the TLB with an address space identifier (ASID) or process identifier. The ASID acts to form a unique global address for each process and avoids the need to purge the TLB on context switch by preventing erroneous matching of a virtual address from one process with a translation owned by another process.

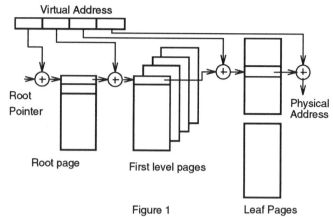

Forward-mapped page table

Figure 1

By duplicating entries on a per process basis, forward-mapped page tables offer a very flexible VM structure to the operating system. It has full support for aliasing, copy-on-write, and independent protection views (different protection mode for different virtual addresses).

Time: Servicing a TLB miss requires the loading of pointers from each of the upper levels of the hierarchy and finally the loading the last entry. The total cost to service a miss involves:

> CPU overhead to suspend execution and step
> through each part of the algorithm,
> Memory and/or cache references to each level,
> Possible TLB miss with virtual tables,
> Possible page fault on the table itself, and
> Possible updates of the dirty and reference bits.

In the earlier example, a TLB miss requires 2 memory references and perhaps additional TLB misses if the page table itself is virtually referenced.

Minimizing the miss time requires careful design of the system. Some multiprocessing systems require bypassing the cache for page structure references to avoid synchronization problems with table management [Appo88]. Even on systems that use the cache, relatively high miss rates occur. Later measurements quantify these values.

The nature of the TLB miss address stream is an important determinant of the system's performance. Largely sequential or densely packed TLB miss addresses match the characteristics of forward-mapped page tables. On the other hand, more sparse and distributed TLB miss addresses can result in longer miss service times.

An interesting variant on the forward-mapped table is a single flat table that is indexed by the virtual page number [DEC83]. The table is very large but only the used pages need to be allocated. From a time standpoint, only one memory reference and potentially one nested TLB miss is possible. For sequential miss patterns the extra TLB miss only occurs on page crossings on the table itself. For sparse accesses, this can require both an expensive memory reference and an expensive nested TLB miss.

In general, the introduction of just a single additional cache miss in TLB miss handling can greatly reduce performance. With cache miss times increasing from 10-20 cycles toward

30-70 cycles, this time could easily double or triple typical TLB miss times. Later measurements quantify some of these effects.

One additional time issue is the hit rate of the TLB itself. Forward-mapped tables generally use address aliasing to share data and require multiple entries in the TLB for the shared pages. This effect reduces the apparent size of the TLB vs a system that uses a single entry to map all access to a shared page. An even more costly approach, requires the purging of translations between every context switch. Programming trends to access mapped files, and shared memory objects will increase the occurrence of this sharing. Forward-mapped systems sometimes allow global sharing with some restrictions on the allowed protection model. For example, the VAX architecture allows all processes to share an address in system address space in the same way, say, read-only.

Space: The space required for page tables is a function of the amount and distribution of allocated virtual memory. In the best case, all entries of the leaf pages are used. In the example, this implies 1 word of overhead for every mapped page (4 bytes/4K bytes $\approx$ .1%). In the worst case, sparse allocation would only utilize one word of a leaf page to map each page (4K/4K = 100%)!

Perhaps a more typical case of the virtual address space requirements for a process:

> 128K of instructions,
> 128K of static and dynamic data, and
> 16K of stack data.

This requires the root page, 1 leaf page for text and data and another leaf page for the stack ($3*4K/272K \approx 4\%$ overhead). The root page might be shared with other root pages and reduce the total overhead.

As the address space grows, the number of table levels needs to grow or the page size needs to increase. Three or four table levels may be needed for even modest growth in the virtual memory range (say 40-48 bits). The best case overhead remains similar. The entry size probably needs to increase to address a large physical address size. In the worst case, the overhead becomes n hundreds of percent with n being the number of table levels. A fully supported 64-bit address space with 4K pages and 8-byte pointers and entries would require roughly 5 page levels. The time and space implications of large address space systems suggest the consideration of alternative structures and approaches.

2.2 Inverted page tables

Implementations of large address space machines have utilized the inverted page table structure [Lee89] [Chan88] [IBM78]. It is a single table with one entry per physical page. Each entry contains the virtual address currently mapped to a physical page as well as some protection and status bits. Discovering the virtual address given a physical address is trivially determined by indexing the table with the physical page number and examining the entry.

To determine the reverse mapping, namely virtual to physical, a hash structure, the hash anchor table (HAT), is first indexed by some function on the virtual address. The HAT provides a pointer to a linked list of potential IPT entries. A quick linear search comparing the desired virtual address with the IPT entry's virtual address completes the look-up. If no match is found, the virtual address is not mapped and page fault handling is initiated. Figure 2 illustrates this structure.

Inverted Page Translation Table

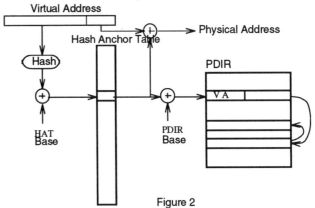

Figure 2

This global table is shared by all the processors. In a sense, the ASID of the forward-mapped table is included in the address itself. Protection in this kind of architecture is either supported by some kind of address isolation or by the use of storage keys.

The biggest difficulty with the IPT is the support for address aliasing. Only one virtual to physical mapping may exist at one time. Whenever aliasing is only used for sharing, most IPT systems accomplish the same function with a global address. To support aliasing for other reasons, the entries must be changed.

Time: TLB miss handling performance is primarily a function of the number of probes to find the translation. The very nature of a hash table suggests one cache miss to reference the HAT pointer. Given a fairly uniform random distribution of virtual to real mappings, each element of the chain is another cache miss. To minimize the average length of the chains, a large HAT is used. Analysis of this type of hash structure allows the designer to trade-off between average hash chain length and number of entries in the HAT. The total cost of the TLB miss involves:

> CPU overhead to suspend execution and step
>   through each part of the algorithm,
> Memory reference to the HAT pointer,
> Memory reference to the IPT,
> Possible memory references for chain elements, and
> Possible update to the dirty and reference bits.

It is possible to minimize some of the HAT cache misses for sequential TLB misses, but generally the memory references have high cache miss rates. Later measurements quantify this parameter.

When sharing with global addresses, it is sometimes possible to reduce the total number of TLB misses. Multiple processes can re-use the same TLB entry and avoid misses.

Space: The size of storage for the mappings is a linear function of the amount of physical memory, with an overhead of roughly (size of entry)/(size of page). Independent of the amount of allocated virtual memory, the physical memory overhead for the mappings remains constant. This storage must be contiguous. *Holes* in the physical address space wastes entries in the IPT in order to preserve the index as the physical address. Memory mapped I/O systems can waste significant storage in an IPT if it cannot be efficiently packed.

For example, to map a 32Mbyte physical memory system with 4Kbyte pages, a HAT of 16K entries is used to index a 8K entry IPT. Assume 32-bit physical addresses. 64-bit virtual

addresses can be nicely packed into a 16byte entry for a:
$$(8 \times 16\text{Kbyte} + 16\text{K} \times 4\text{byte})/4\text{K} \approx .6\% \text{ overhead.}$$

2.3 A combined hash table and IPT: The Hashed Page Table

An alternative to the IPT is to combine the hash table and IPT into a single hashed structure, termed - Hashed Page Table (HPT), both time and space improvements to the traditional inverted table are possible. Fewer memory references are required and better utilization of memory is possible. Each entry, HPTE, contains both the virtual address and the physical address. No longer can the physical address be computed from the index. Figure 3 shows the structure of this table.

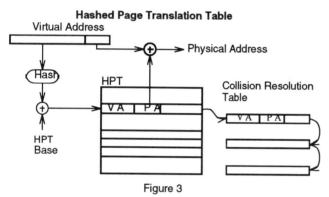

Hashed Page Translation Table

Figure 3

On a TLB miss, some hash of the virtual address is used as an index into the table. The faulting virtual address is compared with the virtual address in the entry. If equal, then the translation is directly loaded. If not equal, then the link is used to chain all of the hash collisions together. Reaching the end of chain indicates a page fault. Collisions can be chained directly into the unused hash entries or chained into an overflow table.

Aliasing is simply supported. Whenever shared global addresses can not be used, the alias is added to the table. This creates multiple dirty and reference bits but does allow different protection attributes. A global address space reduces the need for aliasing and minimizes the number of extra entries.

Time: Servicing a TLB miss requires a reference to the HPT entry and avoids the reference to a separate HAT entry. Eliminating a memory reference is a significant improvement over the IPT structure.

The potential for a chain walk is a function of the size of the HPT. The more entries relative to the number of translations, the lower the likelihood of a chain walk. Choosing a 2 to 1 ratio of entries to physical pages results in average chain lengths of approximately 1.25 entries[Knut73].

Space: Similar to the IPT structure, independent of the virtual memory utilization, there is a fixed overhead that scales with the amount of physical memory. For a table with twice the number of entries as physical pages, the overhead is (16bytes/entry)*2/4Kbytes < 1%. A table with four times the number pages uses < 2% of physical memory.

Address aliasing will reduce the HPT's effectiveness, require a larger size, or require some special handling of certain entries. For example, aliases associated with suspended or swapped processes can migrate to the end of a chain or be deleted and faulted back onto the chain.

The HPT also efficiently handles holes in the physical address space. This has become much more common with graphics adaptors and other I/O devices that take a fixed large amount of address space and use a subset based on the system configuration. This characteristic gives the HPT a significant space advantage over the traditional IPT. For example, a 50 Megabyte un-used segment of physical I/O address space can waste 200Kbytes in unused page directory entries with 4K pages.

Further Discussion: Many variations on the management of a hash table such as the HPT are possible. Collisions can chain to another structure. Secondary hashes could be considered. For example, the MONADS project [Rose85] described a structure similar to the HPT except it was implemented in a separate memory, was managed as a primary TLB, and used internal chaining.

Earlier releases of PA-RISC operating systems, which used the standard IPT structure, had an optional software TLB - swTLB - that is first interrogated using just the low 10 to 12 bits of the virtual page number as an index. An entry in that table was equivalent to an HPT entry for validation purposes, but the swTLB used a secondary hash to resolve collisions into the original IPT. The swTLB proved very effective in early PA-RISC machines for two reasons. The first PA-RISC systems had large direct-mapped hardware TLBs. The software TLB was two-way associative and greatly reduced the cost of thrashing. A slightly later PA-RISC machine had a small two-way associative hardware TLB. The software TLB is very effective since the software TLB had such a high hit rate. This compensated for the lower hit rate in the small hardware TLB, and had faster access because of its simplicity, in CPU overhead, than the IPT table.

By making the HPT very large, it acts as a complete replacement for the older hash table and IPT structure. Alternatively, making the HPT smaller, it acts as a software cache for some other representation of the remainder of the translations. For example, a small HPT can be used in front of a forward-mapped page table.

A final observation: since the HPT entry is nearly identical in form to a TLB entry, it is simple to build a hardware TLB miss handler. It must compute the hash index, accesses the table entry, and faults to software if the entry is not valid or some update to the Such a hardware handler still allows great flexibility for the software. Different page-table policies and organizations are still open to the software since the hardware does not do updates to the table. The designers of a recent PA-RISC CPU chip [Dela92] found the implementation of an HPT hardware miss handler similar to the complexity of the previous generation's 2 level TLB.

By not restricting the size of the HPT or the organization of the overflow table, a VM system has complete flexibility to implement a variety of mechanisms and policies.

3. Data Structures and Implementation

The following sub-sections describe in more detail the format of the measured translation data structures, their requirements, hardware/software interactions, and miss algorithms. Understanding the actual data structures prototyped and simulated along with the operating system environments will aid in the interpretation of the simulation results. This should help the reader to understand how to adapt the results to alternative data structures and search algorithms.

3.1 Operating systems environments

HP's Unix - HP-UX and the proprietary MPE/iX operating system support text and data sharing through a global address model. Objects are shared between different tasks using the same 64-bit virtual address. It is the responsibility of the operating system to manage the address space to enforce the desired level of protection for each application. Copy-on-write is implemented as copy-on-access. In the MPE/iX environment 64-bit pointers may be directly manipulated by end-user applications. Under MPE/iX the database and the file system are memory mapped and accessed directly through a 64-bit address. Each open file is mapped in its entirety within the 64-bit address space. Both HP-UX and MPE/iX originally used an inverted page table as their primary translation data structure. The trace data used in the simulations was obtained from these two operating system environments.

Most Unix implementations use a more traditional sharing model where each task is given it's own private 32-bit flat address space. If two tasks share code or data, it is accomplished through aliasing multiple virtual addresses to the same physical address. A forward mapped page table is commonly used as the primary translation data structure. These per-task page tables are simple to implement and support arbitrary aliasing. The acronym ASM, for aliased sharing model, is used to represent an operating system that uses aliasing and a forward mapped page table. This model is included in the simulation due to its use in existing implementations of the OSF/Mach based operating system.

3.2 Forward-mapped page table model

A two level page table is selected over a three level table to determine a lower bound on TLB miss times for the ASM model. Deeper forward mapped page tables, which are required for larger than 32-bit address spaces, will only increase the miss overhead. The structure of the simulated forward mapped table and search algorithm is based on TLB miss handler code used in an OSF-1/PA-RISC port. The layout of the ASM forward mapped table simulated is as follows:

Root Table entries
RootEntry

real address of leaf PTE
*
*

Leaf table entries

r	x	t	m	x	rpn[0:19]	00000
r	x	t	m	x	rpn[0:19]	00000
r	x	t	m	x	rpn[0:19]	00000

r= Ref bit, m= Modify bit, rpn= Real page number, x= Other unrelated bits

Utilizing a per task 32-bit flat address model reduces the amount of data which must be retained in the tables. Per process protection information and high order address bits (upper 32 bits of 64 bit address) can be maintained in a global or control register, and need not be duplicated in each page table entry. The algorithm to handle a user TLB miss is outlined below. Each step may require one or more instructions. Exact cycle counts attributed to each algorithm are provided in the measurement section.

TLB software miss algorithm (user TLB miss): Move the faulting address to general registers. Determine if the reference is to system or user space. Move the User Root table pointer to a general register. Determine the privilege level. Determine if the reference is to a different process's 32-bit space. Calculate the index into the root table. Load the root table entry. Calculate an index into the leaf page. Load Page table entry. Check reference bit. Form protection information. Insert address, rpn, and protection information into the hardware TLB. Finally, return from interrupt.

There is no need for a valid bit in the page table entry. Invalid entries are initialized with an entry which will generate a protection fault if loaded into the TLB and then accessed. The specified algorithm could have been shortened by several cycles if the hardware were capable of delivering system and user TLB miss exceptions on distinct interrupt vectors.

3.3 Inverted page table model

The inverted page table model supports 64-bit global addressing as follows:

HashTableEntry

word0 rpn&link	h	000000	Next PDE Index	00000

PageDirectoryEntry

word0 rpn&link	h	000000	Next PDE Index		00000
word1 tag1	Upper VA				
word2 tag2	Lower VA			000000000000	
word3 prot	r	x	t	m	b	rights	0000	key(15)	0

r = Ref bit, m = Modify bit, x = Other software bits

TLB Miss Algorithm:

1. Move 64-bit faulting address and hash table base into general registers. Hash the faulting address and compute an address into the hash table.
2. Load hash table entry (word 0).
3. Check H bit to see if end of chain.
4. Calculate the page directory entry from the page directory base, and hash table pde index loaded in step2.
5. Load virtual address tag1 from page directory word1.
6. Compare faulting address with virtual address tag. If not equal load Next Pde index (word0), goto step 3.
7. Load the virtual address tag2 from page directory entry word2.
8. Compare faulting address with virtual address tag. If not equal load Next Pde index (word0) and goto step 3.
9. Load protection fields (word3), and check reference bit.
10. Insert address, rpn, and protection information into the hardware TLB. Return from interrupt.

The layout of the hash table entry and first word of each page directory are identical. Word 0 of the page directory and hash table encodes both the next link and the physical page number (rpn) for the following entry. While this encoding scheme is more compact and saves memory it also restricted the page directory to a physically contiguous table and allows no aliasing. Each page directory entry resides within one 16-byte cache line. The hash function provides an even distribution of addresses over the hash table.

3.4 Hashed page table model

The format of the HPT is the same regardless of whether it is being used as a native translation table or if it is being used as a cache fronting the ASM forward mapped page tables. The structure supports a full 64-bit global address space and is layed out as follows:

HashedPageTableEntry

word 0 tag1	V	offset[0:14]		space[16:31]	
word 1 prot1	rx t mb	rights	0000	key(15)	x
word 2 rpn1	0000000		rpn[0:19]		00000
word 3 link1		real address of next hpt entry			

A second 4 word entry was combined with the first for a 32-byte aligned entry when investigating alternate formats.

word 4 tag2	V	offset[0:14]		space[16:31]	
word 5 prot2	rx t mb	rights	0000	key(15)	x
word 6 rpn2	0000000		rpn[0:19]		00000
word 7 link2		real addres of next hpt entry			

TLB Miss Algorithm:

1. Move 64-bit faulting address and hashed page table base into general registers. Hash the faulting address and compute an address into the HPT.
2. Load HPTE tag word0.
3. Compare faulting address with virtual address tag. If not equal read the next link from word3 and go back to step 2)
4. Load protection fields (word1), and check reference bit. Load the rpn.
5. Insert address, rpn, and protection information into TLB. Return from interrupt.

One or two four word entries are contained in one 32-byte cache line. The preceding data structure was simulated with several variations; two are described in detail:

- 16-byte entries each containing one translation.
- 32-byte entries each containing two independent 16-byte entries which checked in parallel or serially for a match (a 2-way associative HPT).

Each of these was evaluated based on the hardware costs and performance. The best solution for the intermediate hash table will depend, in part, on the hardware organization of the on-chip TLB. A direct mapped on-chip TLB might do better with a two-way associative table.

Optimizations were made to the hash algorithm of both the HPT and inverted page table to further streamline the miss path.

The original software hash function was 5 instructions. It was chosen to give an even distribution of addresses in the hash table. It made no assumptions about the address stream. Since the operating system allocates the ASIDs (on PA-RISC an ASID is the upper 32 bits of the 64-bit address and is stored in a space register), rather then just assigning them in a sequential manner, they can be allocated in a pseudo random sequence. This randomization allows a simpler hash function and still approximates a random uniform distribution in the hash table. A single XOR of the upper virtual address bits and the lower virtual page number bits is effective.

The hardware needs to generate a hash table address, so the hash table is aligned to its size (which is a power of two). Hardware can simply OR in the base HPT table address with the hashed index bits to calculate the effective address of the hash bucket.

To reduce the size of an HPT entry representing a 64-bit address, the tag is compressed from 52 bits to 32 bits. This allows a more compact table and requires less overhead to determine if there is a match. To guarantee that the tag is unique in a hash chain the extra bits which are not a part of the page offset must be used in the hash to generate a unique position within the table. This leads to several restrictions on the table. First it can be no smaller then 32 entries (given the 4K page size) and a 48-bit global address space. Each subsequent bit of virtual address space allocated by the operating system requires a doubling of the table size. Even a modest 4K entry table allows the use of 56 bits of virtual address.

3.5 Hardware HPT and the software interface

A final implementation issue is to properly split hardware and software responsibilities to balance the performance, cost, and flexibility. The term *native* HPT is used to describe the scenario where the operating system's translation tables map directly onto the HPT format. Overflow buckets which are searched by software have the same format as the head HPT bucket. When using a hashed page table with HP-UX, hardware searches the head bucket of the operating system's native translation table. On failure, a trap to software allows HP-UX to continue the search. The term *hybrid* HPT describes a scenario where hardware searches an HPT cache and traps to a software managed table if the entry is not found.

Both approaches can be unified in the same hardware handler. The hardware does the same work to search the first bucket of a hash table in either the native or hybrid HPT. The main difference is the action that software takes on a miss. To maximize the benefit an efficient hand-off mechanism is needed which reduces the amount of re-work required when a software trap occurs.

When using the hashed page table as the native tables, the operating system needs to determine where to continue the search. When using a forward-mapped table in conjunction with the hash table, the operating system needs an efficient mechanism to update the hash table once the normal page walk has finished.

Hardware provides the necessary data to the operating system through a control register when it determines it cannot resolve the TLB fault with the entry stored at the front of the HPT.

On a TLB miss, hardware hashes into the HPT and checks for a hit. If the reference bit and modify bit are set to allow the access then the entry is inserted into the TLB. If there is a virtual tag mismatch then hardware deposits word 3 of the HPTE into a control register. Word 3 is not interpreted by hardware and it's value is maintained by software. In the case where the HPT is a part of the native translation table (e.g. HP-UX) word 3 contains the address of the overflow bucket. When the HPT is being used as a cache in conjunction with a foreign table, word 3 will be written by the operating system to point to the entry itself. This will give the software miss handler a handle on where to write the entry in the HPT cache after installing the translation in the hardware TLB.

If hardware detects an invalid virtual tag, a reference or modify bit exception, it traps to software and deposits the address of the head HPT entry into the control register (rather then word 3). In this scenario software needs to inspect the contents of the head bucket. Software attempts to resolve the fault by setting the appropriate bits in the HPT entry and retrying, or trapping to higher level software.

3.6 Software update of table entries

The task of modifying the translation tables in each model is given to software to simplify hardware and give software more flexibility when modifying an entry. It also allows the operating system to keep track of additional information on the types of accesses which are made to a page.

Allowing the operating system to intervene in the first reference and first modification of a translation allows the operating system to break out the standard reference and dirty bits into additional (modified, accessed, and execute) information bits based on the type of access being performed. On systems which have virtually indexed caches and non-coherent I/O systems, this allows important cache flushing optimizations. Not only can this reduce overhead on the single CPU it can reduce communication overhead in an MP system. Without software management of the reference and modification bits this information would have not been possible to collect. The overhead to manage these bits is small given that they were stored in the HPT and are not manipulated in the typical miss path.

4. Measurements

The HPT analysis suggests that it will perform uniformly better than the inverted table. The performance benefits of the HPT when used to cache a different page table structure is not obvious. This section measures and compares the performance of the HPT with the traditional inverted and forward-mapped page table structures. Measurements of the HPT's performance when used as a cache for a forward-mapped page table are also presented.

Data measurements for events such as TLB misses is a difficult task. This work combines 2 common approaches - hardware monitoring and software simulation - to measure meaningful workloads for systems that were not available [Jain91][Ston88].

The selected benchmarks are executed on a specially modified CPU to trace each cycle of execution. It is possible to hold about 2 million instructions worth of continuous execution before the machine must either be stalled or collection suspended while the data is dumped to permanent storage.

Stalling the processor creates problems in managing the real time clock and perturbs the measurement. For very simple benchmarks, like the SPEC suite, stalling is acceptable. For more complex benchmarks, like the transaction processing and large multi-user suites, the perturbation of the I/O system would be unacceptable. These traces use statistical sampling. While the system is executing the workload, the hardware tracer captures several traces spaced out in time. The trace includes all executed instructions, instruction addresses, and data reference addresses for that interval: operating system state, user state, interruptions, everything. For this study 20 traces were collected for each workload. The trace were stripped of the TLB misses generated by the measurement system since they correspond to a specific hardware organization. The paper by Jog [Jog90] first describes this environment.

The stripped traces are run through a simulator to mimic the various environments. For example, to simply measure the TLB miss rate, the simulator is configured with the desired size, associativity, and replacement algorithm. Each trace is *executed* by the simulator and the data collected from the TLB simulation. The trace is executed in the sense that the data and instruction memory addresses are applied to a simulation of the target system to capture a variety of relevant measures.

A warm start approximation for the caches is utilized which uses the cache state at the end of one trace as the starting point of the next trace. Measurements of actual systems have validated this approach [Call93].

There were 330 million instructions captured in the traces and over 4.7 billion instructions were simulated.

For this study, the simulator is configured to measure the behavior of TLB miss handling. When a TLB miss occurs, the simulator mimics the memory references that the model requires, generates those addresses, and applies them to the cache and memory models. This two step approach allows the measurement of complex and long running workloads and still retain flexibility in cache, TLB, and page table organization.

Generally speaking, a trace's TLB miss rate is unaffected by the underlying translation structure. But the TLB miss rate is effected by the sharing model. Traditionally, IPT based systems have shared data using common global addresses. Shared instruction and memory segments have the potential to reduce the TLB miss rate by finding a translation from the previous process. This only requires a single TLB entry to exist to map the page for all processes. Forward-mapped page table based systems traditionally share data using address aliasing. Each alias requires an additional TLB entry. When little sharing occurs this is not important but environments with large amounts of instruction or data sharing may encounter different miss rates.

All traces labelled *ASM* are HP-UX traces that have been modified to simulate what would have been the address trace in a per-process address space model. The simulator observes when a context switch occurs, and adjusts the instruction and data address stream to appear to be per-process. This approach generates aliases when the original trace is sharing data or instructions. The most common data sharing is by the instruction segment. Some data sharing occurs in the multi-user benchmarks.

Measurements of the original IPT structure were not modeled using the two steps of tracing and simulation since the benefits for using an HPT over the IPT had already been demonstrated with prototype software in the lab. At the time this paper was written, resource constraints prevented re-running the traces against just the IPT model. Instead, the IPT data is generated by using an equivalent sized HPT's first bucket cache hit rate as an approximation to the IPT's hash anchor table cache hit rate. This cache cost plus a fixed overhead in instruction cycles is then added to the equivalent sized HPT's total cost.

The following workloads were collected while executing the HP-UX operating system:

- finite - a large finite element application
- doduc - SPEC
- eqntott - SPEC
- espresso - SPEC
- fpppp - SPEC
- gcc - SPEC
- hilo - circuit simulator
- li - SPEC
- matrix - SPEC
- nasker - SPEC
- spice - SPEC
- tomcatv -SPEC
- OLTP1-ux - A large on-line transaction processing relational database application.
- telcom-ux - A telecommunications benchmark.
- OLTP2-ux - A variation on OLTP1-ux.

Additional workloads were collected while executing the MPE/iX operating system:

- Batch-mpe - Batch hierarchical database application.
- OLTP1-mpe - An on-line transaction processing relational database application.
- OLTP2-mpe - A batch manufacturing database application.
- OLTP3-mpe - A variation on OLTP1-mpe.

All the traces - in particular, the matrix and nasker traces - are from older generation compilers and do not represent the latest optimizations. For most programs, this will have little effect on the TLB miss pattern. For matrix, and to a lesser extent nasker, this is a very significant effect. Consider matrix to represent a program that misses the data TLB on every 16 or so instructions.

The last three traces (OLTP1, telcom, and OLTP2) are large multi-user benchmarks and better represent workloads fully utilizing the available memory.

The simulations modeled a 96 entry fully-associative combined TLB. The TLB requires an extra 1 cycle penalty for each page crossing to validate a mapping for the current instruction address. Additionally, block TLB entries map the static portion of the HP-UX operating system and significantly reduce the number of TLB misses. The MPE/iX operating system is paged and does not utilize block TLB entries.

Penalties consistent with current PA-RISC systems are assumed. The hardware portion of TLB miss handling with an HPT takes a basic 9 cycles. For associative table entries, the hardware requires an extra 2 cycles to examine a second entry. The basic software access to the HPT takes 27 cycles. Chain walking takes an extra 9 cycles per chain element. The basic software forward-mapped table access takes 28 cycles and, if necessary requires 8 cycles to update a HPT cache.

All the measurements use the same hash algorithm cost, and equivalent basic cycle costs such that performance differences only reflect the differences in page table structure.

The cache is a 256K direct-mapped data cache and an equal size instruction cache. The average data cache miss penalty is 30 cycles.

In summary, these measurements are derived from actual traces of significant workloads. The results are measured using a simulation of the desired system using instruction traces as stimulation.

4.1 Key to graph labels

The graphs used in the remaining sections are labeled to identify the environment. The label encodes the base operating system type, software or hardware table walking, page table format, HPT size, and associativity. The HPT size ranges from 1/4 the number of physical pages to 4 times the number of physical pages. For example, with 32Megabytes of memory, 16K table entries are 2 times the number of physical 4Kbyte pages.

Name	Type	HW support	Total # of entries
UX-SW-IPT4x-1w	IPT	All SW	32K
UX-SW-HPT4x-1w	HPT	All SW	32K
UX-HW-HPT4x-1w	HPT	HW-HPT SW-overflow	32K
UX-HW-HPT2x-2w	HPT	HW-HPT SW-overflow	32K
ASM-HW-HPT2x-1w	FMPT	HW-HPT SW-FMPT	16K
ASM-HW-HPT1x-1w	FMPT	HW-HPT SW-FMPT	8K
ASM-HW-HPT.5x-1w	FMPT	HW-HPT SW-FMPT	4K
ASM-HW-HPT.25x-1w	FMPT	HW-HPT SW-FMPT	2K
ASM-SW-FMPT	FMPT	All SW No HPT	-
ASM-HW-FMPT	FMPT	All HW No HPT	-
iX-SW-IPT2x-1w	IPT	All SW	32K
iX-HW-HPT2x-1w	HPT	HW-HPT SW overflow	32K
iX-SW-HPT2x-1w	HPT	All SW	32K

Each HP-UX trace was taken on a machine with 32 Megabytes of memory. The MPE/iX workloads were collected on a 64Megabyte machine.

These measurements represent the management of a 48-bit virtual address space. The HP-UX operating system environment allocates the upper 16 bits in a uniform distribution and the lower 32 bits are allocated in the standard instruction, data, and stack segments.

4.2 TLB Overhead Percentage

Graphs 1 and 2 measure the percentage of total cycles per instruction (CPI) attributed to TLB miss activity when utilizing an HPT or IPT data structure. The graphs give insight into the relative importance of the TLB miss component with respect to various workloads. They also demonstrate the impact of an HPT on overall performance. Graph 1 contains HP-UX trace data from both technical and commercial workloads. Graph 2 contains MPE/iX trace data for commercial workloads.

For example, the OLTP1-ux benchmark spends 12% of its time in TLB miss handling. That benchmark runs 3% faster just due to a software HPT vs. the original IPT structure. Hardware TLB handling gives another 4% improvement. The OLTP3-mpe workload in graph 2 spends 18.5% of its time handling TLB misses under the software IPT model. The software HPT saves 4% and a hardware HPT saves an additional 6%.

Large multi-user programs consistently show the greatest improvement when moving to the HPT. This is to be expected since their more demanding use of address space results in a higher TLB miss rate.

4.3 HPT cache miss rate vs HPT Size

Graph 3 measures the data cache miss rate into the head HPT bucket as a function of the HPT size. Insights into the importance of the cache miss penalty with respect to overall TLB overhead can be obtained by joining data in this graph with graphs 1, 4, and 5. For example, the multi-user workloads show a fairly high TLB overhead in graph 1. From graph 3 these workloads show a cache miss rate of approximately 20% (at 30 cycles per miss). This is a sizeable component of their overall TLB miss penalty given in graph 4.

While the graph does not show the individual cache miss rates for the forward-mapped page table, the following data is presented for comparison. Simulation of the forward mapped page tables under the OLTP1-ux, Telcom, and the OLTP2-ux multi-user workloads showed a 2-3% cache miss rate in the root table, and a 12-15% miss rate in the leaf entry. Under the numeric benchmarks the root table miss rate ranges from a 0-3% while the leaf entries range all the way up to a 25% cache miss rate.

4.4 Original IPT vs HPT

To better understand the TLB miss overheads graph 4 displays the average cycles per TLB miss including cache miss penalties for several configurations all with the same number of total entires. The original software IPT scheme, software 1-way HPT, hardware 1-way HPT, and hardware 2-way HPT are shown. For example, the finite benchmark has a 56 cycle per TLB miss penalty when using a software-only IPT.

The cycles per miss data shows that a software HPT can save a significant number of cycles over the original IPT. The savings can be broken into a static and dynamic component. The HPT saves 6 cycles per miss over the IPT in just basic cycle costs. The remaining difference is attributed to the one less cache line load. The cost of that load is 30 cycles times the cache miss rate into the IPT hash table for the given workload. Those workloads with a modest TLB CPI component, and a high cache miss rate into the translation table, will benefit the most.

In the multi-user benchmarks, the cache penalty cycles accumulated while walking the HPT or IPT amount to 20-35% of the average TLB miss overhead. The use of a hardware HPT miss handler is significantly faster. The basic overhead (not counting cache penalty cycles) is nearly half the software equivalent. The measured dynamic chain lenghts ranged from 1.02 to 1.13 in length.

A 2-way associative HPT performs slightly worse then the 1-way HPT. This was due to the serial compares in hardware (an extra 2 cycles). Had the compares been done in parallel, the higher hit rate in the 2-way table would have made a 2-way table more attractive.

4.5 HPT hybrid vs forward-mapped table

Graph 5 compares various forward-mapped page table (FMPT) results with a native hardware HPT and a small HPT used as a cache for the software managed forward-mapped page tables. The different strategies are compared based on their respective cycles per TLB miss. For example, the small HPT fronting an FMPT is 3 cycles/miss less than a direct hardware FMPT in the *finite* benchmark.

A problem with these HP-UX benchmarks is that they do not use enough of the address space to force the creation of additional levels in the forward-mapped page table (a two level page table is sufficient). A more aggressive use of the 64-bit virtual address space, by the HP-UX operating system, to concurrently map more objects such as is done by MPE/iX would force one or more additional levels to be instantiated in the forward-mapped tables. This would in turn push up the forward-mapped table cycles per miss count.

The results indicate that a small 1-way associative HPT, sitting in front of a forward mapped table, can be effective in reducing the cycles per miss overhead. Under the workloads investigated the combined hybrid strategy gives performance similar to a hardware forward mapped walker, and maintains a simpler hardware structure. This is an important result since it demonstrates that a simple hardware HPT can be designed in a flexible manner which supports/enhances more then one style of page table management.

4.6 TLB miss rate vs sharing Model

With the ASM model, shared memory does not share the same TLB entry. For all the single process benchmarks this makes no difference to the overall TLB miss rate. But with the multi-user benchmarks that share instructions and to a lesser extent data, the TLB miss rate changes significantly.

Graph 6 shows TLB miss rates for the 3 multi-user benchmarks. These small values are magnified by the cost of a miss. The 61% increase in the number of TLB misses for the Telcom-UX benchmark (.35% to .57%) amounts to a proportional change in overall TLB costs from roughly 3.5% to 5%. These numbers do not reflect the use of shared libraries or mapped files that could further increase the sharing of TLB entries across processes.

4.7 Page Table front bucket Hit Rate

Graph 7 measures the hit rate into the head bucket for four different HPT organizations. For example, 82% of the TLB misses are resolved in the front bucket while executing the *doduc* benchmark with the ASM-HW-HPT1x-1w workload.

From the graph, the hit rate into the front bucket is reasonably high. As expected, the larger the table the more likely the first entry holds the desired translation. A 2-way associate HPT achieves a higher hit rate then the 1-way. However as graph 4 demonstrates, the increased hit rate is not enough to offset the extra cycles spent in searching the two entries in series.

The effectiveness of moving an entry to the head bucket on a miss (chain reordering) is apparent when one looks at the hit rate of the much smaller ASM HPT verses the HP-UX HPT (8000 vs 32000 entries). The reason the ASM model can perform almost as well, and occasionally better, is that it is constantly moving the faulting translation into the HPT cache where it is visible to the hardware handler. This suggests that it might be useful to consider reordering the HP-UX HPT under certain workloads.

Graph 8 shows the sensitivity of the miss rate of the front bucket as a function of the HPT cache size. Generally, the cache is effective, but some workloads - especially the multi-user ones - show the need for large caches to hold the translation working set.

5. Conclusions

This paper demonstrates the effectiveness of a hardware HPT which is flexible enough to be used as the primary translation mechanism for large address space machines or as an efficient cache fronting a different page table design. The HPT is designed to maximize the effectiveness of TLB management by minimizing the overhead in handling TLB misses while still allowing complete operating system VM flexibility. Both hardware and software participate in the HPT trade-offs to provide a cost effective solution.

The analysis and data demonstrate that an HPT will out perform the standard IPT. An HPT maintains the same scalable storage properties as the IPT. This is a significant attribute when managing sparse access patterns.

It is shown that the HPT can be configured to operate like a cache in front of a more traditional forward-mapped table. Not all operating system environments can tolerate the limited aliasing capabilities of a "native" HPT. The data demonstrates that under most work loads the hybrid solution exceeds or equals the performance of the hardware forward-mapped walker.

The measurements reflect the behavior of TLBs in large address space machines in the sense that all the virtual memory of each process is being managed as a single sparsely allocated unit. Since the measured systems contained only 32 or 64 megabytes of physical memory, the measurements are only an approximation of future systems which use a larger virtual address space. The HPT's performance is independent of the physical memory size, the amount of allocated virtual memory, and the sparseness of the virtual memory.

The HPT is being used in HP's latest operating system release on PA-RISC hardware platforms.

6. Acknowledgments

Customizations to the simulator and data collection were performed by Joe Martinka. His comments and insights greatly improved the analysis of this paper. We would also like to thank Eric Delano, Greg Snider, Duncan Weir, John Wilkes, and the anonymous reviewers for their detailed suggestions and criticisms.

7. References

[Apol88] Apollo Computer Inc. *Series 10000 Technical Reference Library Volume 1 - Processors and Instruction Set*. Order No. 011720-A00. Apollo, Chelmsford MA, 1988.

[Chan88] Albert Chang and Mark F. Mergen, 801 Storage: Architecture and Programming, *ACM Transactions on Computer Systems*, Vol 6, No 1, February 1988, pp 28-50.

[Clar85] Doug Clark and Joel Emer. Performance of the VAX-11/780 translation buffer: Simulation and measurement. *ACM Transactions on Computer Systems*, 3(1):31-62, February 1985.

[DEC83] Digital Equipment Corporation. *VAX Architecture Reference Manual*. Doc. EK-VAXAR-RM-002. DEC, Bedford, MA, 1983.

[Dela92] Eric Delano, Will Walker, Jeff Yetter, Mark Forsyth. A High Speed Superscalar PA-RISC Processor. *Spring Compcon '92*, February 24-28, 1992, pp. 116-121.

[Call93] Jim Callister. (in HP's PA-RISC performance group). Personal communication.

[IBM78] IBM. IBM System/38 technical developments. Order no. G580-0237, IBM, Atlanta, GA., 1978.

[Jain91] Jain, R. *The Art of Computer Systems Performance Analysis*, pages 98-101, 404-428. John Wiley & Sons, 1991.

[Jog90] Jog,R., Vitale,P., and Callister, J. Performance Evaluation of a Commercial Cache-Coherent Shared Memory Multiprocessor. *ACM SIGMETRICS Conference on Measurement and Modeling of Computer Systems*, pages 173-182, May 1990.

[Knut73] Donald E. Knuth *The Art of Computer Programming - Volume 3: Sorting and Searching*, Addison Wesley, pp 506-549, 1973.

[Lee89] Ruby B. Lee. Precision Architecture. *Computer*, January 1989.

[Rose85] Rosenberg, J. and Abramson, D.A. "MONADS-PC: A Capability Based Workstation to Support Software Engineering", Proc. 18th Hawaii International Conference on System Sciences, 1985, pp. 222-231.

[Ston88] Stone,H., *High-Performance Computer Architecture*, pg. 41-52. Addison-Wesley, 1987.

[Tayl90] George Taylor, P Davies, Mike Farmwald. The TLB slice a low-cost high-speed address translation mechanism. In *The 17th Annual International Symposium on Computer Architecture*. May 1990. pp. 355-363.

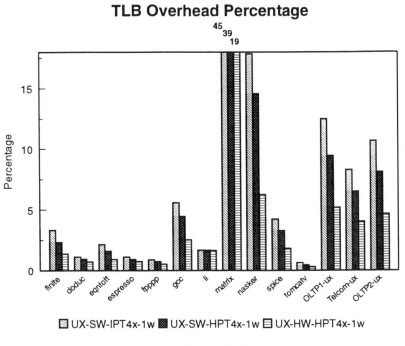

TLB Overhead Percentage

Graph 1

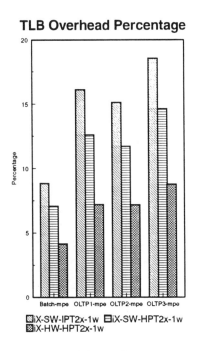

TLB Overhead Percentage

Graph 2

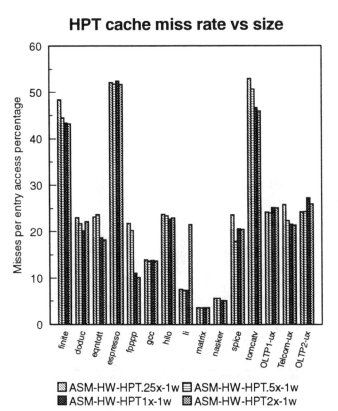

HPT cache miss rate vs size

Graph 3

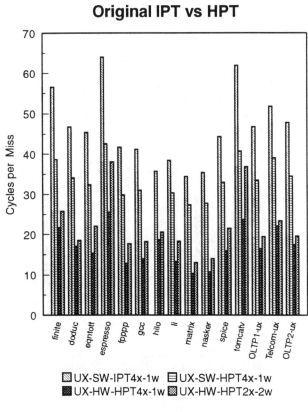

Original IPT vs HPT

Graph 4

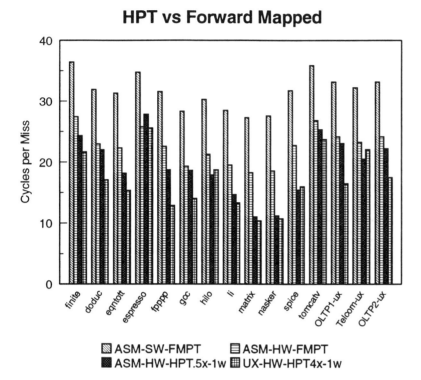

HPT vs Forward Mapped
Cycles per Miss
0
10
20
30
40
finite
doduc
eqntott
espresso
fpppp
gcc
hilo
li
matrix
nasker
spice
tomcatv
OLTP1-ux
Telcom-ux
OLTP2-ux
ASM-SW-FMPT
ASM-HW-FMPT
ASM-HW-HPT.5x-1w
UX-HW-HPT4x-1w

Graph 5

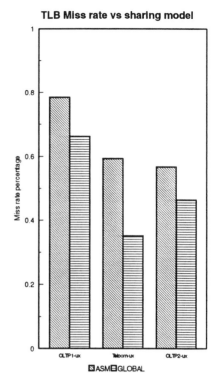

TLB Miss rate vs sharing model
Miss rate percentage
0
0.2
0.4
0.6
0.8
1
OLTP1-ux
Telcom-ux
OLTP2-ux
ASM
GLOBAL

Graph 6

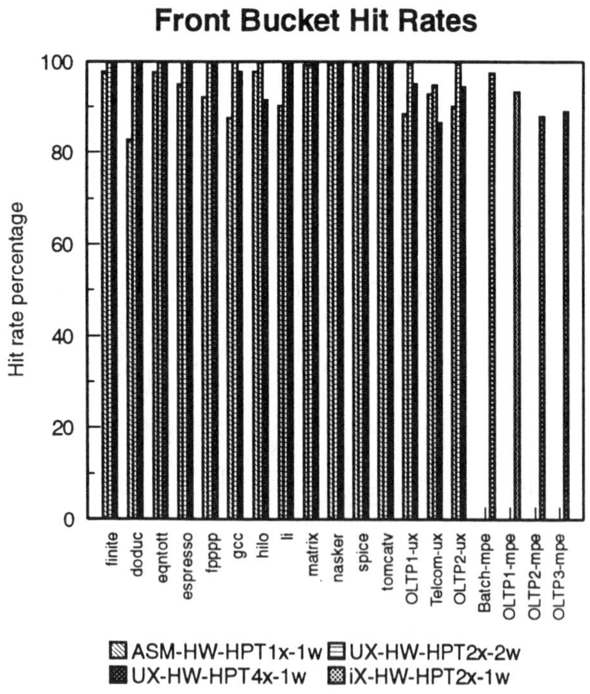

Front Bucket Hit Rates
Hit rate percentage
0
20
40
60
80
100
finite
doduc
eqntott
espresso
fpppp
gcc
hilo
li
matrix
nasker
spice
tomcatv
OLTP1-ux
Telcom-ux
OLTP2-ux
Batch-mpe
OLTP1-mpe
OLTP2-mpe
OLTP3-mpe
ASM-HW-HPT1x-1w
UX-HW-HPT2x-2w
UX-HW-HPT4x-1w
iX-HW-HPT2x-1w

Graph 7

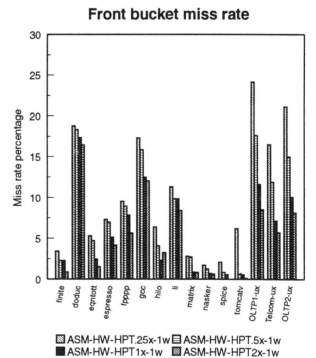

Front bucket miss rate
Miss rate percentage
0
5
10
15
20
25
30
finite
doduc
eqntott
espresso
fpppp
gcc
hilo
li
matrix
nasker
spice
tomcatv
OLTP1-ux
Telcom-ux
OLTP2-ux
ASM-HW-HPT.25x-1w
ASM-HW-HPT.5x-1w
ASM-HW-HPT1x-1w
ASM-HW-HPT2x-1w

Graph 8

SESSION 4:
Input/Output

The TickerTAIP parallel RAID architecture

Pei Cao

Princeton University
Dept. of Computer Science
Princeton, NJ 08540

pc@cs.princeton.edu

Swee Boon Lim

University of Illinois
Dept. of Computer Science
1304 W. Springfield Ave.
Urbana, IL 61801

sblim@cs.uiuc.edu

Shivakumar
Venkataraman

University of Wisconsin
Dept. of Computer Science
1210 West Dayton St.
Madison, WI 53706

venkatar@cs.wisc.edu

John Wilkes

Hewlett-Packard Laboratories

P.O. Box 10490, 1U13
Palo Alto, CA 94303-0969

wilkes@hpl.hp.com

Traditional disk arrays have a centralized architecture, with a single controller through which all requests flow. Such a controller is a single point of failure, and its performance limits the maximum size that the array can grow to. We describe here TickerTAIP, a parallel architecture for disk arrays that distributes the controller functions across several loosely-coupled processors. The result is better scalability, fault tolerance, and flexibility.

This paper presents the TickerTAIP architecture and an evaluation of its behavior. We demonstrate the feasibility by an existence proof; describe a family of distributed algorithms for calculating RAID parity; discuss techniques for establishing request atomicity, sequencing and recovery; and evaluate the performance of the TickerTAIP design in both absolute terms and by comparison to a centralized RAID implementation. We conclude that the TickerTAIP architectural approach is feasible, useful, and effective.

1 Introduction

A disk array is a structure that connects several disks together to extend the cost, power and space advantages of small disks to higher capacity configurations. By providing partial redundancy such as parity, availability can be increased as well. Such *RAIDs* (for Redundant Arrays of Inexpensive Disks) were first described in the early 1980s [Lawlor81, Park86], and popularized by the work of a group at UC Berkeley [Patterson88, Patterson89].

The traditional architecture of a RAID array, shown in Figure 1, has a central controller, one or more disks, and multiple head-of-string disk interfaces. The RAID controller interfaces to the host, processes read and write requests, and carries out parity calculations, block placement, and data recovery after a disk failure.

The RAID controller is crucial to the performance and availability of the system. If its bandwidth, processing power, or capacity are inadequate, the performance of the array as a whole will suffer. (This is increasingly likely to happen: parity calculation is memory-bound, and memory speeds have not kept pace with recent CPU performance improvements [Ousterhout90].) Latency through the controller can reduce the performance of small requests. The single point of failure that the controller represents can also be a concern: published failure rates for disk drives and packaged electronics are now similar. Although some commercial products include spare RAID controllers, they are not normally simultaneously active: one typically acts as a backup for the other, and is held in reserve until it is needed because of failure of the primary. This is expensive: the backup has to have all the capacity of the primary controller.

To address these concerns, we have developed the *TickerTAIP architecture for parallel RAIDs* (Figure 2). In this architecture, there is no central controller: it has been replaced by a cooperating set of *array controller nodes* that together provide all the functions needed. The TickerTAIP architecture offers fault-tolerance (no central controller to break), performance scalability (no central bottleneck), smooth incremental growth (by simply adding another node), and flexibility (it is easy to mix and match components).

This paper provides an evaluation of the TickerTAIP architecture.

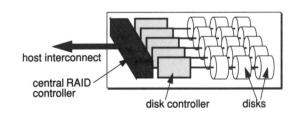

Figure 1: traditional RAID array architecture.

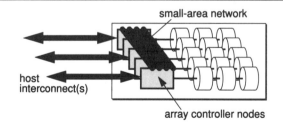

Figure 2: TickerTAIP array architecture.

1.1 Related work

Many papers have been published on RAID reliability, performance, and on design variations for parity placement and recovery schemes, such as [Clark88a, Gibson88, Menon89, Schulze89, Dunphy90, Gray90, Lee90, Muntz90, Holland92]. Our work builds on these studies: we concentrate here on the architectural issues of parallelizing the techniques used in a centralized RAID array, so we take such work as a given—and assume familiarity with basic RAID concepts in what follows.

Something similar to the TickerTAIP physical architecture was realized in the HP7937 family of disks [HPdisks89]. These disks can be connected together by a 10MB/s bus, which allows access to "remote" disks as well as fast switchover between attached hosts in the event of system failure. No multi-disk functions (such as a disk array) were provided, however.

A proposal was made to connect networks of processors to form a widely-distributed RAID controller in [Stonebraker89]. This approach was called RADD—*Redundant Arrays of Distributed Disks*. It proposed using disks spread across a wide-area network to improve availability in the face of a site failure. In contrast to the RADD study, we emphasize the use of parallelism inside a single RAID server; we assume the kind of fast, reliable interconnect that is easily constructed inside a single server cabinet; we closely couple processors and disks, so that a node failure is treated as (one or more) disk failures; and we provide much improved performance analyses—[Stonebraker89] used "all disk operations take 30ms". The result is a new, detailed characterization of the parallel RAID design approach in a significantly different environment.

1.2 Paper outline

We begin this paper by describing the TickerTAIP architecture, including descriptions and evaluations of algorithms for parity calculation, recovery from controller failure, and extensions to provide sequencing of concurrent requests from multiple hosts.

To evaluate TickerTAIP we constructed a working prototype as existence proof and functional testbed, and then built a detailed event-based simulation that we calibrated against the prototype. These tools are presented as background material for the performance analysis of TickerTAIP that follows, with particular emphasis on comparing it against a centralized RAID implementation. We conclude the paper with a summary of our results.

2 The TickerTAIP architecture

A TickerTAIP array is composed of a number of *worker nodes*, which are nodes with one or more local disks connected through a SCSI bus. *Originator nodes* provide connections to host computer clients. The nodes are connected to one another by a high-performance, small-area network with sufficient internal redundancy to survive single failures. (Mesh-based switching fabrics can achieve this with reasonable cost and complexity. A design that would meet the performance, scalability and fault-tolerance needs of a TickerTAIP array is described in [Wilkes91].)

In Figure 2, the nodes are shown as being both workers and originators: that is, they have both host and disk connections. A second design, shown in Figure 3, dedicates separate nodes to the worker and originator functions. Each node might then be of a different type (e.g., SCSI-originator, FDDI-originator, IPI-worker, SCSI-worker). This makes it easy to support a TickerTAIP array that has multiple different kinds of host interface. Since each node is plug-compatible from the point of view of the internal interconnect, it is also easy to configure an array with any desired ratio of worker and originator nodes, a flexibility less easily achieved in the traditional centralized architecture.

Figure 4 shows the environment in which we envision a TickerTAIP array operating. The array provides disk services to one or more *host* computers through the originator nodes. There may be several originator nodes, each connected to a different host; alternatively, a single host can be connected to multiple originators for higher performance and greater failure resilience. For simplicity, we require that all data for a request be returned to the host along the path used to issue the request.

In the context of this model, a traditional RAID array looks like a TickerTAIP array with several unintelligent worker nodes, a single originator node on which all the parity calculations take place, and shared-memory communication between the components.

3 Design issues

This section describes the TickerTAIP design issues in greater detail. It begins with an examination of normal mode

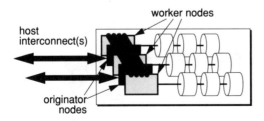

Figure 3: alternative TickerTAIP host interconnection architecture with dedicated originator nodes.

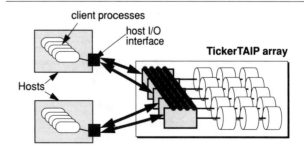

Figure 4: TickerTAIP system environment.

operation (i.e., fault-free) and then examines the support needed to cope with failures.

3.1 Normal-mode reads

In normal mode, read requests are straightforward since no parity computation is required: the data is read at the workers and forwarded to the originator. For multi-stripe requests, we found it beneficial to perform sequential reads of both data and parity, and then to discard the parity blocks, rather than to generate separate requests that omitted reading the parity blocks.

3.2 Normal-mode writes

In a RAID array, writes require calculation or modification of stored parity to maintain the partial data redundancy. Each stripe is considered separately in determining the method and site for parity computation.

3.2.1 How to calculate new parity

The first design choice is how to calculate the new parity. There are three alternatives, which depend on the amount of the stripe being updated (Figure 5):

- *full stripe*: all of the data blocks in the stripes have to be written, and parity can be calculated entirely from the new data;
- *small stripe*: less than half of the data blocks in a stripe are to be written, and parity is calculated by first reading the old data of the blocks which will be written, XORing them with the new data and then XORing the results with the old parity block data;
- *large stripe*: more than half of the data blocks in the stripe are to be written; the new parity block can be computed by reading the data blocks in the stripe that are

not being written and XORing them with the new data (i.e., reducing this to the full-stripe case) [Chen90].

Depending on its size, a single I/O request will involve one or more stripe size types. The effect on performance of enabling the large-stripe mode is discussed later.

3.2.2 Where to calculate new parity

The second design consideration is where the parity is to be calculated. Traditional centralized RAID architectures calculate all parity at the originator node, since only it has the necessary processing capability. In TickerTAIP, every node has a processor, so there are several choices. The key design goal is to load balance the work amongst the nodes—in particular, to spread out the parity calculations over as many nodes as possible. Here are three possibilities (shown in Figure 6):

- *at originator:* all parity calculations are done at the originator;
- *solely-parity*: all parity calculations for a stripe take place at the parity node for that stripe;
- *at parity*: as for solely-parity, except that partial results during a small-stripe write are calculated at the worker nodes and shipped to the parity node.

The solely-parity scheme always uses more messages than the at parity one, so we did not pursue it further. We provide performance comparisons between the other two later in the paper.

3.3 Single failures—request atomicity

We begin with a discussion of single-point failures. One goal of a regular RAID array is to survive single-disk failures. TickerTAIP extends the single-fault-masking semantics to include failure of a part of its distributed controller: we do not

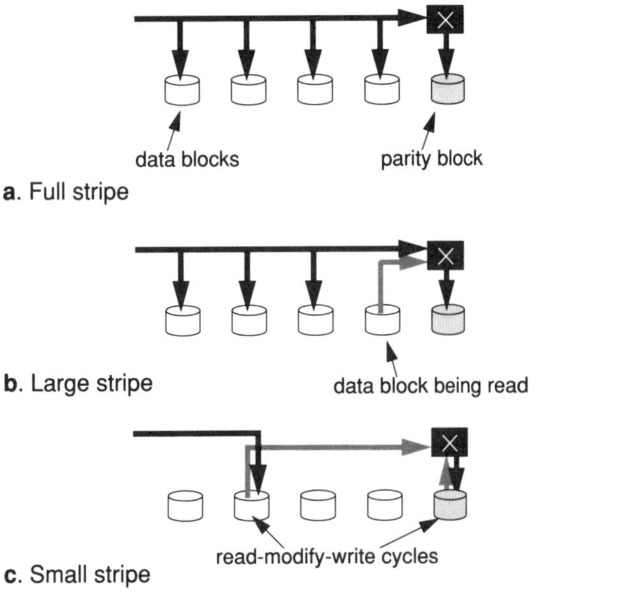

a. Full stripe
data blocks   parity block

b. Large stripe
data block being read

c. Small stripe
read-modify-write cycles

Figure 5: the three different stripe update size policies.

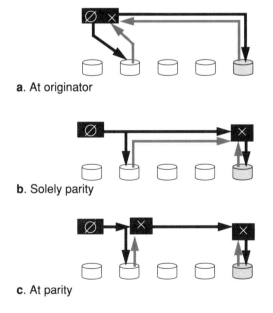

a. At originator

b. Solely parity

c. At parity

Figure 6: three different places to calculate parity.

make the simplifying assumption that the controller is not a possible failure point. (We have legislated internal single-fault-tolerance for the interconnect fabric, so this is not a concern.)

3.3.1 Disk failure

Disk failures are treated in just the same way as in a traditional RAID array: the array continues operation in degraded (failed) mode until the disk is repaired or replaced; the contents of the new disk are reconstructed; and execution resumes in normal mode. From the outside of the array, the effect is as if nothing has happened. Inside, appropriate data reconstructions occur on reads, and I/O operations to the failed disk are suppressed.

3.3.2 Worker failure

A TickerTAIP worker failure is treated just like a disk failure, and is masked in just the same way. (Just as with a regular RAID controller with multiple disks per head-of-string controller, a failing worker means that an entire column of disks is lost at once, but the same recovery algorithms apply.) We assume fail-silent nodes: the isolation offered by the networking protocols used to communicate between nodes is likely to make this assumption realistic in practice for all but the most extreme cases—for which RAID arrays are probably not appropriate choices. A node is suspected to have failed if it does not respond within a reasonable time; the node that detects this initiates a distributed consensus protocol much like two-phase commit, taking the role of coordinator of the consensus protocol. All the remaining nodes reach agreement by this means on the number and identity of the failed node(s). This protocol ensures that all the remaining nodes enter failure mode at the same time. Multiple failures cause the array to shut itself down safely to prevent possible data corruption.

3.3.3 Originator failure and request atomicity

Failure of a node with an originator on it brings new concerns: a channel to a host is lost, any worker on the same node will be lost as well, and the fate of requests that arrived through this node needs to be determined since the failed originator was responsible for coordinating their execution.

Originator failures during reads are fairly simple: the read operation is aborted since there is no longer a route to communicate its results back to the host.

Failures during write operations are more complicated, because different portions of the write could be at different stages unless extra steps are taken to avoid compromising the consistency of the stripes involved in the write. Worst is failure of a node that is both a worker and an originator, since it will be the only one with a copy of the data destined for its own disk. (For example, if such a node fails during a partial-stripe write after some of the blocks in the stripe have been written, it may not be possible to reconstruct the state of the entire stripe, violating the rule that a single failure must be masked.)

Our solution is to both these concerns is to ensure *write atomicity*: that is, either a write operation completes successfully or it makes no changes. To achieve this, we added a two-phase commit protocol to write operations. Before a write can proceed, sufficient data must be replicated in more than one node's memory to let the operation restart and complete—even if an arbitrary node fails. If this cannot be achieved, the request is aborted before it can make any changes.

We identified two approaches to implementing the two phase commit: *early commit* tries to make the decision as quickly as possible; *late commit* delays its commit decision until al that is left to do is the writes.

In *late commit*, the commit point (when it decides whether to continue or not) is reached only after the parity has been computed, and this provides the needed partial redundancy; by this stage, all that is left to do is the writes.

In *early commit*, the goal is for the array to get to its commit point as quickly as possible during the execution of the request. This requires that the new data destined for the originator/worker node has to be replicated elsewhere, in case the originator fails after commit. The same must be done for old data being read as part of a large-stripe write, in case the reading node fails before it can provide the data. We duplicate this data on the parity nodes of the affected stripes—this involves sending no additional data in the case of parity calculations at the parity node (which we will see below is the preferred policy). The commit point is reached as soon as the necessary redundancy has been achieved.

Late commit is much easier to implement, but has lower concurrency and higher request latency. We explore the size of this cost later.

A write operation is aborted if any involved worker does not reach its commit point. When a worker node fails, the originator is responsible for restarting the operation. In the event of an originator failure, a temporary originator is elected to complete or abort the processing of the request, chosen from amongst those nodes that were already participating in the request, since this simplifies recovery. To implement the two-phase commit protocols, new states were added to the worker and originator node state tables. The placement of these additional states determines the commit policy: for early commit, as soon as possible; for late commit, just before the writes.

3.4 Multiple failures—request sequencing

This section discusses measures designed to help limit the effects of multiple concurrent failures. The RAID architecture tolerates any single disk failure. However, it provides no behavior guarantees in the event of multiple failures (especially powerfail), and it does not ensure the independence of overlapping requests that are executing simultaneously. In the terminology of [Lampson81], multiple failures are catastrophes: events outside the covered fault set for RAID. TickerTAIP introduces coverage for partial controller failures; and it goes beyond this by using *request sequencing* to limit the effects of multiple failures in a way that is useful to file system designers. Like a regular RAID, however, a powerfail during a write can corrupt the stripe being written to unless more extensive recovery techniques (such as logging) are used.

3.4.1 Requirements

File system designers typically rely on the presence of ordering invariants to allow them to recover from crashes or power failure. For example, in 4.2BSD-based file systems, metadata (inode and directory) writes must occur before the data to which they refer is allowed to reach the disk [McKusick84]. The simplest way to achieve this is to defer queueing the data write until the metadata write has completed. Unfortunately, this can severely limit concurrency: for example, parity calculations can no longer be overlapped with the execution of the previous request. A better way to achieve the desired invariant is to provide—and preserve—partial write orderings in the I/O subsystem. This technique can significantly improve file system performance. From our perspective as RAID array designers, it also allows the RAID array to make more intelligent decisions about request scheduling, using rotation position information that is not readily available in the host [Jacobson91].

TickerTAIP can support multiple hosts. As a result, some mechanism needs to be provided to let requests from different hosts be serialized without recourse to either sending all requests through a single host, or requiring one request to complete before the next can be issued.

Finally, multiple overlapping requests from a single or multiple hosts can be in flight simultaneously. This could lead to parts of one write replacing parts of another in a non-serializable fashion, which clearly should be prevented. (Our write commit protocols provide atomicity for each request, but no serializability guarantees.)

3.4.2 Request sequencing

To address these requirements, we introduced a request sequencing mechanism using partial orderings for both reads and writes. Internally, these are represented in the form of *directed acyclic graphs* (*DAGs*): each request is represented by a node in the DAG, while the edges of the DAG represent dependencies between requests.

To express the DAG, each request is given a unique identifier. A request is allowed to list one or more requests on which it *explicitly* depends; TickerTAIP guarantees that the effect is *as if* no request begins until the requests on which it depends complete (this allows freedom to perform eager evaluation, some of which we exploit in our current implementation.). If a request is aborted, all requests that explicitly depend on it are also aborted (and so on, transitively). In addition, TickerTAIP will arbitrarily assign sufficient *implicit* dependencies to prevent overlapping requests from executing concurrently. Aborts are not propagated across implicit dependencies. In the absence of explicit dependencies, the order in which requests are serviced is some arbitrary serializable schedule.

3.4.3 Sequencer states

The management of sequencing is performed through a high-level state table, with the following states (diagrammed, with their transitions, in Figure 7):

- **NotIssued**: the request itself has not yet reached TickerTAIP, but another request has referred to this request in its dependency list.
- **Unresolved**: the request has been issued, but it depends on a request that has not yet reached the TickerTAIP array.
- **Resolved**: all of the requests that this one depends on have arrived at the array, but at least one has yet to complete.
- **InProgress**: all of a request's dependencies have been satisfied, so it has begun executing.
- **Completed**: a request has successfully finished.
- **Aborted**: a request was aborted, or a request on which this request explicitly depended has been aborted.

Old request state has to be garbage collected. We do this by requiring that the hosts number their requests sequentially, and by keeping track of the oldest outstanding incomplete request from each host. When this request completes, any older completed requests can be deleted. Any request that

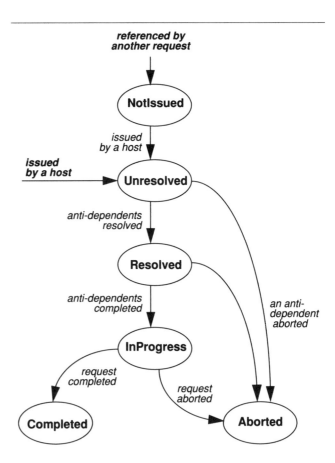

Figure 7: states of a request. An "anti-dependent" is a request that this request is waiting for.

56

depends on an older request than the oldest recorded one can consider the dependency immediately satisfied.

Aborts are an important exception to this mechanism since a request that depends on an aborted request should itself be aborted, whenever it occurred. Unfortunately, there is a race condition between the request being aborted and the host issuing requests that depend on it. Our solution is to maintain state about aborted requests for a guaranteed minimum time—10 seconds in our prototype. Similarly, a time-out on the NotIssued state can be used to detect errors such as a host that never issues a request other requests are waiting for.

3.4.4 Sequencer design alternatives

We considered four designs for the sequencer mechanism:

1. *Fully centralized*: a single, central sequencer manages the state table and its transitions. (A primary and a backup are used to eliminate a single point of failure.) In the absence of contention, each request suffers two additional round-trip message latency times: between the originator and the sequencer, and between the sequencer and its backup. One of these trips is unneeded if the originator is co-located with the sequencer.

2. *Partially centralized*: a centralized sequencer handles the state table until all the dependencies have been resolved, at which point the responsibility is shifted to the worker nodes involved in the request. This requires that the status of every request be sent to all the workers, to allow them to do the resolution of subsequent transitions. This has more concurrency, but requires a broadcast on every request completion.

3. *Originator-driven*: in place of a central sequencer, the originator nodes (since there will typically be fewer of these than the workers) conduct a distributed-consensus protocol to determine the overlaps and sequence constraints, after which the partially-centralized approach is used. This always generates more messages than the centralized schemes.

4. *Worker-driven*: the workers are responsible for all the states and their transitions. This widens the distributed-consensus protocol to every node in the array, and still requires the end-of-request broadcast.

Although the higher-numbered of the above designs potentially increase concurrency, they do so at the cost of increased message traffic and complexity.

We chose to implement the fully centralized model in our prototype, largely because of the complexity of the failure-recovery protocols required for the alternatives. As expected, we measured the resulting latency to be that of two round-trip messages (440µs) plus a few tens of microseconds of state table management. We find the additional overhead to provide request sequencing acceptable for the benefits that it provides, although we also made sequencing optional.

3.5 The RAIDmap

Previous sections have presented the policy issues; this one discusses an implementation technique we found useful. Our first design for sequencing and coordinating requests retained a great deal of centralized authority: the originator tried to coordinate the actions taking place at each of the different nodes (reads and writes, parity calculations). We soon found ourselves faced with the messy problem of coping with a complex set of interdependent actions taking place on multiple remote nodes.

We then developed a new approach: rather than assume that each of the workers need to be told what to do, assume that they would do whatever was necessary without further interaction. Once the workers are told about the original request (its starting point and length, and whether it is a read or a write) and given any data they needed, they can proceed on their own. We call this approach *collaborative execution*: it is characterized by each node assuming that other nodes are *already* doing their part of the request. For example, if node A needs data from node B, A can rely on B to generate and ship the data to A with no further prompting.

To orchestrate the work, we developed a structure known as a *RAIDmap*, a rectangular array with an entry for each column (worker) and each stripe. Each worker builds its column of the RAIDmap, filling in the blanks as a function of the operation (read or write), the layout policy and the execution policy. The *layout policy* determines where data and parity blocks are placed in the RAID array (e.g., mirroring, or RAID 4 or 5). The *execution policy* determines the algorithm used to service the request (e.g., where parity is to be calculated). A simplified RAIDmap is shown in Figure 8.

One component of the RAIDmap is a state table for each block (the states are described in Table 1). It is this table that the layout and execution policies fill out. A request enters the states in order, leaving each one when the associated function has been completed, or immediately if the state is marked as "not needed" for this request. For example, a read request will enter state 1 (to read the data), skip through state 2 to state 3 (to send it to the originator), and then skip through the remaining states.

The RAIDmap proved to be a flexible mechanism, allowing us to test out several different policy alternatives (e.g., whether to calculate partial parity results locally, or whether to send the data to the originator or parity nodes). In addition, the same technique is used in failure mode: the RAIDmap indicates to each node how it is to behave, but now it is filled out in such a way as to reflect the failure mode operations. Finally, the RAIDmap simplified configuring a centralized implementation using the same policies and assumptions as the distributed case.

The goal of any RAID implementation is to maximize disk utilization and minimize request latency. To help achieve this, the RAIDmap computation is overlapped with other operations such as moving data or accessing disks. For the same reason, workers send data needed elsewhere before servicing their own parity computations or local disk transfers.

Table 1: state-space for each block at a worker node

State	Function	Other information
1	Read old data	disk address
2	XOR old with new data	
3	Send old data (or XOR'd old data) to another node	node to send it to
4	Await incoming data (or XOR'd data)	number of blocks to wait for
5	XOR incoming data with local old data/parity	
6	Write new data or parity	disk address

It also proved important to optimize the disk accesses themselves. When we delayed writes in our prototype implementation until the parity data was available, throughput increased by 25–30% because the data and parity writes were coalesced together, reducing the number of disk seeks needed.

4 Evaluating TickerTAIP

This section presents the vehicles we used to evaluate the design choices and performance of the TickerTAIP architecture.

4.1 The prototype

We first constructed a working *prototype implementation* of the TickerTAIP design, including all the fault tolerance features described above. The intent of this implementation was a functional testbed, to help ensure that we had made our design complete. (For example, we were able to test our fault recovery code by telling nodes to "die".) The prototype also let us measure path lengths and get some early performance data.

We implemented the designs on an array of seven storage nodes, each comprised of a Parsytec MSC card with a T800 transputer, 4MB of RAM, and a local SCSI interface, connected to a local SCSI disk drive. The disks were spin-synchronized for these experiments. A stripe unit (the block-level interleave unit) was 4KB. Each node had a local HP79560 SCSI disk with the properties shown in Table 2.

Stripe	node 0	node 1	node 2	node 3	Type
0	–,–,– unused	–,–,– unused	2,0,3 data	–,0,– parity	small stripe
1	4,1,2 data	5,1,2 data	–,1,– parity	3,1,2 data	full stripe
2	–,–,– unused	–,2,– parity	6,2,1 data	7,2,1 data	large stripe

Figure 8: RAIDmap example for a write request spanning logical blocks 2 through 7. Each tuple contains: logical and physical block number, node to send parity data to, and a block type. The rightmost column is discussed in section 3.2.1.

Table 2: characteristics of the HP79560 disk drive

property	value
diameter	5.25"
surfaces/heads	19 data, 1 servo
formatted capacity	1.3GB
track size	72 sectors
sector size	512 bytes
rotation speed	4002 RPM
disk transfer rate	2.2MB/s
SCSI bus transfer rate	5MB/s
controller overhead	1ms
track-to-track switch time	1.67ms
seeks $\leq$ 12 cylinders	$1.28 + 1.15\sqrt{d}$ ms
seeks > 12 cylinders	$4.84 + 0.193\sqrt{d} + 0.00494d$ ms

The prototype was built in C to run on Helios [Perihelion91]: a small, lightweight operating system nucleus. We measured the one-way message latency for short messages between directly-connected nodes to be 110µs, and the peak inter-node bandwidth to be 1.6MB/s. Performance was limited by the relatively slow processors, and because the design of the Parsytec cards means that they cannot overlap computation and data transfer across their SCSI bus. Nevertheless, the prototype provided useful comparative performance data for design choices, and served as the calibration point of our simulator.

Our prototype comprised a total of 13.3k lines of code, including comments and test routines. About 12k lines of this was directly associated with the RAID functionality.

4.2 The simulator

We also built a detailed event driven *simulator* using the AT&T C++ tasking library [ATT89]. This enabled us to explore the effects of changing link and processor speeds, and to experiment with larger configurations than our prototype. Our model encompassed the following components:

- *Workloads*: both *fixed* (all requests of a single type) and *imitative* (patterns that simulate existing workload patterns); we used a closed queueing model, and the method of batched means [Pawlikowski90] to obtain steady-state measurements.

- *Host*: a collection of workloads sharing an access port to the TickerTAIP array; disk driver path lengths were estimated from measurements made on our local HP-UX systems.

- *TickerTAIP nodes (workers and originators)*: code path lengths were derived from measurements of the algorithms running on the working prototype and our HP-UX workstations (we assumed that the Parsytec MSC limitations would not occur in a real design).

58

- *Disk*: we modelled the HP79560 disks as used on the prototype implementation, using data taken from measurements of the real hardware. The disk model included: the seek time profile from Table 2, plus different settling times for reads and writes; track- and cylinder-skews, including track switch times during a data transfer; rotation position; and SCSI bus and controller overheads, including overlapped data transfers from the mechanism into a disk track buffer and transmissions across the SCSI bus: the granularity used was 4KB.

- *Links*: represent communication channels such as the small-area network and the SCSI busses. For simplicity, we report here data from a complete point-to-point interconnect design with a DMA engine per link; however, preliminary studies suggest that similar results would be obtained from mesh-based switching fabrics.

Under the same design choice and performance parameters, our simulation results agreed with the prototype (real) implementation within 3% most of the time, and always within 6%. This gave us confidence in the predictive abilities of the simulator.

The system we evaluate here is a RAID5 disk array with left-symmetric parity [Lee90], 4KB block-level interleave, spin-synchronized disks, FIFO disk scheduling, and with no data replication, spare blocks, floating parity or indirect-writes. The configuration has 4 hosts and 11 worker nodes, each worker with a single HP96760 disk attached to it via a 5MB/s SCSI bus. Four of the nodes were both originators and workers.

The throughput numbers reported here were obtained when the system was driven to saturation; response times with only one request in the system at a time. For the throughput measurements we timed 10000 requests in each run; for latency we timed 2000 requests. Each data point on a graph represents the average of two independent runs, with all variances less than 1.5%, and most less than 0.5%. Each value in a table is the average of five such runs; the variances are reported with each table.

4.3 Read performance

Table 3 shows the performance of our simulated 11-disk array for random read requests across a range of link speeds. There is no significant difference in throughput for any link speed above 1MB/s, but 10MB/s or more is needed to minimize request latencies for the larger transfers.

4.4 Design alternatives: writes

We first consider the effect of the large stripe policy. Figure 9 shows the result: in general, enabling the large write policy for large stripes gives slightly better throughput, so that is what we used for the remainder of the experiments.

Next, we compare the at-originator and at-parity policies for parity calculation. Figure 10 gives the results. At-parity works best because it spreads the work most evenly, so we used it for the remainder of our experiments. As expected,

Table 3: read performance for fixed-size workloads, with varying link speeds. (All variances less than 2%.)

Request size	throughput MB/s	latency (in ms)		
		1MB/s	10MB/s	100MB/s
4KB	0.94	33	31	30
40KB	1.79	38	34	33
1MB	15.2	178	86	76
10MB	21.1	1520	610	520

the difference is greatest for large write requests and slow processors.

The effect of the late commit protocol on performance is shown in Figure 11. (Although not shown, the performance of early commit is slightly better than that of late commit, but not as good as no commit). The effect of the commit protocol on throughput is small (< 2%), but the effect on response time is more marked: the commit point is acting as a synchronization barrier that prevents some of the usual overlaps between disk accesses and other operations. For example, a disk that is only doing writes for a request will not start seeking until the commit message is given. (This could

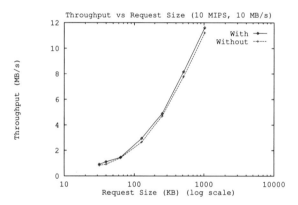

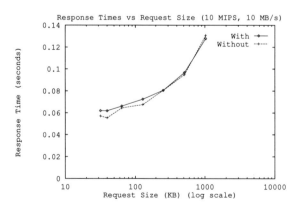

Figure 9: effect of enabling the large-stripe parity computation policy for writes larger than one half the stripe.

be avoided by having it do a seek in parallel with the other pre-commit work.)

Nonetheless, we recommend late commit overall: its throughput is almost as good as no commit protocol at all, and it is much easier to implement than early commit.

4.5 Comparison with centralized RAID array

How would TickerTAIP compare with a traditional centralized RAID array? This section answers that question. We simulated both the same 11-node TickerTAIP system as before and an 11-disk centralized RAID. The simulation components and algorithms used in the two cases were the same: our goal was to provide a direct comparison of the two architectures, as much uncontaminated by other factors as possible. For amusement, we also provide data for a 10-disk non-fault-tolerant striping array implemented using the TickerTAIP architecture.

The results for 10MIPS processors with 10MB/s links are shown in Figure 12. Clearly a non-disk bottleneck is limiting the throughput of the centralized system for request sizes larger than 256KB, and its response time for requests larger than 32KB. The obvious candidate is a CPU bottleneck from parity calculations, and this is indeed what we found. To show this, we plot performance as a function of CPU and link speed (Figure 13), and both varying together (Figure 14).

These graphs show that the TickerTAIP architecture is successfully exploiting load balancing to achieve similar (or better) throughput and response times with less powerful processors than the centralized architecture. For 1MB write requests, TickerTAIP's 5MIPS processors and 2–5MB/s links give comparable throughput to 25MIPS and 5MB/s for the centralized array. The centralized array needs a 50MIPS processor to get similar response times as TickerTAIP.

Finally, we looked at the effect of scaling the number of workers in the array, with both constant request size (400KB) and a varying one with a fixed amount of data per disk (ten full stripes). In these experiments, 4 of the worker nodes were also originators. The results are seen in Figure 12. With varying request size, the TickerTAIP architecture continues to scale linearly over the range we investigated; with constant request size, it degrades somewhat as the disks are kept less busy doing useful work.

4.6 Synthetic workloads

The results reported so far have been from fixed, constant-sized workloads. To test our hypothesis that TickerTAIP performance would scale as well over some other workloads, we tested a number of additional workload mixtures, designed to model "real world" applications:

- *OLTP*: based on the TPC-A database benchmark;

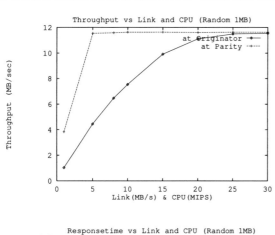

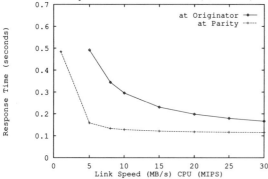

Figure 10: effect of parity calculation policy on throughput and response times for 1MB random writes.

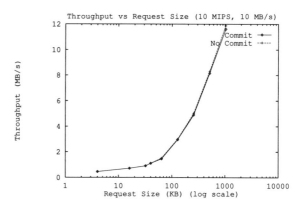

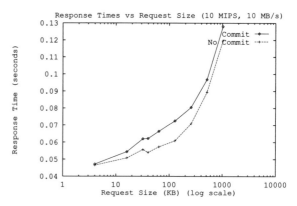

Figure 11: effect of the late commit protocol on write throughput and response time.

- *timeshare*: based on measurements of a local UNIX timesharing system [Ruemmler93];
- *scientific*: based on measurements taken from supercomputer applications running on a Cray [Miller91]; "large" has a mean request size of about 0.3MB, "small" has a mean around 30KB.

Table 4 gives the throughputs of the disk arrays under these workloads for a range of processor and link speeds. As expected, TickerTAIP outperforms the centralized architecture at lower CPU speeds, although both are eventually able to drive the disks to saturation—mostly because the request sizes are quite small. TickerTAIP's availability is still higher, of course.

5 Conclusions

TickerTAIP is a new parallel architecture for RAID arrays. Our experience is that it is eminently practical (for example, our prototype implementation took only 12k lines of commented code). The TickerTAIP architecture exploits its physical redundancy to tolerate any single point of failure, including single failures in its distributed controller; is scalable across a range of system sizes with smooth incremental growth; and the mixed worker/originator node model provides considerable configuration flexibility. Further, we showed how to provide—and prototyped—

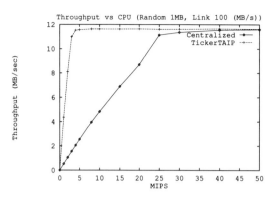

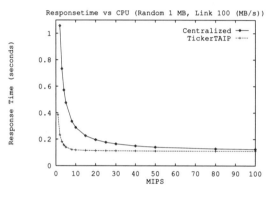

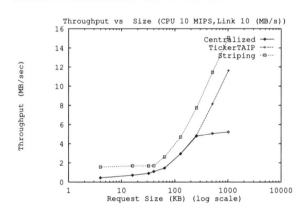

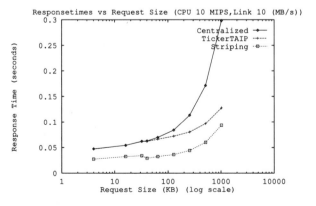

Figure 12: write throughput and response time for three different array architectures.

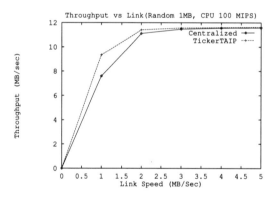

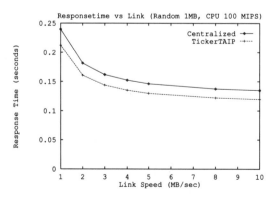

Figure 13: throughput and response time as a function of CPU and link speed. 1MB random writes.

partial write ordering to support clean semantics in the face of multiple outstanding requests and multiple faults, such as power failures. We have also demonstrated that—at least in this application—eleven 5MIPS processors are just as good as a single 50MIPS one, and provided quantitative data on how central and parallel RAID array implementations compare.

Most of the performance differences result from the cost of doing parity calculations, and this turns out to be the main thing that changes with the processor speed: most of the other cpu-intensive work is hidden by disk delays. We suggest that processors are, in fact, cost effective XOR engines—much of the cost is in the memory system, and microprocessors are commodity parts. We believe that designs using dedicated XOR hardware would exhibit similar performance and cost structures to the models presented here.

With small request sizes, it is easy for either architecture to saturate the disks. With larger ones, the difference is more marked as parity calculations become more significant. The difference is also likely to increase as multiple disks are added to each worker, and with better disk scheduling algorithms, which let each disk spend more time doing data transfers [Seltzer90, Jacobson91]. These improvements are obvious upgrade paths for TickerTAIP. And both will make its architecture even more attractive than the centralized model, as the cost of processors increases faster than linearly

with their performance, and the centralized scheme already requires an expensive CPU.

We commend the TickerTAIP parallel RAID architecture to future disk array implementers. We also suggest its consideration for multicomputers with locally attached disks.

Table 4: throughputs, in MB/s, of the three array architectures under different workloads. The shading highlights comparable total-MIPS configurations. (Variances are shown in parentheses after the numbers)

Workload	Speeds		Throughput, in MB/s		
	link MB/s	cpu MIPS	Central RAID	TickerTAIP	Striping
OLTP	10	10	0.59 (1.7%)	0.59 (1.4%)	1.63 (1.0%)
time-share	1	1	0.43 (0.9%)	0.76 (0.8%)	1.69 (1.3%)
	10	10	0.76 (2.5%)	0.76 (1.7%)	1.69 (1.4%)
small scientific	1	1	0.71 (4.2%)	1.20 (1.2%)	1.73 (0.4%)
	10	10	1.20 (2.1%)	1.20 (1.9%)	1.73 (0.2%)
large scientific	10	10	8.23 (4.8%)	8.39 (3.3%)	9.81 (2.1%)

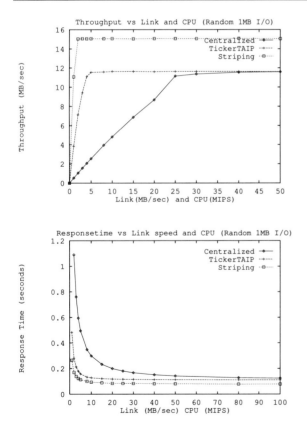

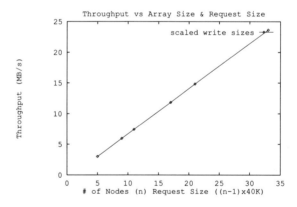

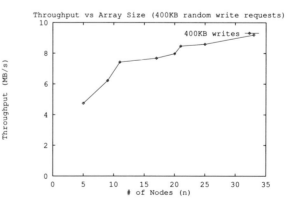

Figure 14: throughput and response time as a function of both CPU and link speeds. 1MB random writes.

Figure 15: effect of TickerTAIP array size on performance.

Acknowledgments

The TickerTAIP work was done as part of the DataMesh research project at Hewlett-Packard Laboratories [Wilkes92]. The implementation is based loosely on a centralized version written by Janet Wiener, and uses the SCSI disk driver developed by Chia Chao. Marjan Wilkes helped edit the paper. Federico Malucelli provided significant input into our understanding of the sequencing options described here, and Chris Ruemmler helped us improve our disk models.

Finally, why the name? *Because tickertaip is used in all the best pa(rallel)raids!*

References

[ATT89] AT&T. *Unix System V AT&T C++ language system release 2.0 selected readings*, Select Code 307-144, 1989.

[Chen90] Peter M. Chen, Garth A. Gibson, Randy H. Katz, and David A. Patterson. An evaluation of redundant arrays of disks using an Amdahl 5890. *Proc. of SIGMETRICS* (Boulder, CO), pp 74–85, May 1990.

[Dunphy90] Robert H. Dunphy, Jr, Robert Walsh, and John H. Bowers. Disk drive memory. United States patent 4 914 656, filed 28 June 1988, granted 3 April 1990.

[Gray90] Jim Gray, Bob Horst, and Mark Walker. Parity striping of disc arrays: low-cost reliable storage with acceptable throughput. *Proc. of the 16th VLDB* (Brisbane, Australia), pp 148–159, August 1990.

[Holland92] Mark Holland and Garth A. Gibson. Parity declustering for continuous operation in redundant disk arrays. *Proc. of 5th ASPLOS* (Boston, MA). In *Computer Architecture News* **20** (special issue):23–35, October 1992.

[HPdisks89] Hewlett-Packard Company. *HP 7936 and HP 7937 disc drives hardware support manual*, part number 07937-90903, July 1989.

[Jacobson91] David M. Jacobson and John Wilkes. *Disk scheduling algorithms based on rotational position.* Technical report HPL–CSP–91–7. Hewlett-Packard Laboratories, 24 February 1991.

[Lampson81] B. W. Lampson and H. E. Sturgis. Atomic transactions. In *Distributed Systems—Architecture and Implementation: an Advanced Course*, volume 105 of Lecture Notes in Computer Science, pp 246–265. Springer-Verlag, New York, 1981.

[Lawlor81] F. D. Lawlor. Efficient mass storage parity recovery mechanism. *IBM Technical Disclosure Bulletin* **24**(2):986–987, July 1981.

[Lee90] Edward K. Lee. Software and performance issues in the implementation of a RAID prototype. UCB/CSD 90/573. University of California at Berkeley, May 1990.

[McKusick84] Marshall K. McKusick, William N. Joy, Samuel J. Leffler, and Robert S. Fabry. A fast file system for UNIX. *ACM Transactions on Computer Systems* **2**(3):181–197, August 1984.

[Miller91] Ethan L. Miller and Randy H. Katz. Analyzing the I/O behavior of supercomputer applications. *Digest of papers, 11th IEEE Symposium on Mass Storage Systems* (Monterey, CA), pp 51–59, October 1991.

[Muntz90] Richard R. Muntz and John C. S. Lui. Performance analysis of disk arrays under failure. *Proc. of 16th VLDB* (Brisbane, Australia), pp 162–173, August 1990.

[Ousterhout90] John K. Ousterhout. Why aren't operating systems getting faster as fast as hardware? *USENIX Summer Conference* (Anaheim, CA), pp 247–56, June 1990.

[Park86] Arvin Park and K. Balasubramanian. *Providing fault tolerance in parallel secondary storage systems.* Technical report CS–TR–057–86. Dept. of Computer Science, Princeton University, November 1986.

[Patterson88] David A. Patterson, Garth Gibson, and Randy H. Katz. A case for redundant arrays of inexpensive disks (RAID). *Proc. of SIGMOD* (Chicago, IL), June 1988.

[Patterson89] David A. Patterson, Peter Chen, Garth Gibson, and Randy H. Katz. Introduction to redundant arrays of inexpensive disks (RAID). *Spring COMPCON'89* (San Francisco, CA), pp 112–17. IEEE, March 1989.

[Pawlikowski90] K. Pawlikowski. Steady-state simulation of queueing processes: a survey of problems and solutions. *Computing Surveys* **22**(2):123–70, June 1990.

[Perihelion91] Perihelion Software. *The Helios parallel operating system*. Prentice-Hall, London, 1991.

[Rosenblum92] Mendel Rosenblum and John K. Ousterhout. The design and implementation of a log-structured file system. *ACM Transactions on Computer Systems* **10**(1):26–52, February 1992.

[Ruemmler93] Chris Ruemmler and John Wilkes. UNIX disk access patterns. *USENIX Winter Technical Conference*. (San Diego, CA), pp 405–420, January 1993.

[Seltzer90] Margo Seltzer, Peter Chen, and John Ousterhout. Disk scheduling revisited. *USENIX Winter Technical Conference* (Washington, DC), pp 313–23, January 1990.

[Stonebraker89] Michael Stonebraker. *Distributed RAID – a new multiple copy algorithm*. UCB/ERL M89/56. University of California at Berkeley, 15 May 1989.

[Wilkes91] John Wilkes. The DataMesh research project. *Transputing'91* (Sunnyvale, CA), volume 2, pp 547–53. IOS Press, Amsterdam, April 1991.

[Wilkes92] John Wilkes. DataMesh research project, phase 1. *USENIX Workshop on File Systems* (Ann Arbor, MI), pp 63–96, May 1992.

Parity Logging
Overcoming the Small Write Problem in Redundant Disk Arrays

Daniel Stodolsky, Garth Gibson, and Mark Holland

School of Computer Science and Department of Electrical and Computer Engineering
Carnegie Mellon University
5000 Forbes Avenue
Pittsburgh, PA 15213-3890
Daniel.Stodolsky@cmu.edu

Abstract

Parity encoded redundant disk arrays provide highly reliable, cost effective secondary storage with high performance for read accesses and large write accesses. Their performance on small writes, however, is much worse than mirrored disks — the traditional, highly reliable, but expensive organization for secondary storage. Unfortunately, small writes are a substantial portion of the I/O workload of many important, demanding applications such as on-line transaction processing. This paper presents parity logging, a novel solution to the small write problem for redundant disk arrays. Parity logging applies journalling techniques to substantially reduce the cost of small writes. We provide a detailed analysis of parity logging and competing schemes — mirroring, floating storage, and RAID level 5 — and verify these models by simulation. Parity logging provides performance competitive with mirroring, the best of the alternative single failure tolerating disk array organizations. However, its overhead cost is close to the minimum offered by RAID level 5. Finally, parity logging can exploit data caching much more effectively than all three alternative approaches.

Section 1:   Introduction

The market for disk arrays, collections of independent magnetic disks linked together as a single data store, is undergoing rapid growth and has been predicted to exceed 7 billion dollars by 1994 [Jones91]. This growth has been driven by three factors. First, the growth in processor speed has outstripped the growth in disk data rates, requiring multiple disks for adequate bandwidth. Second, arrays of small diameter disks often have substantial cost, power, and performance advantages over larger drives. Third, low cost encoding schemes preserve most of these advantages while providing high data reliability (without redundancy, large disk arrays have unacceptably low data reliability because of their large number of component disks). For these three reasons, redundant disk arrays, also known as Redundant Arrays of Inexpensive Disks (RAID), are strong candidates for nearly all on-line secondary storage systems [Gibson92].

Figure 1 presents an overview of RAID systems considered in this paper. The most promising variant employs rotated parity with data striped on a unit that is one or more disk sectors [Lee91]. This configuration is commonly known as the RAID level 5 organization [Patterson88].

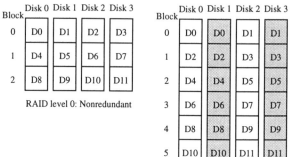

Figure 1   ***Data Layouts***. *In nonredundant disk arrays, data units are simply interleaved across the array. RAID level 1 arrays duplicate every user data unit. RAID level 4 arrays interleave user data blocks across all disks except one. Blocks on the final disk hold the parity (bitwise xor) of the corresponding blocks on the other disks. RAID level 5 arrays distribute the parity blocks uniformly across the disk array. Shaded blocks indicate redundant (parity) information.*

RAID level 5 arrays exploit the low cost of parity encoding to provide high data reliability [Gibson93]. Data is striped over all disks so that large files can be fetched with high bandwidth. By rotating the parity, many small random blocks can also be accessed in parallel without hot spots on any disk. While RAID level 5 disk arrays offer performance and reliability advantages for a wide variety of applications, they are commonly thought to possess at least one critical limitation: their throughput is penalized by a factor of four over nonredundant arrays for workloads of mostly small writes. A small write may require prereading the old value of the user's data, overwriting this with new user data, prereading the old value of the corresponding parity, then overwriting this second disk block with the updated parity. In contrast, mirrored disks simply write the

TPC Benchmark	Scaling to X transactions per second	
get request from terminal		
begin transaction	X*100k	account records (100 bytes each)
update account record	X*10	teller records (100 bytes each)
write history log	X	branch records (100 bytes each)
update teller record	X*10	terminals (1/10 TPS each)
update branch record	X*30K	history records (50 bytes each)
commit transaction	>X*11.5 MB	total online storage
respond to terminal		

*Figure 2   **OLTP Workload Example**. The transaction processing council (TPC) benchmark is an industry standard benchmark for OLTP systems stressing update-intensive database services [TPCA89]. It models the computer processing for customer withdrawals from and deposits to a bank. The primary metric for TPC benchmarks is transactions per second (TPS). Systems are required to complete 90% of the transactions in under 2 seconds and to meet the scaling constraints listed above. Customer account records are selected at random from the local branch 85% of the time and 15% of the time from a different branch. Because history record writes are delayed and grouped into large sequential writes and teller and branch records are easily cached, the disk I/O from this benchmark is dominated by the random account record update. For a 250 TPS system, at least 3GB of storage must concurrently provide more than 250 account record reads and writes per second.*

user's data on two separate disks, and therefore, are only penalized by a factor of two [Bitton88]. This disparity, four accesses per small write instead of two, has been termed the *small write problem* [Gibson92].

Unfortunately, small write performance is important. The performance of on-line transaction processing (OLTP) systems, a substantial segment of the secondary storage market, is largely determined by small write performance. The workload described by Figure 2 is typical of OLTP but nearly the worst possible for RAID level 5; a read-modify-write of an account record will require four or five disk accesses. The same operation would require three accesses on mirrored disks, and only two on a nonredundant array. Because of this limitation, many OLTP systems continue to employ the much more expensive option of mirrored disks.

This paper describes and evaluates a powerful mechanism, *parity logging*, for eliminating this small write penalty. Parity logging exploits well understood techniques for logging or journalling events to transform small random accesses into large sequential accesses. Section 2 of this

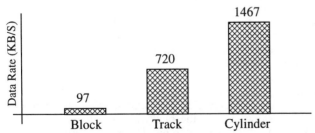

*Figure 3   **Peak I/O Bandwidth**. The figure shows the total kilobytes per second that can be read from or written to a drive using random one block (2KB), one track, and one cylinder access on an IBM 0661 drive (see Figure 12 for disk parameters).*

paper develops the parity logging mechanism. Section 3 introduces a simple model of its performance and cost. Section 4 describes alternative disk system organizations, develops comparable performance models and contrasts them to parity logging. Section 5 introduces our simulation system, describes implementations of parity logging and alternative organizations, and contrasts their performance on a workload of small random writes. Section 6 discusses extensions to multiple failure tolerating systems. Section 7 reviews related work by Bhide and Dias [Bhide92]. Section 8 closes with a summary of current and future work in redundant disk arrays for small write intensive workloads.

Section 2:   Parity Logging

This section evolves the parity logging modification to RAID level 5. Our approach is motivated by the much higher disk bandwidth of large accesses over small. A parity logging disk array accumulates small parity updates until sufficiently large accesses can be used to apply these updates efficiently. The model is introduced in terms of a simple, but impractical RAID level 4 scheme, then refined to the realistic implementation used in the simulations.

A disk access can be broken down into three components: seek time, rotational positioning time, and data transfer time. Small disk writes make inefficient use of disk bandwidth because their data transfer time is much smaller than their seek and rotational positioning times. Figure 3 shows the relative bandwidths of random block, track and cylinder accesses for a modern small diameter disk [IBM0661]. This figure largely bears out the lore of disk bandwidth: random cylinder accesses move data twice as fast as random track accesses which, in turn, move data ten times faster than random block accesses. Parity logging exploits this relationship by replacing many random small parity update accesses with a few large update accesses to log and parity blocks.

Logically, our scheme can be developed beginning with Figure 4. A RAID level 4 disk array (Figure 1) is augmented with one additional disk, a log disk. Initially, this log disk is considered empty. As in RAID level 4, a small write prereads the old user data, then overwrites it. However, instead of similarly updating parity with a preread and overwrite, the parity update image (the result of XOR'ing the old and new user data) is held in a fault tolerant buffer[1]. When enough (one or more tracks) parity update images are buffered to allow for an efficient disk transfer, they are written to the end of the log on the log disk.

When the log disk fills up, the out-of-date parity and the log of parity update information are read into memory with large sequential accesses. The logged parity update images are applied to an in-memory image of the out-of-date parity, and the resulting updated parity is rewritten with large sequential writes. When this completes, the log disk is

---

1. The specific characteristics of the fault tolerant buffers depends on the expected failure modes. If simultaneous controller memory and disk loss is considered to be a single failure, then the fault tolerant buffers must be nonvolatile to provide single failure tolerance. If, however, array controller memory loss and disk failure are independent of each other, then the array can be single failure tolerating without nonvolatile controller buffers. In either case, the software fault tolerance needed to protect these buffers against corruption resulting from software failures is beyond the scope of this paper.

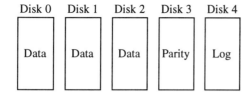

Disk 0   Disk 1   Disk 2   Disk 3   Disk 4

| Data | Data | Data | Parity | Log |

Figure 4   *Basic Parity Logging Model. A RAID level 4 disk array is augmented with a log disk. Parity update records are written sequentially to the log disk at track rates. A full log disk triggers a read of the log and parity disks, computation of the current parity, and a rewrite of the parity disk.*

marked empty, and the logging cycle begins again.

It is straightforward to verify that this scheme preserves data reliability. If a data disk failure occurs, the log disk (and any records in the fault tolerant memory) are first applied to the parity disk, which can then be used to reconstruct the lost data. If the log or parity disk fails, the system can simply recover by reconstructing parity from its data and installing a new empty log disk.

The addition of a log disk allows substantially less disk arm time to be devoted to parity maintenance than in a comparable RAID level 4 or 5 array. This can be shown by computing the average disk busy time devoted to parity updates. Assume there are D blocks on a track, T tracks per cylinder, and V cylinders on a disk (see the glossary in Figure 6). First, every D small writes issued to the array cause one track write to the log to occur. Next, every TVD small writes issued cause the log disk to fill up, which must then be emptied by updating the parity. This requires three full disk accesses, which occur at cylinder data rates. On average, then, for every TVD small writes there are TV sequential track accesses, and $3V$ cylinder accesses for maintenance of the parity information. Track accesses are D times larger than a random small write but about 10 times more efficient. Cylinder accesses are twice as fast and T times larger than track accesses. Thus parity maintenance for TVD small writes consumes about as much disk time as

Region	Disk 0	Disk 1	Disk 2	Disk 3	Disk 4
0	Data	Data	Data	Parity Reg 0	Log Reg 0
1	Data	Data	Data	Parity Reg 1	Log Reg 1
2	Data	Data	Data	Parity Reg 2	Log Reg 2
3	Data	Data	Data	Parity Reg 3	Log Reg 3
4	Data	Data	Data	Parity Reg 4	Log Reg 4

Figure 5   *Parity Logging Regions. Dividing each disk into regions dramatically reduces the required amount of controller buffer space. Each region requires a fault tolerant track buffer to hold its unwritten log records. When a track buffer fills up, the track is written into its regions log with a full track write.*

S	Average seek time
R	Average rotational delay (1/2 disk rotation time)
H	Head switch time
M	Single track seek time
T	Tracks per cylinder
V	Cylinders per disk
N	Disks in the array
K	Tracks buffered per region
C	Cylinders per region
D	Data units per track
L	Log Striping Degree

Figure 6   *Model Parameters. The bandwidth utilization model of Section 3 is presented in terms of these parameters. The majority of the parameters are based on disk geometry. The remainder come from the application or array configuration. The left hand column indicates the symbol used in this text. The same notation also used in Sections 3 and 4.*

$$TV(D/10) + 3V(T/2 \times D/10) = TVD/4$$

random small accesses. In a standard RAID level 4 or 5 disk array, parity maintenance for TVD small writes would consume as much disk time as TVD pairs of random block reads and writes. Thus by logging the parity updates, we have reduced the time consumed by the parity update I/Os by about a factor of eight.

As stated, however, this scheme is completely impractical: an entire disk's capacity of random access memory is required to hold the parity during the application of the parity updates. Figure 5 shows how this limitation can be overcome by dividing the array into regions. Each region is a miniature replica of the array proposed above. Small user writes for a particular region are journalled into that region's log. When a region's log fills up, only that region's log is required to update the region's parity. This reduces the size of the controller memory buffer needed during parity reintegration from the size of a disk to a manageable fraction of a disk. Our models and simulation will use 100 regions per disk (about 3MB per region).

Now, however, each region requires a fault tolerant buffer. Each buffer holds a track (or a few tracks) of parity update images. When one of these buffers fills up, the corresponding region's log is appended with an efficient track (or multitrack) write. Thus the sequential track writes of the single log scheme are replaced with random track writes in the multiple region layout. While random track writes are more expensive than sequential track writes, this more practical implementation still has dramatically lower parity maintenance overhead than RAID levels 4 or 5, as will be shown in the next section.

Similarly to the case of RAID level 4, the log and parity disks may become performance bottlenecks if there are many disks in the array. In particular, the disk bandwidth to all log regions is just the bandwidth of single disk. This limitation can be overcome by distributing parity and logs across all the disks in the array, as indicated in Figure 7. Now the aggregate log bandwidth equals the bandwidth of the array.

Region	Disk 0	Disk 1	Disk 2	Disk 3	Disk 4
0	Data	Data	Data	Parity Reg 0	Log Reg 0
1	Data	Data	Parity Reg 1	Log Reg 1	Data
2	Data	Parity Reg 2	Log Reg 2	Data	Data
3	Parity Reg 3	Log Reg 3	Data	Data	Data
4	Log Reg 4	Data	Data	Data	Parity Reg 4

Figure 7 **Log and Parity Rotation**. *Spreading the log and parity over the entire array increases the parity and log bandwidth to the entire bandwidth of the array. An individual region may still be a hot spot.*

The log and parity bandwidth for a particular region, however, is still that of a single disk. Following the example of RAID level 5, the parity for each region is block striped across the array to increase bandwidth (Figure 8). This also decreases the latency of reintegrating parity updates for a particular region. The log, however, remains a potential bottleneck.

The log bottleneck may also be eliminated by distributing the parity log for each region over multiple disks. Figure 9 shows a parity logging array with the log for each region striped across two disks. Since the parity log is logically part of the parity, it cannot be placed on the same disks as the data is protects. Thus log striping reduces the number

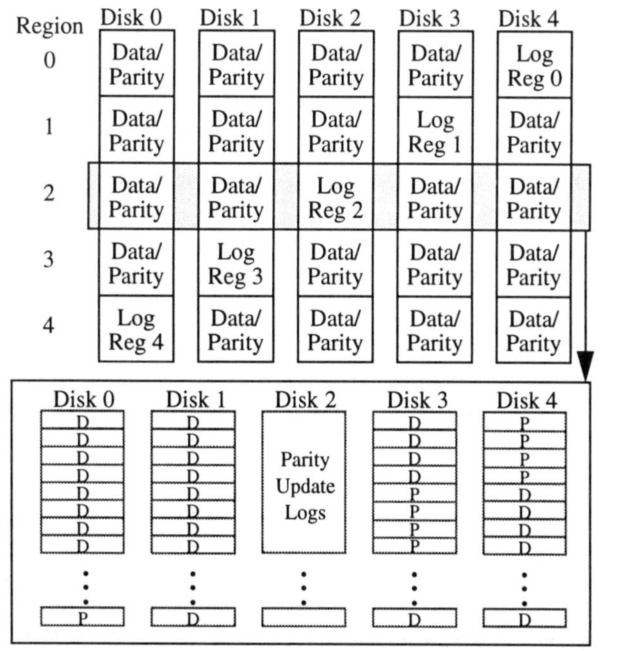

Region	Disk 0	Disk 1	Disk 2	Disk 3	Disk 4
0	Data/Parity	Data/Parity	Data/Parity	Data/Parity	Log Reg 0
1	Data/Parity	Data/Parity	Data/Parity	Log Reg 1	Data/Parity
2	Data/Parity	Data/Parity	Log Reg 2	Data/Parity	Data/Parity
3	Data/Parity	Log Reg 3	Data/Parity	Data/Parity	Data/Parity
4	Log Reg 4	Data/Parity	Data/Parity	Data/Parity	Data/Parity

Figure 8 **Block Parity Striping**. *Parity and data are distributed over all but one disk in each region. The remaining disk contains the parity log. A contiguous layout of parity on each disk allows efficient cylinder rate transfers, while distribution reduces the latency of parity reintegration. The inset shows a detailed layout of a sample region.*

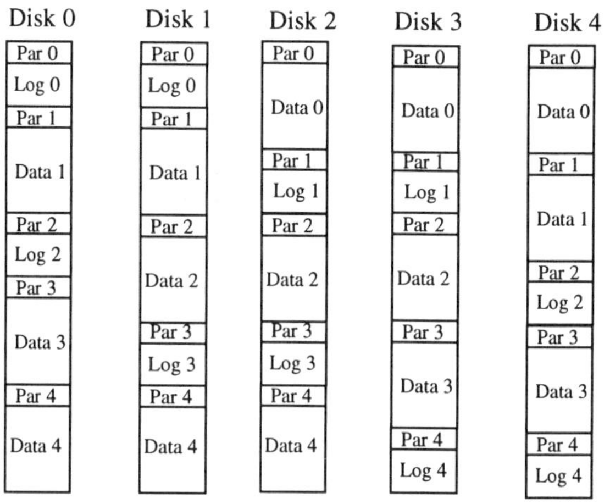

Figure 9 **Distributed Parity Logs**. *To increase the log bandwidth for each region, the log for each region is striped. In this example, each log region is striped over 2 disks. As before, the parity is still spread over on all disks. To preserve single fault tolerance, a parity sublog for a region cannot reside on the same disk as any data for that region. Thus while striping reduces the time for log application for a given region, it increases the space overhead. In addition, if the log is striped over too many disks, the sublogs will become too small and access to them will be inefficient, decreasing performance. When the log is not striped, however, many user data requests queue behind the log reads, which degrades throughput and response time. Fortunately, a moderate degree of striping is beneficial to performance with a small cost increase.*

of disks on which data for a particular region may be placed. Since the disk space overhead is proportional to the number of disks over which data is placed, striping the log increases the disk space overhead. Figure 10 shows the dependence of disk space overhead on the striping degree. As will be shown in Section 5, however, the performance advantages of striping are substantial. The selection of the number of disks over which to stripe the log, the striping degree (L), will also be examined in that section.

The controller memory overhead for this mechanism is fairly modest. With r regions, the controller requires Kr track buffers and another buffer that is VT/r tracks large for the parity reintegration. If a single track is buffered for each of 100 regions, an array of 22 IBM 0661 disks requires 5592KB of buffer space. If memory is assumed to cost 20 times as much as disk per byte, this buffer space costs the equivalent of about 40% of one disk, or about 2% of the 22 disk array.

Section 3: Analytical Modeling

In this section we present a utilization-based analytical model of a disk array. This model predicts sustained array performance in terms of achieved disk utilization, disk geometry, and access size. The parameters and symbols used in this model are listed in Figure 6.

Consider a single small user write in a parity logging array. The user data must be preread, then overwritten. This is done in an I/O which seeks to the cylinder with the user's data, waits for the data to rotate under the head, reads the

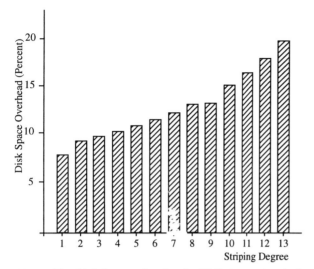

Figure 10 **Disk Storage Overheads.** *While increasing the log striping degree improves array performance, the storage overhead increases. Shown above is the percent of the total disk capacity devoted to storing redundant data in an array with 22 disks. In general, the storage overhead is 2/(N+1-L), where N is the number of disks and L is striping degree. Thus the storage overhead depends only on the total number of disks in the array and the degree of log striping.*

In addition to these disk space overheads, parity logging also requires fault tolerant memory buffer space. With the example disk array of Figure 12, this amounts to 5592 KB, roughly equivalent in cost to 2% of the disk array.

data, waits for the disk to spin around once, then updates the data[2]. On average, such an access will take

disk seconds, which may be simplified to

$$S + (3 + \frac{2}{D}) R = A_0$$

In many cases, it may be possible to predictably avoid prereading user data. For example, in the TPC benchmark the updates of a customer account record is a read modify write operation; a data record is read, modified in memory, then written back to disk. In these cases, the old data value is usually known (cached) at the time of the write, and an additional preread of the data may be skipped. Without pre-reading, the disk busy time needed for a small write access is $S + (1 + 2/D) R$.

Each region has K tracks worth of fault tolerant buffers. Thus, on average, for every KD small user writes, one region's buffers will fill and be written to the region's log in a single K track write. The number of disk seconds needed to do this is

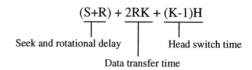

assuming all K tracks are on the same cylinder[3]. This may be rewritten as

$$S + (2K + 1) R + (K - 1) H = A_1.$$

Finally, on average, for every DTC small user writes one region of logged parity must be reintegrated. First, consider the cast of an array that does not stripe its log (Figure 8). The reintegration consists of three steps: a sequential read of C cylinders (one region) from the log, a striped read of the parity from N-1 disks, and a striped write of the parity back onto N-1 disks. The sequential log read requires

$$\underbrace{(S+R)}_{\text{Seek and rotational delay}} + \underbrace{C\ (2RT + (T-1)H)}_{\text{Read Time for 1 Cylinder}} + \underbrace{M(C-1)}_{\text{C-1 single cylinder seeks}}$$

disk seconds, and may be rewritten as

$$S + (2TC + 1) R + (T - 1) HC + (C - 1) M = A_2.$$

The striped accesses each consist of $N - 1$ sequential transfers of $C / (N - 1)$ cylinders. Each of these transfers takes

$$\underbrace{(S+R)}_{\text{First seek and rotational delay}} + \underbrace{(C/(N-1))}_{\text{Cylinders per subaccess}}\underbrace{(2RT+(T-1)H)}_{\text{Read Time for 1 Cylinder}} + \underbrace{(C/(N-1)-1)M}_{\text{Single track seeks per subaccess}}.$$

Rewriting, each striped access takes A_3 disk seconds:

$$(N - 1) (S + R) + C (2RT + (T - 1) H) + M (C - N + 1)$$

$$= A_3$$

Thus, on average, every small user write utilizes disks for

$$A_0 + \frac{1}{KD}A_1 + \frac{1}{DTC} [A_2 + 2A_3] .$$

Figure 11 shows the contributions to disk busy time of the various terms after A_0 in the above equation for the example disk array given in Figure 12.

The analysis for a parity logging disk array with a striped log such as that shown in Figure 9 is similar. When a region's fault tolerant buffers fill, the buffers will be written to one of the regions sublogs in a single K track write. The cost of this operation is the same as in the unstriped case.

---

2. This single access could be separated into two accesses each taking S+R+2R/D for a total of 2S+(2+4/D)R. For most modern disks S is about twice R, so the single access is more efficient.

3. Disks that support zero-latency writes [Salem86] can eliminate the initial rotational positioning delay. If only a single track is buffered (K=1) this can reduce the I/O time by 26%.

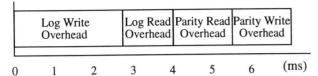

Log Write Overhead	Log Read Overhead	Parity Read Overhead	Parity Write Overhead

```
0    1    2    3    4    5    6    (ms)
```

Figure 11 **Parity Logging Overheads.** *The amortized overhead cost of extra I/Os done in our example parity logging array is shown above. The log writes contribute approximately 40% of the overhead, while the cylinder rate log reads, parity reads and parity writes each contribute about 20%. In contrast, the extra I/Os done by RAID level 5 cost nearly 35 milliseconds per small write.*

Workload Parameters	
Access size:	Fixed at 2 KB
Alignment:	Fixed at 2 KB
Write Ratio:	100%
Spatial Distribution:	Uniform over all data
Temporal Distribution:	66 closed loop processes
	Gaussian think time distribution
Array Parameters	
Stripe Unit:	Fixed at 2KB
Number of Disks:	22 spindle synchronized disks.
Head Scheduling:	FIFO
Power/Cabling:	Disks independently powered/cabled
Disk Parameters	
Geometry:	949 cyls, 14 heads, 48 sectors/track
Sector Size:	512 bytes
Revolution Time:	13.9 ms
Seek Time Model:	$2.0 + 0.01 \cdot dist + 0.46 \cdot \sqrt{dist}$ (ms)
	2 ms min, 12.5 ms avg, 25 ms max
Track Skew:	4 sectors
Head Switch Time:	1.16 ms

Figure 12 **Simulation Parameters.** *The access size alignment and spatial distribution are typical of OLTP workloads, while a 100% write ratio emphasizes the performance differences of the various techniques. Since the disks have independent support hardware, disk failures will be independent, allowing a single parity group [Gibson92]. Disk parameters are modeled on the IBM Lightning drive[IBM0661]. Note that the dist term in the seek time model is the number of cylinders traversed, excluding the destination. As is traditional, the track skew is chosen to equal the head switch time, optimizing data layout for sequential multitrack access. These disks do not support zero latency writes.*

Log reintegration still occurs every DTC small user writes, but now consists of three striped I/Os: a striped (over L disks) read of the log, and a striped read and write of the parity (striped over N disks). The striped log read costs

$$(S+R) + (C/L)(2RT+(T-1)H) + (C/L-1)M$$

Single track seeks per subaccess

Cylinders per subaccess

Read Time for 1 Cylinder

First seek and rotational delay

for a total of

$$L(S+R) + C(2RT + (T-1)H) + (C-L)M$$

disk seconds. Similarly, the striped parity reads and writes will consume

$$N(S+R) + C(2RT + (T-1)H) + (C-N)M$$

disk seconds. Thus striping introduces an additional overhead of $(L+1)(S+R-M)$ disk seconds to the log integration. This increases the parity maintenance overhead per small write by

$$\frac{(L+1)(S+R-M)}{DTC}$$

This increase in parity maintenance work is worthwhile because it reduces long reintegration periods when disk queues grow until the system becomes underutilized which causes maximum performance to fall far short of expectations.

Section 4: Alternative Schemes

Few other authors have addressed the problem of high performance yet reliable disk storage for small write workloads. The most notable of these is floating data and parity [Menon92]. This section reviews and estimates the performance of four configurations: mirrored disks (RAID level 1), nonredundant disk arrays (RAID level 0), distributed N+1 parity (RAID level 5), and floating data and parity. The notation and analysis methodology are the same as used in the previous section.

Small writes in RAID level 5 disk arrays require four I/O's: data preread, data write, parity read, parity write. These can be combined into two read-rotate-write accesses, each of which takes

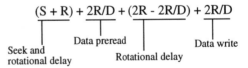

$$(S + R) + 2R/D + (2R - 2R/D) + 2R/D$$

Data preread

Seek and rotational delay

Rotational delay

Data write

disk seconds for a total disk busy time of $2S + (6 + 4/D)R$. No fault tolerant controller storage is required.

The traditional solution to reliable disk storage has been mirroring. In mirrored systems, every data unit is stored on two disks, and all write requests update both copies. No preread is required, however, so each access takes

$$(S + R) + 2R/D$$

Seek and rotational delay

Data write

Hence each small user write utilizes disks for $2S + (2 + 4/D)R$ seconds. While mirrored disks are more efficient than RAID level 5, half their capacity is devoted to redundant data, making them expensive. Similarly to RAID level 5, controllers for mirrored disk arrays do not require

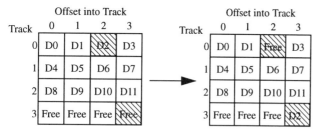

Figure 13 **Floating Data/Parity**. *When updating block D2, the controller searches for a free block within the cylinder that is rotationally close to block D2. In this case, it finds the block at offset 3 into track 3. Immediately following the preread of block D2, the controller writes the new block to the new location, and updates the mapping tables. The preread of the old information and the write of the new are thus effectively done in time of one access.*

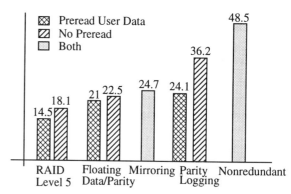

Figure 14 **Model Estimates**. *I/Os per second per disk as predicted by the bandwidth models of Sections 3 and 4. These predictions assume 100% disk utilization, FIFO disk arm scheduling and an unbounded number of requestors. Raid level 5 and parity logging disk arrays both benefit substantially from not having to preread user data. Floating data and parity substantially reduces the overhead of the user preread and therefore achieves less benefit from its elimination. Mirroring and nonredundant disk arrays do not need to preread user data. The parity logging estimates are insensitive to the degree of striping.*

fault tolerant storage.

The *floating data and parity* modification to RAID level 5 was proposed by Menon and Kasson [Mennon92]. This technique organizes data and parity into cylinders that contain either data only or parity only. As illustrated in Figure 13, by maintaining a single track of empty space per cylinder, floating data and parity effectively eliminates the extra rotational delay of RAID level 5 read-rotate-write accesses. Recall that for RAID level 5, the disk busy time for each data and parity update is

$$S + R + 2R/D + (2R - 2R/D) + 2R/D .$$

With floating data and parity, the rotational term $2R - 2R/D$ is replaced with a head switch and a short rotational delay. Using disks similar to those in our sample array Menon and Kasson report an average delay of 0.76 data units. So the expected disk busy time for each access in a floating data and parity array is

$$S + R + 2R/D + H + 0.76 (2R/D) + 2R/D$$

which may be rewritten as $S + (1 + 5.52/D) R + H$. Hence, the total disk busy time for a small random user write in a floating data and parity array is $2S + (2 + 11.04/D) R + 2H$. Note if D is large and H is small, this is close to the performance of mirroring.

Even with a spare track in every cylinder, floating data and parity arrays still have excellent storage overheads. For an N disk array, floating data and parity has a storage overhead[4] of $(T + N - 1) / (TN)$. Floating data and parity arrays, however, require substantial fault-tolerant storage in the array controller to keep track of the current location of data and parity. For each cylinder, an allocation bitmask is maintained. This requires DT bits per cylinder. In addition, a table of current block locations for each cylinder is required. This consumes $D (T - 1) \lceil \log (DT) \rceil$ bits per cylinder. Thus a total of $VD (T + (T - 1) \lceil \log (DT) \rceil)$ bits of fault-tolerant controller storage are required. For the disks in Figure 12, this is 1,343,784 bits (164 KB) per disk,

roughly comparable to parity logging.

While floating data and parity substantially improves the performance of small writes, its performance for other types of accesses is degraded. Within a cylinder, logically contiguous user data units are not likely to be physically contiguous. In the worse case, two consecutive data units may end up at the same rotational position on two different tracks, requiring a complete disk rotation to read both. In addition, the average track has only $D (T - 1) /T$ valid data units. Thus, even on disks with zero-latency reads, the maximum sequential read bandwidth is reduced by $(T - 1) /T$.

Figure 14 compares the model's estimates for maximum throughput of the example arrays based on Figure 12. Throughput at lower utilizations may be calculated by scaling the maximum throughput numbers by the disk utilization. Figure 14 predicts that parity logging and floating data and parity will both substantially improve on RAID level 5, approaching the performance of mirroring, for small random writes.

Section 5:   Simulation

To validate the models presented above and to explore response time for these arrays, we simulated the example array in Figure 12 under five different configurations: nonredundant, mirroring, RAID level 5, floating data and parity, and parity logging. Parity logging was simulated for several different degrees of log striping[5]. The RAIDSIM package, a disk array simulator derived from the Sprite operating system disk array driver [Ousterhout88, Lee91], was extended with implementations of parity logging and float parity and data.

In each simulation, the request stream was generated by 66 processes (i.e, three per disk). Each process requests a

---

4. Each disk gives up 1/T of its capacity for free space and the array gives up 1/N of the remaining space for parity. Thus the array storage efficiency is (T-1)(N-1)/TN and the array storage overhead is 1-(T-1)(N-1)/TN = (T+N-1)/TN.

5. A single track was buffered per region in all parity logging simulations.

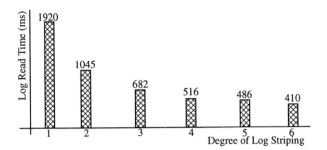

Figure 15 **Sublog Read Times**. *This figure presents the sublog read time for low degrees of log striping for the example disk array. When the sublog reads are very long, many user requests queue behind the read, increasing response time and decreasing array utilization.*

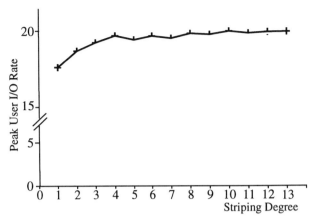

Figure 16(a): Peak User I/Os

small write from a disk selected at random, then waits for acknowledgment from the disk array. Process think time has a Gaussian distribution, but the mean is dynamically adjusted until the desired system throughput is achieved. If the disk array is unable to sustain the offered load, think time is driven to zero. Simulations were run until the 90% confidence interval of the response time is less than 5% of the mean.

Figure 16 shows peak throughput, response time[6] and response time variance as the degree of log striping (L) is varied from 1 (unstriped) to 13. When the log is striped over a small number of disks, performance is substantially lower than other configurations. This behavior can be explained in terms of a "convoy effect". The length of the sublog read I/Os is the basis of the convoy effect. Figure 15 shows sublog read times for low log striping degrees. While these long I/O's are efficient, they completely tie up a disk for seconds. During this period, any access to the disk involved in the log read will block, reducing the effective concurrency in the system. This concurrency reduction causes other disks in the array to become idle until the log read completes, reducing peak throughput and utilization.

Figure 16 **Striped Parity Logging**. *Figure 16(a), (b), and (c) show the achieved user I/Os per disk per second, average user response time, and the standard deviation of the response time under peak load for various degrees of parity log striping. All metrics improve substantially as the striping degree is increased from 1 (no striping) to 4. The difference in performance between striping over 4 to 13 disks is slight, indicating the robustness of the technique.*

The metric with the most dramatic improvement is the response time standard deviation. When log reads are long (see Figure 15), many user requests become queued for that disk, leading to a large variance in the response time. Striping reduces the length of the log reads, reducing this variance.

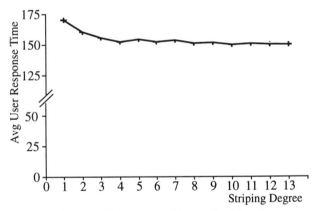

Figure 16(b): Response Time at Peak Load

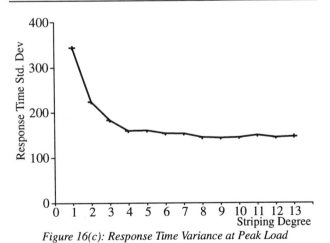

Figure 16(c): Response Time Variance at Peak Load

This convoy effect also has a substantial impact on response time. I/O requests that block behind these long read requests will have very long response times, leading to an increase both average response time and response time variance. A modest degree of striping eliminates the convoy effect. Striping the log over six disks achieves most of the available performance without greatly increasing disk space overhead. Figure 17 compares the performance of this configuration against the alternative organizations presented in Section 4: nonredundant, mirroring, RAID level 5, and floating data and parity. Figure 17(a)-(b) present response time statistics as a function of throughput for simulations that preread user data, and (c) presents the corresponding data for the no preread case.

Because of the relatively small number of simulated pro-

---

6. The simulations reported herein consider a user write in a parity logged array complete when the user data is on disk and the parity update record has been committed to fault tolerant storage. The alternatives consider a user write complete when data and parity are on disk.

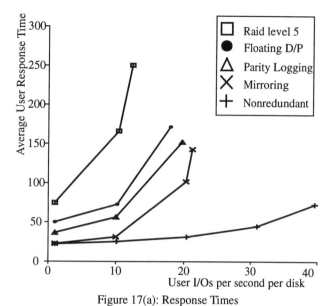

Figure 17(a): Response Times

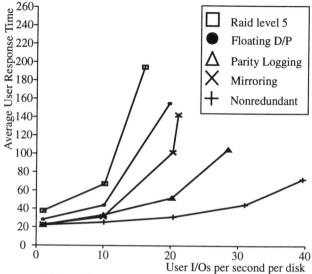

Figure 17(c): Response Times without prereads

*Figure 17 **Response Times and Utilization**. Figure 17(a)-(c) present the average user response times and response time standard deviations as a function of the number of small random writes achieved per disk per second. Figure 17(a) and (b) present the results when the user data must be preread, while the results in Figure 17(c) assume the user data was cached, making the pread of the user data unnecessary. In addition to reducing the amount of I/O required, cached user data allows the user write and parity update to occur concurrently, significantly reducing response time for RAID level 5 and floating data and parity. The reported times are in milliseconds. The response time standard deviation for the no pread case is essentially identical to Figure 17(b).*

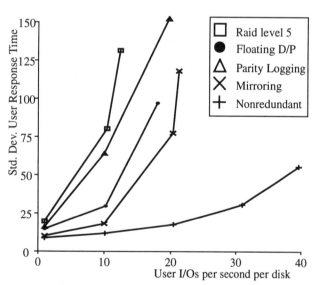

Figure 17(b): Response Time Standard Deviation

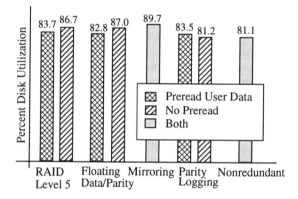

*Figure 18 **Disk Utilization at Peak Load**. The figure above presents the average disk utilization at maximum load for the array simulated in Figure 17. In every configuration disk utilization grew linearly with throughput.*

disk utilization varies from configuration to configuration. Figure 18 shows the disk utilization at peak load for the configurations simulated. Parity logging, floating data and parity, RAID level 5, and nonredundant disk arrays are about equally affected since each system presents only one disk access request at a time per process. Mirroring, on the other hand, presents two write requests simultaneously and is therefore impacted the least[7]. Nonetheless, Figure 19 shows that simulation agreement with the model is good when the model results (Figure 14) are scaled by the achieved disk utilizations in Figure 18.

The simulation response time results may be summarized as follows. Nonredundant disk arrays perform a single disk access per user write, so they have the lowest and most slowly growing response time. Mirroring shows a similar

cesses, the array saturates while some disks are less than fully utilized. That is, because the number of requesting processes is fixed, one overloaded disk can cause other disks to be underutilized. The impact of this effect on peak

7. In many systems, writes to mirrored disks are serialized. One disk in each pair is considered primary, and the write to that disk must complete before the write to the second disk begins. Such serialization would reduce mirroring's disk utilization to the same as the nonredundant case while approximately doubling response time.

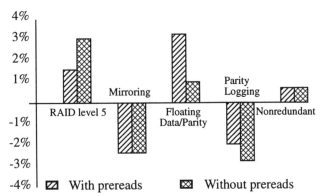

Figure 19 **Model errors.** *The figure shows the percent error between the models and the simulations. The model predictions have been scaled by the achieved disk utilizations. In all cases, the disagreement between the simulation and the models is less than four percent. Note that the 90% confidence interval of the simulation response time is ±5% of the mean.*

behavior, but is driven into saturation with half as much load. In contrast, each small user write in RAID level 5, in the user data preread case, must complete two slow read-rotate-write accesses sequentially. Unloaded system response time is thus quite high and queuing effects cause it to grow quite rapidly with load. While the response time for parity logging on a lightly loaded system is approximately 20ms higher than mirroring, the peak sustainable I/O rate and response time are quite similar. Similar to RAID level 5, floating data and parity arrays require two read-rotate-write accesses per user write. But by removing the rotational delays, floating data and parity achieves peak IO rates similar to parity logging and mirroring. Response time, however, is significantly longer.[8]

Figure 17(c) shows the performance of all configurations without data preread. As expected, this has no effect on mirrored or nonredundant systems and the performance of the other three configurations improves. RAID level 5 benefits substantially from the elimination of the full rotation delay incurred by the data preread. In addition, the user data write and parity update can be issued concurrently, further improving the response time and array utilization. Floating data and parity achieves a lesser benefit from elimination of the preread because its preread overhead is much less. Response time does drop, however, because of the ability to issue the user write and parity update accesses simultaneously. The response time of parity logging improves by a full rotational delay (13.9 ms) due to the elimination of the preread rotate, providing a unloaded response time comparable to a nonredundant array. This also reduces the actuator time per I/O by nearly one third, and the I/O rate and response time improve proportionately.

The variance in user response time, however, is larger with parity logging than with mirroring or floating data and parity, although it is not as large as with RAID level 5. This results from the basic structure of parity logging. Most accesses are fast because inefficient work is delayed. However, some accesses see long response times as delayed work is efficiently completed. Nonetheless, the response

Disk 0	Disk 1	Disk 2	Parity Row 0
Disk 3	Disk 4	Disk 5	Parity Row 1
Disk 5	Disk 6	Disk 7	Parity Row 2
Parity Column 0	Parity Column 1	Parity Column 2	

Figure 20 **Two dimensional parity.** *One disk array organization that achieves double failure tolerance is two dimensional parity. Parity disks hold the parity for the corresponding row or column. In the example above, the parity disk for column 0 holds the parity of disks 0, 3 and 5. Whenever a data disk is written, the corresponding row and column parity disks are also updated. Thus a write to disk 1, in the example above, would require updating the parity on the shaded parity disks.*

time estimates show that parity logging is a viable and much lower cost alternative to mirroring for small write workloads.

Section 6:   Multiple failure tolerating arrays

Another significant advantage of parity logging is its efficient extension to multiple failure tolerating arrays. Multiple failure tolerance provides much longer mean time to data loss and greater tolerance for bad blocks discovered during reconstruction [Gibson89]. Using codes more powerful than parity, RAID level 5 and its variants, floating data and parity and parity logging, can all be extended to tolerate f concurrent failures. Figure 20 gives an example of one of the more easily understood double failure tolerant disk array organizations. This paper does not consider the choice of codes that might be used for f failure protection, except to note that these codes all have one property important to small random write performance [Gibson89]: each small write updates $f + 1$ disks — f disks containing check information (generalized parity) and the disk containing the user's data. This check maintenance work, which scales up with the number of failures tolerated, is exactly the work that parity logging is designed to handle more efficiently.

In an f failure tolerating array using parity logging, the single striped log per region is replaced with f striped logs per region, each on a separate set of disks. When a region's fault tolerant buffers fill up, the corresponding parity update records are written to all logs for that region. When a region's logs fill up, one copy of the log is read in, all check data for the region is read in, updated in memory, and rewritten[9].

The other configurations also extend straightforwardly. Mirroring becomes f-copy shadowing. RAID level 5 and

---

8. In parity logging arrays that are not driven into saturation, making the log accesses preemptible by user access should substantially improve response time and response time variance.

9. Instead of reading all the parity updates from one of the logs, a different subset of the parity update records could be read from each log, effectively further striping the parity update record read.

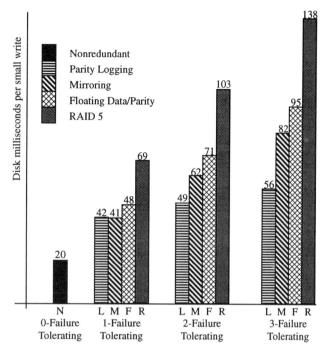

Figure 21 Small write costs. This figure shows the amortized disk arm time consumed by a small write for each of the modeled techniques in arrays that tolerate zero, one, two or three failures. Parity logging is competitive with mirroring in the single failure tolerating case and is substantially better than the other methods in arrays that tolerate two or more failures.

its floating data and parity version simply store more parity and issue read-modify-write updates to f check blocks with every small write.

Relative to these other schemes, parity logging has better performance because of its lower nonpreread overhead. The overhead associated with maintaining check information can be divided into two components: preread bandwidth overhead and nonpreread bandwidth overhead. The bandwidth needed to preread the old copy of the user's data is independent of the number of failures to be tolerated. Nonpreread bandwidth, the disk work done to update the check information given a data change, grows linearly with the number of failures to be tolerated. Parity logging has the smallest cost for this latter, linearly growing component of check maintenance overhead because all check information access (log and generalized parity) are done efficiently.

Figure 21 shows the total disk time required per small random write in zero, single, double, and triple failure tolerating arrays using mirroring, RAID level 5, floating data and parity and parity logging. This data is derived from the models of Sections 3 and 4 and applied to the example disk array of Figure 12.

The maximum I/O rate of the parity logging array declines much more slowly than the other configurations because parity logging has a substantially lower nonpreread overhead. For example, while triple failure tolerating parity logging arrays should sustain about 35% of the I/O rate of nonredundant arrays for random small writes, quadruplicated storage (triple failure tolerating mirroring disk arrays) will sustain only 25%.

Section 7:   Related Work

Bhide and Dias [Bhide92] have independently developed a scheme similar to parity logging. Their LRAID-X4 organization maintains separate parity and parity update log disks, and periodically applies the logged updates to the parity disk. In order to allow writes from the user to occur in parallel with log reintegration, they double buffer both the parity and the parity log for a total of four overhead disks. This double buffering scheme, while expensive in disks, can support a fairly large number of data disks without saturating the parity and log disks, so LRAID-X4 does not distribute parity or log information. Instead of breaking down the log disk into regions to reduce the required storage in the controller, LRAID-X4 sorts parity updates in memory according to the parity block to which they apply. This allows LRAID-X4 to write a "run" of updates for ascending parity blocks to a log disk. When this log disk is full, further updates are sorted and written to the second log disk while the first log disk reintegrates its updates with the parity by reading from one parity disk and writing to the other. The reintegration of a full log disk uses an external sorting algorithm to collect subsequences applying to one area of parity from each run on the log disk. If this area is large, all log reads and parity reads and writes will be efficient.

The model derived by Bhide and Dias assumes user data does not need to be preread. It shows that throughput is limited by the rate at which subsequences of runs are collected for integration with the parity. In a 100% write workload, the peak throughput is $1/T_{seqr}$, where T_{seqr} is the amortized time taken to read a block in a subsequence of a run on the log disk. Bhide and Dias approximate this by

$$(T_{fewtrackseek} + R + tracksr(2R + H))/(tracksr \times D)$$

where $T_{fewtrackseek}$ is the time to seek across 5 to 10 tracks and $tracksr$ is the average size in tracks of a subsequence (constrained to one cylinder). While $tracksr$ is dependent on the amount of controller memory, their array achieves about 80% of its maximum throughput with the about 2% of a disk's worth of memory. With this much memory, $tracksr$ is 2.4. Using the array parameters in Figure 12 and taking $T_{fewtrackseek}$ to be the time of a 5 track seek, one obtains a peak throughput of 624 accesses per second, or an average of 28.4 I/Os per disk per second. With 5% of a disk's worth of memory, LRAID-X4 achieves its maximum of 760 I/Os, or 34.5 I/Os per disk per second. However, LRAID-X4 reaches this performance maximum with 20 disks (16 data, 2 parity, 2 log) for a 100% write workload. Additional disks do not increase performance. In comparison, the parity logging disk array simulated in Section 5, whose controller requires about 2% of a disk's worth of memory, is predicted to achieve 36.2 I/Os per disk per second on the same workload and its performance increases with increasing numbers of disks.

Section 8:   Concluding Remarks

This paper presents a novel solution to the small write problem in redundant disk arrays based on a distributed (and possibly replicated) log. Analytical models of the peak bandwidth of this scheme and alternatives from the literature were derived and validated by simulation. The proposed technique achieves substantially better performance than RAID level 5 arrays. When data must be preread before being overwritten, parity logging achieves performance comparable to floating parity and data without compromising sequential access performance or application control of data placement. Performance is superior to mirroring and floating parity and data when the data to be overwritten is cached. This performance is obtained without the 50% disk storage space overhead of mirroring. For extremely reliable environments, the advantage of parity logging systems is shown to be even more pronounced.

While the parity logging scheme presented in this paper is effective, several optimizations should be explored. The effects of log length on on-line reconstruction performance should be investigated and detailed simulations of multiple failure tolerating configurations should be undertaken. More dynamic assignment of fault tolerant controller memory should allow higher performance to be achieved or a substantial reduction in the amount of memory required. Application of data compression to the parity log should be very profitable. A comparison of the log structured filesystem [Rosenblum 91], which completely avoids small writes, and parity logging should be undertaken. The interaction of parity logging and parity declustering [Holland92] merits particular exploration. Parity declustering provides high performance during reconstruction while parity logging provides high performance during fault free operation. The combination of the two should provide a particularly attractive system for OLTP environments.

Section 9: Acknowledgments

We would like to thank Ed Lee for the original version of Raidsim, and Brian Bershad, Peter Chen, Hugo Patterson, and Jody Prival for early reviews. This research was supported by the Defense Advanced Research Projects Agency monitored by DARPA/CMO under contract MDA 972-90-C-0035 and by an IBM graduate fellowship.

References

[Bhide92] A. Bhide and D. Dias, "Raid Architectures for OLTP," IBM Computer Science Research Report RC 17879, 1992.

[Bitton88] D. Bitton and J. Gray, "Disk Shadowing," *Proceedings of the 14th Conference on Very Large Data Bases*, 1988, pp. 331-338.

[Gibson89] G. Gibson, L. Hellerstein, R. M. Karp, R. H. Katz, and D. A. Patterson, "Coding Techniques for Handling Failures in Large Disk Arrays," *Third International Conference on Architectural Support for Programming Languages and Operating Systems (ASPLOS III)*, ACM Press, 1989, pp 123-132.

[Gibson92] G. Gibson, *Redundant Disk Arrays: Reliable, Parallel Secondary Storage*, MIT Press, 1992.

[Gibson93] G. Gibson and D. Patterson, "Designing Disk Arrays for High Data Reliability," *Journal of Parallel and Distributed Computing*, January, 1993, pp. 4-27

[Holland92] M. Holland and G. Gibson, "Parity Declustering for Continuous Operation in Redundant Disk Arrays," *Proceedings of ASPLOS-V*, 1992, pp. 23-35.

[IBM0661] IBM Corporation, IBM 0661 Disk Drive Product Description, Model 370, First Edition, Low End Storage Products, 504/114-2, 1989.

[Jones91] J. Jones, Jr., and T. Liu, "RAID: A Technology Poised for Explosive Growth," Montgomery Securities Industry Report, Montgomery Securities, San Francisco, 1991

[Lee91] E. Lee and R. Katz, "Performance Consequences of Parity Placement in Disk Arrays," *Proceedings of ASPLOS-IV*, 1991, pp. 190-199.

[Menon92] J. Menon and J. Kasson, "Methods for Improved Update Performance of Disk Arrays," *Proceedings of the Hawaii International Conference on System Sciences*, 1992, pp. 74-83.

[Ousterhout88] J. Ousterhout, et. al., "The Sprite Network Operating System," *IEEE Computer*, February 1988, pp. 23-36.

[Patterson88] D. Patterson, G. Gibson, and R. Katz, "A Case for Redundant Arrays of Inexpensive Disks (RAID)," *Proceedings of the ACM SIGMOD Conference*, 1988, pp. 109-116.

[Rosenblum91] M. Rosenblum and J. Ousterhout, "The Design and Implementation of a Log-Structured File System," *Proceedings of the 13th ACM Symposium on Operating System Principles*, 1991, pp. 1-15.

[Salem86] K. Salem, H. Garcia-Molina, "Disk Striping," *Proceedings of the 2nd IEEE International Conference on Data Engineering*, 1986.

[TPCA89] *The TPC-A Benchmark: A Standard Specification*, Transaction Processing Performance Council, 1989.

The Architecture of a Fault-Tolerant Cached RAID Controller

Jai Menon and Jim Cortney

IBM Almaden Research Center
San Jose, California 95120-6099
Telephone: (408) 927-2070   E-Mail: menonjm@almaden.ibm.com

Abstract— RAID-5 arrays need 4 disk accesses to update a data block -- 2 to read old data and parity, and 2 to write new data and parity. Schemes previously proposed to improve the update performance of such arrays are the Log-Structured File System [10] and the Floating Parity Approach [6]. Here, we consider a third approach, called Fast Write, which eliminates disk time from the host response time to a write, by using a Non-Volatile Cache in the disk array controller. We examine three alternatives for handling Fast Writes and describe a hierarchy of destage algorithms with increasing robustness to failures. These destage algorithms are compared against those that would be used by a disk controller employing mirroring. We show that array controllers require considerably more (2 to 3 times more) bus bandwidth and memory bandwidth than do disk controllers that employ mirroring. So, array controllers that use parity are likely to be more expensive than controllers that do mirroring, though mirroring is more expensive when both controllers and disks are considered.

1. Introduction

A *disk array* is a set of disk drives (and controller) which can automatically recover data when one (or more) drives in the set fails by using redundant data that is maintained by the controller on the drives. [8] describes five types of disk arrays called RAID-1 through RAID-5 and [2] describes a sixth type called a parity striped disk array. In this paper, our focus is on RAID-5 and/or parity striped disk arrays which employ a parity technique described in [1,8]. This technique requires fewer disks than mirroring and is therefore more acceptable in many situations.

The main drawback of such arrays are that they need four disk accesses to update a data block -- two to read old data and parity, and two to write new data and parity. [5] showed that the performance degradation can be quite severe in transaction processing environments. Two schemes that have been previously proposed to improve array update performance

are the Log-Structured File System [10] and the Floating Parity Approach [6]. In this paper, we consider a third approach, called *Fast Write*, which eliminates disk time from the host response time to a write, by using Non-Volatile Storage (NVS) in the disk array controller. A block received from a host system is initially written to NVS in the disk array controller and a completion message is sent to the host system at this time. Actual destage of the block from NVS to disk is done asynchronously at a later time. We call a disk array that uses the Fast Write technique a *Cached RAID*.

The rest of this paper is organized as follows. We first review the parity technique. Then, we describe Fast Write. Next, we give an overview of the architecture of Hagar, a disk array controller prototype developed at the IBM Almaden Research Center. Hagar uses Fast Write. In the last sections of this report, we then analyze several alternatives for destaging blocks from NVS to disk. We show that destage algorithms must be carefully developed because of complex trade-offs between availability and performance goals.

2. Review of Parity Technique

We illustrate the parity technique on a disk array of six data disks and a parity disk. In this diagram, Pi is a parity block that protects the six data blocks labelled Di. Pi and the 6 Dis together constitute a *parity group*. The Pi of a parity group must always be equal to the parity of the 6 Di blocks in the same parity group as Pi.

```
Data Disk 1    D1 D2 D3 D4
Data Disk 2    D1 D2 D3 D4
Data Disk 3    D1 D2 D3 D4
Data Disk 4    D1 D2 D3 D4
Data Disk 5    D1 D2 D3 D4
Data Disk 6    D1 D2 D3 D4
Parity Disk    P1 P2 P3 P4
```

We show only one track (of 4 blocks) from each of the disks. In all, we show four parity groups. P1 contains the parity or exclusive OR of the blocks labeled D1 on all the data disks, P2 the exclusive OR

D2s, and so on. Such an array is robust against single disk crashes; if disk 1 were to fail, data on it can be recreated by reading data from the remaining five data disks and the parity disk and performing the appropriate exclusive OR operations.

Whenever the controller receives a request to write a data block, it must also update the corresponding parity block for consistency. If D1 is to be altered, the new value of P1 is calculated as:

`new P1 = (old D1 XOR new D1 XOR old P1)`

Since the parity must be altered each time the data is modified, these arrays require four disk accesses to write a data block - two to read old data and parity, two to write new data and parity.

3. Overview of the Fast Write Technique

In this technique, all disk array controller hardware such as processors, data memory (memory containing cached data blocks and other data buffers), control memory (memory containing control structures such as request control blocks, cache directories, etc..) are divided into at least two disjoint sets, each set on a different power boundary. The data memory and the control memory are either battery-backed or built using NVS so they can survive power failures. When a disk block to be written to the disk array is received, the block is first written to data memory in the array controller, in two separate locations, on two different power boundaries. At this point, the disk array controller returns successful completion of the write to the host. In this way, from the host's point of view, the write has been completed quickly without requiring any disk access. Since two separate copies of the disk block are made in the disk array controller, no single hardware or power failure can cause a loss of data.

Disk blocks in array controller cache memory that need to be written to disk are called *dirty*. Such dirty blocks are written to disk in a process we call *destaging*. When a block is destaged to disk, it is also necessary to update, on disk, the parity block for the data block. This may require the array controller to read the old values of the data block and the parity block from disk, XOR them with the new value of the data block in cache, then write the new value of the data block and of the parity block to disk. Since many applications first read data before updating them, we expect that the old value of the data block might already be in array controller cache. Therefore, the more typical destage operation is expected to require one disk read and two disk writes.

3.1. Overview of Destage

Typically, the disk blocks in the disk array controller (both dirty and clean disk blocks) are organized in Least-Recently-Used (LRU) fashion. When space for a new disk block is needed in the cache, the LRU disk block in cache is examined. If it is clean, the space occupied by that disk block can be immediately used; if it is dirty, the disk block must be destaged before it can be used. While it is not necessary to postpone destaging a dirty block until it becomes the LRU block in the cache, the argument for doing so is that it could avoid unnecessary work. Consider that a particular disk block has the value d. If the host later writes to this disk block and changes its value to d', we would have a dirty block (d') in cache which would have to be destaged later. However, if the host writes to this disk block again, changing its value to d'', before d' became LRU and was destaged, we no longer need to destage d', thus avoiding some work.[1]

When a block is ready to be destaged, the disk array controller may also decide to destage other dirty blocks in the cache that need to be written to the same track, or the same cylinder. This helps minimize disk arm motion, by clustering together many destages to the same disk arm position. However, this also means that some dirty blocks are destaged before they become the LRU disk block, since they will be destaged at the same time as some other dirty block that became LRU and that happened to be on the same track or cylinder. Therefore, the destage algorithm must be carefully chosen to trade-off the reduction in destages that can be caused by overwrites of dirty blocks if we wait until dirty blocks become LRU versus the reduction in seeks that can be achieved if we destage multiple blocks at the same track or cylinder position together. An example compromise might be along the following lines: when a dirty block becomes LRU, destage it and all other dirty blocks on the same track (cylinder) as long as these other blocks are in the LRU half of the LRU chain of cached disk blocks.

In a practical implementation, we may have a background destage process that continually destages dirty blocks near the LRU end of the LRU list (and others on the same track or cylinder) so that a request that requires cache space (such as a host write that misses in the cache) does not have to wait for destaging to complete in order to find space in the cache. Another option is to trigger destages based on the fraction of dirty blocks in the cache. For example, if the fraction of dirty blocks in the cache exceeds some threshold (say 50%), we may trigger a destage of dirty blocks that are near the LRU end of the LRU chain (and

---

1   On the other hand, there are two copies of every dirty disk block in the cache. The longer we delay destaging the dirty blocks, the longer they occupy two cache locations.

of other dirty blocks on the same tracks as these blocks). This destaging may continue until the number of dirty blocks in cache drops below some reverse threshold (say 40%).

Since read requests to the disk are synchronous while destages to the disk are asynchronous, the best destage policy is one that minimizes any impact on read performance. Therefore, the disk controller might delay starting a destage until all waiting reads have completed to the disk and it may even consider pre-empting a destage (particularly long destages of many tracks) for subsequent reads.

3.2. Summary of Fast Write Benefits

To summarize, Fast Write: will eliminate disk time from write response time as seen by the host; will eliminate some disk writes due to overwrites caused by later host writes to dirty blocks in cache; will reduce disk seeks because destages will be postponed until many destages can be done to a track or cylinder; and can convert small writes (single block) to large writes (all blocks in parity group) and thus eliminate many disk accesses. Work done by Joe Hyde [3] indicates that, for high-end IBM 370 processor workloads, anywhere from 30% to 60% of the writes to the disk controller cause overwrites of dirty blocks in cache. His work also indicates that even though the host predominantly issues single block writes, anywhere from 2 to 7 dirty blocks can be destaged together when a track is destaged. Together, these results indicate that Fast Write can be an effective technique for improving the write performance of disk arrays that use the parity technique.

4. Overview of Hagar

The Hagar prototype is designed to support very large amounts of disk storage (up to 1 Terabyte); to provide high bandwidth (100 MB/sec); to provide high IOs/sec (5000 IOs/sec at 4 Kbyte transfers); and to provide high availability. It provides for continuous operation through use of battery-backed memory, duplexed hardware components, multiple power boundaries, hot sparing of disks, on-the-fly-rebuilding of data lost in a disk crash to a hot spare and by permitting nondisruptive installation and removal of disks and hardware components.

Hagar is organized around checked and reliable control and data buses on a backplane. The structure of Hagar is shown in Figure 1. The data bus is optimized for high throughput on large data transfers and the control bus is optimized for efficient movement of small control transfers. The Hagar data bus is a multi-destination bus; a block received from the host system or from the disks can be placed in multiple data memory locations even though only one copy of the data block travels on the data bus.

In the idealized Hagar implementation, we would have processor cards; host interface cards; global data memory cards; global control memory cards and disk controller cards attached to the reliable data and control buses. Cards of each type are divided into at least 2 disjoint sets; each set is on a different power boundary. The disk controller cards would attach to multiple disk strings over a serial link using a logical command structure such as SCSI. For availability reasons, the disks would be dual-ported and would each attach to two serial links originating from two different disk controllers. The data memory cards would provide battery-backed memory, accessible to all processors, for caching, fast write and data buffering. The control memory cards also provide battery-backed memory, accessible to all processors, used for control structures such as cache directories and lock tables. Unlike the data memory, the control memory provides efficient access to small amounts of data (bytes) and supports atomic operations necessary for synchronization between multiple processors.

The XOR hardware needed for performing parity operations is integrated with the data memory. We chose to integrate the XOR logic with the data memory to avoid bus bandwidth during XOR operations to a separate XOR unit such as that used in the Berkeley RAID-II design ([9]). The data memory in Hagar supports two kinds of store operations: a regular store operation and a special store & XOR operation. A store & XOR to location X, takes the incoming data, XORs it with data at location X, and stores the result of the XOR back into location X.

5. Data Memory Management Algorithms

5.1. Four Logical Regions of Data Memory

The data memory in the disk array controller is divided into four logical regions: the free pool, the data cache, the parity cache and the buffer pool. When a block is written by the host, it is placed in the buffer pool, in two separate power boundaries. Subsequently, the two data blocks are moved into the data cache (this is a logical, not a physical move; that is, the cache directories are updated to reflect the fact that the disk block is in cache). After this logical move of the blocks into the data cache, the array controller returns "done" to the host system that did the write. At some subsequent time, the block D is destaged to disk. The data cache region of the data memory contains data blocks from disk and the parity cache region of the data memory contains parity blocks from disk. The parity blocks are useful during destage, since the presence of a parity block in the

Logical Architecture of Array Controller

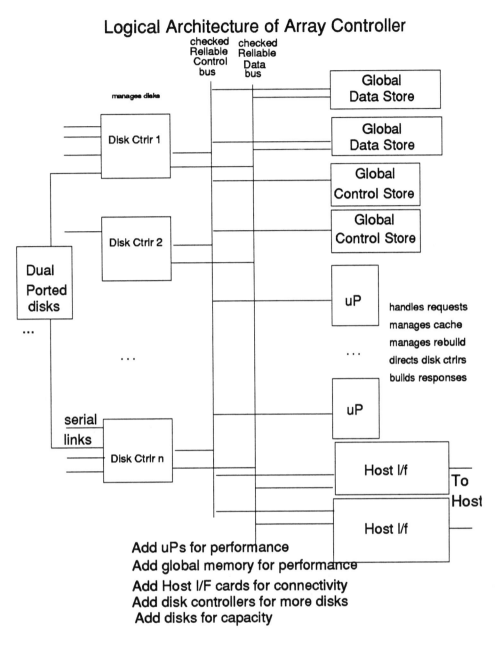

Figure 1: Hagar Array Controller

parity cache would eliminate the need to read it from disk at destage time. There is some argument for not having a parity cache at all and to make the data cache larger. This is because parity blocks in the parity cache only help destage performance, whereas data blocks in the data cache can help both read performance (due to cache hits) and destage performance

(by eliminating the need to read old data from disk). Furthermore, data blocks are brought into the data cache naturally as a result of host block requests; parity blocks, on the other hand, must be specially brought into the cache when a particular data block is read in the hope that the host will subsequently write the data block.

5.2. *Details of Write Request Handling*

When a block (value Y2 say) is written by the host, it is placed in the buffer pool, in two separate locations. Subsequently, the two copies of Y2 are moved into the data cache. At this point, it is possible that a previous clean version of this block, say Y1, is already in data cache. In this case, there are three different possibilities for what action to take.

The first possibility, which is the one we assume in the rest of this paper, is to leave the old value Y1 in data cache and also create two copies of the new value Y2, for a total of three data cache locations occupied. We call this the *save old data method*. The old value Y1 is not removed because it will be useful to us in calculating new parity when we are ready to destage Y2. Since the destage of Y2 may not happen until much later, we may be consuming an extra memory location for Y1 for a long time. We have found from simulations that the disk array controller will need about a 20% larger cache to hold the old values of data. A second possibility we considered was to remove Y1 from cache when Y2 is received, giving us a 20% larger effective cache. We call this the *overwrite old data method*. The drawback is that now, when we are ready to destage Y2, we will need to reaccess Y1 from disk. This possibility may be attractive if the increase in performance from the 20% larger effective data cache offsets the loss in performance due to need to reaccess old data at destage time.

Finally, we considered and rejected the following third possibility. Instead of leaving the old value (say Y1) of the block in cache and creating two copies of the new value (say Y2) of the block (for a total of three memory locations occupied), XOR the old and new values of the block and store (Y1 XOR Y2) in one memory location and Y2 in a second memory location. We call this the *save partial parity method*. This has the advantage of requiring only 2 memory locations instead of 3; also we would have already done one of the XOR operations needed to generate new parity. At destage time, we would only need to read old parity, XOR it with (Y1 XOR Y2) to generate new parity, then write new parity to disk. However, the results of [3] indicate that there is a very high probability of receiving another write (say Y3) to the same disk location before we have had a chance to destage Y2. With our currently assumed approach (save old data method), we would merely overwrite the 2 memory locations containing Y2 with the new value Y3. However, if we went with an approach in which we had already XORed Y1 with Y2, we would need to first XOR Y2 to this result to get back Y1, then XOR the new value Y3 to get (Y1 XOR Y3).

Because of this complication, we decided not to go with the save partial parity approach.

5.3. *Organization of Data Cache*

There are three types of disk blocks in the data cache - type d, type d′, and type d″. A particular block in the data cache is of type d if its value is the same as the value of this block on the disk - in other words, it is a clean block. Blocks of type d′ and of type d″ are both dirty blocks. If a block of type d is in the cache and a new block is written by the host to the same disk location, we will create two new blocks of type d′; that is, the cache now contains a block of type d (old value of block) and 2 blocks of type d′ (2 copies of new value of block). Only blocks of type d′ are destaged from cache to disk. Type d″ is a temporary classification to deal with new host writes received while a block of type d′ is being destaged. When a block of type d′ is being destaged, it is possible to receive another write from the host to the same disk location. If the host write had been received before the destage started, we would have merely overwritten the dirty block in cache with the new one received, and made the new one received of type d′. However, once we have started the destage and are committed to doing the destage, we mark any new block received to the same disk location as being of type d″ (alternatively, we could reject the request). Once a block of type d′ is destaged, it becomes a block of type d. At this time, any blocks of type d″ for the disk location just destaged may be reclassified as blocks of type d′.

6. Destage Algorithms

If a dirty disk block is destaged to disk, we must also calculate and write the corresponding parity block in order to keep the parity group consistent. When a disk block from a parity group is to be destaged, we lock the parity group for the duration of the destage. The parity group is unlocked only after the disk block and the parity block are both written to disk and the parity group is consistent on disk. The parity group lock prevents more than one destage to be in progress simultaneously to any one parity group. While not explicitly referred to in the algorithms that follow, a parity group is locked before a destage begins and is unlocked after the destage completes.

We begin by considering the case where only one of the data blocks of a parity group is dirty in the data cache and needs to be destaged; later we will also consider cases where more than one block of a parity group needs to be destaged. To simplify the discussion, we assume that when a dirty block is to be destaged, other blocks of the parity group are not in the data cache even in clean form. We also assume that the old value of the dirty block is not in cache and needs to be read from disk. Both these assumptions will be relaxed in later sections of this paper.

6.1. Two Data Copies Method (Method 1)

The first part of Figure 2 shows the simplest option available to us in order to destage a dirty block (labelled D1′ in the figure). In this figure, the dotted line separates two different power boundaries in the array controller, and we see that the two different copies of D1′ are on two different power boundaries. Also, the solid horizontal line separates the array controller from the disk drives themselves. The figure shows six data disk blocks D1, D2, ... D6, on six different disks and a seventh parity disk block P on a seventh disk drive. These seven disk blocks on seven different disks constitute the parity group of interest. D1′ is an updated value of block D1 which is to be destaged to disk.

In this option, block D1 and block P are both read from disk and XORed directly into one of the two D1′ locations in controller memory (this would use the store & XOR feature of the data memory we had described earlier). Because the XOR operation is commutative, the XOR of D1 and the XOR of P may happen in either order; this means that we may actually start the two different disk operations in parallel and do not need to serialize the two different disk seeks on the two different disks. D1′ may be written to disk anytime after D1 has been read and XORed. When both D1 and P have been read and XORed to one of the two copies of D1′, this location now contains P′ the new value of P which may now be written to disk.

From the first part of Figure 2, we also see that the entire destage operation consumes 4X bytes of controller data bus bandwidth, where X is the number of bytes in a disk block. This is because there are 2 read and 2 write operations for a total of four disk block movements on the controller data bus. The figure also shows that 6X bytes of memory bandwidth is consumed (each XOR operation requires 2X bytes of memory bandwidth, X to read and X to write). On the other hand, a disk controller that does mirroring which only needs 2X bytes of bus bandwidth and 2X bytes of memory bandwidth.

The simple destage algorithm described above is robust in that no single error can cause it to fail. However, it would not be considered robust enough for many situations, since there are multiple failures that can cause loss of data. For example, a transient error during the process of XORing D1 into one of the two D1′ locations, coupled with a hard failure or loss of the other copy of D1′ results in a situation where D1′ is lost by the array controller (both copies are damaged). Since the array controller had previously assured the host system that the write of D1′ was done as part of the Fast Write operation, this loss of D1′ may be unacceptable in many kinds of situations. Below, we describe a more robust destage algorithm that avoids this situation.

6.2. Two Data Copies and One Parity Copy Method (Method 2)

The algorithm is graphically shown in the second part of Figure 2. The first step in the algorithm is a memory to memory copy operation that creates a third copy of D1′. The rest of the steps of the algorithm are identical to that described previously. New parity is created at the location where the third copy of D1′ is made (location Y). Compared to the earlier algorithm, the new algorithm temporarily occupies one additional disk block in controller memory (location Y), it uses X bytes more of bus bandwidth and 2X bytes more of memory bandwidth, for a total of 5X bytes of bus bandwidth and 8X bytes of memory bandwidth.

The algorithm described above is robust enough for most situations. However, it is not as robust as a disk controller that does mirroring. When the disk controller doing mirroring begins a destage, it writes one copy of the disk block to one disk, another copy of the disk block to the mirror disk. The destage can complete even if a disk other than the two involved in the destage were to fail and, concurrently, a memory failure on one power boundary were to occur. In other words, it can survive two hard failures.

Consider the same set of failures for the disk array controller. Consider that we have just completed writing D1′ and that we have started to write new P′ when there is a hard error in the memory location containing new P′ (location Y). Therefore, we have damaged the disk location that was to contain new P′. It used to contain the old value of P, but it now contains neither P nor P′. To complete the destage correctly, we must recalculate P′ and write P′ to this disk location. Since we already wrote D1′ to disk, we can no longer calculate P′ the way we did before, which was by reading D1 and using D1 to calculate P′. Since D1 on disk has already been overwritten with D1′, we must recalculate P′ by reading D2, D3, ..., D6 and XORing them all together and with D1′. If one of the disks containing D2, D3, ..., D6 also fails, we are unable to recalculate new P′. Therefore, a set of failures that did not prevent a mirrored disk controller from destaging could not be handled by the array controller using the destage algorithm we have described in this section. In the next section, we de-

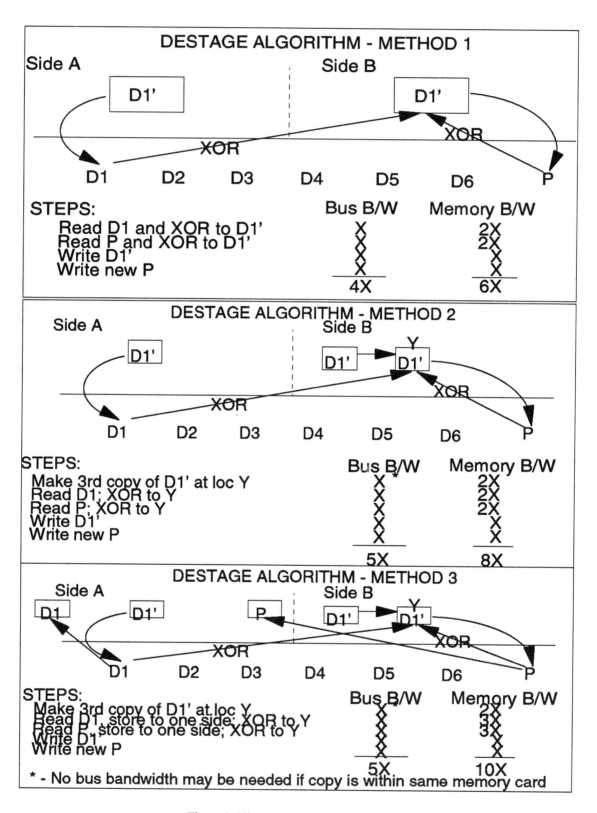

Figure 2: Hierarchy of Destage Algorithms

scribe a destage algorithm that makes the array controller as robust as a disk controller that uses mirroring.

6.3. Two Data Copies and Two Parity Copies Method (Method 3)

The third part of Figure 2 graphically demonstrates the most robust of our destage algorithms. (See [7] for other robust algorithms.). The steps are: make a third copy of D1′ at location Y; in any order, read D1 from disk and XOR it to Y and also make a copy of D1 on the other power boundary, read P from disk and XOR it to Y and also make a copy of P on the other power boundary; after all reads and XORs are done, write D1′ and new P′ (from location Y) to disks in any order. By waiting for all reads and XOR operations to complete before beginning any writes, this algorithm is robust against a combination of three failures; the hard failure of one of the two memory cards, the failure of one of the disks containing D2, D3, ..., D6, and a transient failure while reading and XORing D1 or P. Key to achieving this robustness is ensuring that old values of D1 and P are read into a different power boundary than location Y which contains the third copy of D1′. This, in effect, means that two copies of new parity are present in cache before we begin writing to the disks; one at location Y and one which can be created on the other power boundary by XORing D1′, D1 and P. The price to be paid for the increased robustness of the destage algorithm is performance (since writes must wait until all reads are done) and resource consumption (since it now needs two more temporary locations in memory, uses 10X bytes of memory bandwidth and 5X bytes of bus bandwidth).

6.4. Arrays Versus Mirroring Comparison

We compare a disk controller that performs mirroring to one that implements a RAID-5 array using one of the three different destage algorithms described in the previous section. The comparison is in terms of resources consumed (internal bus bandwidth, internal memory bandwidth and number of internal memory locations occupied) for write operations. It is assumed that all disk controllers use the fast write technique so that write operations proceed in two stages; one stage in which the write is received and buffered and a second stage in which the dirty pages are destaged.

Type of ctlr	Stage 1		Stage 2		Total		Mem Locs
	Bus B/W	Mem B/W	Bus B/W	Mem B/W	Bus B/W	Mem B/W	
Mirror	X	2X	2X	2X	3X	4X	2
Method 1	X	2X	4X	6X	5X	8X	2
Method 2	X	2X	5X	8X	6X	10X	3
Method 3	X	2X	5X	10X	6X	12X	5

From the above table, we see that the simplest parity array controllers require 67% more bus bandwidth and twice as much memory bandwidth as disk controllers that employ mirroring. The most robust parity array controllers need twice the bus bandwidth and thrice the memory bandwidth of disk controllers that perform mirroring. Furthermore, during the destage process, the most robust parity array controllers require 2.5 times as much temporary cache space as disk controllers that perform mirroring.

6.5. Other Destage Cases

It turns out that we have only considered one of four possible destage situations that may arise. Figure 3 shows all the four cases and indicates that which case applies depends on how many data blocks of the parity group are to be destaged and how many of them are in cache (by definition, all the blocks to be destaged are in cache in two separate locations). In the figure, all blocks in cache that are dirty are designated by Di′. These are the blocks to be destaged. The four cases are:

- Destage entire parity group
- Destage part of parity group; entire parity group in cache
- Destage part of parity group; read remaining members of parity group to create new parity
- Destage part of parity group; read old values of data and parity to create new parity

These four cases are described below. In general, we describe the most robust forms of the destage algorithms to be used in each case.

6.5.1. Destage Entire Parity Group

In this case, we first allocate a buffer (P1) to hold parity and initialize it to zero. Each block in the parity group is written to disk and simultaneously XORed with P1. After all data blocks have been written, write P1 (which contains the new parity) to disk.

6.5.2. Destage Part of Parity Group; Entire Parity Group in Cache

We first make a copy of one of the data blocks in the parity group that is not to be destaged at location P1. P1 will eventually contain the new parity to be written to disk. Each dirty block in the parity group is written to disk and simultaneously XORed with

Destaging a Parity Group - Four Cases

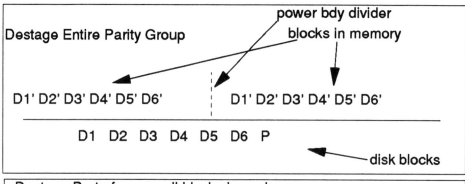

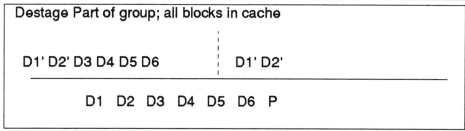

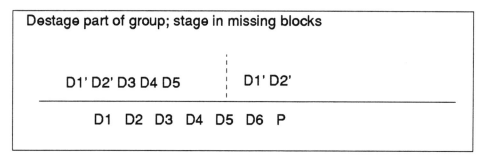

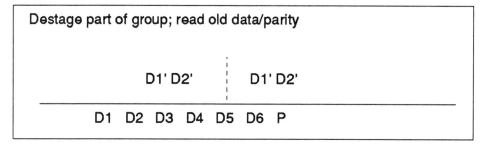

dstgrj6 3/3/91

Figure 3: Cases for Destaging a Parity Group

P1. The other blocks of the parity group are only XORed with P1. After all XORing is completed, write P1 (which contains the new parity) to disk.

The above approach has a small exposure. Consider that we have completed writing one or more of the dirty blocks to disk, but have not yet completed generation of new parity in P1. Now, consider that we lose a memory card that contains a clean data block that was going to be used to generate the new parity in P1. We will now need to read this block from disk, and an exposure arises if we cannot do so. The exposure is small, since the fact that this block was in the data cache most likely implies that we were able to either read or write this disk block in the recent past. If the exposure is considered large, we have the following alternative destage policy.

First make a copy of one of the data blocks in the parity group that is not to be destaged at location P1. XOR all non-dirty data blocks of the parity group into P1. Make copy of result in P1 in other power boundary at P2. Now, write each dirty data block to disk while XORing simultaneously with P1. After all XORing is complete, write P1 which contains the new parity. If we lose a memory card during destage, the copy of the result we saved in P2 can be used to complete the generation of new parity without need to read any disk block.

6.5.3. Destage Part of Parity Group; Read rest from disk

The assumption here is that only a very few of the blocks of the parity group are not in cache, so that it is faster to read these missing members in to generate the new parity than it is to read the old values of the blocks to be destaged.

In this case, we first allocate and zero out a buffer P1. Every data block of the parity group that is missing in cache is read in from disk and XORed into location P1. After all reads have completed, each dirty block in the parity group is both written to disk and XORed with P1 simultaneously. Other blocks of the parity group that were neither dirty, nor missing in cache originally, are XORed with P1 but not written to disk. Eventually, write new parity in P1 to disk.

The reason for first completing the reads of the data blocks missing in cache before allowing any writes to take place is to ensure that all such missing data blocks are readable. If one of these data blocks is unreadable, a different algorithm (the one to be described next) would be used for destage.

6.5.4. Destage Part of Parity Group; Read Old Values from Disk

We first create a third copy of one of the data blocks (say D) to be destaged (say at location C). The old value of every data block to be destaged to disk is read in from disk to a location on a different power boundary from C, and it is also simultaneously XORed into location C. The old value of parity is also read in from disk to a location on a different power boundary from C and simultaneously XORed with C. As before, the reading of old data blocks and the reading of the old parity block can proceed in parallel. After the old value of a block has been read and XORed, its new value can be written to disk and XORed with C (if needed; block D does not need to be XORed with C since we started with a copy of block D in location C) at any subsequent time. After all data blocks have been written and the old parity

block has been read, write C which contains the new parity.

7. Conclusions

In this paper, we have described a technique called Fast Write to improve the performance of disk arrays that use the parity technique. This technique involves use of battery-backed or Non-Volatile Store in the array controller to hold blocks written by the host system. These host-written blocks are destaged to disk asynchronously. Fast Write is expected to have four advantages: it can eliminate disk time from the write response time as seen by the host; it can eliminate some disk writes due to overwrites caused by later host writes to dirty blocks in cache; it can reduce disk seeks because destages will be postponed until many destages can be done to a track or cylinder; it can convert small writes to large writes.

We used an array controller organization which places the XOR logic (needed for parity generation) close to the cache memory in the controller and not as a separate XOR unit as has been proposed for other array controller designs ([9]). We showed that such an approach can reduce internal bus bandwidth requirements for array controllers. We described an organization of the data memory in the disk controller to support Fast Write which involved caching both data and parity blocks. We proposed that the data cache needs to support three different kinds of disk data blocks for efficiently handling Fast Writes. We articulated three alternatives for handling Fast Write hits - save old data, overwrite old data, save partial parity - and examined their pros and cons. For what appears to be the preferred alternative, we estimated that the disk controller would need a 20% larger cache than traditional or mirrored disk controllers that use Fast Write (to achieve the same hit ratios). We showed that parity group locking is an effective technique to avoid incorrect calculation of parity during concurrent destage and rebuild activity. Finally, we described the destage of disk blocks from the data cache in great detail. Four different destage cases were identified. By using one of the destage cases as an example, we described a hierarchy of three different destage algorithms of increasing degrees of robustness to failures in the disk subsystem. These three algorithms were the *two data copies method*, the *two data copies and one parity copy method* and the *two data copies and two parity copies method*. These destage algorithms were compared against those that would be used by a disk controller employing mirroring instead of the parity technique. We were able to show that the least robust array controllers require 67% more bus bandwidth and twice as much memory bandwidth as disk controllers that employ mirroring. The most robust parity array controllers, on the other hand, need twice the bus bandwidth and thrice the memory bandwidth of disk controllers that perform mirroring. These results indicate that while mirroring is more expensive overall (because of the need for more disks), disk array controllers are likely to be somewhat more expensive than controllers that do mirroring.

We also posed the following questions for future research:

- How much of the cache should be devoted to hold parity blocks instead of data blocks? Parity blocks are useful during destage, but data blocks can help both read performance (through read hits in the cache) and destage performance (by eliminating the need to read old data from disk at destage time). Furthermore, data blocks are brought into the data cache naturally as a result of user requests; parity blocks, on the other hand, must be specially brought into the cache when a particular data block is read in the hope that the host will subsequently write the data block.

- When a particular data block is selected for destage, should we also destage other blocks on the same track? or on the same cylinder? If these other blocks were only recently received from the host, then it may be better not to destage them immediately, since we might expect the host to write these blocks again. Therefore, the destage policy must be carefully chosen to trade-off the reduction in destages that can be caused by overwrites of dirty blocks if we wait until dirty blocks become LRU versus the reduction in seeks that can be achieved if we destage multiple blocks at the same track or cylinder position together. Should we also take into account the utilization of devices so that destages are begun to devices that are currently under-utilized?

- Since every dirty block in the controller cache occupies two memory locations until the block is destaged, the sooner we destage the dirty block, the sooner we can reclaim two memory locations. How do we trade-off this requirement for a quick destage of dirty blocks versus the requirement to hold off the destage in the expectation of overwrites that reduce the number of destages needed?

- What is the appropriate method for handling write hits? Should we leave the old data in cache since it is needed at destage time and take the attendant drop in effective cache size, or should we overwrite the old data in cache and reaccess it from disk at destage time?

- What is the appropriate granularity at which to do locking? We have proposed parity group locking be used, but is either a coarser or finer granularity more reasonable? What should the duration of locking be? Is it better to hold the lock until both data and parity are written to disk as proposed in this paper, or should we release the lock sooner.

8. Acknowledgements

Jim Brady originated the idea that we build the XOR hardware close to the memory in the controller.

9. References

1. Clark, B. E. et. al., Parity Spreading to Enhance Storage Access, *United States Patent* **4,761,785** (Aug. 1988).
2. Gray, J. N. et. al., Parity Striping of Disk Arrays: Low-Cost Reliable Storage With Acceptable Throughput, *Tandem Computers Technical Report* **TR 90.2** (January 1990).
3. Hyde, J., Cache Analysis Results, *Personal Communication* (1991).
4. Menon, J. M. and Hartung, M., The IBM 3990 Disk Cache, *Compcon 1988* (San Francisco, June 1988).
5. Menon, J. and Mattson, D., Performance of Disk Arrays in Transaction Processing Environment, *12th International Conference on Distributed Computing Systems* (1992) pp. 302–309.
6. Menon, J., Roche, J. and Kasson, J., Floating Parity and Data Disk Arrays, *Journal of Parallel and Distributed Computing* (Jan. 1993).
7. Menon, J. and Cortney, J., The Architecture of a Fault-Tolerant Cached RAID Controller, *IBM Research Report* **RJ 9187** (Jan. 1993).
8. Patterson, D. A., Gibson, G. and Katz, R. H., A Case for Redundant Arrays of Inexpensive Disks (RAID), *ACM SIGMOD Conference* (Chicago, Illinois, June 1988).
9. Lee, Ed, Hardware Overview of RAID-II, *UC Berkeley RAID Retreat* (Lake Tahoe, Jan 1991).
10. Ousterhout, J. and Douglis, F., Beating the I-O Bottleneck: Case for Log-Structured File Systems, *UC Berkeley Research Report* **UCB-CSD-88-467** (Berkeley, CA, October 1988).

SESSION 5:
Multiprocessor Caches

The Detection and Elimination of Useless Misses in Multiprocessors

Michel Dubois, Jonas Skeppstedt[*], Livio Ricciulli,
Krishnan Ramamurthy, and Per Stenström[*]

Dept. of Electrical Engineering - Systems
University of Southern California
Los Angeles, CA 90089-2562, U.S.A.

[*]Department of Computer Engineering
Lund University
P.O. Box 118, S-221 00 LUND, Sweden

Abstract

In this paper we introduce a new classification of misses in shared-memory multiprocessors based on interprocessor communication. We identify the set of essential misses, i.e., the smallest set of misses necessary for correct execution. Essential misses include cold misses and true sharing misses. All other misses are useless misses and can be ignored without affecting the correctness of program execution. Based on the new classification we compare the effectiveness of five different protocols which delay and combine invalidations leading to useless misses. In cache-based systems the protocols are very effective and have miss rates close to the essential miss rate. In virtual shared memory systems the techniques are also effective but leave room for improvements.

1.0 Introduction

The design of efficient memory hierarchies for shared-memory multiprocessors is an important problem in computer architecture today. With current interconnection and memory technologies, the shared-memory access time is usually too large to maintain good processor efficiency. As the number and the speed of processors increase, it becomes critical to keep instructions and data close to each processor.

These considerations have led to two types of systems, cache-based systems [5,15] and virtual shared memory systems [1,2], in which multiple copies of the same data may exist and coherence must be maintained among them. Cache-based systems are shared memory systems in which each processor has a private cache with a block size typically less than 256 bytes. A virtual shared memory system is a shared memory system built on top of a distributed (message-passing) multicomputer, through software management of virtual memory; coherence is maintained on pages of size larger than 512 bytes.

Write invalidate protocols are the most widely used protocols to enforce consistency among the copies of a particular block or page. In such protocols, multiple processors may have a copy of a block or page provided no one modifies it, i.e., the copy is *shared*. When a processor needs to write into a copy, it must first acquire *ownership*, i.e., it must have the sole copy among all caches. Acquiring ownership implies that copies in remote caches must be invalidated. While an invalidation or miss request is pending in a processor, the processor must often be blocked. The processor blocking time during a memory request is called the *penalty* of the request. Whereas invalidation penalties can be easily eliminated through more aggressive consistency models [9,13], load miss latencies are much harder to hide.

In write invalidate protocols, misses can be classified in cold, replacement, and coherence misses. A cold miss occurs at the first reference to a given block by a given processor. Subsequent misses to the block by the processor are either caused by invalidations (coherence misses) or by replacements (replacement misses). A large number of the coherence misses are not needed for the correct execution of a parallel program. Intuitively, only coherence misses which communicate new values to a processor are essential; all other coherence misses are useless.

Our first contribution is to identify the sets of essential and useless misses in an execution. This new classification is important in general because we cannot compare approaches to reduce miss rates without good measures of miss rate components. For example, in compiler-based approaches to miss reduction it is important to understand how much improvement is due to the elimination of useless misses and how much is due to better locality. Moreover, by identifying the minimum miss rate for an execution, we can understand how close we are to the minimum miss rate and whether further improvements are possible.

This research was supported by the National Science Foundation under Grant No. CCR-9115725

Our second contribution consists of applying the classification to evaluate effects of invalidation timing — or *scheduling* — on the miss rate and its components. Aggressive techniques to tolerate memory latency tend to alter the timing of invalidations. For example, in the DASH machine [13], stores are issued by the processor immediately in a store buffer and are executed later on in the cache and in the system. Therefore invalidations are delayed both in the local processor and later on when they are propagated in the system. These delays can cut the number of useless misses. We show an invalidation schedule which yields the minimum possible miss rate for a trace (called the *essential* miss rate). In practice, it is difficult to reach that minimum but we compare the effectiveness of attempts to do so. We also present results for a worst-case propagation of invalidations consistent with release consistency [13] and which, in some cases, causes a large number of misses.

The paper is structured as follows. Section 2 covers the classification and is followed by the description of various protocols to eliminate useless misses and of the worst-case schedule of invalidations in section 3. In section 4, we present and justify the experimental methodology. Finally, in sections 5, 6 and 7 we analyze our simulation results.

2.0 Classification of Misses

In contrast with previous attempts to classify coherence misses in multiprocessors [11,16] our classification is based on interprocessor communication. We will restrict ourselves to infinite caches and write invalidate protocols. We define the *lifetime* of a block in the cache following a miss as the time interval during which the block remains valid in the cache (from the occurrence of the miss until its invalidation or until the end of the simulation).We then define the following classes of misses.

Cold miss: The first miss to a given block by a processor.

Essential miss: The first miss to a given block by one processor (cold miss) is an essential miss. A miss is also an essential miss if, during the *lifetime* of the block in the cache, the processor *accesses* (Important note: an *access* can be a load or a store[1]) a value *defined* by a different processor since the last essential miss experienced by the same processor to the same block.

Pure True Sharing miss (PTS): An essential miss which is not cold.

Pure False Sharing miss (PFS): A miss which is not

---

1. Strictly speaking, the value of the data is not needed for the correct execution of a store. However, shared memory systems require that the value is accessed for the store to complete.

essential (useless miss).

The first miss in a processor for a given block is a cold miss. This miss communicates all the initial values plus all the values modified by other processors since the start of the simulation. Assume that, after this cold miss, other processors change the value of word(s) in the block. The first true sharing miss is detected when the processor *accesses* one of the new values during the lifetime of the block following the miss; at the occurrence of this first true sharing miss all values modified in the block since the cold miss are also communicated to the processor. Between the cold miss and the first true sharing miss there may have been several false sharing misses. These intervening false sharing misses are useless in the sense that the execution from the cache would still be correct if the block had not been loaded and the processor had kept accessing the values loaded on the cold miss instead. True sharing misses are detected one after the other by detecting the first access to a value modified since the previous essential miss.

In some cases it may be useful to refine the definition of cold misses as follows.

Pure Cold miss (PC): Cold miss on a block which has not been modified since the start of the simulation.

Cold and True Sharing miss (CTS): Cold miss on a block modified since the start of the simulation; moreover, during the subsequent lifetime of the block in the cache, the processor *accesses* one of the modified values. Fig. 1 and 2 show examples of CTS misses.

Cold and False Sharing miss (CFS): Cold miss on a block modified since the start of the simulation; however, during the lifetime of the block in the cache, the processor does not access any one of these modified values. Fig. 3 shows an example of a CFS miss.

PC misses can be eliminated by preloading blocks in the cache. CFS misses can be eliminated by preloading blocks in the cache if we also have a technique to detect and eliminate false sharing misses. CTS misses cannot be eliminated. The classification algorithm for PTS, PFS and cold misses (PC+CTS+CFS) is shown in Appendix A.

2.1 Effect of Block Size

The number of essential misses observed in a trace cannot increase when the block size increases, for the following reasons. Cache block sizes increase in power of two. If a referenced word is in a block of size B_1 and in a block of size B_2 such that B_1 is smaller than B_2, then B_1 is included in B_2. The ith essential miss for a system with block size B_1 cannot happen after the ith essential miss for a system with block size B_2, because each miss in a system with block size B_2 brings more values into the cache than in a system with block size B_1. Similarly the total number of cold misses cannot increase with the block size because more values are brought in on each miss in systems with larger block sizes.

The number of PTS misses decreases with the block size in general, but this is by no means certain. Consider the sequence in Fig. 1, where `Load i` and `Store i` correspond to a load and store in word i and different lines correspond to successive references in the trace. When the block size goes from one word to two words, the number of essential misses decreases, the number of cold misses decreases, and the number of PTS misses increases. In general, when the block size increases, some CTS misses turn into PTS misses; however, the total number of CTS plus PTS misses cannot grow, for the same reason as for the essential misses, i.e., more values are communicated at each essential miss.

Figure 1: Effect of the block size on the number of PTS misses. Words 0 and 1 are in the same block of size 2.

Ref.	P1	P2	B= 1 word	B= 2 words
T0:	Store 0		PC	PC
T1:		Load 0	CTS	CTS
T2:	Store 1	INV	PC	–
T3:		Load 1	CTS	PTS

2.2 Detection and Elimination of Useless Misses

In this section we introduce a simple write-through protocol (with allocation on write misses), which totally eliminates useless misses. On a store into the block, the address of the modified word is propagated to all processors with a copy of the block and is buffered in an invalidation buffer; a local access to a word whose address is present in the buffer invalidates the block copy and triggers a PTS miss. (The invalidation buffer could be implemented by a dirty bit associated with each word in each block of the cache.) This implementation "mimics" the essential miss detection algorithm and its miss rate is the essential miss rate of the trace.

Write-through caches generate an unacceptable amount of write traffic. To make the protocol write back we need to maintain ownership. Stores accessing non-owned blocks with a pending invalidation for ANY one of its words in the local invalidation buffer must trigger a miss. These additional misses are the cost of maintaining ownership.

2.3 Invalidation Delaying and Combining

In the above protocols, invalidations are *delayed* and *combined* in the invalidation buffer until an invalidation

leading to an essential miss is detected. Invalidation combining can be done at both ends: before it is sent out and after it is received. Delaying the sending of a store may increase the false sharing miss rate when, for example, the store is delayed across an essential miss in the receiving processor (without the delay, it would have been combined with that essential miss, but after the delay it may create a new miss.) Actually, it may even increase the essential miss rate as shown in Fig. 2. By delaying the second store of P1 from T1 to T2, a new PTS miss is created. Delaying stores at the sending end can only help if the delays lead to the combining of invalidations. Combining invalidations at the receiving end is more effective because the references causing essential misses can easily be detected and combined invalidations originate from all processors.

Figure 2: Effect of trace interleaving on the number of essential misses. Words 0 and 1 are in the same block.

Ref.	P1	P2	Class.
T0:	Store 0		PC
T1:		Load 0	CTS
T2:	Store 1	INV	–
T3:		Load 1	PTS

Ref.	P1	P2	Class.
T0:	Store 0		PC
T1:	Store 1		–
T2:		Load 0	CTS
T3:		Load 1	–

Finally, the essential miss rate is not an intrinsic property of an application, but only a property of an execution (or of an interleaved trace). For example, the two sequences in Fig. 2 are possible and equivalent executions but the second one yields less essential misses.

3.0 Comparison with Previous Classifications

Previous attempts to classify coherence misses, by Eggers and Jeremiassen [11] and by Torrellas, Lam and Hennessy [16][2] did not capture the set of essential misses. We now contrast these two schemes with ours.

3.1 Torrellas' Scheme

In this scheme, a cold miss (CM) is detected if the accessed *word* is referenced for the first time by a given processor. A True Sharing Miss (TSM) is detected on a reference which misses in the cache, accesses a word accessed before, and misses in a system with a block size

_____

2. In the rest of the paper we will refer to these two proposed classifications as "Eggers" and "Torrellas", whereas we will refer to our classification as "ours".

of one. All other misses are False Sharing Misses (FSM).

This approach has several drawbacks. The way cold misses are detected is not conventional. As it is, the classification is only applicable to iterative algorithms in which words are accessed more than once. Many important parallel algorithms, such as FFT and matrix multiply, do not belong to this class.

Figure 3: Basic shortcoming of current schemes. (1):Torrellas. (2):Eggers. (3):Ours.

Ref.	P1	P2	(1)	(2)	(3)
T0:	Store 1		CM	CM	PC
T1:		Load 0	CM	CM	CFS
T2:	Load 1		-	-	-
T3:	Load 0		-	-	-
T4:	INV	Store 0	-	-	-
T5:	Load 1		FSM	FSM	PTS
T6:	Load 0		-	-	-

The major drawback of the classification however is that it depends on which word of the block is accessed first on a miss. Consider the sequence in Fig. 3. The miss at reference T5 brings a new value defined at T4 and accessed at T6 in the cache of processor P1, and yet it is classified as a false sharing miss. If we did not execute the miss at T5 (or equivalently ignored the invalidation at T4) and kept the old block in the cache instead, P1 would read a stale value at T6. In their paper, Torrellas et al. introduce the notion of *prefetching effects*; however they do not attempt to quantify these effects.

3.2 Eggers' Scheme

A cold miss (CM) occurs at the first reference to a given block by a given processor and all following misses to the same block by the same processor are classified as invalidation misses. Invalidation misses are then classified as True Sharing Misses (TSM) if the word accessed on the miss has been modified since (and including) the reference causing the invalidation. All other invalidation misses are classified as False Sharing Misses (FSM).

Figure 4: Differences between Eggers' and Torrellas' classifications. (1):Torrellas. (2):Eggers. (3):Ours.

Ref.	P1	P2	(1)	(2)	(3)
T0:	Load 1		CM	CM	PC
T1:		Load 0	CM	CM	PC
T2:	INV	Store 1	-	-	-
T3:	Load 0		CM	FSM	PFS
T4:	INV	Store 0	-	-	-
T5:	Load 1		TSM	FSM	PTS
T6:	Load 0		-	-	-

Clearly, any true sharing miss in Eggers' classification must also be a true sharing miss in Torrellas'. Fig. 4 shows a sequence such that more true sharing misses are counted by Torrellas' method and illustrates the differences in counting cold misses.

3.3 Comparison Between the Three Classifications

We have run a few traces to see whether there was a significant difference between the different classifications for real data. Table 1 shows some results for some benchmark runs with the larger data set sizes (see section 5), namely LU200 and MP3D10000 for block sizes of 32 bytes and 1,024 bytes. As can be seen from Table 1, current measures of false and true sharing are unreliable. Eggers' scheme exaggerates the amount of false sharing and underestimates true sharing, because it ignores the possibility of communicating new values in references following the miss.

Table 1: Comparison between the classifications

BENCH.	LU	LU	MP3D	MP3D
Block(bytes)	32	1024	32	1024
PTS-ours	5,769	7,941	188,120	82,125
TSM-Eggers	2,845	2,558	178,206	67,447
TSM-Torrellas	597	183	177,272	112,562
COLD-ours	110,955	5,545	46,242	4,058
COLD-Eggers	110,955	5,545	46,242	4,058
COLD-Torrellas	113,812	9,827	52,264	26,011
PFS-ours	11,839	79,882	31,206	266,245
FSM-Eggers	14,763	85,265	41,120	280,923
FSM-Torrellas	14,154	83,358	36,032	213,855

In Torrellas' scheme, this effect is partially compensated by the fact that a new value can cause a true sharing miss even if it has been loaded in a cache on a previous true sharing miss. Torrellas' classification also classifies a large number of true and false sharing misses as cold misses. The numbers in Table 1 indicate that the net effect tends to be an overestimation of the number of false sharing misses as well.

In sections 2.2 and 2.3 approaches to reduce the miss rate were derived from the classification. In general, the times at which invalidations are scheduled can affect the miss rate and the components of the miss rate, as we argued in the introduction. In the rest of the paper, we present simulation results to quantify these effects.

4.0 Scheduling of Invalidations

We have simulated the following schedules of invalidations.

MIN (Write-through with Word Invalidation): This is the write-through protocol of section 2.2 using a dirty bit per word. It has no false sharing and yields the essential miss rate of the trace.

OTF (On-The-Fly Protocol): Each reference is scheduled one by one in the simulation. The miss rate of the OTF protocol is the miss rate usually derived when using trace-driven simulations.

RD (Receive Delayed Protocol): Invalidations are sent without delay and stored in an invalidation buffer when they are received. When a processor executes an *acquire* all blocks for which there is a pending received invalidation are invalidated [8].

SD (Send Delayed Protocol): If the processor is the owner at the time of a store, the store is completed without delay. Otherwise, the store is buffered. Pending stores in the buffer are sent at the execution of a *release*. A received invalidation is immediately executed in the cache [8].

SRD (Send and Receive Delayed Protocol): This protocol combines the features of RD and SD above [8].

WBWI (Write-back with Word Invalidate Protocol): This protocol is a special case of protocols with partial block invalidations [6]. It is similar to the MIN algorithm, but it maintains ownership in order to reduce the write traffic, as described in section 2.2. WBWI is also similar to RD except that it relies on a dirty bit per word to schedule invalidations instead of relying on releases and acquires.

MAX (Worst-case Invalidation Propagation): MAX is not a protocol. Rather, it corresponds to a worst-case scenario for scheduling invalidations, consistent with the release consistency model. Stores from a given processor can be performed at any time between the time they are issued by the processor and the next release in that processor and they can be performed out of program order. Within these limits, we schedule the invalidations of each store so as to maximize the miss rate [10].

In the next section, we describe and justify the experimental methodology used to compare the effects of various schedules of invalidations.

5.0 Simulation Methodology and Benchmarks

Early on in this project we used execution-driven simulation. We quickly ran into problems because modifying the schedule of invalidations resulted in different executions of the benchmarks. Benchmarks would yield different traces due to different scheduling of threads or would even yield different results. The effects of different scheduling of invalidations were buried into the effects of altered executions in unpredictable ways. Therefore, we decided to use trace-driven simulation instead and collected traces for four benchmark programs and two different data set sizes. All benchmarks were run for 16 processors and infinite caches.

In order to evaluate the effects of delayed protocols, applications must be free of data races and conform to the release consistency model. The first three benchmarks are parallel applications developed at Stanford University (MP3D, WATER, and LU) of which the first two are also in the SPLASH suite [14]. These applications are written in C using the Argonne National Laboratory macro package [3] and are compiled with the `gcc` compiler (version 2.0) using optimization level -O2. Traces from these benchmarks were captured by the CacheMire Test Bench, a tracing and simulation tool for shared-memory multiprocessors [4].

MP3D is a 3-dimensional particle simulator used by aerospace researchers to study the pressure and temperature profiles created as an object flies at hypersonic speeds through the upper atmosphere. The overall computation consists of calculating the positions and velocities of particles during a number of time steps. In each iteration (a time step) each processor updates the positions and velocities of each of its particles. When a collision occurs, the processor updates the attributes of the particle colliding with its own. We have run MP3D with 1,000 particles for 20 time steps (referred to as MP3D1000) and with 10,000 for 10 time steps (referred to as MP3D10000). In both cases, the locking option was switched on, to eliminate data races.

WATER performs an N-body molecular dynamics simulation of the forces and potentials in a system of water molecules in the liquid state. The overall computation consists of calculating the interaction of the atoms within each molecule and of the molecules with each other during a number of time steps. As in MP3D, each processor updates its objects in each iteration (time step). Interactions of its molecules with other molecules involve modifying the data structures of the other molecules. We have run WATER with 16 molecules for 10 time steps (WATER16) and with 288 molecules for 4 time steps (WATER288).

LU performs the LU-decomposition of a dense matrix. The overall computation consists of modifying each column based on the values in all columns to its left. Columns are modified from left to right. They are statically assigned to processors in a finely interleaved fashion. Each processor waits until a column has been produced and then uses it to modify all its columns. We have run LU with a 32x32 (LU32) and a 200x200 random matrix (LU200).

Finally, **JACOBI** [12] was written by us using the ANL macros [3] provided with the SPLASH benchmark suite. It is an iterative algorithm for solving partial differential equations. Two 64x64 grid arrays of double precision floating point numbers (8 bytes each) are modified in turn in each iteration. A component in one grid is updated by taking the average of the four neighbors of the same component in the other grid. After each iteration, the processors synchronize through a barrier synchronization, a test for convergence is done and the two arrays are switched. In each iteration, one array is read only and the other one is write only but across consecutive iterations all components are accessed read/write. Each of the 16 processors is assigned to the update of a 16x16 subgrid.

Table 2: Characteristics of the benchmarks.

BENCH-MARK	SPEED UP	WRITES (000's)	READS (000's)	ACQ/ REL (000's)	DATA SET (KB)
MP3D1000	10.9	357	948	90	36
MP3D10000	14.9	1,510	2,561	411	360
WATER16	12.3	83	973	9	10
ATER288	14.9	5,114	71,134	531	195
LU32	5.7	37	136	4	8
LU200	14.9	5,663	11,764	10	320
JACOBI	15	280	2,407	4	65

In Table 2, we show the characteristics of the benchmarks in the parallel section. The speedup derivation assumes a perfect memory system (single-cycle latencies). We first show the classification for each benchmark with the smaller problem sizes.

6.0 Miss Classification

In LU32, each column goes through two phases. In the first phase, it is accessed exclusively by a single processor whereas, in the second phase, it is read by many. As a result, the column distribution causes CTS misses which show up for small block sizes in Fig. 5. This component drops until the block size reaches 512 bytes because the largest columns occupy 512 bytes each. As the block size increases the CTS misses turn into PTS misses, an effect identified in Fig. 1. As for false sharing, LU works on triangular matrices and columns are interleaved among processors. False sharing starts to appear for the smaller columns and is significant even for small block sizes.

Figure 5: Miss rate classification for the four benchmarks with small data sets.(Miss rates are in %.)

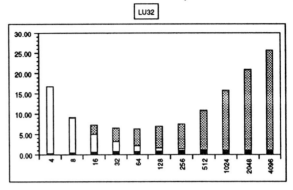

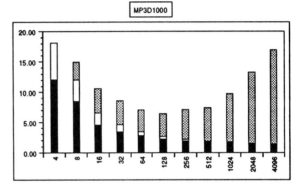

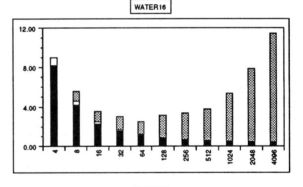

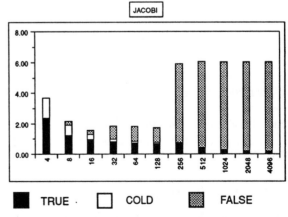

■ TRUE □ COLD ▨ FALSE

In MP3D1000, two data structures contribute to the coherence miss rate: the particle and the space-cell

93

structures. Particle objects occupy 36 bytes each and are finely interleaved among processors. Space cell objects occupy 48 bytes each. In each iteration, all particles are moved. Moving a particle means that its position and the corresponding cell data structures are updated. Occasionally, a particle collides with another particle. This causes true sharing misses if the two colliding particles are allocated to different processors. During a collision five words (20 bytes) of the data structures of the two particles are updated. Consequently, the true sharing miss rate component decreases dramatically up to 32 bytes. False sharing misses are due to modifications of particles and of space cells. False sharing starts to appear for a block size of eight bytes because the object size is 36 bytes and consecutive particle objects belong to different processors. Additional false sharing due to the space-cells appears for blocks larger than 16 bytes because the space-cell object size is 48 bytes.

In WATER16, each processor calculates both intra-molecular and inter-molecular interactions. True sharing is caused by inter-molecular interactions. During this calculation, a part of the other molecule's data structure, corresponding to nine double words (72 bytes), is modified. Consequently, the true sharing miss component decreases rapidly up until a block size of 128 bytes. False sharing mainly results from accesses to two consecutively allocated molecules belonging to different processors. The false sharing rate starts to grow significantly when the block size approaches the size of the molecule data structure (680 bytes).

In JACOBI, each matrix element is a double word (8 bytes) and we would expect true sharing to go down abruptly to half as we move from a block size of 4 to 8 bytes. After that point, it should decrease more slowly. We see these effects in Fig. 5. False sharing appears when a block partly covers the data partitions of two processors. Since the size of a row in the submatrix is 16 elements (128 bytes), false sharing abruptly goes up for a block size of 256 bytes as can be seen in Fig. 5. False sharing starts to appear for a block size of 8 bytes because of the large number of barrier synchronizations in the program (one after each iteration) and also because of the particular implementation of barriers in the ANL macros. In this implementation, two words (a counter and a flag) are stored in consecutive memory locations. The same effect also explains parts of the false sharing present in WATER16 and MP3D1000 for a block size of 8 bytes.

7.0 Effects of Invalidation Scheduling

In Fig. 6 we show the comparison between the miss rates of LU32, MP3D1000, WATER16 and JACOBI for block sizes of 64 (Fig. 6a) and 1,024 bytes (Fig. 6b). These block sizes correspond to cache-based systems and virtual shared memory systems, respectively. The decomposition into PTS, COLD and PFS misses is shown except for MIN (which has no false sharing), WBWI and MAX, for which we only display the total miss rate.

All protocols except MIN suffer from the cost of maintaining ownership. The importance of this effect can be understood by comparing WBWI and MIN, because the only difference between these protocols is ownership. Remarkably, Fig. 6a shows that the cost of ownership is very low for B=64 bytes. This can be explained easily: For small block sizes, the probability that several processors are writing into different parts of the same block at the same time is very low. By contrast the plots for B=1,024 bytes (Fig. 6b) show a large difference between the miss rates of WBWI (or RD) and MIN.

The differences between the essential miss rates of OTF (equal to the miss rate of MIN), RD, SD and SRD are negligible. This shows that the delays do not affect the essential miss count. Store combining at the sending end occurs seldom for B=64 because the blocks are too small. In general, our simulations show that pure send delayed protocols are not very effective for caches and that their miss rate is still far from the essential miss rate. There are much more opportunities for store combining in systems with B=1,024 and the effectiveness of pure SD protocols is much better.

For RD protocols, we expect more false sharing than for the WBWI protocol because the synchronization access causing the invalidation may be very far from the access to the stale word and may even not protect the stale word. For B=64 and B=1,024 it appears from the simulations that this effect is negligible. The invalidation rate of RD is also expected to be lower than that of WBWI because invalidations target entire blocks instead of words. Moreover, WBWI requires one dirty bit per word whereas RD only needs 1 stale bit per block [6,8]. From these results it appears that RD is preferable to WBWI provided that relaxed consistency models are acceptable (WBWI is valid for systems with any consistency model.)

Overall, for B=64, the miss rates of the protocols (except for OTF and SD) are very close to the essential miss rate of the trace and therefore there is little room for improvements. We want to stress here the importance of a correct classification. For example, for LU32 and for B=64 bytes, Eggers' classification yields an essential miss rate (CM+TSM) of 1.68%, whereas our classification yields an essential miss rate of 2.14%. The miss rate of WBWI is 2.37% and therefore is very close to the minimum possible. Eggers' classification would have led us to believe that significant additional reductions of the miss rate were still

Figure 6: Effect of invalidation scheduling on the miss rate (%).

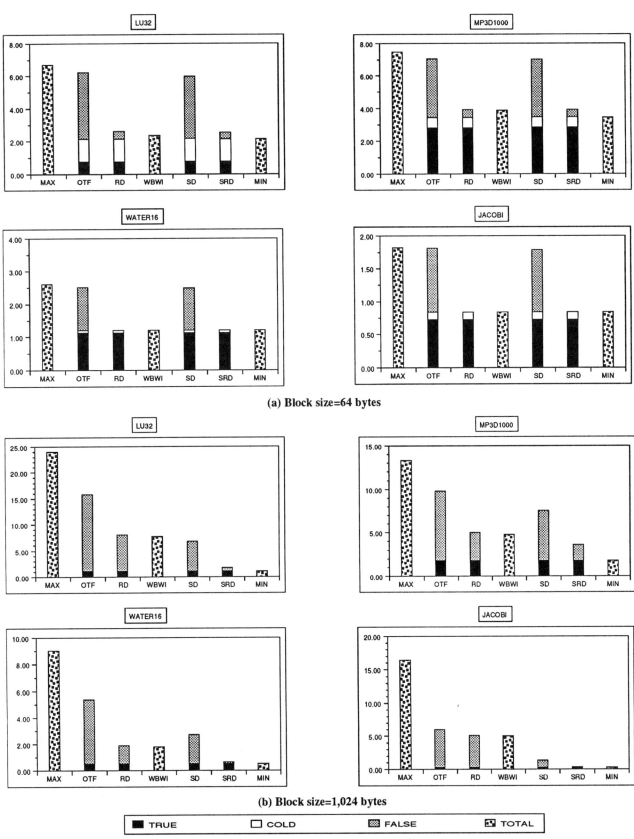

(a) Block size=64 bytes

(b) Block size=1,024 bytes

■ TRUE   □ COLD   ▨ FALSE   ▧ TOTAL

possible beyond the reduction provided by WBWI.

The simulations for B=1,024 show that further improvement is possible because the best protocol (SRD) does not always reach the essential miss rate of the trace, especially in the cases of LU and MP3D. Because of the discrepancy between the miss rates of WBWI and MIN (but not between RD and WBWI), it appears that any improvement will have to deal with the problem of block ownership. This line of thought leads to systems with multiple block sizes [7], or even systems in which coherence is maintained on individual words.

The MAX scheduling of invalidations always yields more misses than any other schedule, including OTF. For smaller block sizes the worst-case schedule gave a miss rate almost equal to OTF: because of the small block size, there are few opportunities to create ping-ponging among multiple processors accessing the same block at the same time. However, for larger block sizes, the worst-case miss rate may be significantly higher than OTF. Delaying invalidations at the receiving end should also help avoid worst-case situations such as the one in MAX.

We were able to run some simulations for the larger data set sizes namely for LU200, MP3D10000 and WATER288. In these traces, the effect of false sharing moves to larger block sizes. We do not show the curves for lack of space. The reader can find more details in [10]. The effects of invalidation schedules are similar to the case of small data sets, but these effects are much reduced for B=64 since the difference between the on-the-fly miss rate and the essential miss rate is always less than 20%. For B=1,024, the false sharing components are very large and the protocols are still quite far from the essential miss rate, as in the case of the smaller data set sizes. We have also observed a very large miss rate for MAX in the case of LU.

8.0 Conclusion

In this paper, we have introduced a classification of multiprocessor cache misses based on the fundamental concept of interprocessor communication. We have defined essential misses as the minimum number of misses for a given trace and a given block size so that the trace receives all the data inputs that it needs to execute correctly. Essential misses include cold misses, which communicate initial values to the processor, and true sharing misses, which communicate updates from other processors. The rest of the misses are useless misses in the sense that the trace would execute correctly even if they (or alternatively the invalidations leading to them) were not executed in the cache.

We have shown that previous classifications tend to overestimate the amount of false sharing. For the small

data set sizes (fine granularity of parallelism) and the four benchmarks the false sharing component is significant even for 16-byte blocks. For larger data sets, false sharing effects are moved to larger blocks.

We have also simulated several approaches to effectively detect and eliminate useless misses by dynamically delaying and combining invalidations. For B=64 (caches), all these techniques were very effective, except for the pure send delayed protocol; there is little room for improvement. Considering hardware complexity, protocols with partial block invalidations such as WBWI may be preferable for small block sizes whereas a pure receive delayed protocol is probably preferable for large block sizes. For B=1,024, the techniques addressed in this paper are particularly needed. In this case, delaying and combining invalidations at both the sending and receiving end is useful but not sufficient to remove all useless misses.The main reason is the need to maintain ownership.

We have not displayed the amount of memory traffic generated by these protocols. The protocols with reduced miss rates also have reduced miss traffic. However, the traffic is very high for large block sizes. At this level of traffic, delayed write-broadcast or delayed protocols with competitive updates, which can reduce the number of essential misses, may become attractive.

Finally, the current classification is applicable to infinite caches only. However, it can easily be extended to finite caches by introducing replacement misses. A replacement miss is an essential miss since the value is needed to execute the program. Coherence misses can then be classified into PFS and PTS misses according to the algorithm in this paper. We expect that the fraction of essential misses will increase in systems with finite caches. This effect will depend on the cache size, cache organization and replacement policy.

9.0 References

[1] Bennett, J.K., Carter, J.B., and Zwaenepoel, W., "Adaptive Software Cache Management for Distributed Shared Memory Architectures," *Proc. of the 17th Ann. Int. Symp. on Comp. Arch.*, pp. 125-134, Jun. 1990.

[2] Borrmann, L., and Herdieckerhoff, M., "A Coherency Model for Virtual Shared Memory," *Proc. of Int. Conf. on Parallel Proc.*, Vol. 2, pp.252-257, Jun. 1990.

[3] Boyle, J., et al., "Portable Programs for Parallel Processors". Holt, Rinehart, and Winston Inc.,1987.

[4] Brorsson, M., Dahlgren, F., Nilsson, H., and Stenström, P.,"The CacheMire Test Bench — A Flexible and Effective Approach for Simulation of Multiprocessors," *Proc. of the 26th Annual Simulation Symposium*, March 1993.

[5] Censier, L.M., and Feautrier, P., "A New Solution to Coherence Problems in Multicache Systems," *IEEE Trans. on Comp.*, Vol. C-27, No. 12, pp. 1112-1118, Dec. 1978.

[6] Chen, Y-S, and Dubois, M., "Cache Protocols with Partial Block Invalidations," *Int. Symp. on Parallel Proc.*, Apr. 1993.

[7] Dubnicki, C., and LeBlanc, T.J.,"Adjustable Block Size Coherent Caches," *Proc. of the 19th Ann. Int. Symp. on Comp. Arch.*, pp. 170-180, May 1991.

[8] Dubois, M., Barroso, L., Wang, J.C., and Chen, Y.S., "Delayed Consistency and its Effects on the Miss Rate of Parallel Programs," *Supercomputing'91*, pp. 197-206, Nov. 1991.

[9] Dubois, M., and Scheurich, C., "Memory Access Dependencies in Shared Memory Multiprocessors," *IEEE Trans. on Soft. Eng.*, 16(6), pp. 660-674, Jun. 1990.

[10] Dubois, M., Skeppstedt, J., Ricciulli, L., Ramamurthy, K., and Stenström, P., "The Detection and Elimination of Useless Misses in Multiprocessors," USC Tech. Rep. No. CENG-93-2, Jan.1993.

[11] Eggers, S. J., and Jeremiassen, T. E., "Eliminating False Sharing," *Proc. of the 1991 Int. Conf. on Par. Proc.*, pp. I-377-I-381, Aug. 1991. Also published as TR 90-12-01, Univ. of Washington, Dept. of Comp. Sc. and Eng, Seattle, Washington.

[12] Ekstrand, M., "Parallel Applications for Architectural Evaluations of Shared-Memory Multiprocessors." Master's thesis, Dept. of Comp. Eng., Lund Univ., Sweden, Feb. 1993.

[13] Lenoski, D., Laudon, J.P., Gharachorloo, K., Gupta, A., and Hennessy, J.L.,"The Directory-based Cache Coherence Protocol for the DASH Multiprocessor," *Proc. of the 17th Ann. Int. Symp. on Comp. Arch.*, pp. 148-159, Jun. 1990.

[14] Singh, J. P., Weber, W-D, and Gupta., A.,"SPLASH: Stanford Parallel Applications for Shared-Memory". Computer Architecture News, 20(1):5-44, March 1992.

[15] Stenström, P., "A Survey of Cache Coherence Schemes for Multiprocessors," *IEEE Computer*, Vol. 23, No. 6, pp. 12-24, Jun. 1990.

[16] Torrellas, J., Lam, M.S., and Hennessy, J.L., "Shared Data Placement Optimizations to Reduce Multiprocessor Cache Misses," *Proc. of the 1990 Int. Conf. on Parallel Proc.*, pp. 266-270, Aug 1990. Also published as "Measurement, Analysis, and Improvement of the Cache Behavior of Shared Data in Cache Coherent Multiprocessors" Tech. Rep. CSL-TR-90-412, Stanford University, Stanford, CA, Feb. 1990.

Appendix A — Classification Algorithm

A miss is classified at the end of the lifetime of the block (either at the time it is invalidated or at the end of the simulation). The classification algorithm uses the following flags associated with each processor: one Presence flag (P), one Essential Miss flag (EM), and one First Reference flag (FR) per block plus one communication flag (C) per word. We specify the actions that are needed for each load (read_action) and store (write_action) in the trace and actions taken at the end of the simulation (end_of_simulation).

Below we show Pascal-like code for the algorithm. N denotes the number of processors, T and F denote logical True and False, and block_ad and word_ad denote the block and word address, respectively:

```
read_action(proc_id,block_ad,word_ad):
  if not P[block_ad,proc_id]then
    begin
      EM[block_ad,proc_id]:=F;
      P[block_ad,proc_id]:=T;
    end;
  if C[word_ad, proc_id]then
    begin
      EM[block_ad, proc_id]:=T;
      for i:=0 until block_len-1 do
        C[block_ad*block_len+i,proc_id]:=F;
    end;

write_action(proc_id, block_ad,word_ad):
  read_action(proc_id,block_ad,word_ad);
  classify(proc_id,block_id,F);
  for i:=0 until N-1 do
    if i<>proc_id then
      begin
        C[word_ad,i]:=T;
        P[block_ad,i]:=F;
      end;

classify(proc_id,block_ad,my_block):
  for i:=0 to N-1 do
    if P[block_ad,i]and
        (my_block or (i<>proc_id)) then
      begin
        if not FR[block_ad,i] then CM:=CM+1;
        else if EM[block_ad,i] then PTS:=PTS+1;
        else PFS:=PFS+1;
        FR[block_ad,i]:=T;
      end;

end_of_simulation:
  for "each processor i and block j" do
    classify(i,j,T);
```

Adaptive Cache Coherency for Detecting Migratory Shared Data

Alan L. Cox
Department of Computer Science
Rice University

Robert J. Fowler
Department of Computer Science
University of Rochester

Abstract

Parallel programs exhibit a small number of distinct data-sharing patterns. A common data-sharing pattern, *migratory access*, is characterized by exclusive read and write access by one processor at a time to a shared datum. We describe a family of adaptive cache coherency protocols that dynamically identify migratory shared data in order to reduce the cost of moving them. The protocols use a standard memory model and processor-cache interface. They do not require any compile-time or run-time software support. We describe implementations for bus-based multiprocessors and for shared-memory multiprocessors that use directory-based caches. These implementations are simple and would not significantly increase hardware cost. We use trace- and execution-driven simulation to compare the performance of the adaptive protocols to standard write-invalidate protocols. These simulations indicate that, compared to conventional protocols, the use of the adaptive protocol can almost halve the number of inter-node messages on some applications. Since cache coherency traffic represents a larger part of the total communication as cache size increases, the relative benefit of using the adaptive protocol also increases.

1 Introduction

Parallel programs exhibit a small number of distinct data-sharing patterns [1, 23]. In one of the most common patterns, *migratory access*, the life of a shared datum consists of a sequence of time intervals. During each interval a single processor both reads and writes the datum. In successive intervals the migratory datum is accessed by different processors. Several common programming techniques give rise to the migratory access pattern, including the use of read/write data structures protected by locks or monitors and the use of shared task queues to distribute work among the nodes of a multiprocessor.

We present and evaluate both snooping and directory-based cache coherence protocols that automatically classify cached memory blocks as *migratory* or *other* and that adaptively switch between a sub-protocol optimized for migratory access and one appropriate for other data-sharing patterns. Since the optimized sub-protocol can halve the number of coherency transactions needed to manage migratory data and since migratory data are very common, the use of these adaptive protocols yields a substantial perfor-

mance improvement for many programs. The magnitude of the improvement depends, of course, on the fraction of total execution time spent waiting for memory coherency operations.

The adaptive caching protocols presented in this paper are distinguished from previous work in three ways. The migratory access pattern is identified using simple on-line algorithms that react quickly to changes in data-sharing pattern. The mechanisms and policies are simple enough to build into hardware cache controllers without a large cost or complexity increase. The adaptive protocols do not change the memory model seen by the programmer and compiler, nor do they add any special requirements to the processor-cache interface. Thus, our adaptive protocols are transparently compatible with existing language, compiler, and processor designs.

In general, multiprocessor cache coherence protocols use either a "write-update" strategy or a "write-invalidate" strategy. The write-update strategy entails interprocessor communication on every write operation to shared data. In contrast, the write-invalidate strategy entails communication only on the first write operation. In this case, the purpose of the communication is to request all other caches to invalidate their copies of the data. Until the data is accessed by another processor, subsequent write operations can be completed locally, without communication. Since migratory data is characterized by a temporal clustering of operations on a single processor, write-invalidate outperforms write-update for this data-sharing pattern. Furthermore, it is difficult to build an efficient implementation of write-update for non-broadcast-based interconnects. Therefore, write-update is generally regarded as unsuitable for use in a scaleable multiprocessor. For these reasons, our work starts from a write-invalidate protocol.

On a read miss, most write-invalidate protocols create a new copy of the block in the cache of the the processor that initiated the miss. Known as "replicate-on-read-miss", this policy is used because it allows read-shared blocks to be replicated at all of the processors that share them. Unfortunately, if a migratory block is read before it is written, the replicate-on-read-miss policy uses two separate inter-cache operations to move the block from one cache to another. For example, assume the block is initially dirty in processor P_i's cache. A read miss by P_j copies the block to P_j's cache and changes its state in P_i's cache to read-only. Later, when P_j writes to the block it is necessary to invalidate the copy in P_i's cache. In contrast, if the cache used a "migrate-on-read-miss" policy, the copying of the block to P_j and the

---

This work is supported in part by NSF Grant CCR-9211004.

invalidation of P_i's copy could be done in one transaction, thereby halving the number of inter-cache operations used to move the migratory block. If the first access from P_j is a write, both policies incur the same amount of overhead since they handle write-misses the same way.

On the other hand, a pure migrate-on-read-miss policy performs poorly for other data-sharing patterns. For example, if the data are read-shared, the cache block will migrate on every read request rather than becoming replicated in the caches of the processors accessing it. In this case, the replicate-on-read-miss policy of standard coherency protocols is appropriate.

Since neither "pure" policy is ideal for both data-sharing patterns, we have developed a scheme in which the two policies co-exist. In Section 2, we present a family of simple cache coherency protocols that (1) efficiently and dynamically differentiate migratory access from other data-sharing patterns and (2) use this information to adaptively switch between the policies. In Section 3, we describe our methodology for evaluating and comparing these adaptive protocols to conventional protocols. Our results appear in Section 4. Briefly, we have found that the adaptive protocols can reduce the number of inter-node messages by almost half for some applications. In Section 5, we compare the adaptive protocols and our results to related work. Finally, in Section 6, we present our conclusions.

2 Identifying and Handling Migratory Data

We first address the issue of distinguishing migratory blocks from read-shared blocks. Under the replicate-on-read-miss policy, a cache block containing migratory data is transported from processor P_i to P_j in two stages.

1. Since the block is migratory by assumption, processor P_i has written it. The block is dirty in P_i's cache and is invalid in P_j's cache. Thus, P_j's first access to the block is a read that misses. To service the read miss, P_j's cache controller sends a read request for the the block. In response, P_i's cache controller provides the modified block, and changes the state of the block to "Shared", a non-exclusive state that permits the block to be read but not written. At the end of this stage, there are valid Shared copies of the block in both caches.

2. P_j's first attempt to write to the block finds it in the Shared state. The operation cannot complete until all other copies of the block have been invalidated, so P_j's cache controller sends an invalidation request. On receiving the request, processor P_i's cache invalidates its copy of the block. To ensure that write operations are serialized correctly, the write operation at P_j is not allowed to proceed until there is a guarantee that there are no other write requests that can precede this one. This guarantee requires either explicit acknowledgement messages or some mechanism, such as a shared bus, that automatically serializes operations.

If a block is currently managed using the replicate-on-read-miss policy, the adaptive protocols use the above pattern of cache coherency operations as evidence that the block is migratory. Specifically, a block appears to be migratory if, at the time of a write-hit to a block in a Shared

state, (1) there are exactly two cached copies of the block, and (2) the processor currently requesting the invalidation operation is not the processor that requested the previous invalidation operation. An alternative statement of the second condition is that originator of the invalidation request has the more recently created copy of the block. A write-miss on a block for which there is a single cached copy can also be used as evidence that the block is migratory.

If a block is currently classified as migratory, the adaptive protocol expects that the block will be modified at every processor it visits. Thus, if the block is not modified before it moves to another processor, this is used as evidence that the block is not currently migratory.

All members of our family of adaptive protocols use these tests as evidence that a given block is migratory or not. In addition to the fundamental implementation differences between snooping and directory-based coherence protocols, family members differ from each other in three ways:

1. How quickly does the protocol adapt to changes in access pattern? Given the set of events used as evidence that a block is migratory or not, a protocol can reclassify a block immediately or it can introduce hysteresis by requiring several successive occurrences of these events.

2. How accurately does the protocol keep track of the classification of and the number of copies of each block? Bus-based snooping protocols and some directory-based protocols [15] do not retain any state for uncached blocks, while other directory protocols can track a block over the long term. Classification information can therefore be lost for blocks that become uncached. To eliminate extraneous communication, a protocol might not keep an accurate count of the number of copies of each block. Typically a cache is allowed to silently evict a clean block without communicating with other caches or with a directory manager.

3. Is the block initially classified as migratory, or non-migratory? This affects cold-start costs. Since many coherency protocols do not keep any state for uncached blocks, the initial classification decision can also affect the cost of managing any block that becomes uncached.

Capacity (and conflict) misses occur because real caches are finite. The choices expressed by the last two items above affect how well an adaptive protocol performs in the presence of such misses.

2.1 A Snooping, Bus-based Implementation

To implement an adaptive protocol on a bus-based multiprocessor, one could extend any of several well-known snoopy cache protocols based on write-invalidate [18]. In this example, we extend the common MESI protocol. In the base protocol, a cache entry can be in one of four states. Invalid (I) means that the block is not currently valid in this cache. Exclusive (E) means that this entry is the only cached copy of the block and that main memory is up to date. Dirty[1] (D) means that this is the only cached copy of the block and that the copy in main memory not current. Shared (S) means that this is one of multiple cached copies and that

---

[1] This state is usually called "Modified". We renamed it to allow us to use M to denote "Migratory" in the extended protocol.

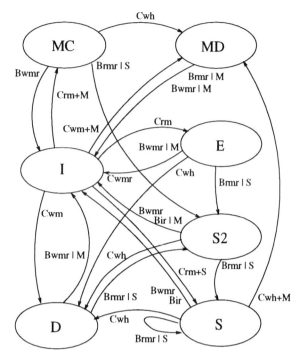

Figure 1: Transition diagram for an adaptive snooping protocol. Each transition is annotated by the event that triggers the transition and by any protocol-specific signals that are asserted on the bus as part of the transaction. The cache itself generates read miss (Crm), write miss (Cwm), and write hit (Cwh) events. Read miss requests (Brmr), write miss requests (Bwmr), and invalidation requests (Bir) are requests coming from other caches on the bus. For example, "Crm+M" labels a transition that occurs when the local cache has a read miss and "Migratory" has been asserted in the response. "Brmr | S" labels a transition triggered by a read miss request. In response, this cache asserts "Shared" on the bus.

memory is up to date. We assume that main memory also snoops, so it is updated on any coherency operations that contain data as well as on any explicit writeback operations. In both the base protocol and in the adaptive extension, any data transferred in a transaction comes from main memory unless the data was dirty in some cache at the start of a transaction.

As part of the bus transaction used to respond to a read miss, the base protocol has a mechanism for a cache to signal that a data block is Shared. The adaptive extension also needs to be able to signal that a block is Migratory in the bus transactions used to respond to read misses, write misses, and invalidation requests. We describe the protocol as though an additional *Migratory* line is added to the bus. It may be possible, however, to encode the new bus transaction type without adding any additional wires.

Figure 1 shows the transition diagram of the adaptive protocol. Figure 2 presents it in tabular form. The lower half of the diagram uses a replicate-on-read-miss policy. It corresponds to a slightly modified version of the base protocol. The main new feature is that the Shared state has been split. A new Shared-2 (S2) state means that there are no more than two cached copies of the block. This condi-

tion is guaranteed because the only transitions into S2 are from states in which there is exactly one cached copy. Thus, transitions from the Exclusive and Dirty states in response to read miss requests from the bus (Brmr) go to S2. This implies that when there are two cached copies of a block that only the older cache entry can be in the S2 state. On subsequent read miss requests, the block enters and stays in the Shared state.

The upper part of Figure 1 corresponds to the subprotocol for handling migratory data. A migratory block can be in either the Migratory-Clean (MC) or Migratory-Dirty (MD) states, depending on whether or not it has been modified at its current location. The transitions among the Invalid, Migratory-Clean, and Migratory-Dirty states implement the migrate-on-read-miss policy.

There are two ways that the protocol can shift from the replicate-on-read-miss policy to the migrate-on-read-miss policy. If processor P_j has a read miss on a block that is currently cached only at P_i in either the Exclusive or Dirty state, then P_i's cache controller changes the state of the local cache entry to Shared-2 and asserts on the bus that the block is Shared. Since Shared is asserted in the the response, the cache entry at P_j will be created in the Shared state. A subsequent write hit at P_j issues an invalidation request on the bus (Bir). In response, P_i's controller invalidates its local entry and asserts Migratory in the acknowledgement. At P_j the protocol takes the transition labelled "Cwh+M" in Figure 1 from Shared to Modified-Dirty.

This aggressive protocol also switches from the replicate-on-read-miss policy to migrate-on-read-miss if a processor has a write miss to a block with a single cached copy in either the Exclusive or Dirty states.

The switch from migrate-on-read-miss to replicate-on-read-miss occurs when a cache with a Migratory-Clean entry for the block receives any miss request from the bus.

The snooping protocol as we have described it uses replicate-on-read-miss as the initial policy for each block. It also switches between policies with no hysteresis. A possible variation is to use migrate-on-read-miss as the initial policy. If this change is made, then the Exclusive state would no longer have any in-transitions and could thus be eliminated as a "dead" state.

Adding hysteresis to the adaptive protocol would multiplicatively increase the number of states, complicating its representation as either a state machine or a transition table. In practice, however, the additional states would be efficiently encoded as a small (one or two bits) counter field.

2.2 A Directory-based Implementation

In this description of a directory-based protocol, we assume that the underlying system is a distributed shared-memory multiprocessor with coherent caches, also known as a *cache-coherent non-uniform memory access* (CC-NUMA) multiprocessor. This type of architecture is based on a collection of *nodes* joined by a logically complete point-to-point network. Each node is a processing element consisting of a processor with its local cache, a memory module, and a memory controller that handles all inter-node memory references going into or out of the node. Each memory controller also maintains directory entries and implements the coherency protocol for all of the blocks in main memory at that node. This node is called the *home node* for those blocks.

Adding an adaptive protocol to an existing directory-based protocol increases the size of each directory entry.

Transitions on Local Cache Events				
State	Event	Request	Reply	New State
I	Crm	Brmr	$\neg M \wedge \neg S$	E
	Crm	Brmr	M	MC
	Crm	Brmr	S	S
	Cwm	Bwmr	$\neg M$	D
	Cwm	Bwmr	M	MD
E	Cwh			D
S2	Cwh	Bir		D
S	Cwh	Bir	$\neg M$	D
	Cwh	Bir	M	MD
MC	Cwh			MD

Transitions on Bus Requests				
State	Request	New State	Assert	Data
E	Brmr	S2	S	
	Bwmr	I	M	
Dirty	Brmr	S2	S	Provide
	Bwmr	I	M	Provide
S2	Brmr	S	S	
	Bwmr	I		
	Bir	I	M	
S	Brmr	S	S	
	Bwmr	I		
	Bir	I		
MC	Brmr	S2	S	
	Bwmr	I		
MD	Brmr	I	M	Provide
	Bwmr	I	M	Provide

Figure 2: State transition tables for the adaptive snooping protocol.

The amount of extra storage depends on both the design of the original protocol and the properties of the particular adaptive policy chosen. For example, if the *copy set*, the data structure that lists the nodes at which a block is cached, allows the memory controller to determine the order in which the cached copies of a block were created, then extra storage to hold the last invalidator is not required. Furthermore, although it is only necessary to add one new state to the protocol to indicate that a block is migratory, it may be convenient to add additional states. In particular, while one could test whether the cardinality (*copy set*) is equal to two as an approximation to the decision rule, this will classify a block as migratory even though there used to be three copies, but one copy was dropped from some cache. To more accurately capture the notion of migratory access, the state encodes the number of copies that have been created rather than the number of copies that currently exist.

Adding hysteresis to the protocol will further expand the size of a directory entry.

Figure 3 presents a pseudo-code implementation of one possible implementation. (Only those parts of the protocol directly related to the adaptive protocol are illustrated.) This implementation initially uses replicate-on-read-miss for each block and requires two successive events to classify a block as migratory, while the switch in the other direction occurs immediately. In this example, the identity of the last invalidator is represented explicitly. Furthermore, this version retains the classification of a block as migratory or other even when the block is not cached. The state of a block is

```
read miss:
    switch ( state )
        case UNCACHED:
            state ← ONE COPY ;
        case UNCACHED/MIGRATORY:
            state ← ONE COPY/MIGRATORY ;
        case ONE COPY:
            state ← TWO COPIES ;
        case ONE COPY/MIGRATORY:
            if dirty = FALSE then
                state ← TWO COPIES ;
                one migration ← FALSE ;
        case TWO COPIES:
            state ← THREE OR MORE COPIES ;
        case THREE OR MORE COPIES:
            null statement ;
    if state = ONE COPY/MIGRATORY then
        migrate the block ;
    else one migration ← FALSE ;
        replicate the block ;

write miss invalidating one or more copies of a block:
    if state = ONE COPY/MIGRATORY then
        if dirty = FALSE then
            state ← ONE COPY ;
            one migration ← FALSE ;
    elsif last invalidator ≠ current processor
                and state = ONE COPY then
        if one migration then
            state ← ONE COPY/MIGRATORY ;
        else one migration ← TRUE ;
    else state ← ONE COPY ;
    last invalidator ← current processor ;
    migrate the block ;

write hit invalidating one or more copies of a block:
    if last invalidator ≠ current processor
                and state = TWO COPIES then
        if one migration then
            state ← ONE COPY/MIGRATORY ;
        else one migration ← TRUE ;
    else state ← ONE COPY ;
        one migration ← FALSE ;
    last invalidator ← current processor ;
    perform the invalidations ;

write hit on a clean, exclusively-held block:
    if last invalidator ≠ current processor
                and state = ONE COPY then
        if one migration then
            state ← ONE COPY/MIGRATORY ;
        else one migration ← TRUE ;
    last invalidator ← current processor ;
```

Figure 3: Pseudo-code for part of an adaptive directory-based coherency protocol. This conservative protocol initially uses replicate-on-read-miss and requires two successive "migratory events" to classify a block as migratory.

represented in two parts. First, the variable *state* indicates how many copies of the block have been made since the last time it was held exclusively by one node. *State* also specifies whether the block is migratory or not. Second, the *dirty* flag indicates whether the block has been modified if its state is "ONE COPY" or "ONE COPY/MIGRATORY".

For the purposes of this example, we have assumed that the directory entry for a memory block, particularly the *last invalidator* and *one migration* fields, is preserved even when the block is not present in any cache. Thus, on a write-hit on a clean, exclusively-held block the protocol checks to see whether the block exhibits migratory behavior spanning the most recent interval in which the block was uncached. This is particularly useful in systems with small caches. It means that when a migratory block is reloaded with a read miss that the cache does not have to send a message back to the memory controller to obtain write permission. This is still a big savings even if there are relatively few coherency messages.

3 Methodology

3.1 Benchmark Suite

We used five of the SPLASH programs for our benchmark suite: Cholesky, Locus Route, MP3D, Pthor, and Water. We refer the reader to Singh *et al.* [19] for a detailed description of each program. We ran the programs using the standard inputs provided with the suite: Cholesky using bcstk14, Locus Route using Primary2.grin, MP3D for 10 iterations with 10,000 particles using a 14x24x7 space array, Pthor using risc, and Water using LWI12. Given these inputs, the amount of shared memory used by each program was 1476 KBytes by Cholesky, 1232 KBytes by Locus Route, 552 KBytes by MP3D, 2676 KBytes by Pthor, and 200 KBytes by Water.

3.2 Simulation Techniques

Given the modest problem sizes, we simulated executions for a sixteen processor system. We used Tango [8] to perform execution-driven simulation and to generate shared-memory access traces for each program in our benchmark suite. To estimate the impact on execution time for one architecture, we performed execution-driven simulation using a version of *dixie*, a Tango memory system simulator for DASH, that implements the adaptive protocol. Lenoski *et al.* [15] provides a detailed description of this architecture.

To evaluate the impact of the adaptive protocols on message traffic for a wide variety of cache and block sizes, we used Tango to generate shared-memory access traces. These traces were used to drive a less-detailed but faster memory system simulator. The traces include accesses to ordinary shared data, but exclude accesses to synchronization variables, private data, and instructions. The traces varied in length from 3,734,816 shared-memory accesses for MP3D to 18,088,572 shared-memory accesses for Water.

3.3 Simplified Architectural Model

In the simplified model, cache coherence is enforced by a directory-based, write-invalidate protocol using a delayed write-back policy. Each processor has a 4-way set-associative cache that uses an LRU replacement strategy.

A modified cache block is written back to main memory when it is replaced in the cache by another block, or when the data is accessed by another processor.

The intended purpose of using an adaptive protocol is to reduce the amount of interprocessor communication required by programs with migratory data. Our machine simulator is therefore designed to compare the amount of interprocessor communication required by the adaptive protocol to the amount required by a replicate-on-read-miss protocol. The model has two types of message. Short messages do not contain the contents of data blocks. They are used for requests and acknowledgements. Long messages, such as responses to miss requests, contain the contents of a data block. The number of messages necessary to perform an operation varies depending on the placement of the directory entry and of any existing cached copies of the block. Table 1 summarizes the number of inter-node messages that we charge to perform a cache operation. For each kind of operation, the number of messages depends on whether or not the home node of the block is the same as the node that initiated the operation, on the current state of the block, and on the cardinality of the set *DistantCopies*, the set of nodes other than the initiator and home nodes at which copies of the block are cached. For example, if a block is dirty there will be exactly one cached copy of the block, but $\|DistantCopies\|$ will be zero if that copy is at either the initiator or the home nodes.

We assume that when a node drops a clean entry from its cache that a message is sent to the block's home node to notify the directory of this action. If such a message is not sent, then later when the block is written by another node it would be necessary to send an invalidation request message that requires an acknowledgement. One could argue that the notification message is a cheap, low-priority "maintenance" message that can be sent asynchronously and that therefore it should not be charged for on the same basis as messages whose latency are on the critical path that determines the execution time of any operation. Nonetheless, we charge the same for these messages as for the other messages.

The assignment of data pages to specific nodes affects the performance of cache coherency protocols in two ways. If page placement is poor then a higher fraction of all coherency operations will require inter-node communication and a higher fraction of the operations requiring communication will require more messages. Although these effects are minimal for migratory data, using a poor page placement algorithm would result in a overall inflated estimate of the total number of messages needed. The simulator therefore attempts to find a reasonable page placement. Rather than attempting to simulate a general dynamic NUMA page-placement protocol [7], we use a simple dynamic technique for finding a good static placement that is similar to those used by Bolosky *et al.* [3] and Stenström *et al.* [21]. We assume that private data and code could have been placed and replicated perfectly to eliminate inter-node message traffic.

In contrast, our execution-driven simulations with *dixie* use the standard round-robin memory allocation. In both the trace-driven and the execution-driven simulations, the page size was 4 Kbytes.

Block size was varied from 16 to 256 bytes to evaluate the effects of larger block sizes on the amount of migratory data and on the ability of the adaptive protocols to deal with it.

The size of the local caches can be expected to affect the benefits of adaptive protocols in two ways. First, with

	home node	block status	inter-node messages without data	inter-node acknowledgements containing a data block
read miss	local	clean	0	0
read miss	local	dirty	1	1
read miss	remote	clean	1	1
read miss	remote	dirty	$1 + \|DistantCopies\|$	$1 + \|DistantCopies\|$
write miss	local	clean	$2 \times \|DistantCopies\|$	0
write miss	local	dirty	1	1
write miss	remote	clean	$1 + 2 \times \|DistantCopies\|$	1
write miss	remote	dirty	$1 + \|DistantCopies\|$	$1 + \|DistantCopies\|$
write hit	local	clean	$2 \times \|DistantCopies\|$	0
write hit	remote	clean	$2 + 2 \times \|DistantCopies\|$	0

Table 1: The number of inter-node messages generated by each type of cache operation requiring communication between the cache and memory controllers. *Home node* is the location of the directory entry for the block. It can either be the the the node that initiated the operation (local) or some other node (remote). *DistantCopies* is the set of cached copies that are located at neither the local nor the home node. It is therefore a subset of *CopySet*.

smaller caches the replacement rate will be higher and therefore the time spent in coherency operations will be a smaller fraction of the total execution time. Since adapting to migratory access is a strategy that reduces the number of coherency operations, this limits potential benefits to be a fraction of an already small cost. Second, replacements interfere with the ability of the adaptive policies to effectively identify migratory data. To examine these effects, we simulated caches ranging from 4K bytes to 1M bytes.

4 Evaluation

4.1 Trace-Driven Simulation of the Directory-based Protocol

We evaluated three adaptive protocols. The *conservative* protocol corresponds to the implementation discussed in Section 2.2. This version initially manages each cache block under the copy-on-read-miss policy and it has a built in delay that requires that a cache block to migrate twice under the conventional copy-on-read-miss policy before it is classified as migratory. The *basic* protocol also starts each block under copy-on-read-miss, and classifies a block as migratory or other after a single event. The *aggressive* protocol initially classifies all blocks as migratory and will reclassify them based on a single event.

Since our simulations are based on traces of references to shared data, our evaluations of the three protocols are cast in terms of how they impact on the cost of managing shared data. Table 2 presents the number of memory system messages used. Using a fixed 16-byte block size, message counts are tabulated by application and by protocol for cache sizes ranging from four kilobytes per node up to one megabyte per node. For every combination of cache size and application, the number of non-data-carrying messages decreases substantially as each of the more aggressive adaptive protocols is used. For example, for MP3D and 1 M caches the most aggressive protocol uses 64.5 percent fewer of these messages than the conventional protocol. This indicates that, as intended, the protocols are successfully identifying migratory data and are realizing the expected elimination of most of the protocol messages. The fact that as more aggressive protocols are used, the number of data-carrying messages is constant or shows a very slight increase is an indication

that the effect of mis-classifying data is small.

Table 2 also tabulates the percentage reduction in total message count. If all messages cost the same, this measures the percentage reduction in the cost of accessing shared data. For example, with large caches the most aggressive protocol yields a cost reduction of between 40 and 50 percent for Cholesky, MP3D, and Water and more modest cost reductions of between 10 and 20 percent for Locus Route, and Pthor. If data-carrying messages are charged twice as much as the other messages, the cost reductions will be less. For example, for one megabyte caches and the aggressive protocol the cost reductions for MP3D and Locus Route are still 38 and 10 percent, respectively, if the ratio of costs is two to one for the two kinds of message. With a four to one ratio of costs these figures decrease to 27 and 6.4 percent, respectively.

Note that the relative effectiveness of the adaptive protocols improves as the cache size increases. This is caused by two related effects. First, with larger caches there are fewer misses and writebacks due to capacity and conflict constraints, so coherency operations represent a larger proportion of the overall communication. Second, classifying a block as migratory is useful only if it allows one to use a more efficient mechanism to migrate it between caches. The higher replacement rates of small caches increase the probability that although a block exhibits the migratory pattern, its movement will be back and forth between main memory and a cache rather than between caches.

Choosing a larger block size can be expected to have an adverse effect on the effectiveness of the adaptive protocols, especially the more aggressive variants. One reason is that for larger blocks there are fewer opportunities to use the mechanism. Furthermore, as block size increases, fewer blocks will be migratory because of false sharing; even though there may be a lot of migratory variables, as block size increases more of them will be stored in blocks that will exhibit other sharing patterns. We evaluated the effect of increasing the cache block size by measuring the cache activity when there are no collisions in the cache or capacity induced misses.

Table 3 summarizes the reduction in the number of cache coherency messages for each of the applications as the cache blocks size changes. Measured in terms of the total number of messages sent, the effectiveness of the adaptive protocol decreases for MP3D as the block size increases. In fact, for

Table 2:

Cache Size	conventional		conservative			basic			aggressive		
	w/o data	w/ data	w/o data	w/ data	%	w/o data	w/ data	%	w/o data	w/ data	%
4 Kbyte											
Cholesky	4549	2429	3921	2429	9.01	3820	2429	10.5	3617	2429	13.4
Locus Route	2052	1126	1864	1127	5.90	1778	1128	8.57	1687	1128	11.4
MP3D	2092	934	896	935	39.5	855	936	40.8	784	936	43.1
Pthor	2041	1018	1666	1022	12.1	1606	1024	14.1	1549	1024	15.9
Water	3290	1644	2535	1644	15.3	2527	1644	15.5	2515	1644	15.7
16 Kbyte											
Cholesky	2074	941	1225	941	28.1	1096	942	32.4	872	942	39.8
Locus Route	1403	660	1268	662	6.43	1220	667	8.54	1131	667	12.8
MP3D	2236	921	946	923	40.8	905	923	42.1	836	923	44.3
Pthor	1942	912	1568	916	13.0	1508	918	15.0	1457	918	16.7
Water	2542	1121	1557	1121	26.9	1550	1121	27.1	1537	1121	27.4
64 Kbyte											
Cholesky	2426	908	1421	908	30.1	1244	908	35.5	974	908	43.5
Locus Route	1302	531	1175	535	6.75	1134	541	8.66	1058	542	12.8
MP3D	1779	612	703	613	45.0	682	614	45.8	634	614	47.8
Pthor	1848	825	1471	829	13.9	1405	833	16.3	1360	833	18.0
Water	1695	584	698	584	43.8	692	584	44.0	683	584	44.4
256 Kbyte											
Cholesky	2451	893	1416	893	31.0	1227	893	36.6	972	893	44.2
Locus Route	1270	472	1139	476	7.32	1091	485	9.56	1020	485	13.6
MP3D	1769	596	690	598	45.6	670	598	46.4	628	598	48.1
Pthor	1744	761	1365	766	14.9	1300	770	17.3	1262	771	18.9
Water	1687	575	686	575	44.3	681	575	44.5	674	575	44.8
1024 Kbyte											
Cholesky	2356	856	1239	856	34.8	1029	856	41.3	870	856	46.3
Locus Route	1268	470	1136	474	7.35	1076	483	10.4	1018	483	13.7
MP3D	1769	596	686	598	45.7	665	598	46.6	629	598	48.1
Pthor	1732	755	1359	760	14.8	1291	764	17.3	1257	764	18.7
Water	1687	574	685	574	44.3	680	574	44.5	673	574	44.8

Table 2: Message counts (in thousands) by cache size, application, and protocol. The column labelled % under each of the adaptive protocols (conservative, basic, and aggressive) is the percentage reduction in total messages used compared with the conventional protocol.

MP3D, false sharing causes the number of invalidations to increase as the block size increases from 64 bytes to 128 bytes. This indicates that the data ping-pongs between processors. The effectiveness of the adaptive protocol increases for Cholesky and Locus Route as the block size increases. The effectiveness of the adaptive protocol increases for Pthor and Water until the block size is 128 bytes. Using the most aggressive adaptive protocol is still the correct strategy for all of the applications and for all of the block sizes for which simulations were done.

The disadvantages of using large block sizes with adaptive protocols become apparent if one applies cost models that charge more for messages that transport data than those that do not. If the ratio of costs is two to one, then for all applications except Cholesky the savings decline substantially for block sizes over 64 bytes[2] Cholesky does show minor improvement. If one applies a cost model that charges one unit per message plus one unit for each sixteen bytes of data transmitted to the data in Table 3, the savings decline even faster and any advantages of the adaptive protocol are close to zero for 256-byte blocks. Cholesky shows a savings

of 7.5% for the conservative protocol and 8% for the aggressive protocol, while Locus Route shows a savings of 0.9% for the conservative protocol but a *penalty* of 0.4% for using the aggressive protocol.

4.2 Execution-Driven Simulation of the Directory-based Protocol

In order to determine the impact that the reduced communication by the adaptive protocol has on execution time, we performed execution-driven simulations of the three programs exhibiting the largest reductions: Cholesky, MP3D, and Water. The basic adaptive protocol reduced the execution times of the parallel sections of these programs by 19.3%, 10.4%, and 3.5%, respectively. As expected, most of the savings are from reduced write-hit latencies. MP3D showed the greatest improvement because it generates the most intense inter-cache traffic of the programs simulated. Even then, there was almost negligible added latency observed due to contention for either the interconnection network or for the local bus of each node. Surprisingly, eliminating the extra invalidation operations decreases the average latency of primary cache read misses by 20%. It ac-

---

[2] Due to space limitations this table is omitted from the paper, but it will appear in a TR. Although it is inconvenient, the costs can be constructed from the data in the tables presented here.

Block Size	conventional		conservative			basic			aggressive		
16-byte	w/o data	w/ data	w/o data	w/ data	%	w/o data	w/ data	%	w/o data	w/ data	%
Cholesky	2337	846	1183	846	36.2	961	846	43.2	849	846	46.7
Locus Route	1268	470	1136	474	7.35	1076	483	10.4	1018	483	13.7
MP3D	1769	596	686	598	45.7	665	598	46.6	629	598	48.1
Pthor	1731	754	1357	760	14.8	1287	764	17.5	1258	764	18.6
Water	1687	574	685	574	44.3	680	574	44.5	673	574	44.8
32-byte											
Cholesky	1294	465	637	466	37.3	525	466	43.7	469	466	46.9
Locus Route	812	300	720	304	7.90	674	310	11.5	638	310	14.7
MP3D	1219	413	484	416	44.8	464	417	46.0	443	417	47.3
Pthor	1835	789	1382	795	17.0	1311	799	19.6	1291	799	20.4
Water	1007	342	406	342	44.6	403	342	44.8	399	342	45.1
64-byte											
Cholesky	773	275	365	275	38.9	307	275	44.4	280	275	47.0
Locus Route	609	225	525	229	9.51	488	233	13.5	468	233	15.8
MP3D	1011	364	461	372	39.5	446	376	40.2	435	376	41.0
Pthor	1777	736	1330	742	17.5	1261	748	20.1	1246	748	20.7
Water	667	226	266	226	44.9	264	227	45.1	262	227	45.3
128-byte											
Cholesky	506	178	228	178	40.6	198	179	44.9	184	179	46.9
Locus Route	479	180	401	183	11.3	376	187	14.6	366	187	16.1
MP3D	959	363	494	375	34.3	472	379	35.7	466	379	36.1
Pthor	1774	726	1337	733	17.2	1266	738	19.8	1255	738	20.3
Water	517	175	248	175	38.9	232	176	41.1	231	176	41.3
256-byte											
Cholesky	373	130	165	131	41.2	148	132	44.4	142	132	45.7
Locus Route	451	171	373	174	12.2	356	177	14.2	352	177	14.9
MP3D	1024	401	594	419	28.9	562	426	31.0	559	426	30.9
Pthor	1803	738	1396	745	15.7	1320	751	18.5	1314	751	18.7
Water	481	162	311	163	26.3	275	165	31.5	275	165	31.7

Table 3: Message counts (in thousands) by block size, application, and protocol. The caches are large enough to eliminate capacity misses. The column labelled % under each of the adaptive protocols is the percentage reduction in total messages used compared with the conventional protocol.

complishes this by nearly eliminating contention at the secondary cache.

We did not observe as large a reduction in the number of messages for the execution-driven simulations as for the trace-driven simulations; for example, 32% versus 46%, respectively, for MP3D. The reason for this difference is largely unrelated to the protocol: The trace-driven simulator used a better page placement policy, reducing the amount of internode communication for the other types of data. Poor page placement has a smaller effect on the number of messages used for migratory data.

4.3 Bus-based Protocol

Due to space limitations, we present only a brief summary of our evaluation of the bus-based protocols.

In terms of the power of the different kinds of protocol, the main difference is that the snooping protocol can not retain the classification of a block across time intervals in which the block is not cached. In terms of costs, the main advantage of the bus-based protocols is the ability to broadcast requests and the freedom from having to wait for individual acknowledgements to invalidation requests. Thus, on the bus-based system the cost of executing a coherency protocol will be proportional to the number of bus operations rather than the number of messages needed to implement While cache misses in a directory scheme can generate a variable number of messages (See Table 1.) that depends on where the data and directory are located, an operation in a cache-based system will generate at most one split bus transaction. Despite these differences, the two classes of protocol behave similarly.

We considered two cost models for the bus-based system. In the first model all memory or coherency operations take one bus transaction and thus have unit cost. In the second model, operations that require replies (misses and adaptive invalidations) are charged two units of cost, while operations that do not require replies (writebacks and invalidations in the conventional protocol) are charged one unit. Using these cost models we see cost reductions similar to those found in the directory-based protocols. Using the first model, programs such as Water and MP3D have savings of over 40 percent for caches of 64 K and larger. In contrast, Pthor gets a savings of 7 percent for 64K caches and 10 percent for one megabyte caches. Using the second model results predicted savings in the 25 to 30 percent range for the Water and MP3D. For Pthor the savings are 3.9 and 5 percent for the two cache sizes.

The variations among the adaptive protocols are similar to those observed for the directory protocols, but the magnitudes of the differences are less. For all cache sizes the programs that do best using adaptive protocols also do best with the more aggressive ones. The other applications show comparatively less benefit from an aggressive protocol, and for large cache sizes the aggressive protocols do slightly worse than the conservative ones.

5   Related Work

Software caching approaches to page placement on NUMA multiprocessors have used several techniques for handling migratory data. In an experimental study that compared a large number of page caching protocols, LaRowe and Ellis [13] concluded that always using a migrate-on-read-miss policy is inferior to always using replicate-on-read-miss. Recognizing the potential advantages of using an adaptive policy, LaRowe *et al.* [14] described a technique for detecting migratory data, but found it to be ineffective. PLATINUM [7, 6] uses the classification technique described in this paper. Because page movement has a cost several times that of a coherency operation, that system uses a conservative protocol with high hysteresis in classifying a page as migratory. Unfortunately, the relative benefit of an adaptive protocol for migratory data is considerably less under these software systems than it is for hardware caches. First, the adaptive protocol saves only coherency transactions, but because they are so much cheaper than page movement transactions the protocol can save only a small fraction of the cost of managing each migratory page. Second, because these systems work at a virtual page granularity, false sharing tends to hide migratory data, providing the adaptive protocol fewer opportunities to apply the migrate-on-read-miss policy.

Several software distributed shared-memory systems have used lock acquisition to indicate the intent to access migratory data. Midway requires the programmer to associate shared data with synchronization [2]. Munin permits, but does not require, the programmer to associate shared data with synchronization [4]. Our results suggest that more data is migratory at a fine grain than may be recognized by a programmer at a coarse grain.

The Sequent Symmetry multiprocessor (model B) [16] has a non-adaptive snooping protocol that uses a migrate-on-read-miss policy for all modified blocks. This policy is also used in the directory-based coherency mechanism of the MIT Alewife [5] system. While this policy is optimal for migratory data, using it on data with other sharing patterns causes additonal read misses. Thakkar [22] observes that read cycles dominate bus traffic on the Sequent and states that the extra read misses caused by this policy contribute significantly to this traffic. Our adaptive protocols avoid this problem. A quantitative comparison between these protocols and the adaptive protocols is needed.

Although the adaptive protocols have the advantages of transparency to user programs and compatibility with a wide range of existing processor architectures, they are on-line and therefore have the disadvantage of being limited to reacting to past and present patterns of access. In contrast, off-line analysis can make predictions about the future behavior of a program and if those predictions are accurate, use them to outperform an on-line algorithm. For example, data identified as migratory could be moved explicitly on a read access if the architecture provides a "load with intent to modify" instruction such as those assumed by the *Read-With-Ownership* operation of the sophisticated version of the "Berkeley Ownership" protocol [12].

The benefit of using either a protocol optimized for migratory data or explicit "load with intent to modify" instructions is the elimination of separate inter-cache invalidation operations. The reduction in traffic can also improve the latency of other operations by decreasing contention. A program using these mechanisms, however, still has to wait for the migratory read operation to complete. This waiting can be decreased using either programmer- or compiler-inserted prefetch requests. Mowry and Gupta [17] studied the effects of inserting non-binding prefetch and prefetch-exclusive requests into three (MP3D, LU, and PTHOR) of the SPLASH programs run on a DASH simulator. With prefetches inserted by hand, their simulations show the same reduction in time spent waiting for invalidations as the the adaptive protocols and they also show a substantial reduction in time spent waiting for read misses. If compilers can be written that achieve the same performance, then a carefully designed prefetching mechanism may be the best approach to the problem. This will require analysis techniques that are powerful enough to insert suffcient prefetches to be effective, but not so many as to generate excessive traffic.

Although support for prefetching appears in some new architectures, not all prefetching mechanisms excel at managing migratory data. The DEC Alpha [9] architecture has prefetch instructions, but they operate on 512-byte blocks. Our results show that even with smaller block sizes a substantial amount of migratory access is masked by false sharing. A more serious problem is that all three of the multiprocessor system architectures designed for the Alpha (Alpha Demonstration Unit, DEC 4000 AXP, and DEC 7000 AXP) are based on a hybrid write-update/write-invalidate coherency protocol that manages migratory data in a very inefficient way. On these machines it can take as many as three inter-cache operations to migrate a block from P_i to P_j: (1) a read miss by P_j that replicates the block, (2) a write hit by P_j that updates the copy in P_i's secondary cache invalidating the copy in the primary cache, and (3) a write hit causing the invalidation of the copy in P_i's secondary cache. These designs do not appear to have a mechanism that would allow the prefetch-exclusive instruction (called "FETCH_M") to bypass this protocol.

A program can be decorated with annotations to enhance cache performance in the Cooperative Shared Memory scheme of Hill *et al.* [11]. The annotation check_in signals when a process is done with a block and other annotations (check_out_X and prefetch_X) mark the points in the program at which a process expects to receive exclusive read/write access. The check_out_S annotation is intended to mark the beginning of an interval in which a block is read shared. These annotations are only advisory; the system still maintains coherence even if they are not used or they are used incorrectly. The "Queue On Sync Bit" (QOSB, called "Queue On Link Bit" in [10]) mechanism implements a similar scheme in hardware.

Stenström *et al.* [20] have developed a directory-based adaptive protocol for migratory data that is very similar to the one we describe. Their rule for shifting into migratory mode is identical to the one we use. Both protocols shift out of migratory mode on read miss to a clean and migratory block. Their protocol also shifts on any write miss to a migratory block. Since there is very little dynamic reclassification in the SPLASH programs, our *dixie* simulations are consistent with their results.

6 Conclusions

The adaptive protocol for identifying and dealing with migratory data appears to be a worthwhile extension to existing directory-based cache coherency protocols. In our trace-driven simulations, it never sent more messages than a standard replicate-on-read-miss protocol. With large caches, an aggressive adaptive protocol reduces the number of memory system messages used by over thirteen percent in the worst case and for three of the five applications we examined, the number of memory system messages saved approaches the theoretical maximum of fifty percent. In our execution-driven simulations of the DASH multiprocessor, a CC-NUMA architecture, we found that the adaptive protocol could reduce execution time by almost 19% for some applications. We expect these results to improve with better page placement.

Our results indicate that for small cache block sizes there is no advantage in being conservative. The aggressive protocol that reclassifies blocks immediately, that initially classifies blocks as migratory, and that remembers classifications over intervals in which data is not cached performs better than any of the more conservative strategies.

One artifact of this study is that the traces used in the simulations contain operations only on ordinary shared data. This may have several effects on the results. If references to private data were included then private and shared data will compete with one another for space in the cache. For a particular actual cache size, the effective cache space available for shared data will be smaller.

While at first blush one might expect that the adaptive protocols would not affect the cost of operations on private data, treating private data as though it is migratory will reduce the cost of process migration.

Acknowledgements

We would like to thank Todd Mowry and Anoop Gupta for providing us with the memory system simulator for DASH, as well as John Carter, David Chaiken, Sandhya Dwarkadas, Mootaz Elnozahy, Pete Keleher, Willy Zwaenepoel and the ISCA referees for their comments.

References

[1] J.K. Bennett, J.B. Carter, and W. Zwaenepoel. Adaptive software cache management for distributed shared memory architectures. In *Proceedings of the 17th Annual International Symposium on Computer Architecture*, pages 125–134, May 1990.

[2] B.N. Bershad and M.J. Zekauskas. Midway: Shared memory parallel programming with entry consistency for distributed memory multiprocessors. Technical Report CMU-CS-91-170, Carnegie-Mellon University, September 1991.

[3] W.J. Bolosky, R.P. Fitzgerald, and M.L. Scott. Simple but effective techniques for NUMA memory management. In *Proceedings of the 12th ACM Symposium on Operating Systems Principles*, pages 19–31, December 1989.

[4] J.B. Carter, J.K. Bennett, and W. Zwaenepoel. Implementation and performance of Munin. In *Proceedings of the 13th ACM Symposium on Operating Systems Principles*, pages 152–164, October 1991.

[5] D. Chaiken, J. Kubiatowicz, and A. Agarwal. Limit-LESS directories: A scalable cache coherence scheme. In *Proceedings of the 4th Symposium on Architectural Support for Programming Languages and Operating Systems*, pages 224–234, April 1991.

[6] A. L. Cox. *The Implementation and Evaluation of a Coherent Memory Abstraction for NUMA Multiprocessors*. PhD thesis, University of Rochester, Rochester, NY, May 1992.

[7] A.L. Cox and R.J. Fowler. The implementation of a coherent memory abstraction on a NUMA multiprocessor: Experiences with PLATINUM. In *Proceedings of the 12th ACM Symposium on Operating Systems Principles*, pages 32–44, December 1989.

[8] H. Davis, S. Goldschmidt, and J. L. Hennessy. Tango: A multiprocessor simulation and tracing system. Technical Report CSL-TR-90-439, Stanford University, 1990.

[9] Alpha AXP architecture and sytems. *Digital Technical Journal*, 4(4), Special Issue 1992.

[10] J. R. Goodman, M. K. Vernon, and P.J. Woest. Efficient synchronization primitives for large-scale cache-coherent multiprocessor. In *Proceedings of the 3rd Symposium on Architectural Support' for Programming Languages and Operating Systems*, pages 64–75, April 1989.

[11] M. D. Hill, J. R. Larus, S. K. Reinhardt, and D. A. Wood. Cooperative shared memory: Software and hardware support for scaleable multiprocessors. In *Proceedings of the 5th Symposium on Architectural Support for Programming Languages and Operating Systems*, pages 262–273, October 1992.

[12] R. Katz, S. Eggers, D. Wood, C.L. Perkins, and R. Sheldon. Implementing a cache consistency protocol. In *Proceedings of the 12th Annual International Symposium on Computer Architecture*, pages 276–283, June 1985.

[13] R. P. LaRowe and C. S. Ellis. Experimental comparison of memory management policies for NUMA multiprocessors. *ACM Transactions on Computer Systems*, 9(4):319–363, November 1991.

[14] R. P. LaRowe, C. S. Ellis, and L. S. Kaplan. The robustness of numa memory management. In *Proceedings of the 13th ACM Symposium on Operating Systems Principles*, pages 110–121, October 1991.

[15] D. Lenoski, J. Laudon, K. Gharachorloo, A. Gupta, and J. Hennessy. The directory-based cache coherence protocol for the DASH multiprocessor. In *Proceedings of the 17th Annual International Symposium on Computer Architecture*, pages 148–159, May 1990.

[16] T. Lovett and S. Thakkar. The Symmetry multiprocessor system. In *Proceedings of the 1988 International Conference on Parallel Processing*, pages 303–310, August 1988.

[17] T. Mowry and A. Gupta. Tolerating latency through software-controlled prefetching in shared-memory multiprocessors. *JPDC*, 12:87–106, June 1991.

[18] M. Papamarcos and J. Patel. A low overhead coherence solution for multiprocessors with private cache memories. In *Proceedings of the 11th Annual International Symposium on Computer Architecture*, pages 348–354, May 1984.

[19] J.P. Singh, W.-D. Weber, and A. Gupta. SPLASH: Stanford parallel applications for shared-memory. Technical Report CSL-TR-91-469, Stanford University, April 1991.

[20] P. Stenström, M. Brorsson, and L. Sandberg. An adaptive cache coherence protocol optimized for migratory sharing. In *Proceedings of the 20th Annual International Symposium on Computer Architecture*, May 1993.

[21] P. Stenström, T. Joe, and A. Gupta. Comparative performance evaluation of cache-coherent NUMA and COMA architectures. In *Proceedings of the 19th Annual International Symposium on Computer Architecture*, pages 80–91, May 1992.

[22] Shreekant S. Thakkar. Performance of Symmetry multiprocessor system. In Michel Dubois and Shreekant S. Thakkar, editors, *Cache and Interconnect Architectures in Multiprocessors*, pages 53–82. Kluwer Academic Publishers, Boston, 1989.

[23] W.-D. Weber and A. Gupta. Analysis of cache invalidation patterns in multiprocessors. In *Proceedings of the 3rd Symposium on Architectural Support' for Programming Languages and Operating Systems*, pages 243–256, April 1989.

An Adaptive Cache Coherence Protocol
Optimized for Migratory Sharing

Per Stenström, Mats Brorsson, and Lars Sandberg
Department of Computer Engineering, Lund University
P.O. Box 118, S-221 00 LUND, Sweden

Abstract

Parallel programs that use critical sections and are executed on a shared-memory multiprocessor with a write-invalidate protocol result in invalidation actions that could be eliminated. For this type of sharing, called migratory sharing, each processor typically causes a cache miss followed by an invalidation request which could be merged with the preceding cache-miss request.

In this paper we propose an adaptive protocol that invokes this optimization dynamically for migratory blocks. For other blocks, the protocol works as an ordinary write-invalidate protocol. We show that the protocol is a simple extension to a write-invalidate protocol.

Based on a program-driven simulation model of an architecture similar to the Stanford DASH, and a set of four benchmarks, we evaluate the potential performance improvements of the protocol. We find that it effectively eliminates most single invalidations which improves the performance by reducing the shared access penalty and the network traffic.

1 Introduction

In order for shared-memory multiprocessors to achieve a high performance, memory system latency and contention must be kept as low as possible. A viable solution to this problem has been to attach private caches to each processing node and maintain cache coherence using a directory-based write-invalidate protocol. Notable examples of real implementations of large-scale multiprocessors that exploit this technique are the Stanford DASH [12], the MIT Alewife [1], the SICS Data Diffusion Machine (the DDM) [9], and the Kendall Square Research's KSR1 [2].

Write-invalidate protocols maintain cache coherence by invalidating copies of a memory block when the block is modified by a processor. The advantage of this is that at most the first write, in a sequence of writes to the same block with no intervening read operations from other processors, causes global interaction. Consequently, write-invalidate protocols perform fairly well for a broad range of sharing patterns. However, there exist common sharing patterns for which all invalidations could have been entirely avoided. A notable example is the invalidation overhead associated with data structures that are accessed within critical sections. Typically, processors read and modify such data structures one at a time. Processors that access data this way cause a cache miss followed by an invalidation request being sent to the cache attached to the processor that most recently exited the critical section. If the cache coherence protocol were aware of this sharing pattern, it would be possible to merge the invalidation request with the preceding read-miss request and thus eliminate all explicit invalidation actions. This sharing behavior, denoted *migratory sharing*, has been previously shown to be the major source of single invalidations by Gupta and Weber in [8].

Eliminating invalidation requests can help performance in many important ways. First, if access requests cannot overlap invalidation requests due to memory consistency model or implementation constraints [6], the access penalty is reduced by reducing the number of global invalidation requests. Second, the network traffic is reduced which, as a secondary effect, may reduce the read and write penalty due to less network contention. Consequently, eliminating the number of invalidation requests may improve the performance significantly.

In this paper, we propose an implementation of an adaptive write-invalidate protocol that effectively eliminates most invalidation requests associated with migratory sharing. The protocol dynamically detects whether a memory block exhibits migratory sharing or not. For blocks deemed migratory, the invalidation request is merged with the preceding read-miss request and for other blocks, it maintains coherence according to the default write-invalidate policy. In addition, the protocol can dynamically, on a per block basis, switch between these operating modes, would the block change sharing behavior. As a case-study, we show that our protocol is a simple extension of a write-invalidate protocol by presenting the modifications needed for a state-of-the-art write-invalidate protocol, in essence the directory-based protocol of the Stanford DASH [11].

To validate the correctness of the protocol and evaluate its performance, we have implemented and evaluated it using a detailed program-driven simulation model of a DASH-like architecture and a set of four benchmarks, of which three are taken from the SPLASH suite [14]. We have found that by eliminating the invalidation requests to

109

migratory blocks, performance can be improved due to less access penalty and network traffic. We show that these factors can improve the performance significantly for high-performance multiprocessors.

The organization of the rest of the paper is as follows. Since the adaptive protocol can be applied to most write-invalidate protocols, we provide in Section 2 a high-level description of the coherence optimization it provides and how it detects migratory sharing. As a base for our implementation and performance study, we use the Stanford DASH protocol. In Section 3, we describe how the DASH protocol can be extended to adaptively detect and optimize migratory sharing. Sections 4 and 5 present the experimental results starting with the architectural assumptions and the benchmarks in Section 4. We finally generalize our findings in Section 6 and conclude the paper in Section 7.

2 The Adaptive Protocol: A High-Level View

In this section, we first identify the type of migratory sharing that incurs invalidation overhead in write-invalidate protocols in Section 2.1. Then in Section 2.2, we present a high-level description of an adaptive protocol that detects such sharing and eliminates its overhead.

2.1 Migratory Sharing

Gupta and Weber classify data structures based on the invalidation pattern they exhibit [8]. According to their definition, data structures manipulated by only a single processor at any given time are called *migratory objects*. Typically, such sharing occurs when a data structure is modified within a critical section. Protecting modifications of shared objects by locks is important to eliminate data races. Therefore, many parallel languages, such as e.g. Modula-2 and Ada, use critical sections (or monitors) as the recommended mechanism to support shared data access. Consequently, reducing access penalties incurred by migratory objects is important.

Assuming a write-invalidate protocol, all blocks that correspond to a migratory object being modified by a processor end up dirty in the processor's cache. When a subsequent processor modifies the migratory object, it causes a single invalidation for each block that belongs to the object. If a migratory block is read and then modified by each processor, the first read access will cause a miss and the first write access will cause a single invalidation, both being sent to the cache associated with the processor that previously modified the block. Clearly, the invalidation request could be merged with the preceding miss request.

To formally define all access sequences that cause such invalidation overhead due to migratory sharing, we use the symbols R_i and W_i to denote a read and write access to a

memory block by processor i. The following regular expression defines all such sequences:

$$(R_i)(R_i)^*(W_i)(R_i \mid W_i)^*(R_j)(R_j)^*(W_j)(R_j \mid W_j)^* \ldots \quad (1)$$

In the above regular expression a '*' succeeding a string designates a string of arbitrary length including the empty string and a '|' denotes the OR-operator. In this sequence, there is one global read followed by a global write access by the same processor before this processor relinquishes exclusive access of the block for another processor. These accesses are marked with boldface.

2.2 Adaptive Detection and Optimization

As a base for the adaptive protocol, we assume a shared-memory multiprocessor that contains a number of processors with associated caches. To maintain coherence, there is an explicit *home* associated with each memory block that keeps track of the global coherence state of the block (e.g. uncached, shared, or dirty). Home dynamically decides whether a block is *migratory*, meaning that it does adhere to the sharing pattern in (1) above, or *ordinary*, meaning it does **not** adhere to (1). Below we describe the coherence actions for migratory and ordinary blocks and the detection algorithm to choose between these coherence policies.

For ordinary blocks, cache coherence is maintained by a write-invalidate protocol as follows. If a read access causes a miss in the cache, a *read-miss request* is sent to home. Depending on whether the memory block is valid or not, either home or the cache that keeps the dirty copy responds with a copy of the block to the local cache. In either case, home will keep a valid copy in state shared. If the local cache copy is shared or invalid, a write access causes an invalidation request, called *read-exclusive request*, to be sent to home. Home is responsible for invalidating all copies of the block.

For migratory blocks, when home receives a read-miss request, it converts this request into a read-exclusive request and forwards it to the cache that has the block in state dirty. This cache gives up its copy for the requesting cache that will load the block in state dirty. As a result, a subsequently issued write access by the requesting processor can be carried out locally and all explicit invalidation actions have been eliminated.

Since all memory blocks are tagged ordinary by default, home can detect migratory sharing based on the fact that it receives the global sequence of read-miss (Rr_i) and read-exclusive (Rxq_i) requests from each processor i for a block. If an ordinary block starts exhibiting migratory sharing, the global sequence is: $Rr_i\ Rxq_i\ Rr_j\ Rxq_j\ Rr_k\ Rxq_k \ldots$ By always keeping track of the identity of the processor that most recently wrote to the block, say i, a block can be nominated as migratory at a point when home receives a read-exclusive request from j given that:

(1) the read-exclusive request comes from a different processor ($j \neq i$) and (2) the number of copies is exactly two.

In summary, the notion of home is important for implementing the adaptive protocol because home sees all read-miss and read-exclusive requests for the block. Cache-coherent NUMA (CC-NUMA) machines [16] constitute an example where home is the memory in which the block is allocated. We will next consider the detailed implementation of the adaptive optimization in an example CC-NUMA machine — the Stanford DASH.

3 An Implementation Study: Stanford DASH

The usefulness of the coherence optimization of migratory blocks as described in the previous section is dictated by the extra hardware complexity required by the protocol and the performance improvements that can be obtained. As a base to address these issues, we have chosen the Stanford DASH protocol [11, 12] because it has been implemented and sufficiently tested and documented. In Section 3.1, we review the Stanford DASH protocol with respect to the actions taken for migratory sharing. In Section 3.2, we describe how these coherence actions are optimized by the adaptive protocol extension. Finally, in Sections 3.3 and 3.4, we present how we extend the DASH protocol to detect and optimize coherence actions for migratory blocks.

3.1 The DASH Write-Invalidate Protocol

In Figure 1, we show the organization of each node. To simplify, we assume that each node contains a single processor. The processor with its associated cache is connected to the local memory module by a local bus. Shared memory is distributed across the processing nodes, which are interconnected by two two-dimensional wormhole-routed mesh networks — one for requests and one for replies.

Cache coherence at the system level is maintained by a directory-based write-invalidate protocol by a directory for each memory module that keeps track of the global state of all memory blocks in this memory module (the home of its blocks). Three global states are associated with each memory block: *Uncached* (not cached by any other node than home), *Shared-Remote* (valid copies exist in other nodes), and *Dirty-Remote* (the block is modified in some other node's cache). Furthermore, if the global state is not Uncached, home keeps track of the nodes that have a copy, the *sharing list*, by a presence-flag vector containing the same number of bits as nodes.

Similarly, each cache keeps track of the local state of its copy by three states: *Invalid* (nonexistent in the cache), *Shared* (valid block in this cache and possibly in other nodes' caches), and *Dirty* (the only copy exists in this cache). We now review the coherence actions taken by the DASH protocol by denoting the issuing node *local* and a

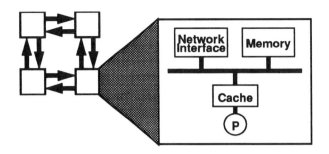

Figure 1: Processing node organization.

2(a)

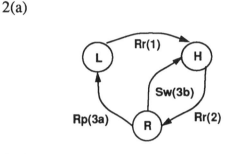

2(b)

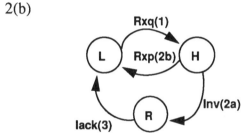

Figure 2: Example coherence actions for DASH. (a) Read-miss and (b) read-exclusive request actions associated with migratory sharing.

node other than the local or the home node *remote*. For simplicity, we will assume that local, home, and remote are distinct nodes.

Processor reads are satisfied by the local cache if the local state is Shared or Dirty. If the state is Invalid, or if there is a tag mismatch, local (L) sends a read-miss request (Rr in Figure 2(a)) to home (H). If the global state of the block is Uncached or Shared-Remote, a copy is returned to the local node and home updates the sharing list to incorporate the new keeper. If the global state is Dirty-Remote (as in Figure 2(a)), home forwards the read request to the node that keeps the dirty copy. This node, the remote node (R), returns the block to local (Rp) and to the home node (Sw) and changes the state of its copy to Shared. The final global state is Shared-Remote.

Moving on to the actions associated with processor writes, we first note that if the local state is Dirty, they can be carried out locally. If the state is Shared or Invalid,

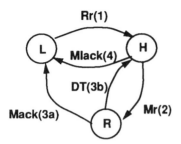

Figure 3: Coherence actions for migratory blocks.

local sends a read-exclusive request to home to acquire ownership as depicted in Figure 2(b) as Rxq. If the global state is Uncached, an exclusive copy is returned to local (Rxp). If the global state is Shared-Remote, however, home also sends invalidations to all remote nodes that have a copy of the block (Inv in Figure 2(b)). When receiving such an invalidation, each node changes the state of its copy to Invalid and sends an acknowledgment to the local node (Iack). The final global state is Dirty-Remote.

In the DASH protocol, coherence of all blocks are maintained according to the actions described in this section. In the adaptive protocol extension we evaluate in this paper, ordinary blocks are handled according to the DASH protocol. How migratory blocks are handled is described next.

3.2 Coherence Maintenance of Migratory Blocks

Recalling the regular expression for global accesses to migratory blocks (1) in Section 2.1, we note that when a new processor starts to access the block, a dirty copy exists in the cache associated with the processor that most recently relinquished exclusive access to the block. Consequently, the read-modify-write access to the migratory block results in a read-miss request (according to the actions in Figure 2(a)) followed by a read-exclusive request (according to the actions in Figure 2(b)) resulting in a single invalidation assuming the DASH protocol.

The adaptive protocol converts these two transactions into a single one that takes place at the time a read-miss request is sent to home according to Figure 3. As in Figure 2(a), local sends a read-miss request to home. Then home forwards the read-miss request to the remote node (depicted Mr in Figure 3). Unlike the actions in Figure 2(a), however, remote gives up ownership of the block by sending its copy to local (Mack). It also notifies home about the ownership change with a request (DT). When local receives the reply message from remote, the cache is filled and the processor is restarted. As a result, the processor stall-time to service the read request, counted in network hops, is the same as in Figure 2(a). However, the local node is not allowed to replace the block until home has updated its directory. This is acknowledged by MIack

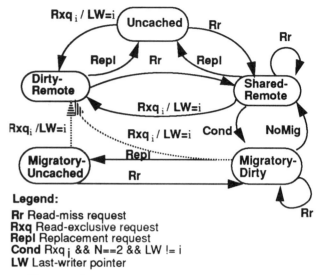

Legend:
Rr Read-miss request
Rxq Read-exclusive request
Repl Replacement request
Cond Rxq_i && N==2 && LW != i
LW Last-writer pointer

Figure 4: State-transition graph for detection of migratory blocks.

in Figure 3. The extra acknowledgment is needed to avoid corrupting the directory.

The performance improvement from this optimization is due to a reduction of write accesses causing global actions, which may reduce the write penalty under sequential consistency [10] and network traffic. The latter can reduce read and write penalty because of a reduction of network contention. In Section 5, we will quantify these effects.

3.3 The Detection Algorithm

The finite-state machine that keeps track of the global state of each block in DASH consists of three states: Uncached, Shared-Remote, and Dirty-Remote. Transitions between these states occur as a result of read-miss, read-exclusive, and replacement requests for ordinary blocks according to Figure 4. In order to detect and keep track of migratory blocks, we have augmented the finite-state machine with two states: *Migratory-Dirty* and *Migratory-Uncached*.

To detect migratory blocks, we recall from Section 2.2 that we have to keep track of the identity of the processor that most recently modified the block. This is done by associating a pointer, the *last-writer* pointer (LW), with each memory block which is updated at each transition to Dirty-Remote in Figure 4 (LW=i). In addition, we must detect when there are exactly two copies. In the DASH protocol this is known from the presence-flag vector.

According to condition Cond in Figure 4, an ordinary block is now nominated as migratory at the time home receives a read-exclusive request from processor i (Rxq_i in Figure 4) and (1) the number of cached copies is two (N==2), and (2) the writing processor is not the same as the previous writer (LW != i). Requirement (1) prevents a state transition as a result of intervening read-miss requests from other processors while the global state is Shared-Remote. Otherwise, the following sequence could be detected as migratory: $Rxq_i\, Rr_j\, Rr_k\, Rxq_j$. Requirement (2) prevents a producer-consumer sequence, such as $Rxq_i\, Rr_j\, Rxq_i\, Rr_j$, from being detected as migratory. Note also that we must associate a valid bit with the last-writer pointer, which is initially reset. It must also be reset as soon as the size of the sharing list exceeds two to prevent an erroneous transition to Migratory-Dirty as a result of replacements such as in: $Rr_i\, Rxq_i\, Rr_j\, Rr_k\, Repl_k\, Rxq_j$, where $Repl_k$ denotes that the block is replaced in cache k.

Once the block has been nominated as migratory, the memory controller will handle all subsequent read-miss requests according to the actions depicted in Figure 3; a read request will result in an ownership to be obtained. Consequently, there is only a single copy in the system and invalidations for migratory blocks are eliminated. To avoid having to re-detect a block as migratory when it is written back to memory as a result of replacement, we have added the state Migratory-Uncached.

3.4 Adaptivity to Alterations in Sharing Behavior

To cope with alterations in the sharing behavior, the protocol can perform transitions between the write-invalidate and the migratory policy. We study below a few situations our protocol supports.

The fact that the memory controller sees only read-miss requests for migratory blocks means that it cannot detect if a block starts to be read-only. For example, if processors i and j alternately read from a migratory block, the memory controller will see the following sequence of read requests: $Rr_i\, Rr_j\, Rr_i\, Rr_j...$ Clearly, the block will ping-pong back and forth between cache i and j. To avoid this, we have added a local cache state denoted *Migrating* which is used as follows. When processor i reads the block, the initial local cache state is Migrating instead of Dirty. A subsequent write to the block results in a transition to Dirty without any global action being taken. However, if the cache receives a migratory read request (Mr in Figure 3) and the local state is Migrating, then instead of giving up ownership, it performs the same actions as in Figure 2(a) by notifying the memory controller with a NoMig request (see Figure 4). The block is also written back to home and the global state is Shared-Remote. The block is considered as ordinary from this point.

We have assumed that the first access to a migratory block by a processor is always a read. If it is a write, however, should we still regard it as migratory, or should we make a transition to Dirty-Remote? As a default policy, we still consider the block as migratory but we have also evaluated the heuristic of making a transition to Dirty-Remote when home receives a read-exclusive request, which is depicted with dashed arrows in Figure 4.

In summary, the adaptive extension to the DASH protocol consists of a pointer per block with $\log_2 N$ bits assuming N nodes, two global and one local cache state in addition to the mechanisms that are already there. In the next two sections, we will see what this extra hardware complexity can buy us in terms of increased performance.

4 Evaluation Methodology

To validate the correctness of the adaptive cache coherence protocol and its potential performance benefits, we have used a simulation methodology using detailed architectural models in conjunction with a suite of parallel applications. We next present the simulation environment, the architectural parameters, and the benchmark programs used.

4.1 Simulation Environment

The simulation platform used is the CacheMire test bench [4] — a program-driven simulator of multiple SPARC processors on top of which it is possible to run parallel applications written in C using the Argonne National Laboratory's macro package to express parallelism [3]. The test bench consists of two parts: (i) a functional simulator and (ii) an architectural simulator. The functional simulator generates memory references that are performed in the architectural simulator. In order to maintain a correct interleaving of memory references, the architectural simulator maintains the global time and delays the processors according to its timing model. As a result, a correct interleaving of events in the architectural model is maintained. This is in contrast to e.g. trace-driven simulation, where the memory reference trace is not affected by timing.

4.2 Architectural Model and Assumptions

The basic architectural model is similar to the Stanford DASH and we show the overall organization of the architecture in Figure 1. Although we present results for architectural variations, we will only focus on the default assumptions in this section.

We assume a 16 node configuration interconnected by two 4x4 wormhole-routed meshes — one for requests and one for replies. Each processing node contains a memory module and a 64 Kbyte, direct-mapped, copy-back cache with a line size of 16 bytes. As for the memory allocation, we allocate shared data pages in a round-robin fashion with the least significant bits of the virtual page number designating the node number. The page size is 4 Kbytes. For simplicity, we only model shared data references; instruction and private data references are assumed to always hit in the on-chip processor caches.

The cache and the memory module are connected by a 128-bit wide split-transaction bus which also provides a connection to the network interface. The network interface

Table 1: Latency numbers (1 pclock = 10 ns).

Latency for Read and Write Requests	Time
Hit in Cache	1 pclock
Fill from Local Memory	22 pclocks
Fill from Remote (2-hop)	54 pclocks
Fill from Remote (3-hop)	73 pclocks
Read-Exclusive Request to Remote (2-hop)	51 pclocks
Read-Exclusive Request to Remote (3-hop)	70 pclocks

routes requests and replies to the corresponding mesh network. It also keeps track of all outstanding requests from the node by means of a mechanism similar in function to the remote-access cache (RAC) in DASH [11].

The two wormhole-routed meshes have a link width of 16 bits. The node fall-through time corresponds to three pipeline stages: arbitrate, route, and send. Infinite buffers are associated with each of the four inputs (X+1 X-1, Y+1, and Y-1) to each network router.

As for the timing model parameters, we assume that the processors are clocked at 100 MHz (1 pclock = 10 ns) and that the cache access time is 10 ns. Moreover, the local bus is assumed to be clocked at 50 MHz — it takes 20 ns for arbitration and 20 ns for the bus transfer. The memory cycle time is assumed to be 100 ns including buffering. Finally, we assume a fairly aggressive mesh implementation that is synchronously clocked at 100 MHz which results in a peak bandwidth of 400 Mbytes/sec out from and into each node.

We model contention correctly at the memory modules, the local buses, and the mesh networks. In Table 1, we list the latencies for processor reads and writes depending on where in the memory hierarchy they are serviced. A 2-hop remote latency means that the request is serviced in two network traversals, e.g. a read to a block that is clean at home and home is not the local node. The remote latencies we model depend on where in the mesh the interacting nodes are situated and on contention. For the latency numbers in Table 1, however, we assume no contention and an average distance of 2.67 links for a network traversal between two arbitrary nodes (the mean distance in a 4x4 mesh).

As far as the memory consistency model is concerned, we assume sequential consistency (SC) [10]. We implement SC by stalling the processor on every read-exclusive request to a cache copy that is Shared or Invalid until the write has been performed. Finally, for simplicity we handle synchronization requests (locks and barriers) ideally with a single-cycle delay outside the architecture model because we feel that their implementations are orthogonal issues to the focus of this study.

4.3 Benchmark Programs

In order to study the relative performance of the DASH protocol with and without the adaptive extension, we have used a set of four scientific applications developed at Stanford University of which three (MP3D, Cholesky, and Water) are from the SPLASH suite [14]. A summary of these applications is given in Table 2. We picked this set of applications to show different aspects of migratory sharing.

Table 2: Benchmark programs.

Benchmark	Description
MP3D	Particle-based wind-tunnel simulator
Cholesky	Cholesky factorization of sparse matrices
Water	Water molecular dynamics simulation
LU	LU decomposition of dense matrices

MP3D was run with 10K particles for 10 time steps. Cholesky was run using the `bcsstk14` benchmark matrix. Water was run with 288 molecules for 4 time steps, and finally, LU uses a 200x200 matrix.

The applications were compiled using `gcc` (version 2.0) with the optimization level -O2. Statistics acquisition is started when the applications enter the parallel section to study steady-state behavior.

5 Experimental Results

In this section, we study the performance improvements provided by the adaptive protocol. In Section 5.1, we compare the execution times of the benchmarks for the adaptive and the write-invalidate protocol by analyzing the occurrence of migratory sharing. Then we move on to see how the adaptive protocol can help performance by reducing the network traffic in Section 5.2. Section 5.3 deals with the impact of cache size on performance, and finally, in Section 5.4, we study the stability of the detection algorithm.

5.1 Performance of Write-invalidate and Adaptive

The performance improvement of the adaptive protocol is dictated by the occurrence of migratory objects in the applications. In Figure 5, we show the execution time under the adaptive protocol (AD) normalized to the execution time without the adaptive extension (W-I).

We observe that the adaptive protocol performs consistently better than write-invalidate by examining the execution-time ratio (ETR) of W-I relative to AD. For example, the adaptive protocol results in 54% better performance (ETR=1.54) for MP3D. The reason for this is that the processors have to stall less as a result of invalidation requests since the adaptive protocol reduces the number of read-exclusive requests. To see this, we have broken down

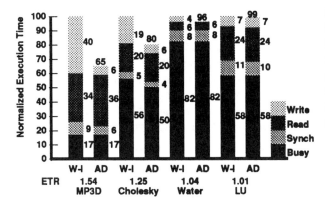

Figure 5: Relative performance of W-I and AD.

the execution time into the contributions due to busy time, synchronization (time waiting for a lock or at a barrier), read, and write stall-time from the bottom to the top. For example, the busy time for W-I running MP3D is 17%, while the synchronization stall-time is 9%. We see that the write stall-time has been significantly reduced for most applications under the adaptive protocol. We therefore review each application below with respect to the occurrence of migratory sharing.

In a previous work, Gupta and Weber [8] studied the invalidation pattern for two of the applications we use. They observed for MP3D and Water that more than 98% of the read-exclusive requests resulted in single invalidations. In MP3D, most accesses to shared data are caused by reading and modifying the particle and space-array entries. Even though the modifications are not protected by locks, they behave as migratory because a modification by a processor follows closely after the read access. In Table 3, we show the reduction of read-exclusive requests for each application. As expected, we see a reduction of read-exclusive requests for MP3D by as much as 87%.

Cholesky performs factorization using supernodal modifications. Supernodes are groups of columns with a similar structure. The computation is mastered by a global task queue that keeps track of all supernodal modifications that are to be done. Typically, a processor pulls a supernode off the task queue and performs modifications on other super-nodes which are protected by locks. The migratory sharing that shows up is due to the task queue and to the supernodal modifications themselves. As expected, the number of read-exclusive requests is reduced by 69% (see Table 3), which results in 25% better performance for AD according to Figure 5.

Since Cholesky dynamically schedules work among the processors, there is a discrepancy in the busy time for W-I and AD. It should therefore be noted that not all of the performance improvements are due to a write-stall reduction.

In Water, the molecule array is statically split among processors. Each processor calculates the pair-wise inter-

action between its molecules and those of others. These modifications are protected by locks and result in migratory sharing. As a result, virtually all read-exclusive requests are eliminated by the adaptive protocol (a 96% reduction). Surprisingly, the execution time is reduced by only 4%. As we easily can make out from Figure 5, the reason is that there is not more to gain — the write stall-time is 4%.

Table 3: Reduction of read-excl. requests and traffic.

Application	Read-excl. Reduction	Traffic Reduction
MP3D	87%	32%
Cholesky	69%	22%
Water	96%	31%
LU	5%	1%

In LU there are virtually no migratory objects, and consequently, no performance improvement. However, LU demonstrates that the adaptive protocol does not impact adversely on the performance as a result of erroneous detections.

In summary, we have seen that the adaptive protocol is successful in reducing the number of read-exclusive requests to migratory blocks. The execution-time reduction is due to the reduced write penalty associated with the sequential consistency model.

5.2 Network Traffic Reduction Effects

The adaptive protocol can also reduce the access penalty by reducing network contention as a result of traffic reduction which is the focus of this section. The reduced traffic is due to the fact that the messages associated with a read-miss request (according to Figure 2(a) in Section 3.1) and a read-exclusive request (according to Figure 2(b)) under W-I have been replaced by the messages according to Figure 3 under AD. To get a feel for the traffic reduction, we review how many bits these messages occupy.

Requests and replies contain the identity of the issuing and receiving node (assuming 16 processors this corresponds to 4 + 4 = 8 bits), the block address (28 bits, assuming 16 bytes blocks and 32-bit addresses), and a command (4 bits). In addition, all replies contain data (16 bytes = 128 bits). For the read-miss request under W-I, two requests (2 × Rr) and two replies containing data (Sw + Rp) are sent. As for the read-exclusive request, we note that a single invalidation is sent which results in three requests (Rxq + Inv + Iack) and one reply (Rxp). Altogether, five requests and three replies are sent. Under AD, four requests (Rr + Mr + DT + MIack) and one reply (Mack) are sent. Thus, the total number of bits sent under W-I to serve a read-miss request and a subsequent read-exclusive request is 704 bits. This number should be compared to 328 bits that are required under AD. To conclude,

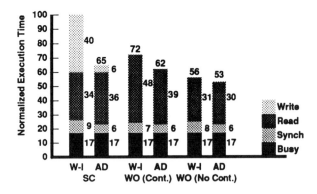

Figure 6: Normalized execution time for AD relative to W-I under SC, assuming sequential consistency (SC) and weak ordering (WO) for the MP3D application.

there is a 53% traffic reduction for each read-miss request to a migratory block under AD. We next study how this reduction affects the overall traffic for the four applications we have run.

In Table 3, we show the traffic reduction data. In MP3D and Water, which contain the largest amount of migratory sharing, traffic is reduced by more than 30%. The traffic reduction in Cholesky, although not as spectacular, is 22% because of a smaller reduction in the number of read-exclusive requests. As we will show, this traffic reduction can have a dramatic impact on performance, even for aggressive network implementations as we assume in this study.

Relaxed consistency models, such as weak ordering [5] and release consistency [6] can hide write stall-time by allowing global requests to overlap each other and local computation. Therefore, one would expect W-I and AD to perform the same under relaxed consistency models. However, as we allow global requests to overlap, the applications will require more bandwidth because the global request rate then increases. Since the adaptive protocol reduces the number of invalidation requests, it is expected to exhibit a lower global access rate. To see this, we measured the execution time for MP3D under weak ordering. We implemented weak ordering by assuming a lockup-free cache [15] that allows an infinite number of global requests to be outstanding as long as synchronizations are respected.

In Figure 6, we show the execution time for MP3D for two consistency model implementations relative to the execution time of W-I under sequential consistency (SC). To the right of SC, we show the execution time under the aggressive weak ordering implementation (WO Cont.). As we would expect, weak ordering manages to hide all write latency for W-I and AD. However, because of a higher global access rate, the read penalty has increased substantially for W-I. As a result, AD performs 16% better under

WO. Surprisingly, AD even performs better under SC than does W-I under WO. To confirm that the read penalty increase is because of network contention we ran the same experiments assuming infinite network bandwidth but the same latency. The results are demonstrated by the two rightmost bars in Figure 6 (WO No Cont.). As expected, the performance of W-I and AD are now nearly identical. We also studied the relative performance of AD and W-I

Table 4: Write penalty reduction (WPR) of W-I by AD and repl. miss-rates (MR) for 64 and 4Kbyte caches.

	MP3D	Cholesky	Water	LU
64 Kbyte — MR	3%	3%	3%	3%
4 Kbyte — MR	7%	18%	9%	21%
64 Kbyte — WPR	86%	67%	94%	3.7%
4 Kbyte — WPR	67%	32%	85%	0.2%

under WO for the other applications but did not see any significant differences. The reason for this is that they do not have the same bandwidth requirements as MP3D which can be seen from the larger busy time fractions in Figure 5. Remember that we have assumed a fairly aggressive network implementation (100 MHz synchronous meshes). Therefore, for large system configurations, or networks with less bandwidth such as buses, these effects can show up for applications with less bandwidth requirements than MP3D. A smaller but significant effect from Figure 6 is that the synchronization stall-time is shorter for AD than W-I. The reason for this is due to less contention for critical sections because of global write request reductions.

The bottom-line of these experiments is that while WO can hide the write latency it cannot reduce its traffic. The adaptive technique reduces write latency **and** traffic. This is critical to performance for applications with larger bandwidth requirements than the network can sustain.

5.3 Impact of Cache Size on Improvements

In the experiments in the previous sections, we have used a cache size of 64 Kbyte. Since the data sets for our applications are quite small, we end up having virtually no replacement misses as shown in Table 4. To study how the adaptive protocol performs when the replacement miss-rate is higher, we scaled down the cache size to 4 Kbytes.

The effect of replacement misses on migratory sharing is as follows. When a processor has relinquished exclusive access to the block, the block may be replaced from the cache if it is not accessed sufficiently soon by the same processor or invalidated by another processor. As a result, the block is written back to home and the global state becomes Migratory-Uncached under AD and Uncached under W-I. Since the copy is now at home, a subsequent read-exclusive request is performed in at most two network hops, instead of at most three, were the block dirty in a remote node. As a result, the reduction of write penalty under sequential consistency is expected to be smaller.

In Table 4, we show how much of the write penalty of W-I that is reduced by the adaptive technique for 64 and 4 Kbyte caches. As expected, the performance improvement of AD is now smaller. For example, while AD reduces the write penalty for MP3D by 86% at 64 Kbyte caches, the write penalty reduction drops to 67% at 4 Kbyte. Cholesky shows an even more dramatic change which has to do with the larger increase in replacement miss-rate. Nevertheless, the adaptive protocol still turned out to be effective in detecting migratory sharing.

5.4 Adaptivity to Sharing Behavior Alterations

After a block has been deemed migratory, it will stay in that state unless it starts to be read-only. According to Section 3.4, read-only sharing is detected by the local cache if it receives a migratory read request and the local processor has not written to the block. When this happens, the local cache notifies home by sending a NoMig request (see Figure 1). One could ask whether a block stays migratory for a long time, meaning that NoMig requests are rare. To see this, we measured the fraction of migratory read requests that trigger a NoMig request. We found that these numbers were 0.5%, 0.09%, and 0.01% for MP3D, Cholesky, and Water, respectively. In other words, the migratory sharing that shows up in these applications turns out to be stable. However, we also found that if we disabled this transition, it impacted significantly on the performance which means that this mechanism is needed. Another possibility to make a transition back to write-invalidate depicted in Figure 1 is when home receives read-exclusive requests for blocks nominated as migratory. For all experiments presented in this section, we did not use this heuristic because it did not provide consistent performance improvements.

In summary, the quantitative evaluation has shown that the adaptive protocol can improve performance of a write-invalidate protocol as a result of write-penalty reduction under sequential consistency and read-penalty reduction under relaxed consistency models if the application consumes a lot of bandwidth. We generalize our contributions in the next section.

6 Discussion

We have presented the implementation and evaluation of an adaptive protocol that dynamically can optimize coherence actions due to migratory sharing. Based on the experiments in the previous section, we have found that the adaptive protocol can improve performance of a DASH-like system by reducing the access penalty and network traffic. In this section, we generalize the results to other system organizations and a wider class of applications.

Our implementation is based on a specific cache coherence protocol, in essence the Stanford DASH protocol. However, the adaptive protocol can be built on top of any write-invalidate protocol provided that there is an explicit notion of a home of the coherence state. The detection mechanism relies on the fact that all global read and write requests must interrogate the home directory. In fact, even a COMA architecture that have an explicit home directory for the coherence state, such as the Flat-COMA proposal [16], can use the adaptive protocol. Note also that the protocol is applicable to bus-based systems with snoopy-cache protocols. In such systems a primary concern is to reduce network traffic rather than reducing latency. The adaptive technique is an adequate candidate for such systems.

In our experiments, we considered a rather small system configuration of 16 processors. The implications of our results for larger system configurations are as follows. First, for larger system configurations it will be more difficult to obtain a scalable bandwidth. Secondly, latencies will be larger and thus, the access penalty due to invalidation requests will be higher. The adaptive technique can help performance by reducing both problems.

A limitation of the scope of our results is due to the small number of applications. We found two types of shared data usage that contributed to migratory sharing (i) shared data access protected by locks and (ii) tight read-modify-write operations to shared data. The first type is expected to be common since protected data access is a means to promote correctness. The second type is not so unusual either and happens when a variable is read and modified in the same high-level language statement. It is also interesting to note that migratory sharing is independent of system size. Gupta's and Weber's data of invalidation patterns for 8, 16, and 32 processors [8] support this. They found that the single invalidation numbers for MP3D and Water did not change significantly with system size.

An alternative to the adaptive technique is to use software-controlled, non-binding read-exclusive prefetching [13]. Under this scheme, the programmer/compiler inserts prefetch-instructions so as to get ownership of the block prior to the point when it is accessed. Although this technique can be as effective, it relies on the programmer/compiler to detect the occurrence of read-modify-write operations on shared data which in general can be difficult.

7 Conclusions

The focus of this paper has been to optimize cache coherence actions that arise as a result of migratory objects causing migratory sharing.

We have proposed an adaptive cache coherence protocol that can detect migratory sharing and eliminate all invalidation actions associated with migratory blocks. We have shown that the mechanisms to support this technique add little to the complexity of coherence mechanisms of directory-based write-invalidate protocols such as the Stanford DASH. Based on a simulation study and four parallel applications, we have found that the adaptive technique can help performance in many important respects. First, because it reduces the number of read-exclusive requests, the write stall-time can be reduced under sequential consistency. Second, even when we go to relaxed consistency models, the read-stall time can be reduced because of contention reduction, especially for applications that require a substantial communication bandwidth. Third, the network traffic was reduced by more than 20% for the studied applications that exhibit migratory sharing, which is as critical for small bus-based as large system configurations.

Because of the limited availability of parallel applications, it is an open question what type of sharing behavior is common and worthwhile to optimize. However, on the premise that migratory objects are common, we feel that the adaptive technique is important because of its simplicity and consistent performance improvements.

Acknowledgments

The authors are deeply indebted to Magnus Karlsson who implemented the DASH simulator. We would also like to thank Kourosh Gharachorloo of Stanford University, Fredrik Dahlgren and Jonas Skeppstedt of Lund University, and the anonymous reviewers for helpful comments. Thanks are also directed to Jeff McDonald, Ed Rothberg, and Jaswinder Pal Singh, who provided us with the parallel applications which made our experiments possible.

This research has been sponsored by the Swedish National Board for Industrial and Technical Development (NUTEK) under the contract number 9001797.

References

[1] Anant Agarwal, Beng-Hong Lim, David Kranz, and John Kubiatowicz. APRIL: A Processor Architecture for Multiprocessing. In *Proceedings of the 17th Annual International Symposium on Computer Architecture*, pages 104-114, May 1990.

[2] Kendall Square Research. Kendall Square Research1 (KSR1) Technical Summary. 1992.

[3] J. Boyle et al. Portable Programs for Parallel Processors. Holt, Rinehart, and Winston Inc. 1987.

[4] Mats Brorsson, Fredrik Dahlgren, Håkan Nilsson and Per Stenström. The CacheMire Test Bench — A Flexible and Effective Approach for Simulation of Multiprocessors. In *Proceedings of the 26th Annual Simulation Symposium*, to appear, March 1993.

[5] Michel Dubois, Christoph Scheurich, and Faye Briggs. Memory Access Buffering in Multiprocessors. In *Proceedings of the 13th Annual International Symposium on Computer Architecture*, pages 434-442, 1986.

[6] Kourosh Gharachorloo, Anoop Gupta, John L. Hennessy. Performance Evaluation of Memory Consistency Models for Shared-Memory Multiprocessors. In *Fourth ASPLOS*, pages 245-257, April 1991.

[7] Kourosh Gharachorloo, Daniel E. Lenoski, James P. Laudon, Philip Gibbons, Anoop Gupta, and John L. Hennessy. Memory Consistency and Event Ordering in Scalable Shared-Memory Multiprocessors. In *Proceedings of the 17th Annual International Symposium on Computer Architecture*, pages 15-26, May 1990.

[8] Anoop Gupta and Wolf-Dietrich Weber. Cache Invalidation Patterns in Shared-Memory Multiprocessors. *Transactions on Computers*, Volume 41, Number 7, pages 794-810, July 1992.

[9] Erik Hagersten, Anders Landin, and Seif Haridi. DDM — A Cache-Only Memory Architecture. *IEEE Computer Magazine*, pages 44-54, September 1992.

[10] Leslie Lamport. How to make a Multiprocessor Computer That Correctly Executes Multiprocess Programs. *Transactions on Computers*. C-28(9), pages 241-248, September 1979.

[11] Daniel E. Lenoski, James P. Laudon, Kourosh Gharachorloo, Anoop Gupta, and John L. Hennessy. The Directory-Based Cache Coherence Protocol for the DASH Multiprocessor. In *Proceedings of the 17th Annual International Symposium on Computer Architecture*, pages 148-159, May 1990.

[12] Daniel E. Lenoski, James P. Laudon, Kourosh Gharachorloo, Wolf-Dietrich Weber, Anoop Gupta, John L. Hennessy, Mark Horowitz, and Monica S. Lam. The Stanford DASH Multiprocessor. *IEEE Computer Magazine*, pages 63-79, March 1992.

[13] Todd Mowry and Anoop Gupta. Tolerating Latency Through Software-Controlled Prefetching in Shared-Memory Multiprocessors. *Journal of Parallel and Distributed Computing*, 2(4), pages 87-106, June 1991.

[14] Jaswinder P. Singh, Wolf-Dietrich Weber, and Anoop Gupta. SPLASH: Stanford Parallel Applications for Shared-Memory. *Computer Architecture News*, 20(1). pages 5-44, March 1992.

[15] Per Stenström, Fredrik Dahlgren, and Lars Lundberg. A Lockup-free Multiprocessor Cache Design. In *Proceedings of 1991 International Conference on Parallel Processing*, Vol. I, pages 246-250, August 1991.

[16] Per Stenström, Truman Joe, and Anoop Gupta. Comparative Performance Evaluation of Cache-Coherent NUMA and COMA Architectures. In *Proceedings of the 19th Annual International Symposium on Computer Architecture*, pages 80-91, May 1992.

SESSION 7:
Multithreading
Support

Register Relocation: Flexible Contexts for Multithreading

Carl A. Waldspurger *   William E. Weihl *

MIT Laboratory for Computer Science
Cambridge, MA 02139

Abstract

Multithreading is an important technique that improves processor utilization by allowing computation to be overlapped with the long latency operations that commonly occur in multiprocessor systems. This paper presents *register relocation*, a new mechanism that efficiently supports flexible partitioning of the register file into variable-size contexts with minimal hardware support. Since the number of registers required by thread contexts varies, this flexibility permits a better utilization of scarce registers, allowing more contexts to be resident, which in turn allows applications to tolerate shorter run lengths and longer latencies. Our experiments show that compared to fixed-size hardware contexts, register relocation can improve processor utilization by a factor of two for many workloads.

1 Introduction

Multithreading is an important technique for tolerating latency in multiprocessor systems [3, 7, 19, 21]. Support for multiple contexts and rapid context switching permits high latency operations such as remote memory references and synchronization events to be overlapped with computation, which improves processor utilization. Because the number of registers required by thread contexts varies across applications and among threads within a single application, the ability to partition the register file into contexts of varying sizes enables more efficient use of the available registers. We present *register relocation*, a

*E-mail: {carl,weihl}@lcs.mit.edu. The first author was supported by an AT&T USL Fellowship and a grant by the MIT X Consortium. This research was also supported by the National Science Foundation under grant CCR-8716884, by the Defense Advanced Research Projects Agency (DARPA) under contract N00014-91-J-1698, by grants from AT&T and IBM, and by an equipment grant from DEC. The views and conclusions contained in this document are those of the authors and should not be interpreted as representing the official policies, either expressed or implied, of the U.S. government.

simple mechanism that efficiently supports flexible, variable-size processor contexts with minimal hardware support. The register relocation hardware should affect only the instruction decode stage of the processor pipeline, and would be a simple addition to many existing architectures.

Existing multithreaded architectures typically provide several separate, fixed-size contexts managed in hardware. This fixed, inflexible division of the register file often results in a significant waste of scarce high-speed registers. More efficient partitioning of the register file would permit a larger number of resident contexts. Since the optimal number of contexts is both application- and machine-dependent [19], enabling more resident contexts will allow programs with sufficient parallelism to tolerate longer latencies and shorter run lengths. Alternatively, better utilization of the register file would permit a smaller register file to support a given number of contexts, which has architectural advantages in terms of chip area and processor cycle-time [11].

Register relocation adheres to the RISC philosophy [17] by maintaining a simple processor architecture and relying upon the compiler and runtime system to manage the allocation and use of contexts. We discuss several runtime-level software techniques that exploit the register relocation hardware, managing the division of the register file into contexts in software. Because the size of contexts is not dictated by the hardware, there is considerable flexibility in the use of the register file to support multithreading. Possible organizations range from *static* partitioning into contexts with fixed or varying sizes to *dynamic* allocation of contexts with varying sizes as needed. The flexibility to provide a better match between application requirements and the organization of the register file into contexts enables better utilization of scarce registers, which allows more resident contexts and higher processor utilization. Our experiments show that register relocation can improve performance by a factor of two or more for many workloads.

Improvements in processor utilization can be expected whenever more contexts are able to remain loaded through an efficient partitioning of the register file. This is likely to be a common case, since many threads cannot make effective use of a large number of registers. Moreover, most programs exhibit decreasing marginal performance improvements as the number of available registers is increased. For example, one performance study [9] revealed a pattern of decreasing marginal savings in memory references as the number of available registers is increased. Another [5] found that even in workloads containing programs with large basic blocks, the degradation in execution time given 16 registers instead of 32 averaged only 12%; the improvement given more than 32 registers averaged only 1%. This study also showed that sophisticated code generation strategies require fewer registers. We believe that these effects are likely to be even more pronounced in systems with many fine-grained threads and sophisticated optimizing compilers.

In the next section, we discuss the hardware and software support required for register relocation. Section 3 discusses the results of several quantitative experiments comparing register relocation to conventional multithreaded architectures. In Section 4, we examine related work. Extensions and directions for future research are discussed in Section 5. Finally, we summarize our conclusions in Section 6.

2 Register Relocation

The register relocation mechanism is very simple. Instruction operands specify *context-relative* register numbers, which are numbered consecutively starting with register 0. These context-relative register numbers are dynamically combined with a special *register relocation mask* (RRM) to form absolute register numbers that are used during instruction execution. A bitwise OR is used as the combining operation.

The OR operation permits a flexible division between the number of RRM bits treated as the register relocation *base*, and the number of register operand bits treated as the register relocation *offset*, as shown in Figure 1. This simple mechanism allows the register file to be partitioned into a collection of variable-size contexts. For example, the register file can be divided into a small number of large contexts, as is conventionally done in hardware. Alternatively, the register file can be divided into a large number of small contexts, providing support for many fine-grained threads. The register file can also be divided, statically or dynami-

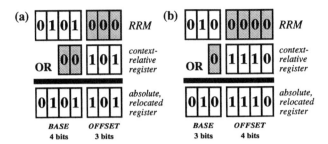

Figure 1: Register Relocation Examples. In both examples, there are a total of 128 general registers, the RRM is 7 bits wide, and register operands are 5 bits wide. The shaded portions of registers are effectively unused. (a) The RRM provides relocation for a context of size 8. Context-relative register 5 is relocated to absolute register 45. (b) The RRM provides relocation for a context of size 16. Context-relative register 14 is relocated to absolute register 46.

cally, into different combinations of context sizes, supporting a mix of both coarse and fine-grained threads.

2.1 Hardware Support

A *register relocation mask* (RRM) is maintained in a special hardware register. The RRM register requires $\lceil \lg n \rceil$ bits for a processor architecture with n general registers. A special LDRRM R instruction is used to set the RRM from the low-order $\lceil \lg n \rceil$ bits of register R. Depending on the organization of the processor pipeline, there may be one or more delay slots following a LDRRM instruction.

RISC architectures typically employ a *fixed-field decoding* scheme in which register operands are always specified at the same location within an instruction [18]. During every instruction decode, a bitwise OR operation is performed with each of the instruction's register operand fields and the RRM, yielding *relocated* register operand fields, as shown in Figure 2. After the instruction decode phase, no additional work needs to be performed.

Another hardware change that would be necessary in some architectures is to widen the internal paths that carry the register operands specified by an instruction. This is because a relocated register operand requires $\lceil \lg n \rceil$ bits to address the entire register file, while a register operand field in an instruction may only be able to address a smaller portion of the register file, due to limitations on the width of a machine instruction. We will denote the width of an instruction

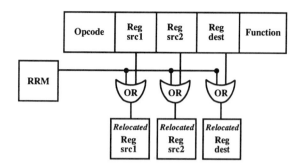

Figure 2: Register Relocation Hardware. During instruction decode, a bitwise **OR** is performed with each of the instruction's operands and the **RRM**, yielding relocated register operands.

register operand by w, which constrains the number of addressable registers and places an upper bound of 2^w on the size of a single context.

2.2 Context Scheduling

Unlike multithreaded architectures with hardware control over scheduling [2, 10, 12, 22], we schedule contexts entirely in software. We have developed an approach for very fast context switching that does not require hardware support or the use of a separate scheduler context. Sample assembly-language code for this fast context switch is listed in Figure 3. The scheduler "ready queue" for loaded contexts is implemented as a circular linked list of register relocation masks. This list is maintained by storing a **NextRRM** mask in each resident context. A transfer of control to the next runnable thread context is implemented as follows:

- Store the current program counter in a register associated with the current context. In the listed code, context-relative register **R0** is used to store the **PC**.

- Execute a **LDRRM** instruction to install the register relocation mask for the next thread context. Depending on the organization of the processor pipeline, there may be one or more delay slots following this instruction. In the listed code, **R2** is used to store the **NextRRM** relocation mask, and there is one delay slot.

- If necessary, save any processor state that must be restored when the current thread is resumed. When the newly installed **RRM** becomes active, restore any processor state associated with the new

```
|  Context-Relative Register Conventions
|
|     R0:   thread program counter (PC)
|     R1:   processor status word (PSW)
|     R2:   mask for next thread (NextRRM)

fault:  |  jump and link; save next PC in r0
        jalr    yield, r0
        :

yield:  |  install new relocation mask,
        |  save old status register
        |  (single ldrrm delay slot)
        ldrrm   r2
        mov     PSW, r1


        |  restore new status register,
        |  execute code in new context
        mov     r1, PSW
        jmp     r0
```

Figure 3: Context Switch Code. The instruction labelled **fault** may be explicit (as shown), or the result of a trap. The register move (**mov**), unconditional jump (**jmp**), and jump and link (**jalr**) instructions are similar to those found in many RISC architectures. The **LDRRM** instruction is described in Section 2.1.

context.[1] In the listed code, a processor status word (PSW) is stored in **R1**.

- Jump to the program counter associated with the new context.

This approach requires approximately 4 to 6 RISC cycles, depending on the number of **LDRRM** delay slots and the need to save and restore processor status information. More sophisticated scheduling policies can also be implemented by altering the order in which contexts are linked together by their **NextRRM** masks. For example, separate linked lists of register relocation masks could be maintained to implement different thread classes or priorities. Such flexibility is possible because context scheduling is under software control.

---

[1]On some architectures, condition codes such as carry flags must be preserved. This is unnecessary on architectures which don't use condition codes, such as the MIPS R3000. At the other extreme, architectures such as the SPARC may require expensive traps to manipulate this state.

2.3 Context Allocation

The register relocation mechanism can allocate a context with size 2^k registers, for $0 \leq k \leq w$; the maximum context size is limited to 2^w by the number of address bits used for register operands. However, the minimum context size should be large enough to maintain some state other than a program counter. For example, practical context sizes for an architecture with 256 registers and 6-bit register operands would be 4, 8, 16, 32, and 64 registers.

Context allocation is performed entirely in software, and is thus extremely flexible. One option is to partition the register file statically into contexts (with identical or differing sizes) for a particular application, which makes allocation and deallocation extremely inexpensive. Another option is to partition the register file dynamically into contexts of varying sizes as needed.

For the experiments discussed in Section 3, we coded general-purpose dynamic context allocation and deallocation routines for a RISC architecture with 128 registers. The implementation employs simple shift and mask operations to search an allocation bitmap for available contexts. Linear search is used for some context sizes, and binary search is used for others. General-purpose allocation executes in approximately 25 RISC cycles, and general-purpose deallocation requires fewer than 5 RISC cycles.[2] Sample C code for general-purpose allocation is listed in Appendix A.

2.4 Compiler Support

Compilers can generate code as usual, and may assume that the available registers are numbered from 0 to $2^w - 1$. Although the compiler is permitted to use all 2^w registers, many threads will require fewer registers. For each thread, the compiler must inform the runtime system about the number of registers that the thread requires, which can be determined by traversing the thread call graph. In systems that support separate compilation, the compiler will need to provide this information to the linker. However, this should not present any difficult challenges; more sophisticated cooperation between compilers and linkers has already been demonstrated for register allocation [23].

The register relocation mechanism also presents some interesting opportunities for compiler optimizations. As noted in Section 1, most programs real-

ize decreasing marginal improvements from additional registers. A compiler can thus make tradeoffs between allocating additional registers to a thread or using fewer registers to enable more resident contexts. For example, a compiler may normally achieve some marginal benefit by allocating 17 (versus 16) registers to a thread; there is no reason to conserve registers if they would otherwise be wasted. However, due to the power-of-two constraint on context sizes, a thread that uses 17 registers will require a context of size 32. The 15 extra registers that are consumed could instead be used to support a higher degree of multithreading, and the corresponding increase in processor utilization is likely to exceed the original gain from using an extra register.

Finally, by guaranteeing not to use any additional registers, the compiler – not the hardware – is responsible for ensuring protection among thread contexts. However, similar protection issues arise for memory locations due to the execution of multiple threads within a single address space. Note that we are assuming that threads are associated with a single application, and hence are logically related. Thus, erroneous register overwrites are not inherently more problematic than memory overwrites; they simply occur at different levels in the memory hierarchy. In order to facilitate low-level debugging of compilers and runtime system routines, a separate tool could be used to statically check executables or object files for most violations of context boundaries.[3]

2.5 Context Loading

The register relocation mechanism requires the compiler to determine the number of registers needed by each thread, as described in Section 2.4. This information can also be exploited to save or restore the exact number of registers used by a thread when its context is loaded or unloaded. The runtime system can provide one context unload routine that successively stores registers numbered $2^w - 1$ to 0 to memory, with 2^w separate entry points corresponding to every possible number of context registers used by threads. Similarly, a single context load routine with multiple entry points can be provided to successively load registers from memory.

---

[2] If an operation such as the Motorola MC88000's FF1 instruction is available that can find the first bit set in a word, then general-purpose allocation can be performed in approximately 15 RISC cycles.

[3] One of the referees suggested the use of MUXs to select each bit from either the RRM or the register operand; this might be faster in CMOS than an OR, and would also prevent a thread from accessing registers outside its allocated context. Alternatively, hardware could be added for "bounds checking" on contexts.

Parameter	Description	(units)
R	average run length	(cycles)
L	average fault latency	(cycles)
S	context switch cost	(cycles)
F	register file size	(registers)
C	required context size	(registers)

	Cost (cycles)	
Operation	Flexible	Fixed
context allocate (succeed)	25	0
context allocate (fail)	15	0
context deallocate	5	0
context load/unload	C	C
thread queue insert/remove	10	10

Figure 4: Parameters and Assumptions. The first table describes the experimental parameters. The second table lists the cost assumptions used for both the register relocation (*Flexible*) and conventional fixed-size contexts (*Fixed*) architectures.

3 Experiments

We ran a large number of experiments, over a wide range of system parameters, to evaluate the register relocation mechanism. The experiments focus on a single multiprocessor node executing multiple threads with stochastic run lengths and varying fault latencies. We assume a coarsely multithreaded processor architecture similar to APRIL [2], which switches contexts only when a high-latency operation such as a remote cache miss or synchronization fault occurs. We conducted our experiments using PROTEUS [6], a high-performance parallel architecture simulator, which we modified to support multiple contexts.

Below we discuss several experiments involving only cache faults, and others involving only synchronization faults. We also ran experiments involving both types of faults, with similar results; the main effect was to increase the overall fault rate. The data presented in this paper is representative of our experimental results; additional experiments appear in [24].

3.1 Parameters and Assumptions

In each experiment, a supply of synthetic threads was created with particular fault rates and fault service latencies. All threads executed until completion, and statistics were extracted over a substantial fraction of the execution that avoided transient startup

and completion effects.[4] Our experimental parameters are summarized in Figure 4.

For each set of parameters, we performed two experiments: one to simulate a conventional multithreaded processor architecture with fixed hardware contexts, each containing 32 registers, and another to simulate an architecture using the register relocation mechanism. In both experiments, local thread queue insertion and removal operations cost 10 cycles, and loading contexts from memory and unloading contexts to memory cost 1 cycle per register. An additional charge of 10 cycles was assessed for the software overhead of blocking and unblocking contexts when loading and unloading.

For register relocation, successful context allocation and deallocation cost 25 and 5 cycles, respectively, and unsuccessful context allocation was charged 15 cycles. These costs are consistent with the general-purpose dynamic allocation routines listed in Appendix A. For the conventional hardware architecture with fixed contexts, these costs were all set to 0, assuming some hardware support for context scheduling. This assumption was deliberately conservative for comparison with the register relocation approach.

3.2 Tolerating Cache Faults

The experiments described in this section explore the use of multithreading to hide the latency associated with remote memory references. In each experiment, the average run length between cache faults (R) is geometrically distributed, and the average cache fault latency (L) is constant. Thus, there is a fixed probability of a cache miss on each execution cycle, and network response time is uniform, which is reasonable for lightly loaded networks. These distributions are also consistent with the assumptions and models used in earlier studies [3, 19]. The context switch cost is set to $S = 6$ cycles, which is consistent with the code presented in Figure 3, and better than the 11 cycle cost incurred by the current APRIL implementation [2]. To avoid effects due to the selection of a particular thread unloading policy, contexts are never unloaded.

Figure 5 summarizes many experiments; each data point represents a separate simulation. The graphs plot *efficiency* (i.e., processor utilization) vs. memory latency for a family of curves corresponding to various run lengths. The solid curves denote results for fixed-size hardware contexts, and the dotted curves denote

---

[4] We also collected statistics from entire runs; these differed only slightly from the statistics that excluded transients.

results for register relocation. For these experiments, the number of registers required by each context (C) is uniformly distributed between 6 and 24 registers. Due to the power-of-two constraint on context sizes for register relocation, these experiments are biased toward large contexts. Despite this bias, register relocation consistently outperforms conventional fixed-size contexts, resulting in significantly higher efficiencies over a wide range of values for L and R. Thus, even for workloads consisting of many large contexts and few small contexts, more contexts remain resident, improving processor utilization.

3.3 Tolerating Synchronization Faults

This section describes experiments that examine the use of multithreading to hide the latency associated with synchronization events. In each experiment, the average run length between synchronization faults (R) is geometrically distributed, and the average synchronization fault latency (L) is exponentially distributed. Thus, there is a fixed probability of a synchronization fault on each execution cycle, and wait times for synchronization are exponentially distributed, which is reasonable for producer-consumer synchronization [14]. The context switch cost is set to $S = 8$ cycles, which is 2 cycles more than the cost used in Section 3.2. This allows for simple bookkeeping and test operations (e.g., an add and conditional branch) which can be used to implement a thread unloading policy. The thread unloading policy used in these experiments is a competitive, two-phase algorithm [14]. A context is unloaded when the cost of repeated, unsuccessful attempts to continue execution equals the cost of unloading and blocking the context. Note that the cost assessed for loading and unloading a context is based on C, the number of registers *required* by the context (see Section 2.5), not on the size of the *allocated* context; this is true for all our simulations. Since conventional architectures with fixed-size contexts typically save and restore all registers allocated to a context, including unused ones, our experiments conservatively overestimate the performance of conventional approaches using hardware contexts.

Figure 6 summarizes the results for synchronization faults; each data point represents a separate simulation. The graphs plot efficiency vs. synchronization latency for a family of curves corresponding to various run lengths. The solid curves denote results for fixed-size hardware contexts, and the dotted curves denote results using register relocation. For these experiments, the number of registers required by each context (C) is uniformly distributed between 6 and

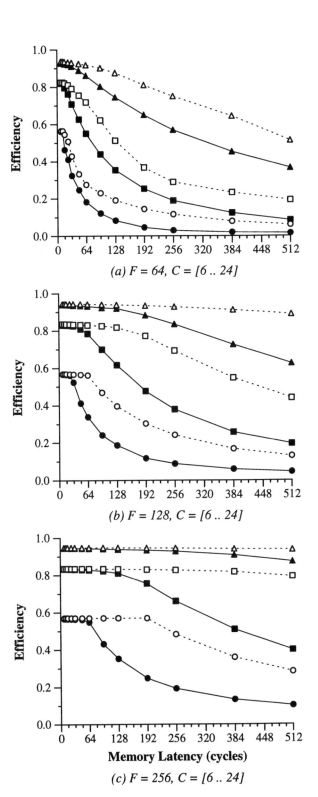

(a) F = 64, C = [6 .. 24]

(b) F = 128, C = [6 .. 24]

(c) F = 256, C = [6 .. 24]

Figure 5: Cache Faults. Efficiency for $F = 64$, 128, and 256 registers, and C uniformly distributed from 6 to 24 registers. Curves: solid – fixed-size contexts, dotted – register relocation. Data points: circles – $R = 8$, squares – $R = 32$, triangles – $R = 128$.

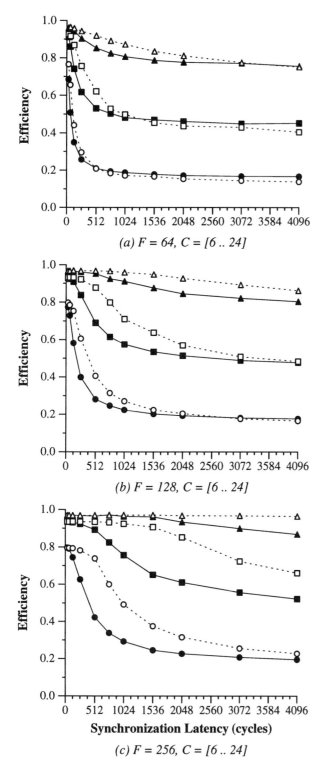

(a) F = 64, C = [6 .. 24]

(b) F = 128, C = [6 .. 24]

Synchronization Latency (cycles)

(c) F = 256, C = [6 .. 24]

Figure 6: Synchronization Faults. Efficiency for $F =$ 64, 128, and 256 registers, and C uniformly distributed from 6 to 24 registers. Curves: solid – fixed-size contexts, dotted – register relocation. Data points: circles – $R = 32$, squares – $R = 128$, triangles – $R = 512$.

24 registers. As explained earlier, this distribution is biased toward large contexts.

Register relocation improves processor utilization for virtually all parameter values. The only notable exception is provided by Figure 6(a), in which relatively large contexts are competing for a small register file ($F = 64$). As L increases, the advantages provided by register relocation diminish, and fixed-size hardware contexts marginally outperform register relocation for large L. This is due to the software overhead associated with context allocation in the register relocation approach. When the register file is small and contexts are large, contexts are continually loaded and unloaded for small R and large L, resulting in a large number of allocation operations. Re-executing the experiments in Figure 6(a) with lower allocation costs confirmed this explanation; in this case register relocation consistently outperformed the fixed-size contexts. Recall that allocation costs were set to 0 for the fixed-size hardware contexts in order to conservatively overestimate the performance of conventional approaches. If workload parameters similar to those in Figure 6(a) were common, a different, specialized allocation policy could be adopted. For example, two sets of context sizes could be implemented extremely cheaply; an allocation bitmap for contexts of size 16 and 32 can be encoded in four bits, and a direct lookup table indexed by this bitmap could be used to allocate contexts. The flexibility of performing allocation in software makes such schemes possible.

Nevertheless, even with a general-purpose dynamic allocation policy, register relocation still results in substantial efficiency gains over a wide range of values for L and R. Thus, for most workloads, we expect register relocation to enable more resident contexts, making it possible to improve processor utilization by tolerating long synchronization latencies.

3.4 Discussion

We also performed numerous experiments similar to those presented above, using homogeneous context sizes $C = 8$ and $C = 16$. The results were similar to those presented in Figures 5 and 6, but the relative improvements due to register relocation were often substantially larger [24]. This is not surprising, since the primary effect of smaller context sizes is to increase the number of contexts that can be supported by a given register file.

Register relocation significantly outperforms fixed-size hardware contexts over a wide range of system parameters, sometimes by huge margins. By providing the flexibility to efficiently partition the register file, scarce register resources are better utilized, allowing more contexts to remain resident. The number of resident contexts has a dramatic impact on processor utilization. As run lengths decrease and latencies increase, more contexts are needed to prevent the processor from idling. This trend is clearly indicated by the data presented in Figures 5 through 6, and can also be explained analytically.

A simple mathematical analysis of multithreaded architectures [19] reveals that for constant run lengths and latencies, processor efficiency can be determined from the parameters R, L, and S.[5] When there is always a resident context that is ready to execute, the processor is *saturated*, and its efficiency is independent of L: $\mathcal{E}_{sat} = \frac{R}{R+S}$. When the number of resident contexts is below the saturation point, the processor will not be fully utilized, and its efficiency is *linear* in the number of resident contexts (N): $\mathcal{E}_{lin} = \frac{NR}{R+S+L}$.

Thus, processor efficiency increases linearly in the number of resident contexts until saturation, after which it remains constant. From these two equations, we find that for $N < 1 + \frac{L}{R+S}$, processor efficiency is in the linear region. Given current trends toward large parallel machines and extremely fast processors, we expect R to decrease and L to increase, requiring a large number of contexts before processor efficiency saturates. Thus, systems with a small number of hardware contexts are likely to operate in the linear regime, where register relocation can substantially improve performance.

Some earlier studies have suggested that only a small number of contexts (2 to 4) is required to achieve high processor utilization [2, 25]. Although it is true that a small number of contexts significantly boosts efficiency for relatively low L and sufficiently high R, the optimal number of contexts is both application- and machine-dependent [19]. For example, the Horizon architecture [22] provides 128 hardware contexts in order to tolerate long latencies and short run lengths. Moreover, even proponents of a small number of hardware contexts agree that a large supply of runnable, loaded contexts is needed to tolerate synchronization latencies, which are typically much longer than latencies for remote memory access. For example, additional hardware for *dribbling registers* is currently being explored by the APRIL designers for tolerating longer latencies [20].[6] Our register relocation mechanism provides a simple, effective alternative to increasingly complex and specialized hardware solutions.

4   Related Work

Most multithreaded processor architectures employ hardware-intensive and inflexible mechanisms for multithreading. Our approach is software-intensive, and attempts to minimize the hardware required to support multithreading efficiently and flexibly. In this section we compare register relocation in more detail to other approaches.

A number of processor architectures with multiple hardware contexts have been proposed. *Finely* multithreaded processors, such as the Denelcor HEP [21], execute an instruction from a different thread on each cycle. A drawback to this approach is that the interleaving of threads in the processor pipeline degrades single-thread performance. Also, these processors require a steady supply of runnable threads that can be interleaved cycle-by-cycle to keep the processor pipeline busy. The more recent MASA architecture [10] also suffers from this problem. The Horizon and Tera architectures [4, 22] also switch among instruction streams on every cycle, but allow several instructions from the same thread to co-exist in the pipeline.

Coarsely multithreaded processors, such as APRIL [2], execute larger blocks of instructions from each thread, and typically switch contexts only when a high-latency operation occurs. A drawback to this approach is that a context switch typically bubbles the processor pipeline, degrading multithreaded performance. Hybrid dataflow / von-Neumann architectures [12, 15] also have pipelines that only contain instructions from a single thread, and typically provide support for hardware task queues.

Most of the architectures described above maintain a fixed, inflexible division of high-speed register resources into multiple contexts. Our register relocation mechanism supports coarse multithreading, but permits unusual flexibility in the organization of the register file by managing contexts in software. Context scheduling is also performed entirely in software, yet only a few RISC cycles are required to implement a context switch.

The AMD Am29000 processor [1] implements a base plus offset form of register addressing[7] that could be used to support multiple variable-size contexts. An ADD operation for register addressing is more general than our proposed OR operation for register relocation,

---

[5] A considerably more complex analysis is also presented in [19] that accounts for stochastic run lengths. However, the simpler equations for the deterministic case still provide a reasonable approximation for processor efficiency.

[6] The dribbling registers idea is completely orthogonal to the register relocation mechanism.

[7] The Denelcor HEP provided a similar capability.

and eliminates the power-of-two constraint on context sizes. However, an `ADD` is much more expensive than an `OR` in terms of hardware and time on the critical path. Moreover, the software for managing arbitrary-size contexts is likely to be more complex.

A completely different approach is the Named State Processor [16], which replaces a conventional register file with a *context cache*. The context cache binds variable names to individual registers in a fully associative register file, and spills registers only when they are immediately needed for another purpose. Our register relocation mechanism supports a binding of variable names to contexts that is finer than conventional multithreaded processors, but coarser than the context cache approach.

5 Extensions and Future Work

We are currently exploring a variety of issues related to register relocation and multithreading.

5.1 Software-Only Approach

We have devised a related approach for multi-threading that requires *no* hardware support, and can be used with many existing processors. The basic idea is to have the compiler generate *multiple versions* of code that use disjoint subsets of the register file. Thus, register relocation is effectively performed at compile-time. This scheme has the obvious disadvantage of code expansion. However, the restrictions on context sizes no longer apply, and *any* partitioning of the register file is possible.

We performed some simple experiments by modifying `gcc`, the GNU C compiler, to investigate this scheme on a uniprocessor using the MIPS R3000 architecture. Our preliminary results were encouraging, but because of the limited number of general registers on the MIPS architecture, the technique was not practical for more than two contexts.[8]

5.2 Cache Interference Effects

Threads sharing a common cache can interfere with each other. Several studies have indicated that most cache interference is destructive, increasing the cache miss ratio [19, 25]. However, Agarwal has observed that the working set size of fine-grained threads tends

to decrease with increasing parallelism, reducing cache interference [3].

There is a tradeoff between improving processor utilization and exacerbating cache interference as the number of contexts is increased. Limiting the number of contexts to improve cache performance is analogous to the problem of controlling the degree of multiprogramming to improve virtual memory performance. Starting with some of the literature on multiprogramming, thrashing, and working sets [8], we are currently investigating methods for adaptively limiting the number of resident contexts at runtime.

5.3 Multiple Active Contexts

We are also examining extensions to the basic register relocation hardware primitive. One powerful extension is to provide *multiple* register relocation masks that can be selected during instruction execution. As with the basic mechanism, this extension should only impact the instruction decode stage of the processor pipeline.

For example, the high-order bit of each register operand in a machine instruction could be used to select among two different `RRM`s. This would permit instructions to perform inter-context operations such as `ADD C0.R3, C0.R4, C1.R6`. The resulting instruction set would make an interesting compilation target for a concurrent intermediate language such as TAM [7], which attempts to minimize context switches by scheduling threads to share activation frames. This mechanism is also sufficiently powerful to emulate fixed-size, overlapping register windows.

Since an `RRM` requires only $\lceil \lg n \rceil$ bits for an architecture with n general registers, allowing multiple `RRM`s would require little additional hardware; the `LDRRM` instruction could simultaneously load several masks from a single general register. The most costly aspect of allowing multiple relocation masks is likely to be the need for multiplexers to permit each register operand to select the desired `RRM` for relocation.

6 Conclusions

We have presented a new mechanism that efficiently supports multiple variable-size processor contexts with minimal hardware support. Simple register relocation hardware, combined with appropriate software support, provides significant flexibility in the use of the register file to support multithreading. This flexibility enables better utilization of scarce register resources, allowing more contexts to remain resident

---

[8] The MIPS architecture has only 32 integer registers, and several are reserved for the operating system and standard calling conventions [13].

than is possible with conventional fixed-size hardware contexts.

A larger number of resident contexts makes it feasible to tolerate shorter run lengths and longer latencies, improving processor utilization over a wide range of system parameters. We have presented and analyzed a collection of experiments that demonstrates that register relocation can achieve substantial performance gains over fixed-size hardware contexts; a factor of two improvement is possible for many workloads. We are currently exploring the effects of multithreading on cache interference, and are examining extensions to the basic register relocation primitive.

Acknowledgements

We would like to thank Anant Agarwal, Eric Brewer, Bill Dally, Wilson Hsieh, Bruce Leban, Beng-Hong Lim, Peter Nuth, Greg Papadopoulos, and Paige Parsons for their comments and assistance. Thanks also to the anonymous reviewers for their many helpful suggestions.

References

[1] Advanced Micro Devices. *Am29000 User's Manual*, 1990.

[2] A. Agarwal, *et al.* "APRIL: A Processor Architecture for Multiprocessing", *Proc. 17th Annual Intl. Symp. on Comp. Arch.*, June 1990.

[3] A. Agarwal. "Performance Tradeoffs in Multithreaded Processors", *IEEE Trans. on Parallel and Distributed Systems*, September 1992.

[4] R. Alverson, *et al.* "The Tera Computer System", *Intl. Conf. on Supercomputing*, 1990.

[5] D. Bradlee, S. Eggers, R. Henry. "The Effect on RISC Performance of Register Set Size and Structure Versus Code Generation Strategy", *Proc. 18th Annual Intl. Symp. on Comp. Arch.*, 1991.

[6] E. Brewer, C. Dellarocas, A. Colbrook, and W. Weihl. "Proteus: A High-Performance Parallel Architecture Simulator", Tech. Rep. MIT/LCS/TR-516, MIT Lab. for Comp. Sci., September 1991.

[7] D. Culler, *et al.* "Fine-grain Parallelism with Minimal Hardware Support: A Compiler-Controlled Threaded Abstract Machine", *Proc. 4th Intl. Conf. on Architectural Support for Programming Languages and Operating Systems*, April 1991.

[8] P. J. Denning. "Working Sets Past and Present", *IEEE Trans. on Software Engineering*, January 1980.

[9] R. Eickemeyer and J. Patel. "Performance Evaluation of Multiple Register Sets", *Proc. 14th Annual Intl. Symp. on Comp. Arch.*, 1987.

[10] R. H. Halstead, Jr. and T. Fujita. "MASA: A Multithreaded Processor Architecture for Parallel Symbolic Computing", *Proc. 15th Annual Intl. Symp. on Comp. Arch.*, 1988.

[11] J. Hennessy. "VLSI Processor Architecture", *IEEE Trans. on Computers*, December 1984.

[12] R. A. Iannucci. "Toward a Dataflow / von Neumann Hybrid Architecture", *Proc. 15th Annual Intl. Symp. on Comp. Arch.*, 1988.

[13] G. Kane. *Mips RISC Architecture*, Prentice-Hall, 1989.

[14] B. H. Lim and A. Agarwal. "Waiting Algorithms for Synchronization in Large-Scale Multiprocessors", MIT VLSI Memo #91-632, July 1991.

[15] R. S. Nikhil and Arvind. "Can Dataflow subsume Von Neumann Computing?", *Proc. 16th Annual Intl. Symp. on Comp. Arch.*, May 1989.

[16] P. Nuth and W. Dally. "A Mechanism for Efficient Context Switching", *Proc. IEEE Conf. on Computer Design*, October 1991.

[17] D. Patterson. "Reduced Instruction Set Computers", *Communications of the ACM*, January 1985.

[18] D. Patterson and J. Hennessy. *Computer Architecture: A Quantitative Approach*, Morgan Kaufmann, 1990.

[19] R. H. Saavedra-Barrera, D. E. Culler, and T. von Eicken. "Analysis of Multithreaded Architectures for Parallel Computing", *ACM Symp. on Parallel Algorithms and Architecture*, July 1990.

[20] V. Soundararajan. *Dribble-Back Registers: A Technique for Latency Tolerance in Multiprocessors*, Bachelor's thesis, MIT, 1992. Supervised by A. Agarwal.

[21] B. J. Smith. "A Pipelined, Shared Resource MIMD Computer", *Proc. Intl. Conf. on Parallel Processing*, 1978.

[22] M. R. Thistle and B. J. Smith. "A Processor Architecture for Horizon", *Proc. Supercomputing '88*, November, 1988.

[23] D. W. Wall. "Global Register Allocation at Link Time", *Proc. ACM SIGPLAN '86 Symp. on Compiler Construction*, 1986.

[24] C. A. Waldspurger and W. E. Weihl. "Register Relocation: Flexible Contexts for Multithreading", Tech. Rep., MIT Lab. for Comp. Sci. (to appear).

[25] W. D. Weber and A. Gupta. "Exploring the Benefits of Multiple Hardware Contexts in a Multiprocessor Architecture: Preliminary Results", *Proc. 16th Annual Intl. Symp. on Comp. Arch.*, June 1989.

A Context Allocation Code

```
/*
 * AllocMap is an allocation bitmap, represented by
 * a 32-bit integer. Each bit represents a 'chunk' of
 * 4 contiguous registers in a register file with 128
 * general registers. A set bit (1) denotes an unused
 * chunk; an unset bit (0) denotes a used chunk.
 *
 */
int AllocMap;

void ContextDealloc(Thread *t)
{
  /* Update bitmap to reclaim thread context. */
  AllocMap |= t->allocMask;
}

int ContextAlloc64(Thread *t)
{
  /*
   * Attempt to allocate a context for thread t
   * with 64 registers (16 'chunks'). Uses linear
   * search. Returns SUCCESS or FAILURE.
   *
   */
  int tempMap;

  /* check low-order halfword */
  tempMap = AllocMap & 0xffff;
  if (tempMap == 0xffff)
    {
      /* success: update bitmap, thread state */
      AllocMap &= ~tempMap;
      t->rrm = 0;
      t->allocMask = 0xffff;
      return(SUCCESS);
    }

  /* check high-order halfword */
  tempMap = AllocMap >> 16;
  if (tempMap == 0xffff)
    {
      /* success: update bitmap, thread state */
      AllocMap &= 0xffff;
      t->rrm = (16 << 2);
      t->allocMask = (0xffff << 16);
      return(SUCCESS);
    }

  /* fail: unable to alloc context */
  return(FAILURE);
}
```

```
int ContextAlloc16(Thread *t)
{
  /*
   * Attempt to allocate a context for thread t
   * with 16 registers (4 'chunks'). Uses binary
   * search. Returns SUCCESS or FAILURE.
   *
   */
  int rrm, tempMap;

  /*
   * Construct bitmap for blocks of chunks.
   * Use bit-parallel prefix scan. Combine to form
   * map of size-2 blocks, then map of size-4 blocks.
   * Then mask out irrelevant unaligned bits.
   *
   */

  tempMap  = AllocMap & (AllocMap >> 1);
  tempMap &= tempMap >> 2;
  tempMap &= 0x11111111;

  /* fail quickly if unable to alloc context */
  if (tempMap == 0)
    return(FAILURE);

  /*
   * Search bitmap for free block of chunks, setting
   * the rrm. Use binary search. First choose a 16-bit
   * block with an unused chunk, then an 8-bit block,
   * and finally a 4-bit block. A 'find first bit'
   * instruction could eliminate most of this code.
   *
   */

  rrm = 0;
  if ((tempMap & 0xffff) == 0)
    { rrm |= 16; tempMap >>= 16; }
  if ((tempMap & 0x00ff) == 0)
    { rrm |=  8; tempMap >>=  8; }
  if ((tempMap & 0x000f) == 0)
    { rrm |=  4; }

  /* success: update bitmap, thread state */
  tempMap = 0x000f << rrm;
  AllocMap &= ~tempMap;
  t->rrm = (rrm << 2);
  t->allocMask = tempMap;
  return(SUCCESS);
}
```

Multiple Threads in Cyclic Register Windows

Yasuo Hidaka   Hanpei Koike   Hidehiko Tanaka

Department of Electrical Engineering, The University of Tokyo
7-3-1 Hongo, Bunkyo-ku, Tokyo 113 Japan
E-mail : {hidaka,koike,tanaka}@mtl.t.u-tokyo.ac.jp

Abstract

Multi-threading is often used to compile logic and functional languages, and implement parallel C libraries. Fine-grain multi-threading requires rapid context switching, which can be slow on architectures with register windows. In past, researchers have either proposed new hardware support for dynamic allocation of windows to threads, or have sacrificed fast procedure calls by fixed allocation of windows to threads.

In this paper, a novel window management algorithm, which retains both fast procedure calls and fast context switching, is proposed. The algorithm has been implemented on the SPARC processor by modifying window trap handlers. A quantitative evaluation of the scheme using a multi-threaded application with various concurrency and granularity levels is given. The evaluation shows that the proposed scheme always does better than the other schemes. Some implications for multi-threaded architectures are also presented.

1 Introduction

Overlapping register windows have been incorporated into RISC architectures[9] to speed up procedure calls by reducing the number of register saves and restores. While register windows have proven quite effective in improving the sequential program performance, it has resulted in lengthening context switching time. Slow context switching is usually quite detrimental to the performance of multi-threaded applications, which are becoming increasingly important. For instance, distributed operating systems, object-oriented programming languages, functional and logic languages, all demand good multi-threading performance[2]. Furthermore, good multi-threading performance is essential for medium-grained and fine-grained parallel machines.

In this paper, a novel algorithm for managing register windows is proposed. It enables both *fast context switching* by sharing windows among threads, and *fast procedure calls* by allowing multiple windows to be used by a thread. Since the algorithm relies on cyclic window allocation, there is no need of special hardware support for dynamic window allocation. A key to the algorithm is the treatment of *window underflow trap*, which occurs on a procedure return when the caller's window has been spilt into memory. In the conventional algorithm, the caller's window is restored into the same place where the window resided before being spilt. If windows were to be allocated among several threads, the conventional algorithm would not work as is discussed in Section 3.

In our algorithm, the caller's window is restored in the same place that the *callee* had used. This always works because the caller's window is needed only when the callee terminates and thus, the callee's window is no longer needed. This simple idea avoids all the problems of window sharing in the conventional algorithm. Thus, it becomes possible to share simple cyclic register windows among several threads, and fast context switching is attained without totally sacrificing fast procedure calls.

Though the idea is quite simple, we have not seen any publications on this algorithm. In fact, SunOS on SPARC does not use this algorithm[6], and most researchers believe that overlapping register windows have lengthy context switching[2, 5, 10, 16]. In the following, we briefly discuss some published techniques for implementing multi-threading.

Cypress Semiconductor Co. have suggested a technique in their user's guide[12] for fast context switching for register windows. Agarwal et al. have used this technique in the implementation of APRIL[1]. In this method, one window is statically assigned to each thread. Though it enables fast context switching, the advantage of fast procedure calls is lost, because each thread can use only the assigned window.

Quammen, Kearns and Soffa have suggested another way to share register windows among multiple

131

threads. They use register windows to hold temporary values in expression evaluation in a single stack for all the threads[11]. However, activation records of procedures are not held in registers, and thus, windows are not used to speed up procedure calls.

In the MASA architecture, proposed by Halstead and Fujita, *task frames* are provided for fast context switching, fast procedure calls and fast trap handling[4]. Task frames are non-overlapped multiple register sets, and a task can access at most three task frames – that of the current task, its child and its parent tasks. However, task frames are dynamically allocated for each task by sophisticated hardware.

Threaded windows proposed by Quammen and Miller are non-overlapping windows, which can be used in various manners, e.g. a register window-stack, a single register set, or a dynamically sized global area[10]. Though multiple threads can share threaded windows, sophisticated hardware is needed for dynamic window allocation.

Thus, all these approaches are quite different from ours. Namely, some researchers sacrifice the advantage of fast procedure calls for the sake of static window allocation for fast context switching, and the others require special hardware support for dynamic window allocation. Our algorithm maintains the advantage of fast procedure calls, without dynamic window allocation. In fact, we have implemented it on SPARC[3] which has simple cyclic window organization. It is of great benefit, because SPARC is widely used in workstations all over the world, and further, SPARC is already used in many parallel machines, e.g. CM5, EDS[14] and AP1000[13], in which multi-threading performance is especially important.

An implementation of the algorithm, and its evaluation are described in this paper. The evaluation was done quantitatively using real hardware, and a real multi-threaded application program with controllable concurrency and granularity levels. The evaluation was done also for various number of windows under fair scheduling and adaptive scheduling. Under adaptive scheduling, the proposed scheme works well even for a small number of windows.

The paper is organized as follows: Section 2 describes a basic management algorithm of register windows. In Section 3, problems in sharing windows among threads using the conventional window management algorithm, along with a solution, are presented. Section 4 discusses variations of the proposed algorithm, and Section 5 gives a discussion of the program behaviors which should be taken into account in the evaluation. The evaluation of the scheme is de-

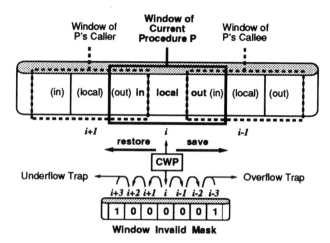

Figure 1: Organization of register windows of SPARC. The currently used window is indicated by CWP, which is changed by save and restore instructions. WIM is used to detect *window overflow* and *underflow*.

scribed in Section 6, and conclusions are presented in Section 7.

2 Basic register window management

Overlapping register windows were first introduced by Berkeley RISC machines[9], and then they were incorporated in the SPARC architecture[3]. Since our method was developed for SPARC, the terminology of SPARC is used in the paper. However, the proposed algorithm should be applicable to other processors with register windows.

Figure 1 shows the organization of the register windows of SPARC. The Current Window Pointer (CWP) indicates the window of the current procedure, which consists of three parts; 1) eight **in** registers shared with the caller (the parent procedure), 2) eight **out** registers shared with a callee (a child procedure), and 3) eight **local** registers which are private to the current procedure. **Save** and restore instructions are provided to change the CWP. On procedure entry, a **save** instruction is executed, which decreases CWP by one. Similarly the restore instruction on a procedure return increases CWP by one. In this paper, we regard window *i-1* as being *above* window *i*, and window *i+1* as being *below* window *i*.

Since the number of the windows on a processor is limited, only some contiguous windows near the stack top are held in the processor, and the rest of the stack is saved in memory (see **Figure 2**). The two ends of the contiguous windows in the processor are called *stack-top* window and *stack-bottom* window in this paper. The window buffer is managed in a cyclic manner

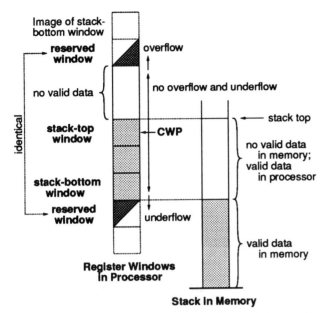

Figure 2: Mapping of stack onto register windows. At least one window has to be reserved to detect *window overflow* and *underflow*.

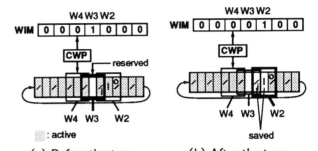

(a) Before the trap.   (b) After the trap.

Figure 3: An *overflow trap*. W4 is the current window. The trap occurs because W3 has been reserved. The **in** and **local** registers in W2 are saved, and W2 becomes the new reserved window.

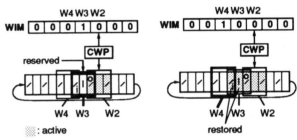

(a) Before the trap.   (b) After the trap.

Figure 4: An *underflow trap*. W2 is the current window. The trap occurs because W3 has been reserved. The **in** and **local** registers in W3 are restored, and W4 becomes the new reserved window.

with the help of a *reserved* window, which indicates the limit of growth for the stack-top window. Window Invalid Mask (WIM) register shows whether each window is reserved or not. If the **save** instruction encounters a reserved window, an *overflow trap* occurs, and the trap handler saves some windows "above" the reserved window in the memory. Similarly, if a **restore** instruction encounters a reserved window, an *underflow trap* occurs, and the trap handler restores some windows from the memory. Tamir and Sequin studied the effect of the number of windows to be saved or restored for each *overflow* or *underflow trap*, and showed that transferring one window is the best in most cases[15].

Figure 3 shows an example of an *overflow trap*. Since CWP indicates window W4, and the window above is reserved, **save** causes an *overflow trap*. The trap handler saves **in** and **local** registers of window W2 in memory, and makes W2 the reserved window[6]. **Figure 4** shows an example of an *underflow trap*. Since CWP indicates window W2, and the window below is reserved, **restore** causes an *underflow trap*. The trap handler restores **in** and **local** registers of window W3 from memory, and makes W4 the reserved window. In this way, **in** and **local** registers are handled together, and **out** registers are handled as **in** registers in the window above. Since the alias of **in** and **out** makes window borders ambiguous, the term "window" means only **in** and **local** registers in the

following sections and figures, unless the term **out** is explicitly mentioned. While the figures look like non-overlapping windows, actual windows are overlapped.

3 Multiple threads in register windows

3.1 Problems

Figure 5 shows the basic idea of multiple threads in register windows. We may indicate the windows of the currently active thread by setting the corresponding WIM bits to 0, while setting all other WIM bits to 1. In order to minimize extra overhead, it is desirable

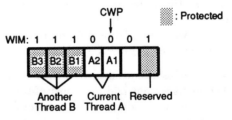

Figure 5: Multiple threads in register windows. Windows of the other threads are protected by setting the corresponding WIM bits to 1.

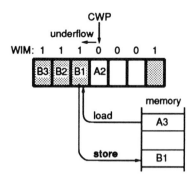

Figure 6: Window spillage on an *underflow trap*. Thread A demands window A3. Restoration of A3 requires saving window B1, which is the stack-top window of thread B.

that all windows of a thread be contiguous, and represent the top fraction of the real stack of the thread. The basic window management algorithm needs to be modified to solve the following problems:

1. In the basic window management algorithm, window spillage can occur only on an *overflow trap*. However, if windows belonging to other threads were allowed, it could also occur on an *underflow trap*. That is, it might be required to save *another* thread's window before restoring the missing window of the current thread (see **Figure 6**).

2. In **Figure 6**, an *underflow trap* from thread A would cause the stack-top window of thread B to spill. Accordingly, windows of thread B would be no longer the top fraction of the real stack of thread B. However, since any thread demands its stack-top window first, and its stack-bottom window last, it is much more desirable to spill windows from the stack-bottom than the stack-top.

3. If windows were spilt from the stack-top window, windows of the thread may become non-contiguous, complicating context switching and trap handling. As an example of this, consider switching from thread A to B in **Figure 7 (a)**. The stack-top window B1 would have to be restored in the same place as A3, because of the relative position of window B1 to B3. As can be seen, the windows of thread A and B are no longer contiguous (see **Figure 7 (b)**).

These problems would involve awful complications in window management and lose most of the benefits of sharing windows among threads. A notable point is that all the above problems are caused by window spillage at *underflow traps*; there is no such problem for *overflow traps*. While a window spilt by an

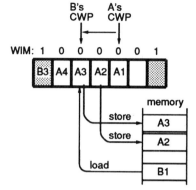

(a) Context switching from thread A to B.

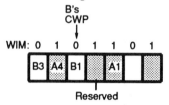

(b) After context switching.

Figure 7: Complicated context switching, and scattered windows. The stack-top window B1 would have to be restored in the same place as A3. The windows of thread A and B are no longer contiguous.

overflow trap may be another thread's window, there is no significant change in the window management, because the spillage is always from the stack-bottom window. Hence, if *underflow traps* could be handled without any window spillage, all the above problems may disappear.

3.2 Solution

Though *overflow* and *underflow* are handled symmetrically in the basic management algorithm, is this symmetry necessary? Suppose on an *underflow trap*, the missing window is restored in the same place as the current window (see **Figure 8**). This will involve the extra work of copying the active **in** registers of the current window (W3) into the **out** registers (into the **in** registers of W2), before the missing window can be restored. Though the current window does not physically move between before and after **restore**, it virtually goes back to the window below. In this way, window spillage is no longer needed at *underflow traps*, and all the problems mentioned earlier are successfully solved.

It should be noted that not all **in** registers of A2 need to be copied. The registers to be copied are usually only the values returned from the procedure, and the stack pointer. However, partial copying changes

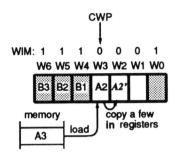

Figure 8: *Underflow trap* handling without any window spillage. Window A3 can be restored in W3, because most registers in A2 are no longer needed.

the semantics of the `restore` instruction. If other features of `restore` are used by the compiler, it may be necessary to copy all the **in** registers. Still the overhead is small.

4 Variations of the algorithm

The above description of the algorithm is not complete, because there are still several choices left to be made regarding reserved windows, window allocation and thread scheduling. We discuss these issues next.

4.1 With or without private reserved windows (PRW)

The proposed algorithm has two possibilities for the reserved window as shown in **Figure 9**; whether there is only one reserved window, or each thread keeps its own private reserved window (PRW).

Remember that actual windows are overlapped and **out** registers of the stack-top window may be held in the reserved window. In Figures 5 through 8, it was assumed that there is only one reserved window. Since the current thread must have a reserved window on the top, some extra work is required at the time of context switching. Suppose we want to switch to thread B in **Figure 9 (a)**. Window A2, the stack-bottom window of thread A, must be spilt into memory to make it into a reserved window for thread B. Also **out** registers of the stack-top window always have to be saved and restored on context switches.

On the other hand, if each thread keeps its own PRW as shown in **Figure 9 (b)**, **out** registers of the stack-top window need not be saved and restored on context switches. Furthermore, switching to another thread already resident in the windows never causes any window transfer. A minor technical point is that, on a context switch, if the suspended thread has some free windows above the stack-top, the PRW of the suspended thread is moved immediately above the stack-

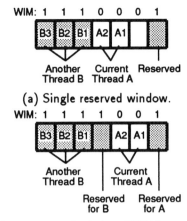

(a) Single reserved window.

(b) Private reserved window (PRW) per thread.
Figure 9: Alternative algorithm.

top. However, since the reserved window has no information to be copied, there is no overhead in doing so.

Since extra space is required to keep PRW for every thread, the rate of window spillage would potentially increase. Moreover, if a scheduled thread has no windows, two windows may have to be saved to allocate one for the new stack-top window, and another one for the new PRW. In the former scheme without PRW, only one window may have to be saved, because the old reserved window is available.

Both schemes are evaluated in later sections.

4.2 Window allocation

When a scheduled thread has no windows on a context switch, two windows have to be allocated. A simple allocation scheme is to allocate windows above the suspended-thread's windows. However, if it is used in conjunction with the scheme without PRW, one can imagine an undesirable case. Suppose a context switch occurs from thread A to thread B, and B does not have a window. B's window will be allocated above A's windows. Then, B immediately suspends without any procedure calls, and A is scheduled again. In order to make space for the reserved window of A, B's window will be spilt into memory. If there is repeated switching between threads A and B, this process may repeat itself causing unnecessary spillage and restoration.

It may be worth the extra cost to search for a free window, or to select the least-recently-used stack-bottom window when all windows are in use. Another concern is that there is external fragmentation of free windows. In our evaluations, we have only considered the simple allocation scheme.

4.3 Semantics of restore instruction

If only a few **in** registers are copied on an *underflow trap*, semantics of **restore** may be changed. However, even if all **in** registers are copied, there is still a potential problem, because the **restore** instruction on SPARC also acts as a kind of **add** instruction. Compilers often use this feature in a peephole optimization; if the instruction immediately before the **restore** instruction is an **add**, **sub**, or **move** instruction to set the return value in the particular register, that instruction and the **restore** instruction can be replaced by a single **restore** instruction which also performs the calculation.

There are two solutions for this problem. One is not to do the peephole optimization. In this way, one extra instruction may be occasionally added at the end of a procedure. The other solution is to interpret and emulate the trapped **restore** instruction by the *underflow trap* handler. This can be done with a small overhead, because the instruction format is simple and the destination register is either the particular return-value register if the adding function is used, or the zero register if it is not used. We used this emulation technique in our implementation.

4.4 Two types of context switching

If a suspended thread is known to sleep for a long time, it is sometimes more efficient to flush all the windows of the suspended thread. This is so because flushing a window at the time of context switch is cheaper than causing an *overflow trap* to save the window, that is, the overhead of entering and leaving the trap handler can be avoided.

Even if the proposed scheme is employed, it is a good idea to provide for both types of context switching; one that leaves windows of the suspended thread in situ, and the other, that completely flushes them. The reason for the suspension of a thread may be helpful in choosing the type of context switching. For instance, if a thread suspends on a cache miss and waits for the completion of a remote memory load, the thread is likely to wake up soon, and it may be better to leave its windows. On the other hand, if a thread suspends for the completion of a disk read, it may be better to flush its windows.

In the following evaluation, it is assumed that all threads are likely to wake up soon, and hence no flushing of windows is done in the sharing scheme.

4.5 Evaluated schemes

We have implemented and evaluated the following three schemes:

NS : Non-sharing scheme
Windows are not shared among threads like the conventional algorithm. All active windows are flushed on a context switch.

SNP : Sharing scheme without PRW
Windows are shared. There is no private reserved window for each thread, but only one reserved window. If the newly-scheduled thread has no windows, the window above the suspended thread's is allocated.

SP : Sharing scheme with PRW
Windows are shared. Each thread has its own private reserved window, which is located immediately above its active windows. If the newly-scheduled thread has no windows, the window above the reserved window of the suspended thread is allocated.

The scheduling is non-preemptive in all the evaluation. Besides, it is first-in-first-out (FIFO) except in the evaluation of the working set concept described below.

4.6 Working set concept on register windows

If there are insufficient number of windows, it is also possible for the sharing schemes to incorporate the working set concept of the virtual memory into register windows[8]. In the virtual memory, multiprogramming level is controlled so that the working set memory of all concurrently active programs fits in the available physical memory. This avoids thrashing.

Similarly in register windows, concurrency level can be controlled so that the working set of windows of all concurrently scheduled threads fits in the available physical windows. It can be done by changing the scheduling policy to give higher priority to the threads whose windows remain on the processor. Thus, the probability of window spillage is reduced, and the probability of fast context switching is increased.

The extra overhead in scheduling can be avoided by selecting threads *only* when a thread is awoken by somebody else. If the thread just awoken still has windows, it is enqueued in front of the ready queue; otherwise, it is enqueued at the back. This can be done with little overhead. Thus, the basic scheduler still remains FIFO, and no additional overhead is added to the time of context switching.

5 Program behavior

Evaluation of almost any aspect of processor architecture requires an understanding of the behaviors of the programs to be run[5]. In this section, we discuss what aspects of program behavior are likely to affect the performance of the proposed window management scheme.

The performance of the proposed scheme depends on how often a scheduled thread finds windows that were allocated to it prior to its suspension. If most windows are often spilt before the thread is scheduled again, the proposed schemes would be ineffective, because saving windows by *overflow traps* is more expensive than flushing them on context switches. This frequency crucially depends upon the total number of windows concurrently used by all threads. Here, we define several terms which concern us:

- **Total window activity:** The number of windows used during a given period, assuming there are infinite number of windows, (that is, assuming there are no window *overflows* and *underflows*). A repeatedly-used window is counted as one.

- **Window activity per thread:** The number of windows used between two successive context switches, assuming there are infinite number of windows. A repeatedly-used window is counted as one.

- **Concurrency:** The number of threads which are concurrently scheduled, at least once, during a given period. A repeatedly-scheduled thread is counted as one.

- **Granularity:** Execution run length between two successive context switches. The shorter the run length, the finer the granularity.

- **Parallel slackness:** The number of threads available for execution at a given time, excepting currently executed threads. (Length of the ready queue.)

Efficiency of the proposed scheme is directly affected by the *total window activity*; if it is smaller than the number of physical windows, the proposed scheme works well. Therefore, it is important to understand the *total window activity* of a given application, and how it is affected by other characteristics.

Total window activity is the product of *window activity per thread* and *concurrency*. The *window activity per thread* varies according to *granularity*. As the *granularity* becomes finer, the *window activity per thread* will decrease, and the *total window activity* will decrease, provided the *concurrency* is unchanged.

Concurrency is determined primarily by the characteristics of applications, but it also varies according to the scheduling policy. As an example, suppose threads are divided into two groups according to some criterion, and threads in different groups are scheduled in disjoint periods. Then, the *concurrency* will be less than that in the FIFO scheduling. The *total window activity* will also decrease, provided the *window activity per thread* is unchanged. In the working set concept, the scheduling policy reduces *concurrency* so as to make *total window activity* below the number of physical windows.

Parallel slackness represents how much leeway scheduling policy has in controlling *concurrency*. If the *parallel slackness* is always zero or one, the execution order of the threads is completely deterministic, regardless of scheduling policy; the working set concept will not work. On the contrary, if the *parallel slackness* is high, the scheduling policy can reduce *concurrency*, choosing a desirable thread at the time. Thus, higher *parallel slackness* is better for the working set concept.

The *granularity* greatly affects the frequency of context switching, and thus, has first order influence on performance. But it does not directly affect whether the proposed scheme works well or not. However, it does have an indirect effect on the success of the scheme through *window activity per thread* and *concurrency*.

Next, we will show how we generated various *granularity* and *concurrency* levels from a single application program. The application has realistic *window activity*, and this activity varies according to the *concurrency* and *granularity*. The application also has sufficient *parallel slackness*. The evaluation was done on a single processor, since the scheduling effects are difficult to understand on a parallel machine.

5.1 The application program: a multi-threaded spell checker

We used a spell checker for LaTeX source files as our application program. It is a multi-threaded version of the spell checker commonly used on UNIX systems. A draft version of this paper was used as the input in the evaluation. The draft used was 40500 bytes long.

Figure 10 shows the basic organization of the program. T1 through T7 are threads, and S1 through S6 are streams. T1 through T3 behave like UNIX filters, and constitute the main part of the program. T1 removes LaTeX commands from the input, and makes each line have just one word. T2 and T3 are spell-check threads. T3 filters out correct words, and feeds incorrect words to T5, taking account of derivatives of words in the dictionary. T2 picks up and feeds incorrect derivatives to T5, and feeds other words to T3; otherwise, those derivatives would be filtered out as correct words by T3.

File input and output are *simulated* by T4 through T7. These threads, instead of actually reading (writing) disks, merely copy data from (to) their internal memory buffers into (from) the stream. These threads correspond to OS kernel threads, and their internal buffers correspond to disk cache.

T1 is written in lex (lexical analyzer generator) on UNIX, and the rest of the program is written in C. There are two primary differences in our program from the UNIX version; UNIX one has "deroff" for roff files instead of T1, and there is "sort -u" between T1 and T2 to reject duplicates of words. We omitted sort, because it accumulates the whole input, and it will be an obstacle to the concurrent execution of threads. However, the spell-checking algorithm is similar to the UNIX version. The *window activity* depends on the input, which has highly irregular patterns. Such *window activity* is much more complex and realistic than that of simple artificial benchmarks.

Each stream is FIFO, and is organized as a cyclic buffer. The buffers of S1 and S4 through S6 are each M bytes long, and those of S2 and S3 are each N bytes long. Since the scheduling is non-preemptive, a thread execution continues until an input (output) buffer becomes empty (full). Thus, there is usually more than one thread available for scheduling, and *parallel slackness* is sufficient.

Granularity and *concurrency* of the program can be changed as follows:

- **Granularity can be changed by the absolute value of M and N.**

- **Concurrency can be changed by the relative value of M and N.**

The *granularity* of a thread is determined by the size of the smallest input or output buffer related to the thread; the smaller the size, the finer the *granularity*. Besides, the overall *granularity* is determined by the smaller value of M and N.

If M and N are equal and rather small, many threads will be scheduled concurrently, and contribute to the *concurrency*. Thus, the *concurrency* will be *high*.

On the other hand, suppose M is much bigger than N, and N has a rather small value. T4 through T7 will have greater *granularity* and less frequent context switches than T1 through T3. Under such as-

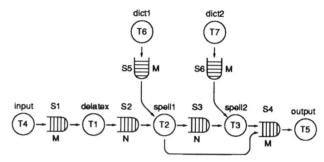

Figure 10: Organization of the application program. Threads are connected by streams. Each stream has an M or N bytes long buffer.

sumptions, the *concurrency* during execution of T4 through T7 will be almost one, and only T1 through T3 will contribute to the *concurrency*. Accordingly, the *concurrency* will be *low*.

In this way, relative value of M and N provide a good way to control the *concurrency* in this application.

5.2 Evaluated program behavior

We have evaluated six kinds of behavior. Though it is difficult to show *concurrency* and *granularity* directly, one can realize them somewhat from **Table 1**. The reason of showing these numbers is that they are completely independent of the window management schemes and the number of physical windows, provided the scheduling is FIFO. Besides, the dynamic count of **save** instructions is independent of the buffer size and scheduling strategy, i.e. there are always the same number of function calls.

It is rather easy to understand *granularity*; the more the context switches, the finer the *granularity*. To understand *concurrency*, some consideration has to be given to the execution phases of the program; not all threads can be active in all phases due to various dependencies. Execution of the spell checker consists of two phases: reading the dictionaries and doing the spell check. During the first phase, the *concurrency* can be varied from a high value of four (all of T2, T3, T6 and T7) to the low value of one (one of T2, T3, T6 and T7). During the second phase, the high *concurrency* is between four and five (T1 through T4 and occasionally T5), and the low case is between three and four (T1 through T3 and occasionally T4 and T5).

It should be noticed that the change in *granularity* and *concurrency* are not completely independent. The *concurrency* is rather constant for different *granularity*, except in the second phase of the computation,

Table 1: Controlling *granularity* and *concurrency* by buffer sizes.

Program behavior							Dynamic count of
Concurrency	high			low			
Granularity	fine	medium	coarse	fine	medium	coarse	
Buffer size (bytes)							
M	1	4	16	1024	1024	1024	
N	1	4	16	1	4	16	
Number of context switches (FIFO scheduling)							Dynamic count of save instructions
T1 (delatex)	60566	12680	2653	29838	8925	2001	113015
T2 (spell1)	102447	23497	5400	49952	9983	2049	110740
T3 (spell2)	80578	21327	5400	29887	8791	2049	75526
T4 (input)	40501	11548	2653	4817	4612	1974	10127
T5 (output)	1005	314	146	197	196	135	262
T6 (dict1)	50001	12501	3126	49	49	49	12502
T7 (dict2)	50001	12501	3126	49	49	49	12502
Total	385099	94368	22504	114789	32605	8306	334674

when the buffers are set for low *concurrency*. There finer *granularity* results in lower *concurrency*. However, the *granularity* is not constant for different *concurrency*. Therefore, care must be taken in comparing such cases.

When the working set concept is incorporated, the number of context switches is still within ±10% of the numbers in Table 1. Thus, the change in the *granularity* is also within ±10%. We have not measured the *concurrency* directly, because it is difficult to determine adequate length for a measurement period, which in turn depends on the *granularity*. However, the following result will show that the *concurrency* was definitely reduced in comparison with the FIFO scheduling.

6 Evaluation

6.1 Environment

Since implementing the window management schemes involves modification to trap handlers, it is difficult to evaluate them on a SPARC-based Unix system without deep understanding of the operating system. Fortunately, we are developing a parallel computer, PIE64[7], in which each processing element has a version of SPARC, S-20 made by Fujitsu. Therefore, this evaluation was done on a processing element of PIE64. As an aside, the algorithm described in this paper was discovered while developing a multi-tasking monitor for PIE64!

In order to evaluate performance at various numbers of physical windows, we have also developed a register window emulator. In this emulator, usual instructions are executed at real speed, but instructions

which concern windows are trapped and emulated. A cycle counter for measurement is stopped during the emulation, so that the exact result is obtained.

6.2 Number of cycles for a context switch

Before showing performance evaluation, we begin with the number of cycles for a context switch in each scheme. While this measurement is rather static one, it is not merely instruction counts, but takes account of all cycles on S-20; i.e. cycles for instruction fetch, data transfer, pipeline stall, and pipeline flush. It was done by monitoring SPARC's bus traffic with a dedicated logic analyzer of PIE64.

Table 2 shows the result. The number of windows transferred on a context switch is dependent on the scheme and the situation of windows at the time. In addition to the window transfer, there is other overhead such as calculation of the WIM and scheduling, because everything is implemented in software.

In the NS scheme, as the number of active windows increases, the cost grows substantially high. Besides, even in the best case, two windows have to be transferred. Furthermore, the cost is terrible in the worst case, in which all windows except a reserved one have to be saved; this is an undesirable characteristic in hard real time systems.

The NS scheme has also hidden overhead of *underflow traps*; if two or more windows are saved at a context switch, some of the saved windows will have to be restored by *underflow traps*. (More precisely the stack-top window is restored on the context switch.)

On the contrary, the sharing schemes take less cycles in many cases than the NS scheme. In the best case, no windows have to be transferred. Though there

Table 2: Number of cycles for a context switch.

Scheme	Window Transfer		Cycles
	save	restore	
NS	1	1	145 - 149
	2	1	181 - 185
	3	1	217 - 221
	4	1	253 - 257
	5	1	289 - 293
	6	1	325 - 329
	...	...	...
SNP	0	0	113 - 118
	0	1	142 - 147
	1	0	162 - 171
	1	1	187 - 196
SP	0	0	93 - 98
	0	1	136 - 141
	1	1	180 - 197
	2	1	220 - 237

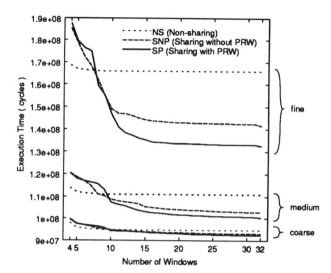

Figure 11: Performance at *high concurrency*. With sufficient number of windows, SP is best. *Total window activity* varies according to *granularity*.

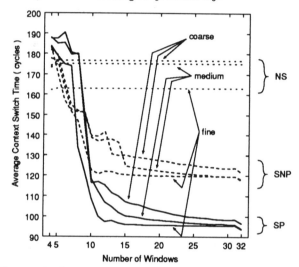

Figure 12: Average context switch time at *high concurrency*. With sufficient number of windows, the result of SP and SNP is very close to the best case (see Table 2).

is still software overhead in the best case, it will be reduced to zero or a few cycles, if the proposed algorithm is implemented in multi-threaded architecture.

The SP scheme takes less cycles in the best case than the SNP scheme, because **out** registers in the stack-top window and program counters can be held in PRW. However, the SP scheme is more expensive in the worst case than the SNP scheme, because two windows have to be saved in the worst case.

6.3 High-concurrency case

Figure 11 shows performance comparison among the schemes in the *high-concurrency* case. Execution time of each scheme was evaluated for three levels of *granularity* at various numbers of windows. The range of the number of windows was from four to thirty two.

If there are sufficient number of windows, the best scheme is SP, and if the number of windows is small, the NS scheme is best; there is no region where the SNP scheme outperforms both the SP and NS schemes. Besides, as the *granularity* becomes fine, the advantage of the sharing schemes increases.

Variation in *total window activity* is also observed in this figure. Look at the number of windows where the effect of more windows is saturated in the sharing schemes. That number is proportional to the *total window activity*. Thus, as the *granularity* becomes fine, the *total window activity* decreases.

Figure 12 shows average time of a context switch in the *high-concurrency* case. Compare this figure with Table 2. If there are sufficient number of windows, context switch time of the SP and SNP schemes, is very close to the best case, especially in the fine

granularity. It means most context switches are done without any window transfer.

This fact is very important to multi-threaded architecture. Since such frequency of the best case is independent of the implementation, this fact suggests that multi-threaded architecture with the proposed algorithm will have excellent multi-threading performance.

Figure 13 is the probability of *window overflow* and *underflow traps*. Since the number of function calls is constant, it shows that the SP and SNP scheme is also very effective for fast procedure calls with sufficient number of windows.

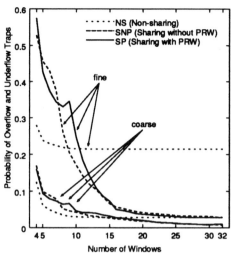

Figure 13: Probability of *window traps* at *high concurrency*. The number of *window overflow* and *underflow traps* divided with the number of executed **save** and **restore** instructions.

6.4 Low-concurrency case

Figure 14 is the performance comparison in the *low-concurrency* case. The SNP scheme has strange behavior at fine *granularity*. It is probably caused by the undesirable effect of the simple window allocation mentioned before, because the order of threads in windows is affected by the number of windows. The variation in *total window activity* is greater than the *high-concurrency* case, and 20 or more windows are required for the SP scheme at the coarse *granularity*.

Thus, *total window activity* greatly varies according to *granularity* and *concurrency*. Though the variation in *concurrency* is rather small in this evaluation, it is natural to imagine that other programs have quite-different *concurrency*, and hence, quite-different *total window activity*. Therefore, unless the working set concept is incorporated, the proposed scheme works well only for applications whose *total window activity* is low enough for the number of available physical windows.

6.5 Working set concept on register windows

Figure 15 is the performance comparison when the working set concept is incorporated into the *high-concurrency* case. The performance at a small number of windows is much improved, and the sharing schemes work well with even seven or eight windows. Besides, there is no significant performance loss from the FIFO scheduling at a large number of windows.

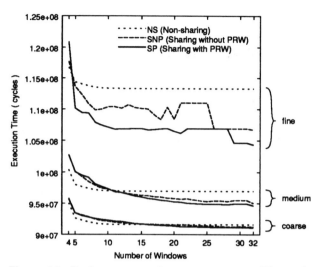

Figure 14: Performance at *low concurrency*. The variation in *total window activity* is greater than the *high-concurrency* case. 20 or more windows are required for SP at *coarse granularity*.

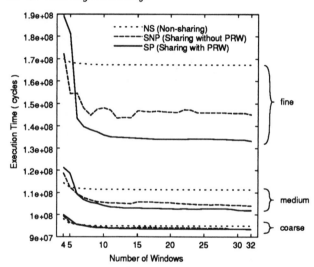

Figure 15: Performance at *high concurrency* with the working set concept. *Total window activity* is reduced to the number of available windows unless the available windows are extremely limited.

The fact that the sharing schemes do not work well at four or five windows means that the scheduling cannot reduce the *total window activity* to such low level. If an application program has little *parallel slackness* but high *concurrency*, this lower limit of *total window activity* will be high. In order to deal with such applications, *it is worth having as many windows as possible*.

However, a reason for lack of *parallel slackness* is bad program design; too much invocation of threads which cannot be executed in parallel actually. For such an application, it may be possible to rewrite the program to have lower *concurrency* and lower *total window activity*. Thus, the sharing scheme with private reserved windows together with the working set concept always works well.

7 Conclusion

A new management algorithm of cyclic register windows was described. It enabled multiple threads to share windows, and improved multi-threading performance by converting the drawback of lots of registers to a benefit. If the working set concept is incorporated in register windows, *the proposed scheme always works well*.

The following are the most important implications of our study:

1. The proposed algorithm will improve the performance for a certain class of applications on stock processors which have a small number of windows.

2. Since, according to our algorithm, the advantage of fast procedure calls is not at the expense of lengthy context switching, it is possible to use more register windows profitably. The trade-off in new processor design will be between the advantage of fast context switching and the lengthening of register-access time.

3. The proposed algorithm is also applicable to multi-threaded architecture, where excellent multi-threading performance as well as excellent sequential performance can be obtained without any sophisticated hardware support for dynamic window allocation.

Acknowledgements

We are deeply indebted to Professor Arvind of MIT for his help in writing this paper. We had useful discussions with Mr. Hosaka of Soum Corporation in Japan. We are also thankful to Mrs. Gita Mithal for editing an earlier draft of this paper. This work is supported by Grant-in-Aid for Scientific Research (No.03555071, No.03003891) from the Ministry of Education, Science and Culture. One of the authors, Hidaka, is supported by JSPS Fellowships for Japanese Junior Scientists.

References

[1] A. Agarwal, B. H. Lim, D. Kranz, and J. Kubiatowicz, "APRIL: A Processor Architecture for Multiprocessing," *Proc. of 17th Annual Intl. Symp. on Comp. Arch.*, pp. 104-114, 1990.

[2] T. E. Anderson, H. M. Levy, B. N. Bershad, and E. D. Lazowska, "The Interaction of Architecture and Operating System Design," *Proc. of ASPLOS-IV*, pp. 108-120, 1991.

[3] R. B. Garner, et al., "The Scalable Processor Architecture (SPARC)," *Proc. of COMPCON88*, pp. 278-283, 1988.

[4] R. H. Halstead and T. Fujita, "MASA: A Multi-threaded Processor Architecture for Parallel Symbolic Computing," *Proc. of 15th Annual Intl. Symp. on Comp. Arch.*, pp. 443-451, 1988.

[5] J. L. Hennessy and D. A. Patterson, *Computer Architecture : A Quantitative Approach*, Morgan Kaufmann Publishers, 1990.

[6] S. R. Kleiman and D. Williams, "SunOS on SPARC," *Proc. of COMPCON88*, pp. 289-293, 1988.

[7] H. Koike and H. Tanaka, "Overview of the Parallel Inference Engine: PIE64," *Annual Report of Engineering Research Institute*, Faculty of Eng., Univ. of Tokyo, Vol.48, pp. 63-68, 1990.

[8] M. Maekawa, A. Oldehoeft, and R. Oldehoeft, *Operating Systems – Advanced Concepts*, The Benjamin/Cummings Publishing Co., Inc., 1987.

[9] D. A. Patterson and C. H. Sequin, "RISC I: A Reduced Instruction Set VLSI Computer," *Proc. of 8th Annual Intl. Symp. on Comp. Arch.*, pp. 443-457, 1981.

[10] D. J. Quammen and D. R. Miller, "Flexible Register Management for Sequential Programs," *Proc. of 18th Annual Intl. Symp. on Comp. Arch.*, pp. 320-329, 1991.

[11] D. Quammen, J. P. Kearns, and M. L. Soffa, "Efficient Storage Management for Temporary Values in Concurrent Programming Languages," *Trans. on Comp.*, Vol.C-34, No.9, pp. 832-840, 1985.

[12] ROSS Technology, Inc., *SPARC RISC USER'S GUIDE, 2nd Edition*, Cypress Semiconductor Corporation, 1990.

[13] T. Shimizu, et al., "Low-Latency Message Communication Support for the AP1000," *Proc. of 19th Annual Intl. Symp. on Comp. Arch.*, pp.288-297, 1992.

[14] C. J. Skelton, et al., "EDS: A Parallel Computer System for Advanced Information Processing," *Proc. of the 4th International PARLE Conference*, LNCS 605, Springer-Verlag, pp. 3-18, 1992.

[15] Y. Tamir and C. H. Sequin, "Strategies for Managing the Register File in RISC," *Trans. on Comp.*, Vol.C-32, No.11, pp. 977-988, 1983.

[16] M. Weiser, A. Demers, and C. Hauser, "The Portable Common Runtime Approach to Interoperability," *Proc. of the Twelfth ACM Symposium on Operating Systems Principles*, pp. 114-122, 1989.

SESSION 8:

Mechanisms for Creating Shared Memory

Evaluation of Release Consistent Software Distributed Shared Memory on Emerging Network Technology

Sandhya Dwarkadas, Pete Keleher, Alan L. Cox, and Willy Zwaenepoel
Department of Computer Science
Rice University *

Abstract

We evaluate the effect of processor speed, network characteristics, and software overhead on the performance of release-consistent software distributed shared memory. We examine five different protocols for implementing release consistency: eager update, eager invalidate, lazy update, lazy invalidate, and a new protocol called *lazy hybrid*. This lazy hybrid protocol combines the benefits of both lazy update and lazy invalidate.

Our simulations indicate that with the processors and networks that are becoming available, coarse-grained applications such as Jacobi and TSP perform well, more or less independent of the protocol used. Medium-grained applications, such as Water, can achieve good performance, but the choice of protocol is critical. For sixteen processors, the best protocol, lazy hybrid, performed more than three times better than the worst, the eager update. Fine-grained applications such as Cholesky achieve little speedup regardless of the protocol used because of the frequency of synchronization operations and the high latency involved.

While the use of relaxed memory models, lazy implementations, and multiple-writer protocols has reduced the impact of false sharing, synchronization latency remains a serious problem for software distributed shared memory systems. These results suggest that future work on software DSMs should concentrate on reducing the amount of synchronization or its effect.

1 Introduction

Although several models and algorithms for software distributed shared memory (DSM) have been published, performance reports have been relatively rare. The few performance results that have been published consist of measurements of a particular implementation in a particular hardware and software environment [3, 5, 6, 13]. Since the cost of communication is very important to the performance of a DSM, these results are highly sensitive to the implementation of the communication software. Furthermore, the hardware environments of many of these implementations are by now obsolete. Much faster processors are commonplace, and much faster networks are becoming available.

We are focusing on DSMs that support release consistency [9], i.e., where memory is guaranteed to be consistent only following certain synchronization operations. The goals of this paper are two-fold: (1) to gain an understanding of how the performance of release consistent software DSM depends on processor speed, network characteristics, and software overhead, and (2) to compare the performance of several protocols for supporting release consistency in a software DSM.

The evaluation is done by execution-driven simulation [7]. The application programs we use have been written for (hardware) shared memory multiprocessors. Our results may therefore be viewed as an indication of the possibility of "porting" shared memory programs to software DSMs, but it should be recognized that better results may be obtained by tuning the programs to a DSM environment. The application programs are Jacobi, Traveling Salesman Problem (TSP), and Water and Cholesky from the SPLASH benchmark suite [14]. Jacobi and TSP exhibit coarse-grained parallelism, with little synchronization relative to the amount of computation, whereas Water may be characterized as medium-grained, and Cholesky as fine-grained.

We find that, with current processors, the bandwidth of the 10-megabit Ethernet becomes a bottleneck, limiting the speedups even for a coarse-grained application such as Jacobi to about 5 on 16 processors. With a 100-megabit point-to-point network, representative of the ATM LANs now appearing on the market, we get good speedups even for small sizes of coarse-grained prob-

*This work was supported in part by NSF Grants CCR-9116343 and CCR-9211004, Texas ATP Grant No. 0036404013 and by a NASA Graduate Fellowship.

lems such as Jacobi and TSP, moderate speedups for Water, and very little speedup for Cholesky. Regardless of the considerable bandwidth available on these networks, Cholesky's performance is constrained by the very high number of synchronization operations.

Among the protocols for implementing software release consistency, we distinguish between *eager* and *lazy* protocols. *Eager* protocols push modifications to all cachers at synchronization variable releases [5]. In contrast, *lazy* protocols [11] pull the modifications at synchronization variable acquires, and communicate only with the acquirer. Both eager and lazy release consistency can be implemented using either invalidate or update protocols. We present a new *lazy hybrid* protocol that combines the benefits of update and invalidate: few access misses, low data and message counts, and low lock acquisition latency.

Our simulations indicate that the lazy algorithm and the hybrid protocol significantly improve the performance of medium-grained programs, those on the boundary of what can be supported efficiently by a software DSM. Communication in coarse-grained programs is sufficiently rare that the choice of protocols becomes less important. The eager algorithms perform slightly better for TSP because the branch-and-bound algorithm benefits from the early updates in the eager protocols (see Section 6.2). For the fine-grained programs, lazy release consistency and the hybrid protocol reduce the number of messages and the amount of data drastically, but the communication requirements are still beyond what can be supported efficiently on a software DSM. For these kinds of applications, techniques such as multithreading and code restructuring may prove useful.

The outline of the rest of this paper is as follows. Section 2 briefly reviews release consistency, and the eager and lazy implementation algorithms. Section 3 describes the hybrid protocol. Section 4 details the implementation of the protocols we simulated. Section 5 discusses our simulation methodology, and Section 6 presents the simulation results. We briefly survey related work in Section 7 and conclude in Section 8.

2 Release Consistency

For completeness, we reiterate in this section the main concepts behind release consistency (RC) [9], eager release consistency (ERC) [5], and lazy release consistency (LRC) [11].

RC [9] is a form of relaxed memory consistency that allows the effects of shared memory accesses to be delayed until selected synchronization accesses occur. Simplifying matters somewhat, shared memory accesses

are labeled either as *ordinary* or as *synchronization* accesses, with the latter category further divided into *acquire* and *release* accesses. Acquires and releases may be thought of as conventional synchronization operations on a lock, but other synchronization mechanisms can be mapped on to this model as well. Essentially, RC requires ordinary shared memory accesses to be performed only when a subsequent release by the same processor is performed. RC implementations can delay the effects of shared memory accesses as long as they meet this constraint.

For instance, the DASH [12] implementation of RC buffers and pipelines writes without blocking the processor. A subsequent release is not allowed to perform (i.e., the corresponding lock cannot be granted to another processor) until acknowledgments have been received for all outstanding invalidations. While this strategy masks latency, in a software implementation it is also important to reduce the *number* of messages sent because of the high per message cost.

In an *eager* software implementation of RC such as Munin's multiple-writer protocol [5], a processor delays propagating its modifications of shared data until it executes a release (see Figures 1 and 2). *Lazy* implementations of RC further delay the propagation of modifications until the acquire. At that time, the last releaser piggybacks a set of *write notices* on the lock grant message sent to the acquirer. These write notices describe the shared data modifications that precede the acquire according to the *happened-before-1* partial order [1]. The *happened-before-1* partial order is essentially the union of the total processor order of the memory accesses on each individual processor and the partial order of release-acquire pairs. The *happened-before-1* partial order can be represented efficiently by tagging write notices with vector timestamps [11]. At acquire time, the acquiring processor determines the pages for which the incoming write notices contain vector timestamps larger than the timestamp of its copy of that page in memory. For those pages, the shared data modifications described in the write notices must be reflected in the acquirer's copy either by invalidating or by updating that copy. The tradeoffs between invalidate and update and a new *hybrid* protocol are discussed in the next section.

3 A Hybrid Protocol for LRC

A lazy invalidate protocol invalidates the local copy of a page for which a write notice with a larger timestamp is received (see Figure 3). The lazy update protocol never invalidates pages to maintain consistency. Instead, acquiring processes retrieve all modifications named by

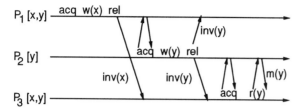

Figure 1 Eager Invalidate

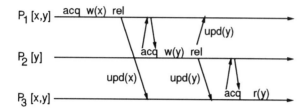

Figure 2 Eager Update

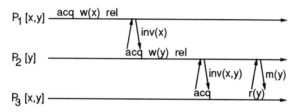

Figure 3 Lazy Invalidate

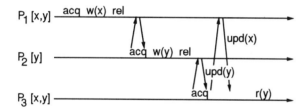

Figure 4 Lazy Update

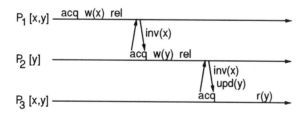

Figure 5 Lazy Hybrid

incoming write notices for any page that is cached locally (see Figure 4). As an optimization, the releaser piggybacks the modifications it has available locally on the lock grant message.

In the lazy *hybrid* protocol, as in the lazy update protocol, the releaser piggybacks on the lock grant message, in addition to write notices, the modifications to those pages that it believes the acquirer has a copy of in its memory. However, unlike in the lazy update protocol, the acquirer does not make any attempt to obtain any other modifications. Instead, it invalidates the pages for which it received write notices but for which no modifications were included in the lock grant message.

Previous simulations [11] indicate that (1) the lazy protocols send fewer messages and less data than the eager protocols, and (2) the lazy update protocol send fewer messages in most cases than the lazy invalidate protocol, while the lazy invalidate protocol sends less data than the lazy update protocol. The reduction in the number of access misses outweighs the extra messages exchanged at the time of synchronization. Also, the reduced access misses result in reduced latency, thus favoring the update protocol.

However, the choice of a lazy or an eager algorithm, and furthermore the choice between an update or an invalidate protocol also affects the lock acquisition latency. We distinguish two cases.

1. The lock request is pending at the time of the release. The lazy invalidate protocol has the shortest lock acquisition latency, since a single message from the releaser to the acquirer suffices, followed by the invalidations at the acquirer, a purely local operation. In contrast, the eager algorithms must update or invalidate all other cachers of pages that have been modified at the releaser, and the lazy update protocol must retrieve all the modifications that precede the acquire, again potentially a multi-host operation.

2. The lock request is not yet pending at the time of the release. The eager algorithms have the lowest lock acquisition latency, followed closely by the lazy invalidate protocol. All require a single message exchange between the releaser and the acquirer, but the lazy invalidate protocol also needs to invalidate any local pages that have been modified. The lazy update protocol potentially requires a multi-host operation, resulting in higher lock acquisition latency.

The lazy hybrid protocol combines the advantages of lazy update and lazy invalidate protocols. First, like the invalidate protocol, the hybrid only exchanges a single pair of messages between the acquiring and the releasing processor. As a result, lock acquisition latency for the lazy hybrid protocol is close to that of the lazy invalidate protocol. The only additional overhead comes from the need to send and process the modifications piggybacked on the lock grant message. Second, the amount of data exchanged is smaller than for the update protocol. Finally, the hybrid sends updates for recently modified pages cached by the acquirer. It is likely that these pages will be accessed by the acquirer, thus reducing the number of access misses, and, as a result, reducing the latency and the number of miss messages.

4 Protocol Implementations

In this section we describe the details of the five protocols that we simulated: lazy hybrid (LH), lazy invalidate (LI), lazy update (LU), eager invalidate (EI), and eager update (EU).

All five are *multiple-writer* protocols. Multiple processors can concurrently write to their own copy of a page with their separate modifications being merged at a subsequent release, in accordance with the RC model. This contrasts with the exclusive-writer protocol used, for instance, in DASH [9], where a processor must obtain exclusive access to a cache line before it can be modified. Experience with Munin [5] indicates that multiple-writer protocols perform well in software DSMs, because they can handle false sharing without generating large amounts of message traffic between synchronization points.

All of the protocols support the use of exclusive locks and global barriers to synchronize access to shared memory. Processors acquire locks by sending a request to the statically assigned owner, who forwards the request on to the current holder of the lock. "Locks" and "unlocks" are mapped onto acquires and releases in a straightforward manner. Barriers are implemented using a *barrier master* that collects arrival messages and distributes departure messages. In terms of consistency information, a barrier arrival is modeled as a release, while a departure is modeled as an acquire on each of the other processors.

Processes exchange three types of information at locks and barriers: synchronization information, consistency information, and data. The consistency information is a collection of *write notices*, each of which contains the processor identification and the vector timestamp of the modification. Consistency information can be piggybacked on synchronization messages, but often the data comprising the modifications to shared memory can not. Most shared data exchanged in the protocols is in the form of *diffs*, which are runlength encodings of the modified data of a single page. Sending diffs instead of entire pages greatly reduces data traffic, and allows multiple concurrent modifications to be merged into a single version.

Each shared page has a unique, statically assigned owner. Each processor keeps an approximate copyset for every shared memory page. The copyset is initialized to the owner's copyset when a page is initially received, and updated according to subsequent write notices and diff requests. The copysets are used in the eager protocols to flush invalidations or updates to all other processors at releases. Since the copyset is only approximate, multiple rounds are sometimes needed to ensure that the consistency information reaches every cacher of the modified pages. The copysets are used by LH to determine which write notices should be accompanied by diffs.

Table 1 summarizes the message counts for locks, barriers, and access misses for each of the protocols. In this table, the *concurrent last modifiers* for a page are the processors that created modifications that do not precede, according to *happened-before-1*, any other known modifications to that page.

4.1 The Eager Protocols

4.1.1 Locks

We base our eager RC algorithms on Munin's multiple-writer protocol [5]. A processor delays propagating its modifications of shared data until it comes to a release. At that time, write notices, together with diffs in the EU protocol, are sent to all other processors that cache the modified pages, possibly taking multiple rounds if the local copysets are not up to date.

A lock release is delayed until all modifications have been acknowledged by the remote cachers. An acquire consists solely of locating the processor that executed the corresponding release and transferring the synchronization variable. No consistency-related operations occur at lock acquires.

4.1.2 Barriers

At barrier arrivals, the EI protocol sends synchronization and consistency information to the master in a single message. However, the EI barrier protocol has a slight complication in that multiple processors may invalidate the same page at a barrier. In order to prevent all copies of a page from being invalidated, the master designates one processor as the "winner" for each page. Only the winner retains a valid copy for a given concurrently modified page. The losers forward their modifications to the winner and invalidate their local copies.

In the EU protocol, each processor flushes modifications to all other cachers of locally modified pages before sending a synchronization message to the barrier master.

4.1.3 Access Misses

Access misses are treated identically for both protocols. A message is sent to the owner of the page. The owner forwards the request to a processor that has a valid copy. This processor then sends the page to the processor that incurred the access miss.

4.2 The Lazy Protocols

4.2.1 Locks

At an acquire, the protocol locates the processor that last executed a release on the same variable. The releaser sends both synchronization and consistency information to the acquirer in a single message. The consistency information consists of write notices for all modifications that have been performed at the releaser but not the acquirer. While LI moves data only in response to access misses, both the LH and LU protocols send diffs along with the synchronization and consistency information. However, LH moves diffs only from the releaser to the acquirer, and hence can append them to an already existing message. The releaser sends all diffs that correspond to modifications being performed at the acquire for the first time, such that for each diff the acquirer is in the releaser's copyset for the page named by the diff. Pages named by write notices that arrive without diffs are invalidated.

The LU protocol *never* invalidates pages. An acquire does not succeed until all of the diffs described by the new write notices have been obtained. In general, the acquirer must talk to other processors in order to pick up all of the required diffs. However, the number of processors with which the acquirer needs to communicate can be reduced because of the following observation. If processor p modifies a page at time t, then all diffs of that page that precede the modification according to *happened-before-1* can be obtained from processor p.

4.2.2 Barriers

At barrier arrivals, the LI protocol sends synchronization information and write notices to the master in a single message. When all processors have arrived, the barrier master sends a single message to each processors that contains the barrier release as well as all the write notices that it has collected.

LH and LU barrier arrivals are handled similarly. In both cases, each processor pushes updates to all processors that cache pages that have been modified locally, before sending a barrier arrival message to the master. The only difference is that in LU, the processes must wait on the arrival of the data before departing from the barrier.

4.2.3 Access Misses

Access misses are handled identically by LH, LI, and LU. At a miss, a copy of the page and a number of diffs may have to be retrieved. The number of sites that need to be queried for diffs can be reduced through the same logic as in Section 4.2.1. The new diffs are then merged into the page and the processor is allowed to proceed. The lazy protocols determine the location of a page or updates to the page entirely on the basis of local information. No additional messages are required, unlike in other DSM systems [13].

5 Methodology

5.1 Application Suite

We simulated four programs, from three different classes of applications. Jacobi and TSP are coarse-grained programs with a large amount of computation relative to synchronization (323,840 and 18,092,000 cycles per processor between off-node synchronization operations, respectively, at 16 processors). Our Jacobi program is a simple Successive Over-Relaxation program that works on grids of 512 by 512 elements. TSP solves the traveling salesman problem for 18-city tours. Water, from the SPLASH suite[14], is a medium grained molecular dynamics simulation (19200 cycles per processor between off-node synchronization operations). We ran Water with the default parameters: 288 molecules for 2 steps. Cholesky performs parallel factorization of sparse positive definite matrices, and is an example of a program with fine-grained parallelism from the SPLASH benchmark suite (4,000 cycles per processor between off-node synchronization operations). Cholesky was run with the default input file, 'bcsstk14'. TSP and Cholesky use only locks for synchronization, Jacobi uses only barriers, and Water uses both.

5.2 Architectural Model

We used two basic architectural models, an *Ethernet* model and an *ATM* switch model. Both models assume 40MHz RISC processors with 64 Kbyte direct-mapped caches and a 12 cycle memory latency, 4096 byte pages, and an infinite local memory (no capacity misses). The ethernet is modeled as a 10 MBit/sec broadcast network, while the ATM is modeled as a 100 MBit/sec cross-bar switch.

5.3 Protocol Simulation

Each message exchanged by the protocols was modeled by the wire time consumed by sending the mes-

	Access Miss	Lock	Unlock	Barrier
LH	2m	3	0	2(n-1)+u
LI	2m	3	0	2(n-1)
LU	2m	3+2h	0	2(n-1)+2u
EI	2 or 3	3	2c	2(n-1) + v
EU	2	3	2c	2(n-1) + 2u

m = # concurrent last modifiers for the missing page

h = # other concurrent last modifiers for any local page

c = # other cachers of the page

n = # processors in system

p = # pages in system

$u = \sum_{i=1}^{n}$(# other procs caching pages modified by i)

$v = \sum_{i=1}^{p}$(# excess invalidators of page i)

Table 1 Shared Memory Operation Message Costs

sage, any inherent network latency, contention for the network, and a *software overhead* that represents the operating system cost of calling a user-level handler for incoming messages, creating and reading the messages in the DSM software, and the cost of the DSM protocol implementation. This cost is set at (1000 + message length $*$ 1.5/4) processor cycles at both the destination and source of each message. These figures were modeled after the Peregrine [10] implementation overheads. Peregrine is an RPC system that provides performance close to optimal by avoiding intermediate copying. The lazy implementation's extra complexity is modeled by doubling the per-byte message overhead both at the sender and at the receiver. Diffs are modeled by charging four cycles per word per page for each modified page at the time of diff creation. Although all messages are simulated, protocol-specific consistency information is not reflected in the amount of data sent. Only the actual shared data moved by the protocols is included in message lengths.

6 Simulation Results

6.1 DSM on an Ethernet

Although prior work [5] showed that Ethernet-based software DSMs can achieve significant speedups, we find that for modern processors the Ethernet is no longer a viable option. Figure 6 shows the speedup of Jacobi, a coarse-grained program. Jacobi's speedup peaks at 5.2 for eight processors, and declines rapidly thereafter. While Jacobi's communication needs are modest in comparison with other programs, the individual pro-

cessors execute identical code and therefore create significant network contention at each barrier. This contention is especially significant for the update protocols, in which each processor sends updates to its neighbors prior to the barrier. In an 8-processor run, processors on average wait more than 3 milliseconds before gaining control of the Ethernet.

6.2 DSM on an ATM

The emerging ATM networks have several advantages over the Ethernet. Foremost among these are increased bandwidth and reduced opportunity for contention. Unlike the Ethernet, in which all processors seeking to communicate contend with each other, processors in an ATM network can communicate concurrently and interfere only when they try to send to a common destination.

Figures 7-9 summarize the performance of the Jacobi program on an ATM. While the Ethernet simulation of Jacobi achieved a speedup of about 5, the ATM version reaches 14. Part of this increase is due to the increased bandwidth, but much of it is due to the fact that no more than two competing updates (from each of a processor's two neighbors) ever arrive at a single destination during one interval. The performance of all five protocols is roughly the same for this program because of the regular nearest-neighbor sharing. The invalidate protocols fare slightly worse than the update protocols because pages on the edge of a processor's assigned data are invalidated at barriers, and have to be paged across the network. The lazy protocols perform slightly worse than the eager protocols because of the extra overhead

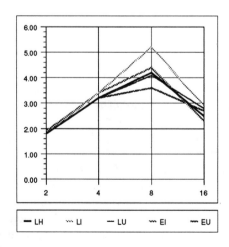

Figure 6 Speedup for Jacobi on Ethernet

149

added in the simulation for message processing. This overhead is probably unjustified for Jacobi because of the nature of communication involved. As will be seen in all of the simulations, EI moves significantly more data than the other protocols because its access misses cause entire pages to be transmitted, rather than diffs.

Like Jacobi, TSP is a coarse-grained program with modest amounts of communication. Much of TSP's inefficiency results from contention for a global tour queue. Fully 10% of a 16-processor execution is wasted waiting for the queue lock. In order to prevent repeated acquires because of unpromising tours, each acquirer holds the queue's lock while making a preliminary check on the topmost tour. If the tour is promising, the queue's lock is released. Otherwise, the acquirer removes another tour from the queue.

Figures 10-12 present TSP's performance. There is little variation among the lazy protocols and among the eager protocols because of the large granularity and the contention for the queue lock. However, the speedup for the eager protocols is better than for the lazy protocols. TSP uses a branch-and-bound algorithm, using a global minimum to prune recursive searches. Read access to the current minimum is not synchronized. A processor may therefore read a stale version of the minimum. The lock protecting the minimum is acquired only when the length of the tour just explored is smaller than (the potentially stale value of) the minimum. The length is then rechecked against the value of the minimum, which is now guaranteed to be up to date, and the minimum is updated, if necessary. The eager protocols push out the new value of the minimum at each release, and therefore local copies of the minimum are frequently updated. It is thus unlikely that a processor would read a stale value, unlike with the lazy protocols where the local copy is only updated as a result of an acquire. Since the algorithm uses the global minimum to prune searches, such stale values may cause TSP to explore more unpromising tours with the lazy protocols.

Water is a medium-grained program that uses both locks and barriers. Water's data consists primarily of an array of molecules, each protected by a lock. During each iteration, the force vectors of all molecules with a spherical cutoff range of a molecule are updated to reflect the molecule's influence. In combination with the relatively small size of the molecule structure in comparison with the size of a page, this creates a large amount of false sharing. The simulation results for Water can be seen in Figures 13-15. LH performs better than the other protocols because the molecules' migratory behavior during the force modification phase allows the protocol to have far fewer cache misses, and hence messages, than the other protocols. The lazy protocols perform better than the eager protocols, and

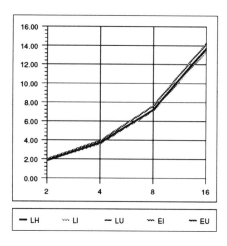

Figure 7 Speedup for Jacobi

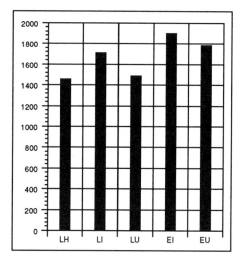

Figure 8 Message Count in Jacobi

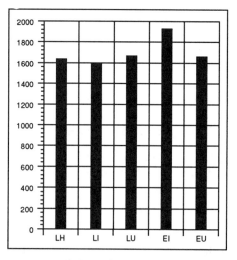

Figure 9 Data (Kbytes) Transmitted in Jacobi

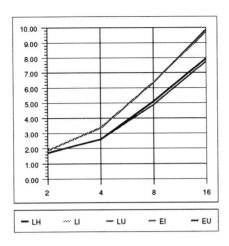

Figure 10 Speedup for TSP

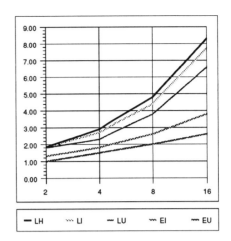

Figure 13 Speedup for Water

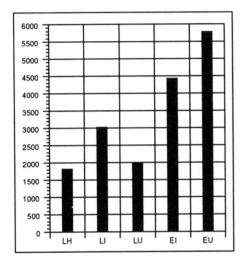

Figure 11 Message Count in TSP

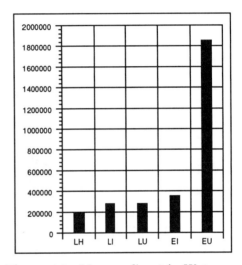

Figure 14 Message Count in Water

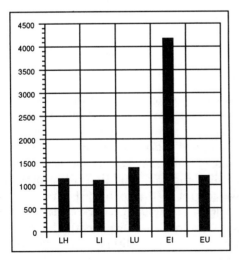

Figure 12 Data (Kbytes) Transmitted in TSP

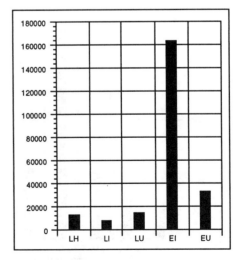

Figure 15 Data (Kbytes) Transmitted in Water

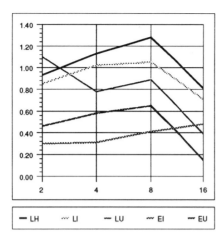

Figure 16 Speedup for Cholesky

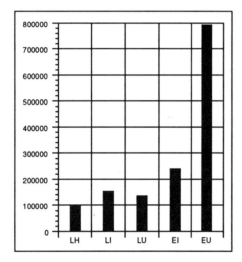

Figure 17 Message Count in Cholesky

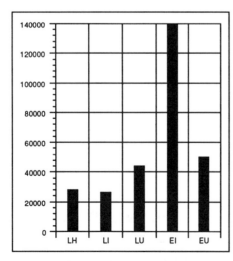

Figure 18 Data (Kbytes) Transmitted in Cholesky

invalidate performs better than update. EU sends an order of magnitude more messages than any of the other protocols because releases cause updates to be sent to many other processors. Ninety-one percent of EU's messages are updates sent during lock releases. The invalidate protocols send fewer messages because fewer processors cache each page.

Cholesky is a program with fine-grained synchronization that uses a task queue approach to parallelism. Locks are used to dequeue tasks as well as to protect access to multiple columns of data. Figures 16-18 summarize Cholesky's performance. The large amount of synchronization limits the speedup to no more than 1.3 for any of the protocols. The eager protocols suffer from excessive updates and invalidations caused by false sharing. The lazy protocols, and in particular LH, fare better because communication is largely localized to the synchronizing processors, leading to much better handling of false sharing.

Our simulations indicate that synchronization is a major obstacle to achieving good performance on DSM systems. For example, 83% of the messages required by Water running on the 16-processor *ATM* model under the hybrid protocol were for synchronization. For Cholesky running on 2 processors, 96% of the messages were used for synchronization. All but a few of these synchronization messages were for lock acquisition. Moreover, 84% of each processor's time was spent acquiring locks in the 16-processor LH Cholesky run. While approximately one third of the lock acquisition messages carried data, the rest were solely for synchronization purposes. When a lock is reacquired by the same processor before another processor acquires it, the lazy protocols have an advantage over the eager protocols. An eager protocol must distribute diffs at every lock release. Lazy release consistency permits us to avoid external communication when the same lock is reacquired.

6.3 The Effect of Network Characteristics

The network is a shared resource that can be a performance bottleneck. We can break down the network's effect on performance into three categories: *bandwidth*, *serialization*, and *collisions*. Bandwidth affects the total amount of data that can be moved. Serialization refers to the processor wait time when other processors have control of the contended network link. By *collisions* we mean actual network collisions as well as the effect of protocols like exponential backoff that are used to avoid network collisions in the case of an ethernet network. Table 2 summarizes speedup for Jacobi and Water on five different networks.

	Jacobi	Water
10 Mbit Ethernet w/ Coll.	2.5	0.7
10 Mbit Ethernet w/o Coll.	4.1	1.3
10 Mbit ATM	10.1	4.0
100 Mbit ATM	13.7	8.3
1 GBit ATM	13.8	8.8

Table 2 Speedups With Different Network Characteristics (LH, 16 processors)

Prog.	Overhd.	LH	LI	LU	EI	EU
Jacobi	Zero	15.1	15.3	15.1	14.9	15.4
	Normal	13.7	13.4	13.7	14.2	13.4
	Double	12.9	12.6	12.8	12.7	12.5
TSP	Zero	7.8	7.8	7.8	10.3	10.3
	Normal	7.9	7.9	7.8	9.7	9.8
	Double	8.7	8.7	7.4	10.3	10.3
Water	Zero	13.1	13.1	12.8	5.2	10.5
	Normal	8.3	7.7	6.6	3.8	2.6
	Double	6.9	6.0	5.2	3.3	1.5
Chol.	Zero	2.4	2.6	1.2	0.7	1.3
	Normal	0.8	0.7	0.4	0.5	0.2
	Double	0.4	0.4	0.2	0.3	0.1

Table 3 Speedups With Varying Software Overhead (16 processors)

Jacobi communicates with neighbors at a barrier. Both the implementation of barriers and the access pattern (regular, to fixed neighbors) benefit from a point-to-point network that eliminates most serialization. Hence, most of the benefits of ATM for this program are from the concurrency in the network. Water's access pattern is much less regular because molecules move. The potential for communication to be completed entirely in parallel is significantly reduced. As a result, Water benefits as much from network concurrency as from increased bandwidth. Increasing the network bandwidth to 1 Gbit/sec does not improve performance significantly with a 40 MHz processor, since at this point, the software overhead is the major performance bottleneck.

6.4 The Effect of Software Overheads

Software overheads have a significant impact on performance. Table 3 shows the simulated performance of an ATM network in the 16-processor case, with no software overhead, with software overhead identical to that used in the previous simulations, and with double that amount.

We first removed the overhead in order to find an upper bound on DSM performance for the given network and processor architecture, regardless of the operating system and DSM implementation. The large speedups indicate the performance potential for the protocols, and the potential gains to be had from hardware support.

With software overhead removed, there is no longer a significant per-message penalty on a crossbar network. This lessens the importance of access misses, and favors protocols that reduce the amount of data moved for improved performance. For instance, the LI protocol outperforms LH on a 16-processor Cholesky run even though the LH protocol sends 30% fewer messages and has 75% fewer access misses than the LI protocol. The reason is that the hybrid protocol attempts to find a compromise between low message counts, low numbers of access misses, and low amounts of data, but the data total is more significant if software overhead is removed.

The significance of software overhead can be seen most clearly in comparing the speedups of Water with and without overhead. The lazy protocols improve by an average of 80% when the overhead is removed. EI still performs badly because the amount of data it moves, five times more than any of the other protocols. EU, which runs three times slower than the LH protocol when software overhead is included, speeds up by more than 400% when software overhead is removed.

In order to determine the variation in performance that might occur due to an increase in software overhead, we determined speedups when the overhead per message was doubled. The performance decreases by 20% to 40% for Water. The decrease in performance is not as large as when going from zero to normal overhead since the normal overhead includes the per diff overhead, which is significant. In general, the lazy protocols, and in particular the lazy hybrid, perform better as communication becomes more expensive.

6.5 The Effect of Processor Speeds

Processor speeds affect the ratio of computation time to communication time. However, the software overhead is proportional to the processor speed. We varied the processor speeds from 20 to 80 MHz. Table 4 shows the variation in speedup for the 16-processor case when using the lazy hybrid protocol in the case of Jacobi, TSP and Water, and the 8-processor case for Cholesky. For Jacobi and TSP, the variations are negligible because the low message counts for these programs results in little variation in the computation to communication ratio. Water and Cholesky show a more significant variation in speedup due to the larger amount of communication. In the latter two cases, communication latency is as much of a bottleneck as the software overheads, and hence an increased processor speed reduces speedup. However, some of the improvements are masked by the corresponding changes in software overheads.

6.6 The Effect of Page Size

The large page sizes in common use in software DSMs result in a high probability of false sharing. Prior work has developed implementations of relaxed memory consistency models for DSM that reduce but do not totally eliminate the effects of false sharing. For example, Munin's eager implementation of release consistency eliminates the "ping-pong" effect of a page bouncing between two writing processors [5]. However, modifications to falsely shared pages still have to be distributed to all processors caching the page at a release. The lazy hybrid protocol further reduces the effect of false sharing because data movement only occurs between synchronizing processors. In other words, false sharing in LH increases the amount of data movement but *not* the number of messages.

The results we have reported are for a page size of 4096 bytes. To obtain a measure of the effects of false sharing, we ran simulations using a page size of 1024 bytes. While going to a 1024-byte page reduces false sharing, we found that we need to communicate with approximately the same number of processors to maintain consistency. Furthermore, the resulting reduction in communication is often partially counterbalanced by the increased number of access misses (see Table 5, which presents data for the lazy hybrid protocol). While reducing the page size has a limited effect on performance, restructuring the program may prove more beneficial.

7 Related Work

This work draws on the large body of research in relaxed memory consistency models (e.g., [2, 4, 8, 9]). We

Procs	Page Size (bytes)	Jac.	TSP	Wat.	Chol.
2	1024	1.8	1.7	1.9	1.0
	4096	1.8	1.7	1.8	0.9
4	1024	3.7	2.6	3.1	1.2
	4096	3.7	2.6	2.9	1.1
8	1024	7.2	5.1	5.1	1.4
	4096	7.2	5.1	4.8	1.3
16	1024	13.7	8.5	8.7	0.9
	4096	13.7	7.9	8.3	0.8

Table 5 Effect on Speedup of Reducing the Page Size to 1024 bytes (LH)

have chosen as our basic model the release consistency model introduced by the DASH project at Stanford [12], because it requires little or no change to existing shared memory programs. An interesting alternative is *entry consistency* (EC), defined by Bershad and Zekauskas [4]. EC differs from RC because it requires all shared data to be explicitly associated with some synchronization variable. On a lock acquisition EC only needs to propagate the shared data associated with the lock. EC, however, requires the programmer to insert additional synchronization in shared memory programs to execute correctly on an EC memory. Typically, RC does not require additional synchronization.

Ivy [13] and Munin [5] are two implementations of software DSMs for which performance measurements have been published. Both achieve good speedups on many of the applications studied. The slow processors used in the implementations prevented the network from becoming a bottleneck in achieving these speedups. With faster processors, faster networks are needed and more sophisticated methods are required. In addition, synchronization latency becomes a major issue. Performance measurements are also available for the DASH hardware DSM multiprocessor. Comparison between these numbers and our simulation results indicates the benefits of a dedicated high-speed interconnect for fine-grained parallel applications.

8 Conclusions

With the advent of faster processors, the performance of DSM that can be achieved on an Ethernet network is limited. Serialization of messages, collisions, and low bandwidth severely constrain speedups, even for coarse-grained problems. Higher-bandwidth point-to-point networks, such as the ATM LANs appearing on

Pr. Spd (MHz)	Jacobi	TSP	Water	Chol.
80	13.7	10.5	7.7	0.9
40	13.7	9.8	8.3	1.3
20	13.4	10.0	8.6	1.4

Table 4 Speedups with Different Processor Speeds (LH, 16 processors)

the market, allow much better performance, with good speedups even for medium-grained applications. Fine-grained applications still perform poorly even on such networks because of the frequency and cost of synchronization operations.

Lazy hybrid is a new consistency protocol that combines the benefits of invalidate protocols (relatively little data) and update protocols (fewer access misses and fewer messages). In addition, the lazy hybrid shortens the lock acquisition latency considerably compared to a lazy update protocol. The hybrid protocol outperforms the other lazy protocols under a model that takes into account software overhead for communication. For medium-grained applications the differences are quite significant.

The latency of synchronization remains a major problem for software DSMs. Without resorting to broadcast, it appears impossible to reduce the number of messages required for lock acquisition. Therefore, the only possible approach may be to hide the latency of lock acquisition. Multithreading is a common technique for masking the latency of expensive operations, but the attendant increase in communication could prove prohibitive in software DSMs. Program restructuring to reduce the amount of synchronization may be a more viable approach.

References

[1] S. V. Adve and M. D. Hill. A unified formalization of four shared-memory models. Technical Report CS-1051, University of Wisconsin, Madison, September 1991.

[2] M. Ahamad, P.W. Hutto, and R. John. Implementing and programming causal distributed shared memory. In *Proceedings of the 11th International Conference on Distributed Computing Systems*, pages 274–281, May 1991.

[3] H.E. Bal and A.S. Tanenbaum. Distributed programming with shared data. In *Proceedings of the 1988 International Conference on Computer Languages*, pages 82–91, October 1988.

[4] B.N. Bershad and M.J. Zekauskas. Midway: Shared memory parallel programming with entry consistency for distributed memory multiprocessors. Technical Report CMU-CS-91-170, Carnegie-Mellon University, September 1991.

[5] J.B. Carter, J.K. Bennett, and W. Zwaenepoel. Implementation and performance of Munin. In *Proceedings of the 13th ACM Symposium on Operating Systems Principles*, pages 152–164, October 1991.

[6] J.S. Chase, F.G. Amador, E.D. Lazowska, H.M. Levy, and R.J. Littlefield. The Amber system: Parallel programming on a network of multiprocessors. In *Proceedings of the 12th ACM Symposium on Operating Systems Principles*, pages 147–158, December 1989.

[7] R. G. Covington, S. Dwarkadas, J. R. Jump, S. Madala, and J. B. Sinclair. The Efficient Simulation of Parallel Computer Systems. *International Journal in Computer Simulation*, 1:31–58, January 1991.

[8] M. Dubois and C. Scheurich. Memory access dependencies in shared-memory multiprocessors. *IEEE Transactions on Computers*, 16(6):660–673, June 1990.

[9] K. Gharachorloo, D. Lenoski, J. Laudon, P. Gibbons, A. Gupta, and J. Hennessy. Memory consistency and event ordering in scalable shared-memory multiprocessors. In *Proceedings of the 17th Annual International Symposium on Computer Architecture*, pages 15–26, May 1990.

[10] D.B. Johnson and W. Zwaenepoel. The Peregrine high-performance RPC system. *Software: Practice and Experience*, 23(2):201–221, February 1993.

[11] P. Keleher, A. L. Cox, and W. Zwaenepoel. Lazy release consistency for software distributed shared memory. In *Proceedings of the 19th Annual International Symposium on Computer Architecture*, pages 13–21, May 1992.

[12] D. Lenoski, J. Laudon, K. Gharachorloo, A. Gupta, and J. Hennessy. The directory-based cache coherence protocol for the DASH multiprocessor. In *Proceedings of the 17th Annual International Symposium on Computer Architecture*, pages 148–159, May 1990.

[13] K. Li and P. Hudak. Memory coherence in shared virtual memory systems. *ACM Transactions on Computer Systems*, 7(4):321–359, November 1989.

[14] J.P. Singh, W.-D. Weber, and A. Gupta. SPLASH: Stanford parallel applications for shared-memory. Technical Report CSL-TR-91-469, Stanford University, April 1991.

Mechanisms for Cooperative Shared Memory*

David A. Wood, Satish Chandra, Babak Falsafi, Mark D. Hill, James R. Larus,

Alvin R. Lebeck, James C. Lewis, Shubhendu S. Mukherjee, Subbarao Palacharla, Steven K. Reinhardt

wwt@cs.wisc.edu

Computer Sciences Department

University of Wisconsin–Madison

1210 West Dayton Street

Madison, WI 53706 USA

Abstract

This paper explores the complexity of implementing directory protocols by examining their *mechanisms*— primitive operations on directories, caches, and network interfaces. We compare the following protocols: Dir_1B, Dir_4B, Dir_4NB, Dir_nNB [2], Dir_1SW [9] and an improved version of Dir_1SW (Dir_1SW^+). The comparison shows that the mechanisms and mechanism sequencing of Dir_1SW and Dir_1SW^+ are simpler than those for other protocols.

We also compare protocol performance by running eight benchmarks on 32 processor systems. Simulations show that Dir_1SW^+'s performance is comparable to more complex directory protocols. The significant disparity in hardware complexity and the small difference in performance argue that Dir_1SW^+ may be a more effective use of resources. The small performance difference is attributable to two factors: the low degree of sharing in the benchmarks and Check-In/Check-Out (CICO) directives [9].

Keywords: Shared-memory multiprocessors, memory systems, cache coherence, directory protocols, and hardware mechanisms.

*This work is supported in part by NSF PYI Awards CCR-9157366 and MIPS-8957278, NSF Grant CCR-9101035, Univ. of Wisconsin Graduate School Grant, Wisconsin Alumni Research Foundation Fellowship and donations from A.T.&T. Bell Laboratories and Digital Equipment Corporation. Our Thinking Machines CM-5 was purchased through NSF Institutional Infrastructure Grant No. CDA-9024618 with matching funding from the Univ. of Wisconsin Graduate School.

1 Introduction

Directory protocols are a technique used to implement cache coherence on large-scale shared-memory parallel computers [2]. Directory protocols logically associate a directory entry with each aligned block in main memory. This entry records that the block is idle (no cached copies), one writable copy exists, or one or more read-only copies exist. We only consider write-invalidate protocols that invalidate outstanding copies of a block in other processors when a processor wishes to write into it. To facilitate invalidations, each directory entry also contains logical pointers to some or all of the processor(s) that hold copies of the block. Agarwal et al. [2] use the notation Dir_iB to denote protocols that explicitly record the i processors that share a block and rely on broadcasts to invalidate more than i processors. Dir_iNB denotes protocols that avoid broadcast by preventing more than i processors from sharing a block.

We examine Dir_nNB, Dir_4B, Dir_4NB, Dir_1B, Dir_1SW, and Dir_1SW^+. The Stanford DASH project and IEEE Scalable Coherent Interface (SCI) implement Dir_nNB [13, 8]. DASH uses a bit vector pointing to a maximum of 16 clusters, while SCI uses a linked-list whose head is stored in the directory and other list elements are associated with blocks in a maximum of 64K processor caches.

Dir_4B and Dir_4NB were inspired by empirical data suggesting that, in many sharing patterns, the number of readers is lower than four, regardless of the system size [17]. MIT Alewife's [4] LimitLESS directory contains four hardware pointers and uses software to record additional pointers. LimitLESS's software can implement Dir_4B, Dir_4NB, Dir_nNB, and other alternatives.

Dir_1B, and our protocols, Dir_1SW and Dir_1SW^+, record only one writer or reader. The limited state reduces implementation complexity, but can cause many broadcasts. Dir_1SW [9] (reviewed in Section 2) and Dir_1SW^+ (introduced in Section 3.6.3) count the readers so they can return the directory to idle when all readers return the block, thereby avoiding an unnecessary broadcast. Programmers or compilers can also produce more desirable sharing patterns by reasoning about the shared-memory communication in a program with the *Check-In/Check-Out (CICO)* programming model. Furthermore, CICO primitives also serve as memory system directives that improve performance. We review this approach—*cooperative shared memory*—in Section 2 [9].

Many directory protocols are complex and require considerable hardware, which reduces the attractiveness of shared-memory machines. A directory protocol *policy* describes its response to program events, such as loads and stores, and the interactions among directories and caches on different processors. At the next lower level of abstraction, these policies are implemented with *mechanisms*—operations on directories, caches, and network interfaces—such as updating a directory pointer, replacing a cache block, and sending a point-to-point message. Describing a directory protocol at the mechanism level exposes disparities in protocol complexity that are not apparent at the policy level. Most protocols, for example, have policy transitions from many readers to one writer and from one writer to another writer. The shared-exclusive transition is more complex to implement than the exclusive-exclusive transition. The difference becomes clear at the mechanism level. Most systems synthesize the shared-exclusive transition by sending a sequence of invalidate and acknowledgement messages. An implementation must (a) sequence through a large number of message sends, (b) count the acknowledgements, (c) ensure concurrent requests to the same directory entry are serialized, and (d) guarantee that the interaction of these messages with messages for the node's processor, cache, and other directory entries cannot cause network deadlock. On the other hand, for an exclusive-exclusive transition, the directory only sends a single invalidation, which greatly simplifies these considerations.

The first contribution of this paper is to explore the complexity of Dir_1B, Dir_4B, Dir_4NB, Dir_nNB [2], and Dir_1SW [9] at the mechanism level of abstraction (Section 3). The mechanisms and mechanism sequencing of Dir_1SW are significantly simpler than these other protocols because the shared-to-exclusive transition is not handled by hardware (MIT LimitLESS is more complex that Dir_1SW, but much simpler than the other protocols). Dir_1SW's mechanisms can also be used to implement a protocol with higher performance. We call the best extended protocol Dir_1SW^+.

However, this comparison is an academic exercise if simpler protocols perform poorly. Several papers have examined directory protocol performance. Agarwal et al. [2] presented event counts for four-processor VAX traces less than two million instructions long (half-million per processor). Weber and Gupta [17] used five benchmarks, more processors (up to 16), and longer traces (4 million instructions). A major contribution of their paper is a classification of shared objects (into read-only, migratory, synchronization, mostly-read, and frequently read/written). In addition, for migratory data, they suggested flushing data from a cache. Their second paper [7] switched to the MIPS architecture, ran the applications to completion (up to 2–48 million references—instruction counts not given), and extended results to 32 processors. This change may be due to longer traces and different synchronization assumptions. Lenoski et al. [13] presented speedup measurements from the Stanford DASH prototype running three applications. Since prototypes of other directory systems were unavailable, the paper could not compare DASH against alternatives. Chaiken [5] compared LimitLESS against Dir_4NB and Dir_nNB, using several applications on 16 and 64 processors with 7 to 30 million references per application. His principal result was that LimitLESS's performance is comparable to Dir_nNB and better than Dir_4NB (even though he assumes read-only data is handled separately). Hill et al. [9] measured the performance of Dir_1SW by recording event counts, but did not compare their results with other protocols.

The second contribution of this paper is a comparison of directory protocol performance that extends previous work in three ways (Section 4). First, our results come from executing billions, not millions, of instructions. Second, we evaluate performance with execution time, not event counts. Third, we present results for Dir_1B, Dir_4NB, Dir_4B, Dir_nNB, Dir_1SW, and Dir_1SW^+ together. Our simulations show that Dir_1SW^+'s performance is similar to more complex directory protocols for seven of eight benchmarks on a system of 32 processors (Dir_nNB preforms better on mp3d due to unscalable, unsynchronized sharing). If this result holds for other applications and larger systems, the significant disparity in hardware complexity and the small difference in performance argue that Dir_1SW^+ may be a more effective use of resources. The small performance difference between Dir_1SW^+ and the more complex protocols is attributable to two factors. First, as Weber and Gupta's measurements show, the number of outstanding shared copies is typically close to one and rarely much greater [17]. This small amount of sharing means that directory protocols that track many outstanding copies provide functionality that is not fully utilized and their additional hardware rarely improves performance. Second, CICO memory system directives reduce sharing even further.

After the principal results in Sections 3 and 4, Section 5 discusses the implication of technology trends and directions for future work, while Section 6 draws conclusions.

2 CICO and Dir_1SW

This section reviews cooperative shared memory, CICO and Dir_1SW, originally presented in Hill et al. [9]. The *Check-In/Check-Out (CICO)* programming performance model allows a programmer both (1) to reason about the communications caused by shared-memory references and (2) to pass performance directives to the memory system. Neither the programming model or the directives are specific to Dir_1SW. Elsewhere, we demonstrate that the annotations can be used to improve program performance by increasing cache reuse and reducing program sharing [12]. This paper examines the effect on directory protocol behavior of using CICO annotations as memory system directives. We do not discuss the cooperative prefetch mechanism.

In CICO, programmers bracket uses of shared data with a check_out annotation marking the expected first use and a check_in annotation terminating the expected use of the data. In programs conforming to the model, processors coordinate access to exclusive (writable) cache blocks to avoid expensive invalidates. The primary effect of using CICO annotations as memory system directives is to have check_in's flush cache blocks back to memory.

The base Dir_1SW protocol associates two state bits, a trap bit, and a pointer/counter with each block in memory. A directory entry can be in one of three states: Dir_X, Dir_S, and Dir_Idle. State Dir_X implies that the directory has given an exclusive copy of the block to the processor pointed to by the pointer/counter. State Dir_S implies that the directory has given out N shared copies, where N is the number in the pointer/counter. State Dir_Idle implies that the directory owns the only valid copy of the block.

Figure 1 illustrates state transitions for the base Dir_1SW protocol. Msg_Get_X (Msg_Get_S, respectively) is a message to the directory requesting an exclusive (shared) copy of a block. Msg_Put is a message relinquishing a copy. Processors send a Msg_Get_X

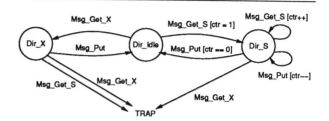

Figure 1: Base Dir_1SW Protocol

(Msg_Get_S) message when a local program references a block that is not in the local cache or performs an explicit check_out. In the common case, a directory responds by sending the data. A processor sends a Msg_Put message on an explicit check_in or a cache replacement of the block.

Several state transitions in Figure 1 set a trap bit and trap to a software trap handler running on the directory processor (not the requesting processor), as in MIT LimitLESS [4]. The trap bit serializes traps from multiple references to a block. The software trap handler reads directory entries from the hardware and sends explicit messages to other processors to complete the request that trapped and then restarts the program that faulted. Traps only occur on memory accesses that violate the CICO model. Thus, programs conforming to this model run at full hardware speed. Traps on blocks in state Dir_X interact with one processor, while *traps in state Dir_S must broadcast to recall all read-only copies.* While broadcast cannot be used in infinitely large systems, it is acceptable in finite systems if the frequency of broadcast times the cost of the broadcast is small.

3 Directory Mechanisms

The hardware base of cache-coherent shared memory is similar to a message-passing machine. Each processor node contains a microprocessor, a cache, and a memory module. Nodes are connected with a fast point-to-point network. Shared memory differs because each memory module is addressed in a global address space and each processor node contains additional hardware to implement a directory protocol. Moreover, many directory protocols are complex and require considerable hardware, which reduces the attractiveness of shared-memory machines.

A directory protocol can be decomposed into three levels of abstraction. *Policy* describes its response to program events, such as loads and stores, and the interactions among directories and caches on different processors. At the next lower level of abstraction, policies are implemented with *mechanisms*—operations on directories, caches, and network interfaces—such as updating a directory pointer, replacing a cache block, and sending a point-to-point message. Mechanisms are further decomposed into primitive operations on a particular hardware *implementation*, which is the lowest level of abstraction. For example, $Dir_1 SW$ requires a mechanism to increment the directory's pointer/counter and has a policy to increment this counter on a `Msg_Get_S` message that finds a block in state `Dir_S`. This mechanism may, in turn, be implemented as an atomic sequence of primitive hardware operations that read, add one to, and write the counter.

Policy and mechanisms can be implemented in either hardware or software. Most directory protocols implement both policy and mechanisms in hardware. However, both LimitLESS [4] and $Dir_1 SW$ [9] implement policy with a combination of software and hardware.

Previous work has concentrated on developing new protocols, that is, policies. This section focuses, instead, on the mechanisms required to implement these protocols. Describing a directory protocol at the mechanism level exposes disparities in protocol complexity that are not apparent at the policy level. Most protocols, for example, have policy transitions from many readers to one writer and from one writer to another. When examined at the mechanism level, the shared-exclusive transition is clearly harder to implement than the exclusive-exclusive transition. Most systems synthesize the shared-exclusive transition by sending a sequence of invalidate and acknowledgement messages. An implementation must (a) sequence through a large number of message sends, (b) count the acknowledgements, (c) ensure concurrent requests to the same directory entry are serialized, and (d) guarantee that the interaction of these messages with messages for the node's processor, cache, and other directory entries cannot cause network deadlock. On the other hand, for an exclusive-exclusive transition, the directory only sends a single invalidation, which greatly simplifies these considerations. By examining protocols' mechanisms, we can compare the cost and complexity of implementing different protocols and explore the appropriate boundary between hardware and software.

3.1 Message-Passing Hardware

All parallel machines provide message-passing mechanisms. Message-passing machines, such as the Intel Paragon, simply expose these mechanisms directly to the programmer. Shared-memory machines, such as

Stanford DASH and the Kendell Square KSR1, use these mechanisms to implement shared memory but hide the underlying mechanisms from the programmer. We believe that future shared-memory systems will expose the underlying message passing, as done in MIT Alewife [4]. Some statically-partitionable codes achieve maximum performance through explicit message passing. Agarwal, et al., have demonstrated that other codes achieve better performance with a combination of shared-memory and message-passing than by using one or the other alone [11].

Consequently, we assume base hardware includes support to explicitly send and receive messages. Messages contain a 4-bit message type and are sent to an explicitly-specified destination node p. The messages are large enough to contain at least one cache block and an address. The network interface is memory-mapped and resides on the memory bus. A limited DMA capability allows contiguous data to be fetched (stored) directly from (to) memory. When a message arrives at a destination node, it can either wait for an explicit receive operation (i.e., polling) or interrupt the processor and invoke a software trap handler.

The network interface and routers constitute a significant fraction of a parallel machine's design. Our focus in this paper is supporting shared memory without greatly increasing the overall design effort.

3.2 General Directory Mechanisms

This section identifies the primary directory mechanisms needed to implement other protocols: $Dir_i B$, $Dir_i NB$, and $Dir_n NB$ (collectively called $Dir_i X$). Rather than formally describing the protocols, we abstract these mechanisms from several recently proposed machines that use these protocols or minor variants of them. Where the published literature lacks details, we made reasonable design choices. We also concentrate exclusively on directory mechanisms since these protocols require identical cache mechanisms.

The $Dir_i X$ directory protocols require numerous additions to the underlying message-passing mechanisms, as Table 1 illustrates. The fundamental change is that some messages, based on the message type, invoke directory operations. The basic directory mechanisms are:

1. Send a single point-to-point message from a directory controller to a processor cache controller.

2. Read/write a pointer field.

3. Increment/decrement/zero a counter.

4. Test for counter equal to zero.

MsgP	Dir_iX	Dir_1SW	Mechanisms	Description
			Message Receive	
•	•	•	poll	Wait for processor to poll for message
•	•	•	interrupt	Interrupt processor and invoke software trap handler
	•	•	directory	Invoke directory operation
			Message Send	Send message to processor
•	•	•	explicit send	Memory mapped interface for explicit sends
	•	•	implicit send	Integrated support for directory controller
•	•	•	dest = p	Send message to node p
	•	•	dest = PTR	Send message to node in pointer/counter
	i (NB) n (B)	1	max. messages	Maximum messages sent in response to single message
	•	•	Update State	Update directory state field with new value
	•	•	new_state	New state value
	•	•	Update PTR/CTR	Update directory entry pointer/counter
	•	•	op = Incr	Increment counter by one
	•	•	op = Decr	Decrement counter by one
	•	•	op = Zero	Reset counter to zero
	•	•	op = Set	Set pointer to source node id
	•	•	Test PTR/CTR	
	•	•	CTR = 0	Test if counter equals 0
	•		PTR = p	Test if pointer points to node p
	•		PTR is valid	Test if field contains a valid pointer
			Sequence through PTR/CTR	Sequence through pointer/counter fields
	•		test	Test pointer/counter field
	•		update	Update pointer/counter field
	•		send	Send message to node in pointer field
	$i < n$ (NB)		Select victim for replacement	Select pointer field to be invalidated

Table 1: Mechanisms Summary

This table summarizes the mechanisms need for underlying message-passing hardware (MsgP), the general directory protocols Dir_iX, and our protocol Dir_1SW. The parameters for each mechanism are listed below it. A • in the appropriate column indicates when a particular protocol requires a mechanism. A directory is invoked in response to a message originating at a processor cache controller (possibly the local one).

When Dir_iX protocols send invalidation messages, they must keep track of acknowledgements in order to maintain sequential consistency (or weaker models). Although a counter is not strictly required (one could invalidate a pointer at each acknowledgement and test for no valid pointers), a counter is far easier to implement.

In general, Dir_iX protocols also need the following mechanisms:

1. Identify valid pointer fields.

2. Compare pointer fields against a node ID.

3. Sequence through the pointers.

Dir_iNB protocols, $i < n$, use a replacement policy to select a victim when the $i + 1^{st}$ shared copy is requested. This policy, in turn, requires an additional mechanism.

The mechanisms for Dir_nNB protocols are slightly different because they can employ bit vectors instead of explicit pointers.

1. Decode node ID and test/set/clear bit in vector.

2. Sequence through bit vector.

All Dir_iX protocols for $i > 1$ require the ability to sequence through either a set of pointers or a bit vector and send multiple invalidations.

3.3 Dir_1SW Mechanisms

The Dir_1SW column of Table 1 lists the subset of directory mechanisms required by Dir_1SW. Dir_1SW requires mechanisms to update state, send a single message, and test and update a single pointer/counter field. However, because Dir_1SW has only a single pointer/counter field, it does not need the sequencing logic used by Dir_iX ($i > 1$). Similarly, Dir_1SW sends at most one message in response to an incoming request; protocol transitions requiring multiple messages are handled by software.

160

3.4 Design Cost

In our view, the ultimate measure of directory protocol complexity is *design cost*—how long a protocol takes to implement. Unfortunately, differences in design teams, tools, and project goals prevent any concrete comparison of design cost.

For this reason, this section considers indirect measures of design cost that arise from sequencing directory mechanisms. A key goal of Dir_1SW was to reduce the cost and complexity of shared-memory hardware by using a protocol where the most frequent policy transitions can be implemented with simple, short sequences of mechanisms (e.g., a single invalidate message). More complex sequencing—involving many messages—is done by system software (trap handlers). Avoiding complex hardware sequencing eliminates the complexity that arises from transient states, ensuring new policy requests are serialized, and avoiding network deadlock.

One indirect measure of protocol complexity that has some value is the number of state/event pairs that must be handled in hardware, where events can be messages or processor actions (e.g., loads and stores). This measure is useful, because it quantifies the number of cases that the designer must consider and test for correctness. By this measure, Dir_1SW is fundamentally simpler than any of the Dir_iX protocols (with the exception of Dir_1NB) because it does not require sequencing, sends at most one message in response to any message, and requires only a simple datapath. Since much of this simplicity comes from pushing the complexity into software trap handlers, other hardware/software protocols such as LimitLESS, share this advantage.

All Dir_iX protocols for $i > 1$ require the ability to sequence through either a set of pointers or a bit vector and send multiple invalidations. To implement this mechanism as an atomic sequence, all invalidations must be sent before receiving any other messages. Unfortunately, deadlock avoidance then becomes a major consideration. If the maximum number of messages is bounded by a small constant, as in Dir_iNB, deadlock can be avoided with sufficient output buffering. The directory controller simply waits until its output FIFO has room for i messages before sending the first. However, this is not a scalable solution[1] for protocols that may send large numbers of messages, such as Dir_iB and Dir_nNB, since the maximum number of messages is proportional to system size.

---

[1] This solution can be used for any system with a *fixed* maximum size, provided each node has output buffering at least as large as this size.

The alternative is to make this mechanism non-atomic, and process incoming messages between sends. This facilitates deadlock avoidance, however, the sequencer's state becomes an additional, transient part of the cache block's state, greatly increasing the number of state/message interactions. In addition, multiple cache blocks may need to be sequenced simultaneously (in order to avoid deadlock), requiring some form of preemptive scheduling. Although this complexity can be managed, architects must expend considerable effort designing, building, and testing complex hardware rather than improving the performance of simpler hardware.

3.5 Manufacturing Cost

Comparing the manufacturing cost of mechanisms is relatively straight-forward. *Manufacturing cost* is ultimately measured in dollars, but is commonly estimated with other measures such as transistor count, bits of memory, datapath width, etc. For directory protocols, the dominant cost is memory overhead: number of bits of state stored per block of memory. All protocols need a small number of bits (e.g., 3 or 4) to represent the block's state. The Dir_iX protocols other than Dir_nNB require i pointers of log_2n bits each; Dir_nNB protocols require n bits. By contrast, Dir_1SW requires only one log_2n-bit pointer/counter field. Consider a system that supports up to 1024 nodes and has 32-byte cache blocks. If we assume 4 bits can describe the state of each block, then Dir_4NB incurs a 16% memory overhead (44 bits/256 bits), Dir_nNB incurs a 402% overhead, while Dir_1SW incurs only 5% overhead.

After memory, the next greatest cost is the directory datapath. For the Dir_iX protocols other than Dir_nNB, the comparison of a node ID with i pointer fields requires either a wide datapath with i comparators or a sequential search. A Dir_nNB implementation will require an n-bit datapath and priority decoder. By contrast, the Dir_1SW state machine requires only a log_2n-bit datapath with the ability to increment, decrement, test for zero, and select the ALU result, the message source ID, or a small constant for writing into the pointer/counter.

The absence of sequencing in the Dir_1SW mechanisms also allows a regular structure: in response to each message, the state associated with the cache block is read, modified, and written back, and optionally a single message is sent. Beyond its inherent simplicity, this regularity leads naturally to a pipelined implementation with increased throughput. While other schemes can also be pipelined, as for example, in the Stanford DASH [14], the increased datapath complexity requires additional designer time that could otherwise be spent elsewhere.

3.6 Improvements to Dir_1SW

The base Dir_1SW protocol described above performs as well as any feasible directory coherence protocol for programs that exactly follow the CICO programming model (see Section 2). However, rigidly adhering to this model is not possible or desirable for all programs. This section examines several extensions to the Dir_1SW protocol that improve its performance for programs that do not conform precisely to CICO. With one exception, these extensions use *exactly* the same mechanisms as base Dir_1SW and require minor changes to the policy implemented in hardware and software. The new mechanism, which is very simple, sets the counter in a directory entry to the value 1.

3.6.1 Dir_1SW+NPT: No Pairwise Traps

The base Dir_1SW protocol traps to software whenever a CICO violation occurs; that is, whenever the directory receiving a Msg_Get message cannot immediately respond with the requested data. However, the Dir_1SW mechanisms permit directory hardware to send a single message to an arbitrary processor in response to a message from another processor. The NPT extension modifies the hardware policy to directly send an invalidation message and forward the block to the requesting processor when the Msg_Put message arrives. This extension moves a common, but more complex policy from software to hardware, which may reduce execution time.

3.6.2 Dir_1SW+RO1: One Shared Copy

The Dir_1SW mechanisms permit a protocol to maintain either a pointer to a processor node or a counter. The base Dir_1SW protocol maintains a pointer for exclusive copies and a count of shared copies. However, many of the shared-to-exclusive state transitions occur when only a single shared copy is outstanding: over 50% for 6 of the 8 applications, and over 85% for 4 of them. An obvious extension of Dir_1SW is to add a new state Dir_S_One that maintains a pointer to a single shared copy. The benefit of this change is that it reduces the number of traps that broadcast an invalidate to all processors.

3.6.3 Dir_1SW+RO1+NPT: Dir_1SW^+

This extension, called Dir_1SW^+, combines the changes from Section 3.6.2 and Section 3.6.1. In this

Name	Input Data Set	Cycles (billions)
barnes	2048 bodies, 10 iter.	3.3
ocean	98 × 98 2 days	1.5
sparse	256 × 256 dense	2.5
pthor	5000 elem, 50 cycles	20.9
cholesky	bcsstk15	21.0
water	256 mols, 10 iter	9.8
mp3d	50000 mols, 50 iter	24.6
tomcatv	1024 × 1024, 10 iter	8.5

Table 2: Application Programs

This table describes the benchmarks used in this paper. *Sparse* is a locally-written program that solves $AX = B$ for a sparse matrix A. *Tomcatv* is a parallel version of the SPEC benchmark. All other benchmarks are from the SPLASH benchmark suite [16].

protocol, the trap handler is only invoked to broadcast an invalidation for a block that was shared by more than one processor.

4 Directory Performance

This sections presents our experimental methods, compares the performance of Dir_1SW variants, and compares the best Dir_1SW variant with alternative protocols.

4.1 Methods

The measurements in this paper came from the eight explicitly parallel programs listed in Table 2 running on the Wisconsin Wind Tunnel (WWT), a virtual prototype for cache-coherent, shared-memory computers [15]. WWT runs parallel shared-memory programs on a parallel message-passing computer (a Thinking Machines CM-5) and uses a distributed, discrete-event simulation to concurrently calculate the programs' execution times on a proposed target machine.

The simulated parallel computer (the target system) used in this paper consists of 32 processor nodes, each containing a processor, shared-memory module, cache, and network interface. Processors execute SPARC binaries. The execution time for each instruction is fixed. Instruction fetches and stack references require no additional cycles beyond the basic instruction time. Other memory locations are cached in a node's cache. A cache hit takes no additional cycles, while a cache miss invokes a coherence protocol that sends messages, accesses a directory entry, etc. Each message, cache or directory transition has a cost. Caches and directories process messages in first-

Cache	256 KB, 4-way set-associative
Block size	32 bytes
TLB	64 entries, fully associative, FIFO replacement
Page size	4 KB
Message latency	100 cycles remote, 10 cycles to self
Barrier latency	100 cycles from last arrival
Cache miss	19 cycles + 5 if block is replaced + 8 if replaced block was exclusive copy
Cache invalidate	3 cycles + 5 if block is invalidated + 8 if invalidated block was exclusive copy
check_out	Same as cache miss, plus 1 cycle for check_out issue
check_in	Same as cache invalidate, plus 1 cycle for check_in issue
Directory	10 cycles + 8 if cache block is received + 5 if message is sent + 8 if cache block is sent
Trap	255 cycles + 5 for each message sent + 8 for each block sent (directory hardware locked out for first 55 cycles)

Table 3: Baseline System Assumptions

Factor	Var. Due (%)	Mean Effect (%)	90% Confidence Interval
Benchmarks	67.45	n/a	n/a
NPT	24.29	-15.86	[-21.77, -9.96]
RO1	0.14	-1.19	[-7.10, 4.71]
NPT+RO1	0.04	-0.68	[-6.59, 5.22]
/CICO	6.05	-7.92	[-13.82, -2.02]
NPT/CICO	1.94	4.48	[-1.42, 10.38]
RO1/CICO	0.08	0.90	[-5.01, 6.80]
NPT+RO1/CICO	0.00	0.01	[-5.89, 5.92]

Table 4: Analysis of Variance of Dir_1SW Extensions

These numbers were collected from a full factorial experiment using the benchmarks for replication and NPT, RO1, and CICO as factors [10, Chapter 18]. Column "Variation Due" lists the percent of performance variation in the 64 runs ($8 * 2^3$) caused by benchmark, factors, and interactions between factors. The results show that the benchmark, NPT, and CICO are the most important factors. Column "Mean Effect" gives the relative change in normalized execution time caused by factors and interaction terms. NPT and CICO reduce running time the most. (The benchmark row is marked "n/a" because a replication factor is assumed to have no systematic effect.) The final column gives the 90% confidence intervals for each factor and interaction term. The range of all intervals extends up and down from the mean effect by $t_{[0.95;2^3*(8-1)]} * SSE/(2^3 * 8 * 2^3 * (8-1))$, where SSE is the sum of the squares of the residuals (errors)—the difference between an actual value and the corresponding prediction using the mean effect. Use of the t-distribution is meaningful if these differences are distributed normally with zero mean. A normal quantile-quantile plot of the 64 residuals (not shown) reveals that this assumption is approximately true.

come-first-serve order. Queuing delay is included in the cost of a cache miss. Network topology and contention are ignored, and all messages are assumed a fixed latency. Table 3 lists the basic system parameter values.

4.2 Dir_1SW Variants

This section discusses the performance of Dir_1SW variants on 32 processors for the benchmarks in Table 2. The variants are: no-pairwise-traps (NPT), one-shared-copy (RO1), and CICO directives. We examine all eight combinations (2^3). Figure 2 displays execution times for seven cases, normalized to the execution time of the base case (without NPT, RO1, and CICO). Since the normalized execution times are less than 1.0, the extensions all improve performance relative to base Dir_1SW. However, the extensions affect the benchmarks by varying amounts. They matter little to *water* and *tomcatv*, for example, because both perform little communication relative to their computation. (The same effect is apparent for the other protocols compared in Figure 3 of Section 4.3.) For *mp3d*, however, NPT and CICO reduce execution time by 52% and 21%, respectively, by mitigating the effect of this program's unsynchronized sharing in its cell data structure.

To get more insight from the many numbers in Figure 2, we use an analysis of variance to charac-

terize mean behavior. This aggregation is meaningful only if the eight benchmarks are representative of some interesting workload. Table 4 reports results and the table's caption describes the analysis of variance method in more detail. The results show that most of the variation between runs is caused by the benchmarks themselves. Nevertheless, NPT and CICO caused statistically significant variation. The mean relative improvement from NPT was 16%, while CICO yielded 8%.

Using CICO primitives as memory system directives affects sharing behavior and improves performance. Table 5 examines the effect on sharing behavior of using CICO check_in's to flush cache blocks (rather than allowing them to be replaced or invalidated).[2] A check_in improves performance if it enables another processor to find a block at the directory instead of requiring additional messages be sent

---

[2] We also examined check_out's but found their effect to be small.

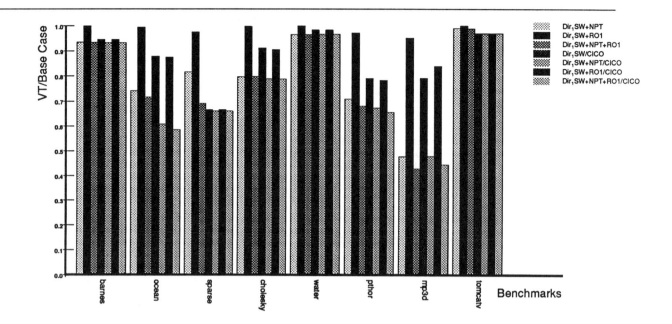

Figure 2: Performance of $Dir_1 SW$ Extensions

This figure shows the time to run the benchmarks with and without no-pairwise-traps (NPT), one-shared-copy (RO1), and CICO, relative to the time to run the same program under base $Dir_1 SW$ without CICO.

Benchmark	Indirections Avoided (%)	Counter Productive check-in's (%)
barnes	84	52
ocean	45	14
sparse	99	51
pthor	61	61
cholesky	94	27
water	97	6
mp3d	74	58
tomcatv	100	65

Table 5: CICO Effects

This table displays the effect on each benchmark's sharing behavior of using check_in's to flush cache blocks (rather than allowing them to be replaced or invalidated). Column "Indirections Avoided" shows the relative reduction in the frequency of indirections. An indirection occurs when a processor cannot obtain a block from the directory, but must send messages to one or more processors. Column "Counter-productive check_in's" gives the fraction of check_in for which the same processor is the next user of a checked-in block.

to other processors. The results show that check_in reduces the frequency of indirections by 45%–100%. A check_in hurts performance if the same processor is the next user of the block, which we found to occur in 6%–65% of the check_in'x.

Together, NPT and CICO ran programs 19% faster, implying NPT makes CICO less important. With NPT, CICO has a more modest impact on indirections to previously exclusive blocks (e.g., migratory data). Without NPT or CICO, migrating a block costs four network traversals and two traps. Adding NPT or CICO eliminates the traps, while CICO also reduces the network traversals to two. Thus, at best, adding CICO to NPT improves performance by a factor of two. In practice, the effect is much smaller, because programs do not spend much time migrating data.

Finally, we would like to estimate how the effects of NPT and CICO vary from benchmark to benchmark. To do this, we calculate 90% confidence intervals assuming the residuals—the performance not explained by average effects—are normally distributed with mean zero. This calculation—explained further in the caption of Table 4—reveals $[-22\%, -10\%]$ for NPT and $[-14\%, -2\%]$ for CICO. With eight benchmarks and not-exactly-normally distributed residuals, our confidence intervals are best taken with a grain of salt.

In summary, NPT and CICO improve performance of almost all programs, while RO1 helps a little. Since

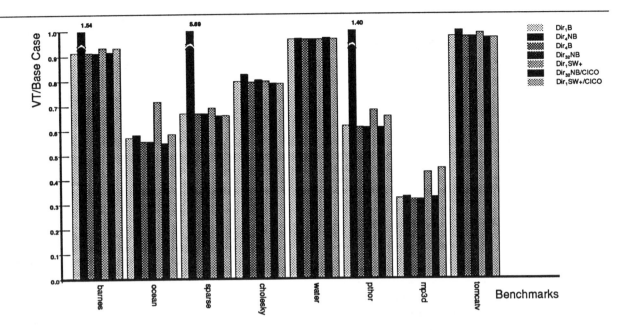

Figure 3: Performance of Other Protocols

This figure displays the normalized execution times (with respect to base Dir_1SW without CICO) for several protocols. Three runs of Dir_4NB are broken bars, because their normalized execution was much longer than Dir_1SW's.

NPT and RO1 use the same mechanisms as the base protocol, we incorporated them in a new protocol called Dir_1SW^+.

4.3 Comparison to Other Protocols

This section compares Dir_1SW^+ without and with CICO, denoted Dir_1SW^+ and Dir_1SW^+/CICO, against several other protocols. Figure 3 displays normalized execution time for the eight benchmarks running on 32 processors under several protocols. The principal result is that Dir_1SW^+ and Dir_1SW^+/CICO perform comparably to $Dir_{32}NB$—well within 10%—even when $Dir_{32}NB$ uses CICO, except for mp3d with its unscalable, unsynchronized sharing. The data also show that Dir_4NB is an unstable protocol, at least, when no special mechanism handles read-only data.

These conclusions do not seem to be sensitive to the key system parameters of network and directory latency. (We also measured runs with 64 processors, but do not report these results because they did not differ qualitatively.) Table 6 shows the normalized execution time results from varying interconnection network latency from 100 processor cycles (the default) to 400 cycles. A 400-cycle network slowed all protocols by about a factor of two, but it has little ef-

fect on the performance difference between $Dir_{32}NB$ and Dir_1SW^+.

Increasing the latency of a directory operation to 100 cycles approximates the effect of using an auxiliary processor, rather than a finite state machine, to perform directory operations. Increasing the directory cost from 10 to 100 cycles slowed the benchmarks by an average of 40% with no obvious trends favoring one protocol over another. Finally, we looked at performance with larger values for both network and directory latency. With the slower network, increasing directory latency only decreased performance slightly (15%).

5 Discussion

While quantitative results are useful, it is important to step back and look at what they mean. The data shows that:

- Memory system directives, such as CICO, can alter program behavior to make simple directory hardware more attractive.

- Elucidating the mechanisms underlying a coherence protocol can lead to new protocols that per-

Directory Access Cost	Network Latency	$Dir_{32}NB$		$Dir_1 SW^+$		$Dir_1 SW^+/CICO$	
		Mean	Deviation	Mean	Deviation	Mean	Deviation
10	100	0.7261	0.2155	0.7756	0.1759	0.7503	0.1829
10	400	1.3285	0.3286	1.3777	0.3210	1.3348	0.2914
100	100	1.0096	0.2035	1.0803	0.1535	1.0332	0.1452
100	400	1.5403	0.4142	1.5857	0.4076	1.5179	0.3636

Table 6: Varying System Assumptions

This table displays the arithmetic mean and standard deviation of the normalized execution times (with respect to base $Dir_1 SW$ without CICO) for eight benchmarks under several protocols with different assumptions of directory cost and network latency. The arithmetic mean listed for each specific system is proportional to the execution time of the eight benchmarks on that system, provided each benchmarks ran for the same amount of time under the base case.

form better without significantly increasing implementation complexity.

- For the system assumptions and benchmarks, most protocols performed similarly. The significant disparity in hardware complexity and the small difference in performance argue that $Dir_1 SW^+$ may be a more effective use of resources.

Although our results have immediate import, they also apply to future computers. These machines are moving toward large-scale ($\geq 1K$-processors) systems of fast microprocessors (≥ 1 GIPS). The network latencies of these machines (measured in processor cycles) will be much larger than today's machines. The data in Table 6 for 400 cycle network latency shows that larger networks do not affect $Dir_1 SW$ more than other protocols such as $Dir_n NB$ (assuming that programs infrequently cause broadcasts).

A perhaps more important implication of the data is that performance in machines with long network latencies is not sensitive to directory latency. This suggests that moving protocol sequencing to software running on a node's main processor, an auxiliary processor (as in the Intel Paragon), or a processor in the network interface may be practical [1]. The obvious drawback of this approach is that a processor sequences a protocol slower than a hardware finite state machine. A secondary drawback is that slower directories increase directory contention. The data shows that increasing directory latency from 10 to 100 cycles degrades execution time by 15%. This degradation can be mitigated or reversed by reducing directory contention (e.g., with greater interleaving) and by using protocols that send fewer messages.

On the other hand, software sequencing offers many advantages and opportunities:

- System design time can be reduced because less hardware must be designed. In addition, field-

upgrades of protocols are possible. Thus, the design time and hardware for shared-memory machines could be similar to message-passing computers.

- Protocols can adapt to dynamic program behavior since buffering and analyzing recent behavior is practical in software.

- Protocols can be statically tailored by compilers, program libraries, or application programs to behave differently for different objects [3]. For example, update protocols could distribute widely-used data (e.g., the vector x in $x := Ax + b$) and help in synchronization (a barrier wakeup) [6].

- Protocols can support higher-level operations such as fetching an entire row of a matrix or a scatter-gather operator.

- Collecting information for performance monitoring is much easier.

Regrettably, we leave evaluation of these ideas to future work. Our benchmarks were written for small scale systems. Running these programs on more than 32 or 64 processors exposes bottlenecks and yields poor speedup. We plan to use the CICO programming model [12] to construct programs that manage communication more effectively and use these programs to evaluate these ideas.

6 Conclusions

Shared memory offers many advantages, such as a uniform address space and referential transparency, that are difficult to replicate in today's massively-parallel, message-passing computers. The key to effective, scalable, shared-memory parallel computers is to address the software and hardware issues together.

This paper explored the complexity of implementing directory protocols by examining their *mechanisms*—primitive operations on directories, caches, and network interfaces. We compare the following protocols: Dir_1B, Dir_4B, Dir_4NB, Dir_nNB [2], Dir_1SW [9] and an improved version of Dir_1SW (Dir_1SW^+). The comparison shows that the mechanisms and mechanism sequencing of Dir_1SW and Dir_1SW^+ are simpler than those for other protocols. Simulation results for eight benchmarks on 32-processor systems show that Dir_1SW^+'s performance is comparable to more complex directory protocols. The small performance difference between Dir_1SW^+ and the more complex protocols is attributable to two factors: the small degree of sharing in programs and CICO directives. The significant disparity in hardware complexity and the small difference in performance argue that Dir_1SW^+ may be a more effective use of resources.

As network latencies increase, the performance effect of directory operation overhead decreases, which provides the opportunity to sequence directory operations in a processor rather than a state machine. This change, in turn, permits high-level directory operations that have the potential to hide more of the increased communication cost. Evaluating these alternatives for kiloprocessor systems will require new benchmarks and an evaluation platform that simulate more processors than current machines contain.

7 Acknowledgements

Dave Douglas, Danny Hillis, Roger Lee, and Steve Swartz of Thinking Machines provided invaluable advice and assistance in building the Wisconsin Wind Tunnel. Glen Ecklund and Alain Kägi helped develop the Wisconsin Wind Tunnel and applications. Singh et al. [16] wrote and distributed the SPLASH benchmarks.

References

[1] Anant Agarwal, Beng-Hong Lim, David Kranz, and John Kubiatowicz. APRIL: A Processor Architecture for Multiprocessing. In *Proceedings of the 17th Annual International Symposium on Computer Architecture*, pages 104–114, June 1990.

[2] Anant Agarwal, Richard Simoni, Mark Horowitz, and John Hennessy. An Evaluation of Directory Schemes for Cache Coherence. In *Proceedings of the 15th Annual International Symposium on Computer Architecture*, pages 280–289, 1988.

[3] John K. Bennett, John B. Carter, and Willy Zwanepoel. Munin: Distributed Shared Memory Based on Type-Specific Memory Coherence. In *Second ACM SIGPLAN Symposium on Principles & Practice of Parallel Programming (PPOPP)*, pages 168–176, February 1990.

[4] David Chaiken, John Kubiatowicz, and Anant Agarwal. LimitLESS Directories: A Scalable Cache Coherence Scheme. In *Proceedings of the Fourth International Conference on Architectural Support for Programming Languages and Operating Systems (ASPLOS IV)*, pages 224–234, April 1991.

[5] David Lars Chaiken. Cache Coherence Protocols for Large-Scale Multiprocessors. Technical Report MIT/LCS/TR-489, MIT Laboratory for Computer Science, September 1990.

[6] James R. Goodman, Mary K. Vernon, and Philip J. Woest. Efficient Synchronization Primitives for Large-Scale Cache-Coherent Multiprocessors. In *Proceedings of the Third International Conference on Architectural Support for Programming Languages and Operating Systems (ASPLOS III)*, pages 64–77, April 1989.

[7] Anoop Gupta and Wolf-Dietrich Weber. Cache Invalidation Patterns in Shared-Memory Multiprocessors. *IEEE Transactions on Computers*, 41(7):794–810, July 1992.

[8] David B. Gustavson. The Scalable Coherent Interface and Related Standards Projects. *IEEE Micro*, 12(2):10–22, February 1992.

[9] Mark D. Hill, James R. Larus, Steven K. Reinhardt, and David A. Wood. Cooperative Shared Memory: Software and Hardware for Scalable Multiprocessors. In *Proceedings of the Fifth International Conference on Architectural Support for Programming Languages and Operating Systems (ASPLOS V)*, pages 262–273, October 1992.

[10] Raj Jain. *The Art of Computer Systems Performance Analysis: Techniques for Experimental Design, Measurement, Simulation, and Modeling*. John Wiley & Sons, 1991.

[11] David Kranz, Kirk Johnson, Anant Agarwal, Kubiatowicz, and Beng-Hong Lim. Integrating Message-Passing and Shared-Memory: Early Experience. In *Fourth ACM SIGPLAN Symposium on Principles & Practice of Parallel Programming (PPOPP)*, May 1993. To appear.

[12] James R. Larus, Satish Chandra, and David A Wood. CICO: A Shared-Memory Programming Performance Model. Submitted for publication., January 1993.

[13] Daniel Lenoski, James Laudon, Kourosh Gharachorloo, Wolf-Dietrich Weber, Anoop Gupta, John Hennessy, Mark Horowitz, and Monica Lam. The Stanford DASH Multiprocessor. *IEEE Computer*, 25(3):63–79, March 1992.

[14] Daniel E. Lenoski. *The Design and Analysis of DASH: A Scalable Directory-Based Multiprocessor*. PhD thesis, Stanford University, February 1992. CSL-TR-92-507.

[15] Steven K. Reinhardt, Mark D. Hill, James R. Larus, Alvin R. Lebeck, James C. Lewis, , and David A. Wood. The Wisconsin Wind Tunnel: Virtual Prototyping of Parallel Computers. In *Proceedings of the 1993 ACM SIGMETRICS Conference on Measuring and Modeling of Computer Systems*, page ?, May 1993. To appear.

[16] Jaswinder Pal Singh, Wolf-Dietrich Weber, and Anoop Gupta. SPLASH: Stanford Parallel Applications for Shared Memory. *Computer Architecture News*, 20(1):5–44, March 1992.

[17] Wolf-Dietrich Weber and Anoop Gupta. Analysis of Cache Invalidation Patterns in Multiprocessors. In *Proceedings of the Third International Conference on Architectural Support for Programming Languages and Operating Systems (ASPLOS III)*, pages 243–256, April 1989.

SESSION 9:

Cache
Design

A case for two-way skewed-associative caches*

André Seznec

IRISA, Campus de Beaulieu

35042 Rennes Cedex, FRANCE

e-mail : seznec@irisa.fr

Abstract

We introduce a new organization for multi-bank caches: the skewed-associative cache. A two-way skewed-associative cache has the same hardware complexity as a two-way set-associative cache, yet simulations show that it typically exhibits the same hit ratio as a four-way set associative cache with the same size. Then skewed-associative caches must be preferred to set-associative caches.

Until the three last years external caches were used and their size could be relatively large. Previous studies have showed that, for cache sizes larger than 64 Kbytes, direct-mapped caches exhibit hit ratios nearly as good as set-associative caches at a lower hardware cost. Moreover, the cache hit time on a direct-mapped cache may be quite smaller than the cache hit time on a set-associative cache, because optimistic use of data flowing out from the cache is quite natural.

But now, microprocessors are designed with small on-chip caches. Performance of low-end microprocessor systems highly depends on cache behavior. Simulations show that using some associativity in on-chip caches allows to boost the performance of these low-end systems.

When considering optimistic use of data (or instruction) flowing out from the cache, the cache hit time of a two-way skewed-associative (or set-associative) cache is very close to the cache hit time of a direct-mapped cache. Therefore two-way skewed associative caches represent the best tradeoff for today microprocessors with on-chip caches whose sizes are in the range of 4-8K bytes.

Keywords: *microprocessors, cache, set-associative cache, skewed-associative cache.*

1 Introduction

For a few years, the direct-mapped cache organization has been considered as the best organization for microprocessor caches [7, 14]. But technology has changed, large external caches which *were* associated with first generation RISC microprocessors are now replaced by small on-chip caches.

In section 2.1, we introduce a new organization for multi-bank cache: the skewed-associative cache. A two-way skewed-associative cache has the same hardware complexity as a two-way set-associative cache. Simulations presented in section 3 show that a two-way skewed-associative cache typically exhibits the same hit ratio as a four-way set associative cache with the same size: two-way skewed-associative caches must be preferred to two-way or four-way set-associative caches.

Then we compare using on-chip two-way skewed-associative caches in place of on-chip direct-mapped caches. In low-end microprocessor systems, the miss penalty is high; increasing clock frequency does not lead to a significant performance improvement. Using a two-way skewed associative cache rather than a direct-mapped cache improves the performance of the system even when it slightly reduces the clock frequency.

On high-end microprocessor systems, a fast second-level cache is used; the performance depends more directly on the clock frequency. In order to reduce cycle time, optimistic use of data flowing out from the caches may be used. Using this technic on microprocessors with on-chip two-way skewed-associative caches will lead to better performance than using on-chip direct-mapped caches.

Finally, we show that skewed-associative caches may be used for implementing physically indexed caches as well as virtually indexed caches.

2 Skewed-associative caches

In this section, we present a new organization for a multi-bank cache: the *skewed-associative cache*.

2.1 Background

High-end microprocessors based systems are built with a secondary external cache: a miss on the primary cache will be served in a few cycles when the line is present in the secondary cache. As the cost of a fast secondary cache is prohibitive, there will not be secondary caches in low-end systems; the miss penalty will be very high (20 or even 50 CPU cycles) (see Figure 1).

Let us recall some technological parameters:

1. Access time to the first word of a line in main memory is generally higher than 250 ns.

2. Access time to the first word of a line in the second level cache is around 60 ns (assuming 12-15ns static memory chips): a throughput of one word per 20 ns may then be obtained.[1]

---

*This work was partially supported by CNRS (PRC-ANM)

[1]This corresponds to TI SuperSparc second-level cache specification[19]

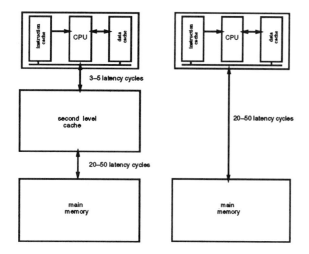

Figure 1: Basic implementations of microprocessor based systems

processor	Freq Mhz	Inst per cycles	WITH	NO
DEC 21064	200	2	24	100
MIPS R4000	100	1	6	25
TI SuperSparc	50	3	9	37
PowerPC	66	2	8	32

WITH: miss penalty with a second level cache
NO: miss penalty without second level cache

Figure 2: Miss penalties converted in Instruction Delays

Figure 2 shows the miss penalties converted in Instruction Delays for some of the recently announced microprocessors when assuming these access delays.

Reducing miss ratio on on-chip caches has become a key issue for performance on all microprocessor systems.

2.2 Skewing on caches: principle

A set-associative cache is illustrated by Figure 3: a X way set-associative cache is built with X distinct banks. A line of data with base address D may be physically mapped on physical line $f(D)$ in any of the distinct banks. This vision of a set-associative cache fits with its physical implementation: X banks of static memory RAMs.

We propose a very slight modification in this design as illustrated in Figure 4:

> Different mapping functions are used for the distinct cache banks i.e., a line of data with base address D may be mapped on physical line $f_0(D)$ in cache bank 0 or in $f_1(D)$ in cache bank 1, etc.

We call a multi-bank cache with such a mapping of the lines onto the distinct banks: a *skewed-associative cache*.

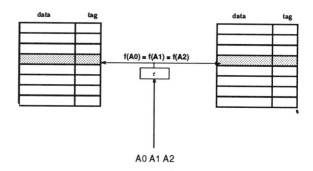

Figure 3: 3 data conflicting for a single set on a two-way set-associative cache

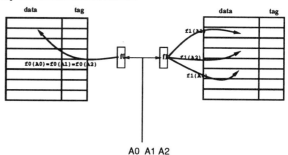

Figure 4: Data conflicting for a cache line on bank 0, but not on bank 1 on a skewed-associative cache

This hardware modification incurs a very small hardware over cost when designing a new microprocessor with on-chip caches since the mapping functions can be chosen so that the implementation uses a very few gates. But we shall see that this may help to increase the hit ratio of caches and then to increase the overall performance of a microprocessor using a multi-bank cache structure.

Related works

In 1977, Smith [15] considered set-associative caches and suggested selecting the set by hashing the main memory address; this approach corresponds to figure 3: a *single* hashing function is used.

More recently Agarwal [2] (Chapter 6.7.2) studied hash-rehash caches.

> As in a conventional cache, the address indexes into a cache set, and the word of data is sent to the processor if it is valid in the set. This case is called a first time hit. On a miss, the address again indexes into the cache but using a different hashing function. If the second access is also unsuccessful, the data must be fetched from memory.

Hash-rehash caches present better overall hit ratios than direct-mapped caches. But Agarwal remarked that for a 64 Kbytes cache, hash-rehash caches induce longer execution time than two-way set-associative caches.

In hash-rehash caches, the primary cache itself is used as a secondary cache after a first time miss. However in skewed-associative caches, different hashing functions are used *at the same time* for indexing the distinct cache banks.

2.3 Choosing the skewing functions

In this section, we give some insight on the properties that might exhibit functions chosen for skewing the lines in the distinct cache banks in order to obtain a good hit ratio.

2.3.1 Equitability

First of all like in classical caches, for each line in the cache, the numbers of lines of data in the main memory that may be mapped onto this cache line must be equal.

2.3.2 Inter-bank dispersion

In a usual X-way set-associative cache, when $(X+1)$ lines of data contend for the same set in the cache, they are all conflicting for the same place in the X cache banks: one of the lines must be rejected from the cache (Figure 3).

We have introduced skewed-associative caches to avoid this situation by scattering the data: mapping functions can be chosen such that whenever two lines of data conflict for a single location in cache bank i, they have very low probability to conflict for a location in cache bank j (Figure 4).

Ideally, mapping functions may be chosen such as the set of lines that might be mapped on a cache line of bank i will be equaly distributed over all the lines in the other cache banks.

2.3.3 Local dispersion in a single bank

Many applications exhibit spatial locality, therefore the mapping functions must be chosen so as to avoid having two "almost" neighbor lines of data conflicting for the same physical line in cache bank i.

The different mapping functions must respect a certain form of local dispersion on a single bank; the mapping functions f_i must limit the number of conflicts when mapping any region of consecutive lines of data in a single cache bank i.

2.3.4 Simple hardware implementation

A key issue for the overall performance of a microprocessor is the pipeline length. Using distinct mapping functions on the distinct cache banks will have no effects on the performance, as long as the computations of the mapping functions can be added to a non critical stage in the pipeline and do not lengthen the pipeline cycle. Let us notice that in most of the new generation microprocessors, the address computation stage is not the critical stage in the pipeline (e.g. in TI Super-Sparc, two cascaded ALU operations may be executed in a single cycle).

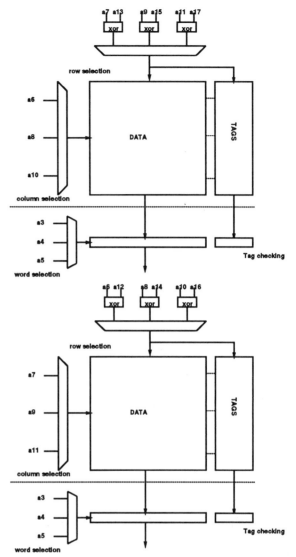

Figure 5: An example of a two-way skewed-associative cache

In order to achieve this, we have to chose mapping functions whose hardware implementations are very simple: as few gate delays as possible.

In [20], we exhibited a family of four functions f_i mapping which respects the previous properties. For an address A, each bit of $f_i(A)$ is obtained by Exclusive-ORing at most 4 bits of the binary decomposition of A.

2.4 Skewing on two-way associative caches

In this paper, we focus only on two-way skewed-associative caches. Our basic goals here are to minimize hardware implementation cost and extra delay on cache hit time.

An example

Let us consider the particular case of 64 bytes lines and 4096 bytes cache banks. $(a_n, .. , a_0)$ is the binary representation of the address. A possible organization for a two-way skewed associative cache is illustrated in Figure 5.

The skewing functions used in this example verify the previously mentioned criterions for "good" skewing functions.

On this example, only three two entries XOR gates are added to the classical cache bank design. In the proposed design, the access time to the cache bank is only slightly increased by the delay for crossing a XOR gate when using skewing functions.

We believe that the access time may even be exactly the same as in a classical two-way set-associative cache:

1. In a microprocessor, when using a one-cycle access cache, the cache hit time generally determines the machine cycle. The address computation is performed in a less critical stage: the XOR gates may be added at the end of that stage.

2. When using a pipelined cache, row selection may be done in the second cycle.

A formal description of the family of skewing functions

Let 2^c be the size of the line.

Let 2^n be the number of cache lines in a cache bank and let us consider the decomposition of a binary representation of an address A in bit substrings A = (A_3 ,A_2, A_1, A_0), A_0 is a c bit string: the displacement in the line. A_1 and A_2 are two n bits strings and A_3 is the string of the $q - (2*n+c)$ most significant bits.

Let us consider T an integer such that $0 \leq T < 2^n$ and $\bar{T}$ its binary opposite,($\bar{T} = 2^n - 1 - T$).

Let ϕ be a Bit Permute Permutation on the set $\{0, .., 2^n - 1\}$ (e.g. Identity, Perfect Shuffle, Bit Reversal).

We consider the mapping functions defined respectively by:

$$F_0^{T,\phi} : \quad S \quad \longrightarrow \quad \{0, .., 2^{n+c} - 1\}$$
$$(A_3, A_2, A_1, A_0) \quad \longrightarrow \quad (A_1 \oplus (\phi(A_2) \bullet T), A_0)$$

$$F_1^{T,\phi} : \quad S \quad \longrightarrow \quad \{0, .., 2^{n+c} - 1\}$$
$$(A_3, A_2, A_1, A_0) \quad \longrightarrow \quad (A_1 \oplus (\phi(A_2) \bullet \bar{T}), A_0)$$

$\oplus$ is the exclusive OR and $\bullet$ is the bitwise product.

These functions satisfy the criterions for "good" skewing functions defined in the paper (Equitability, inter-bank dispersion and local dispersion).

Each bit of the $F_0^{T,\phi}(A)$ or $F_1^{T,\phi}(A)$ is either directly a bit of the binary representation of address A or the XOR of two bits of this binary representation.

T may be chosen in order to allow symmetric design of the two cache banks: when n is even, having the same number of bits equal to one and zero seems an interesting approach.

In the previous example in figure 5, T= 44 (binary decomposition 101010) and the Bit Permute Permutation is the identity.

2.5 Replacement policy on a two-way skewed-associative cache

When a miss occurs on a X-bank cache, the line of data to be replaced must be chosen among X lines. Different replacement policies may be used. LRU replacement policy or pseudo-random replacement policy are generally used in set-associative caches.

The pseudo-random replacement policy is the simplest to implement. But LRU replacement policy generally works better and may be implemented at a reasonable hardware cost. Implementing a LRU replacement policy on a two-way set-associative cache is quite simple: a single bit tag per set sufficient. More generally a LRU replacement policy for a X-way associative is feasible with adding only $X * (X - 1)/2$ bit tags to each set.

Unfortunately, we have not been able to find concise information to associate with a cache line which would allow a simple hardware implementation of a LRU replacement policy on a skewed-associative cache.

Nevertheless, for two-way skewed-associative caches, a pseudo-LRU replacement policy may work fine:

> A tag bit is associated with each line in bank 0: when the line is indexed, the tag bit is asserted when the data was in bank 0 and deasserted when the data is in bank 1.

> On a miss, the tag of the line selected in bank 0 is read: when this tag is 1, the missing line is written in bank 1 otherwise the missing line is written in bank 0

Notice that implementing this replacement policy on a two-way skewed-associative cache requires the same hardware as implementing a LRU replacement policy on a two-way set-associative cache.

3 Simulations

Cache simulations have been conducted in order to compare skewed-associative caches with usual cache organizations.

Presented results show that for equal sizes, a two-way skewed-associative cache exhibits approximately the same miss ratio as a four-way set-associative cache.

3.1 Traces

Our set of traces is composed with two distinct sets.

The first set is composed with the three traces from the Hennessy-Patterson software obtained from the DLX simulator [5] (gcc, TeX and Spice).

Seven other traces were generated using the SparcSim simulator facility [18]; this set was composed with:

- RESEAU: the simulator of a particular interconnection network

- POISSON : a Poisson solver

- STRASSEN: a matrix-matrix multiply using the Strassen algorithm.

- LINPACKUD: part of the LINPACK benchmark

- CACHE : The cache simulator itself

- CPTC : A Pascal-to-C translator

- SPARSE: multiply of a sparse matrix by a full vector.

In the results presented in the paper, all the benchmarks were valued with the same weight.

For direct-mapped caches, a victim cache of four lines was assumed. A similar mechanism was evaluated for multi-way associative caches, but as it did not bring significant hit improvement, we do not consider it in the paper.

Virtual indexing of the cache was assumed for the simulations. Physical indexing will be discussed in section 5.

3.2 Miss ratios

Different cache configurations have been simulated: mixed data/instructions and split caches. Results for a 16 bytes line size are reported in figures 6 to 9. Notice that the reported miss ratios are certainly very optimistic: single process traces, exceptions not simulated (TLB miss, etc.), no system, .. Effective miss ratios will certainly be higher.

For separate instruction and data caches, the microprocessor is assumed to execute one instruction per cycle. The miss ratios reported in Figures 8 and 9 is the average number of misses per sequenced instruction (i.e $\frac{Instruction\ Misses+Data\ Misses}{Number\ of\ Instructions}$).

For direct-mapped caches, a victim buffer [9] of four lines was assumed. The ratio of misses which effectively induce an access on memory or on a second level cache is reported in column "Miss-Vict"[2].

LRU replacement policy was used for set-associative caches. The pseudo-LRU replacement policy described in the previous section was used for two-way skewed-associative caches.

These results show that at equal sizes a two-way skewed-associative cache exhibits approximately the same miss ratio as a four-way set-associative cache. Figures 10 and 11 shows that this conclusion is valid on the two sets of traces. Experiments were also conducted with larger line sizes and lead to the same conclusion.

At this point of the study, we make the following recommendation:

> A two-way skewed associative cache must be preferred to a usual two-way or four-way set-associative caches.

Remark 1: Other simulations were conducted assuming a LRU policy replacement on a two-way skewed-associative cache. Better hit ratios than with the

---

[2]Victim caching does not lead to significant hit improvement for skewed-associative or set-associative caches

Organization	Miss	Miss - Vict
Direct mapped	0.074086	0.064618
2-way set-associative	0.050133	
4-way set-associative	0.041690	
2-way skewed-associative	0.043938	

Figure 6: mixed data/instruction cache: 4096 bytes

Organization	Miss	Miss - Vict
Direct mapped	0.046719	0.041846
2-way set-associative	0.029362	
4-way set-associative	0.024265	
2-way skewed-associative	0.024287	

Figure 7: mixed data/instruction cache: 8192 bytes

Organization	Miss	Miss - Vict
Direct mapped	0.058757	0.054152
2-way set-associative	0.041994	
4-way set-associative	0.036830	
2-way skewed-associative	0.037562	

Figure 8: two 4096 bytes split caches

Organization	Miss	Miss - Vict
Direct mapped	0.037876	0.034900
2-way set-associative	0.025992	
4-way set-associative	0.021844	
2-way skewed-associative	0.020865	

Figure 9: two 8192 bytes split caches

pseudo-LRU policy were obtained, but unfortunately LRU policy cannot be implemented at a reasonable hardware cost.

3.3 Skewing versus hashing

Hewlett-Packard recently introduced the HP7100 microprocessor. In this microprocessor, addresses are hashed before accessing a direct-mapped cache. On the HP7100, the whole virtual address including process number is hashed and a very large *external* cache is used (greater than 128 Kbytes); the microprocessor designers claimed that this technic improves the average hit ratio on a virtually-indexed large cache when running multiprocess workloads. This phenomenum was also observed by Agarwal [2].

Set-associative caches indexed with the function f_0 instead of the usual bit-selection have been simulated for associativity degree 1,2 and 4. Results for split 8192 bytes caches are shown in figure 12. On our benchmark set and for a small cache size, hashing the addresses does not lead to very significant hit ratio

Organization	Miss	Miss - Vict
Direct mapped	0.033929	0.031123
2-way set-associative	0.022641	
4-way set-associative	0.018305	
2-way skewed-associative	0.016981	

Figure 10: SparcSim traces

Organization	Miss	Miss - Vict
Direct mapped	0.047087	0.043712
2-way set-associative	0.033811	
4-way set-associative	0.030103	
2-way skewed-associative	0.029928	

Figure 11: DLX traces

improvement.

These results show that the improveement of performance of skewed-associative over set-associative caches is mostly due to the inter-bank dispersion property (see section 2.3.2) and not to a simple hashing on the addresses.

3.4 Local dispersion

In order to illustrate why, the local dispersion property (see section 2.3.3) is very important, we simulated a two-way skewed-associative cache where skewing functions f_0 and f_1 are two independent random functions. Average miss ratio for these simulations are given in figure 12 in row "skewed-assoc. RAND". As f_0 and f_1 are independant random functions, there may be local interferences on a single cache bank. These interferences affect a lot the hit ratio.

Organization	Miss	Miss - Vict
Direct mapped	0.037876	0.034900
Direct mapped hashed	0.037586	0.032970
2-way set-assoc.	0.025992	
2-way set-assoc. hashed	0.025632	
4-way set-assoc.	0.021844	
4-way set-assoc. hashed	0.020895	
2-way skewed-assoc.	0.020865	
2-way skewed-assoc. RAND	0.024202	

Figure 12: Skewing versus hashing

4 Influence on performance

In this section, we show that, for 8K bytes cache, using an associative cache structure will lead to better performance than using a direct-mapped cache structure.

4.1 Caches for low-end microprocessor systems

In this section, we consider low-end microprocessor systems.

When cache hit time does not determine the microprocessor clock

From now, we resent performance using *Cycle Per Instruction* or *Time per Instruction* assuming separate instruction cache and data cache.

Figure 13 illustrates the performance in Cycle Per Instruction on our benchmark set for different memory latencies. Both cache sizes are 8192 bytes and length of a cache line is 16 bytes.

Formula (1) is used for deriving Figure 13 from Figure 9.

$$3 * (miss - vict) * Cycle + vict + Lat * (miss - vict) \quad (1)$$

where *miss* is the miss ratio of the cache, *vict* is is the ratio of misses that hits in the victim cache [3] and *Lat* is the latency for accessing the missing line in the main memory (or second level cache). The internal delay in the microprocessor is assumed to be 3 cycles.

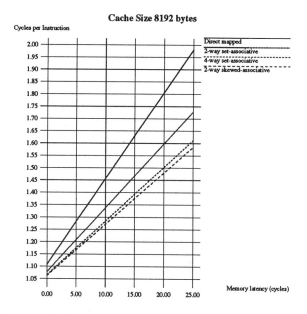

Figure 13: Separate instruction cache and data cache

When the cache hit time does not determine directly the clock frequency of the microprocessor (e.g. when cache access is pipelined), then an associative structure must be used for the cache: performance benefits for memory latency of the order of 20 cycles is about 20 %.

Unfortunately, on many microprocessors, the cache hit time is determined by the clock frequency of the microprocessor.

---

[3]for direct mapped caches only

When cache hit time determines the microprocessor clock

For illustrating why on-chip caches used in low-end microprocessors must be associative, we consider two microprocessors directly accessing a main memory with a 250 ns access time [4]:

- Processor P1 is a single-issue RISC microprocessor with two on-chip 8K bytes direct-mapped caches.

- Processor P2 is a single-issue RISC microprocessor with two on-chip 8K bytes two-way skewed-associative caches.

Figure 14 illustrates the clock needed on each of the two processors for achieving a performance of one instruction per X ns on our set of benchmarks.

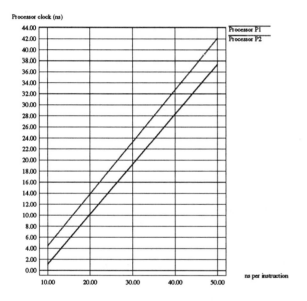

Figure 14: Comparing P1 and P2 connected to main memory

Remark that Processor P2 achieved one instruction per 20 ns with a 14 ns clock, while Processor P1 needs a 10 ns clock to achieve the same performance level.

This example clearly indicates that for low-end microprocessor systems, the structure of the caches have to be associative:

> Using a two-way skewed-associative cache is the reasonable choice.

4.2 Caches for high-end microprocessor systems

In high-end microprocessor systems, second level caches will be used. For getting back the first word of

data of a missing line from this second level cache, a delay around 60 ns seems realistic with today technology.

As for low-end microprocessor systems, an associative structure of cache must be used when the cache hit time does not determine the basic clock of the processor (see Figure 13).

As in the previous section, in Figure 15, we compare the clocks needed on the hypothetic processors P1 and P2 for achieving a constant performance when they are connected to a second level cache [5]

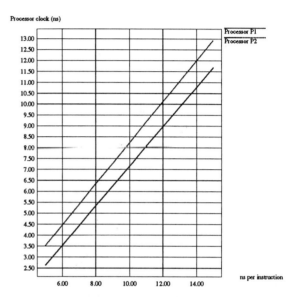

Figure 15: Comparing P1 and P2 both connected with a second level cache

On this figure, one will notice that the *effective* performance of processor P1 and processor P2 at a given frequency are quite close:

> With a 10 ns clock, processor P2 achieves one instruction per 12 ns, while processor P1 achieves this level of performance with a 9 ns clock.

When data flowing out from the cache cannot be used before tag check, the cache hit time on a two-way skewed-associative cache and on a direct mapped cache are within a very few per cent [6], then using two-way skewed-associative caches will lead to slightly better overall performance of the system than using direct-mapped caches.

Optimistic execution

In order to increase clock frequency, data flowing out from the cache may be used before tag check with direct-mapped caches. Checking the validity of the data word may be executed in parallel with the other activities in the pipeline. The current cycle in the

---

[4] In this example, the important parameter is the sequencing rate, a single-issue microprocessor at frequency F may be replace by a dual-issue microprocessor at frequency F/2

[5] For simplicity, we do not consider second level cache misses.
[6] 2 % was reported by Hill [6]

pipeline will be canceled if the data (or instruction) is found to be unvalid.

We shall refer to this technic as *optimistic execution*.

Optimistic execution was also proposed for a set-associative cache: the most-recently-used data (MRU) in the selected set [3] can be systematically used.

> For a 128 Kbytes cache, assuming a 12 cycles penalty on a global miss, and a one cycle penalty on a miss on the MRU region, but a hit on the global cache, the cache access time was shown to be within 4% of the performance of a true one-cycle 4-way set-associative cache[7].

Although a 32-way set-associative cache was initially considered,, the authors claimed that reducing associativity degree to four and using the optimistic MRU policy dramatically reduce the cache hit time in the range of 30-35%.

Using optimistic execution on a direct-mapped cache and on a set-associative (or skewed-associative) cache seem to lead to very close cache hit times.

When using a skewed-associative associative cache, the (pseudo) Most Recently Used data is selected. We assume that a miss on pseudo MRU region which hits in the other cache bank costs one stall cycle on the processor [8].

Notice that, on a four-way set-associative cache, the hit ratio on the MRU region corresponds to the hit ratio on a direct-mapped cache which size is only the fourth of the original cache size, while on a two-way skewed-associative cache, this hit ratio corresponds approximately to the hit ratio on a direct-mapped cache which size is half of the original cache size. There a two-way skewed-associative cache will achieve better performance than a four-way set-associative cache.

In Figure 16, we compare the clocks needed on the hypothetic processors P1 and P2 for achieving a constant performance, but here we assume optimistic execution on both processors.

Performance of processor P1 and performance of processor P2 are quite close:

> With a 8 ns clock, processor P2 achieves one instruction per 10 ns, while processor P1 achieves this performance with a 7.2 ns clock.

As, cache hit times for the two processors would be in a very few per cent (may be 5 %), using a two-way skewed associative cache would lead to slightly better performance.

5 Skewed-associative caches and virtual memory

5.1 Virtual indexing or physical indexing

As already mentionned, cache hit time is one of the critical path in the microprocessor. Caches may be

---

[7] considering a constant cycle

[8] This assumption is quite pessimistic, when the read data (or instruction) is not used directly by the next instruction, no cycle is lost

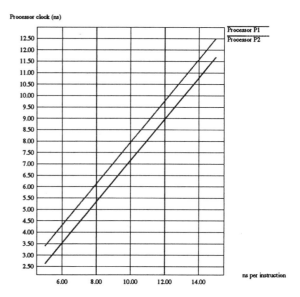

Figure 16: Optimistic execution on P1 and P2, both connected with a second level cache

virtually or physically indexed. When sharing pages between processes, physical addressing of the cache allows to avoid multiple copies of the same line of data in the cache and then the data in the cache always remain coherent; physical addressing of the cache may be considered as very desirable. Unfortunately, for physically indexed caches, the virtual-to-physical address translation must precede the cache indexing, thus increasing the overall cache hit time.

Virtually indexed caches are used in HP7xxx, MIPS R4000 for example. When the cache is virtually indexed, using a skewed-associative cache in place of a set-associative cache will not lenghten the cache hit time.

5.1.1 An artifice for physical indexed caches

Physically indexed caches are used in Dec 21064, TI SuperSparc, IBM Power for example. When the virtual-to-physical address translation effectively precedes the cache indexing, using a skewed-associative cache in place of a set-associative cache would not lenghten the overall hit time.

But, on the Dec 21064 and the TI SuperSparc, an artifice has been used in order to allow to execute in parallel the indexing of the cache and the virtual-to-physical address translation. The size of the cache bank is chosen equal to (or inferior than) the minimum size of a page of the virtual memory; on a direct-mapped or a set-associative cache, the bits required for indexing the cache are not translated: virtual-to-physical address translation and cache indexing may be executed in parallel.

Such an artifice cannot be used for skewed-associative caches: in order to enable inter-bank dispersion, some extra bits of th address are used for computing the distinct mapping functions for the distinct cache banks e.g. for computing the skewing functions F_0 and F_1 proposed in section 2.4 for a 8Kbytes two-way skewed-associative cache with a 16 bytes cache line, the 20 lowest significant bits of the address must be known!

5.1.2 Uncomplete address translation

Some recent works [13, 12] have shown that, when the page allocation algorithm is implemented in such a way that virtual-to-physical address translation does not affect the lowest significant bits of the virtual page number, the miss ratio on a physically indexed cache is lower than when usual page allocation algorithm is used.

This result holds for medium range primary caches (16 KB to 512 KB) [13], as well as for large secondary caches [12]. On the other hand, a too large number of untranslated bits would lead to a significant increase of page faults, particularly on low-end microprocessor systems; e.g. on a 8 Megabyte system, having 20 bits untranslated is not realistic.

But keeping 15 or even 18 bits untranslated, even on a low-end system would not lead to a significant increase of the number of page faults:

Let us consider a 8 Megabytes physical memory and a virtual page size of 4Kbytes, with the usual page allocation, the physical memory acts as a 2048 lines fully-associative cache, while if the 15 lowest significant bits must not be affected by the virtual-to-physical address translation, it would act as a 256-way set-associative cache. It is well known that the behavior of these two structures of caches are very close!

5.2 Partial skewing

In this section, we assume that the page allocation algorithm is implemented in such a way that it does not affect a few of the lowest significant bits of the page number.

If the computation of mapping functions on the cache banks uses only the untranslated address bits, then the artifice described in section 5.1.1 may be used for executing in parallel the indexing of a skewed-associative cache and the virtual-to-physical address translation.

In this section, we show that skewed-associative cache may also perform well in the case where only a limited number of bits are skewed.

A case study Let us consider that the 15 lowest significant bits of the virtual addresses not translated i.e the virtual address and the physical address are equal modulo 32K.

Let us consider the mapping functions defined by:

if $X = 2^{15}X_4 + 2^{12}X_3 + 2^9 X_2 + 2^4 X_1 + X_0$ then

$$f_0 : \quad S \quad \longrightarrow \quad \{0, .., 4095\}$$
$$(X_4, X_3, X_2, X_1, X_0) \quad \longrightarrow \quad (X_2, X_1, X_0)$$

$$f_1 : \quad S \quad \longrightarrow \quad \{0, .., 4095\}$$
$$(X_4, X_3, X_2, X_1, X_0) \quad \longrightarrow \quad (X_3 \oplus X_2, X_1, X_0)$$

f_0 is the usual bit truncation; f_1 does not change the nine lowest significant bits, and the three highest significant bits are simply obtained a XOR.

f_0 and f_1 may be used as mapping functions for a two-way 8Kbytes skewed-associative cache.

Notice that when using these functions, the inter-bank dispersion of data will only be partial: the set of data that can be mapped (by mapping function f_0) onto a given line in bank 0 is distributed among only 8 lines on cache bank 1 by mapping function f_1.

Simulations were conducted using these skewing functions for 8K bytes two-way skewed-associative caches; miss ratios are reported in figure 17. The miss ratios obtained when using this partial skewing are in the same range as the miss ratios observed when using the complete skewing described in section 2.1.

Organization	Miss
Unified 2-way partial skewed-assoc.	0.024503
Unified 2-way complete skewed-assoc.	0.024287
Split 2-way partial skewed-assoc.	0.020891
Split 2-way complete skewed-assoc.	0.020865

Figure 17: Partial versus Complete skewing

Our simulation results tend to show that there is no significative hit ratio improvement when increasing the inter-bank dispersion degree over 8 on a two-way skewed-associative cache as there is no significative hit ratio improvement when increasing the associativity degree over 4 or 8 on a set-associative cache.

This result associated with the results presented in [13, 12] may encourage microprocessor designers to implement physically indexed skewed-associative caches and to impose implementing operating systems with page allocation algorithms respecting the 15 or may be 18 lowest significant bits of the virtual address.

6 Conclusion

We have introduced a new multi-bank cache organization: the skewed-associative cache. The two-way skewed-associative cache has the same hardware complexity as a two-way set-associative, but exhibits a miss ratio close to the miss ratio of a four-way set-associative cache:

A two-way skewed-associative cache must be preferred to a two-way or four-way set associative cache.

Today, microprocessors are built with relatively small on-chip caches. In 1992, 8 Kbytes is the current size for on-chip caches. For this size, miss ratios on direct-mapped caches are significantly higher than on associative caches. In section 4, we have pointed out that, for low-end microprocessor systems, some associativity on on-chip cache(s) will enhance performance: using direct-mapped cache may allow to increase clock frequency, but when the miss penalty becomes high, using a skewed associative cache with a slower clock will lead to a better over all system performance.

Peak performance on high-end systems is a major commercial argument for microprocessor vendors. In high-end systems, large very fast second level caches are used. Performance in these systems highly depends on the clock frequency. In order to reduce the clock frequency, the cache access may be pipelined (e.g. in MIPS R4000 [10] or in DEC 21064[4]) and optimistic execution may be used (e.g. MIPS R4000). Optimistic execution on skewed-associative caches will allow to reach a clock frequency within a few per cent of the clock reachable when using direct-mapped caches. In section 4.2, we have pointed that using such an optimistic execution will lead to slightly better performance when using a two-way skewed associative cache.

At last, in section 5, we have shown that skewed-associative caches may be used for implementing physical caches as well as virtual caches without lenghtening the cache hit time.

As most of the microprocessor chips are designed to built both high-end microprocessor systems and low-end microprocessor systems, using two-way skewed-associative cache structure seems a very interesting trade-off.

Further work on skewed-associative caches will include studies on higher degree of associativity, using skewed-associative caches as second-level caches and for TLBs.

Acknowledgement

The author is endebted with Francois Bodin of IRISA who wrote the first version of the cache simulator and Daniel Windheiser, currently with the University of Michigan who carefully read a draft version of the paper.

References

[1] A. Agarwal, M. Horowitz, J. Hennesy "Cache performance of operating systems and multi-programming workloads" ACM Transactions on Computer Systems, Nov. 1988

[2] A. Agarwal *Analysis of Cache Performance for Operating Systems and Multiprogramming*, Kluwer Academic Publishers, 1989

[3] J.H. Chang, H. Chao, and K. So "Cache Design of A Sub-Micro CMOS System/370" pp208-213, Proceedings of the 14th International Symposium on Computer Architecture (IEEE-ACM), May 1987.

[4] "DECChip 21064-AA RISC Microprocessor, Preliminary Data Sheet" Digital Equipment Corporation, 1992

[5] J.L. Hennessy, D.A. Patterson *Computer Architecture a Quantitative Approach*, Morgan Kaufmann Publishers, Inc. 1990

[6] M.D. Hill, "Aspects of Cache Memory and Instruction Buffer Performance", Ph.D Thesis, University of Berkeley, 1987

[7] M.D. Hill, "A case for direct-mapped caches", IEEE Computer, Dec 1988

[8] M.D.Hill, A.J. Smith "Evaluating Associativity in CPU Caches" IEEE Transactions on Computers, Dec. 1989

[9] N.P. Jouppi, "Improving Direct-Mapped Cache Performance by the addition of a Small Fully-Associative Cache and Prefetch Buffers" Proceedings of the 17th International Symposium on Computer Architecture, June 1990

[10] G. Kane *MIPS RISC Architecture* Prentice-Hall, 1988

[11] G. Kane, J. Heinrich *MIPS RISC Architecture* Prentice-Hall, 1992

[12] R.Kessler, M. Hill "Miss Reduction in Large Real-Indexed Caches," Technical Report No 940, Dpt of Computer Science, University of Wisconsin-Madison, June 90.

[13] W.L. Lynch, B.K. Bray, M.J. Flynn "The Effect of Page Allocations on Caches" Proceedings of MICRO 25 , December 1992

[14] S.A. Przysbylski "Performance-Directed Memory Hierarchy design" PhD Thesis, Stanford University, 1988

[15] A.J. Smith "A Comparative Study of Set Associative Memory Mapping Algorithms and Their Use for Cache and Main Memory" IEEE Transactions on Sofware Engineering, March 1978

[16] A.J. Smith "Cache memories" ACM Computing Surveys, Sept. 1982

[17] A.J. Smith "Line (block) size choice for CPU cache memories" IEEE Transactions on Computers, Sept. 1987

[18] SparcSim Manual, SUN Inc, Dec 1989

[19] "TMS390Z55 Cache Controller, Data Sheet", Texas Instrument, 1992

[20] "Skewed Associative Caches" A. Seznec, F. Bodin INRIA Report 1655, March 1992

Column-Associative Caches:
A Technique for Reducing the Miss Rate of Direct-Mapped Caches

Anant Agarwal and Steven D. Pudar
Laboratory for Computer Science
Massachusetts Institute of Technology
Cambridge, MA 02139

Abstract

Direct-mapped caches are a popular design choice for high-performance processors; unfortunately, direct-mapped caches suffer systematic interference misses when more than one address maps into the same cache set. This paper describes the design of *column-associative* caches, which minimize the conflicts that arise in direct-mapped accesses by allowing conflicting addresses to dynamically choose alternate hashing functions, so that most of the conflicting data can reside in the cache. At the same time, however, the critical hit access path is unchanged. The key to implementing this scheme efficiently is the addition of a *rehash bit* to each cache set, which indicates whether that set stores data that is referenced by an alternate hashing function. When multiple addresses map into the same location, these *rehashed locations* are preferentially replaced. Using trace-driven simulations and an analytical model, we demonstrate that a column-associative cache removes virtually all interference misses for large caches, without altering the critical hit access time.

1 Introduction

The cache is an important component of the memory system of workstations and mainframe computers, and its performance is often a critical factor in the overall performance of the system. The advent of RISC processors and VLSI technology have driven down processor cycle times and made frequent references to main memory unacceptable.

Caches are characterized by several parameters, such as their size, their replacement algorithm, their block size, and their degree of associativity [1]. For cache accesses, a typical address *a* is divided into at least two fields, the tag field (typically the high-order bits) and the index field (the low-order bits), as shown in Figure 1. The index field is used to reference one of the sets, and the tag field is compared to the tags of the data blocks within that set. If the tag field of the address matches one of tag fields of the referenced set, then we have a *hit*, and the data can be obtained from

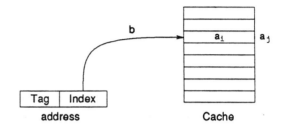

Figure 1: Indexing into a direct-mapped cache using bit-selection hashing.

the block that exhibited the hit.[1] In a *d-way set-associative cache*, each set contains *d* distinct blocks of data accessed by addresses with common index fields but different tags. When the degree of associativity is reduced to one, each set can then hold no more than one block of data. This configuration is called a *direct-mapped cache*.

For a cache of given size, the choice of its degree of associativity influences many performance parameters such as the silicon area (or, alternatively, the number of chips) required to implement the cache, the cache access time, and the miss rate. Because a direct-mapped cache allows only one data block to reside in the cache set that is directly specified by the address index field, its *miss rate* (the ratio of misses to total references) tends to be worse than that of a set-associative cache of the same total size. However, the higher miss rate of direct-mapped caches is mitigated by their smaller *hit access time* [2, 3]. A set-associative cache of the same total size always displays a higher hit access time because an associative search of a set is required during each reference, followed by a multiplexing of the appropriate data word to the processor. Furthermore, direct-mapped caches are simpler and easier to design, and they require less area. Overall, direct-mapped caches are often the most economical choice for use in workstations, where cost-performance is the most important criterion.

1.1 The Problem

Unfortunately, the large number of interference misses that occur in direct-mapped caches are still a major problem. An *interference miss* (also known as a *conflict miss*) occurs when two addresses map into the same cache set in a direct-mapped cache, as shown

---

[1]In most caches, more than one data word can reside in a data block. In this case, an *offset* is the third and lowest-order field in the address, and it is used to select the appropriate data word.

in Figure 1. Consider referencing a cache with two addresses, a_i and a_j, that differ only in some of the higher-order bits (which often occurs in multiprogramming environments). In this case, the addresses will have different tags but identical index fields; therefore, they will reference the same set. If we denote the set that is selected by choosing the low-order bits of an address a as $b[a]$, then we have $b[a_i] = b[a_j]$ for conflicting addresses. The name b comes from the bit-selection operation performed on the bits to obtain the index.

Assume the following reference pattern: a_i a_j a_i a_j a_i a_j $\cdots$. A set-associative cache will not suffer a miss if the program issues the above sequence of references because the data referenced by a_i and a_j can co-reside in a set. In a direct-mapped cache, however, the reference to a_j will result in an interference miss because the data from a_i occupies the selected cache block. The percentage of misses that are due to conflicts varies widely among different applications, but it is often a substantial portion of the overall miss rate.

We believe these interference misses can be largely eliminated by implementing control logic which makes better use of cache area. The challenge, then, is determining a simple, area-efficient cache control algorithm to reduce the number of interference misses and to boost the performance without increasing the degree of associativity.

1.2 Contributions of This Paper

This paper presents the design of a column-associative cache that resolves conflicts by allowing alternate hashing functions, which results in significantly better use of cache area. Using trace-driven simulation, we demonstrate that its miss rate is much better than that of Jouppi's victim cache [4] and the hash-rehash cache of Agarwal, Horowitz, and Hennessy [5], and virtually the same as that of a two-way set-associative cache. Furthermore, its hit access time is the same as that of a direct-mapped cache. To help explain the behavior of the column-associative cache, we also develop and validate an analytical model for this cache.

The rest of this paper is organized as follows. The next section discusses other efforts with similar goals. Section 3 presents the column-associative cache, and Section 4 develops an analytical model for this cache. Section 5 presents the results of trace-driven simulations comparing the performance of several cache designs, and Section 6 concludes the paper.

2 Previous Work

Several schemes have been proposed for reducing the number of interference misses. A general approach to improving direct-mapped cache access is Jouppi's victim cache [4]. A victim cache is a small, fully-associative cache that provides some extra cache lines for data removed from the direct-mapped cache due to misses. Thus, for a reference stream of conflicting addresses, such as a_i a_j a_i a_j ..., the second reference, a_j, will miss and force the data indexed by a_i out of the set. The data that is forced out is placed in the victim cache. Consequently, the third reference, a_i, will not require accessing main memory because the data can be found in the victim cache.

However, this scheme requires a sizable victim cache for adequate performance because it must store all conflicting data blocks. Like the column-associative cache, it requires two or more access

times to fetch a conflicting datum. (One cycle is needed to check the primary cache, the second to check the victim cache, and a possible third to store the datum into the primary cache.) Because of its fixed size relative to the primary direct-mapped cache, both our results and those presented by Jouppi (see Figure 3-6 in [4]) show that it is not very effective at resolving conflicts for large primary caches. On the other hand, because the area available to resolve conflicts in the column-associative cache increases with primary cache size, it resolves virtually all conflicts in large caches.

The scheme in [6] is proposed for instruction caches and uses two instruction buffers (of size equal to a cache line) between the instruction cache and the instruction register, and an instruction encoding that makes it easy to detect the presence of branch instructions in the buffers.

Kessler et al. [7] propose inexpensive implementations of set-associative caches by placing the multiple blocks in a set in sequential locations of cache memory. Tag checks, done serially, avoid the wide datapath requirements of conventional set-associative caches. The principle focus of this study was a reduction in implementation cost. The performance (measured in terms of average access time) of this scheme could often be worse than a direct-mapped cache for long strings of consecutive addresses, which occur commonly. For example, a long sequential reference stream of length equal to the cache size would fit into a direct-mapped cache, and subsequent references to any of these locations would result in a first-time hit. However, in a d-way set-associative implementation of this scheme, only $1/d$ of the references would succeed in the first access.

A similar problem exists in the MRU scheme proposed by So et al. [8]. The MRU scheme is a means for speeding up set-associative cache accesses. It maintains a few bits with each cache set indicating the most recently used block in the set. An access to a given set immediately reads out its MRU block, betting on the likelihood that it is the desired block. If it isn't, then an associative search accompanies a second access. Clearly, a two-way set-associative cache does not require an associate search, but does require a second access. Unfortunately, only $1/d$ of the references in a long sequential address stream would result in first-time hits into a d-way set-associative cache using this scheme.

A more desirable cache design would reduce the interference miss rate to the same extent as a set-associative cache, but at the same time, it would maintain the critical hit access path of the direct-mapped cache. The hash-rehash cache [5] had similar goals, but in Section 3.1 we demonstrate that it has one serious drawback. The technique introduced in Section 3 removes this drawback and largely eliminates interference misses by implementing slightly more complex control logic to make better use of the cache area. By maintaining direct-mapped cache access, these schemes do not affect the critical hit access time. With proper design, the few additional cycles required to execute the algorithms in case of a miss are balanced by the decrease in the miss rate due to fewer conflicts. This decrease in the interference miss rate is achieved not by set associativity but by exploiting temporal locality to make more efficient use of the given cache area—a notion called *column associativity*.

3 Column-Associative Caches

The fundamental idea behind a column-associative cache is to resolve conflicts by dynamically choosing different locations (accessed by different hashing functions) in which conflicting data

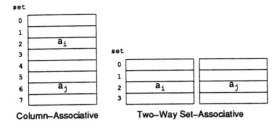

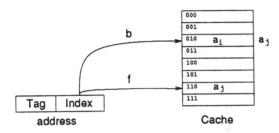

Figure 2: Comparison of column-associative and two-way set-associative caches of equal size. The conflict $b[a_i] = b[a_j]$ is resolved by both schemes.

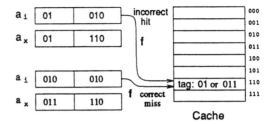

Figure 4: Appending the high-order bit of the index to the tag. This technique is necessary when bit flipping is implemented.

Figure 3: Indexing into a cache by bit selection and by bit flipping. The conflict $b[a_i] = b[a_j]$ is resolved by the bit-flipping rehash.

to the need for an associative search and for the logic to maintain a least-recently-used replacement policy. Of course, storing conflicting data within the cache—instead of in a separate victim cache—very likely results in the loss of useful data, but this effect (henceforth referred to as *clobbering*) can be minimized as discussed in Section 3.2.

The remainder of our discussion proceeds in two steps. First, we describe a basic system that uses multiple hashing functions and discuss its drawbacks. Then, we add rehash bits to this design to alleviate its problems.

3.1 Multiple Hashing Functions

can reside. Figure 2 compares the column-associative cache with a two-way set-associative cache of equal size. When presented with conflicting addresses ($b[a_i] = b[a_j]$), the set-associative cache resolves the conflict statically by referencing another location within the same set. On the other hand, the column-associative cache is direct-mapped, and when presented with conflicting addresses, a different hashing function is dynamically applied in order to place or locate the data in a *different* set. One simple choice for this other hashing function is bit selection with the highest-order bit inverted, which we term *bit flipping*. If $b[a] = 010$, then $f[a] = 110$, as illustrated in Figure 3. Therefore, conflicts are resolved not within a set but within the entire cache, which can be thought of as a column of sets—thus the name *column associativity*.

Column associativity can obviously improve upon direct-mapped caching by resolving a large number of the conflicts encountered in an address stream. In addition, as long as the control logic used to implement column associativity is simple and fast, then the benefits of direct-mapped caches over set-associative caches (as discussed in Section 1) are maintained, especially the lower hit access time. Because hits are much more frequent than misses, the extra cycles required to implement the column-associative algorithm on a miss can be easily balanced by the small improvement in hit access time on every hit, resulting in a smaller *average* memory access time when compared to a two-way set-associative cache. Of course, column associativity could be extended to emulate degrees of associativity higher than two, but it is likely that the complexity of implementing such an algorithm would add little to the performance and might even degrade it.

Additionally, the column-associative implementation uses sets within the cache itself to store conflicting data; only a simple rehash of the address is required to access this data. By comparison, a victim-cache implementation requires an entirely separate, fully-associative cache to store the conflicting data. Not only does the victim cache consume extra area, but it can also be quite slow due

Like the hash-rehash cache in [5], column-associative caches use two (or possibly more) distinct hashing functions, h_1 and h_2, to access the cache, where $h_1[a]$ denotes the index obtained by applying hashing function h_1 to the address a. If $h_1[a_i]$ indexes to valid data, a *first-time* hit occurs; if it misses, $h_2[a_i]$ is then used to access the cache. If a *second-time* hit occurs, the data is retrieved. The data in the two cache lines are then swapped so that the next access will likely result in a first-time hit. However, if the second access also misses, then the data is retrieved from main memory, placed in the cache line indexed by $h_2[a_i]$, and swapped with the data in the first location.

Using two or more hashing functions mimics set associativity, because for conflicting addresses (that is, a_i and a_j for which $h_1[a_i] = h_1[a_j]$), rehashing a_j with h_2 resolves the conflict with a high probability (that is, $h_1[a_i] \neq h_2[a_j]$). However, notice that the hit access time of a first-time hit remains unchanged. For simplicity and for speed, the first-time access is performed with bit selection (that is, $h_1 = b$), and bit flipping is often used for h_2 (that is, $h_2 = f$).

The use of bit flipping as a second hashing function results in a potential problem. Consider two addresses, a_i and a_x, which differ only in the high-order bit of the index field (that is, $f[a_i] = b[a_x]$). These two addresses are distinct; however, the tag fields are identical, thus a rehash access with $f[a_i]$ results in a hit with a data block that should only be accessed by $b[a_x]$. This is unacceptable, because a data block must have a one-to-one correspondence with a unique address. For addresses whose indexes are the same and which thus reference the same set, the tags are compared in order to determine whether an address should access the data block. This suggests a simple solution to the situation, appending the high-order bit of the index field to the tag, as illustrated in Figure 4. The rehash with $f[a_i]$ will correctly fail because the data block is once again referenced by a unique address, a_x. This scheme is assumed to be in place whenever bit flipping is used.

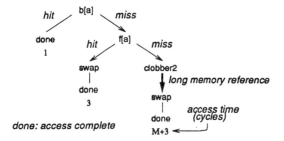

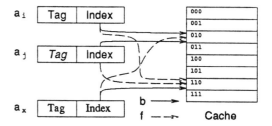

Figure 5: Decision tree for the hash-rehash algorithm.

mnemonic	action	cycles
b[a]	bit-selection access	1
f[a]	bit-flipping access	1
swap	swap data in sets accessed by $b[a]$ and $f[a]$	2
clobber2	get data from memory, place in set $f[a]$	M
clobber1	get data from memory, place in set $b[a]$	M
Rbit=1?	check if set $b[a]$ is a rehashed location	0

Table 1: Decision tree mnemonics and cycle times for each action.

To illustrate the operations more clearly, the hash-rehash algorithm has been expressed as the *decision tree* in Figure 5, simply a translation of the verbal description of the hash-rehash algorithm into a tree structure. Table 1 explains the mnemonics used in this decision tree and in the others which are introduced in this paper. The table also includes the number of cycles required to complete an action, which is necessary for the calculation of average access time.

In the decision tree, note that after a first-time miss and a second-time hit, which require two cycles to complete, a swap is performed. According to Table 1, the swap requires an additional two cycles to complete. The design requirements for accomplishing a swap in two cycles is discussed in Section A of the appendix. However, given an extra buffer for the cache, this swap need not involve the processor, which may be able to do other useful work while waiting for the cache to become available again. If this is the case half of the time, then the time wasted by a swap is one cycle. Therefore, for all decision trees in this paper, we assume that a swap adds only one cycle to the execution time. (However, we provide access time results for both one and two cycle swaps.) Thus, the three cycles indicated in the swap branch of Figure 5 results from one cycle for the initial cache access, one cycle for the rehash access, and one cycle wasted during the swap.

Unfortunately, the hash-rehash cache has a serious drawback, which often reduces its performance to that of a direct-mapped cache, as can be seen in Section 5.3. The source of its problems is that a rehash is attempted after *every* first-time miss, which can replace potentially useful data in the rehashed location, even when the primary location had an inactive block. Consider the following reference pattern: $a_i \; a_j \; a_x \; a_j \; a_x \; a_j \; a_x \; \cdots$, where the addresses a_i and a_j map into the same cache location with bit selection, and a_x is an address which maps into the same location with bit flipping (that is, where $b[a_i] = b[a_j]$, and $f[a_i] = b[a_x]$). This situation is illustrated in Figure 6. After the first two references, both the hash-rehash and the column-associative algorithms will have the data referenced by a_j (which will be called j for brevity) and the data i

Figure 6: The potential for secondary thrashing in a reference stream of the form $a_i \; a_j \; a_x \; a_j \; a_x \; a_j \; a_x \; \cdots$. Different fonts are used to indicate different index fields and tags. In this case, $b[a_i] = b[a_j]$ and $f[a_i] = b[a_x]$.

in the non-rehashed and rehashed locations, respectively. When the next address, a_x, is encountered, both algorithms attempt to access the set $b[a_x]$, which contains the rehashed data i. But when this first-time miss occurs, the hash-rehash algorithm next tries to access $f[a_x]$, which results in a second-time miss and the clobbering of the data j. This pattern continues as long as a_j and a_x alternate; the data referenced by one of them is clobbered as the inactive data block i is swapped back and forth but never replaced. We will refer to this negative effect as *secondary thrashing* in the future.

The following section describes how the use of a rehash bit can lessen the effects of these limitations.

3.2 Rehash Bits

The key to implementing column associativity effectively is inhibiting a rehash access if the location reached by the first-time access itself contains a rehashed data block. This idea can be implemented as follows. Every cache set contains an extra bit which indicates whether the set is a *rehashed location*, that is, whether the data in this set is indexed by $f[a]$. This algorithm, which is illustrated as a decision tree in Figure 7, is similar to that of the hash-rehash cache; however, the key difference lies in the fact that when a cache set must be replaced, a rehashed location is always chosen—immediately if possible. Thus, if the first-time access is a miss, then the rehashed-location bit (or *rehash bit* for short) of that set is checked (Rbit=1?, as listed in Table 1). If it has been set to one, then no rehash access will be attempted, and the data retrieved from memory is placed in that location. Then the rehash bit is reset to zero to indicate that the data in this set is to be indexed by $b[a]$ in the future. On the other hand, if the rehash bit is already a zero, then upon a first-time miss the rehash access will continue as described in Section 3.1. Note that if a second-time miss occurs, then the set whose data will be replaced is again a rehashed location, as desired.

Of course, at start-up (or after a cache flush), all of the empty cache locations should have their rehash bits set to one. The reason that this algorithm can correctly replace a location with a set rehash bit immediately after a first-time miss is based on the fact that bit flipping is used as the second hashing function. Given two addresses a_i and a_x, if $f[a_i] = b[a_x]$, then it must be true that $f[a_x] = b[a_i]$. Therefore, if a_i accesses a location using $b[a_i]$ whose rehash bit is set to one, then there are only two possibilities.

1. The accessed location is an empty location from start-up, or

2. there exists a non-rehashed location at $f[a_i]$ (or $b[a_x]$) which previously encountered a conflict and placed the data in *its*

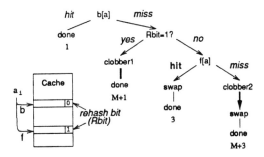

Figure 7: Decision tree for a column-associative cache.

rehashed location, $f[a_x]$.

In both cases, it makes sense to replace the location reached during the first-time access that had its rehash bit set to one.

However, it must be proven that a third possibility does not exist, namely, the location $b[a_i]$ has its rehash bit set to one, but the data referenced by a_i actually resides in $f[a_i]$ simultaneously. Consider the actions taken by the algorithm when one of the conditions precedes the other. First, if $b[a_i]$ is a rehashed location, then any first-time miss results in the immediate clobbering of that location and the resetting of the rehash bit to zero. Therefore, it is not possible for the placement of the data into $f[a_i]$ to follow this condition.

On the other hand, if the data referenced by a_i already resides in $f[a_i]$ due to a conflict, then the rehash bit of $b[a_i]$ must be a zero, because it contains the most recently accessed data. The only way to change this bit is if $b[a_i]$ were to be used as a rehashed location in order to resolve a different conflict. However, because bit flipping is the rehashing function, the only location for which this situation can occur is $f[a_i]$ itself. A first-time access to this location, though, would automatically clobber the rehashed data. Therefore, it is clear that the two conditions for this third possibility can never occur simultaneously. This important property could not be utilized in the column-associative algorithm if bit flipping was not the second hashing function or if more than two hashing functions were included.

Like the hash-rehash cache, the column-associative algorithm attempts to exploit temporal locality by swapping the most recently accessed data into the non-rehashed location, if a rehash is indeed attempted. The use of the rehash bit helps utilize cache area more efficiently because it immediately indicates whether a location is rehashed and should be replaced in preference over a non-rehashed location.

In addition to limiting rehash accesses and clobbering, the rehash bits in the column-associative cache eliminate secondary thrashing. Referring to the reference stream, $a_i\ a_j\ a_x\ a_j\ a_x\ a_j\ a_x\ \cdots$, in Figure 6, the third reference accesses $b[a_x]$, but it finds the rehash bit set to one. Thus, the data i is replaced immediately by x, the desired action. Of course, this column-associative cache suffers thrashing if three or more conflicting addresses alternate, as in $a_i\ a_j\ a_x\ a_i\ a_j\ a_x\ a_i\ \cdots$, but this case is much less probable than two alternating addresses.

4 A Simple Analytical Model for Column-Associative Caches

We have developed a simple analytical model for the column-associative cache that predicts the percentage of interference misses removed from a direct-mapped cache using only one measured parameter—the size of the program's working set—from an address trace. Our model builds on the self-interference component of the direct-mapped cache model of Agarwal, Horowitz, and Hennessy [9], and it estimates the percentage of interference misses removed by computing the percentage of cache block conflicts removed by the rehash algorithm. Because the behavior is captured in a simple, closed-form expression, our model yields valuable insights into the behavior of the column-associative cache. Validations against empirically derived cache miss rates suggest that the model's predictions are fairly accurate as well.

Like the self-interference model in [9], the percentage reduction in cache block conflicts in the column-associative cache is captured by two parameters: S and u. The parameter S represents the number of cache sets; in direct-mapped caches, the product of S and the block size yields the cache size. The parameter u denotes the working-set size of the program, and must be measured from an address trace of a program. The *working set* of a program is the set of distinct blocks a program accesses within some interval of time.

The model makes the assumption that blocks have a uniform probability of mapping to any cache set, and that the mappings for different blocks are independent of each other. The same assumption is also made for the rehash accesses. This assumption is commonly made in cache modeling studies [10, 11, 9]. Although this assumption makes the models generally overestimate miss rates, its effect is less severe when we are interested in the *ratios* of the number of conflicting blocks in direct-mapped caches and column-associative caches.

A detailed derivation of the model appears in [12]; this section summarizes the major results. Let c_d denote the number of conflicting blocks in a direct-mapped cache, and c_{cac} the corresponding number of conflicting blocks in a column-associative cache. Blocks are said to conflict when multiple blocks from the working set of a program map to a given cache set. In a column-associative cache, conflicting blocks are blocks that conflict even after a rehash is attempted. Section 5.1 provides further discussion on the notion of conflicts.

Expressions are derived in [12] for the number of conflicting blocks in direct-mapped and column-associative caches in terms of $P(d)$, which is the probability that d program blocks (out of a total of u) map to a given cache set. Because blocks are assumed to map with equal likelihood to any cache set, the distribution of the number of blocks in a cache set is binomial, which yields

$$P(d) = \binom{u}{d} \left(\frac{1}{S}\right)^d \left(1 - \frac{1}{S}\right)^{u-d} \qquad (1)$$

The following are expressions for the number of conflicting blocks.

$$c_d = u - SP(1)$$

$$c_{cac} = u - SP(1) - SP(2)(1 + P(0) - P(1) - P(2))$$

183

We estimate the percentage of interference misses removed by the percentage reduction in the number of conflicting blocks. Our validation experiments indicate that this is a good approximation. Thus, the percentage of interference misses removed,

$$\frac{c_d - c_{cac}}{c_d} = \frac{SP(2)\left(1 + P(0) - P(1) - P(2)\right)}{u - SP(1)} \quad (2)$$

It is instructive to take the first-order approximations of the expression in Equation 2 after substituting for $P(d)$ from Equation 1 and simplifying the resulting expression. The first-order approximation is valid when $S \gg u$ and $u \gg 1$, which allow us to use $\left(1 - 1/S\right)^{u-1} \approx \left(1 - u/S\right)$. Proceeding along these lines, we obtain

$$\frac{c_d - c_{cac}}{c_d} \approx \left(1 - \frac{2u}{S}\right) \quad (3)$$

It is easy to see from the above equation that the percentage of conflicts removed by rehashing will approach unity as the cache size is increased. Similarly, roughly 50% of the conflicts are removed when the cache is four times larger than the working set of the program.

To demonstrate the accuracy of the model, we plot in Figure 13 the measured values of the average percentages of interference misses removed and the values obtained using Equation 2 for our traces. The predictions for each of the individual traces is also fairly accurate, as displayed in Figures 8 and 9. Both the model and the simulations use a block size of 16 bytes. The analytical model uses only one parameter—the working-set size, u—measured from each trace. Table 3 shows the working set sizes for each of our traces.

5   Results

This section presents the data obtained through simulation of the various caches and an analysis of these results. First, the metrics which have been used to evaluate the performance of the caches must be described.

5.1   Cache Performance Metrics

We use three cache performance metrics in our results: the cache miss rate, the percentage of interference misses removed, and the average memory access time.

The *miss rate* is the ratio of the number of misses to the total number of references.

The *percentage of interference misses removed* is the percentage by which the number of interference misses in the cache under consideration is reduced over those in a direct-mapped cache. An interference miss is defined as a miss that results when a block that was previously displaced from the cache is subsequently referenced. In a single processor environment, the total number of misses minus the misses due to first-time references is the number of interference misses.[2]

---

[2]A similar parameter was used by Jouppi [4] as a useful measure of the performance of victim caches. We note that our interference metric measures the sum of the intrinsic interference misses and the extrinsic interference misses in the classification of Agarwal, Horowitz, and Hennessy [9], and the sum of the capacity, conflict, and context-switching misses in the terminology of Hill and Smith [13].

This metric is particularly useful for determining the success of a particular scheme because all cache implementations must share the same compulsory or first-time miss rate for a given reference stream, but they may have different interference miss rates. The percentage of interference misses removed is calculated by the equation

$$\frac{direct\ miss\ rate - miss\ rate}{direct\ miss\ rate - compulsory\ miss\ rate} \times 100\%$$

where, for a given address trace and cache size, the miss rate is that of the particular cache design, and the direct miss rate is that of a direct-mapped cache of equal size. The compulsory miss rate is the ratio of unique references to total references for that trace.

Finally, the *average memory access time* is defined as the average number of cycles required to complete one reference in a particular address stream. This metric is useful in assessing the performance of a specific caching scheme because although a particular cache design may demonstrate a lower miss rate than a direct-mapped cache, it may do so at the expense of the hit access time. As mentioned earlier, our graphs include access time results for both one-cycle and two-cycle swaps.

Let the cache access time for a hit be one cycle, and let M represent the number of cycles required to service a miss from the main memory (in our simulations, $M = 20$). If R is the total number of references in the trace, H_1 is the total number of hits on a first-time access, and H_2 is the total number of hits on a second-time access, then the average memory access time for the various schemes can be computed from the decision trees of Section 3 as shown below.

For direct-mapped caches, the access time is one for hits, and one plus M for misses. Thus,

$$t_{ave} = \frac{1}{R}\left[H_1 + (M+1)(R - H_1)\right]$$

For hash-rehash caches, the access time is one for first-time hits, 3 for rehash hits (Every first-time miss is followed by a rehash.), and $(M+3)$ otherwise.

$$t_{ave} = \frac{1}{R}\left[H_1 + 3H_2 + (M+3)(R - H_1 - H_2)\right]$$

For column-associative caches, we need an additional parameter R_2, which is the total number of second time accesses. (Recall that second-time accesses are attempted only when the rehash bit is zero.) Thus the access time is one for first-time hits, and three for the H_2 hits during a rehash attempt. If a rehash is not attempted, then $(M+1)$ cycles are spent. Rehash attempts that miss suffer a penalty of $(M+3)$ cycles. Therefore,[3]

$$t_{ave} = \frac{1}{R}\left[H_1 + 3H_2 + (M+1)(R - H_1 - R_2) + (M+3)(R_2 - H_2)\right]$$

The simulator described in the next section measures R, R_2, H_1, and H_2 for each of the cache types, and it derives average memory access times from the above equations.

---

[3]The cycles per instruction (or CPI) assuming single-cycle instruction execution can be calculated easily from the average access time. For a unified instruction and data cache with a single cycle access time, the CPI with a 100% hit rate is $(1 + l)$, where l is the fraction of instructions that are loads or stores. In the presence of cache misses, however, the average access time becomes t_{ave}, and the CPI becomes $(1 + l)t_{ave}$.

name	trace description
LISP0	LISP runs of BOYER (a theorem prover)
DEC0.1	Behavioral simulator of cache hardware, DECSIM
SPIC0	SPICE simulating a 2-input tristate NAND buffer
IVEX0	Interconnect verify, a DEC program checking net lists in a VLSI chip
FORL0	FORTRAN compile of LINPACK

Table 2: Description of uniprocessor traces used during simulation.

trace	no. of references			compulsory miss rate (%)
	u	unique	total	
LISP0	392	1,789	262,760	0.6808
DEC0.1	463	2,418	334,775	0.7223
SPIC0	740	2,834	358,168	0.7912
IVEX0	774	11,087	307,172	3.6097
FORL0	826	6,787	314,110	2.1607
MUL6.0		5,267	400,698	1.3145

Table 3: Number of references (both instructions and data) and compulsory miss rate for each of the address traces simulated. The block size for measuring u and *unique* is set to 16 bytes (four words).

5.2 Simulator and Trace Descriptions

We wrote trace-driven simulators for direct-mapped, set-associative, victim, hash-rehash, and column-associative caches. Multiprogrammed simulations assume that a process identifier is associated with each reference to distinguish between the data of different processes. All caches are assumed to be combined instruction and data caches.

The traces used in this study come from the ATUM experiment of Sites and Agarwal [14]. The ATUM traces comprise realistic workloads and include both operating system and multiprogramming activity. The five uniprocessor traces, derived from large programs running under VMS, are described in Table 2. We also use a multiprogramming trace called MUL6.0, which includes activity from six processes including a FORTRAN compile, a directory search, and a microcode address allocator. Each trace length is on the order of a half million references. We believe these lengths are adequate for our purposes, since we explicitly subtract the number of first-time misses and present the percentage of interference misses removed, and because it is possible to differentiate the performance of the various caching methods without resorting to measurement methods that yield cache miss rates with a degree of accuracy exceeding the first or second decimal place. The compulsory miss rates and other parameters for these traces are listed in Table 3. In the table, u is the average number of unique blocks in 10,000 reference windows, while *unique* is the total number of unique blocks in the entire trace.

5.3 Measurements and Analysis

In this section, the results of the trace-driven simulations are plotted and interpreted. Before introducing the plots, a few of their features must be explained. If the miss rate of a cache happens to be worse than that of a direct-mapped cache for the particular cache size, as is occasionally the case for a hash-rehash cache, then the percentage of interference misses removed becomes a negative quantity. On the graph, this is instead indicated by a point at zero percent.[4]

The victim cache size has been set to 16 entries. This is based on simulation data which suggests that the removal of conflicts quickly saturates beyond this size. In addition, remember that each victim-cache entry is a complete cache line, storing the tag, status bits, and the data block, which contains four words in these simulations.

5.3.1 Miss Rates and Interference Misses Removed

LISP0 and DEC0.1 The results for the LISP0 and DEC0.1 traces are very similar, so only LISP0 results are plotted in Figure 8. It is evident that all of the cache designs exhibit much lower miss rates than the direct-mapped cache. The lowest miss rates are achieved by the two-way set-associative and the column-associative caches. The victim and hash-rehash caches have higher miss rates.

A striking feature of the miss rate plots is the relationship between the direct-mapped and hash-rehash caches. Whenever doubling the cache size results in a sharp decrease in the direct-mapped miss rate, the same change in cache size yields a sharp and similarly sized *increase* of the hash-rehash miss rate. This effect makes sense intuitively—a hash-rehash cache is designed to resolve conflicts through the use of alternate cache locations. It is successful as long as the the number of conflicts decreases only slightly as the cache size increases. However, if an increase in cache size itself suddenly removes a large portion of the conflicts, then the hash-rehash algorithm clobbers many locations and suffers a sharp drop in the second-time hit rate because it is attempting to resolve conflicts which no longer exist.[5] Notice that the column-associative cache does not suffer from this degradation because its access algorithm is designed specifically to alleviate the problems of clobbering and low second-time hit rates.

Referring to the percentages of interference misses removed in Figure 8, notice that the dashed curve corresponding to the predictions of the model is very close to the curve obtained from simulations. The LISP0 trace has a small working set compared to the other traces (see Table 3), and therefore the percentage of interference misses removed quickly approaches 100% for all but the victim cache, which is a phenomenon readily explained by the approximate analytical expression for this metric: $(1 - 2u/S)$.

SPIC0, IVEX0, and FORL0 The results for these traces are also similar enough to be grouped together. The data for the SPIC0 trace has been plotted in Figure 9. Nearly all of the results from the previous section apply to the simulations with these three traces, but there are several important differences. Because the working-set sizes of these traces are larger than the LISP0 trace, the percentages of interference misses removed by column associativity start at much lower values and approach 100% more slowly. Because the victim cache is much more sensitive to working set size, it does not attain the same percentages found for LISP0 and DEC0.1; for these traces, the victim cache lies around 25% or less for this metric. Recall that the victim cache size remains constant, while the column-associative and the set-associative caches can devote larger areas to resolve conflicts as cache size increases.

---

[4]This is why the points for the hash-rehash cache are not connected in the graphs showing percentage of interference misses removed.

[5]The addition of one, high-order bit to the index could separate two groups of addresses which conflict often because they differ for the first time in that bit.

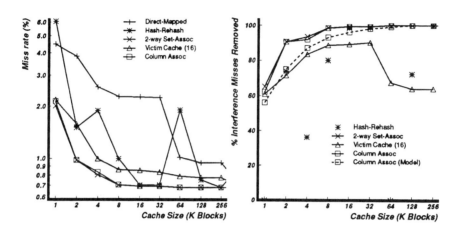

Figure 8: Miss rates and percentages of interference misses removed versus cache size for LISP0. Block size is 16 bytes.

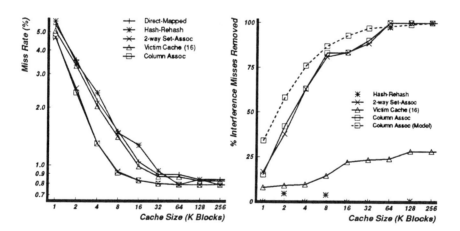

Figure 9: Miss rates and percentages of interference misses removed versus cache size for SPIC0. Block size is 16 bytes.

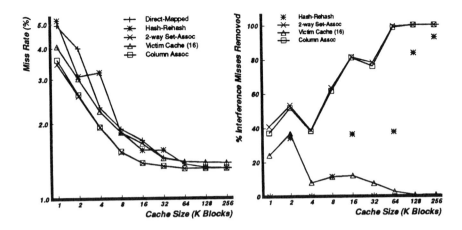

Figure 10: Miss rates and percentages of interference misses removed versus cache size for MUL6.0. Block size is 16 bytes.

The plots for SPIC0 in Figure 9 reveal another interesting fact: the column-associative cache outperforms the two-way set-associative cache for some of the cache sizes. A hypothesis that explains this behavior is based on the fact that when comparing the two caches at an equal cache size, the set-associative cache has only half that number of cache sets. As seen before, doubling the cache size and thus adding a high-order bit to the index may eliminate a large number of conflicts that have been occurring because many addresses differ for the first time in that bit. For example, consider the addresses 0001111, 0101111, and 1011111. All three result in multiple conflicts (thrashing) if only the four, low-order bits are used as the index. This is a cache size of 2^4 or 16 for the column-associative cache, but the total cache size is 32 for the two-way set-associative cache, and it still exhibits thrashing. Note that both caches have 16 sets. A 32-set column-associative cache, however, uses five bits for the index. In this case, the conflicts between 0101111 and 1011111 are automatically eliminated because of the different fifth bits.

MUL6.0 The miss rates and percentages of interference misses removed for the multiprogramming trace are plotted in Figure 10. Once again, many of the observations made for the other trace results apply to MUL6.0. Perhaps the most telling result is the relatively poor performance of the victim cache. Its miss rate is virtually the same as that of the direct-mapped cache (for cache sizes greater than 2K blocks). The large working sets of multiprogramming workloads make the fixed size of the victim cache a serious liability. The larger available area for storing conflicts in the column-associative cache is clearly a big win in this situation.

5.3.2 Average Memory Access Times

Two key factors must be considered when interpreting the access time data. First, although the average memory access times of set-associative caches are in reality increased due to their higher hit access times, the graphs in this paper assume their hit access times are the same as that of direct-mapped caches. If realistic access times of two-way set-associative caches are considered, their average memory access times might well become greater that those of column associative caches. (This is why the corresponding curves are labeled "Ideal").

Second, the average memory access time is very sensitive to the time required to service a miss (M). The results assume $M = 20$ cycles. For larger (and still reasonable) miss penalties, the designs such as column-associative caches which reduce the number of accesses to main memory ($R - H_1 - H_2$) will look even more impressive than indicated by our results.

The results for the LISP0 and SPIC0 traces are presented together in Figure 11. As before, DEC0.1 is similar to LISP0, while IVEX0 and FORL0 are similar to SPIC0. All the average memory access time plots are largely similar in shape to the miss rate plots, which is expected, because t_{ave} is a linear function of the miss rate.

The graph for LISP0 shows that column associativity achieves much lower average memory access times than a direct-mapped cache. The improvement is about 0.3 cycles for most cache sizes. For SPIC0, the column-associative cache exceeds 0.2 cycle improvements only for small caches. This fact is confirmed when the miss rate plot is considered—the direct-mapped interference miss rate is not much higher than the compulsory miss rate, unlike the case for LISP0. The results for MUL6.0 are largely similar: the column-associative cache saves about 0.2 cycles over direct-mapped caches, and the two-way set associative cache saves a further 0.1 cycle, when the caches are less than 4K blocks. (With a 16-byte block, the cache size is 64K bytes.) The savings are smaller for larger caches.

Perhaps most important, however, is the fact that the column-associative cache achieves an average access time close to the two-way set-associative cache, even though the hit access time of the set-associative cache was (unrealistically) kept the same as that of a direct-mapped cache.

5.4 Summary

This section presents data for each of the metrics averaged over all of the traces. The resulting plots serve as excellent examples for reviewing the major points made in this section.

When the miss rates of all six traces are averaged for each cache size, the plot in Figure 12 is the result. The direct-mapped miss rate is the baseline for comparison and falls quickly from 6.0% to 2.0%, before settling toward the average compulsory miss rate of about 1.5%.

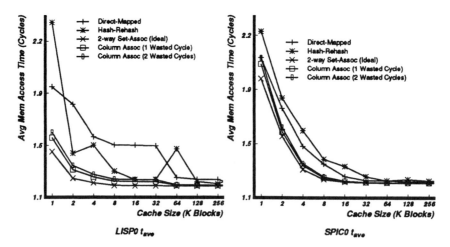

LISP0 t_{ave} SPIC0 t_{ave}

Figure 11: Average memory access times (in cycles) versus cache size for LISP0 and SPIC0. Block size is 16 bytes. The hit access time of two-way set-associative caches is assumed to be the same as that of a direct-mapped cache.

The other cache designs can be split into two groups, based not only on their similar miss rate curves but also on the relationships among their access algorithms. The first group contains the hash-rehash cache and the victim cache, which have similar control algorithms. The hash-rehash cache is usually an improvement upon direct-mapped caching; the miss rate drops more quickly from 6.0% to about 1.7%. However, at the transition point, the hash-rehash miss rate increases about as much as the direct-mapped miss rate decreases. This is due to the fact that once the cache size exceeds the working-set size, the interference miss rate drops markedly. The many rehash accesses performed by the hash-rehash algorithm now are more likely to clobber live data than to resolve conflicts. The victim cache does not suffer from this effect, because it is designed to alleviate the main problems with the hash-rehash algorithm: clobbering and low second-time hit rates.

The second group consists of the two-way set-associative and the column-associative caches. The miss rates of these caches are almost 2.0% lower than direct-mapped miss rates for small caches, just under 1.0% near the transition, and right at the compulsory miss rate for large caches. As predicted in Section 3, the column-associative cache achieves two-way set-associative miss rates.

The plot in Figure 13 shows the average percentages of interference misses removed. (This average does not include the MUL6.0 numbers, so that we could compare the simulation averages with the model.) The curves for set-associative and column-associative caches are almost identical, starting at about 40% and climbing to 100% when the cache size reaches 256 K blocks. As predicted in Section 2, the performance of the victim cache relative to the column-associative cache degrades with cache size. Finally, the dashed curve for the model is seen to be surprisingly close to simulation results when the individual trace anomalies are averaged out.

The average memory access time (t_{ave}) data for the six traces have been averaged and plotted in Figure 14. Based on this average plot and on most of the other data, the column-associative cache appears to be good choice under most operating conditions. In this example, t_{ave} is reduced by over 0.2 cycles for small to moderate caches, and by about 0.1 cycles for moderate to large caches.

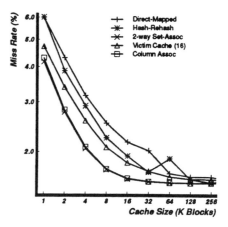

Figure 12: Miss rates versus cache size, averaged over all six traces. Block size is 16 bytes.

6 Conclusions

The goal of this research has been to develop area-efficient cache control algorithms for improved cache performance. The main metrics used to evaluate cache performance have been the miss rate and average memory access time; unfortunately, minimizing one of them usually affects the other adversely. The optimal cache design would remove interference misses as well as a two-way set-associative cache but would maintain the fast hit access times of a direct-mapped cache.

Two previous solutions which attempted to achieve this are the hash-rehash cache and the victim cache. Although some performance gain is achieved by both these schemes, the success of the hash-rehash cache is very erratic and is hampered by clobbering and low second-time hit rates. The drawbacks of the victim cache include the need for a large, fully-associative buffer and its lack of robust performance (in terms of its miss rate) as the size of the primary cache increases.

This paper proposed the design of a column-associative cache

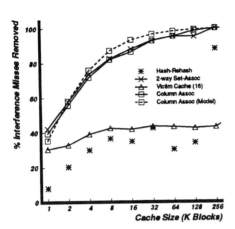

Figure 13: Percentages of interference misses removed versus cache size, averaged over the single process traces. Block size is 16 bytes.

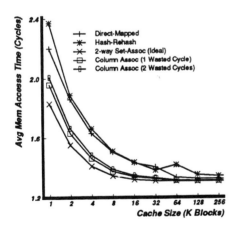

Figure 14: Average memory access times versus cache size, averaged over all six traces. Block size is 16 bytes. The hit access time of two-way set-associative caches is assumed to be the same as that of a direct-mapped cache.

that has the good hit access time of a direct-mapped cache and the high hit rate of a set-associative cache. The fundamental idea behind column associativity is to resolve conflicts by dynamically choosing different locations in which the conflicting data can reside. The key aspect which distinguishes the column-associative cache is the use of a rehash bit to indicate whether a cache set is a rehashed location.

Trace-driven simulations confirm that the column-associative cache removes almost as many interference misses as does the two-way set-associative cache. In addition, the average memory access times for this cache are close to that of an ideal two-way set-associative cache, even when access time of the two-way set-associative cache is assumed to be the same as that of a direct-mapped cache. Finally, the hardware costs of implementing this scheme are minor, and almost negligible if the state represented by the rehash bit could be encoded into the existing status bits of many practical cache designs.

7 Acknowledgments

The research reported in this paper is funded by NSF grant # MIP-9012773 and DARPA contract # N00014-87-K-0825.

References

[1] Alan Jay Smith. Cache Memories. *Computing Surveys*, 14(4):473–530, September 1982.

[2] Steven Przybylski, Mark Horowitz, and John Hennessy. Performance Tradeoffs in Cache Design. In *Proceedings of the 15th Annual Symposium on Computer Architecture*, pages 290–298. IEEE Computer Society Press, June 1988.

[3] Mark D. Hill. A Case for Direct-Mapped Caches. *IEEE Computer*, 21(12):25–40, December 1988.

[4] Norman P. Jouppi. Improving Direct-Mapped Cache Performance by the Addition of a Small Fully-Associative Cache and Prefetch Buffers. In *Proceedings of the 17th Annual Symposium on Computer Architecture*, pages 364–373. IEEE Computer Society Press, August 1990.

[5] Anant Agarwal, John Hennessy, and Mark Horowitz. Cache Performance of Operating Systems and Multiprogramming. *ACM Transactions on Computer Systems*, 6(4):393–431, November 1988.

[6] Matthew K. Farrens and Andrew R. Pleszkun. Improving Performance of Small On-Chip Instruction Caches. In *Proceedings of the 16th Annual Symposium on Computer Architecture*, pages 234–241. IEEE Computer Society Press, May 1989.

[7] R.E. Kessler, Richard Jooss, Alvin Lebeck, and Mark D. Hill. Inexpensive Implementations of Set-Associativity. In *Proceedings of the 16th Annual Symposium on Computer Architecture*, pages 131–139. IEEE Computer Society Press, May 1989.

[8] Kimming So and Rudolph N. Rechtschaffen. Cache Operations by MRU Change. Technical Report RC 11613, IBM T.J. Watson Research Center, November 1985.

[9] Anant Agarwal, Mark Horowitz, and John Hennessy. An Analytical Cache Model. *ACM Transactions on Computer Systems*, 7(2):184–215, May 1989.

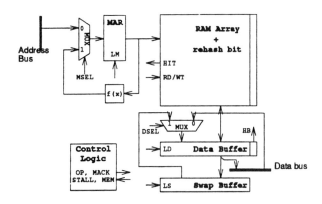

Figure 15: Column-associative cache implementation. Every cache set must have a rehash bit appended to it.

state	input	output	next state
IDLE	OP	LM, RD	b[a]
b[a]	HIT		IDLE
	!HIT, !HB	STALL,MSEL,LM,RD,LS	f1[a]
	!HIT, HB	MEM, STALL	XWAIT
f1[a]	HIT	MSEL, LM, WT DSEL, LD	f2[a]
	!HIT	MEM	WAIT1
f2[a]		MSEL, LM, WT	IDLE
WAIT1	MACK	MSEL, LM, WT DSEL, LD	WAIT2
WAIT2		MSEL, LM, WT	IDLE
XWAIT	MACK	LD, WT	IDLE

Table 4: State flow table for the control logic of a column-associative cache. In constructing the state flow table all cache accesses are assumed to be reads.

[10] Alan Jay Smith. A Comparative Study of Set Associative Memory Mapping Algorithms And Their Use for Cache and Main Memory. *IEEE Transactions on Software Engineering*, SE-4(2):121–130, March 1978.

[11] Dominique Thiebaut and Harold S. Stone. Footprints in the Cache. *ACM Transactions on Computer Systems*, 5(4):305–329, November 1987.

[12] Anant Agarwal and Steven Pudar. Column-Associative Caches: A Technique for Reducing the Miss Rate of Direct-Mapped Caches. Technical Report LCS TM 484, MIT, March 1993.

[13] M. D. Hill and A. J. Smith. Evaluating Associativity in CPU Caches. *IEEE Transactions on Computers*, 38(12):1612–1630, December 1989.

[14] Richard L. Sites and Anant Agarwal. Multiprocessor Cache Analysis using ATUM. In *Proceedings of the 15th International Symposium on Computer Architecture*, pages 186–195, New York, June 1988. IEEE.

A Cache Implementation Example

The datapaths required for a column-associative cache are displayed in Figure 15. Since the rehashing function used is bit flipping, the functional block $f(x)$ is simply an inverter. In order to accomplish the swap of conflicting data, a data buffer is required. All buffers are assumed to be edge triggered. An n-bit multiplexor can be used to switch the current contents of the memory address register (MAR) between the two conflicting addresses. A MUX is also needed at the input of the data buffer, so that it may read data from either the swap buffer or the data bus. Finally, a rehash bit is added to each cache set; when this bit is read out into the data buffer, it then serves as a control signal. In some implementations the rehash state can be encoded using the existing state bits associated with each cache line, thus eliminating the need for an extra bit.

First-time hits proceed as in direct-mapped caches; however, if there is a first-time miss and the rehash bit of this location is a one, then the column-associative algorithm requires that this location be replaced by the data from memory, which is accomplished in the XWAIT state. When the memory acknowledges completion (MACK), the data is taken off the data bus (LD) and written back into the cache (WT). On the other hand, if the first location is not rehashed (!HB), then a rehash is to be performed. The processor

is stalled (STALL), MSEL and LM are asserted to load the MAR with $f[a]$, the second-time access is begun (RD), LS is asserted to move the first datum into the swap buffer, and the state changes to f1[a].

If there is a second-time hit, then the correct datum resides in the data buffer. In order to perform the swap, state f1[a] loads the MAR with the original address, $f(f(a))$, and issues a write (WT). State f1[a] also moves the datum accessed the first time from the swap buffer to the data buffer (by asserting DSEL and LD), where it can be written back into the rehashed location in the next state, f2[a]. A second time miss is handled similarly by states WAIT1 and WAIT2, except that the correct datum to be swapped into the non-rehashed location comes from the memory.

190

Cache Write Policies and Performance

Norman P. Jouppi

Digital Equipment Corporation Western Research Lab

250 University Avenue

Palo Alto, CA 94301

Abstract

This paper investigates issues involving writes and caches. First, tradeoffs on writes that miss in the cache are investigated. In particular, whether the missed cache block is fetched on a write miss, whether the missed cache block is allocated in the cache, and whether the cache line is written before hit or miss is known are considered. Depending on the combination of these polices chosen, the entire cache miss rate can vary by a factor of two on some applications. The combination of no-fetch-on-write and write-allocate can provide better performance than cache line allocation instructions. Second, tradeoffs between write-through and write-back caching when writes hit in a cache are considered. A mixture of these two alternatives, called *write caching* is proposed. *Write caching* places a small fully-associative cache behind a write-through cache. A write cache can eliminate almost as much write traffic as a write-back cache.

1. Introduction

Most of the extensive literature on caches has concentrated on read issues (e.g., miss rates when treating stores as reads), or writes in the context of multiprocessor cache consistency. However, uniprocessor[1] write issues are in many ways more complicated than read issues, since writes require additional work beyond that for a cache hit (e.g., writing the data back to the memory system).

The cache write policies investigated in this paper fall into two broad categories: write hit policies, and write miss policies.

Unlike instruction fetches and data loads, where reducing latency is the prime goal, the primary goal for writes that hit in the cache is reducing the bandwidth requirements (i.e., write traffic). This is especially important if the cycle time of the CPU is faster than that of the interface to the

second-level cache, and if multiple instruction issue allows store traffic approaching one per cycle to be sustained in many applications. The write traffic into the second-level cache primarily depends on whether the first-level cache is *write-through* (also called *store-through*) or *write-back* (also called *store-in* or *copy-back*). Write-back caches take advantage of the temporal and spatial locality of writes (and reads) to reduce the write traffic leaving the cache.

Write miss policies, although they do affect bandwidth, focus foremost on latency. Write miss policies include three semi-dependent variables. First, writes that miss in the cache may or may not have a line allocated in the cache (*write-allocate* vs. *no-write-allocate*). If a cache uses a no-write-allocate policy, when reads occur to recently written data, they must wait for the data to be fetched back from a lower level in the memory hierarchy. Second, writes that miss in the cache may or may not fetch the block being written (*fetch-on-write* vs. *no-fetch-on-write*). A cache that uses a fetch-on-write policy must wait for a missed cache line to be fetched from a lower level of the memory hierarchy, while a cache using no-fetch-on-write can proceed immediately. We emphasize that write-allocate and fetch-on-write are not synonymous as commonly assumed. This paper investigates the combination of write-allocate but no-fetch-on-write which has superior performance over other policies. A new third variable of write policy, *write-before-hit*, is also investigated in this paper. If writes use the same pipeline timing as reads to reduce structural hazards in the pipeline, writes will occur before hit or miss is known. Obviously write-before-hit is only useful with write-through caches; if used with a write-back cache unique dirty data will be overwritten. Writes using write-before-hit that miss in the cache may simply invalidate cache lines "erroneously" written and pass the data written on to lower levels in the memory hierarchy. Different combinations of these three write-miss policy variables can result in a 2:1 range in cache miss rates for some applications.

Out of the hundreds of papers on caches in the last 15 years [14, 15], Smith [12] was the only paper to exclusively deal with write issues. This paper discussed write buffer

---

[1]By uniprocessor we include non-coherency issues in multiprocessor cache memories, as well as uniprocessor cache memories.

performance for write-through caches, but did not investigate merging of pending writes to the same cache line by a write buffer. Smith [13] and Goodman [6] both have a section on write-back versus write-through caching, but they study only mixed first-level caches with traces under a million references. Among the more recent work in uniprocessor cache issues, Agarwal [1] and Hill [7] assumed write references were identical to read references in their analysis. Przybylski [10] includes write overheads in his analysis, but only considers the case of write-back caches at all levels. Write miss policies have been even less investigated. Almost all of the known results in the literature have been for the combination of write-allocate and fetch-on-write. The VAX 11/780 [2] and 8800 [3] were notable exceptions to this and used no-write-allocate. An unpublished paper by Smith [16] has a section that considers tradeoffs between write-allocate and no-write-allocate. It uses traces up to ten million references, but investigates only 4KB data caches with 16B lines.

Section 2 briefly describes the simulation environment and benchmarks used in this study. Policies for write misses, specifically fetch-on-write, write-allocate, and write-before-hit are investigated in Section 3. Section 4 investigates write hit tradeoffs between write-back and write-through caching, as well as ways of reducing write-through traffic. Section 5 summarizes the results of the paper.

2. Experimental Environment

This paper investigates write policies in the context of a modern memory hierarchy. One or more levels of on-chip caching are assumed, although the data in the paper is for the effects of these policies on the first-level cache performance. Because one or more levels of on-chip caching are assumed, the first-level cache sizes studied are from 1KB to 128KB, which are suitable for implementation on a VLSI chip.

Separate instruction and data caches are assumed at the first level, since these are necessary for superscalar and other types of high performance machine design. Only direct-mapped first-level data caches are studied.

The results in this paper were obtained by modifying a simulator for the MultiTitan [8] architecture. The MultiTitan architecture does not support byte loads and stores, so byte writes appear as word read-modify-writes. However, the number of byte operations in the programs studied are insignificant, so this does not significantly affect the results presented. Each experiment involved simulating the benchmarks, and not analyzing trace tapes.

The characteristics of the test programs used in this study are given in Table 2-1. Although six is a small number of benchmarks, the programs chosen are quite diverse, with two numeric programs, two CAD tools, and two Unix utilities. However, operating system execution, transaction-processing code, commercial workloads (e.g., COBOL), and multiprocessing were beyond the scope of

program name	dynamic instr.	data reads	data writes	total refs.	program type
ccom	31.5M	8.3M	5.7M	45.5M	C compiler
grr	134.2M	42.1M	17.1M	193.4M	PC board CAD
yacc	51.0M	12.9M	3.8M	67.7M	Unix utility
met	99.4M	36.4M	13.8M	149.7M	PC board CAD
linpack	144.8M	28.1M	12.1M	185.5M	100x100
livermore	23.6M	5.0M	2.3M	31.0M	loops 1-14
total	484.5M	132.8M	54.8M	672.8M	

Table 2-1: Test program characteristics

this study. The benchmarks used are reasonably long in comparison with most traces in use today.

3. Write Misses: Fetch-on-Write, Write-Allocate, and Write-Before-Hit

The policy used on a write that misses in the cache (i.e., "write miss") can significantly affect the total amount of cache refill traffic, as well as the amount of time spent waiting during cache misses. The number of cache misses due to writes varies dramatically depending on the benchmark used. Figure 3-1 shows the percentage of misses that are due to writes for various cache sizes with 16B lines, using write-allocate with fetch-on-write. Figure 3-2 shows the percentage of misses that are due to writes for an 8KB cache with various line sizes. On average over all the cache configurations, write misses account for about one-third of all cache misses. Since loads outnumber stores in these benchmarks by roughly 2.4:1 (see Table 2-1), this means that stores are about as likely to cause a miss as loads.

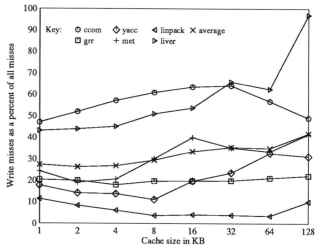

Figure 3-1: Write misses vs. cache size for 16B lines

There are four combinations of three write-miss policies from which to choose (see Figure 3-3).

In systems implementing a *fetch-on-write* policy, on a write miss the line containing the write address is fetched. In systems implementing a *write-allocate* policy, the address written to by the write miss is allocated in the cache. Note that it is possible to have a write-allocate policy without using fetch-on-write: here the data being written is writ-

192

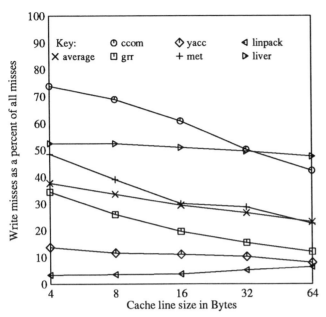

Figure 3-2: Write misses vs. line size for 8KB caches

Fetch-on-write?

		Yes	No		Write-before-hit?
Write-allocate?	Yes	Fetch-on-write	Write-validate	No	
		Fetch-on-write	Write-validate	Yes	
	No		Write-around	No	
			Write-invalidate	Yes	

Figure 3-3: Write miss alternatives

ten into the cache without fetching the old contents of the cache line. As compared to systems with non-blocking writes [17] which just write into a write buffer on a write miss, this combination can give significant performance improvement because the data written into the cache can be read later without a cache miss.

If a direct-mapped write-through cache is being used, the data can be written concurrently with the tag check. We call this a *write-before-hit* policy. If the tag does not match, the data portion of the line has been corrupted (i.e., assuming the line size is larger than the amount of data being written, the data is a mixture of information from two cache lines). If the system is fetch-on-write or write-allocate, the normal miss processing will restore the cache line to a consistent state. However, if the system is no-fetch-on-write and no-write-allocate, the line can simply be marked invalid, since the data is being written to a lower level in the memory hierarchy anyway. This invalidation can usually be done in a single cycle, or sometimes even in parallel with subsequent cache accesses, and so it is much faster than fetching the correct contents of the cache line being written.

A combination of fetch-on-write and no-write-allocate policies is not useful, since the old data at the write miss address is fetched but is discarded instead of being written into the cache. When referring to caching policies, fetch-on-write has been used to imply write-allocate in the literature. A fetch-on-write policy has the same result whether or not write-before-hit is used. If the old data at the write miss address is not fetched (i.e., no-fetch-on-write), three distinct options are possible. We call the combination of no-fetch-on-write and write-allocate *write-validate*. With write-validate, the line containing the write is not fetched. The data is written into a cache line with valid bits turned off for all but the data which is being written. For write-validate polices with write-before-hit, the valid bits for the old data must be turned off with an additional write operation once miss is detected. We call the combination of no-fetch-on-write, no-write-allocate, and no-write-before-hit *write-around*, since write misses do not go into the cache but go around it to the next lower level in the memory hierarchy, leaving the old contents of the line in place. Note that writes that hit in the cache still write into the cache with a write-around policy; here we are only considering write miss alternatives. The combination of write-before-hit, no-fetch-on-write, and no-write-allocate we call write-invalidate, because the line must be invalidated on a miss. Note that this is not the same as the *write-purge* of [16] which invalidates the cache line on a write hit. As defined here, write-invalidate only invalidates lines when it misses. Thus, write hits still write into the cache as usual with a write-invalidate write miss policy.

We call write misses that that do not result in any data being fetched with a write-validate, write-around, or write-invalidate policy *eliminated misses*. For example, with write-validate if the invalid part of a line is never read, the fetch of the data (and the attendant stalling of the processor) is eliminated. Only if the invalid portion of a line resulting from the write-validate strategy is read without first being written or the line being replaced, is this counted as a miss. Similarly, with write-invalidate only if the line being written or the old contents of the cache line are read before another address mapping to the same cache line misses is it counted as a miss. Finally, with write-around, only if the data being written is read before any other data which maps to the same cache line is read is the miss counted. This terminology neglects the time required to set the valid bits on an eliminated miss. However, if maintenance of the valid bits cannot be done in parallel with other operations, it typically takes at most a cycle, which is insignificant compared to cache miss penalties.

The write miss policy used is sometimes dependent on the write hit policy chosen. Write-around and write-invalidate (i.e., policies with no-write-allocate) are only useful with write-through caches, since writes are not entered into the cache. Fetch-on-write and write-validate can be used with either write-through or write-back caching.

Write-validate requires the addition of valid bits within a cache line. Valid bits could be added on a word basis, so that words can be written and the remainder of the line marked invalid. In systems that allow byte writes or un-aligned word writes, byte valid bits would be required for a pure write-validate strategy. However, the addition of byte valid bits is a significant overhead (one bit per byte, or 12.5%) in comparison to a valid bit per word (3.1%). Thus, in practice machines with byte writes that have write-validate capability for aligned word and double-word writes would probably provide fetch-on-write for byte writes. Write-validate also requires that lower levels in the memory system support writes of partial cache lines.

In multiprocessor systems with cache consistency, write misses require traffic to gain exclusive write ownership of the block being written. In a multiprocessor using write-validate with an ownership protocol, a fetch with owner-ship still needs to be sent to the coherency point. When the fetched data returns it can be merged with the cache line which has been allocated based on the word valid bits. Thus extra coherency transactions required by write-validate can negate its traffic advantages over fetch-on-write in multiprocessor configurations. However, to the extent that the processor can continue execution with relaxed consistency models, including use of data which has been previously written but for which the rest of the line has not returned, improved performance would still be possible with write-validate as compared to a simple fetch-on-write policy.

The choice of write miss policy can make a significant difference in the performance of certain operations. For example, consider copying a block of information. If fetch-on-write is used, each write of the destination must hit in the cache. In other words, the original contents of the target of the copy will be fetched even though they are never used and are only overwritten with write data. This will reduce the bandwidth of the copy by wasting fetch bandwidth. Given a total bandwidth available for reads and writes, a fetch-on-write strategy would have only two-thirds of the performance on large block copies as a no-fetch-on-write policy since half of the items fetched would be discarded.

Some architectures have added instructions to allocate a cache line in cases where programmer directives specify or the compiler can guarantee that the entire cache line will be written and the old contents of the corresponding memory locations will not be read [11, 8, 4]. These instructions are limited to situations where new data spaces are being al-located, such as a new activation record on a process stack, or a new output buffer is obtained from the operating sys-tem. Unfortunately there are a number of problems that prevent broader application of software cache line alloca-tion:
1. The entire cache line must be known to be written at compile time, or if some of the line is not written its old contents must not need to be saved. (In contrast, write-validate can allow partial lines to written, and is not

subject to optimization limitations such as incomplete alias information, etc.)
2. Cache line sizes vary from implementation to im-plementation, limiting object code using these instruc-tions to the machines with cache line sizes equal to or smaller than that assumed in the allocate instructions.
3. Context switches after a line has been allocated and partially written but before it has been completely writ-ten result in dirty and incorrect cache lines. (One way around this would be to add valid bits to each write quantum in the line, but this provides the hardware sup-port needed for write-validate).
4. There is extra instruction execution overhead for the cache allocation instructions, or extra opcode space is used if they are merged with store instructions.

Thus, the use of cache line allocation instructions is limited to situations such as new data allocation and buffer copies. Write-validate can provide better performance than cache line allocation instructions since it is also applicable in cases where only part of a line is being written or it is not possible to guarantee that an entire line is written at com-pile time. Write-validate works for machines with various line sizes, and does not add instruction execution overhead to the program. Finally, since write-validate has word valid bits there are no problems with cache lines being left in an incorrect state on context switches.

A technique that has recently become popular in the literature is non-blocking (also called lock-up-free) caches [17]. Typically a cache with non-blocking writes implements what we have called a write-around policy. Some practical implementations of non-blocking writes may need to use write-invalidate, however, for timing reasons.

Figure 3-4 shows the reduction in write misses for write-validate, write-around, and write-invalidate for caches with 16B lines. We define the reduction in *misses as a percent-age of write misses* (M%WM) for a policy X as follows:

$$M\%WM_{reduction} = 100 \times \frac{Misses_{fetch-on-write} - Misses_X}{WriteMisses_{fetch-on-write}}$$

Note that we take the difference in *total* misses (both read and write) and divide it by the number of *write* misses of fetch-on-write. When policies other than fetch-on-write are used this takes into account extra read misses that occur as a result of not using fetch-on-write. Since fetch-on-write fetches a cache line on every write miss, it corresponds to the X axis (0% reduction) in Figure 3-4. In general write-validate performs the best, averaging more than a 90% reduction in misses as a percentage of write misses. The two no-write-allocate strategies, write-around and write-invalidate, have an average reduction in misses as a per-centage of write misses of 40-65% and 30-50% respec-tively. Write-around has a greater than 100% reduction in misses as a percentage of write misses for 32KB and 64KB caches when running *liver, because it saves read misses as well. liver* is a synthetic benchmark made from a series of loop kernels, and the results of loop kernels are not read by successive kernels. However, successive loop kernels read the original matrices again. The range of cache sizes from 32KB to 64KB is big enough to hold the initial inputs, but not the results too. Since write-around does not place the results in the cache but keeps the old contents of the cache line unchanged, it can also result in fewer read misses since the initial data is not replaced with write data or in-validated.

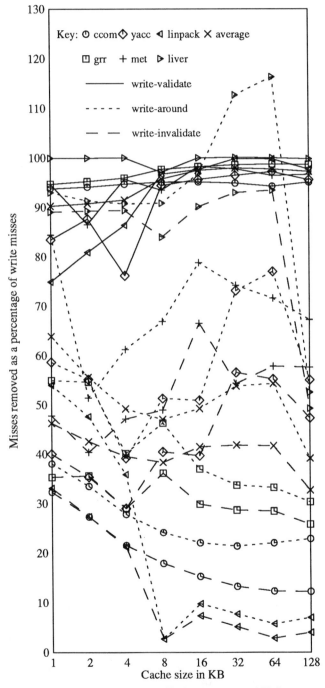

Figure 3-4: Miss reduction as % of write misses, 16B lines

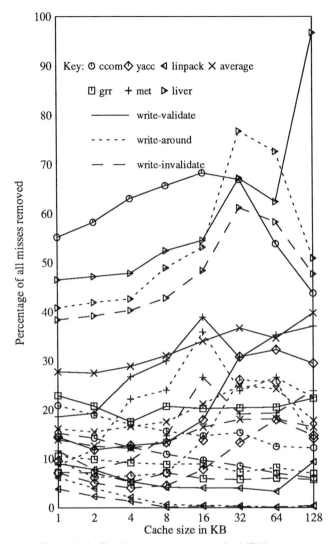

Figure 3-5: Total miss rate reductions for 16B lines

Figure 3-5 shows the reduction in data cache misses (including both read and write) for write-validate, write-around, and write-invalidate for caches with 16B lines. The overall reduction in miss rate (MOverall) is computed as folows:

$$MOverall_{reduction} = 100 \times \frac{Misses_{fetch-on-write} - Misses_X}{Misses_{fetch-on-write}}$$

Figure 3-5 is basically Figure 3-4 multiplied by Figure 3-1. *ccom* and *liver* benefit the most from a write-validate policy. This can be explained as follows. Many of the operations in *ccom* and *liver* are similar to copies: data is read but other data is written. For example, array operations of the form "for j := 1 to 1000 do A[j] := B[j] + C[j]" only write data which is never read before being written. Similarly, write-validate would be useful for a compiler if it has a number of sequential passes, each one reading the data structure written by the last pass and writing a dif-

195

ferent one. The other programs have more read-modify-write behavior. The best example of this is *linpack*. The inner loop of *linpack*, saxpy, loads a matrix row and adds to it another row multiplied by a scalar. The result of this computation is placed into the old row. Here write-validate would be of very little benefit since almost all writes are preceded by reads of the data anyway. On average over the six programs write-validate reduced the total number of data cache misses (over both read and write) by 31% for an 8KB data cache with 16B line size.

Write-around performs well when the data being written by the processor is not read by it soon or ever. This is the situation in *liver* with a 32KB or 64KB cache, the only benchmark that performs better with write-around than write-validate. In general, however, most programs are more likely to read what they have just written than they are to re-read the old contents of a cache line. For all other cases the performance of write-around is worse than that of write-validate.

Write-invalidate does not show as much improvement over fetch-on-write as the other two strategies, but it still performs surprisingly well. *livermore* has about a 40% reduction in misses, and the six benchmarks on average have a 10-20% total reduction in misses compared to fetch-on-write. Moreover, write-invalidate is very simple to implement. In a write-through cache using write-invalidate the data can be written at the same time the tags are probed. If the access misses, the line has been corrupted so it can be simply marked invalid, often without inserting any machine stall cycles.

Figure 3-6 shows the reduction in misses as a percentage of write misses for write-validate, write-around, and write-invalidate for 8KB caches with various line sizes. Since fetch-on-write fetches a cache line on every write miss, it corresponds to the X axis (0% reduction) in Figure 3-6. Write-validate, write-around, and write-invalidate have the highest benefit for small lines. If the line size is the same as the item being written, any old data fetched by fetch-on-write is merely discarded when the write occurs. As the line size gets larger, the odds that some old data on the line will be needed increases, so the advantage of write-validate decreases. The miss rate reduction of write-around also decreases with increasing line size for similar reasons. The performance advantage of write-invalidate decreases with increasing line sizes because more information is being thrown away. Again write-validate performs the best, averaging more than a 90% reduction in misses as a percentage of write misses except at the longest line sizes. The two no-write-allocate strategies, write-around and write-invalidate, have an average reduction in misses as a percentage of write misses of 40-70% and 35-50% respectively.

Figure 3-7 shows the overall reduction in total misses for write-validate, write-around, and write-invalidate for 8KB caches. (This graph is basically Figure 3-6 multiplied by Figure 3-2.) Again write-around generally performs worse

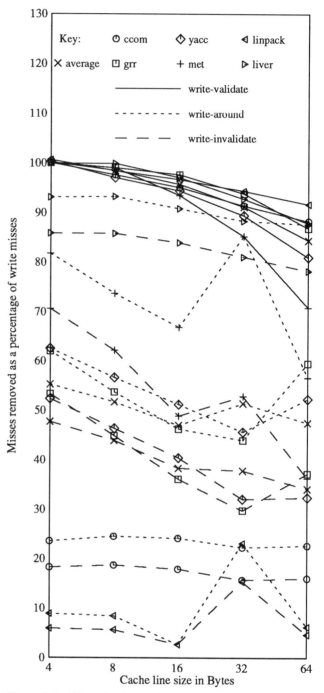

Figure 3-6: Miss reduction as % of write misses, 8KB caches

than write-validate, because most programs are more likely to read the data that was just written than the old contents of the cache line. Both write-validate and write-around perform better than write-invalidate, but again write-invalidate performs surprisingly well.

We can generate a partial order of the relative total read and write miss traffic between these four write-miss policy combinations (see Figure 3-8). Fetch-on-write always has the most lines fetched, since it fetches a line on every miss.

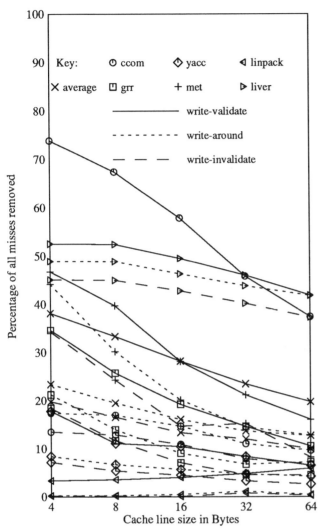

Figure 3-7: Total miss rate reduction for 8KB caches

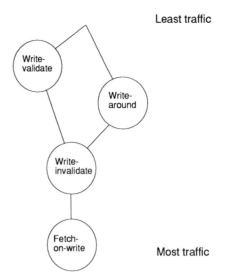

Figure 3-8: Relative order of total fetch traffic

Write-invalidate avoids misses in the case where neither the line containing the data being written nor the old contents of the cache line are read before some other line mapping to the same location in the cache is read. This saves some misses over fetch-on-write. Write-around and write-validate always have fewer misses than write-invalidate. Write-around avoids fetching data in the same cases as write-invalidate, as well as cases where the old contents of the cache line are accessed next. Write-validate avoids fetching data in the same cases as write-invalidate, as well as cases where the data just written is accessed next. Usually the data just written (i.e., write-validate) is more useful than the old contents of the cache line (i.e., write-around), but this is not always the case. Also, the ratio of miss rate reduction of write-validate to write-around decreases as the line size increases since write-validate invalidates an increasing number of bytes while write-around leaves all the bytes on the line valid.

4. Write Hits: Write-Through vs. Write-Back

When a write hits in a cache, two possible policy choices exist. First, the data can be written both into the cache and passed on to the next lower level in the memory hierarchy. This policy is called write-through. A second possible policy on write hits is to only write the data to the first-level cache. Only when a dirty line (i.e., a line that has been written to) is replaced in the cache is the data transferred to a lower level in the memory hierarchy. This policy is called write-back. Write-back caching takes advantage of the locality of reference of writes to reduce the amount of write traffic going to the next lower level in the memory hierarchy.

Although the conventional wisdom may be that write-back caching is always preferred over write-through caching, in multilevel cache hierarchies there are a number of significant advantages of write-through caching for first-level caches. In the common case where the first-level caches are on-chip, the second-level cache is typically write-back.

One advantage of write-through caching is the write bandwidth into the cache (i.e., the number of cycles required per write). A write-back cache must probe the tag store for a hit before the corresponding data is written. This is because if the write access misses and the victim is dirty, unique dirty data will be lost if the cache line is written before the probe. However, a direct-mapped write-through cache can always write a cache line of data at the same time as probing the address tag for a hit. If the access misses, the line is never dirty and will be replaced anyway so there is no problem. If the data cache is set-associative, the probe must occur before the write whether the cache is write-back or write-through. However, a large and increasing number of first-level data caches are direct-mapped, for reasons discussed in [7, 10]. The two-cycle access of straightforward write-back and set-associative cache implementations (i.e., a probe cycle followed by a write cycle) provides more limited store bandwidth at the input to the cache than a direct-mapped write-through cache, in order to reduce the write bandwidth required on the output side of the cache. In machines that can issue multiple instructions per cycle, the incoming load/store bandwidth of the cache can be a limiting factor to machine performance. Although stores are about half as frequent as loads on average, if each store requires two cycles this will result in a 33% reduction in effective first-level cache bandwidth as compared to a machine that only requires one cycle per store. There are also more complicated methods for reducing write-hits to a single cycle in write-back and set-associative write-through caches [5] which are beyond the scope of this work.

A second advantage of write-through caching over write-back caching is the ease with which stores and their attendant writes are integrated into the machine pipeline (see Figure 4-1). In a direct-mapped write-through cache writes can always be performed in the pipestage where loads read the cache. If the access turns out to be a miss the conventional miss-recovery hardware provided for load misses can be used, and the store write cycle is simply repeated. However, a simple write-back or set-associative write-through cache can require two cycles of cache access per store: the first cycle probes the cache tags, and the second sets the appropriate dirty bits and writes the data. This will require interlocks when loads immediately follow stores, since the stores would be accessing the data section at the same time as the next (load) instruction is accessing the data section of the cache (i.e., without interlocks the WB pipestage of the store would be at the same time as the MEM pipestage of the load.) Note that if load latency weren't important, loads could delay their data access until WB after hit or miss were already known. Then stores and loads would access the cache with the same timing and could be issued one per cycle in any order. However, since load latency is of critical importance in machine design, this is not a viable option. Although in Figure 4-1 stores into a write-through cache would commit a pipestage earlier than loads or other operations (which commit in WB), the cache line written by the store can be flushed a pipestage after its write without adverse consequences. This allows exceptions to be handled precisely. Similarly, data going into the write buffer in the MEM pipestage of Figure 4-1 can be aged one cycle until the instruction is known to have completed without exception.

A third advantage of write-through caching over write-back caching is error-tolerance, for both manufacturing or hard defects and soft defects. A write-through cache can function with either hard or soft single-bit errors, if parity is provided. This is because the write-through cache contains no unique dirty data, and reads of data with errors can be turned into cache misses. A write-back cache can not tolerate a single-bit error of any type unless ECC is provided. ECC must usually be computed on at least a 32

pipestage	load timing	store timing write-through$	store timing write-back*
instr fetch			
register fetch			
address calc.			
cache access	read data read tags	write data read tags	read tags
write registers			write data if tags hit

$ Also assumes direct-mapped.
* Also applies if set-associative write-through.

Figure 4-1: Direct-mapped write pipelines

bit data word to be economical. For example, single bit detection and correction (but not double detection) ECC requires 6 bits per 32 bit word versus 4 bits per 8 bit byte giving 16 bits per 4 bytes. Thus operations like byte store must first read and ECC-decode a word before being able to write a byte. Moreover, byte parity on a four-byte word would allow four single-bit errors to be corrected by refetching a write-through line in comparison to only one error for an ECC-protected write-back cache word. This is true even though byte parity requires only two-thirds of the overhead of word ECC. Thus write-through caches with parity have better error-tolerance at a smaller cost than write-back caches with ECC.

The primary problem with write-through caches is their higher write traffic as compared to write-back caches. One way to reduce this traffic is to use a *coalescing write buffer*, where writes to addresses already in the write buffer are combined.

Figure 4-2 shows the simulation results for an 8-entry coalescing write buffer. Each write buffer entry is a cache line (16B) wide. The data presented are the results of the six benchmarks averaged together. Simulations were performed where the write buffer emptied out an entry every n cycles, with n varying from 0 to 48 cycles. In practice the number of cycles between retirement of write buffer entries will depend on intervening cache miss service and other system factors. However, as on-chip processor cycle times become much faster than the off-chip cycle times, and processors issue more than one instruction per cycle, the number of off-chip cycles between writes can become very large (e.g., more than 12). Since cache miss service effectively stops processor execution in many processors, cache misses were ignored in Figure 4-2. This allows a fixed time between writes to be used as a reasonable model of the write buffer operation. If dirty write buffer entries are written back quickly, they do not stay in the write buffer for many cycles and hence relatively little merging takes place. For example, if write buffer entries are retired every 5 cycles, the write traffic is reduced by only 10%. The only way that a significant number of writes are merged (e.g., 50% or more) is if the write buffer is almost always full. But in this case stores almost always stall because no write buffer entries are available. For example, to attain a write traffic reduction of 50%, writes must be retired no more frequently than every 38 cycles, resulting in a CPI burden of 7! Since much of current computer research is focused on achieving machines with CPIs of less than one, write buffer stalls should be well under 0.1 CPI. This means that only a small percentage of writes (e.g., less than 20%) can be merged with simple coalescing write buffers. The extra traffic resulting from this lack of coalescing wastes cache bandwidth that could otherwise be used for prefetching or other uses.

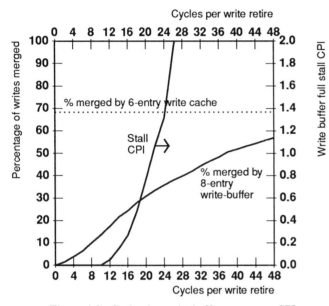

Figure 4-2: Coalescing write buffer merges vs. CPI

Instead of having writes enter and leave the write buffer as soon as possible, we can add a *write cache* in front of the write buffer and behind the data cache. A write cache is a small fully-associative cache (see Figure 4-3). With a small number of entries we can try to coalesce the majority of writes and decrease the write traffic exiting the chip. When a write misses in the write cache, the LRU entry is transferred to the write buffer to make room for the current write. In actual implementation, the write cache can be merged with a coalescing write buffer. Here a write buffer of *m* entries would only empty an entry if it has more than *n* valid entries, where *n* is the number of entries conceptually in the write cache (with $m > n$). A write cache can also be implemented with the additional functionality of a victim cache [9], in which case not all entries in the small fully-associative cache would be dirty. Note that whereas a first-level data cache which can probed and written in one cycle is very difficult to achieve (for an interesting cycle time), a several-entry fully-associative write-cache could be easily implemented within a machine cycle. This is because each tag in the write cache must has its own comparator. Thus there is no tag RAM access time before the tag comparisons can begin, as would be the case in a ordinary data cache.

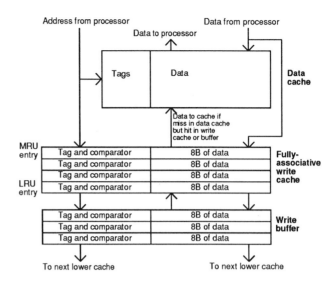

Figure 4-3: Write cache organization

Figure 4-4 gives the number of writes removed by a write cache with varying numbers of 8B lines. (8B was chosen as the write cache line size since no writes larger than 8B exist in most architectures, and write paths leaving chips are often 8B.) A write cache of only five 8B lines can eliminate 50% of the writes for most programs. Two notable exceptions to this are *linpack* and *liver*. Because these programs sequentially travel through large arrays, even a write-back cache of modest size (less than 32KB) removes very few writes. In order to get a better idea of how write caches compare with write-back caches, the write traffic reduction of a write cache is given relative to a 4KB write-back cache in Figure 4-5. In Figure 4-5 a write cache of only four 8B entries removes over 50% of the writes removed by a 4KB write-back cache on all of the benchmarks except *met*. Another interesting result is that a write cache with eight or more 8B entries actually outperforms a 4KB direct-mapped write-back cache on *liver*. This is because mapping conflicts within the write reference stream prevent a direct-mapped write-back cache from being as effective at removing write traffic as the fully-associative write cache.

Figures 4-4 and 4-5 also give the average traffic reduction of write caches in absolute terms and relative to a write-back cache. The two most interesting points on these curves are probably a five-entry write cache, since it seems to be at the knee of the traffic reduction curve, and a one-entry write cache, since it is the simplest to implement. The five-entry write cache can remove 40% of all writes, or 63% of those removed by a 4KB write-back cache. The single-entry write cache can remove 16% of all writes on average, which is 21% of the writes removed by a write-back cache.

Of course the relative traffic reduction of a write cache varies as the size of the write-back cache used in the comparison varies (see Figure 4-6). Compared to a 1KB write-back cache, a five-entry write cache removes 72% of the

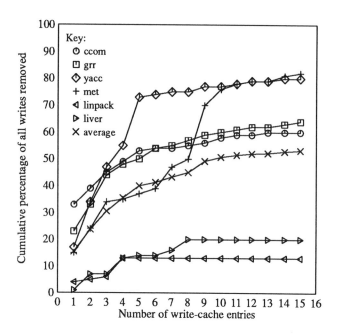

Figure 4-4: Write cache absolute traffic reduction

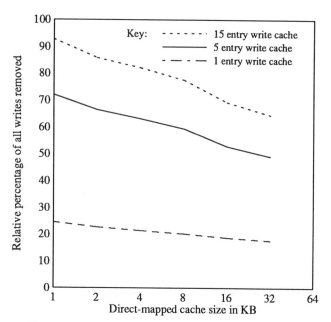

Figure 4-6: Write cache traffic reduction vs. cache size

5. Conclusions

An important performance issue involving writes is the policy for handling write data on a write miss. Four options exist: either fetch the line before writing (i.e., fetch-on-write), allocate a cache line and write the data while turning off valid bits for the remainder of the line (i.e., write-validate), just write the data into the next lower level of the memory hierarchy leaving the old contexts of the cache line intact (i.e., write-around), or invalidate the cache line and pass the data on to the next lower level in the memory hierarchy (i.e., write-invalidate). Write-invalidate is useful when writes occur in a direct-mapped write-through cache before hit or miss is known, and the line is corrupted on a miss. Of course if a write hits in the cache, the cache is written into as usual independent of the write miss policy. Systems with lock-up-free caches in the literature typically provide a write-around policy, although write-invalidate may need to be implemented in some machines due to timing constraints. Write-validate and write-around always outperform fetch-on-write. In general write-validate outperforms write-around since data just written is more likely to be accessed soon again than data read previously. Write-invalidate always performs worse than write-validate or write-around, but always outperforms fetch-on-write. For systems with caches in the range of 8KB to 128KB with 16B lines, write validate reduced the total number of misses by 30 to 35% on average over the six benchmarks studied as compared to fetch-on-write, write-around reduced the total number of misses by 15 to 25%, and write-invalidate reduced the total number of misses by 10 to 20%. Unlike cache line allocation instructions, write-validate is applicable to all write operations.

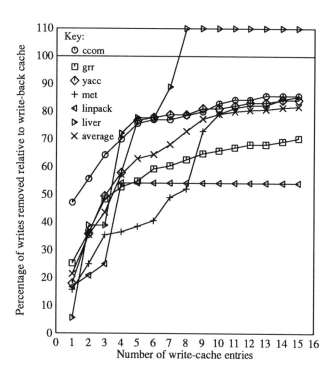

Figure 4-5: Write cache traffic relative to 4KB write-back

write traffic but compared to a 32KB write-back cache it only removes 49% of the write traffic. This change is surprisingly small considering the 32:1 ratio in write-back cache size, and is due to the write cache's good absolute traffic reduction. The reduction in write cache relative effectiveness is fairly uniform as the write-back cache size used for comparison increases in size.

Moreover, it does not require compiler analysis or program directives, works with various line sizes, does not add any instruction execution overhead, and through the use of word valid bits allows a consistent and correct view of memory to be maintained.

An important write policy issue for writes that hit in a cache is write-through versus write-back caching. *Write caching*, a technique for reducing the traffic of write-through caches, was studied. It was found that a small fully-associative write cache of five 8B entries could remove 40% of the write traffic on average. This compares favorably to the 58% reduction obtained by a 4KB write-back cache. Since write-through caches have the advantage of only requiring parity for fault tolerance and recovery, while write-back caches require ECC, write-through caches seem preferable for small and moderate sized on-chip caches. Only when cache sizes reach 32KB does the additional traffic reduction provided by write-back caches over write-through caches become significant.

Acknowledgments

The author would like to thank the referees for their helpful comments, and those at DECWRL who had helpful comments on early drafts of this paper.

References

1. Agarwal, Anant. *Analysis of Cache Performance for Operating Systems and Multiprogramming.* Ph.D. Th., Stanford University, 1987.

2. Clark, Douglas W. "Cache Performance in the VAX 11/780". *ACM Transactions on Computer Systems 1*, 1 (February 1983), 24-37.

3. Clark, Douglas W., Bannon, Peter J., and Keller, James B. Measuring VAX 8800 Performance with a Histogram Hardware Monitor. The 15th Annual Symposium on Computer Architecture, IEEE Computer Society Press, June, 1988, pp. 176-185.

4. DeLano, Eric, Walker, Will, Yetter, Jeff, and Forsyth, Mark. A High-Speed Superscalar PA-RISC Processor. Compcon Spring, IEEE Computer Society Press, February, 1992, pp. 116-121.

5. Fu, John, Keller, James B., and Haduch, Kenneth J. "Aspects of the VAX 8800 C Box Design". *Digital Technical Journal 1*, 6 (February 1987), 41-51.

6. Goodman, James R. Using Cache Memory to Reduce Processor-Memory Traffic . The 10th Annual Symposium on Computer Architecture, IEEE Computer Society Press, June, 1983, pp. 124-131.

7. Hill, Mark D. *Aspects of Cache Memory and Instruction Buffer Performance.* Ph.D. Th., University of California, Berkeley, 1987.

8. Jouppi, Norman P. Architectural and Organizational Tradeoffs in the Design of the MultiTitan CPU. The 16th Annual Symposium on Computer Architecture, IEEE Computer Society Press, May, 1989, pp. 281-289.

9. Jouppi, Norman P. Improving Direct-Mapped Cache Performance by the Addition of a Small Fully-Associative Cache and Prefetch Buffers . The 17th Annual Symposium on Computer Architecture, IEEE Computer Society Press, May, 1990, pp. 364-373.

10. Przybylski, S.A. *Cache Design: A Performance-Directed Approach.* Morgan-Kaufmann, San Mateo, CA, 1990.

11. Radin, George. The 801 Minicomputer. (The First) Symposium on Architectural Support for Programming Languages and Operating Systems, IEEE Computer Society Press, March, 1982, pp. 39-47.

12. Smith, Alan J. "Characterizing the Storage Process and Its Effect on the Update of Main Memory by Write-Through". *Journal of the ACM 26*, 1 (January 1979), 6-27.

13. Smith, Alan J. "Cache Memories". *Computing Surveys 14*, 3 (September 1982), 473-530.

14. Smith, Alan J. "Bibliography and Readings on CPU Cache Memories". *Computer Architecture News 14*, 1 (January 1986), 22-42.

15. Smith, Alan J. "Second Bibliography on Cache Memories". *Computer Architecture News 19*, 4 (June 1991), 154-182.

16. Smith, Alan J. CPU Cache Memories. unpublished, draft of April 24, 1984.

17. Sohi, Gurindar, and Franklin, Manoj. High-Bandwidth Data Memory Systems for Superscalar Processors. Fourth International Conference on Architectural Support for Programming Languages and Operating Systems, IEEE Computer Society Press, April, 1991, pp. 53-62.

SESSION 10:
Evaluation
of
Machines I

Hierarchical Performance Modeling with MACS:
A Case Study of the Convex C-240

Eric L. Boyd and Edward S. Davidson

Advanced Computer Architecture Laboratory
Department of Electrical Engineering and Computer Science
University of Michigan

Abstract

The MACS performance model introduced here can be applied to a Machine and Application of interest, the Compiler-generated workload, and the Scheduling of the workload by the compiler. The MA, MAC, and MACS bounds each fix the named subset of M, A, C, and S while freeing the bound from the constraints imposed by the others. A/X performance measurement is used to measure access-only and execute-only code performance. Such hierarchical performance modeling exposes the gaps between the various bounds, the A/X measurements, and the actual performance, thereby focusing performance optimization at the appropriate levels in a systematic and goal-directed manner. A simple, but detailed, case study of the Convex C-240 vector mini-supercomputer illustrates the method.

1. Introduction

The MACS performance modeling techniques described in this paper facilitate critiquing an architecture, its implementation, and its compiler, as well as providing suggestions for their improvement. The model is based on a Machine and high–level Application code of interest, the Compiler-generated workload, and the Scheduling of the workload by the compiler. We define a hierarchy of bounds equations (MA, MAC, and MACS), each of which fixes the named subset of M, A, C, and S while allowing the others to be idealized. The MAC bound thus poses a limit on what the best possible schedule could achieve on the compiled code while the MA bound may be approachable by the best compiler/scheduler for the specified Machine-Application pair. In contrast, the peak floating point performance claimed for a machine (an "M" bound) bounds the minimum number of cycles per floating point operation (CPF) ever attained by any application. Total application performance measurements are contrasted with these bounds. We also employ A/X performance measurements [1] by which actual performance is measured with floating-point or

memory accessing operations removed from the code.

Ascending through this hierarchy of models and measurements refines a machine's "best possible" performance on an application by successively adding constraints on its performance. Hierarchical bounds-based performance modeling thus exposes and explains the specific gap for each pair of bounds equations and measurements. With this understanding, performance optimization can proceed in a systematic and goal–directed manner to minimize the gap between delivered and deliverable performance.

The MACS models are improvements of models originally developed for the Cray vector supercomputer systems [2] [3], the Decoupled Access-Execute (DAE) architecture Astronautics ZS-1 [1] [4], and the superscalar IBM RS/6000 [4] [5]. We have significantly expanded the functionality of this general performance modeling approach, and illustrate its utility with a detailed case study of the Convex C-240 vector mini-supercomputer [6] [7].

As with all vector machines, the delivered performance of the Convex C-240 on a well–vectorized scientific code is primarily related to the efficiency of implementation of inner loops, the architectural flexibility, and the bandwidths and latencies of the machine implementation. Although parallel processes can be executed on the Convex C-240, the throughput penalty of running parallel jobs on a heavily loaded machine makes single-threaded vectorized processes the most common mode of operation.

Our performance study of the Convex C-240 focuses on modeling the steady-state performance of the vector processor on vectorized inner loops, which is the first portion of the code to optimize for running a well-suited application on a vector machine. Ten of the Lawrence Livermore Fortran Kernels (LFKs) [8] are used as workloads in this case study. This benchmark set contains a variety of inner loops, each small enough to be considered in detail, yet representative of many vectorizable scientific codes.

0884-7495/93 $3.00 © 1993 IEEE

2. Overview of the Convex C-240 Architecture

The Convex C-240 has four CPUs sharing the same physical memory and I/O subsystems. The effective system clock period is 40 ns. Each CPU is self-allocating, taking a task for itself when ready. Processes can be run in scalar mode, vector mode, or parallel vector mode. CPUs are single-issue; instructions are issued in order with hardware interlocks. Each CPU contains an Address/Scalar Unit (ASU) and a Vector Processor (VP).

The ASU contains the scalar function units, scalar registers, and cache. It controls all machine instruction execution and executes all scalar instructions, addressing functions for scalar operations, and most addressing functions for vector operations.

The VP concentrates solely on the execution of all vector operations. The VP data path includes eight vector registers of 128 elements each, a memory interface, the scalar processor interface, the vector merge register, and the three pipelined function units (load/store, add, multiply) used to perform all vector operations. The load/store function pipe is its only interface to memory. The add function pipe handles all types of adds, population counts, shifts, logical functions, and data type conversions. The multiply function pipe executes multiplications, divisions, square root operations, and vector edits. The three function pipes may execute different instructions concurrently. Operand chaining permits the output of one pipeline to be fed directly into the input of another pipeline.[1] The VP accesses memory directly, bypassing the scalar unit data cache. The Convex C-240 is a load/store architecture with eight vector registers.

The memory subsystem has five ports: one for I/O operations, and one for each of the four independent CPUs. Memory contention is typically minimal assuming a reasonable pattern of memory accesses among different processes. The memory system consists of 32 banks in the standard system configuration. Each memory word is eight bytes and the bank cycle time is eight clock cycles. Under an ideal no-conflict situation, the four processors can request and the 32 memory banks can satisfy one memory access per processor per cycle.

3. Hierarchy of Performance Models and Measurements

We analyze the performance of a target architecture using the hierarchy of performance bound models and measurements shown in Figure 1. The performance models are

constructed using selected parameters of the machine and static analysis of the high-level application code (A) of interest, the compiler-generated workload (C), and the scheduling (S) of the workload by the compiler. In ascending through the bounds hierarchy from t_{MA}, the model becomes increasingly constrained as it moves in several steps from potentially deliverable toward actually delivered performance, t_p. Each step quantifies a performance gap associated with a particular cause. The model is constrained to fit a specific compiler-generated workload in t_{MAC}, and then to fit a specific schedule for that workload in t_{MACS}.

The several t_f and t_m parameters bound the minimum time for executing only the associated vector floating point operations and memory load/store operations, respectively. We extend the model analysis by measuring actual performance of the execute-only portion of the code, t_x, the access-only portion, t_a, and the entire code t_p. Note that t_{MAC} and t_{MA} are simply the maximum of their f and m components, while t_{MACS} and t_p are influenced by more complex interactions of the floating point and memory units, as discussed in Sections 3.4 and 3.6.

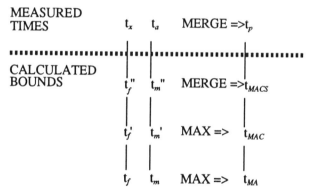

Figure 1: Hierarchy of Performance Models and Measurements

3.1. MA and MAC Performance Models

Performance analysis can be simplified by focusing on bottleneck functional units. In scalar machines such as the Astronautics ZS-1 and the IBM RS/6000, common bottleneck units include the instruction issue unit, the memory interface (load/store) unit, the floating point arithmetic unit (additions/multiplications), and a dependence pseudo-unit to model loop-carried dependence. [4] For vector machines such as the Cray-1, the instruction issue unit is not a bottleneck and can be ignored. [2] [3] No true loop-carried dependence cycle appears in the ten LFKs of the case study workload and most memory accesses are unit stride. We thus focus our model of the Convex C-240 exclusively on bottlenecks caused by operations in the vector load/store, add, and multiply function pipes. The multiply and add pipes each have a peak rate of 1 floating point operation per

---

[1] Superscalar machines such as the IBM RS/6000 mimic chaining in single-port vector machines by employing "combined multiply-add" instructions which can be issued simultaneously with one memory load or store (with address update), and test and branch. [4] [5]

clock cycle. The single memory port per CPU has a peak rate of 1 memory operation per clock cycle. The peak memory rate could be reduced for nonunit stride accesses by defining a fifth degree of freedom, D, after M, A, C and S to bind the allocation (decomposition) of the data structures in memory.

The MA bound, t_{MA}, is a lower bound on *Cycles Per inner Loop iteration*, CPL, which models the application and the target machine. The application is defined by a particular high level code. Modifications to the high level code that may alter the essential workload are considered as creating a new application. The machine model characterizes the bottlenecks of interest in the target architecture. The MA bound for the Convex C-240 is calculated by counting the number of additions (f_a) and multiplications (f_m) that appear in the loop body of the high level code, and the necessary number of loads (l_{fl}), and stores (s_{fl}) of floating point data assuming perfect index analysis that eliminates reaccessing memory when data is reused among the iterations. The MA bound ignores additional operations introduced by the compiler and schedule-specific effects including dependence within and between iterations, enforcing Fortran precedence, register spilling, and bank conflicts due to nonunit stride memory accesses. The MA machine model assumes that the f_a, f_m, and $l_{fl} + s_{fl}$ operations can each be executed at one per clock. Hence $t_f = MAX\{f_a, f_m\}$, $t_m = l_{fl} + s_{fl}$, and $t_{MA} = MAX\{t_m, t_f\}$ in units of CPL.

The MAC bound, t_{MAC}, also models the compiler (not including the scheduler) by counting all the operations of the classes of interest (f_a', f_m', l_{fl}', and s_{fl}') in the compiler-generated assembly code rather than in the high-level source code. The MAC bound thus includes the effects of added operations, particularly from poor data reuse in the vector registers and spilling. Hence $t_f' = MAX\{f_a', f_m'\}$, $t_m' = l_{fl}' + s_{fl}'$, and $t_{MAC} = MAX\{t_m', t_f'\}$ in units of CPL.

Bounds and measurements in units of CPL can be converted to Clocks Per Floating point operation (CPF) by dividing by ($f_a + f_m$), the number of floating point arithmetic operations in the loop body of the high level code:

$$t_{MA} (CPF) := MAX (t_m, t_f) / (f_a + f_m) \qquad (2)$$

$$t_{MAC} (CPF) := MAX (t_m', t_f') / (f_a + f_m) \qquad (3)$$

The average CPF over a set of applications yields their harmonic mean performance in megaflops as:

$$HMEAN\ (MFLOPS)\ =\ \frac{clock\ rate\ (MHz)}{average\ CPF} \qquad (4)$$

3.2. Pipeline and Memory Effects

The MA and MAC bounds model a single vector instruction as taking VL clock cycles (1 clock cycle per vector element) to complete. Unmodeled effects may, however, significantly reduce delivered performance. These include

pipeline start-up, memory access conflicts, cache miss and page fault effects, and the time that a dynamic memory needs periodically to refresh its contents. These bounds thus produce performance goals to strive for, but better explanations of delivered performance require assessing schedule-specific phenomena, and a more detailed machine model.

Specially constructed *calibration loops* were used to verify specific aspects of machine performance and to confirm and clarify the start-up overheads claimed in [7]. Calibration loops are simple test loops constructed specifically for evaluating such parameters for a particular machine when detailed knowledge of the machine implementation or its minimum specifications is unavailable or needs to be confirmed. A similar approach is used in [9][10] to characterize memory hierarchy performance. The time to execute a single independent vector instruction can be expressed as:

$$X + Y + Z * VL \qquad (5)$$

where for any vector instruction:

X = # of clock cycles for initial overhead. (6)

Y = # of additional clock cycles until the first element result is available. (7)

Z = # of additional clock cycles per vector element to complete the instruction. (8)

VL = Vector Length (9)

The Convex-specified X, Y, and Z parameters (listed in Table 1) were compared to the results of running calibration loops for several common vector instructions. To achieve a

Instruction	Format	X	Y	Z	B
vector load	ld.l 0(a5),v0	2	10	1.00	2
vector store	st.l v0,0(a5)	2	10	1.00	4
vector add	add.d v0,v1,v2	2	10	1.00	1
vector multiply	mul.d v0,v1,v2	2	12	1.00	1
vector subtract	sub.d v0,v1,v2	2	10	1.00	1
vector divide[a]	div.d v0,v1,v2	2	72	4.00	21
vector reduction[b]	sum.d v0	2	10	1.35	0
vector negation	neg.d v0	2	10	1.00	1

Table 1: Vector Instruction Execution Times (VL = 128)
a. The extended number of cycles for a vector divide instruction may be masked by other instructions if no resource conflict exists.
b. It is claimed in [7] that for vector reduction, Z = 1.0. According to Patrick McGehearty at Convex Computer Corporation, Z ≈ 1.5 for vector reduction instructions. Calibration loops determined that for vector reduction Z ranged between 1.39 and 1.43. For purposes of the MACS bounds equations, Z was set conservatively at 1.35. B is set to zero due to the uncertainty in Z. Equivalently, we could set Z = 1, B = 45.

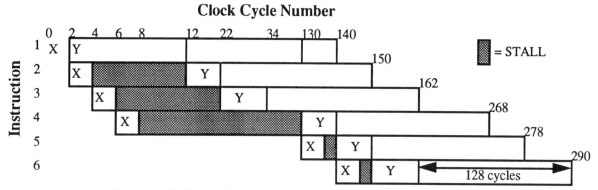

Figure 2: Chaining with Perfect Tailgating in the Function Unit Pipelines

fit with measured calibration loop performance, we introduce an additional parameter, a bubble of B cycles, as described in Section 3.3.

Periodically the Convex C-240 memory must refresh itself. A memory refresh occurs every 16 μs (400 cycles) and lasts 8 cycles, a possible 2% performance penalty. If four vector memory accesses appear at the memory in succession, taking over 500 cycles total to complete, a memory refresh will force the VP to stall for eight cycles. If the vector memory accesses are not successive, the memory refresh might be masked during a time when no memory access operation is accessing memory. Memory refreshes that might be masked are never included in the bound. Some of the parameters given in Table 1 vary slightly when VL < 128, and in particular run time no longer improves when VL drops below some operation-specific threshold.

3.3. Vector Chime Effects

Vector computers such as the Convex C-240 have multiple function pipes and allow vector instructions with non-conflicting resource requirements to be issued in quick succession and executed concurrently. We refer to such a group of concurrent vector instructions as a *chime*. (*Chime* commonly refers to the unit of time taken by such a group of concurrent vector instructions.) Most vector computers, with the notable exception of the Cray-2, are designed to let multiple *dependent* vector instructions *chain* together. Chaining occurs when the output of one vector pipeline feeds directly into the pipeline of another vector function unit, so the two dependent vector instructions are executed concurrently in the same chime. For example, consider the following three instructions:

ld.l 0(a5), v0;   V0 := values starting at a5   (10)

add.d v0,v1,v2;   V2 := V0 + V1   (11)

mul.d v2,v3,v5;   V5 := V2 * V3   (12)

Assume V1 and V3 already contain valid vectors and the vector length VL = 128. If the vector instructions did not chain, the first and second instructions would each take 2+10+VL cycles, and the third would take 2+12+VL cycles for a total of 422 cycles. With chaining, vector processor performance improves dramatically and the same three chained instructions take 162 cycles to complete, as shown in Figure 2.

The interaction of successive chimes yields an even larger improvement over the non-chaining approach. Assume that the chime in the above example is followed by an identical copy of the same three vector instructions in the same order (with a5 appropriately incremented). The first instruction of the second chain would begin at time 6, complete its initial overhead at time 8 and then immediately block, since the load/store pipe is busy. At time 130, the first instruction of the first chime begins to empty the load/store pipe. The first instruction of the second chime can now enter the load/store pipe (beginning its Y time). Its first element will be available at time 140, and that instruction will finish at time 140+VL = 268. Thus its X and Y parameters are essentially masked. The second instruction of the second chime will finish at time 150+VL = 278, and the third at time 290. The total time for the second chime is 290 - 162 = 128 = VL. This process can repeat many times, and even wrap around loop iterations. Most scalar instructions will be masked, and thus the average chime will asymptotically approach VL = 128 cycles to complete.

Tailgating occurs in a pipelined function unit as the first vector instruction begins to drain the pipeline (its last element leaves the first pipeline stage) and the first element of the next vector instruction using that pipeline follows it right in. The tailgating assumed in the above example does not actually work quite as smoothly as described. Results of our calibration experiments indicate that a bubble of one or more cycles in length occurs between successive instructions. We define B to be the number of cycles in a bubble. B is an empirical parameter not mentioned in [6][7], but observed in the calibration loops. The experimentally derived values of B are defined in Table 1 for each type of instruction and are summed over all the instructions in a loop iteration. We conjecture that B may represent a handshaking restart penalty for a stalled instruction. Hence for one chime of instructions, Equation (5) is incorrect; the corrected formula to calculate the number of clock cycles to execute a chime (preceded by at least one chime) is given as:

$$(Z)\ (VL)\ +\ \left(\sum_i B_i\right) \tag{13}$$

where B is summed over the instructions in the chime. In the previous example, the B values add 4 cycles to each chime, resulting in 166 cycles for the first chime and 132 cycles per successive chime.

Chaining on the Convex C-240 has some inherent limitations, but it appears to be much more flexible than the Cray-1 or even the Cray–XMP. [3] A chime can include at most one vector operation on each of the three pipelines; regardless of dependence, chimes are also limited by which vector registers are utilized. The Convex C-240 permits at most two reads and one write to each vector register pair during a single chime of two or three instructions. The vector registers {v0, v4} are a vector register pair, as are {v1, v5}, {v2, v6}, and {v3, v7}. The following example sequence of operations will not execute in the same chime since there are more than two read references to the vector pair {v2, v6}. [7]

$$\text{add.d v2,v6,v6;}\quad V6 := V2 + V6 \tag{14}$$

$$\text{mul.d v6,v1,v4;}\quad V4 := V6 * V1 \tag{15}$$

Likewise, the following sequence of operations will not execute in the same chime since there is more than one write reference to the vector pair {v2, v6}. [7]

$$\text{add.d v1,v0,v2;}\quad V2 := V1 + V0 \tag{16}$$

$$\text{mul.d v2,v1,v6;}\quad V6 := V2 * V1 \tag{17}$$

If scalar instructions are interspersed among vector instructions, chimes of vector instructions will often mask the scalar instructions as there is no resource contention between the ASU and the VP. However, since there is only one port between the CPU and memory, both vector loads and stores and scalar loads and stores must compete for that resource. As a result, a chime including a vector memory access cannot span a scalar memory access instruction. The chime will be terminated just before the scalar or vector memory reference instruction, whichever comes later. A new chime will begin with the next vector instruction. Although it is unclear from [6] [7], some vector instructions utilizing a scalar register as an operand may exhibit resource contention with purely scalar instructions. This effect was not observed in the loops we studied.

3.4. MACS Performance Model

The MACS performance model attempts to accurately incorporate the effects of the application, the compiler-generated assembly instruction counts, and the compiler-generated instruction schedule (specifically including the effects of the architectural details discussed in Sections 3.2 and 3.3) to bound steady-state loop performance on a machine. By definition, the MACS bound is specific to a particular code schedule. Reordering the sequence of instructions or reallocating the registers may change the MACS bound, but it will not change the MA or MAC bounds.

The general approach taken in developing the MACS model is to add the number of cycles it takes to execute each chime and divide by VL to achieve a new bound, t_{MACS}, in units of CPL. In contrast, the MA and MAC bounds equations assume that it takes one clock cycle to operate on each element of a vector instruction and that all possible parallelism between functional pipes is exploited. Thus in the MA and MAC bound models, one iteration of a vectorized loop is assigned a number of cycles equal to VL times the maximum of the number of vector additions, vector multiplications, and vector memory access operations counted.

To calculate the MACS bound, the vectorized inner loop of the compiled code is first partitioned into chimes, according to the rules described in Section 3.3. In most applications that fully exploit functional unit parallelism, the number of chimes will equal the maximum of the number of vector additions, multiplications, and memory access operations. The first vector instruction of a chime contributes B + VL cycles to the total number of cycles for the chime. The second and third instructions of the chime, if they exist, each add B cycles to the time for the chime. The interaction between chimes is effectively modeled by including the bubble B associated with the last instruction in each chime. The interaction of the last chime in the loop followed by the first chime in the loop must also be considered.

The number of cycles for all chimes in one iteration of the inner loop is then totaled. For each group of four or more successive chimes that include one memory operation per chime, the total number of cycles for the group is multiplied by 1.02 to account for the memory refresh penalty. This total is then divided by VL to determine t_{MACS} in units of CPL. To obtain the CPF–bound, t_{MACS} is divided by $(f_a + f_m)$.

Additional insight may be obtained by applying the MACS bound calculation algorithm to a reduced instruction list. In particular, t_f'' is calculated by applying the MACS algorithm to the compiled application code with all the vector memory access operations deleted. Likewise, t_m'' is calculated by applying it to the compiled application code with all the vector floating point operations deleted. t_{MACS} is not simply the maximum of t_f'' and t_m'' due to resource conflicts and bursts of f–only and m–only operations that prohibit a perfect merging of the *f* and *m* instructions into chimes for the total code.

Calculation of MACS bounds for chimes involving reductions and/or divisions is somewhat more complicated, involving numerous special cases, and is not discussed.

3.5. Example: Calculating MA, MAC, and MACS Bounds

As an example, LFK1 is analyzed using the MACS performance model. The code for LFK1 is relatively straightforward and easily vectorizable. The Fortran listing is as follows:

```
1001   DO 1 k = 1,n
   1      X(k)=Q+Y(k)*(R * ZX(k+10)+ T*ZX(k+11))
```

The resulting assembly code for the inner loop is:

Chime	Line	L7:		
	01:	mov	s0,VL	; #145
1	02:	ld.l	space1+40120(a5),v0	; #146, ZX
1	03:	mul.d	v0,s1,v1	; #146
2	04:	ld.l	space1+40128(a5),v2	; #146, ZX
2	05:	mul.d	v2,s3,v0	; #146
2	06:	add.d	v1,v0,v3	; #146
3	07:	ld.l	space1+32032(a5),v1	; #146, Y
3	08:	mul.d	v1,v3,v2	; #146
3	09:	add.d	v2,s7,v0	; #146
4	10:	st.l	v0,space1+24024(a5)	; #146, X
	11:	add.w	#1024,a5	; #146, 0x400
	12:	add.w	#-128,s0	; #146, 0xffffff80
	13:	lt.w	#0,s0	; #146, 0x0
	14:	jbrs.t L7		; #146

A vector instruction is taken to be any instruction that accesses at least one of the eight vector registers $\{v0,..., v7\}$. The workload parameters for LFK1 are given in Table 2, including MAC counts only when they differ from MA counts. Thus $t_{MA} = 3$ CPL $= 0.6$ CPF and $t_{MAC} = 4$ CPL $= 0.8$ CPF. To evaluate the MACS bound, we partition the loop into chimes as shown above.

- Chime 1 contains two vector instructions (load followed by multiply). Chaining will occur since there are one read and one write to the $\{v0, v4\}$ array, and zero reads and one write to the $\{v1, v5\}$ array. The vector load is assigned 2+128 cycles and the vector multiply adds an additional cycle for a total of 131 cycles. A calibration loop duplicating chime 1 yields a time of 131.93 cycles.
- Chime 2 contains three instructions that chain together. VL + the sum of the B values for this chain is 128 + 4 = 132 cycles. A calibration loop duplicating chime 2 yields 133.33 cycles.
- Chime 3 is also assessed 132 cycles. Its calibration

loop also yields 133.33 cycles.
- Chime 4 contains a single store instruction with B = 4, resulting in 132 cycles. Its calibration loop yields 132.35 cycles.

The sum of the MACS time bounds for all four chimes is 527 cycles. The sum of the individual experimental timings for all four chimes is 530.94 cycles. When the full LFK1 code is run (all four chimes in sequential order repeatedly), the measured time is 545.28 cycles. Each of the four chimes contains one memory access operation resulting in an additional 2% performance penalty. The t_{MACS} bound is thus 537.54 cycles for one iteration of vectorized code. Thus $t_{MACS} = 537.54 / 128 = 4.200$ CPL $= 0.840$ CPF for LFK1. The actual measured time is 0.852 CPF.

3.6. A/X Performance Measurements

To achieve the goal of decreasing the actual run time toward t_{MA} (or less aggressively t_{MAC} or t_{MACS}) or to tighten the bounds toward actually achievable performance, a simple approach to locating problematic sections of code is required. Additional information on the potential performance of an application may be gleaned by measuring the actual performance of modified versions of the application.

A logical division of the code into memory access operations and floating point operations suggests itself naturally. [1] This view springs from the Decoupled Access–Execute (DAE) view of computing as two distinct concurrent processes. The access process (A) is responsible for accessing memory. The execute process (X), is responsible for executing functional operations on program data.

In essence, the performance of the A-process, t_a, is determined by actually running the application code with all of the vector floating point operations removed. Since scalars are unchanged, control flow is unaffected,[2] but the incremental effect on run time caused by the floating point vector functional units over the time required by A-process instructions alone is removed. Likewise, the performance of the X-process, t_x, is determined by running the application code with all of the vector memory access instructions removed. Again control flow is unaffected, but the incremental effect on run time caused by servicing memory requests over the time required by the X-process alone is removed.

The A/X performance measurements are not performance bounds *per se*, but rather they measure actual machine performance with certain potential bottlenecks entirely eliminated. Normally we would expect:

$$\text{MAX} (t_x, t_a) \le t_p \le (t_x + t_a) \qquad (18)$$

---

[2] Control flow is preserved in the kernels under observation since vectorization does not occur over operations on data that affect conditional control flow. The loop counter is not modified by vector operations and no floating point data dependent conditional branches occur in these loops.

where t_p is the actual total application performance. The numerical program outputs obtained when timing either the A-process or the X-process alone are nonsense, but the timing results indicate the degree of access-execute overlap according to where t_p lies in the range shown above. Overlap is poor when t_x and t_a are both far from t_p. Performance is bottlenecked on X or A when t_p is close to MAX$\{t_x, t_a\}$ and t_x and t_a differ significantly. The performance evaluation hierarchy in Figure 1 also relates t_x to t_f'' and t_a to t_m''. Gaps between them can indicate unmodeled system effects that may need attention within the X or A-processes themselves.

We have developed tools that automatically generate both A-process and X-process executable codes given the assembly code listing of the original compiled code. Although generating the A-process testing code is relatively straightforward, the process of generating the X-process testing code must prime all registers with large, relatively prime, nonzero, floating-point numbers in order to avoid floating point exceptions induced by performing illegal calculations on nonsense data.

4. Timing and Model Evaluation

The MA, MAC, and MACS performance models and the A/X performance measurements have been evaluated for the Convex C-240 using ten of the first twelve kernels of the LFKs as a case study. Insights on each kernel's performance are developed by examining the gaps between the various bounds and measurements within the hierarchy.

4.1. Derivation of the MA, MAC, and MACS Bounds

In Table 2, the MA workload for each kernel as well as the MAC workload generated by the C-240 fc Fortran compiler V6.1 are presented. The MAC values, shown in columns f_a' and l_{fl}', show the MAC count of vector adds and loads only where they differ from the MA counts. A dashed line represents no change from the MA counts. No difference was observed between f_m and f_m' or between s_{fl} and s_{fl}' in the kernels examined. These MA and MAC values serve as parameters for the model given in Section 3.1 which yields the MA and MAC performance bounds shown in Table 3.

The actual number of memory access operations per cycle, t_m', dominates the MAC bound in all 10 LFKs, and the "excess" memory operations inserted by the compiler cause some significant increases in the MAC bound over the MA bound. The MA bound is itself memory limited except for LFKs 7 and 8.

The MACS performance bounds are also shown in Table 3. A bound for each kernel is calculated by a direct examination of the compiler-generated assembly language source code, as shown for LFK1 in Section 3.5. Fractional values are a result of fixed B overheads for each vector instruction (which are later divided by VL) and from memory refresh. The MACS bounds vary from moderately to significantly greater than the MA and MAC bounds.

LFK	f_m	f_a	f_a'	l_{fl}	s_{fl}	l_{fl}'
1	3	2	-	2	1	3
2	2	2	-	4	1	5
3	1	1	-	2	0	-
4	1	1	2	2	0	-
6	1	1	-	2	0	-
7	8	8	-	3	1	9
8	15	21	-	9	6	15
9	8	9	-	10	1	-
10	0	9	-	10	10	-
12	0	1	-	1	1	2

Table 2: LFK Work Load[a]

a. The additional vector instruction using the add functional unit in LFK4 is a vector negation instruction which is necessary due to limitations in the C-240 instruction set and constraints imposed by the vector reduction operation.

LFK	CPL–Bound			Workload					
	t_{MA}	t_{MAC}	t_{MACS}	t_f	t_f'	t_f''	t_m	t_m'	t_m''
1	3	4	4.20	3	-	3.04	3	4	**4.14**
2	5	6	6.26	2	-	2.03	5	6	**6.22**
3	2	-	2.08	1	-	1.37	2	-	**2.07**
4	2	-	2.45	1	2	2.37	2	-	**2.07**
6	2	-	2.46	1	-	1.37	2	-	**2.07**
7	8	10	10.50	8	-	9.13	4	10	**10.37**
8	21	-	30.15	21	-	21.28	15	21	**21.85**
9	11	-	11.55	9	-	9.13	11	-	**11.41**
10	20	-	20.95	9	-	9.07	**20**	-	**20.88**
12	2	3	3.13	1	-	1.01	2	3	**3.12**

Table 3: Performance Bounds (boldfaced entries dominate the equations for t_{MA}, t_{MAC}, and t_{MACS})

As shown in Table 3, $(t_f'' - t_f') > 1$ in LFK7, implying that f_m and f_a are not perfectly overlapped in the chimes. This would degrade performance, however, only after t_m' is reduced closer to t_m. Also of interest in Table 3 is the fact that $t_{MACS} \gg t_m''$ in LFK8. This is caused by scalar loads splitting potential chimes (as discussed in Section 3.3), resulting in poor overlap of vector instructions.

209

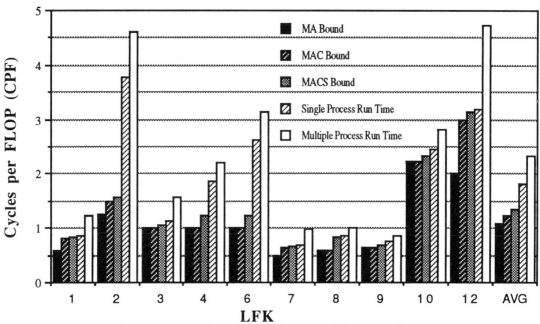

Figure 3: Comparison of CPF–Bounds and Actual Performance

LFK	t_{MA} (CPF)	t_{MAC} (CPF)	t_{MACS} (CPF)	t_p (CPF)	% of MA Bnd(t_{MA}/t_p)	% of MAC Bnd(t_{MAC}/t_p)	% of MACS Bnd(t_{MACS}/t_p)
1	0.600	0.800	0.840	0.852	70.4%	93.9%	98.6%
2	1.250	1.500	1.566	3.773	33.1%	39.8%	41.5%
3	1.000	1.000	1.044	1.128	88.7%	88.7%	92.6%
4	1.000	1.000	1.226	1.863	53.7%	53.7%	65.8%
6	1.000	1.000	1.222	2.632	38.0%	38.0%	46.4%
7	0.500	0.625	0.656	0.681	73.4%	91.8%	96.4%
8	0.583	0.583	0.824	0.858	67.9%	67.9%	97.7%
9	0.647	0.647	0.679	0.749	86.4%	86.4%	90.7%
10	2.222	2.222	2.328	2.442	91.0%	91.0%	95.3%
12	2.000	3.000	3.132	3.182	62.9%	94.3%	98.4%
AVG	1.080	1.238	1.352	1.900	66.6%	74.6%	82.3%
MFLOPS	23.15	20.19	17.79	13.16			

Table 4: Comparison of Bounds with Measured Performance

4.2. Using the MA, MAC, and MACS Bounds as Indicators of Performance

Comparing the MA, MAC, and MACS bounds and the actual CPF performance t_p in Table 4 and Figure 3 demonstrates first the effect of extra workload inserted by the compiler over the ideal, then the schedule-specific added run time effects as modeled by t_{MACS}, and finally the incremental effect of all unmodeled run time seen in t_p. The simple, highly idealized MA bound explains 80% or more of actual measured run time only in LFKs 3, 9, and 10. The MAC bound does likewise for all but LFKs 2, 4, 6, and 8. The MACS bound is at least 90% of t_p for all but LFKs 2, 4, and 6. Explanations for the various gaps are discussed in Section 4.4.

The single process run times were measured by running

210

on a single processor while making the other three processors idle. Figure 3 also shows multiple process run times which were calculated by measuring the run time for the kernel of interest on one processor while an uncontrolled normal workload (from other users) was running on the other processors. The load average at this time was 5.1, which is greater than the number of processors. In all cases the effects of memory contention when multiple processes are running simultaneously leads to noticeable performance degradation.

A rough rule of thumb is that if all four processors are running different programs simultaneously, memory contention will typically cause a 20% performance degradation. If all four processors are executing different processes for the same executable, the programs will tend to fall into lockstep, typically causing only a 5% to 10% performance degradation. Although memory access instructions can theoretically achieve a peak performance of one access per 40 ns cycle, in practice typical memory contention reduces the performance to one access every 56 to 64 ns. Performance will not, however, degrade proportionately because some of the degradation in memory access performance is masked by other operations. More of this degradation will be exposed, however, as performance is improved toward the bound. Timing experiments designed to reduce contention do allow performance to approach the 40 ns peak. However this is not a realistic set of working conditions for running standard applications.

4.3. A/X Performance Measurements

Measurements of the A-process and the X-process alone for the ten LFK kernels are presented in Table 5. Except for LFKs 2, 4, and 6 the calculated t_f'' and t_m'' closely model the measured results of t_x and t_a, respectively. The t_m' bound explains at least 95% of the measured t_a, except for LFKs 2, 4, and 6. The measured t_a is larger than t_x except for LFKs 4, 6, and 8. The gap between t_x and t_p is always large, although this is of little concern if $t_a \gg t_x$ as that indicates that the chief performance bottleneck is within the A-process. In LFKs 2, 4, 6, and 8, $t_p \gg MAX\{t_a, t_x\}$, and thus the existing code does not overlap the A-process and the X-process well. In this workload t_a is usually larger than t_x and when it is not both are significantly smaller than t_p. As a result, the Convex C-240 performance on these loops is dominated either by memory accesses or by bad coupling between the access and execute processes.

4.4. Evaluation of Performance on Benchmark Set

Examining the performance gaps in the hierarchy between pairs of performance bounds and measurements for the ten LFKs yields insights on where run time is spent and

LFK	t_p	t_{MACS}	t_x	t_f''	t_a	t_m''
1	4.26	4.20	3.13	3.04	**4.20**	4.14
2	15.09	6.26	9.05	2.03	13.39	6.22
3	2.26	2.09	1.47	1.37	**2.07**	2.07
4	3.73	2.45	2.91	2.37	2.44	2.07
6	5.26	2.44	3.74	1.37	3.29	2.07
7	10.89	10.50	9.55	9.13	**10.35**	10.37
8	30.90	30.15	22.77	21.28	22.53	21.85
9	12.73	11.55	9.61	9.13	**11.62**	11.41
10	21.97	20.95	9.95	9.07	**21.62**	20.88
12	3.18	3.13	1.05	1.01	**3.15**	3.12

Table 5: MACS Bounds and Measurements (in CPL) (boldfaced entries indicate that t_a is within 10% of t_p)

how it might be reduced.

- LFK1,7,12: The gap between the MA bound and the MAC bound is caused by the extra $t_m' - t_m$ memory references inserted by the compiler. Vector elements reused in the next iteration are shifted by the loop index increment. This misalignment typically forces a vector reload (or theoretically a vector shift). A scalar processor could keep reused array elements in registers. In LFK7, $(t_f'' - t_f') > 1$ implies that the floating point vector additions and multiplications are not perfectly overlapped thus creating a ninth chime. This has little impact, however, since $t_m' = 10$.

- LFK2: Large gaps in Table 5 between t_a and t_m'', t_x and t_f'', and t_p and t_{MACS} indicate that unmodeled activity dominates the performance of this kernel. The conspicuous t_{MACS} to t_p gap raises an appropriate warning flag for this loop. Indead, this loop has significant outer loop overhead, nonuniform memory access strides, and difficulty in vectorizing due to its multiple exits. Outer loop overhead and scalar code could be modeled as in [5].

- LFK3,9,10: The small gap in Table 4 between t_{MA} and t_p indicates that 86% to 91% of the ideally deliverable performance has been achieved. $t_{MACS} - t_{MA}$ explains 1/3 to 1/2 of the $t_p - t_{MA}$ gap. The remainder is primarily due to access-execute overlap effects, as shown by $t_p - t_a$.

- LFK4, 6: Since $t_p \gg t_x > t_a$, we can conclude that the interaction of the vector reduction operator with vector memory accesses is a significant bottleneck. Since $t_x \gg t_f''$, and $t_a \gg t_m''$, we can conclude that significant run time is spent on the substantial amount of scalar code which is not removed from either the X or A-process code and which is not modeled by either t_f'' or t_m''. In LFK4, the gap between t_f and t_f' is explained by the footnote to Table 2.

- LFK8: Since $t_p \gg t_x \approx t_a$, we can conclude that the A-process and the X-process are poorly overlapped. This is due to the large number of scalar loads splitting potential chimes. This effect is captured by t_{MACS}, but not by t_f'' or t_m'', since a scalar load will split a potential load-add-multiply chime (t_{MACS}) but not an add-multiply chime (t_f'') or a load chime (t_m''). As a result, t_{MACS} explains all but 2.3% of t_p.

The ability to pinpoint the causes of performance degradation through the use of the hierarchy of performance bounds and measurements in these ten LFKs demonstrates the viability of the MACS hierarchical approach to performance analysis.

5. Conclusion

The MACS performance modeling and measurement approach provides a coherent framework for analyzing and improving performance. The hierarchy of performance models and measurements allow a user, compiler-writer, or computer architect to pinpoint areas where performance is lost and to identify what improvements might be most effective in the application, compiler, or machine.

A case study of the Convex C-240 using the ten vector loop kernels was used to illustrate the power of this approach. The relative magnitude of the hierarchy of MACS bounds, their component terms, and the A/X and total code performance measurements clearly, and fairly automatically, identified for each kernel the factors that contributed to its run time and prevented it from achieving its ideal performance.

We believe that this approach can be generalized and automated to assess a broad range of machines and scientific applications. Aspects of the MACS bounds hierarchy could be incorporated within a goal-directed optimizing compiler that would efficiently assess where and how best to spend its time.

Acknowledgments

We are grateful for many illuminating discussions of the C-240 generously provided by Patrick McGehearty, Greg Astfalk, Aaron Pottler, and Carl Jackson of the Convex Computer Corporation.

References

[1] D. Windheiser and W. Jalby. "Behavioral Characterization of Decoupled Access/Execute Architectures," *Proceedings of the International Conference on Supercomputing 1991*, pp. 28-39, 1991.

[2] J-H. Tang, E. S. Davidson, and J. Tong. "Polycyclic Vector Scheduling vs. Chaining on 1-Port Vector Supercomputers," *Proceedings of Supercomputing 1988 Conference*, pp. 122-129, November, 1988.

[3] J-H. Tang and E. S. Davidson. "An Evaluation of Cray-1 and Cray X-MP Performance on Vectorizable Livermore Fortran Kernels," *Proceedings of the 1988 International Conference on Supercomputing*, pp. 510-518, July, 1988.

[4] W. Mangione–Smith, S. G. Abraham, E.S. Davidson, "Architectural vs. Delivered Performance of the IBM RS/6000 and the Astronautics ZS-1," *Computer*, pp. 39-46, January, 1991.

[5] W. Mangione–Smith, T.P. Shih, S. G. Abraham and E. S. Davidson. "Approaching a Machine-Application Bound in Delivered Performance on Scientific Code," *IEEE Proceedings Special Issue on Performance Evaluation,* to appear September, 1993.

[6] "CONVEX Theory of Operation (C200 Series)", CONVEX Computer Corporation Document No. 081-005030-000, Second Edition, September 1990.

[7] "CONVEX Architecture Reference (C200 Series)", CONVEX Computer Corporation Document No. 081-009330-000, Fifth Edition, September 1990.

[8] F. H. McMahon, "The Livermore Fortran Kernels: A Computer Test of the Numerical Performance Range," Technical Report UCRL-5375, Lawrence Livermore National Laboratory, December 1986.

[9] K. Gallivan, D. Gannon, W. Jalby, A. Malony, and H. Wijshoff, "Behavioral characterization of multiprocessor memory systems," *Proceedings of the 1989 ACM SIGMETRICS Conference on Measuring and Modeling Computer Systems*, pp. 79-89, ACM Press, New York, 1989.

[10] K. Gallivan, W. Jalby, A. Malony, and H. Wijshoff, "Performance Prediction of Loop Constructs on Multiprocessor Hierarchical Memory Systems," *Proceedings of the 1989 International Conference on Supercomputing*, pp. 433-442, ACM Press, New York, 1989.

The Cedar System and an Initial Performance Study*

D. Kuck, E. Davidson† D. Lawrie † A. Sameh
C.-Q Zhu† A. Veidenbaum, J. Konicek, P. Yew,
K. Gallivan, W. Jalby† H. Wijshoff† R. Bramley† U.M. Yang
P. Emrath, D. Padua, R. Eigenmann, J. Hoeflinger, G. Jaxon† Z. Li†
T. Murphy, J. Andrews, S. Turner

Center for Supercomputing Research and Development
University of Illinois
Urbana, IL, 61801

Abstract

In this paper, we give an overview of the Cedar mutliprocessor and present recent performance results. These include the performance of some computational kernels and the Perfect Benchmarks® . We also present a methodology for judging parallel system performance and apply this methodology to Cedar, Cray YMP-8, and Thinking Machines CM-5.

1 Introduction

Tremendous progress in VLSI technology today has made it possible to build large-scale parallel systems with dazzling peak performances. Several such systems have even been commercialized over the last 5 years. However, the goal of building a general-purpose large-scale parallel system remains quite elusive. Many of the systems still have very little software support and are very difficult to program. The sustainable performance from various real applications running on those machines remains erratic and unpredictable. These phenomena show that we still do not know how to build parallel machines, how to program such machines, or how to characterize the performance of such machines for writing good application codes. The difficulties stem from the fact that in order to build a large-scale parallel machines that can deliver "practical parallelism," we need to understand the interactions among system architecture, system software and parallel application codes.

The Cedar project brought together a group of people in the areas of computer architecture, parallelizing compilers, operating systems, and parallel algorithms/applications to help solve the real problems associated with building a "complete" parallel system, and to study the effects of interaction among these components on such a machine [GKLS83, KDLS86]. The machine has been in full operation since late 1990. The Cedar experience includes the architecture, compiler, OS, and application perspectives and this paper attempts to summarize these for the architecture community.

We describe the machine organization in Section 2, concentrating on the unique aspects of Cedar. Programming and compilation for Cedar are discussed in Section 3. Performance measurements of the systems and the interpretation of those results are presented in Section 4.

2 The Organization of Cedar

Cedar is a cluster-based shared memory multiprocessor. The system consists of four clusters connected through two unidirectional interconnection networks to a globally shared memory (Fig. 1). Each cluster is a slightly modified Alliant FX/8 system with eight processors. In this section we first summarize the features of these clusters and then describe the unique features of Cedar. For a more detailed overall description of Cedar see [KTVZ91].

*This research was supported by the Department of Energy under Grant No. DE-FG02-85ER25001 and by the National Science Foundation under Grants No. US NSF-MIP-8410110 and NSF-MIP-89-20891, IBM Corporation, and the State of Illinois.

†Affiliated with CSRD for a portion of the project.

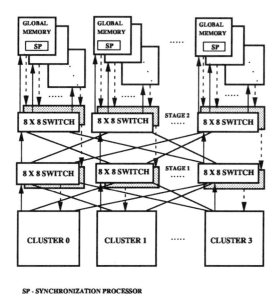

Figure 1: Cedar Architecture

SP - SYNCHRONIZATION PROCESSOR

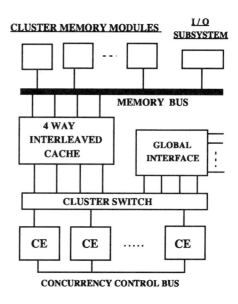

Figure 2: Cluster Architecture

Alliant clusters The organization of an Alliant FX/8 cluster is shown in Figure 2. Each Alliant FX/8 contains 8 *computational elements* (CEs). The CEs are connected to a 4-way interleaved *shared cache* which in turn is connected to an interleaved cluster memory. The FX/8 also includes *interactive processors* (IPs) and IP caches. IPs perform input/output and various other tasks.

The CE is a pipelined implementation of the 68020 instruction set augmented with vector instructions. The CE instruction cycle is 170ns. The vector unit implements 64-bit floating-point as well as integer operations. Vector instructions can have a register-memory format with one memory operand. The vector unit contains eight 32-word registers. The peak performance of each CE is 11.8 Mflops on 64-bit vector operations.

Each CE is connected to a *concurrency control bus* designed to support efficient execution of parallel loops. Concurrency control instructions implement fast fork, join and synchronization operations. For example: concurrent start is a single instruction that "spreads" the iterations of a parallel loop from one to all the CEs in a cluster by broadcasting the program counter and setting up private, per processor stacks. The whole cluster is thus "gang-scheduled." CEs within a cluster can then "self-schedule" iterations of the parallel loop among themselves.

Each Alliant FX/8 has 32MB of cluster memory. All references to data in cluster memory first check the 512KB physically addressed shared cache. Cache line

size is 32 bytes. The cache is write-back and lockup-free, allowing each CE to have two outstanding cache misses. Writes do not stall a CE. The cache bandwidth is eight 64-bit words per instruction cycle, sufficient to supply one input stream to a vector instruction in each processor. This equals 48MB/sec per processor or 384MB/sec per cluster. The cluster memory bandwidth is half of that or 192MB/sec.

Memory Hierarchy The Cedar memory hierarchy consists of 64MB of shared global memory and four cluster memories with caches. It supports a virtual memory system with a 4KB page size. The physical address space is divided into two equal halves: cluster memory is in the lower half and shared memory is in the upper half. Global memory is directly addressable and shared by all CEs. Cluster memory is only accessible to the CEs within that cluster. Data can be moved between cluster and global shared memory only via explicit moves under software control. It can be said that cluster memories form a distributed memory system in addition to the global shared memory. Coherence between multiple copies of globally shared data residing in cluster memory is maintained in software. The global memory system is weakly ordered. Global memory is double-word (8byte) interleaved and aligned. The peak global memory bandwidth is 768MB/sec or 24MB/sec per processor.

Global Network The Cedar network was designed to support simultaneous vector loads/stores from global memory by all processors. It is a multistage shuffle-exchange network as shown in Figure 1. The network is self-routing, buffered and packet-switched. Routing is based on the tag control scheme proposed in [Lawr75], and provides a unique path between any pair of input/output ports. Each network packet consists of one to four 64-bit words, the first word containing routing and control information and the memory address. The network is constructed with 8 × 8 crossbar switches with 64-bit wide data paths. A two word queue is used on each crossbar input and output port and flow control between stages prevents queue overflow. The network bandwidth is 768MB/sec for the entire system or 24MB/sec per processor, which matches the global memory bandwidth.

Data Prefetch The Cedar *data prefetch unit* (PFU) is designed to mask the long global memory latency and to overcome the limit of two outstanding requests per Alliant CE. Each CE has its own individual PFU. Each PFU supports one vector load from global memory. A PFU is "armed" by giving it the length, the stride and the mask of the vector to be fetched. It is then "fired" by the physical address of the first word to be fetched. This starting address can be supplied by a special prefetch instruction or by the first address of a vector load. In the former case the prefetch is completely autonomous and can be overlapped with computation or cluster memory accesses. In the latter case it is only overlapped with the current vector instruction. When a prefetch crosses a page boundary the PFU suspends until the processor supplies the first address in the new page because only physical addresses are available to the PFU. In the absence of page crossings the PFU issues up to 512 requests without pausing. The data returns to a 512-word prefetch buffer which is invalidated when another prefetch is started. It is possible to keep prefetched data in that buffer and reuse it from there. Data can enter the prefetch buffer from the global network out of order due to memory and network conflicts. A full/empty bit per word allows the CE both to access the buffer without waiting for the prefetch to be complete and to get the data in same order as requested.

Memory-based Synchronization requires read-modify-write operations on global memory. However, given multistage interconnection networks it is impossible to provide standard lock cycles and very inefficient to perform multiple memory accesses for synchronization. Cedar implements a set of indivisible synchronization instructions in each memory module. These include Test-And-Set and Cedar synchronization instructions based on [ZhYe87], which are performed by a special processor in each memory module. Cedar synchronization instructions implement Test-

And-Operate, where Test is any relational operation on 32-bit data (e.g. $\geq$) and Operate is a Read, Write, Add, Subtract, or Logical operation on 32-bit data. Synchronization instructions are accessible from a CE via memory-mapped instructions initiated by a Test-And-Set to a global memory address.

Performance monitoring The Cedar approach to performance monitoring relies on external hardware to collect time-stamped event traces and histograms of various hardware signals. The event tracers can each collect 1M events and the histogrammers have 64K 32-bit counters. These can be cascaded to capture more events. Each of the major Cedar units has several important signals available for external monitoring. Any other accessible hardware signal can also be monitored. Software tools start and stop the experiments and move the data collected by the performance hardware to workstations for analysis. It is also possible to post events to the performance hardware from programs executing on Cedar, which allows software event tracing.

3   Programming Cedar

Cedar programs can be written using the CEDAR FORTRAN language, Xylem assembler or C. All of these make use of the abstractions provided by the Xylem kernel [EABM91] which links the four separate operating systems in Alliant clusters into the Cedar OS. Xylem exports virtual memory, scheduling, and file system services for Cedar.

A program for Cedar can be written using explicit parallelism and memory hierarchy placement directives. Parallelism can be in the form of DOALL loops or concurrent tasks. Alternatively, programs written in Fortran 77 can be translated automatically into CEDAR FORTRAN by the "Parallelizing Restructurer". The overall compilation and program execution process is simple and identical to the same process on a single-processor workstation. Writing programs that extract all of Cedar performance is a more challenging task.

The CEDAR FORTRAN language is a dialect of FORTRAN77 that includes parallel and vector extensions. CEDAR FORTRAN is translated into ALLIANT FORTRAN and Alliant's compiler performs code generation. Programming in FORTRAN77 provides a simpler user interface and better portability, although sometimes at the expense of performance.

CEDAR FORTRAN offers an application programmer explicit access to all the key features of the

Cedar system: the memory hierarchy, the prefetching capability from global memory, the global memory synchronization hardware, and cluster features including concurrency control. This access is supported by language extensions and run-time library functions. The CEDAR FORTRAN language extensions and compilation for Cedar are described next. CEDAR FORTRAN is fully described in [Hoef91] and description of the Cedar Compiler project can be found in [EHJL91, EHLP91, EHJP92].

3.1 Fortran Extensions

Parallel Loops A programmer can express parallelism using DOALL loop constructs. A DOALL is a loop in which iterations are independent and therefore can be executed in parallel. Several flavors of DOALLs are provided in order to better control load balancing, data placement, and scheduling overhead. These include CDOALL, SDOALL, and XDOALL which will be described below.

Data Placement and Sharing Data can be placed in either cluster or shared global memory on Cedar. A user can control this using a GLOBAL attribute. Variable placement is in cluster memory by default. A variable can also be declared inside a parallel loop. The loop-local declaration of a variable makes a private copy for each processor which is placed in cluster memory.

3.2 Compilation for Cedar

Parallel Loops XDOALL makes use of all the processors in the machine and schedules each iteration on a processor. The processors get started, terminated, and scheduled through functions of the run-time library. Since these operations work through the global memory there is a typical loop startup latency of 90 μs and fetching the next iteration takes about 30 μs. The second type of parallel loop is the SDOALL which schedules each iteration on an entire cluster. Each iteration starts executing on one processor of the cluster. The other processors in the cluster remain idle until a CDOALL is executed within the body of the SDOALL. The CDOALL makes use of the concurrency control bus to schedule loops on all processors in a cluster and can typically start in a few microseconds. The XDOALL has more scheduling flexibility but also higher overhead. An SDOALL/CDOALL nest has a lower scheduling cost due to the use of the concurrency control bus. Both SDOALL and XDOALL loops

can be statically scheduled or self-scheduled via run-time library options. CDOALL loops are used to exploit the faster loop control and shared cluster memory and cache in a cluster. Data that is private to an SDOALL iteration but shared by all cluster processors will be placed in the cluster memory.

Data Prefetching The compiler backend inserts an explicit prefetch instruction, of length 32 words or less, before each vector operation which has a global memory operand. The compiler then attempts to float the prefetch instructions in order to overlap prefetch operations with computation. This rarely succeeds and thus most of the time prefetch is started immediately before the vector instruction. More aggressive methods are being investigated [GoGV90].

Data privatization CEDAR FORTRAN uses data declared local to a loop in place of scalar and array expansion. In all Perfect programs we have found loop-local data placement to be an important factor in reducing data access latencies. In addition to loop-local declaration, data can be localized by partitioning and distributing them to the cluster memories. Subsequent loops can operate on these data by distributing iterations to clusters according to the data partitions. CEDAR FORTRAN supports this by scheduling iterations of successive SDOALLs on the same clusters.

Global Synchronization The Cedar synchronization instructions have been mainly used in the implementation of the runtime library, where they have proven useful to control loop self-scheduling. They are also available to a Fortran programmer via run-time library routines.

3.3 Program Restructuring

The parallelizing compiler project has two parts. In the first phase we retargeted an early copy of KAP restructurer to Cedar (KAP from KAI as released in 1988) and evaluated its performance. In the second phase we searched for restructuring techniques that improved the performance of real application programs significantly. We did these experiments by manually restructuring the suite of Perfect Benchmarks® programs, using techniques that may be automated in an eventual implementation of the parallelizer. The results are summarized in Table 3.

The table lists speed improvements over the serial execution time of two versions of the Perfect programs. The results in column "Compiled by Kap/Cedar" show that with the original compiler most programs have very limited performance improvement. This happened even though we set compiler options according to the Perfect Benchmarks rules. Specifically, in a few cases program execution was confined to a single cluster to avoid intercluster overhead.

The *Automatable* column presents the performance of the programs to which we applied compiler transformations by hand. The name automatable is somewhat optimistic because we have not yet implemented these transformations in an actual parallelizer. However we believe that most of the applied transformations are realizable. These transformations include array privatization, parallel reductions, advanced induction variable substitution, runtime data dependence tests, balanced stripmining, and parallelization in the presence of SAVE and RETURN statements. Many of these transformations require advanced symbolic and interprocedural analysis methods. The transformations have been described in more detail in [EHLP91, EHJL91, EHJP92]

4 Cedar Performance

Examples of Cedar performance are discussed in this section. Given the complexity of the Cedar architecture, compilers, OS, and of the codes themselves it is very difficult to isolate the performance effects of various architectural features at the level of full codes. Therefore, we start by considering data from well-understood algorithms and kernels which are much smaller and can be modified easily to explore the system. We continue with the performance of the Perfect codes achieved via automated and automatable restructuring transformations. Next we comment on the performance improvements possible for some of the codes when algorithmic and architectural knowledge is used to transform the codes in nonautomatable ways. Finally, we present a methodology for judging parallel system performance and apply this methodology to Cedar, Cray YMP-8, and Thinking Machines CM-5.

4.1 Memory System Performance

The effect of the memory system on performance can be demonstrated by considering three versions of a matrix primitive which computes a rank-64 update to an $n \times n$ matrix. For all versions the matrices reside in global memory. The difference between the versions lies in the mode of access of the data and the transfer of subblocks to cluster cache. Specifically: in the GM/no-pref version all vector accesses are to global

memory and do not use prefetching, the GM/pref version is identical with the exception that prefetching is used and the GM/cache version transfers a submatrix to a cached work array in each cluster and all vector accesses are made to the work array. All versions chain two operations per memory request.

The performance difference for a matrix of size $n = 1K$ (see Table 1) between the three versions is solely due to memory latency. The table shows megaflops achieved for the three versions. The performance of the GM/no-pref version is determined by the 13 cycle latency of the global memory and the two outstanding requests allowed per CE, and is typical of codes that cannot effectively exploit prefetching in their global accesses. The aggressive use of prefetch can mitigate this latency effectively for up to 16 CEs. The GM/pref version demonstrates this with performance improvement factors of 3.5 and 2.9 on 8 and 16 CEs respectively. For three and four clusters, the effectiveness of prefetching is reduced and improvements of only 2.2 and 1.9 are observed. To achieve a significant fraction of the 376 MFLOPS absolute peak performance (or the 274 MFLOPS effective peak due to unavoidable vector startup) the caches in each cluster must be used. The GM/cache version achieves improvements over GM/no-pref that range from 3.5 on one cluster (identical to the effect of prefetch) to 3.8 on four clusters. The 32 CE observed performance yields 74 % efficiency compared to the effective peak and is consistent with the observed maximum bandwidth of memory system characterization benchmarks [GJTV91].

	1 cl.	2 cl.	3 cl.	4 cl.
GM/no pref	14.5	29.0	43.0	55.0
GM/pref	50.0	84.0	96.0	104.0
GM/Cache	52.0	104.0	152.0	208.0

Table 1: MFLOPS for rank-64 update on Cedar

To explore the cause of the degradation of the effectiveness of prefetch for more than two clusters we analyze the performance of four computational kernels using the hardware performance monitor. We consider a vector load (VL), a tridiagonal matrix-vector multiply (TM), the rank-64 update of a matrix (RK), and a simple conjugate gradient algorithm (CG) to show directly the behavior of the global memory and networks in Table 2. The codes use 8, 16, and 32 processors, global data only, and prefetching. The RK kernel prefetches blocks of 256 words and aggressively overlaps it with computation, the other codes use compiler-generated 32-word prefetches. The metrics used are first word Latency and Interarrival time between the remaining words in the block, in instruction cycles. These are measured for every prefetch request by recording when an address from the prefetch unit is issued to the forward network and when each datum returns to the prefetch buffer via the reverse networks from memory. Minimal Latency is 8 cycles and minimal Interarrival time is 1 cycle. The cycles needed to move data between the CE and prefetch buffer complete the 13 cycle latency mentioned above. Monitoring these times required access to internal hardware signals and is not possible on all processors. As a result, we monitored all requests of a single processor and compared repeated experiments for consistency. The results of all experiments were within 10% of each other.

# CEs	Prefetch Speedup			Latency (cycles)			Interarrival (cycles)		
	8	16	32	8	16	32	8	16	32
TM	2.1	2.0	1.5	9.4	10.2	14.2	1.1	1.2	2.1
CG	2.4	2.2	1.5	9.4	10.3	15.1	1.1	1.2	2.1
VF	1.8	1.7	1.5	9.6	11.0	16.7	1.2	1.4	2.2
RK	3.4	2.9	1.8	12.9	15.3	18.3	1.2	1.8	3.2

Table 2: Global memory performance

The results in Table 2 show that global memory degradation due to contention causes the reduction in the effectiveness of prefetching as the number of CEs used increases. For one cluster both the latency and interarrival time are near their minimums. RK degrades most quickly due to the fact that it uses the longest prefetch block and overlaps all operations with memory accesses. VF is also dominated by memory accesses but degrades less quickly due to the smaller prefetch block which reduces access intensity. The TM and CG kernels suffer approximately the same degradation and are affected less than the others due to the presence of register-register vector operations which reduce the demand on the memory system. We have shown via detailed simulations that this degradation is not inherent in the type of network used but is a result of specific implementation constraints [Turn93].

4.2 Cedar Performance Using the Perfect Codes

All the results presented in this section were collected in single-user mode to avoid the non-determinism of multiprogramming. The results are shown in Table 3 and have speed improvements versus uniprocessor scalar versions of the same codes. Comparison of automatic restructuring with automatable transformations was given is Section 3.3.

Effect of Cedar Features. The results for the versions derived from automatable transformations in Table 3 assume the use of compiler-generated prefetch and Cedar synchronization in the runtime library. "Slowdown" with respect to "Automatable" results for some of these codes when Cedar synchronization is not used for loop scheduling is due to parallel loops with relatively small granularity requiring low-overhead self-scheduling support, e.g., DYFESM and OCEAN. "Slowdown" without the use of prefetching (given with respect to "No Synchronization" results) for many of the codes is typically due to one of two reasons. The first is a domination of scalar accesses, e.g., TRACK. The second is the presence of a large amount of short-lived loop-local data that is placed in cluster memory. The automatable version of the code DYFESM benefits significantly from prefetch due to the large number of vector fetches from global memory on a small number of processors (due to the limited parallelism available).

Hand Optimization. It is possible to improve the execution time of the Perfect codes using knowledge of their main algorithms and of Cedar.[1] Table 4 contains the execution times for these updated codes. Some of the codes were analyzed resulting in changes that ranged in complexity from a simple modification of I/O (BDNA) to a complete rewriting (TRFD).

The execution time for BDNA is reduced to 70 secs. by simply replacing formatted with unformatted I/O. Careful consideration of ARC2D reveals a substantial number of unnecessary computations. Primarily due to their elimination but also due to aggressive data distribution into cluster memory the execution time is reduced to 68 secs. [BrBo91]. If a hand-coded parallel random number generator is used, QCD can be improved to yield a speed improvement of 20.8 rather than the 1.8 reported for the automatable code.

FLO52, DYFESM, and TRFD require more elaborate analyses and modifications. Four of the five major

---

[1] We use prefetch but not Cedar synchronization.

Program	Compiled by Kap/Cedar time (Improvement)	Auto. transforms time (Improvement)	W/o Cedar Synchronization time (% slowdown)	W/o prefetch time (% slowdown)	MFLOPS (YMP-8/Cedar)
ADM	689 (1.2)	73 (10.8)	81 (11%)	83 (2%)	6.9 (3.4)
ARC2D	218 (13.5)	141 (20.8)	141 (0%)	157 (11%)	13.1 (34.2)
BDNA	502 (1.9)	111 (8.7)	118 (6%)	122 (3%)	8.2 (18.4)
DYFESM	167 (3.9)	60 (11.0)	67 (12%)	100 (49%)	9.2 (6.5)
FLO52	100 (9.0)	63 (14.3)	64 (1%)	79 (23%)	8.7 (37.8)
MDG	3200 (1.3)	182 (22.7)	202 (11%)	202 (0%)	18.9 (1.1)
MG3D [a]	7929 (1.5)	348 (35.2)	346 (0%)	350 (1%)	31.7 (3.6)
OCEAN	2158 (1.4)	148 (19.8)	174 (18%)	187 (7%)	11.2 (7.4)
QCD	369 (1.1)	239 (1.8)	239 (0%)	246 (3%)	1.1 (11.8)
SPEC77	973 (2.4)	156 (15.2)	156 (0%)	165 (6%)	11.9 (4.8)
SPICE	95.1 (1.02)	NA	NA	NA	0.5 (11.4)
TRACK	126 (1.1)	26 (5.3)	28 (8%)	28 (0%)	3.1 (2.7)
TRFD	273 (3.2)	21 (41.1)	21 (0%)	21 (0%)	20.5 (2.8)

[a] This version of MG3D includes the elimination of file I/O.

Table 3: Cedar execution time, megaflops, and speed improvement for Perfect Benchmarks

Code	Time	Improvement
ARC2D	68	2.1
BDNA	70	1.7
DYFESM	31	2.2
FLO52	33	1.9
SPICE	26	3.7
TRFD	7.5	2.8
QCD	21	11.4

Table 4: Execution times (secs.) for manually altered Perfect Codes and improvement over automatable w/ prefetch and w/o Cedar synchronization

routines in FLO52 require a series of multicluster barriers. Unfortunately, the associated synchronization overhead degrades performance for problems that are not sufficiently large, e.g., the Perfect data set. Analysis of the algorithms reveals that by introducing a small amount of redundancy, we can transform the sequence of multicluster barriers into a single multicluster barrier and four independent sequences of barriers that can exploit the concurrency control hardware in each cluster. This along with eliminating several recurrences in the remaining major routine results in an execution time of 33 secs.

The major problem with DYFESM is the very small problem size used in the benchmark. If some of the data structures are reshaped and certain key kernels are reimplemented, aggressively using Cedar's

prefetch unit via Xylem assembler, the execution time drops to around 40 secs. If we change the algorithm used in the code and exploit the hierarchical SDOALL/CDOALL control structure an execution time of 31 secs. results [YaGa93].

The execution time of TRFD was reduced to 11.5 secs. by implementing high performance kernels to efficiently exploit the clusters' caches and vector registers [AnGa93]. The improved version was shown to have almost four times the number of page faults relative to the one-cluster version and was spending close to 50% of the time in virtual memory activity. The extra faults are TLB miss faults as each additional cluster of a multicluster version first accesses pages for which a valid PTE exists in global memory. Based on analysis of the virtual memory performance of Cedar, [MaEG92], a distributed memory version of the code was developed to mitigate this problem and yielded a final execution time of 7.5 secs.

SPICE also benefits significantly from algorithmic attention. After considering all of the major phases of the application and developing new approaches where needed the time is reduced to approximately 26 secs.

4.3 Judging Parallelism

In this section we present a performance evaluation methodology for parallel systems. We will cast this discussion in general terms and will compare initial Cedar performance data to commercially available systems. However, our goal is not to argue that system X is better than system Y, but rather to shed light on how to understand performance and thereby to make parallel processing a practical real-world technology in the future. We first define five practical parallelism tests, then some performance metrics, and finally discuss acceptable performance levels.

The Practical Parallelism Tests

Practical parallelism has not yet been demonstrated; in fact, no standard definition of it exists. It seems clear that there should be "laboratory level" and "commercial level" criteria for judging practical parallelism, and we will now propose five criteria that form a Practical Parallelism Test.

At the laboratory level, we will use as our criterion for the success of parallelism,

The Fundamental Principle of Parallel Processing (FPPP): Clock speed is interchangeable with parallelism while (A) maintaining delivered performance, that is (B) stable over a certain class of computations.

There are really three statements in the FPPP: first, the well-established point that high peak speeds are possible through parallelism, and then two important constraints that we shall use as Practical Parallelism Tests (PPT's) 1 and 2.

Practical Parallelism Test 1. Delivered Performance: The parallel system delivers performance, as measured in speedup or computational rate, for a useful set of codes.

Practical Parallelism Test 2. Stable Performance: The performance demonstrated in Test 1 is within a specified stability range as the computations vary with respect to certain program structures, data structures, and data sizes.

Next we discuss two additional tests that must be met if one has demonstrated the FPPP and wants to use it in a commercially viable product.

Practical Parallelism Test 3. Portability and Programmability: The computer system is easy to port codes to and to program, for many applications.

Practical Parallelism Test 4. Code and Architecture Scalability: The computer system effectively runs each code/data size on a range of processor counts, and each code's data size can be scaled up or down on a given architecture.

Finally, if the first system is a success and the company is to survive over time, the system must demonstrate:

Practical Parallelism Test 5. Technology and Scalable Reimplementability: The system architecture must be capable of being reimplemented (scaled up) with much larger processor counts in the current technology or in new, faster or less expensive technologies as they emerge.

In what follows, we will expand these ideas and illustrate methods by which we can observe the PPT's and track progress toward satisfying them over time. Despite the great enthusiasm for parallel processing today, not even the Fundamental Principle of Parallel Processing has been demonstrated generally. Substantial amounts of work will be required before the remaining three PPT's are passed.

For at least twenty years we have used speedup and efficiency as abstract measures of performance. In addition, we now define stability, St, on P processors of an ensemble of computations over K codes as follows:

$$St(P, N_i, K, e) = \frac{min\ performance(K, e)}{max\ performance(K, e)},$$

where N_i is the problem size of i-th code, and e computations are excluded from the ensemble because their results are outliers from the ensemble (and each code may have a different number of data sets). Instability, In, is defined as the inverse of Stability. The traditional megaflops (millions of floating-point operations per second) are used as our rate measure. We avoid debating how to define floating-point operation counts by simply using the floating-point counts obtained from the Cray Hardware Performance Monitor.

Acceptable Performance Levels Given a speedup we are confronted with the question of "how good is good?" We should answer this using some function of the total number of processors P. Most people experienced with running a variety of real codes on parallel machines would be pleased if they could achieve some fraction of P or even $P/\log P$, especially as P grows to hundreds or thousands of processors. Note that in terms of the 10X/7 years performance improvement achieved over the history of supercomputing, which has mainly been due to hardware speed increases, such a 1000 processor machine would provide about 15 equivalent years of electronics-advancement speed improvement. Thus, if we knew how to build machines that met all five of the PPT's, $O(P/\log P)$ would be a good performance level. For this discussion, we shall use $P/2$ and $P/2\log P$, for $P \geq 8$, as levels that denote **high performance** and **acceptable performance**, respectively. We refer to speedups in the three bands defined by these two levels as high, intermediate, or unacceptable.

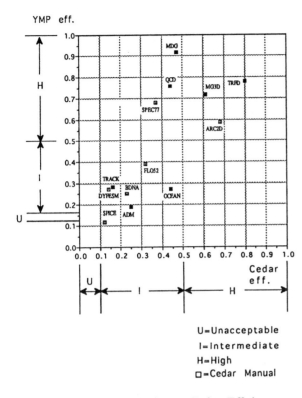

YMP eff.

U=Unacceptable
I=Intermediate
H=High
□=Cedar Manual

Figure 3: Cray YMP/8 vs. Cedar Efficiency

Applying the Methodology

In this section we apply the ideas of the previous section by using the first four PPT's to analyze Cedar and compare it to other systems.

Practical Parallelism Test 1 is the easiest of the PPT's to meet, and has been demonstrated many times by showing that one code or another runs well on a parallel machine. Figure 3 shows a scatter plot of Cray YMP/8 vs. Cedar efficiencies for the manually optimized Perfect codes. The 8-processor YMP has about half high and half intermediate levels of performance, while the 32-processor Cedar has about one-quarter high and three-quarters intermediate. Note that the YMP has one unacceptable performance, while Cedar has none. We conclude from this that both the Cray YMP and Cedar are on the average acceptable, delivering intermediate parallel performance and thus pass PPT1 for the Perfect codes.

Practical Parallelism Test 2 is much more difficult to meet than PPT1, as it requires that a whole set of programs runs well on some parallel machine. To show the world that it really is a practical system, a parallel machine should be demonstrated on a wide range of program structures, data structures and data sizes. What stability range can one expect on

supercomputers in general, and, at the other extreme, what could one expect on workstations? For the past 20 years, from the VAX 780 through various modern workstations (Sun SPARC2, IBM RS6000), an instability of about 5 has been common for the Perfect benchmarks. Users are evidently not concerned with such computational rate variations on workstations, so we will define a system as **stable** if $\frac{1}{6} \leq St(K, e)$, for small e, and as unstable, otherwise. However, if on some architecture, the computational rate varied by substantially more, the net effect could be noticed by many users.

Table 5 shows that Cedar and the Cray YMP/8 both have terrible instabilities for their baseline-automatable computations. This is generally caused by several very poor performers (e.g., SPICE) and several very high performers. So we are led to examining the number of exceptions required to achieve workstation-level stability. We find that two exceptions are sufficient on the Cray 1 and Cedar, whereas the YMP needs six – about half of the Perfect codes. Thus, the YMP cannot be judged as passing PPT2 for the Perfect codes, i.e., it is unstable, while the other two systems do pass with two exceptions.

	$In(13,0)$	$In(13,2)$	$In(13,6)$
Cedar	63.4	5.8	–
Cray 1 [a]	10.9	4.6	–
YMP/8	75.3	29.0	5.3

[a] with modern compiler

Table 5: Instability for Perfect codes

It may be regarded as absurd to invoke a test that can be passed by ignoring codes that give top performance. On the other hand, consider two points. First, it can be argued that if a few codes have very high performance, then users should expect that (eventually) all codes will perform well, as is the case with workstations. Secondly, the Perfect codes have relatively small data sizes and stability is a measure that can focus us on the class of codes that are well matched to the system, so varying the data size and observing stability would be instructive. Both of these points indicate that the general purpose abilities of a system are related to its stability.

Practical Parallelism Test 3 Automatic compilation will go a long way towards portability and programmability of parallel systems. Our discussion of PPT3 will thus center on the performance levels that can be obtained by using compilers on parallel systems. As we discussed earlier, fully automatic compilation is not yet available on Cedar. However, we have developed several compiler enhancements that have not yet been implemented but have been applied manually to the Perfect codes. These "automatable" results are reported together with automatic results for CRAY YMP/8 in Table 6 . We conclude from this that the state of today's compiler art indicates that acceptable levels for the Perfect codes may be reached in the next few years. Thus, we can expect PPT3 to be passed by parallel systems in the near future.

Performance Level	Cedar	Cray YMP
High ($E_p \geq .5$)	1 Codes	0 Codes
Intermediate ($E_p \geq 1/2 \log P$)	9 Codes	6 Codes
Unacceptable ($E_p < 1/2 \log P$)	3 Codes	7 Codes

Table 6: Restructuring Efficiency

Absolute Performance: Cray YMP/8 vs. Cedar The previous discussion has ignored absolute performance in terms of time or megaflops. Table 3 shows the megaflops generated by Cedar automatable versions [Add1], as well as Cray YMP/8 baseline compiler MFLOPS to Cedar MFLOPS ratios. The harmonic mean for the MFLOPS on the YMP/8 is 23.7, 7.4 times that of Cedar. It should be remembered that the ratios of clock speeds of the two systems is 170ns/6ns = 28.33.

Practical Parallelism Test 4 Parallel system performance can vary widely as a function of both the number of processors used and the size of the problems being solved. We shall use the High and Intermediate efficiency (see Table 6) and stability range of $.5 \leq St(P, N, 1, 0) \leq 1$ as acceptability criteria. The system is scalable in a range of processor counts and problem sizes where these criteria are satisfied. We are being more restrictive here than we were in PPT 2. This is reasonable because one should expect less variation in performance when varying data size alone than when varying data size as well as program and data structures, as is done across any benchmark suite. Furthermore, based on a number of measurements (not shown here) an Instability of 2 seems reasonable to expect on workstations as data size varies. It is difficult to vary the problem sizes and col-

lect scalability information for the Perfect codes, so we drop to the level of algorithm studies here, and use the Thinking Machines, Inc. CM-5 for comparison because it has a larger number of processors than CRAY YMP/8. The performance of a conjugate gradient (CG) iterative linear system solver was measured on Cedar while varying the number of processors from 2 to 32. This computation involves 5-diagonal matrix-vector products as well as vector and reduction operations of size N, $1K \leq N \leq 172K$. Cedar exhibits scalable high performance for matrices larger than something between 10K and 16K, and on up to the largest problems run. Cedar exhibits scalable intermediate performance for smaller matrices, evidently ranging well below the smallest actual runs of $N = 1K$. No unacceptable performance was observed in the data that was gathered.

In [FWPS92], a number of linear algebra experiments are reported on the CM-5. For comparison, we quote data for matrix-vector products with bandwidths 3 and 11. The CM-5 used does not have floating-point accelerators. For problem sizes run, $16K \leq N \leq 256K$, high performance was not achieved relative to 32, 256, or 512 processors. The communication structure of the CM-5 evidently causes these performance difficulties [FWPS92]. The CM-5 exhibits scalable intermediate performance with these three processor counts for problems evidently smaller than 16K for bandwidth 11 and evidently much smaller problems for bandwidth 3. No unacceptable performance was observed in the ranges reported.

Thus we conclude that, for these problems and for the number of processors studied, CM-5 is scalable with intermediate performance, while for up to 32 processors Cedar is scalable with high performance for many problem sizes and with intermediate performane for debugging sized runs.

Absolute Performance: The 32-processor Cedar delivers between 34 and 48 MFLOPS as the CG problem size ranges from 10K to 172K. On the banded matrix-vector product, the 32-processor CM-5 delivers between 28 and 32 MFLOPS for BW=3 and between 58 and 67 MFLOPS for BW=11, as the problem sizes range from 16K to 256K. Thus, the per-processor MFLOPS of the two systems on these problems are roughly equivalent.

We are in the process of collecting detailed simulation data for various computations on scaled-up Cedar-like systems. This takes us into the realm of PPT 5 which we shall not deal with further, in this paper.

Acknowledgments.

We acknowledge the contributions of D. Gajski, R. Downing, T. Tilton, M. Haney, R. McGrath, R. Barton, M. Sharma, D. Lavery, A. Malony, M. Farmwald, S. Midkiff, M. Guzzi, V. Guarna, C. Polychronopoulos, L. Harrison and T. Beck.

References

[Add1]   CSRD Staff. *Perfect Report 2: Addendum 1.* Center for Supercomputing Research and Development, University of Illinois, 1991.

[AnGa93] J. Andrews and K. Gallivan. *Analysis of a Cedar Implementation of* TRFD, CSRD Report in preparation, University of Illinois.

[BrBo91] R. Bramley and J. Bordner. *Sequential Optimization and Data Distribution for* ARC2D *on the Cedar Hierarchical Multiprocessor,* CSRD Report No. 1128, University of Illinois, 1991.

[EABM91] Emrath, P., et al. *The Xylem Operating System.* Procs. of ICPP'91, vol. 1, pg. 67-70, 1991.

[EHJL91] Eigenmann, et al. *Restructuring Fortran Programs for Cedar.* Procs. of ICPP'91, vol. 1, pp. 57-66, 1991.

[EHJP92] Eigenmann, et al. *The Cedar Fortran Project.* CSRD Report No. 1262, University of Illinois, 1992.

[EHLP91] Eigenmann, et al. *Experience in the automatic Parallelization of Four Perfect-Benchmark Programs.* Proceedings of the Fourth Workshop on Languages and Compilers for Parallel Computing, pp. 65-83, 1991.

[FWPS92] Ferng, W., et al. *Basic Sparse Matrix Computations on Massively Parallel Computers.* AHPCRC Preprint 92-084, University of Minnesota, July, 1992.

[GJTV91] K. Gallivan, et al. *Preliminary Performance Analysis of the Cedar Multiprocessor Memory System.* Proc. 1991 ICPP, Vol. I, pp. 71-75, 1991.

[GJWY93] K. Gallivan, et al. *Comments on a Cedar Implementation of* FLO52, CSRD Report in preparation, University of Illinois.

[GKLS83] Gajski, D., et al. *CEDAR – a Large Scale Multiprocessor,* Procs. 1983 ICPP, pp. 524-529, 1983.

[GoGV90] Gornish, E., et al. *Compiler-directed Data Prefetching in Multiprocessors with Memory Hierarchies.* Procs. ICS'90, Amsterdam, The Netherlands, vol. 1, pp. 342-353, 1990.

[Hoef91] Hoeflinger, J. *Cedar Fortran Programmer's Handbook.* Center for Supercomputing Research and Development, University of Illinois, 1991.

[KDLS86] Kuck, D., et al. *Parallel Supercomputing Today and the Cedar Approach,* Science, vol. 231, pp. 967-974, Feb. 28, 1986.

[KTVZ91] Konicek, J., et al. *The Organization of the Cedar System.* Procs. ICPP'91, vol. 1, pg. 49-56, 1991.

[Lawr75] Lawrie, D., *Access and Alignment of Data in an Array Processor.* IEEE Trans. on Computers, vol. C-24, no. 12, pp. 1145-1155, Dec. 1975.

[MaEG92] B. Marsolf, P. Emrath, and K. Gallivan. *Investigation of the Page Fault Performance of Cedar,* CSRD Report No. 1263, University of Illinois, 1992.

[Turn93] S. Turner. *Performance Analysis of Interconnection Networks,* PhD Thesis in preparation, 1993.

[YaGa93] U. M. Yang and K. Gallivan. *Analysis of a Cedar Implementation of* DYFESM, CSRD Report No. 1284, University of Illinois, 1993.

[ZhYe87] Zhu, C-Q. and Yew, P-C., *A Scheme to Enforce Data Dependence on Large Multiprocessor Systems.* IEEE Transactions on Software Engineering, vol. SE-13, no. 6, pp. 726-739, June 1987.

The J-Machine Multicomputer: An Architectural Evaluation*

Michael D. Noakes, Deborah A. Wallach, and William J. Dally
Artificial Intelligence Laboratory and Laboratory for Computer Science
Massachusetts Institute of Technology
Cambridge, Massachusetts 02139
noakes@ai.mit.edu, kerr@ai.mit.edu, billd@ai.mit.edu

Abstract

The MIT J-Machine multicomputer has been constructed to study the role of a set of primitive mechanisms in providing efficient support for parallel computing. Each J-Machine node consists of an integrated multicomputer component, the Message-Driven Processor (MDP), and 1 MByte of DRAM. The MDP provides mechanisms to support efficient communication, synchronization, and naming. A 512 node J-Machine is operational and is due to be expanded to 1024 nodes in March 1993. In this paper we discuss the design of the J-Machine and evaluate the effectiveness of the mechanisms incorporated into the MDP. We measure the performance of the communication and synchronization mechanisms directly and investigate the behavior of four complete applications.

1 Introduction

Over the past 40 years, sequential von Neumann processors have evolved a set of mechanisms appropriate for supporting most sequential programming models. It is clear, however, from efforts to build concurrent machines by connecting many sequential processors, that these highly-evolved sequential mechanisms are not adequate to support most parallel models of computation. These mechanisms do not efficiently support synchronization of threads, communication of data, or global naming of objects. As a result, these functions, inherent to any parallel model of computation, must be implemented largely in software with prohibitive overhead.

The J-Machine project [5] was developed to study how to best apply modern VLSI technology to construct a multicomputer. Each processing node of the J-Machine consists of a Message-Driven Processor (MDP) and 1 MByte of DRAM. The MDP incorporates a 36-bit integer processor (32 bits of data augmented with 4 bits of tag), a memory

management unit, a router for a 3-D mesh network, a network interface, a 4K-word $\times$ 36-bit SRAM, and an ECC DRAM controller in a single 1.1M transistor VLSI chip. Rather than being specialized for a single model of computation, the MDP incorporates primitive mechanisms for communication, synchronization, and naming that permit it to efficiently support threads with 50 to 150 instructions which exchange small data objects frequently with low-latency and synchronize quickly. A 512 node J-Machine is in daily use at MIT and will be expanded to 1024 nodes in March 1993.

This paper describes a range of experiments performed on the J-Machine to study the effectiveness of the selected mechanisms in supporting parallel applications. These experiments are divided into micro-benchmarks, designed to isolate the effects of the primitive mechanisms, and macro-benchmarks, to demonstrate the cumulative effect of the mechanisms on application level codes. We investigate the sequential performance of the MDP, the message-passing mechanisms, the performance of the 3D-mesh network, and the behavior of parallel applications running on the J-Machine.

We use these studies to critique the effectiveness of the mechanisms and reflect on the impact of these design decisions in developing programming systems for the J-Machine. We contrast the effectiveness of the J-Machine with comparable multicomputers and consider the impact of alternative mechanisms to further enhance efficiency.

2 The J-Machine

This section describes the architecture of the J-Machine and the hardware prototype on which the studies were performed.

2.1 Architecture

The instruction set of the MDP includes the usual arithmetic, data movement, and control instructions. The MDP is unique in providing special support for communication, synchronization, and naming.

*The research described in this paper was supported in part by the Defense Advanced Research Projects Agency under contracts N00014-88K-0738 and F19628-92C-0045, and by a National Science Foundation Presidential Young Investigator Award, grant MIP-8657531, with matching funds from General Electric Corporation, IBM Corporation, and AT&T.

The MDP supports communication using a set of `send` instructions for message formatting, a fast network for delivery, automatic message buffering, and task creation upon message arrival. A series of `send` instructions is used to inject messages at a rate of up to 2 words per cycle. The format of a message is arbitrary except that the first word must contain the address of the code to run at the destination and the length of the message. Messages are routed through the 3D-mesh network using deterministic, e-cube, wormhole routing [4]. The channel bandwidth is 0.5 words/cycle and the minimum latency is 1 cycle/hop. Upon arrival, messages are buffered in a hardware queue. When a message arrives at the head of the queue, a task is dispatched to handle it in four processor cycles. During these cycles the Instruction Pointer is loaded from the message header, an address register is set to point to the new message so that the thread's arguments may be accessed, and the thread's first instruction is fetched and decoded.

Messages may be issued to one of two priorities. Priority one messages receive preference during channel arbitration, are buffered in a separate queue at the destination, and are dispatched before pending priority zero messages. Priority one threads may interrupt executing priority zero threads. There is also a background priority that runs whenever both message queues are empty. Fast interrupt processing is achieved through the use of three distinct register sets.

Synchronization is provided by the ability to signal events effectively using the low-latency communication primitives and by the use of data-tagging in both the register file and memory. Two of the possible sixteen data types, `cfut` and `fut`, are used to mark slots for values that have not yet been computed. If a thread attempts to read a slot before the value has been supplied, the processor will trap to a system routine to suspend the thread until the value is delivered. In this event, the arrival of the value is used to restart the thread. The `cfut` type provides inexpensive synchronization on a single slot, much like a full-empty bit. The `fut` type may be copied without faulting and thus supports the more flexible, but more expensive, future datatype [2]. Futures are first-class data objects and references to them may be returned from functions and stored in arrays, for example.

The MDP supports a global namespace with segmented memory management and with name translation instructions. Local memory is referenced using indexed accesses via segment descriptors that specify the base and length of each memory object. These objects may be relocated at will, to implement local heap compaction, for example, if we ensure that only global virtual addresses of objects are exported from nodes. A hardware name-translation table is provided to accelerate virtual address to physical segment descriptor conversion. Virtual-physical pairs are inserted in the table using the `enter` instruction and extracted using `xlate`. A successful `xlate` takes three cycles.

The register file includes four data registers and four address registers per priority. The instruction set of the MDP permits most operators to read one of the operands from memory to help reduce access pressure on the register file. The MDP instruction encodes two 17 bit instructions in each word. Most instructions can operate in one cycle if both operands are in registers and in two cycles if one operand is in internal memory. The peak execution rate is therefore 12.5 million instructions per second. Branch instructions, prefetching stalls, operands in memory, and instruction alignment issues reduce this rate to a typical value of 5.5 million instructions per second if code and data are in internal memory. This can fall to fewer than 2 million instructions per second if all code and data are in external memory.

2.2 Prototype

Each processing node of the J-Machine is composed of a single Message-Driven Processor (MDP) chip and three $1M \times 4$ DRAM chips. The resulting node is 2" by 3". Each J-Machine processor board contains 64 MDP chips along with their external memories. The board measures 26" by 20.5". Each pair of nodes shares a set of elastomeric conductors to communicate with the corresponding nodes on the boards above and below in the board stack. A total of 48 elastomeric connectors held in four connector holders provide 1420 electrical connections between adjacent boards. Of these connections, 960 are used for signalling and the remaining 460 are ground returns. The use of elastomeric conductors enables the J-Machine to achieve a very high network bisection bandwidth (a peak rate of 14.4 Gbits/sec) in a very small cross sectional area (2 ft^2) and at the same time keep the length of the longest channel wire in a 1024-node machine under four inches. A stack of sixteen processor boards contains 1024 processing nodes (12,500 MIPS peak) and 1Gbyte of DRAM memory in a volume of 4 ft^3, and dissipates 1500W (1.5W per node).

Figure 1 shows a pair of J-Machine cabinets. The cover has been removed from the cabinet on the left to reveal a partial processor board stack at the top and a pair of peripheral interface cards below. Cards will soon be available to connect to SCSI devices, a Sun Sparc host, and a distributed graphics frame-buffer. The maximum possible bandwidth into this peripheral stack is 3.2 Gbyte/sec using just one of the faces of the cube. The base of the cabinet holds an array of up to 80 3.5-inch disk-drives, power supplies, and the host.

The experiments reported in this paper were run on a 512-node machine arranged as an $8 \times 8 \times 8$ mesh, operating at a processor clock rate of 12.5Mhz (derived from a 25Mhz input clock).

225

Figure 1: J-Machine.

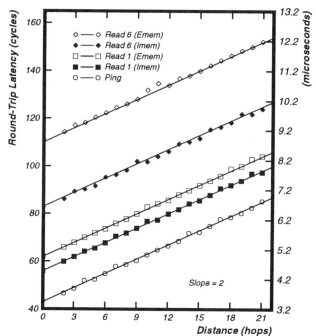

Figure 2: Round Trip Latency vs Distance for different types of remote reads, explained in Section 3.1.

3 Micro-Benchmark performance

To characterize the performance of the J-Machine's communication and synchronization mechanisms, we have written a number of small, synthetic programs designed to measure various aspects of J-Machine performance. Our studies focus on the tight coupling between the processor core and the network to support fine-grained communication, the impact of the differing communication bandwidths among the modules of the MDP, and the variation of message latency with network load.

3.1 Network performance

Communication performance is characterized by throughput, which is the number of messages per unit time that can be delivered, and latency, which is the end-to-end time required to deliver one message. Throughput limits the performance of communication intensive programs with large amounts of parallelism. Latency adds to the length of the critical path through a program with limited parallelism. Both latency and throughput depend on the

end-to-end performance of the communication system, not just on network performance. The performance of the network interface and the coupling between the processor and the network interface are key factors in determining overall communication performance.

Network latency Figure 2 shows the round-trip latency of a null remote procedure call (RPC) as a function of the distance traversed and the data transferred. These measurements are taken on an unloaded network. The indicated data points show measured values for a 512 node machine.

Each line corresponds to a different type and size of data transfer. The line labeled *Ping* gives the latency for sending a two-word request message to the remote node and waiting for and receiving a single word acknowledgment. The remaining lines give the latencies for remote reads of 1 or 6 words from either the on-chip memory (Imem) or the off-chip memory (Emem). The remote read is performed by sending a three-word request message to a remote node. That node reads the specified address and replies with a 2 or 7 word message containing the requested data.

The figure shows that there are four components to round-trip remote-procedure-call latency on the J-Machine. In addition to a base latency, there are components due to distance, message length, and computation. The base latency of 43 cycles is the round-trip latency for a node

Machine		T_s μs/msg	T_b μs/byte	cycles/msg	cycles/byte
nCUBE/2	(Vendor)	160.0	0.45	3200	9
CM-5†	(Vendor)	86.0	0.12	2838	4
DELTA	(Vendor)	72.0	0.08	2880	3
nCUBE/2	(Active)	23.0	0.45	460	9
CM-5	(Active)	3.3	0.12	109	4
J-Machine		0.9	0.04	11	0.5

†: blocking send/receive

Table 1: One-way message overhead. T_s is the sum of the fixed overheads of send and receive. T_b is the injection overhead per byte [6], [17].

---

pinging itself. This latency consists of two trips through the network at a total cost of 24 cycles, and the execution of two threads at a total cost of 19 cycles. All of the lines in the figure have a slope of two, indicating that one-way latency increases by one clock per hop as the distance traveled increases. Increasing the message length also increases the latency proportionally. The time required to compute the result (*i.e.* access the appropriate memory) adds 2 cycles per word for internal memory and 8 cycles per word for external memory.

Table 1 compares the asynchronous send and receive overheads of the J-Machine to those reported for several other current multicomputers. These overheads are generally composed of times to format a message and inject it into the network on the sender side, and to either poll or interrupt the processor and absorb the message on the receiver side. Note that network latency is not included in this table. The first three rows in the table are the times reported by the vendor based on their message libraries. The second set of rows are for tuned implementations of the Active Message system [17] on the same hardware and give a sense of the reduction in overhead that can be achieved when the programming model matches the available hardware more closely. We observe that the J-Machine reduces the overhead per byte by almost an order of magnitude and the overhead per message by up to two orders of magnitude. This is a striking difference whose repercussions have a dramatic impact on communication costs in the machine.

Network latency vs load The latency statistics reported above were measured on an unloaded network. In a loaded network there is an additional component of latency due to contention. We developed an experiment to evaluate the total one-way message latency for messages of different lengths at different average network loads. In this experiment, every node in the 512 node machine repeats a simple loop in which it selects a random destination, sends a message of length N to the target, waits for an N word acknowledgment, and then idles for L cycles. The idle phase simulates computation and its duration has an inverse relation to the average traffic load placed on the network. We run this loop for between 15 and 30 seconds, and then compute the average message rate and thereby the bisection traffic. We establish a base case in which no messages are transmitted in order to determine the number of cycles that execute in the loop itself. This allows us to measure the total number of cycles for the round-trip exchange. We divide this by two to obtain the one-way message latency.

The left-hand side of Figure 3 shows the one-way message latency in a 512 node machine as a function of network bisection traffic. A family of four curves represent messages of length 2, 4, 8, and 16 words, respectively. Again, the difference in latencies for the zero load case is due to both message overhead costs and propagation delays. The idle time L is varied to generate the full range of possible loads. The basic loop of the application takes 45 cycles without any idling. This sets an upper bound on the possible message rate for this experiment that is quite adequate for our purposes. The figure shows that random traffic causes the network of a 512-node J-Machine to saturate with a bisection traffic of 6Gbits/sec, nearly half of the bisection capacity (14.4Gbits/sec). This measurement is consistent with analytical predictions and simulation studies [1] [4]. The figure also shows that the component of latency due to contention increases in the expected manner [1].

The right-hand side of Figure 3 uses the same data to illustrate how network contention affects the achievable ratio of communication to computation. We consider an experiment in which each node picks a random destination within the machine, sends an N word message and receives an N word acknowledgment, performs a computation that is modeled by an idle loop, and then repeats the sequence. The time spent in computation as a fraction of the total

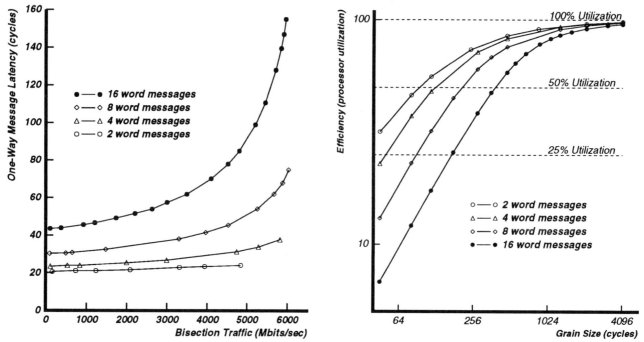

Figure 3: The left side of this figure shows message latency as a function of bisection traffic for an 8x8x8 J-Machine. The right side shows the processor efficiency vs grain size.

time determines the efficiency. The right side of the figure shows the coarse-grain case where efficiency is 100% and performance is determined only by computation. As one moves to the left along each curve, a point is reached where communication latency becomes the limiting factor and the efficiency decreases since increasingly more time is spent awaiting the completion of each message exchange. The *half-power* point, where efficiency reaches 50%, occurs when the computation to communication ratio is between 100 and 300 cycles/message for the message lengths shown.

Throughput Network saturation bandwidth, discussed above, is a limiting factor for programs that perform distant communications. For programs that exploit locality and tend to communicate mainly with neighboring nodes, however, terminal network bandwidth often becomes the limiting factor to performance.

A remote operation incurs overhead due to message setup, channel acquisition, and message invocation. This overhead is traditionally amortized by ensuring that remote accesses transfer relatively large amounts of data [9]. Requiring coarse-grain communication complicates programming in general and makes fine-grained synchronization and effective load-balancing particularly difficult. The efficient communication mechanisms of the J-Machine enable us to approach the effective terminal bandwidth of the network using small messages.

Figure 4 shows the maximum data-transfer rate that can be sustained between two nodes for a given message size. The data is generated at the source by loading dummy data directly from the register file. When the message is dispatched at the destination, it may be discarded, copied into internal memory, or copied into external memory. The figure shows that even for the highest bandwidth case (discarding the delivered data), the bandwidth is already within a 90% of its peak rate with messages as short as eight words. In all of the cases, two word messages achieve a throughput that is more than half of the eventual peak.

3.2 Synchronization

Synchronization involves enforcing the ordering of events in a parallel program. The J-Machine provides hardware support for synchronization via efficient message dispatch and the use of presence tags in the memory and register file. The task that is created and dispatched in response to each arriving message is a natural means to signal a waiting task that the event it is waiting on has occurred. Presence tags on every storage location are used to signal when a value is not yet available. Attempting to read a not-present value raises an exception. Since synchronization is often performed in conjunction with the production of data, it is natural to associate the synchronization tag with the data.

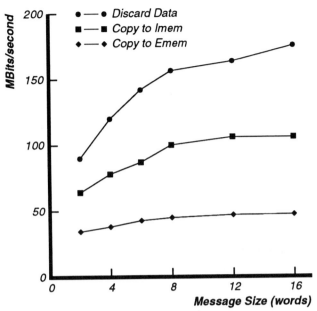

Figure 4: The terminal network bandwidth.

Event	Tags	No Tags	Save/Restore
Success	2	5	
Failure	6	7	30 - 50
Write	4	6	
Restart	0	0	20 - 50

Table 2: A comparison of synchronization times, in cycles, with and without hardware support for presence tags.

Software barrier synchronization (μsec)					
Nodes	EM4	J	KSR	IPSC/860	Delta
2	2.7	4.4	60	111	109
4	3.6	6.5	90	234	248
8	4.7	8.7	180	381	473
16	5.4	11.7	260	546	923
32		14.4	525	692	1816
64	7.4	16.5		847	3587
128		20.7			
256		24.4			
512		27.4			

Table 3: Barrier synchronization [6], [7], [14].

Producer-Consumer synchronization Table 2 compares the cost in cycles of performing a local producer-consumer synchronization both with and without the J-Machine presence tags. In the absence of tags, a separate synchronization variable must be tested before (or set after) accessing data. The table shows the costs of four events: reading data that is ready (Success), attempting to read unavailable data (Failure), writing data without needing to restart a thread (Write), and restarting a thread when the data is available (Restart). All data is stored in on-chip memory. We separate the general cost of thread suspension and restart, for which we provide a range of values reflecting different possible policies within the runtime and compiler system, from the issues directly related to the data operations. This table shows that the use of hardware provides a modest advantage when the test passes and that task suspension and restart overhead, rather than the synchronization overhead itself, is the dominant cost of failure. For the MDP, this synchronization mechanism is naturally integrated with our general mechanisms for runtime data tagging and fault management.

Barrier synchronization To test the ability of the J-Machine to synchronize sets of tasks, we measured the performance of a barrier synchronization library routine written in assembly language. Table 3 indicates the time taken in microseconds per barrier for a range of machine sizes and compares the performance with a number of contemporary parallel computers. It is difficult to compare the

performance of our algorithm to similar routines on other machines as presented in the literature since sufficient detail to determine what is being included is rarely provided. Our numbers represent the time taken from the point at which the current thread calls the barrier routine until the time this single thread is resumed.

The barrier synchronization library routine is implemented in a *scan* [3] style. For an n processor machine, $O(n \log_2 n)$ messages are sent, n per wave. The pattern formed by the messages is that of a butterfly network mapped onto a 3-d grid, with the messages sent each wave representing one stage of the butterfly. Incoming messages invoke a different handler for each wave; this matching is done quickly through the use of the fast hardware dispatch mechanism.

Although faster synchronization times can be achieved by hardware barrier synchronization mechanisms, software routines can be used to synchronize several sets of threads simultaneously.

4 Macro-Benchmark performance

We have implemented a number of programs on the J-Machine and profiled their execution to determine the role that mechanisms play in enhancing performance. We discuss the programming tools we used and the general characteristics of the applications we studied.

4.1 Programming systems

Two J-Machine programming systems were used to conduct the benchmark studies reported in this section: Tuned J and Concurrent Smalltalk (CST). Two other programming systems are also running on the machine: Id [12] [15] and PCN [16].

Tuned J The J language serves as a system-level programming language for the J-Machine. It extends a per-node ANSI C environment with a small number of additional constructs for remote function invocation and synchronization. The user is responsible for data placement and task coordination, providing the ability to tune and to readily understand the runtime behavior of the application at the cost of increased programming effort. The J compiler currently produces inefficient code, so we perform modest hand-tuning of a few of the critical code sequences to reflect the expected future behavior of the compiler. Applications are profiled by static evaluation of the basic blocks of key routines and the addition of counters to determine the dynamic frequencies for each block.

Three of the applications reported here were written in both C and either equivalent hand-tuned J or assembly language. The run times on a single node of the J-machine running at 12.5 MHz varied from 8% faster to 20% slower than the C versions compiled with a C compiler and run on a Intel 386SX processor at 33 MHz.

CST The Concurrent Smalltalk programming system [8] supports object-based abstraction mechanisms and encourages fine-grained program composition. It extends sequential Smalltalk by supporting asynchronous method invocation, distributed objects, and a small repertoire of control constructs for explicit specification of parallel control flow. The compiler and runtime system provide the programmer with a global object namespace. The CST system includes several simple tools for analyzing the dynamic behavior of an application. We augment these tools with hand-placed counters as in Tuned J.

4.2 Parallel applications

Longest Common Subsequence This program determines the longest subsequence of characters common to two source strings, where a subsequence is the string remaining after removing arbitrary characters from a source string. In this implementation, one string is distributed evenly across the nodes of the machine; the other string is placed on Node 0 and the characters are passed across the nodes in a systolic fashion. We studied the application

for the case where the first string is 1024 characters long and the second 4096. This program was written directly in assembly language.

Radix Sort This application sorts a set of integer keys. The keys are sorted one digit at a time, with digits represented by b-bits, from the least-significant to the most-significant digit. A stable, three-phase counting sort was used to sort each digit. In the first phase, a single scan of the source array determines the number of keys that hash to each of the digits (0 to $2^b - 1$). These keys will appear consecutively in the destination array at the end of the iteration. The counts are used to compute the initial offset for each key in the destination array. Finally, the array is scanned again and the data is reordered. In the parallel version, the data is distributed evenly across the machine. The counts computed by each node are combined and the initial offsets are generated using a binary combining/distributing tree. This program is written in Tuned J and sorts a set of 65,536 28-bit integers 4 bits at a time. This data set is small enough that it can be contained entirely within the local memory of one node to serve as a challenging base case.

N-Queens This familiar program determines the number of ways in which N queens may be placed on an $N \times N$ chess board so that no queen may attack another. It represents a range of graph-searching problems, all of whose central challenge is to control the potentially explosive parallelism that is available. This program is written in Tuned J and we explore its behavior as it solves the 13 queens problem.

Traveling Salesperson Problem The Traveling Salesperson Problem (TSP) benchmark is a classic path-searching program which finds the optimal tour in which the nodes of a graph with weighted edges can be traversed. A task is defined as a unique subpath of a given length; the tasks are initially distributed evenly over all the nodes. To process a task, a node explores all possible tours containing the subpath in depth-first order, while maintaining the shortest tour seen so far. If the length of the task's subpath is larger than the current bound, the node does not explore the subpath. This program is written in Concurrent Smalltalk and solves a 14 city configuration.

4.3 Application analysis

We present three sets of results that summarize the behavior of each of these applications. We will use these figures in the more detailed discussions that follow.

Figure 5 shows the speedup of each application. The apparent speedups that occur for a given application are strongly affected by the definitions of speedup used and the base case for the analysis. In all of these experiments we

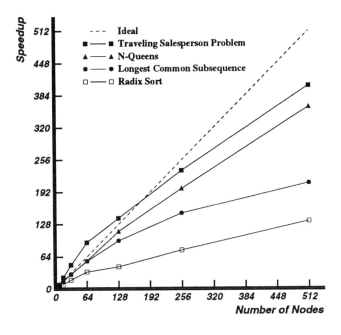

Figure 5: Speedup of applications on the J-Machine.

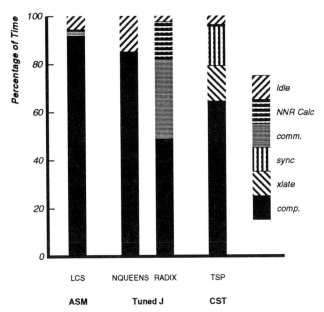

Figure 6: Breakdown of the total functions performed in each application running on a 64 node J-Machine.

hold the problem size constant. The base case for LCS, Radix-Sort, and N-Queens is a good sequential implementation; for TSP it is the parallel code. We view these curves as being primarily useful in directing attention to interesting trends rather than being of significance in themselves.

Figure 6 indicates the coarse breakdown of the functions performed by each node of a 64 processor machine for these applications. The calculations are in terms of cycles for LCS, N-Queens, and Radix Sort, allowing overhead such as the dispatch time to be considered, and in instructions for TSP, de-emphasizing the importance of the disparity between using internal and external memory.

Finally, Table 4 summarizes a number of metrics for the assembly language and Tuned J applications running on the 64 node machine. Each of these applications relies on two major classes of threads, for which the statistics are shown separately. For each application, we present the 64 node machine run time. For each thread, we additionally show the number of times the thread is invoked, the number of instructions run, the average thread length, and the message length used when invoking the thread.

4.3.1 Longest Common Subsequence

With 64 nodes, each node contains 16 characters of the base string and receives 4096 messages, each containing one character of the second string. The application is dominated by the behavior of this single message handler. The

	LCS	NQueens	RadixSort
RunTime (ms)	153	775	63
Thread 1	NxtChar	NQueens	Sort
# Threads	262,000	1,030	64
# K Instr	60,800	305,000	17,600
Instr/Thread	232	296,000	276,000
Msg Length	3	8	8
Thread 2	StartUp	NQDone	Write
# Threads	1	1,180	452,000
# K Instr	86	25	1,810
Instr/Thread	86,000	21	4
Msg Length	1	3	3

Table 4: Application statistics for a 64 node J-Machine.

application is initiated by Node 0 sending 4096 messages to itself, to process each character. After each node handles a character, it sends a message containing the character and the partial match information to its neighbor.

The key message handler consists of a fixed prologue section which generates an index into the state tables that maintain the match information, a loop over each of the characters in the base string on the node, and an epilogue section which forwards the partial result. As the size of the machine is increased, the time spent in the loop scales down proportionally, but the thread entry and exit cost remains constant. At 64 nodes, the handler entry and exit account for 9% of the total time. This overhead grows to 24% and then 33% as the machine grows to 256 and then 512 nodes respectively, becoming the dominant effect on scaling.

Performance is also reduced by idle cycles arising from two effects: load imbalance due to initialization and systolic skew. Work is distributed evenly except that Node 0 generates the initial set of 4096 messages. These messages appear one at a time and begin to traverse the machine almost immediately. Node 0, however, has significantly more work to do than the other nodes, causing them to periodically idle waiting for it to catch up. This load imbalance accounts for 4%, 13%, and 17% of the total runtime for machines of sizes 64, 256, and 512 nodes respectively. Nodes also idle due to systolic skew (pipeline end effects) during which the work front has either not reached a given node or has passed the node but has not reached the final node. This systolic skew represents a maximum of 11% of the total runtime across the range of machines studied.

4.3.2 Radix Sort

Radix sort is composed of two principal functions: the main loop that iterates seven times across the three phases, and the message handler that supports remote writing of values during the reorder phase. We regard the outer function as a single thread which suspends twice per iteration, once at the end of the counting phase and once at the end of each iteration, and each WriteData message as a separate thread. Table 4 shows that the outer-loop threads run for 310,000 instructions on a 64 node machine while the WriteData messages are only 4 instructions (16 cycles) each. We have written this application in a "fine-grained" style in which each value is written to its new slot as soon as the location has been computed. In machines lacking efficient communication primitives, one would need to collect and send large blocks of data to each node in order to amortize the overhead of injection.

Figure 5 shows three regimes of execution. The speedup from the tuned sequential one node version to the parallel two node version is 1.3. This is because the critical path through the inner loop is slightly longer and because the cost

of a remote memory write is over three times greater than a local memory write. The latter effect is the dominant term and becomes even more pronounced as the machine size grows. Between 2 and 64 nodes, the performance is limited by local processor throughput, and the runtime halves for each doubling in machine size. From 64 to 128 nodes, the bisection bandwidth remains constant but the offered traffic is approaching the onset of saturation. This results in the glitch observed. Thereafter, the bisection bandwidth again doubles with each doubling in the number of nodes and the relative runtimes halve accordingly.

The discontinuity between 64 and 128 nodes is also affected by unfairness in the MDP router. Arbitration for output channels occurs at a fixed priority and nodes may be unable to inject a message into the network for an arbitrarily long period of time during periods of high congestion. Network congestion causes back-pressure on the nodes in the form of send-faults that indicate that a word cannot be accepted for injection. We have verified that certain nodes experience fault rates that are as much as two orders of magnitude higher than average. These nodes are correlated with physical position in the machine and logical position within the tree of combining/distributing messages used in the phase immediately preceding the reorder phase. This problem will always be resolved by the inevitable synchronization points that occur in parallel applications, but any nodes that have been blocked will need to catch up with their peers that have been able to make progress.

To achieve good performance our radix sort implementation had to compensate for the MDP's inability to accept and process messages at the peak rate of the network. The peak network to message buffer bandwidth is 0.5 words/cycle. The processor core is able to read words from the message queue at the same rate but it takes at least 3 cycles to relocate the value into internal memory and 6 into external memory. Typically, message handlers also update local data or synchronization state resulting in additional cycles per word. These operations lead to a rate mismatch which can cause the message buffer to experience transient overflows. This problem is especially challenging in an application like this one in which thousands of messages arrive during a single phase. This effect forced us to reduce the amount of work performed in the handler and to relocate this work to a different phase.

4.3.3 N-Queens

N-Queens is a graph search problem, with a state space exponential in the problem size. The key difficulty in an efficient N-Queens implementation is to control the explosive parallelism that tends to cause a large number of threads, overwhelming the machine's buffering resources.

The N-Queens application attacks this problem by expanding the number of boards first in a breadth-first manner, then switching to a depth-first traversal of the rest of the state space. The amount of breadth-first expansion depends on the machine size and the problem size. Most of the N-Queens threads are coarse-grained tasks that perform a depth-first traversal locally. For a 64 node machine running a 13 queens problem size, most threads are 300,000 instructions long, as can be seen in Table 4. Small messages are used to communicate boards to be expanded (eight words) and results from finished computation (three words).

The MDP provides one primitive mechanism for low-level task scheduling: the message queue. This queue can contain no more than 256 minimum-length messages (four words) and is configured for 128 of these messages in Tuned-J. This buffer is only large enough for at most 64 board-distribution messages. In this implementation, all of the work is generated at the start of program and spread relatively evenly across the machine. It is not possible to determine a priori how long each thread will run for and there are insufficient threads to rely on the laws of averages to balance the load. This results in an observed idle time of 15% (Figure 6). We can distribute more task descriptors that represent less work per thread by buffering the messages in memory using a system-level queue overflow fault handler but it is relatively expensive and is intended to be used for transient traffic overruns rather than as a general task management mechanism. Alternatively, we could implement a user-level "scheduler" that spreads the creation of smaller threads across the duration of the application.

4.3.4 Traveling Salesperson Problem

The traveling salesperson algorithm is the only application we discuss that is implemented in CST. As such, there are several key differences between this application and the others, because the style of machine usage that CST and the COSMOS runtime promote is different than that of J. There are no procedure calls per se; all calls become message invocations, either on the local node or a remote node. All data structures are *objects*, which can migrate to other nodes, or even change position on a single node, and are always referred to by a global virtual name which must be translated at every use. Finally, no priority 1 messages may be sent in the current CST/COSMOS system.

Nevertheless, an experienced CST programmer can take steps to eliminate certain sources of overhead. These efforts have led to an implementation that scales well and that has a single-node performance that is comparable to published run times for other implementations. Procedure calls were inlined in many cases to reduce context switching overhead. Data objects were declared to be non-migratable for the duration of the program. Incomplete tours of the cities can be redistributed to balance the load; they are represented,

TSP		
	User	O/S
Run Time (msec)	26300	
# Threads (Msgs)	9.1×10^6	8.9×10^6
# Instructions	2.8×10^9	5.4×10^8
# xlates	5.1×10^8	
# xlate Faults	1.6×10^4	
Instr/Thread (mean)	309	61
Avg Msg Length	5.1	4

Table 5: Major components of cost for TSP.

however, by primitive objects, and as such are not referred to with global IDs.

The TSP algorithm, like the N-Queens algorithm, is a graph-searching problem. The main difference between them is that TSP can prune the amount of work that needs to be done based on the work already done: a shortest path cannot be longer than any already calculated path. Pruning dominates the behavior of the TSP application, as can be seen in the speedup curve shown in Figure 5. The multi-node version happens to find better paths using less total work than the sequential one for this particular city configuration, and therefore exhibits super-linear speedup for the smaller machines. The TSP application's use of dynamic task balancing results in an idle time of only 3.8% as compared to 15% in N-Queens (Figure 6).

The TSP application, also like N-Queens, is very coarse-grained in its current implementation. There are three main types of threads: task-processing, bounds-distributing, and work-requesting. A task-processing thread can run as a single 32,000 instruction task; however, it must be interrupted periodically so that the messages that propagate updated bounds can be processed. These messages could, in principle, be handled using priority one threads but CST/COSMOS does not currently support this. Instead, we cause the path-tracing thread to suspend periodically by performing a null procedure call. Sixteen percent (the synchronization overhead from Figure 6) of the time that TSP runs is currently spent in this operation.

The xlate instruction is used to translate global object names into local physical addresses. The name is generally stored in the current context frame, and xlate places the physical address in the specified address register. Because the instruction takes only three cycles if the name is found in the name-cache, it is also used to reload an address register after a spill. This accounts, in part, for the large number of xlate instructions and the low xlate miss ratio (the percentage of time an xlate misses and thus needs to fault is insignificant) as noted in Table 5.

5 Critique

This paper has reported the results of an experimental evaluation of the J-Machine multicomputer. We have measured the communication and synchronization performance of the J-Machine using synthetic micro-benchmarks and compared these numbers to published figures for other contemporary parallel computers. The behavior of several application programs has also been studied.

The focus of the J-Machine design was on the tight coupling between a conventional integer-processing core and a high-bandwidth, low-latency network. Fast message injection, automatic message buffering, and fast message dispatching form the foundation of a system that offers efficient communication and synchronization. The J-Machine also includes hardware-based presence tags to enhance fine-grained data synchronization and a general name translation mechanism (enter and xlate) to support a global name space.

The communication micro-benchmarks demonstrate that the J-Machine reduces one-way message overhead by one to two orders of magnitude compared to contemporary multicomputers constructed from off-the-shelf processors (Table 1). Combining effective injection and dispatching with a low-latency network enables a node in one corner of a 512-node J-Machine to read a word from the memory of its nearest neighbor in 60 cycles and from the opposite corner node in 98 cycles (Figure 2). Figure 3 shows that threads achieve processor utilization of over 50% with task lengths between 25 and 50 cycles per word of message data even for random message patterns. A terminal network bandwidth of 90% of the eventual peak is achieved with messages as short as 8 words (Figure 4).

The impact of the communication mechanisms and hardware-based message dispatching on synchronization primitives is clearly seen in our implementation of a barrier synchronization library routine (Table 3), in which the J-Machine is again one to two orders of magnitude faster than contemporary microprocessor-based multicomputers.

Each macro-benchmark application has provided insight into the interplay of the mechanisms of the J-Machine and the task of producing effective parallel programs. The performance of N-Queens, LCS, and TSP is set by factors such as the nature of the problem, the length of the sequential path length through the code, and load balancing, rather than by constraints imposed by the low-level mechanisms. The performance of radix sort is limited by the global bandwidth available and by the use of messages to pass every word of data. This is our only application to date that has stressed our fine-grain communication and synchronization mechanisms.

In running these benchmarks we became aware of a number of limitations of the J-Machine and MDP architectures. Including statistics collection hardware in the machine design would have greatly simplified and enhanced the measurement collection process for this paper. The inclusion of a cycle counter, for example, would have enabled the time-stamping of events.

The MDP's external memory bandwidth limits performance. The network can deliver data at a rate three times greater than the external memory can accept it. External memory latency (6 cycles) also limits the sequential performance of each node. This limitation could be addressed by using a RAM technology with a higher bandwidth to capacity ratio and automatically managing the on-chip memory as a cache.

The naming mechanisms of the MDP are inadequate to transparently and inexpensively provide a global name space. CST applications spend time XLATEing virtual addresses to segment descriptors and some applications spend considerable time converting virtual addresses or linear node indices to router addresses. Automatic translation from virtual memory addresses to physical memory address and from virtual node id's to physical router addresses would eliminate the need for explicit name management. This mechanism could be implemented with a pair of TLBs. It would both eliminate much of our current naming overhead and, by protecting the translation of node addresses, provide greater protection between programs running on different partitions of the machine.

A method of applying "backpressure" to sending nodes is needed to avoid overflowing the MDPs on-chip queue into off-chip memory. Such a flow-control mechanism would also avoid blocking the network completely when one node stops accepting messages to handle a queue overflow. One simple method of flow control is to adopt a "return-to-sender" protocol that refuses messages when the queue is above a certain threshold by returning them to the sending node.

Future directions Our experience with the J-Machine has shown that global bandwidth is a critical resource that limits the computation to communication ratio for highly parallel programs. To reduce the demand for bandwidth, we are exploring methods for building parallel software systems that minimize communication by exploiting locality [11].

The MDP's paucity of registers, while reducing context switch time, resulted in more memory references than were necessary. We are currently researching methods of increasing the number of architectural registers without increasing context switch time for short-lived tasks [13].

To extract more parallelism out of an application of a given size, we are exploring ways to combine compile-time and run-time scheduling to exploit inter-thread and instruction-level parallelism [10].

The data presented here demonstrates that the J-Machine's communication, synchronization, and naming mechanisms are effective in supporting programs with small task sizes (150 instructions). These programs also demonstrate that a fast communication facility makes it possible to operate with only a small amount of memory per node (1MB) by fetching instructions and data from remote nodes when needed.

Conventional parallel computers offer no cost/performance benefits when compared to the workstations from which they are derived. Rather, they extend the absolute performance. Providing efficient mechanisms allows the construction of physically small nodes, which would offer the potential of better cost/performance across a range of machine sizes. It would be straightforward to incorporate the J-Machine mechanisms with the improvements described above into a conventional RISC processor core without affecting sequential performance. Combining such a core with a small, high-bandwidth memory and a router would result in an integrated processing node suitable for use in machines ranging from personal workstations (a few nodes) to departmental servers (tens to hundreds of nodes) and supercomputers (thousands of nodes). By reducing the memory and hence cost per node by an order of magnitude, such physically fine-grain machines offer proportionally better cost/performance while retaining the same total memory capacity.

Acknowledgments

The existence of a 512 node J-Machine with an infrastructure for basic performance evaluation is a credit to a large team of researchers; all are extended our gratitude. In addition we wish to acknowledge those people who contributed directly to this paper: Kirk Johnson and Steve Keckler wrote micro-benchmark programs. Shaun Kaneshiro, John Keen, and Kathy Knobe wrote and instrumented macro-benchmark programs. We thank them for their generous assistance.

References

[1] AGARWAL, A. Limits on interconnection network performance. *IEEE Transactions on Parallel and Distributed Systems 2*, 4 (Oct. 1991), 398–412.

[2] BAKER, H. C., AND HEWITT, C. the incremental garbage collection of processes. In *Conference Record of the Conference on AI and Programming Languages* (Rochester, New York, Aug. 1977), ACM, pp. 55–59.

[3] BLELLOCH, G. Scans as primitive parallel operations. In *International Conference on Parallel Processing* (1987), pp. S355–362.

[4] DALLY, W. J. Performance analysis of k-ary n-cube interconnection networks. *IEEE Trans. Comput. 39*, 6 (June 1990).

[5] DALLY, W. J., FISKE, J. S., KEEN, J. S., LETHIN, R. A., NOAKES, M. D., NUTH, P. R., DAVISON, R. E., AND FYLER, G. A. The Message-Driven Processor: A multicomputer processing node with efficient mechanisms. *IEEE Micro 12*, 2 (Apr. 1992), 23–39.

[6] DUNIGAN, T. Communication performance of the Intel Touchstone Delta mesh. Tech. Rep. ORNL/TM-11983, Oak Ridge National Laboratory, Jan. 1992.

[7] DUNIGAN, T. Kendall Square multiprocessor: early experiences and performance. Tech. Rep. ORNL/TM-12065, Oak Ridge National Laboratory, Mar. 1992.

[8] HORWAT, W. A Concurrent Smalltalk compiler for the Message-Driven Processor. AI Memo, MIT, 545 Technology Sq., Cambridge, MA 02139, May 1988. SB Thesis.

[9] HSU, J.-M., AND BANERJEE, P. Performance measurement and trace driven simulation of parallel and numeric applications on a hypercube multicomputer. In *17th Annual International Symposium on Computer Architecture* (1990), IEEE Press, pp. 260–269.

[10] KECKLER, S. W., AND DALLY, W. J. Processor coupling: Integrating compile time and runtime scheduling for parallelism. In *Proceedings of the 19th International Symposium on Computer Architecture* (Queensland, Australia, May 1992), ACM, pp. 202–213.

[11] KNOBE, K., LUKAS, J. D., AND DALLY, W. J. Dynamic alignment on distributed memory systems. In *The Third Workshop on Compilers for Parallel Computers* (Vienna, Austria, July 1992), Austrian Center for Parallel Computation.

[12] NIKHIL, R. S., AND ARVIND. Id language reference manual version 90.1. Tech. Rep. 284-2, Computation Structures Group, MIT, Cambridge, MA 02139, 1991.

[13] NUTH, P. R., AND DALLY, W. J. A mechanism for efficient context switching. In *Proceedings of the International Conference on Computer Design: VLSI in Computers & Processors* (Oct. 1991), IEEE, pp. 301–304.

[14] SHAW, A. Implementing data-parallel software on dataflow hardware. Master's thesis, MIT, Laboratory for Computer Science, 545 Technology Square, Cambridge, MA 02139, January 1993.

[15] SPERTUS, E. Execution of dataflow programs on general-purpose hardware. MS Thesis, Massachusetts Institute of Technology, Department of Electrical Engineering and Computer Science, Aug. 1992.

[16] TAYLOR, S., ET AL. Scalable concurrent programming project. Semiannual technical report, Dept. of Computer Science, California Institute of Technology, Apr. 1992.

[17] VON EICKEN, T., CULLER, D., GOLDSTEIN, S., AND SCHAUSER, K. Active messages: A mechanism for integrated communication and computation. In *Proceedings of 19th Annual International Symposium on Computer Architecture* (1992), IEEE, pp. 256–266.

SESSION 11:

Processor
Architecture
and
Implementation

16-Bit vs. 32-Bit Instructions
for Pipelined Microprocessors

John Bunda,* Don Fussell,
Roy Jenevein
Department of Computer Sciences
The University of Texas at Austin
Austin, Texas 78712

W. C. Athas
Information Sciences Institute
University of Southern California
Marina del Rey, California

Abstract

In any stored-program computer system, information is constantly transferred between the memory and the instruction processor. Machine instructions are a major portion of this traffic. Since transfer bandwidth is a limited resource, inefficiency in the encoding of instruction information (low code density) can have definite hardware and performance costs.

Starting with a parameterized baseline RISC design, we compare performance for two instruction encodings for the same instruction processing core. One is a variant of DLX, a typical 32-bit RISC instruction set. The other is a 16-bit format which sacrifices some expressive power while retaining essential RISC features. Using optimizing compilers and software simulation, we measure code density and path length for a suite of benchmark programs, relating performance differences to specific instruction set features. We measure time to completion performance while varying memory latency and instruction cache size parameters. The 16-bit format is shown to have significant cost-performance advantages over the 32-bit format under typical memory system performance constraints.

1 Introduction

Efficient transfer of instructions between the memory and instruction set processor is a significant issue in any Von Neumann computer system. Since the capacity of a processor to execute instructions typically exceeds the capacity of a memory to provide them, efficiency in the encoding of instruction information can

be expected to have definite hardware and/or performance costs. Such considerations for many years supported the development of CISC processors. CISC instructions provide relatively compact encodings of computations, but this comes at the cost of complex decoding and execution, often requiring multiple processor cycles per instruction. These drawbacks have motivated widespread adoption of the RISC paradigm, which in pure form employs only simple instructions which can be decoded easily, execute in a single machine cycle, and facilitate pipelining of the processor. With the use of instruction caching and advanced compiler technology, RISC machines can provide significant performance advantages over CISC machines.

Most RISC instruction sets contain only 32-bit instructions, allowing simple instruction fetch and decode stages, three operand instructions for flexibility in compiler optimization, and sufficient addressing capability for modern machines. However, such instruction sets require significantly larger numbers of bits to represent object programs than CISC machines and in that sense provide a less efficient encoding of instructions. This means that RISC programs require more main memory for storage and more instruction fetch bandwidth for execution than CISC machines [9, 14]. These considerations are somewhat mitigated by the fact that memory is a relatively inexpensive resource in current technology and through the use of instruction cache to reduce fetch bandwidth requirements. Thus, the RISC paradigm seems better suited to today's technology. A variable-length instruction format [10, 15, 4] increases density, but the performance benefits can be easily offset by higher fetch alignment and instruction decode overhead. The density drawbacks of fixed 32-bit instruction sets appear to be more than offset by other RISC advantages *vis à vis* CISC. However, it is natural to ask whether low code density is really an inherent penalty for RISC performance. In

*This work supported in part by the IBM Corporation through the Graduate Resident Study Program. John Bunda is now at IBM's Somerset Design Center, 9737 Great Hills Trail, Austin, TX 78759.

this paper, we claim that the answer to this question is no.

One strategy for increasing density is to retain a fixed-length format but reduce the instruction size to sixteen bits. By keeping all instructions the same length, fetch and decode simplicity can be maintained. A load/store general register architecture can still be used, but the short instructions will limit the number of registers that can be referenced and the number of operands per instruction. Fewer bits are available for address offsets. These limitations can be expected to limit the ability of compilers to optimize code for these machines, lengthen instruction sequences required for given computations, and thus decrease performance. On the other hand, short instructions allow more fetches for a given memory bandwidth and require smaller instruction caches for a given miss ratio. Thus, it is unclear *a priori* whether the use of 32-bit instructions is the best way to exploit the advantages of the RISC paradigm.

In this paper, we report the results of a set of experiments designed to provide specific, quantitative evaluations of these tradeoffs. We start with a baseline instruction processor with a fixed pipeline architecture and set of operations, and compare performance of a sixteen-bit and a thirty-two bit instruction encoding for the machine. Execution of a suite of benchmark programs is simulated for a processor with a multistage pipeline, executing single instructions at a peak rate of one per clock cycle. The thirty-two bit encoding, DLXe, is a variant of DLX, Hennessy and Patterson's composite RISC instruction set [5]. We compare this to a 16-bit format called D16. An overview of these is given in Section 2.

Our measurements are based on code compiled by GCC 2.1, a portable optimizing C compiler [13]. Optimized code produced by GCC is competitive with the native compilers for commercial workstations. While there are potential advantages to specifically targeted compilers, basing both on the same technology helps ensure a level playing field, where compilation, optimization, and code generation capabilities are as similar as possible. The minor differences between the instruction sets are, for the most part, handled by code generation parameters of the portable compiler.

Using an architecture simulator that executes programs of either instruction encoding, we measure relative code density (size of compiled programs) and path length (total count of executed instructions) for a suite of benchmark programs. We examine in detail the particular restrictions of the 16-bit encoding to determine precisely the effects of these restrictions

on density and path length. Results show that the compiler is able to exploit the expressive power of 32-bit instructions to measurably reduce the number of instructions in the static representation. These results are presented in Section 3.

In Section 4, performance of the instruction sets with respect to memory system parameters is examined briefly. Cache performance advantages of D16 instructions and memory system performance required for a machine to exploit the path length advantages of the 32-bit DLXe format are discussed.

2 D16 and DLXe Instruction Sets

D16 and DLXe are both RISC-inspired load-store instruction sets. They are nearly identical in function and supported on the same pipeline with identical execution resources. Both have the normal complement of ALU, shift, memory, and floating-point operations. The principal differences lie in the size and format of instruction encodings and the size of the register files. D16 instructions are sixteen bits long, DLXe instructions thirty-two. D16 instructions can address sixteen general and sixteen floating-point registers, while DLXe instructions can address thirty-two of each.

DLXe is a variant of the 32-bit DLX RISC instruction set [5], which is a simple RISC design with a strong resemblance to the MIPS R2000 [8]. DLXe differs from DLX only in its floating-point comparison instructions and the lack of direct loads and stores of floating-point registers. These restrictions were incorporated to simplify the FPU interface for a prototype implementation.

Instruction formats are shown in Figures 1 and 2, respectively. Because the information density of 16-bit instructions is higher, a more elaborate encoding scheme is necessary; D16 has five instruction types to DLXe's three. Both instruction sets define general-register machines, though some D16 instructions have fixed, implicit operand and/or destination registers. D16 has four bits for each register address, designating one of sixteen general or sixteen floating-point registers. The DLXe format has five bits per register name, addressing thirty-two of each register class. The set of opcodes for each instruction set is approximately the same, as shown in Table 1. D16 and DLXe instructions are both executed on the five-stage execution pipeline shown in Figure 3. A more complete description of the D16 and DLXe instruction sets appears in [3].

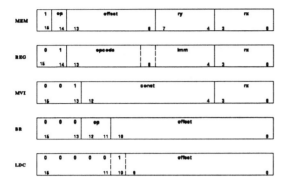

Figure 1: D16 16-bit instructions.

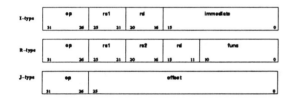

Figure 2: DLX 32-bit instructions.

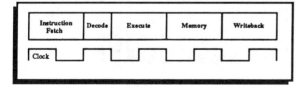

Figure 3: D16-DLXe execution pipeline.

Instructions	Description
ld st ldh ldhu sth ldb ldbu stb	For D16, subword mode addresses must be contained in a register. For word mode load/store, the offset magnitude must be less than 128. The LDC format allows negative offsets to 4096. DLXe allows signed 16-bit offsets for all loads and stores. Loads have one delay slot.
br bz bnz j jz jnz jl	Branches are to PC-relative offsets. The D16 limit is ±1024. Jumps are to an absolute address in the specified register, and the return address is placed in r1. All have one exposed delay slot.
s*cond*	Integer compare. For D16, both operands must be registers. The destination register (for D16, r0) is set to all zeros or ones. *Cond* may be lt, ltu, le, leu, eq, neq. DLXe also allows immediate operands and gt, gtu, ge, geu, with the result going to any GPR destination.
add addi sub subi and or xor neg inv	The D16 immediate range on addi/subi is unsigned 5 bits. DLXe also has andi ori xori, all immediates are signed 16 bits. DLXe omits neg inv since r0 is always zero.
shra shrai shr shri shl shli	D16 immediates are 5 bits unsigned, $0 \leq i < 32$.
mv, mvi mvhi	D16 only, immediate signed 9 bits. DLXe only, sets upper 16 bits.
add.sf sub.sf mul.sf div.sf neg.sf cmp.sf add.df sub.df mul.df div.df neg.df cmp.df	Single and double precision floating-point operations.
si2sf sf2df di2df df2di df2sf	Floating and integer mode conversions.
trap rdsr	Special instructions. The rdsr instruciton reads the status register containing the result of floating-point comparisons.

Table 1: D16 and DLXe opcodes.

3 Instruction Set Performance

One measure of the expressive power of an instruction set is the physical size of compiled programs. The *relative density* of two programs that encode the same computation is the ratio of their sizes. Another measure is *path length*, the total number of instructions in an execution trace. In general, a shorter path length is preferred, though as RISC processors have demonstrated, other performance considerations can offset even large path length differences. A processor achieving higher throughput can execute more instructions in the same number of cycles.

This section compares density and path length for a suite of programs chosen from commonly quoted synthetic benchmarks and real programming tasks. The benchmark suite is summarized in Table 2.

Program	Description
ack	Computes the Ackermann function.
asm	The D16 assembler.
bsrt	Bubblesort from the Stanford suite.
8qns	The Stanford eight-queens program.
qsrt	The Stanford quicksort program.
twrs	The Stanford Towers of Hanoi program.
grep	The Unix utility from BSD sources.
linp	The linpack benchmark.
matr	Gaussian elimination.
dhry	The Dhrystone synthetic benchmark.
pi	Computes digits of pi.
solv	A Newton-Raphson iterative solver.
latex	The typesetter.
ipl	PostScript plotting package.
whet	The Whetstone synthetic benchmark.

Table 2: The benchmark suite.

3.1 Code Density

The relative density of programs of the benchmark suite compiled and linked for DLXe and D16 are shown in Figure 4. The figure shows the relative density of D16 programs with respect to the DLXe equivalent. The programs are compiled with all optimizations enabled, including instruction scheduling. The size measure includes total bytes of instructions and initialized constants.

DLXe programs average approximately 1.5 times the size in bytes of D16 binaries. While D16 instructions are half the size of DLXe, there is a measurable increase in the total number of instructions, reducing relative density to less than two.

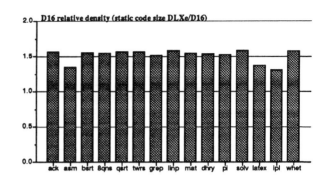

Figure 4: D16 relative density.

3.2 Path Length

The *path length* of a program is the total number of instructions in an execution trace. Relative density is useful in assessing memory requirements, but static instruction counts are only weakly correlated to path length. This is partly because program execution time is dominated by inner loops. Also, some optimization strategies reduce path length at a cost of increased static size [1]. Consequently, few conclusions about performance can be drawn from density alone.

Direct comparison of D16 and DLXe program path lengths is more meaningful than comparisons between arbitrary architectures, because both instruction sets are executed on the same pipeline. If execution resources or computations per instruction for both machines were different, it would be more difficult to make direct cost-performance comparisons.

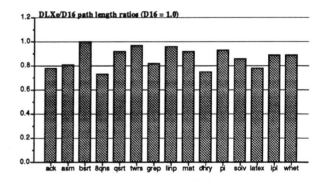

Figure 5: DLXe path length reduction.

The path length ratios of DLXe to D16 for the benchmark suite are shown in Figure 5. The DLXe path length reduction compared to D16 is not proportional to the density differences, averaging 15 percent over all test programs. In the next section, we examine features of the DLXe instruction set to assess the contribution of each to density and path length differences.

3.3 Instruction Set Features

DLXe instructions differ from D16 instructions in several important ways:

1. 32 *vs.* 16 general and floating-point registers.

2. Three-address *vs.* two-address instructions.

3. Larger (16-bit) immediate fields, and more instructions with immediate operands.

4. Larger (16-bit) address displacements, which are also available on halfword and byte loads and stores.

To determine which instruction set features provide the most return in the code density tradeoff, the code generator of the DLXe compiler is selectively restricted to prevent exploitation of a particular feature, and resulting performance is compared.

3.3.1 Register File Size

One of the difficult compromises in the D16 instruction set is reducing the number of addressable registers. The number of registers required depends on both the compiler allocation scheme and the target application. With procedure-level register allocation, sixteen registers has been claimed to be sufficient [12, 7], but with the GCC compiler, we observe measurable differences in both static and dynamic performance between sixteen and thirty-two registers.

For both instruction sets, the register file is fixed and allocated at compile time, as opposed to using a register-windowing scheme. Register windows provide a sliding-window type access to a large register file, which can reduce memory traffic in saving and restoring non-volatile scratch registers on procedure call and return [11]. Schemes for allocating registers statically have been shown to provide performance as good or better than register windows [16], but the the D16 register file is probably too small for these methods to work well. For D16, register windows is perhaps more promising, but we do not address this question here.

All else being equal, reducing the size of the visible register file degrades a program's performance if, at any point in its execution, there are more live values than available registers. When this happens, values needed in registers must be spilled to temporary

variables in memory. An increase in spills increases the total number of instructions, as well as data traffic to memory. This is the bad news; the good news is that in many programming environments (our compiler for one), spills are to stack frame variables, which are extremely likely to hit in a data cache. Spills are therefore generally less expensive than other memory references.

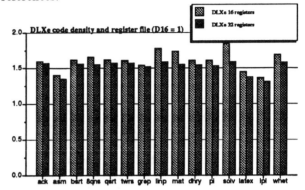

Figure 6: Density effects of 16 *vs.* 32 registers.

To test the effects of the smaller D16 register file in isolation, the DLXe compiler is restricted to generate code using only 16 general and 16 floating-point registers. Again, the code is measured for density, dynamic instruction counts. Figure 6 shows the increase in static code size for the suite of benchmarks. The increase in total instructions to run each program with the smaller register file is shown in Figure 7.

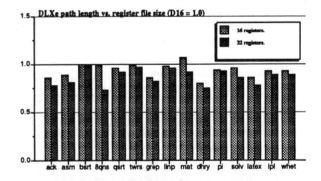

Figure 7: Path length effects, 16 *vs.* 32 registers.

Table 3 gives the relative data traffic increase over DLXe for both D16 and DLXe restricted to a D16-sized register file. D16 does better than the restricted DLXe in some cases, but this is may be due to the fact that DLXe has one fewer register available, since r0 is always zero. However, in general, for the allocation

| Benchmark | Increase% | |
Program	D16	DLXe-16
ack	0.2	1.2
asm	0.0	3.1
bsrt	0.7	1.0
8qns	8.8	2.7
qsrt	15.4	14.7
twrs	-2.0	0.0
grep	54.5	36.5
linp	10.8	10.6
matr	26.3	26.9
dhry	10.9	2.7
pi	1.3	3.2
solv	13.8	10.5
latex	6.2	4.7
ipl	1.6	-2.8
whet	3.0	19.5
Average	10.1	9.0

Table 3: Data traffic increase for smaller register file.

scheme used by the GCC compiler, the data traffic penalty for the smaller register file is about 10 percent.

3.3.2 Three-Address vs. Two-Address Instructions

The ability to specify a destination register distinct from the operand registers appears in many 32-bit RISC instruction sets, despite the fact that it is widely believed to have little tangible benefit. However, the availability of bits when encoding most operations in a fixed 32-bit instruction makes this feature virtually free in most 32-bit RISC instruction sets.

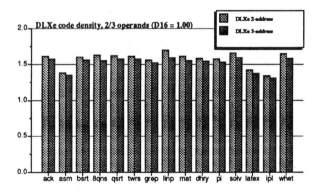

Figure 8: Code density effects, two-address instructions.

Figure 8 shows how density decreases when DLXe instructions are restricted to two operands (the des-

tination register is always required to be the same as the left source operand register). The increase in path length is shown in Figure 9. Both measures show that three-address instructions have a small but measurable advantage for most of the benchmark programs.

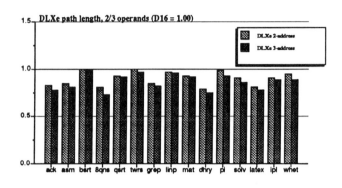

Figure 9: Path length effects, two-address instructions.

3.3.3 Immediate Operands

The limits of 16-bit instructions appear especially acute when confronting the issue of encoding constant operands in an instruction field. Where DLXe allows 16-bit immediate operands and address displacements, the bits available for such operands are very scarce in D16 instructions. As described in Section 2, the only D16 integer instructions supporting immediate operands are add, subtract, and shift instructions, which are limited to (unsigned) 5 bits. The move-immediate instruction has a sign-extended 9-bit immediate operand. Address displacements are limited to word-aligned displacements of ±128 bytes.

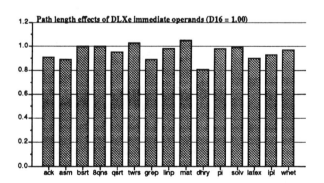

Figure 10: Effect of large immediates on path lengths.

Restricting the DLXe compiler to both a small register file and two-address instructions, we measure a machine that approximates D16 but with the 16-bit immediates and displacements (and appropriate additional opcodes) of DLXe. The reduction in total instructions this provides is shown in figure 10. The figure gives speedup of each program relative to D16= 1.0. Two of the programs are actually measurably slower; this is perhaps due to the sacrifice of a register (r0 permanently zero).

Compare immediate	2.1%
ALU immediate, > 5 bits	2.8%
Memory displacements > 8 bits	4.6%
Total	9.5%

Table 4: Average immediate-field instruction frequencies.

The average speedup provided by immediate fields is about 10 percent, and this is confirmed by the breakdown of the instructions in program traces shown in Table 4, which gives the frequencies of immediate-operand instructions in DLXe programs that exceed D16 immediate field precision. If each has a penalty of one additional D16 instruction, the path length difference is explained.

Half of the total DLXe speedup involves address displacements that exceed 8 bits, and most of these are stack frame references. The GCC compiler assumes that stack frame slots can be addressed cheaply, so this situation could be improved with more sophisticated compiler stack management. For example, common subexpression elimination on stack addresses, or biasing the stack and frame pointers to increase addressability could be used by a compiler to reduce the D16 addressability problem for large stack frames.

3.4 Combined Effects

In doubling the instruction size from sixteen to thirty-two bits, static code size does not double. The compiler is able to exploit larger immediate fields and offsets for memory instructions, yielding a significant reduction in the static measure of the number of instructions. However, the reduction in path length is not nearly as dramatic as density measures might predict. One reason for this is that the execution time of any program is dominated by inner loops. The better a compiler is able to move expensive operations out of inner loops, the less effect these instructions have on ultimate performance. It appears that D16 programs have considerable overhead in manipulating constant operands, but the overhead instructions comprise a proportionally small part of dynamic instruc-

tion traces.

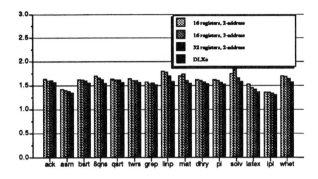

Figure 11: DLXe code density summary (D16 = 1.0).

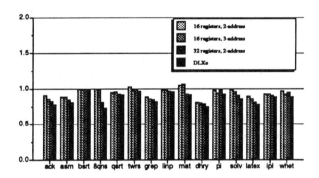

Figure 12: DLXe path length summary (D16 = 1.0).

Figures 11 and 12 summarize the density and path-length differences of all the measured instruction set features and their interactions. Each bar group shows how DLXe density and path length are affected by the corresponding instruction set feature, immediate fields, three-address instructions, a larger register file, and all three combined. Density and path length ratios averaged over all programs in the test suite are shown in Table 5. More detailed performance data is available [2].

4 Memory System Performance

On the average, D16 instructions decrease instruction traffic by about 35 percent while increasing path lengths by about 15 percent. Assessing the impact of these on total system performance requires considering latency of the instruction fetch mechanism on total cycles to execute a program.

Code Size (D16 = 1.00)		
Registers	Two-Address	Three-Address
16	1.62	1.61
32	1.57	1.52
Path Length (D16 = 1.00)		
Registers	Two-Address	Three-Address
16	.95	.94
32	.90	.87

Table 5: Summary of density and path length effects.

With instruction fetch channels of equal width, a D16 machine transfers twice as many instructions per fetch transaction as a DLXe machine. This means that the latency of each fetch is amortized over more D16 instructions, reducing the *average* latency per instruction. Figure 13 shows how performance of D16 and DLXe machines is affected as average fetch varies. Performance is expressed as Cycles Per Instruction (CPI) averaged over all programs in the benchmark suite (lower CPI indicates higher performance). For D16, both raw and *normalized* CPI are shown. Normalized CPI indicates dividing both D16 and DLXe cycle counts by the same "unit of work", in this case the DLXe path length, to make direct comparison meaningful. In this figure, fetch width refers to the unit of memory made available by each fetch request, in this case the aligned word or doubleword containing the requested item. It is assumed the processor buffers this unit and issues instructions from it until an instruction in a different memory unit is needed.

penalty, even with relatively low average latencies. The break-even point is at about .6 cycles for a 32-bit fetch channel, 1.2 cycles for 64 bits; with average latencies above these points, D16 provides superior performance. However, average latency is not a design parameter, it is a measurement of memory system performance, and it depends both on program behavior and code density. With any fixed set of memory resources, D16 instructions yield lower average latency than DLXe instructions.

The real question is whether a D16 machine, in trading increased code density for longer path length, is capable of higher performance than an equivalent DLXe machine if, for example, both are implemented with an instruction cache viable in current technology. Given equal cache hardware, do the additional DLXe miss penalty cycles exceed its path length advantage? Since cache behavior varies widely depending on cache size, organization, and individual program behavior, this question can only be answered with respect to a specific cache design and program execution. The cache design space is large, and evaluation of this question demands a thorough examination with a comprehensive set of benchmarks, which is beyond the scope of this paper.

However, the following examples offer some insight with respect to current-technology cache memory systems. Cache hit rates for the programs of the benchmark suite large enough to have interesting cache behavior, **asm**, **latex**, and **ipl** were measured with the **dinero** cache simulator [6]. The D16/DLXe path length ratios for these programs are 1.24, 1.15, and 1.26 respectively. Figures 14 and 15 give normalized CPI versus miss penalty for the three programs for separate direct-mapped instruction and data caches of 4K and 16K bytes, with double-word cache blocks.

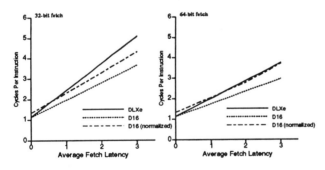

Figure 13: Average fetch latency and CPI.

Figure 13 shows that increased stalls due to latency in a DLXe machine cancel the D16 path length

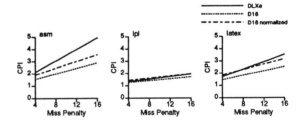

Figure 14: Performance with 4K instruction and data caches.

With 4K caches, D16 performance is superior for

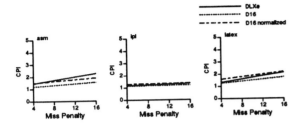

Figure 15: Performance with 16K instruction and data caches.

all three programs, though for **latex** and **ipl**, the advantage is slight. Increasing the caches to 16K allows capture of working sets of these programs in both machines, and here DLXe performs a little better than D16 on **ipl** and **latex**. While neither encoding displays a clear CPI performance advantage in all cases, it is worth noting that D16 performance is achieved with approximately 35-40 percent less cache-memory traffic. Implications of memory system performance are examined in more detail in [3].

5 Conclusions.

Results presented in this paper show that reducing instruction size for a RISC processor to sixteen bits increases code density with respect to processor with a fixed 32-bit format. This approach has measurable costs in terms of expressive power of the instructions, but measurement with optimizing compilers reveals that this sacrifice does not impact dynamic performance as much as static measurements or conventional wisdom might predict. The increased density measured for D16 program compares favorably with CISC encodings, yet the instruction set design does not sacrifice essential advantages of the RISC paradigm. Moreover, architectural trends, such as parallel-issue machines, multiprocessors, and deeply pipelined machines tend to increase rather than decrease concern over instruction traffic as a performance bottleneck.

The principal advantage of the D16 format lies in its more efficient exploitation of instruction fetch resources. It is clear that with an aggressive enough memory hierarchy design, the code density disadvantage of the 32-bit format can be somewhat mitigated, but our results indicate this is more difficult to achieve than one might expect within the technology con-

straints of today's microprocessors. In cost-critical applications such as embedded control or palmtop computers, where the cost of memory speed and capacity is a major concern, the smaller size of D16 programs and higher performance with slow memory are obvious advantages. Even for performance-driven designs where higher-speed memory systems including large caches can be justified, it is difficult to find a clear advantage for DLXe. In current implementation technology, the second-order benefits of a denser 16-bit encoding can easily exceed the path length reduction achieved with the 32-bit format.

Acknowledgments.

Justine Blackmore prototyped the architecture simulator. The assembler is a modified version of one originally written by Rick Simpson. Some of the library code, including the floating point math routines, came from public BSD sources. The linker and C compiler are ports of GNU software from the Free Software Foundation; special thanks to Richard Stallman and Richard Kenner for their invaluable advice in porting GCC. The authors are grateful to the program referees for thoughtful criticism and suggestions.

References

[1] Frances E. Allen and John Cocke. A catalogue of optimizing transformations. In Randall Rustin, editor, *Proceedings Courant Computer Science Symposium 5*. Prentice-Hall, March 1971.

[2] J. D. Bunda, D. K. Fussell, W. C. Athas, and R. M. Jenevein. 16-bit vs. 32-bit instructions for pipelined architectures. Technical Report TR 92-39, Department of Computer Sciences, The University of Texas at Austin, 1992. Available by anonymous ftp at `cs.utexas.edu`.

[3] John D. Bunda. *Instruction-Processing Optimization Techniques for VLSI Microprocessors*. PhD thesis, The University of Texas at Austin, Austin, Texas, 1993.

[4] Michael J. Flynn, Chad L. Mitchell, and Johannes M. Mulder. And now a case for more complex instruction sets. *Computer*, 20(9):71-83, September 1987.

[5] John L. Hennessy and David A. Patterson. *Computer Architecture: A Quantitative Approach*. Morgan Kaufmann Publishers, Inc., Palo Alto, CA, 1990.

[6] Mark D. Hill. Dinero cache simulator, 1992. Available at several internet sites including `max.stanford.edu`.

[7] Jerome C. Huck and Michael J. Flynn. *Analyzing Computer Architectures*. IEEE Computer Society Press, 1989.

[8] Gerry Kane. *Mips RISC Architecture*. Prentice-Hall, 1988.

[9] Chad Leland Mitchell. *Processor Architecture and Cache Performance*. PhD thesis, Stanford University, Stanford, California, 1986. Technical Report CSL-TR-86-296.

[10] David Patterson, Phil Garrison, Mark Hill, Dimitris Lioupis, Chris Nyberg, Tim Sippel, and Korbin Van Dyke. Architecture of a VLSI instruction cache for a RISC. In *Proceedings of the 10th Annual Symposium on Computer Architecture*, pages 108–116, June 1983.

[11] David A. Patterson. Reduced instruction set computers. *CACM*, 28(1), January 1985.

[12] George Radin. The 801 minicomputer. *IBM Journal of Research and Development*, 27(3):237–246, May 1983.

[13] Richard M. Stallman. *Using and Porting GCC Version 2*. Free Software Foundation, 1992.

[14] Peter Steenkiste. The impact of code density on instruction cache performance. In *Conference Proceedings of the 16th Annual International Symposium on Computer Architecture*, pages 252–259, 1989.

[15] D. E. Waldecker and P. Y. Woon. ROMP/MMU technology introduction. In *IBM RT Personal Computer Technology*, pages 44–47. IBM Corporation, 1986. SA23-1057.

[16] David W. Wall. Register windows vs. register allocation. Technical Report 87/5, Digital Western Research Laboratory, Palo Alto, CA, 1987.

Register Connection: A New Approach to Adding Registers into Instruction Set Architectures

Tokuzo Kiyohara

Scott Mahlke, William Chen, Roger Bringmann
Richard Hank, Sadun Anik, Wen-mei Hwu

Media Research Laboratory
Matsushita Electric Industrial Co., Ltd.
Kadoma-shi, Osaka, 571 Japan

Coordinated Science Laboratory
University of Illinois at Urbana-Champaign
Urbana, IL 61801

Abstract

Code optimization and scheduling for superscalar and superpipelined processors often increase the register requirement of programs. For existing instruction sets with a small to moderate number of registers, this increased register requirement can be a factor that limits the effectiveness of the compiler. In this paper, we introduce a new architectural method for adding a set of extended registers into an architecture. Using a novel concept of connection, this method allows the data stored in the extended registers to be accessed by instructions that apparently reference core registers. Furthermore, we address the technical issues involved in applying the new method to an architecture: instruction set extension, procedure call convention, context switching considerations, upward compatibility, efficient implementation, compiler support, and performance. Experimental results based on a prototype compiler and execution driven simulation show that the proposed method can significantly improve the performance of superscalar processors with a small or moderate number of registers.

1 Introduction

Designing high-performance processors often involves exploiting instruction-level parallelism (ILP). An example of such an approach, pipelining, has been widely used, and many pipelined designs are capable of executing nearly one instruction per cycle. Further performance improvement can be achieved either by executing more than one instruction per cycle, or by increasing the depth of pipelining. Superscalar and VLIW processors fetch, decode, and execute more than one instruction per cycle by providing multiple functional units and datapaths. Superpipelined processors divide the pipeline into smaller segments that have less delay, allowing the clock cycle to be shortened and more instructions to overlap with each other.

In order to assist the hardware to achieve performance objectives, compilers for superscalar, VLIW, and superpipelined processors use optimization and code scheduling techniques to exploit ILP. The code optimization techniques for these processors create additional temporary variables to eliminate data and control dependences among instructions. The code scheduling techniques reorder instructions so that instructions that are close to each other tend to be independent of each other. Both can greatly improve the effectiveness of a processor that exploits ILP. However, they also tend to increase the number of variables that are simultaneously live at each point of program execution. For instruction set architectures with small register files, such as the Intel i80X86 and the Motorola 680X0, with 8 and 16 registers respectively, these simultaneously live variables cannot be accommodated in registers. As a result, some of the variables have to be *spilled* to memory. Extra memory loads must be executed before using these spilled variables and extra stores must be executed after modifying them. Spilling tends to add to the latency of computation and consume memory access bandwidth, which reduces the effectiveness of the optimization and scheduling techniques.

A straightforward solution to a shortage of registers is to increase the number of registers in the instruction set architecture. However, major difficulties exist with this approach. In the case of designing a new instruction set, the number of bits required to select among registers may be too large for a given instruction format. For thirty two bit instruction formats, supporting more than thirty two registers imposes a strict limit on the number of bits available to opcodes and constants. For existing architectures, the sizes of the opcodes and constants are already fixed, leaving no room for indexing into an enlarged register file.

In this paper, we introduce a method referred to as *Register Connection (RC)* to add a set of *extended registers* to an architecture. We will refer to the registers in the original architecture as *core registers*. The novel aspect of the RC method is that rather than explicitly moving data between the core and the extended registers, it specifies a small set of opcodes to dynamically *connect* the register indices to a large set of registers. When a register index is connected to a register, all accesses using the register index are automatically directed to the appropriate register of the enlarged register file.

The concept of connecting registers without data movement enables an efficient implementation of our proposed method. The basic idea is to have all the processor function units directly access a enlarged register file. A translation is performed by keeping track of the connection between the addressable registers in the instruction set and the larger number of registers available in the architecture. With this translation, instructions with small register indices end up accessing the large register file before they are issued into the function units. By systematically scheduling the connect instructions, one can achieve a performance level similar to that with a large register file for an architecture with RC support.

Although the basic idea of RC is simple, there are important technical issues involved in applying RC to an instruction set. The rest of this paper is structured to address these issues. Section 2 describes the architectural support for RC. Section 3 discusses register allocation issues. Section 4 addresses upward compatibility. Section 5 reports experiments on the performance advantage of RC using a prototype compiler and execution-driven simulation. Finally, concluding remarks are offered in Section 6.

2 Architecture Support for Register Connection

2.1 Design overview

RC requires several architectural extensions to increase the number of registers in existing instruction sets. The base architecture to which these extensions are applied is a generic, pipelined, superscalar processor with an m-entry register file. A summary of the changes to the base architecture to support RC is presented in Figure 1. First, the base register file is replaced by an n-entry register file, $n > m$. The enlarged register file consists of two logical components, the core section and the extended section. The core section contains the first m registers and corresponds to the original register file of the base architecture. The extended section contains the remaining $n - m$ registers that have been added to the architecture.

The second extension is the addition of an m-entry register mapping table. The register mapping table is used to map between the m addressable registers in the instruction set and the n registers available in

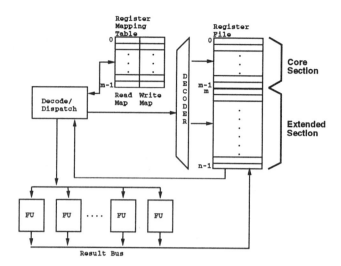

Figure 1: Superscalar processor supporting register connection.

the extended architecture. In order to provide for this mapping, register accesses in the base architecture are converted to indirect accesses through the register mapping table. Therefore, in the extended architecture, each register access consists of the following steps: a register number specified in the operand field of a machine instruction is used to index into the register mapping table. The register mapping table is then accessed to obtain the physical register number. Finally, the register file entry specified by the physical register number is accessed. The register mapping table used for RC is similar to the mapping used in the PDP-11 to map a smaller addressable memory space into a larger physical memory [1].

To make register mapping more flexible, each mapping entry contains both a read map and a write map. The read/write map specifies the physical register to be utilized when the register is specified as a source/destination register. Separate read and write maps allow more efficient use of a limited number of register mapping table entries. This flexibility becomes more important for smaller values of m in the base architecture.

The final extension is a modified decode/dispatch stage in the processor pipeline. Since registers are accessed indirectly, two accesses are required to fetch each register source operand of an instruction. First, the register mapping table is accessed to determine the physical register numbers for all registers utilized by the instruction. Second, the register file is accessed to obtain the register source operand values. A possible side effect of RC is an increased time to perform decode/dispatch. This may require an additional pipeline stage to perform decode/dispatch to prevent an increase in cycle time.

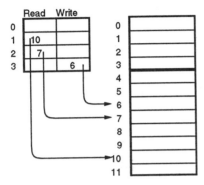

connect-use $Ri1, Rp10$
connect-use $Ri2, Rp7$
connect-def $Ri3, Rp6$
$Ri3 \leftarrow Ri1 + Ri2$

Figure 2: Connection instruction example.

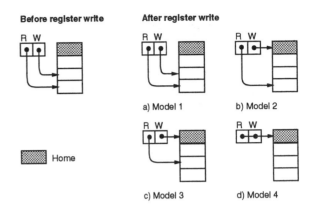

Figure 3: Four RC models. a) The register map is unchanged after a register write. b) The write map is reset to the home location after a register write. c) The write map is reset to the home location after a register write and the read map is replaced by the previous write map entry. d) Both the write and read maps are reset to the home location after a register write.

2.2 Connection instructions

To utilize the enlarged register file, two instructions referred to as *connect-use* and *connect-def* are added to the instruction set. The *connect-use* and *connect-def* instructions change the register mapping information within the register mapping table. Both instructions take two input operands: a register mapping table index Ri and a register number Rp of the physical register file. *Connect-use* inserts the register number into the read map entry referenced by the register mapping table index. All subsequent reads using Ri are redirected to Rp. Similarly, *connect-def* updates the write map entry, and redirects subsequent writes using Ri to Rp.

The functionality of *connect-use* and *connect-def* can be illustrated with the code sequence in Figure 2. The core section has only four registers and the extended section adds another eight registers. The *connect-use* and *connect-def* instructions redirect the accesses made by the add instruction to the extended section of the register file. With the redirection, the add instruction will access $Rp10$ and $Rp7$ for its input operands and deposit its results into $Rp6$.

To reduce the number of connect instructions, it is possible to combine two connects into a single instruction provided the instruction size is large enough. There are three possible combinations: *connect-use-use*, *connect-def-use*, and *connect-def-def*. By incorporating these three new multiple-connect instructions instead of *connect-use* and *connect-def*, a more compact code schedule can be obtained. [1] The function-

---

[1] For illustration purposes, the *connect-use* and *connect-def* model is used for clarity. However, for the experimental results, the *connect-use-use*, *connect-def-use*, and *connect-def-def* model is used.

ality of the multiple-connect instructions remain the same as *connect-use* and *connect-def*; however, the number of operands is four instead of two.

2.3 Alternative techniques for automatic register connection

In order to reduce the number of connect instructions, other instructions can be allowed to perform automatic register connection as a side effect. In this section, four alternative models of automatic register connection are discussed: (1) no reset, (2) write reset, (3) write reset with read update, and (4) read/write reset.

The first model provides for no automatic register connection. Therefore, the register mapping information may only be changed by explicit connect instructions. The other three models perform varying degrees of automatic register connection after an execution of a register write. In all models, only the register mapping table entry corresponding to the destination register is altered. Other strategies for automatic register connection for the source registers are possible; however, they are not considered in this paper. Figure 3 shows the updated register connection information after a register write for the four models.

Model two attempts to avoid an extra *connect-def* instruction by relocating the write map after a register write. When writing into a register pointed to by Rix, Rix_{write} (write map of Rix) is reset to Rpx (referred to as the *home location* of Rix) for subsequent writes. However, to read the written value, a subsequent *connect-use* for Rix is still required.

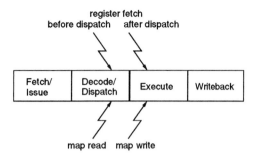

Figure 4: Example pipeline configuration with two variations.

In addition to adjusting the write map done with model two, model three also modifies the read map in an attempt to eliminate an extra *connect-use* instruction. In this model, when writing into a register pointed to by Rix, the automatic reset mechanism sets Rix_{read} to Rix_{write}, and Rix_{write} to Rpx. The automatic adjustment of connections provides the result of the execution for subsequent reads of Rix, and avoids the destruction of the data saved in Rix by subsequent writes of Rpx. Model three is chosen for implementation and performance simulation in this paper. The compiler algorithm to utilize this automatic reset model is discussed in Section 3.

Model four emphasizes the free use of the registers in the core section. When writing into a register pointed to by Rix, both the read map and the write map entries of Rix are set to Rpx. Future reads and writes of Rix are redirected to Rpx without extra connect instructions.

2.4 Zero-cycle execution latency of connect instructions

Since the RC mechanism does not require actual data movement, *connect-use* and *connect-def* can be implemented with zero-cycle execution latency. In order for these instructions to have zero-cycle latency, the implementation must allow them to affect the register accesses of instructions issued at the same cycle. This requires some forwarding logic to update the register accesses with the information contained in the connect instructions issued at the same cycle.

The forwarding that is performed varies slightly with the pipeline configuration. A simple four-stage pipeline to illustrate the necessary forwarding is shown in Figure 4 with two variations: register fetch is performed before dispatch or after dispatch. The register mapping table for both variations of this model is read late during the decode stage and updated at the beginning of the execute stage. Therefore, all connect instructions are ensured to update the register mapping table so that instructions in the next cycle can read the correct value. However, any instructions

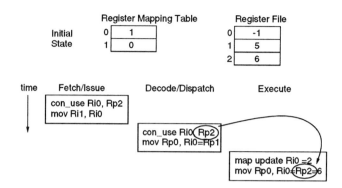

Figure 5: Example of forwarding when register fetch is performed after instruction dispatch.

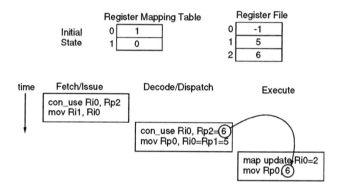

Figure 6: Example of forwarding when register fetch is performed before instruction dispatch.

which utilize connect instructions issued at the same cycle will obtain stale data from the register mapping table.

When register fetch is performed after dispatch, *connect-use* and *connect-def* must forward updated physical register numbers to other instructions during dispatch. Therefore, the correct physical registers are always either fetched during register fetch or available for writeback of the results. This forwarding is illustrated in the example shown in Figure 5. In this example, a 2-entry register mapping table and a 3-entry physical register file with the initial states shown in the figure are assumed. A *connect-use* which updates map location 0 is issued at the same time as a move instruction which utilizes map location 0 as a source operand. During decode, the move instruction reads the register mapping table, however stale data is obtained (Mapping table entry 0 contains a 1 rather than the desired value of 2). The *connect-use*, therefore, forwards the updated physical register number to the move instruction during dispatch, so the correct physical register contents are read during the execution stage.

When register fetch is performed before dispatch, the forwarding mechanism for *connect-def* instructions is not changed. However, *connect-use* instructions must forward the data value of the correct register to other instructions rather than the updated physical register numbers because register fetch has already been performed. The previous example illustrating the modified forwarding is shown in Figure 6. In the decode stage, the move instruction obtains the wrong data for $Ri0$ since map location 0 is stale. In order to properly forward the correct data to the move prior to execution, *connect-use* instructions are required to read the physical register contents which the read map is being set to. Thus in this example, *connect-use* reads the contents of $Rp2$ during the decode stage. During the dispatch stage, a simultaneous use of $Ri0$ is detected, and the correct data is forwarded from the *connect-use* to the move.

The timing constraints of these forwarding mechanisms must be addressed for any processor design. In the case of *connect-def*, there is likely sufficient time to perform to proper updates since the destination register is not required until a late stage in the pipeline. In the case of *connect-use* instructions, there is a more strict timing requirement. For this paper, it is assumed there is sufficient timing freedom prior to instruction dispatch to accommodate the necessary forwarding; however, this may not be the case for all implementations. In Section 5, the performance degradation in the case where an extra pipeline stage is required for RC support is evaluated.

2.5 Comparison with previous work

At the architecture level, the extended registers are similar to the T registers in the CRAY-1 architecture [2]. The similarity is that both techniques provide additional registers to hold more values than may be addressed in the instruction set. However, explicit data movement is necessary in the CRAY-1 architecture to utilize data in the T registers. In contrast, the RC method requires no explicit data movement to utilize data in the core and extended sections of the register file. Dynamic connection through the register mapping table is utilized to access both core and extended sections of the register file.

The register mapping table used in RC is similar to the mapping table used in the IBM RS/6000 [3]. In the RS/6000 the mapping table is utilized to perform dynamic register renaming. Each instruction accesses the mapping table to determine the appropriate physical register to access. In comparison, the RC method provides explicit instructions to modify the mapping table. Therefore, the extended registers are exposed to the code optimizer, code scheduler, and register allocator for use.

3 Register Allocation

The RC method requires a number of changes to the register allocation process [4]. The register allocator now has a much larger register file available with the addition of the extended registers. However, the decision to place a variable in a core register over an extended register depends upon the architectural model of register connection and the register allocation method chosen.

The register allocation method we chose attempts to place the most important variables into the core registers, while storing the less important variables in the extended registers or memory. This method is similar to the caller/callee save convention used in many compilers. The automatic reset RC models can naturally take advantage of this method since its reset mechanism can eliminate many connect instructions. The no-reset model treats all physical registers uniformly. However, if the number of active variables is larger than the number of mapping indices at any time, a large number of connect instructions may be required. The above allocation method automatically minimizes the number of connection instructions by maximizing the use of the core registers.

Once register allocation is complete, appropriate connect instructions must be inserted to enable instructions to access the variables allocated to extended registers. This can be accomplished by emulating the register mapping table and either selecting the index entry currently pointing to the physical register as its index or selecting the least important index as the new index. Consider the code sequence shown below that uses model three (Section 2.3). The core register file size is eight registers (R1-R8). Two variables have been allocated to extended registers, R9 and R10.

	connect_use Ri6,Rp9
1) R2 ← R2 + R9	1) Ri2 ← Ri2 + Ri6
2) R10 ← R3 + 1	*connect_def* Ri7,Rp10
3) R4 ← R10 + R5	2) Ri7 ← Ri3 + 1
	3) Ri4 ← Ri7 + Ri5

If we assume that the register maps for registers R1-R8 are currently pointing to their home locations, the code sequence requires two *connect instructions*. A *connect-use* is required prior to instruction 1 to allow reading of Rp9, in which case we use the register *read* map of Ri6. Also, the destination of instruction 2 was assigned to extended register Rp10, requiring a *connect-def* to set the register *write* map of Ri7 to Rp10. Note that a *connect-use* is not required prior to instruction 3 since the register *read* map of Ri7 is set to the register *write* map as a side affect of writing into the register. The selection of the register map entry used to access an extended register is arbitrary; however, with proper selection, the register allocator can attempt to minimize the artificial dependences introduced by these instructions and maximize the code motion opportunity available to the scheduler.

4 Upward Compatibility

One important reason for extending an architecture with the RC method instead of adding more registers to the operand fields in the instruction set, is to ensure upward compatibility with existing program binaries. On the surface, the RC method should trivially satisfy the upward compatibility requirement. Since the programs compiled for the original architecture will not contain any *connect-use* and *connect-def* instructions, all of the core registers will remain connected to their home locations throughout the program execution. The register access operations will operate as if there were no extended register file. However, there are three situations which must be addressed to completely ensure upward compatibility - subroutine calls, context switching, and trap and interrupt handling.

4.1 Subroutine calls

A typical approach to saving one of the extended registers across subroutine calls is to perform a *connect-use* to the extended register and then store the contents to memory. If the register is not subsequently reconnected to its core register, it is possible for the called subroutine to incorrectly access a register that it treats as a callee save register. For example, assume map entry 5 is connected to extended register 30 prior to the subroutine call so that it can be saved to memory. At the beginning of the called subroutine, core register 5 is saved since it is being treated as a callee-save register. Since the register is still connected to register 30, the wrong register contents are saved. Any subsequent write to register 5 will set the read map to correctly point to register 5. Prior to exiting the subroutine, register 5 must be restored from memory. Unfortunately, the contents of register 30 would be restored to register 5, introducing a possible program error.

This problem could be prevented by first performing a *connect-use* to register 5 and then saving its content. However, programs compiled for the original architecture cannot take advantage of this. It could also be prevented by requiring the calling subroutine to re-connect the core registers. In the worst case scenario, this could introduce one instruction for every core register. A more efficient solution to this problem is to make the *jsr* instruction also reset the map to point to the original core registers. The hardware to perform the reset of the register map is required by the architecture to ensure correct mapping of the core registers after power-up initialization.

A similar problem can also occur when returning from a subroutine. It is possible that a register is connected to an extended register to compute a returned value from the subroutine. Any *connect-use* instructions would be live across the subroutine return. Thus, reading a caller-save core register may actually access the extended set and introduce a program error. This problem can be eliminated by also requiring the *rts* instruction to reset the register map.

4.2 Context switches

A subtle issue of upward compatibility arises in the case of context switching. Programs compiled to use the RC extension require the connection information to be maintained across any context switch point. Therefore, core registers, extended registers and the connection information should be saved and restored. For programs compiled for the original architecture, only core registers need to be saved and restored, although saving and restoring extended registers and connection information would still result in correct operation. Therefore, there is an opportunity to avoid saving the extended registers and the connection information for programs compiled for the original architecture. This optimization would require a flag in the process status word to mark the program as either for the original architecture or for the extended architecture. The context switching routine can use this bit to choose different formats of the process context representation in the process control blocks.

4.3 Traps and Interrupts

Traps and interrupts are slightly more complicated than subroutine calls since they occur outside the control of the program. To permit access to registers, the method discussed for handling context switches can be used. However, traps and interrupts are typically used to implement time critical device drivers and perform instruction emulation. If any register is used, it must be saved and restored. However, to access the correct physical register, the map entry must also be saved, connected to the correct register and finally restored. The addition of the connect instructions could cause a severe performance penalty for device drivers that require few registers. A simple alternative to this approach is to bypass the register map for traps and interrupts. This can be accomplished by adding a register map *enable* flag to the processor status word. A trap or interrupt would disable this flag. Any subsequent register accesses would go directly to the core registers. The return from exception or interrupt condition will restore the original processor status word, which will automatically re-enable the register map.

If the trap or interrupt require more than the core registers, the register map can be re-enabled by writing to the processor status word. The register map

Instruction	Latency	Instruction	Latency
INT ALU	1	FP ALU	3
INT multiply	3	FP conversion	3
INT divide	10	FP multiply	3
branch	1/1-slot	FP divide	10
memory load	2 or 4	memory store	1

Table 1: Instruction latencies.

thus used must be saved, reset and restored prior to the return.

5 Experimental Results

5.1 Compiler support

In order to conduct meaningful experimental evaluation of the RC method, the required register allocation, code scheduling, and code generation support for RC have been implemented in the IMPACT-I compiler. All benchmark programs are compiled with full-scale classical and instruction-level parallelization code optimizations [5]. The register allocator uses a graph coloring algorithm that utilizes profile information in its priority calculations. All compiler optimizations are verified by executing the output code on a DEC-3100 workstation.

For the original architecture, the compiler generates spill code needed to access variables spilled out to memory. For the extended architecture, the compiler manages the register file through the register mapping table and generates *connect-use* and *connect-def* instructions to access variables in the register file. In addition, the compiler generates save and restore code for the registers at procedure call interfaces. The code scheduler is designed to take advantage of the zero-cycle latency of the connect instructions as illustrated in Section 2.4. For all core register file sizes, four integer registers are reserved as spill registers and one integer register is reserved for Stack Pointer.

5.2 Architecture assumptions

The instruction set used in all experiments is the MIPS R2000 instruction set extended with additional branch opcodes to allow general operand comparison and to facilitate static branch prediction. In the experiments, the size of the number of core integer registers is varied from 8 to 64, and the number of the core floating-point registers is varied from 16 to 128 to study the effect of the register file size. Double precision floating point variables use two floating point registers.

In experiments with integer benchmarks, RC support is evaluated only for the integer register file

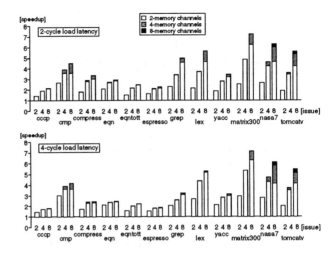

Figure 7: Speedup for processors with an unlimited number of registers, varying issue rates and memory channels.

while a fixed floating point register file of 64 entries is assumed. Conversely, for experiments with floating point benchmarks, RC support is evaluated only for the floating point register file while a fixed integer register file of 64 entries is assumed. Furthermore, in experiments with RC support, the register file is assumed to contain a total of 256 registers with the size of the core section specified in the experiment. The size of the extended section is therefore the difference between the core size and 256. In experiments without RC support, the register file contains only the specified number of core registers.

The underlying microarchitecture is assumed to have deterministic instruction latencies (see Table 1) and CRAY-1 style register interlocking [2]. Given an issue rate, all combinations of instruction patterns are allowed to be executed in parallel assuming homogeneous pipelined function units. The only exception is that memory accesses are restricted to a subset of the function units in the experiments. For 2-issue and 4-issue models, there are two memory channels and in the 8-issue model there are four memory channels.

5.3 Results

The performance of the RC mechanism is evaluated using nine integer and three floating-point benchmarks. The integer benchmarks are *cccp*, *cmp*, *compress*, *eqn*, *eqntott*, *espresso*, *grep*, *lex* and *yacc*, and the floating-point benchmarks are *matrix300*, *nasa7* and *tomcatv*. The execution time of each benchmark, assuming a 100% cache hit rate, is derived using execution-driven simulation. The base configuration for the speedup calculations is a single-issue processor with an unlimited number of registers using conventional compiler scalar optimizations.

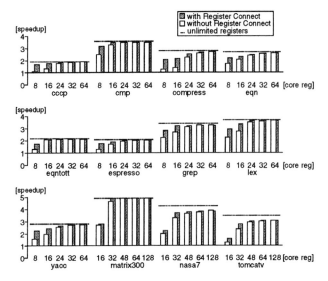

Figure 8: Speedup for a 4-issue processor with 2-cycle load latency and varying number of core registers.

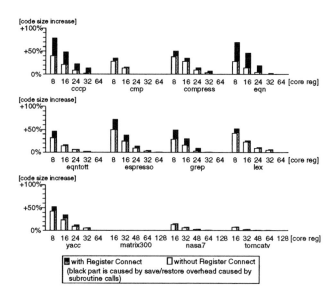

Figure 9: Percentage of code size increase due to spill code for a 4-issue processor with 2-cycle load latency and varying number of core registers.

The speedup for processors with unlimited registers, varying issue rates and memory channels is shown in Figure 7. The goal of the RC method is to approach the unlimited register performance with the combination of a small number of core registers.

Effect of the number of core registers

Figure 8 shows the benefit of the RC method for processors with varying numbers of core registers. The white bars show the speedup of the model without RC support, (referred to as the without-RC model). The shaded bars show the speedup of the model with RC support, (referred to as the with-RC model). All results in this figure assume a 4-issue processor and 2-cycle load latency. The dotted lines show the speedup of the model with the unlimited number of integer registers.

For the integer benchmarks, 32 and 64 core registers for both with-RC and without-RC models achieve almost the same performance level as the unlimited register case. The performance degradation of both models starts in the 24-register case and becomes more severe in the 16-register case. For floating-point benchmarks, performance degradation starts around 32 registers and becomes more severe for 16 registers. All benchmarks run with a small number of core registers demonstrate a large performance advantage using the with-RC model over the without-RC model.

Figure 9 presents the percentage increase of code size after register allocation. The white bars show the percentage of code size increase for the without-RC model. The shaded/black bars show the percentage increase for the with-RC model. The black part corresponds to the percentage increase caused by

save/restore of the extended registers before and after procedure calls.

As expected, with 32 and 64 core registers, the code size increase of both models for integer benchmarks is very small: approximately 10% or less. The code size expansion for both models starts with the 16 register case, which corresponds to the extra spill code or connect instructions inserted by the compiler. Although the code size increase of the with-RC model is significantly more than the without-RC model, the with-RC model achieves higher performance.

Effect of issue rate and load latency

Figures 10 and 11 illustrate the benefit of the RC method for different load latencies and instruction issue rates. The white bars show the speedup of the without-RC model with 16 core integer registers for the integer benchmarks and 32 core floating-point registers for the floating-point benchmarks. The shaded bars show the speedup of the with-RC model with the same number of registers. The dotted lines correspond to the speedup achievable using an unlimited number of registers.

The performance improvement due to the RC method is more significant for higher issue rates, especially in the 8-issue case. The RC method reduces the overhead caused by spill code. This overhead is attributed to the spill load latency and the scheduling restrictions imposed by dependences between spill registers. For higher issue rate processors, the impact of these two factors on the scheduled code and the instruction level parallelism is more significant. Fur-

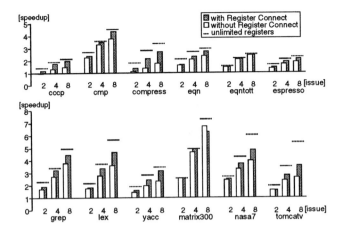

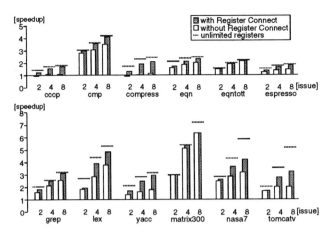

Figure 10: Speedup for 2-cycle load latency, 16 core integer registers for integer benchmarks, 32 core floating-point registers for floating-point benchmarks, and varying issue rate.

Figure 11: Speedup for 4-cycle load latency, 16 core integer registers for integer benchmarks, 32 core floating-point registers for floating-point benchmarks, and varying issue rate.

thermore, in the 8-issue case, the number of empty instruction slots at each clock cycle increases because of the limited instruction level parallelism in the benchmarks. This allows the compiler to hide the adverse effects of the code expansion due to the RC method.

The shorter load latency increases the efficiency of the spill code, so the performance improvement achieved by the RC method is less for two cycle load latency than for four cycle load latency. Nevertheless, there is sizable benefit for both latencies.

Effects of different RC implementations

Figure 12 compares the performance of four possible implementation scenarios for a 4-issue processor with 2-cycle load latency. The most efficient implementation considered is zero-cycle latency connect instructions implemented within an existing processor pipeline. The zero-cycle latency connect instruction and additional pipeline stage scenario considers adding a pipeline stage for accessing the register mapping table, and implementing forwarding to instructions issued in the same cycle. The one-cycle latency implementation of the connect instruction does not require forwarding. Similarly, the additional pipeline stage is evaluated with one-cycle latency connect instructions. The results show that there is very little performance loss when the RC method cannot be implemented within an existing pipeline with zero-cycle latency. This makes the RC method a feasible improvement even for high speed implementations.

Effect of a limited number of memory channels

The number of memory channels can greatly affect the processor implementation cost. Figure 13 shows the

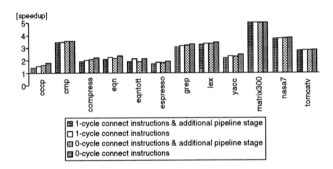

Figure 12: Speedup for an 4-issue processor, 2-cycle load latency, 16 core integer registers for integer benchmarks, 32 core floating-point registers for floating-point benchmarks, and varying architecture support and pipeline implementation.

effect of increasing the the number of memory channels from two to four for a 4-issue processor with 2 and 4-cycle load latency. The white bars show the speedup of the without-RC model and the shaded bars show the speedup of the with-RC model for two memory channels. The upper solid bars show the additional gain in speedup by increasing the memory channels to four for the without-RC model. The dotted lines show the speedup with an unlimited number of registers and two memory channels.

Figure 13 shows that for a 4-issue processor, the benefit of increasing the number of memory channels from two to four is much less than the benefit of implementing the RC method for two memory channels. This demonstrates that the RC method improves performance not only by reducing the frequency of memory accesses but also by providing a more efficient mechanism.

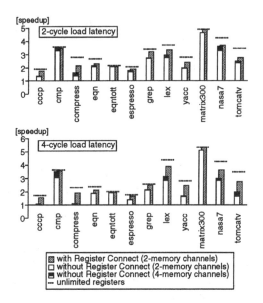

Figure 13: Speedup, varying the number of memory channels and register rename channels, for 4-issue processor with 2 and 4-cycle load latency.

6 Conclusion

The effectiveness of compilers for superscalar and superpipelined processors can be limited by the size of the register files in existing architectures. In this paper, we have introduced the Register Connection (RC) method to add a large number of registers into an architecture. We have shown that the RC method does not require any change to the format of existing instructions. It allows the compiler to take advantage of a large register file which can be conveniently accessed through a small register mapping table. We have also addressed the issues regarding procedure calls and context switches. Overall, the RC method can be added to an existing architecture in an upward compatible manner.

An implementation of the RC method has been described. By overlapping the execution of the connect instructions with the instruction dispatch logic in superscalar processors, one can achieve zero-cycle effective execution latency for the connect instructions. As a result, the connect instructions can affect the immediate subsequent instructions issued in the same clock cycle. This makes it extremely inexpensive for instructions to access the extended register file.

Experimental evaluation shows that the RC method improves the performance of superscalar processors with 16 or fewer core registers. The performance improvement increases with the issue rate. A four-issue processor with 16 core integer registers and 240 extended registers, and a 2 cycle load latency can achieve 90% of the performance of an equivalent

processor with an unlimited number of core registers. This performance result shows that the RC method is a very promising technique to extend existing instruction set architectures for high performance superscalar implementation. As new code parallelization methods become available, we expect that the RC method will become beneficial for architectures with 32 or more registers.

Acknowledgements

The authors would to thank John Gyllenhaal and Grant Haab, along with all members of the IMPACT research group for their comments and suggestions. Special thanks to the anonymous referees whose comments and suggestions helped to improve the quality of this paper significantly. This research has been supported by JSEP under Contract N00014-90-J-1270, Dr. Lee Hoevel at NCR, the AMD 29K Advanced Processor Development Division, Matsushita Electric Industrial Co. Ltd., Hewlett-Packard, and NASA under Contract NASA NAG 1-613 in cooperation with ICLASS. Scott Mahlke is also supported by fellowship provided by Intel Foundation.

References

[1] Digital Equipment Corporation, Marlboro, Massachusetts, *Microcomputers and Memories*, 1982.

[2] R. M. Russell, "The Cray-1 computer system," *Communications of the ACM*, vol. 21, pp. 63–72, January 1978.

[3] G. F. Grohoski, "Machine organization of the IBM RISC System/6000 processor," *IBM Journal of Research and Development*, vol. 34, pp. 37–58, January 1990.

[4] G. J. Chaitin, "Register allocation and spilling via graph coloring," in *Proceedings of the ACM SIGPLAN 82 Symposium on Compiler Construction*, pp. 98–105, June 1982.

[5] W. Hwu, S. Mahlke, W. Chen, P. Chang, N. Warter, R. Bringmann, R. Ouellete, R. Hank, T. Kiyohara, G. Haab, J. Holm, and D. Lavery, "The superblock: An effective technique for VLIW and superscalar compilation," *The Journal of Supercomputing*, January 1993.

A Comparison of Dynamic Branch Predictors that use Two Levels of Branch History

Tse–Yu Yeh and Yale N. Patt
Department of Electrical Engineering and Computer Science
The University of Michigan
Ann Arbor, Michigan 48109-2122

Abstract

Recent attention to speculative execution as a mechanism for increasing performance of single instruction streams has demanded substantially better branch prediction than what has been previously available. We [1, 2] and Pan, So, and Rahmeh [4] have both proposed variations of the same aggressive dynamic branch predictor for handling those needs. We call the basic model Two-Level Adaptive Branch Prediction; Pan, So, and Rahmeh call it Correlation Branch Prediction. In this paper, we adopt the terminology of [2] and show that there are really nine variations of the same basic model. We compare the nine variations with respect to the amount of history information kept. We study the effects of different branch history lengths and pattern history table configurations. Finally, we evaluate the cost effectiveness of the nine variations.

1 Introduction

With the current movement toward deeper pipelines and wider issue rates, extremely high branch prediction accuracy becomes critical because a larger amount of speculative work needs to be thrown away after a branch misprediction. To improve branch prediction, several authors have suggested basing predictions on two levels of branch history information.

Lee and Smith [7] proposed collecting these two levels of history information statically. We [1] introduced the idea of dynamically collecting two levels of branch history, branch execution history and pattern history, to achieve substantially higher accuracy than any other scheme reported in the literature. We call our algorithm *Two-level Adaptive Branch Prediction*. Our predictor adjusts its prediction according to the behavior of the branch instructions at run-time. The first-level branch execution history is the history of the last k branches encountered. The second-level pattern history is the branch behavior for the last j occurrences of the specific pattern of these k branches. Prediction is based on the branch behavior for the last j occurrences of the current branch history pattern. The first-level branch execution history and the second-level pattern history are collected at run-time, eliminating the disadvantages inherent in Lee and Smith's method, that is, the differences in the branch behavior of the profiling data set and the run-time data sets.

In [2] we described three variations of Two-level Adaptive Branch Prediction, differentiating them by the manner in which the first-level of branch history information is kept (G, for global, or P, for per-address) and the manner in which the second-level pattern history tables are associated with this history information (g, for global, or p, for per-address). We suggested that history information can be kept in a single global register, or in separate per-address registers for each address that contains a branch instruction. We further suggested that a single global pattern table could contain the second-level history information, or each address that contains a branch instruction could contain its own second-level per-address pattern table. We identified the three schemes as GAg, PAg, and PAp and showed that PAg is the most cost-effective variation.

Pan, So and Rahmeh [4] proposed a model they called *Correlation Branch Prediction*, because the prediction of a branch depends on the history of other branches. In the terminology introduced in [2], this would be called GAp. They also introduced another variation, which we could label GAs, where the addresses that contain branch instructions are partitioned into subsets, each subset sharing the same second-level pattern table.

This paper describes and characterizes possible variations of the Two-Level Adaptive Branch Prediction model according to the manner in which the first-level branch history information is kept (G, S, or P) and the manner in which the second-level pattern history tables are associated with this history information (g, s, or p). The variation S means addresses that contain branch instructions are partitioned into sets, each set sharing the same first-level branch history register. This yields nine variations of the model: GAg, GAs, GAp, PAg, PAs, PAp, SAg, SAs, and SAp. They are summarized, along with the reference to where they were first introduced, in Table 1.

Variation & Reference		Description
GAg	[2]	Global Adaptive Branch Prediction using one global pattern history table.
GAs	[4]	Global Adaptive Branch Prediction using per-set pattern history tables.
GAp	[4]	Global Adaptive Branch Prediction using per-address pattern history tables.
PAg	[1]	Per-address Adaptive Branch Prediction using one global pattern history table.
PAs	-	Per-address Adaptive Branch Prediction using per-set pattern history tables.
PAp	[2]	Per-address Adaptive Branch Prediction using per-address pattern history tables.
SAg	-	Per-Set Adaptive Branch Prediction using one global pattern history table.
SAs	-	Per-Set Adaptive Branch Prediction using per-set pattern history tables.
SAp	-	Per-Set Adaptive Branch Prediction using per-address pattern history tables.

Table 1: The Nine Variations of Two-Level Adaptive Branch Prediction

In this paper, we focus on comparing the prediction accuracies of the nine variations of Two-Level Adaptive Branch Prediction by using trace-driven simulations of nine of the ten SPEC89 benchmarks [1]. These variations are studied with respect to various history register lengths, branch history table configurations, and implementation costs.

This paper is organized in five sections. Section 2 describes in brief Two-Level Adaptive Branch Prediction and its nine variations. Section 3 discusses the simulation model and traces used in this study. Section 4 reports the simulation results and our analysis. Section 5 contains some concluding remarks.

---

[1] The Nasa7 benchmark was not simulated because this benchmark consists of seven independent loops. It takes too long to simulate the branch behavior of these seven kernels, so we omitted these loops.

2 Two-Level Adaptive Branch Prediction and Its Variations

2.1 Concept Summary

Two-Level Adaptive Branch Prediction uses two levels of branch history information to make predictions. The first level is the history of the last k branches encountered. We call the structure which keeps the history of the last k branches encountered the branch history register (BHR). Depending on which variation of the model we implement, the last k branches can mean the actual last k branches encountered (G), the last k occurrences of the same branch instruction (P), or the last k occurrences of the branch instructions from the same set (S). If several BHRs are used to keep branch history, the collection of BHRs is called the branch history table (BHT). If a branch is taken, then the branch history register records a "1"; if it is not taken, the branch history register records a "0".

The second level of the predictor records the branch behavior for the last j occurrences of the specific pattern of the k branches. Prediction is based on the branch behavior for the last j occurrences of the history pattern in question by using an automaton. Our previous study [2] has shown that a 2-bit counter is the most effective automaton among four-state automata. Since the history register has k bits, at most 2^k different patterns appear in the history register. Each of these 2^k patterns has a corresponding entry in what we have called the pattern history table (PHT).

Both branch history and pattern history are updated dynamically When the prediction of a branch is made, the contents of its history register are recorded. After the branch is resolved, the result is used to update the entry indexed by the previously-recorded branch history register contents. The branch history register, on the other hand, is updated with the prediction right after the prediction is made. Since it usually takes several cycles to resolve a branch, updating the branch history speculatively allows the prediction to be made with up-to-date branch history. When an incorrect branch prediction is made, the branch history register should be restored with correct branch history. More details of the Two-Level Adaptive Branch Predictors are contained in [2] and [4].

2.2 Variations

The nine variations of Two-Level Adaptive Branch Prediction (Table 1) can be classified into three classes according to the way the first-level branch history is collected. These three classes are shown in Figures 1, 2, and 3. They are characterized as follows:

Global History Schemes

In the global history schemes (shown in Figure 1) (also called Correlation Branch Prediction by Pan *et al.* [4]), the first-level branch history means the actual last k branches encountered; therefore, only a single global history register (GHR) is used. The global history register is updated with the results from all the branches. Since the global history register is used by all branch predictions, not only the history of a branch but also the history of other branches influence the prediction of the branch.

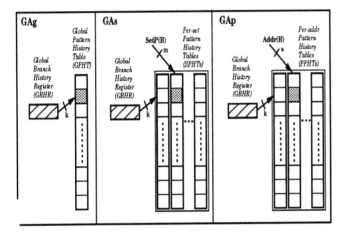

Figure 1: The three variations of global history Two-Level Adaptive Branch Prediction.

Per-address History Schemes

In the per-address history schemes (shown in Figure 2), the first-level branch history refers to the last k occurrences of the same branch instruction; therefore, one history register is associated with each static conditional branch to distinguish the branch history information of each branch. One such history register is called a per-address history register (PBHR). The per-address history registers are contained in a per-address branch history table (PBHT) in which each entry is indexed by the static branch instruction address. In these schemes, only the execution history of the branch itself has an effect on its prediction; therefore, the branch prediction is independent of other branches' execution history.

Per-set History Schemes

In the Per-set history schemes (shown in Figure 3), the first-level branch history means the last k occurrences of the branch instructions from the same subset; therefore, one history register is associated with a

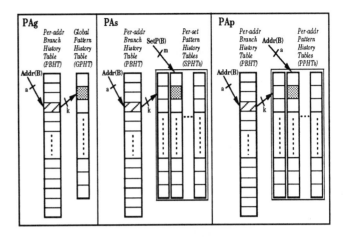

Figure 2: The three variations of per-address history Two-Level Adaptive Branch Prediction.

set of conditional branches. One such history register is called a per-set history register. The set attribute of a branch can be determined by the branch opcode, branch class assigned by a compiler, or branch address. Since the per-set history register is updated with history possibly from all the branches in the same set, the prediction of a branch is influenced by other branches in the same set.

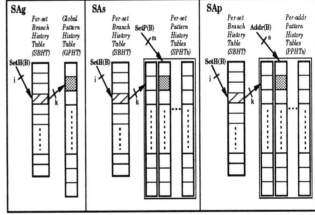

Figure 3: The three variations of per-set history Two-Level Adaptive Branch Prediction.

For each of the above classes, there are three variations when it is further classified by the association of the pattern history tables with branches. The association of the pattern history tables can be one pattern table for each branch (called per-address pattern history table (PPHT)), one pattern table for all the branches (called global pattern history table(GPHT)), or one pattern table for a set of branches (called per-set pattern history table (SPHT)). Indexing into the multiple pattern history tables is done by using the low-order bits of the branch address, branch opcode, or the branch class passed from a compiler.

3 Simulation Methodology

3.1 Description of Traces

Nine benchmarks from the original SPEC89 benchmark suite are used in this branch prediction study. Table 2 lists the benchmark programs, their abbreviations, and testing data sets used in our simulations. These nine programs were compiled using the Green Hills FORTRAN 1.8.5 compiler or the Diab Data C Rel. 2.4 compiler with all optimizations turned on. The integer benchmarks include *eqntott*, *espresso*, *gcc*, and *li*. Since integer programs tend to have a higher branch frequency, each integer program was simulated for twenty million conditional branches or until the program completed execution. The floating point benchmarks include *doduc*, *fpppp*, *matrix300*, *spice2g6*, and *tomcatv*, each one of which was simulated for one hundred million instructions.

Benchmark & Abbreviation		Testing Data Set	Number of Dynamic Conditional Branches
eqntott	eqn	int_pri_3.eqn	20,000,000
espresso	esp	bca	20,000,000
gcc	gcc	dbxout.i	7,326,688
li	li	li-input.lsp	20,000,000
doduc	dod	doducin	7,717,746
fpppp	fpp	natoms	1,139,093
matrix300	mat	Built-in	3,451,457
spice2g6	spi	greycode.in	10,976,668
tomcatv	tom	Built-in	2,926,569

Table 2: Benchmark programs and their data sets.

3.2 Simulation Configurations and Assumptions

Trace-driven simulations were used in this study. A Motorola 88100 instruction level simulator generated instruction traces, which were used as inputs to a branch prediction simulator. The branch prediction simulator decoded instructions, predicted branches, and compared the predictions to the actual outcome to collect statistics of branch prediction accuracy.

A total of nine variations of the Two-Level Adaptive Branch Prediction were simulated with the following methodology:

- Each branch is distinguished by its address. The branch address is used to select a branch history register (BHR) in a branch history table (BHT) and to choose a pattern history table (PHT) in per-address or per-set pattern history tables.

- For GAs and PAs schemes, the low-order bits of the branch address are used as indices to map adjacent branches into different PHTs, so PHT contention is minimized. The low-order bits of the branch address are also used as the index of a BHR in a BHT of limited size to minimize the branch history conflicts between branches.

- For per-set history schemes, we use the branch address to classify branches into sets. The branches in a block of 1K bytes (256 instructions) are members of the same set. Four set history registers are used in our simulations, so that the set index is taken from bits <11:10> of a branch address. These four instruction blocks cover only 4K bytes; therefore, branches from different sets may share the same history register. The index to a pattern table ($SetP(B)$ in Figure 3) is a combination of the set index and the low-order bits of the branch address. We also tried classifying branches by opcode; however, the prediction accuracy is lower than using the branch address.

- Every scheme is configured with a branch history table for storing the instruction fetch addresses [3] of both conditional and unconditional branches. The branch history table is accessed by using the low-order bits of the branch address. For per-address history schemes, each branch history table entry also records branch history. Unless otherwise stated, the default configuration of the branch history table is 1024-entry, 4-way set-associative. The replacement policy of the branch history table is least-recently-used (LRU).

- Two-bit up-down counters are used in all the pattern history table entries for keeping second-level pattern history.

- A pattern history table entry is updated with the information from the trace right after a prediction is made with no delay because the exact branch resolution time is not known in our branch prediction simulator. However, we have shown that various reasonable pipeline delays in the pattern history update have negligible effects on prediction accuracy in [3].

- For the per-address history schemes, a backward taken, forward not-taken scheme is used for making predictions on branch history table misses.

We simplified the hardware cost estimate functions described in [2] and expanded them to all the variations of Two-Level Adaptive Branch Prediction. These functions do not consider the costs for target address fields in the branch history table because all the variations need those fields to store fetch addresses.

Scheme Name	History Register Length	Number of Pattern History Tables	Simplified Hardware Cost
GAg(k)	k	1	$k + 2^k \times 2$
GAs(k,p)	k	p	$k + p \times 2^k \times 2$
GAp(k)	k	b	$k + b \times 2^k \times 2$
PAg(k)	k	1	$b \times k + 2^k \times 2$
PAs(k,p)	k	p	$b \times k + p \times 2^k \times 2$
PAp(k)	k	b	$b \times k + b \times 2^k \times 2$
SAg(k)	k	s×1	$s \times k + s \times 2^k \times 2$
SAs(k,s×p)	k	s×p	$s \times k + s \times p \times 2^k \times 2$
SAp(k)	k	s×b	$s \times k + s \times b \times 2^k \times 2$

b is the number of entries in the BHT and s is the number of branch sets.

Table 3: Conditional branch predictor configurations and their estimated costs.

3.3 Performance Metric

In this paper we use prediction accuracy as the metric to evaluate the performance of branch predictors. The prediction accuracy is the percentage of correctly-predicted conditional branches. The pipeline delays of correct branch predictions on BHT misses are different from the pipeline delays of correct branch predictions on BHT hits. Therefore, prediction accuracy is shown in two major categories: BHT hits and BHT misses. When the branch prediction is correct on a BHT hit, no delay is incurred in instruction fetch after the predicted fetch address is fetched from the BHT. On a BHT miss, even if the conditional branch prediction is correct, the instruction fetch mechanism needs time to decode the branch instruction in order to have the next fetch address if the branch is taken. If the branch is not taken, a prefetch of the next sequential address is assumed. Therefore, there is no penalty for a correctly-predicted fall-through branch on a BHT miss.

When a prediction is incorrect, the processor discards the instructions which are fetched after the branch. Details of the instruction fetch mechanism are contained in [3].

The translation from prediction accuracy to machine performance is not direct [5]. However, higher prediction accuracy means machine pipelines stall less frequently for incorrect branch predictions.

4 Simulation Results

To evaluate the performance of the nine variations of Two-Level Adaptive Branch Prediction schemes, we first study the effects of the branch history length and the number of pattern history tables on their prediction accuracy. Secondly, we show the cost effectiveness of the variations of each class of schemes. Finally, from the schemes with implementation costs of about 8K and about 128K bits, we choose one configuration from each class of the schemes for comparison.

4.1 Effects of Branch History Register Length and Number of Pattern History Tables

4.1.1 Global History Schemes

Figure 4 shows the average prediction accuracy of integer (int) and floating point (fp) programs by using global history schemes with branch history lengths ranging from 2 to 18 bits. Each curve shows the prediction accuracy for a different number of pattern history tables (PHTs). These curves are cut off when the implementation cost exceeds 512K bits.

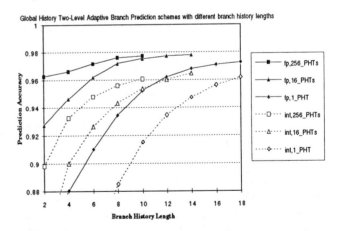

Figure 4: Global history schemes with different branch history lengths.

The performance of the global history schemes is sensitive to the branch history length. This can be seen from the rising trend of the curves. Using one pattern history table, the prediction accuracy of integer programs is still rising when an 18-bit branch history register is used. The prediction accuracy increases about 25 percent by lengthening the branch history from 2 bits to 18 bits. Even when 16 PHTs are used, the prediction accuracy increases over 10 percent by lengthening the history register from 2 bits to 14 bits. When 256 PHTs are used, the prediction accuracy increases over 6 percent from 90 percent to about 96 percent. The prediction accuracy of floating point programs does not increase as much as integer programs, but is still significant.

Figure 5 shows the average prediction accuracy of integer and floating point programs by using global history schemes with the number of pattern history tables ranging from 1 to 1024. Each curve shows the prediction accuracy for a different branch history length.

The performance of the global history schemes is also sensitive to the number of pattern history tables. As the branch history becomes longer, the increase in the number of pattern history tables results in a smaller increase in accuracy.

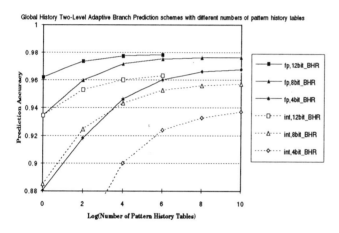

Figure 5: Global history schemes with different number of pattern history tables.

When the global branch history is used, the pattern history of different branches interfere with each other if they map to the same pattern history table. Together, Figures 4 and 5 show that prediction accuracy increases significantly by increasing either the branch history length or the number of pattern history tables. The reasons are that lengthening the global branch history register increases the probability that the history which the current branch depends on remains in the history register, and decreases the possibility of pattern history interference because longer branch history is used. Similarly, adding pattern history tables reduces the possibility of pattern history interference by mapping interfering branches into different tables.

4.1.2 Per-address History Schemes

Figure 6 shows the average prediction accuracy of integer and floating point programs by using per-address history schemes with branch history lengths ranging from 2 to 18 bits. Each curve shows the prediction accuracy for a different number of pattern history tables (PHTs). These curves are cut off when the pattern history table cost exceeds 512K bits.

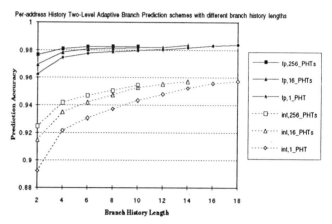

Figure 6: Per-address history schemes with different branch history lengths.

The prediction accuracy of per-address history schemes is not as sensitive to the branch history length as global history schemes. When one pattern history table is used, the average integer prediction accuracy increase is about 6 percent (89.2 percent to 95.7 percent) compared to 25 percent for global history schemes (72.4 percent to 96.1 percent). The curves of average floating point prediction accuracy for per-address history schemes are nearly flat when the branch history length is larger than 6-bit.

Comparing the asymptotic prediction accuracy in Figures 4 and 6, we see that the global history schemes have higher asymptotic averages than the per-address history schemes for integer programs while the per-address history schemes have higher asymptotic average than the global history schemes for floating point programs. This phenomenon is due to the large number of if-then-else statements in integer programs which depend more on the results of adjacent branches; therefore, the global history schemes perform well. The floating point programs, on the other hand, contain more loop-control branches which exhibit periodic branch behavior. This periodic branch behavior is better retained in multiple BHRs, so those branches are more predictable for the per-address history schemes.

Figure 7 shows the average prediction accuracy of integer and floating point programs by using per-address history schemes with the number of pattern history tables ranging from 1 to 1024. Each curve shows the prediction accuracy for a different branch history length.

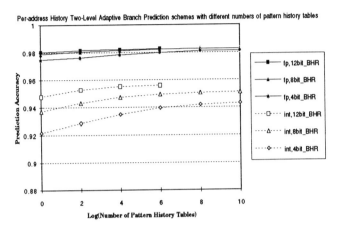

Figure 7: Per-address history schemes with different number of pattern history tables.

When the per-address branch history is used, the pattern history of different branches interfere less with each other when they map to the same pattern history table. As seen from Figure 7, attempting to reduce pattern history interference by increasing the number of pattern history tables results in only a small increase in prediction accuracy. Increasing the branch history length, on the other hand, is more effective in improving the average integer prediction accuracy but not the average floating point prediction accuracy.

4.1.3 Per-set History Schemes

Figure 8 shows the average prediction accuracy of integer and floating point programs by using per-set history schemes with branch history lengths ranging from 2 to 16 bits. Each curve shows the prediction accuracy for a different number of pattern history tables (PHTs). These curves are cut off when the cost of pattern history tables exceeds 512K bits.

By increasing the history register length, the average integer prediction accuracy increases significantly, similar to the behavior of global history schemes. However, the average floating point prediction accuracy does not improve significantly when 4×16 or 4×256 PHTs are used, similar to the behavior of per-address history schemes. The similarity in the behavior of per-address and per-set history schemes is due to the partitioning of branches into sets according to

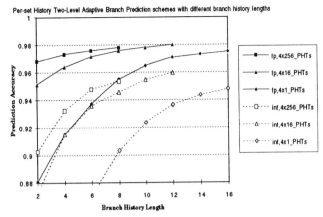

Figure 8: Per-set history schemes with different branch history lengths.

their addresses. The prediction of a branch is dependent on adjacent branches, as in global history schemes. However, the branches involved in the prediction of a branch is limited to the address space a set spans. The instruction block a set covers contains few branches in floating point programs because of their large basic block sizes; therefore, per-set history schemes become similar to per-address history schemes.

Figure 9 shows the average prediction accuracy of integer and floating point programs by using per-set history schemes with the number of pattern history tables in each set ranging from 1 to 1024. Each curve shows the prediction accuracy for a different branch history length.

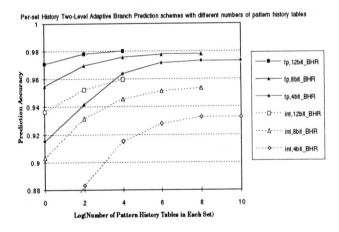

Figure 9: Per-set history schemes with different number of pattern history tables.

The performance improvement of per-set history schemes are less sensitive to the increase in the number of pattern history tables than the global history schemes. However, it is more sensitive than the per-address history schemes. Since branches of the same set use their own pattern history tables to reduce pattern history interference, increasing the number of pattern history tables is not as effective.

4.2 Cost Effectiveness

4.2.1 Three Classes of Schemes

Figures 10, 11, and 12 illustrate the cost effectiveness of the three classes of Two-Level Adaptive Branch Prediction. Each curve shows the total average prediction accuracy for a different pattern history table implementation cost. The pattern history table implementation cost (in bits) of the schemes on each curve is labelled in the legend. On each curve, as the number of pattern history tables doubles, the branch history length is decremented by one bit. To calculate the total cost of a branch predictor, in addition to the pattern history table cost, a global history scheme needs to add the cost of a global history register, a per-address history scheme needs to add the cost of a branch history table, and a per-set history scheme needs to add the cost of a per-set branch history table.

The per-address history schemes are effective with low implementation costs. Their average prediction accuracy is over 96 percent with 2K bits, about 97 percent with 32K bits, and over 97 percent with 128K bits. The prediction accuracy increases about 1 percent at a cost of an extra 126K bits. On each curve, the average prediction accuracy decreases as the number of pattern history tables increases, which shows that the increasing the number of pattern history tables is less beneficial than increasing the branch history

length. The knee is a branch history length of 4 bits.

The global history schemes require high implementation costs to be effective. Their best average prediction accuracy is only 94.5 percent with 2K bits but over 97 percent with 128K bits. The prediction accuracy increases about 2.5 percent at a cost of an extra 126K bits. By comparing the best prediction accuracy achieved with 512K bits, the global history schemes achieve a higher asymptote than the per-address history schemes. On each curve, as the number of pattern history tables increases, the average prediction accuracy initially increases due to the fact that increasing the number of pattern history tables reduces pattern history interference between branches. As the number of pattern history tables continues to increase, the average prediction accuracy levels off, then decreases because the accuracy gained by increasing the number of pattern history tables is more than offset by the accuracy lost by decreasing the branch history length.

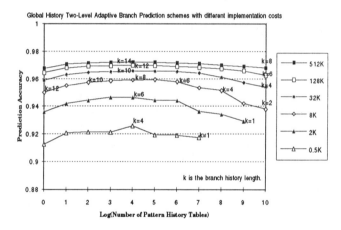

Figure 11: Global history schemes with different implementation costs.

The curves of Per-set history schemes show the same trend as those of global history schemes. However, with the same implementation cost, the per-set history schemes achieve lower prediction accuracy than the global history schemes.

4.2.2 Comparison

Figure 13 compares the cost effectiveness of the three classes of Two-Level Adaptive Branch Prediction given a fixed hardware budget of 8K bits for the costs of both branch history registers and pattern history tables. Each bar graph shows the contributions to prediction accuracy made under four situations: a miss in the BHT which results in the conditional

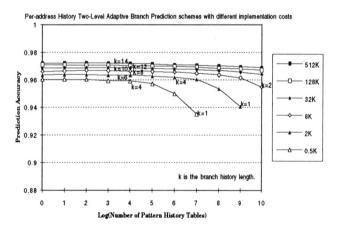

Figure 10: Per-address history schemes with different implementation costs.

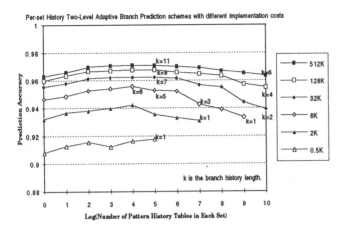

Figure 12: Per-set history schemes with different implementation costs.

branch fall-through (BHT_{miss}, CBR_{ft}), a miss in the BHT which results in the conditional branch taken (BHT_{miss}, CBR_{tk}), a hit in the BHT which results in the conditional branch fall-through (BHT_{hit}, CBR_{ft}), and a hit in the BHT which results in the conditional branch taken (BHT_{hit}, CBR_{tk}).

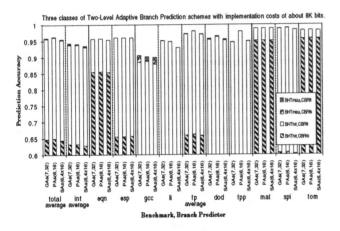

Figure 13: Comparison of the most effective configuration of each class of Two-Level Adaptive Branch Prediction with an implementation cost of 8K bits.

The most cost-effective configuration is chosen from each class. For global history schemes, the most cost-effective configuration is GAs(7,32). For per-address history schemes, the most cost-effective one is PAs(6,16). For per-set history schemes, the most cost-effective one is SAs(6,4×16). All three chosen schemes were simulated with a 1024-entry, 4-way set-associative branch history table.

PAs(6,16) achieves the highest average prediction accuracy among these three configurations. It outper-

forms the other two configurations on all the benchmarks except for *gcc* and *li*. On *gcc* it suffers from low prediction accuracy on BHT misses; however, it performs better than GAs(7,32) on BHT hits. On *li* it performs almost as well as GAs(7,32). GAs(7,32) achieves the second among these three schemes because of its low prediction accuracy of floating point programs. SAs(6,4×16) is the worst with prediction accuracy about 0.8 percent lower than that of PAs(6,16).

Figure 14 compares the cost effectiveness of the three classes of Two-Level Adaptive Branch Prediction given a higher hardware budget of 128K bits for the costs of both branch history registers and pattern history tables. For global history schemes, the most cost-effective configuration is GAs(13,32). For per-address history schemes, the most cost-effective one is PAs(8,256). For per-set history schemes, the most cost-effective one is SAs(9,4×32). All three chosen schemes were also simulated with a 1024-entry, 4-way set-associative branch history table.

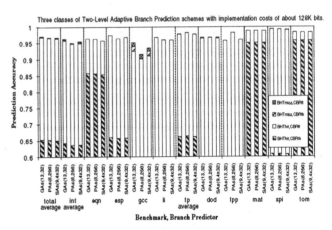

Figure 14: Comparison of the most effective configuration of each class of Two-Level Adaptive Branch Prediction with an implementation cost of 128K bits.

GAs(13,32) achieves the highest prediction accuracy among these three configurations. GAs(13,32) gains the most increase on *gcc* by increasing the history register length at a cost of an extra 120K bits. The increase is substantially better than that gained by PAs(8,256). PAs(8,256) gains little accuracy improvement with the extra bits, whereas SAs(9,4×32) improves its performance to do almost as well as PAs(8,256).

5 Concluding Remarks

We have characterized the global, per-address, and per-set history schemes (GAg, GAs, GAp, PAg, PAs, PAp, SAg, SAs, SAp) and compared them with respect to their branch prediction performance and cost effectiveness.

Global history schemes perform better than other schemes on integer programs but require higher implementation costs to be effective overall. Integer programs contain many if-then-else statements. Global history schemes make effective predictions for if-then-else branches due to their correlation with previous branches. On the other hand, when the global history is used, the pattern history of different branches interfere with each other if they map to the same pattern history table. Therefore, global history schemes require long branch history and/or many pattern history tables to reduce the interference for effective overall performance.

Per-address history schemes perform better than other schemes on floating point programs and require lower implementation costs to be effective overall. Floating point programs contain many frequently-executed loop-control branches which exhibit periodic branch behavior. This periodic behavior is better retained with a per-address branch history table. When the per-address branch history is used, the pattern history of different branches tend to interfere less with each other; therefore, fewer pattern history tables are needed.

Per-set history schemes have performance similar to global history schemes on integer programs; they also have performance similar to per-address history schemes on floating point programs. To be effective, however, per-set history schemes require even higher implementation costs than global history schemes due to the separate pattern history tables of each set.

With respect to the cost-effectiveness of different variations, PAs is the most cost effective among low-cost schemes. If, for example, 8K bits are available to implement the branch predictor, PAs(6,16) outperforms the other variations with an average prediction accuracy of 96.3 percent. However, on *gcc*, GAs(7,32) performs better because the backward taken, forward not-taken default on branch history table misses used in the PAs scheme is not effective. Among high-cost schemes, GAs is the most cost effective. If 128K bits are available to implement the branch predictor, GAs(13,32) achieves the best average prediction accuracy of 97.2 percent.

Acknowledgement

This paper is one result of our ongoing research in high performance computer implementation at the University of Michigan. The support of our industrial partners: Intel, Motorola, NCR, Hal, Hewlett-Packard, and Scientific and Engineering Software is greatly appreciated. In addition, we wish to gratefully acknowledge the other members of our HPS research group for the stimulating environment they provide, and in particular, for their comments and suggestions on this work. We are particularly grateful to Intel and Motorola for technical and financial support, and to NCR for the gift of an NCR 3550, which is a very useful compute server in much of our work.

References

[1] T-Y Yeh and Y.N. Patt, "Two-Level Adaptive Branch Prediction", *Proceedings of the 24th Annual ACM/IEEE International Symposium and Workshop on Microarchitecture*, (Nov. 1991), pp. 51-61.

[2] T-Y Yeh and Y.N. Patt "Alternative Implementations of Two-Level Adaptive Branch Prediction," *Proceedings of the 19th International Symposium on Computer Architecture*, (May. 1992), pp. 124-134.

[3] T-Y Yeh and Y.N. Patt "A Comprehensive Instruction Fetch Mechanism for a Processor Supporting Speculative Execution," *Proceedings of the 25th Annual ACM/IEEE International Symposium on Computer Microarchitecture*, (Dec. 1992), pp. 129-139.

[4] S-T Pan, K. So, and J.T. Rahmeh, "Improving the Accuracy of Dynamic Branch Prediction Using Branch Correlation," *Proceedings of the 5th International Conference on Architectural Support for Programming Languages and Operating Systems*, (Oct. 1992), pp. 76-84.

[5] J.A. Fisher and S.M. Freudenberger, "Predicting Conditional Branch Directions From Previous Runs of a Program," *Proceedings of the 5th International Conference on Architectural Support for Programming Languages and Operating Systems*, (Oct. 1992), pp. 85-95.

[6] J.E. Smith, "A Study of Branch Prediction Strategies", *Proceedings of the 8th International Symposium on Computer Architecture*, (May. 1981), pp.135-148.

[7] J. Lee and A. J. Smith, "Branch Prediction Strategies and Branch Target Buffer Design", *IEEE Computer*, (January 1984), pp.6-22.

SESSION 12:
Multiprocessor Memory Systems

The Performance of Cache-Coherent Ring-based Multiprocessors

Luiz André Barroso and Michel Dubois
barroso@paris.usc.edu; dubois@paris.usc.edu

Department of Electrical Engineering - Systems
University of Southern California
Los Angeles, CA 90089-2562

Abstract

Advances in circuit and integration technology are continuously boosting the speed of microprocessors. One of the main challenges presented by such developments is the effective use of powerful microprocessors in shared memory multiprocessor configurations. We believe that the interconnection problem is not solved even for small scale shared memory multiprocessors, since the speed of shared buses is unlikely to keep up with the bandwidth requirements of new microprocessors. In this paper we evaluate the performance of the unidirectional slotted ring interconnection for small to medium scale shared memory systems, using a hybrid methodology of analytical models and trace-driven simulations. We evaluate both snooping and directory-based coherence protocols for the ring and compare it to high performance split transaction buses.

1.0 Introduction and motivations

In the last decade, parallel processing has become the consensus approach to high-performance computing. Virtually all of today's high-performance machines are shared memory or distributed memory multiprocessors, ranging from a few tens to thousands of processors. Even though much of the research in interconnection networks today aims at connecting thousands of processing elements — the massively parallel processing (MPP) trend — the problem of building interconnections for smaller scale shared memory multiprocessors is still not solved. As new and faster processors are made available each year, it becomes clear that shared buses, the most popular technology for current commercial systems, cannot cope with state-of-the-art RISC microprocessors, such as Digital's 21064 Alpha [8] with a peak performance of 400 MIPS.

Bus bandwidth is not likely to increase at the same pace as processor and circuit technology improves. The major reasons for the poor technological scalability of bus interconnections are severe problems related to the bus topology itself. First of all, the bus is a mutually exclusive resource and only one processor can transmit at any given time. Second, all processors must participate in an arbitration phase before accessing the bus. Third, the bus clock cycle must be long enough so that signals can propagate throughout the entire extension of the bus. Lastly, a transmitter on the bus drives several receivers at the same time, each receiver adding to the characteristic impedance of the bus and reducing the signal propagation speed. Increasing the bus width to transfer more data per bus cycle is an attractive option. However, bus width is constrained by limited pin count and crosstalk interference, and little performance is gained from bus widths surpassing the size of the average data block.

In the past few years, point-to-point unidirectional connections have emerged as a very promising interconnection technology. Point-to-point connection links have only one transmitter and one receiver (one at each end) and can be very short depending on the packaging. Their characteristic impedance is very small and, if they are terminated properly, the transmission speed is much higher than on buses. Additionally, signals can be pipelined: A new transmission can be started on a point-to-point link before the previous one has reached the receiver. Therefore the clocking speed and the throughput are not limited by wire length. Overall, point-to-point connections are much more technologically scalable than bus connections, and we can expect their delivered bandwidth to benefit continuously from improvements in circuit technology. The potential of point-to-point communications is demonstrated by the IEEE Scalable Coherent Interface (SCI) [12] set of standards, based on 500 MHz 16-bit wide links in its first generation of circuits.

This research was supported by the National Science Foundation under Grant No. CCR-9115725. Luiz Barroso is supported by CAPES/MEC, Brazil, Grant No. 1547/89-2.

In this paper we evaluate the unidirectional slotted ring as an alternative to buses for cache-based multiprocessor systems with up to 64 processors and in the context of multitasking. The slotted ring architecture is described in the next section. Section 3 briefly explains a snooping cache coherence protocol first proposed in [1] as well as a directory-based protocol, both for the slotted ring architecture. Quantitative evaluations of the two protocols are shown in section 4, after which the performance of the slotted ring is compared to that of high-end split transaction buses. Related work is discussed in section 5. Final remarks and conclusions are drawn in section 6.

2.0 The slotted ring

The unidirectional ring is the simplest form of point-to-point interconnection. In particular, the unidirectional ring requires the simplest routing mechanism possible: The only routing decision is whether to remove a message from the ring or to forward it to the next node. Store-and-forward is avoided, communication delays are shorter and the raw bandwidth provided by point-to-point links is better utilized. Point-to-point connections are becoming so fast that the board logic will eventually become a performance bottleneck, and therefore simple and fast routing mechanisms are critical.

The general architecture of the unidirectional ring is shown in Figure 1, and consists of a set of processing elements with a CPU, a local cache memory, a fraction of the shared memory space and a ring interface. The data path on the ring interface consists of one input link, a set of latches, and one output link. At each ring clock cycle the contents of a latch are copied to the following latch so that the interconnection behaves as a circular pipeline. The main function of the latches is to hold an incoming message in order to determine whether to forward it or not. The number of latches in each interface should be kept as small as possible so to reduce the latency of messages.

Figure 1: The unidirectional ring interconnect

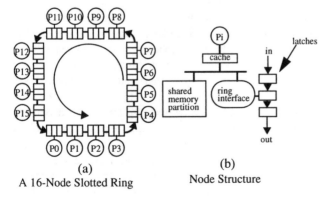

(a)
A 16-Node Slotted Ring

(b)
Node Structure

The ring access control mechanism, which dictates

when a node can send a message, is complicated by the fact that messages can be larger than the width of the data path (latches and links), and may span multiple pipeline stages. Furthermore, messages can have different sizes. In a cache-coherent system there are at least two types of messages, which we call *probe messages* (or probes) and *block messages*. Probes are short messages carrying miss or invalidation requests, and consisting typically of a block address field and other control/routing information. Block messages are made up of a header and a cache block, and are needed for misses and write-backs; the header format is similar to that of a probe.

To avoid breaking messages into packets, the protocol must transmit messages in consecutive pipeline stages and consecutive empty stages must be freed to fit a particular message. There are three main solutions to this problem: token passing rings, register insertion rings and slotted rings. In token passing rings, a special bit pattern, called token, is passed on from node to node and the node with the token is allowed to transmit. The main disadvantage of token passing is that only one message may travel on the ring at a time. In the register insertion approach, chosen for the SCI standard, a bypass FIFO between the input and output stages of the ring interface buffers incoming messages while the local processor is transmitting. When the transmission is completed, the contents of the FIFO are forwarded to the output link and the local processor is not allowed to transmit until the FIFO is emptied. Finally, in the slotted ring, the ring bandwidth is divided into marked message slots with different sizes and a processor ready to transmit a message waits for an empty slot with the same size as the message. The slotted ring restricts the utilization of the ring bandwidth because the mix of message slots is pre-determined. To limit the impact on performance, the mix of slots must match the expected mix of messages.

Which one of slotted or register insertion rings offers the best performance is not clear. Intuitively, under light loads, the register insertion ring has a faster access time since a message does not wait for a proper slot to pass by. Under medium to heavy loads, the simplicity of enforcing fairness on the slotted ring may yield better performance. The delay of transmitting a message in the register insertion ring can vary significantly depending on the activity of other nodes in the message path. A slotted ring interface is also simpler because it does not require a bypass buffer. We chose the slotted ring in our evaluations mainly for its simplicity, but also because it can support both snooping and directory-based protocols. Snooping is not suited for a register insertion ring. An implementation of snooping on a token ring is presented by Delp and others in [7].

3.0 Coherence protocols for the slotted ring

3.1 A snooping protocol

In contrast to other point-to-point interconnections [5,6], the unidirectional slotted ring allows efficient snooping implementations due to its similar cost for broadcasting and for unicasting. Snooping protocols require less state information at the memory modules and arguably are less complex than directory-based protocols.

The snooping cache coherence protocol for the slotted ring, introduced in [1], is a write-invalidate write-back protocol, logically similar to an ownership-based snooping protocol for a split transaction bus. Three cache states, *Invalid* (INV), *Read-Shared* (RS), and *Write-Exclusive* (WE), indicate whether the block is not present in the cache, present in read-only mode, or present in read-write mode respectively. The node to which the address of a cache block maps is called the *home* node of that block. The node which has a WE copy of a block is called the *dirty* node. A *dirty bit* per block in memory indicates when a block is cached in WE state. When the dirty bit is set, the dirty node is the owner and is responsible for responding to coherence requests, whereas, when the dirty bit is reset, the home node responds. Miss and invalidation[1] requests are broadcasted through the ring in probe slots. Probes are inserted and removed by the requester and are "snooped" as they pass through each node in the system. Only the owner acknowledges a probe message. Coherence actions at the snooper are consistent with typical write-invalidate protocols.

The most important feature of this snooping protocol is that no coherence transaction traverses the ring more than once because probes are snooped on without being removed from the ring; the owner simply acknowledges a probe in an acknowledgment field in the following probe slot of the same type. The latency of misses is independent of the relative positions of the requesting node and the owner. Therefore, the slotted ring with a snooping protocol behaves as a uniform memory access (UMA) interconnect, just like a shared bus.

3.2 A directory-based protocol

The full map directory-based protocol has the same cache states as the snooping protocol. The home node knows whether the block is dirty, and which nodes currently have valid copies by maintaining one set of presence bits (one per node in the system) and one dirty bit

---

1. The difference between a write miss and an invalidation is that an invalidation is issued when the node already has a RS copy of the block and it is only requesting permission to write.

per block in a directory [5]. All coherence requests are first sent to the home node, which looks up the directory entry for the block and takes the appropriate coherence actions.

Remote read misses on clean blocks take only one trip around the ring, since they involve the requester and the home node only. Whenever the home node is not the owner, the request is forwarded to the dirty node; if the dirty node is on the path between the requester and the home, one extra trip around the ring is needed, as shown in Figure 2.b. For each write miss and each invalidation for blocks that are cached RS elsewhere, the home node must send a multicast invalidation and wait for the reply before responding; this case also requires one extra ring traversal.

**Figure 2: Read miss on a dirty block:
(a) snooping; (b) directory**

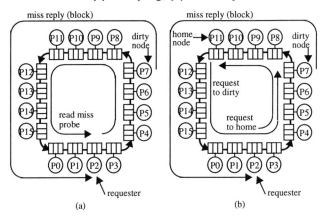

(a)   (b)

We have chosen a full map directory rather than other directory organizations such as limited directory [6] or linked list [12] to compare the snooping scheme with the most efficient directory protocol. Whereas linked-list and limited directory protocols save memory and reduce directory contention especially in large scale systems, they are not likely to outperform full map directories in the context of the slotted ring.

In a linked list protocol such as the one adopted by SCI [12], each blockframe in a cache has one or more pointer fields linking all nodes with cached copies of a block in a *sharing list*. The home node keeps a pointer to the head of the sharing list (the *head* node), which is responsible for maintaining the coherence of the block. Each miss request to a cached block is first transferred to the home node, which then forwards the request to the head node; this transaction requires one or two ring traversals, depending on the relative positions of the requester, the home and the head. Invalidating the sharing list also takes extra ring traversals when the order of the nodes in the sharing list conflicts with the direction of the ring. In the worst case, it may take n traversals to invalidate a block shared by n nodes. Table 1 compares the distribution of remote misses and invalidations requiring 1, 2 and 3 or more ring traversals in the linked list and full map directory protocols and for three 16 processor benchmarks (see Section 4.1.)

Table 1: Distribution of the number of ring traversals full directory vs. linked list (values in %)

Ring Traversals	MP3D 16				WATER 16				CHOLESKY 16			
	Miss		Invalidate		Miss		Invalidate		Miss		Invalidate	
	full	l.list	full	l.list	full	l.list	full	l.list	full	l.list	full	l.list
1	70.5	67.0	12.6	7.1	72.4	53.5	12.6	7.2	84.5	66.5	17.1	5.2
2	29.5	32.0	87.4	87.7	27.6	45.9	87.4	88.6	15.5	31.5	82.9	75.5
3 or more	0.0	1.0	0.0	5.2	0.0	0.6	0.0	4.2	0.0	1.8	0.0	19.3

3.3 Discussion

The performance differences between the snooping and the directory protocols are very dependent on the application sharing patterns. If an application has very little read-write sharing of blocks, the vast majority of misses to shared data are misses on clean blocks, and most invalidations find the block uncached elsewhere. In this case the latencies for the full map and the snooping protocols are similar; the full map protocol also generates less traffic than the snooping protocol since the probes are not broadcasted and it might outperform snooping because of the reduced contention. On the other hand, in applications with a fair amount of read-write block sharing, the coherence transactions in the directory protocol may experience significantly non-uniform and higher latencies. This non-uniformity of latencies cannot be easily avoided by intelligent placement of data or scheduling of processes, as shown Figure 2.b: if processors *P2* and *P7* share a block in read-write mode, the configuration depicted always occurs for either *P2* or *P7*, no matter where the home node of the block is located (unless it is *P2* or *P7*).

Snooping implementations have harder real-time constraints than non-snooping implementations, since the snooper must react to all remote memory operations issued in the system. With today's point-to-point connection speeds of up to 500 MHz, the snooper hardware cannot respond at the maximum rate of incoming probes (which, by the way, makes register insertion rings unsuitable for snooping protocols.) The slotted ring access control mechanism proposed in [1] overcomes this problem. In this scheme, probe slots on the ring are separated by a minimum number of clock cycles by interleaving them with other types of slots, forming *frames*. A frame is composed of one probe slot for even-address blocks, one probe slot for odd-address blocks, and one block slot. If the dual directory in the ring interface is 2-way interleaved, two consecutive probes for the same dual-directory bank are always separated by at least one frame, which is no less than 20 nsec. for a 32-bit wide ring using a 16-byte cache

block size and clocked at 500 MHz (2 nsec.).

The mix of 2 probe slots per block slot is optimum in the snooping protocol because the numbers of probes and of block messages generated in actual simulations are approximately the same, and probes traverse the whole ring whereas block messages are removed by the destination and travel through half the ring on the average. The optimum mix of probe and block slots is not as predictable for the directory scheme, because transactions do not always commit in a single ring traversal. We also chose a mix of 2 probe slots for each block slot for the directory protocol since this was the mix showing the best performance in our simulations.

4.0 Performance evaluation

Our performance evaluation methodology is a hybrid one relying on both trace-driven simulations and analytical models [6,14]. Very detailed trace-driven simulations of a limited number of configurations are first performed to gain better understanding of the interactions between the programs and the architectures. Then simple analytic models are formulated to capture the essential performance characteristics. The input parameters for the models are derived from simulations, and the outcome of each model is validated by simulations. We used an approximate iterative methodology similar to Menasce and Barroso's [14] for the analytical models. In this methodology, an estimate of the average latencies of memory requests is used to calculate an estimate of the program execution time, which in turn is used to estimate new values for the average latencies, iterating until convergence. A detailed description of the models can be found in [2], along with validation results.

This hybrid approach gives us the accuracy expected from detailed simulations as well as the efficiency of analytical models to explore the design space. Each run of our trace-driven simulations takes an average of 6-8 CPU hours to complete on a Sun SparcStation2, generating only one point in the design space for each benchmark whereas the analytical models typically take less than a second of CPU time to produce a complete curve.

All the evaluations reported in this section are performed by first simulating each benchmark for each value of network bandwidth and with 50 MIPS processors; the simulations generate parameter values describing the average behavior of each system, including a count of each type of relevant coherence events. These values are then applied to the analytical models to generate all the curves. All model predictions fall within 15% of the simulated values for latencies, and within 5% for processor and network utilizations.

4.1 Benchmarks

The models and simulations are driven by two sets of benchmarks. The first set is a group of three programs from the Stanford SPLASH benchmark suite [18]: MP3D, WATER and CHOLESKY. These programs were traced using the CacheMire simulator [3] developed by Per Stenstrom's group at Lund University, Sweden, and traces were obtained for systems with 8, 16 and 32 processors. Traces for the second set of benchmarks were obtained from Anant Agarwal's group at MIT [6], and are 64-processor traces of three parallel FORTRAN programs: FFT, WEATHER and SIMPLE. These are all well-known scientific benchmarks and the reader is referred to [18] and [6] for insight into the structure of the programs.

Table 2: Trace characteristics (references in millions)

benchmark	proc	data refs	instr. refs.	private data references	shared data references	total miss rate	shared miss rate
MP3D	8	3.76	7.51	2.48(22% w)	1.27(33% w)	3.29%	9.44%
	16	3.94	8.23	2.50(22% w)	1.43(30% w)	4.54%	12.17%
	32	4.64	11.16	2.51(22% w)	2.08(21% w)	16.55%	35.74%
WATER	8	11.05	25.89	9.54(18% w)	1.50(7% w)	0.21%	1.38%
	16	11.36	27.15	9.55(18% w)	1.81(6% w)	0.32%	1.82%
	32	11.60	28.12	9.56(18% w)	2.03(6% w)	0.73%	3.82%
CHOLESKY	8	6.97	15.00	5.29(21% w)	1.62(14% w)	2.88%	10.61%
	16	8.91	21.26	6.27(20% w)	2.55(9% w)	6.12%	18.96%
	32	13.75	37.84	8.21(18% w)	5.33(5% w)	19.47%	46.71%
FFT	64	4.31	3.12	3.28(27% w)	1.03(50% w)	6.85%	26.12%
WEATHER	64	15.63	13.64	13.11(16% w)	2.52(19% w)	5.25%	30.78%
SIMPLE	64	14.02	11.59	9.94(35% w)	4.07(11% w)	15.97%	54.16%

The main characteristics of the traces derived from each benchmark are shown in Table 2. The miss rate values are derived with 128 Kbytes direct-mapped data caches and a block size of 16 bytes. We further assume that instruction references never miss in order to reduce the simulation times. This assumption does not impact the results since the actual hit rate in the instruction cache is extremely high. The analysis also assumes that a processor blocks on all misses and invalidations and that the time to access a local memory bank is fixed at 140 nsec. for all systems. These assumptions remain fixed throughout the rest of the paper. The simulations of the ring and bus systems were developed using the CSIM package [17] which is a library of C functions for process-oriented simulation.

4.2 Snooping vs. directory for the slotted ring

The comparison between the snooping and the directory-based protocols for the slotted ring is shown in Figures 3 to 5. Processor utilization[2], average ring slot utilization and average miss latency are displayed for systems with 8, 16 and 32 processors for the SPLASH benchmarks, and for systems with 64 processors for the remaining benchmarks. The clock rate of the ring is fixed at 500 MHz (2 nsec.), the links are 32-bit wide, and the processor cycle time varies from 1 to 20 nanoseconds. The processors execute each instruction in one cycle as long as accesses hit in the cache. Hence, a processor cycle of 20 nsec. means 50 MIPS of processing power.

Using 16-byte blocks, a frame composed of two probe slots and one block slot occupies 10 pipeline stages. With a minimum of 3 stages per node, the number of stages in the ring is 24 for an 8-node system. Six extra stages are added to accomodate an integer number of frames (3). As a result, the pure round-trip latency for an 8-node 500 MHz ring is 60 nsec. Figure 5 shows the distribution of the latencies of remote misses for the directory protocol. *1-cycle clean misses* are misses to clean blocks mapping to a remote home and taking one ring traversal; *1-cycle dirty misses* are misses to dirty blocks which also require one ring traversal because of the fortunate relative position of the dirty node with respect to the requester and the home node; *2-cycle misses* are the remaining shared misses taking two ring traversals. The latency of 1-cycle dirty misses is higher than that of 1-cycle clean misses since they need three hops to commit instead of two. For MP3D, WATER and CHOLESKY, the fraction of 1-cycle clean misses increases steadily as the system size increases. This is a result of the random allocation of shared memory pages among the nodes. When the number of processors increases, a smaller fraction of the shared memory is allocated to each node and the fraction of clean misses which are remote goes up.

The snooping protocol outperforms the directory-based protocol for all system sizes in the case of MP3D, because the fraction of 2-cycle misses is significant in all cases. The performance gap between the two schemes is not as wide for the 32 processor system, in which the fraction of 2-cycle misses is smaller. The ring utilization levels are always higher for snooping, as expected. Nevertheless, it takes a ring utilization of over 70% — as is the case for the 32 processor systems with a processor cycle time of less than 5 nsec. — for the latency of snooping to approach the latency of the directory protocol.

For WATER, the high hit ratio hides most differences between the snooping and directory-based protocols in terms of processor and ring utilizations. The average miss latency values confirm the impact of the higher latency of 1-cycle dirty and 2-cycle misses. CHOLESKY has a smaller fraction of 1-cycle dirty and 2-cycle misses than WATER and MP3D for each system size, and the gap between the latencies of misses of the two protocols is not

---

2. Processor utilization is the fraction of time that the processor is busy, instead of waiting for misses or invalidations.

Figure 3. Snooping vs. directories; 500 MHz 32-bit rings

8 processors:
——— snooping
········ directory

16 processors:
– – – snooping
–.–.– directory

32 processors:
++++ snooping
xxxx directory

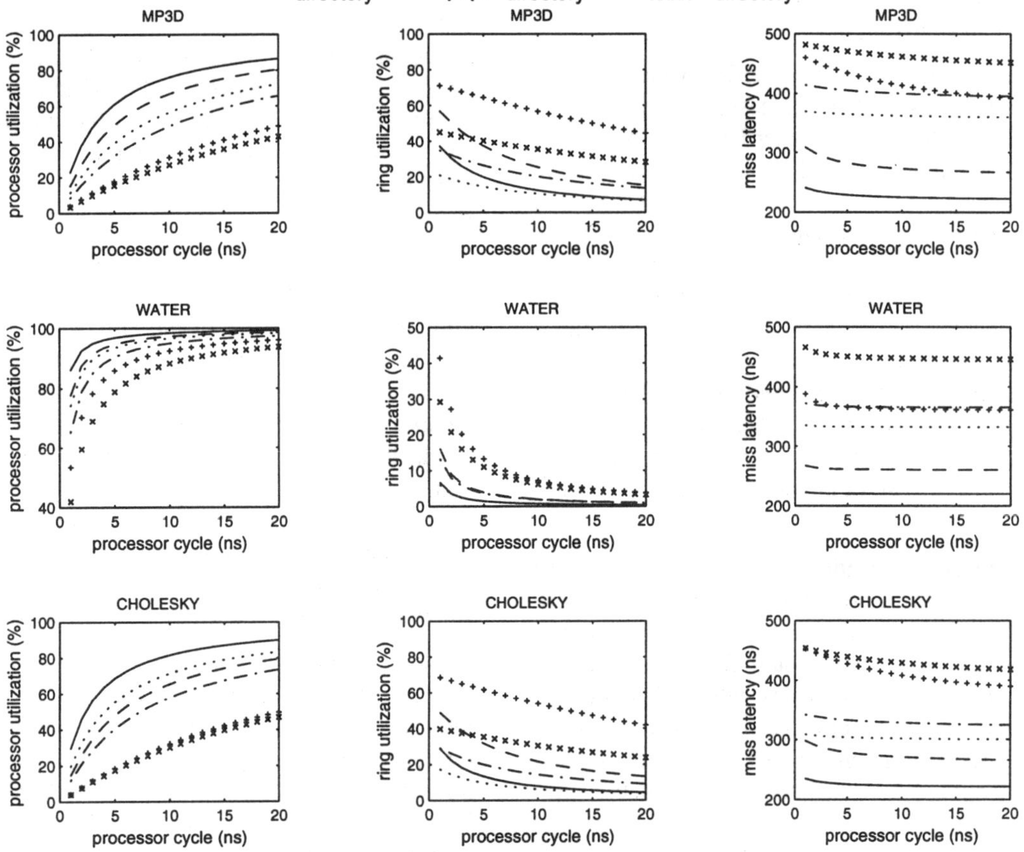

Figure 4. Snooping vs. directories; 500 MHz 32-bit rings

FFT
——— snooping
········ directory

SIMPLE
– – – snooping
–.–.– directory

WEATHER
++++ snooping
xxxx directory

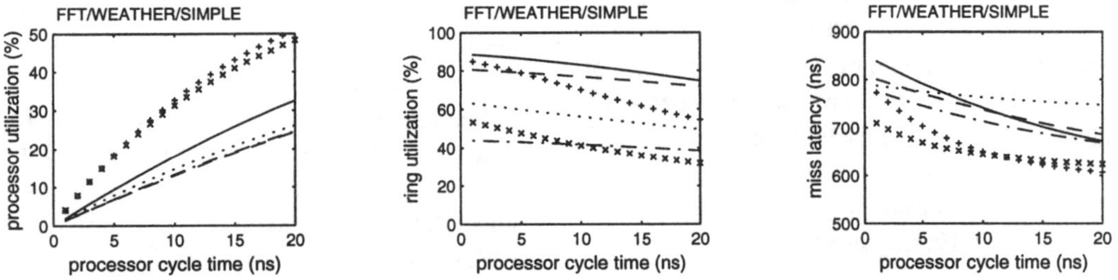

Figure 5. Breakdown of the types of misses in the directory protocol

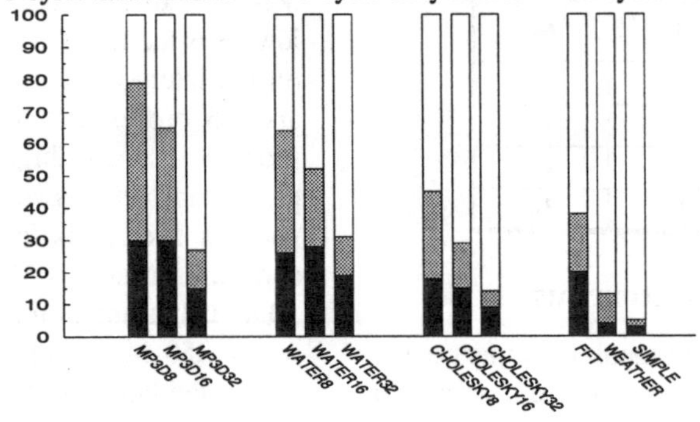

□ 1-cycle clean misses   ▨ 1-cycle dirty misses   ■ 2-cycle misses

as wide. As in MP3D, the only case where the miss latency of the directory protocol approaches the miss latency of snooping is for 32 processors, when the ring utilization for snooping is significantly higher.

For FFT, SIMPLE and WEATHER, which are 64 processor benchmarks, the processor utilization is considerably lower because of higher latencies. Again, the correlation between the mix of remote misses and the differences in performance between the two protocols is obvious. Among the three benchmarks, FFT is the only one that shows a significant number of 1-cycle dirty and 2-cycle misses; consequently, the average miss latency of the snooping protocol is shorter than for the directory-based protocol when ring utilization values are relatively low. This is in contrast with SIMPLE and WEATHER, which exhibit a very small fraction of higher latency misses. In WEATHER, as the processor cycle decreases, the latencies of snooping surpass those of directory because of network contention.

In general, for ring utilizations below 70%, the latencies of the snooping protocol are lower than for the directory protocol. Only when the ring utilization for snooping is high the average miss delays could favor the directory scheme. Our simulation experiments with a 64-bit parallel slotted ring (not shown here) agree with this assessment. With 64-bit parallel rings, utilization levels never surpass 50% and snooping performs significantly better than directory in all cases.

The snooping implementation requires faster ring interface logic, which may be more costly than for the directory protocol. Therefore, in design regions where the performance gap is not very significant, a directory implementation may be preferred. The cost of snooping is mainly affected by the minimum inter-arrival time of probes to a given dual-directory bank, which depends on the ring width, clock cycle, and cache block size. Table 3 displays the probe inter-arrival times for various ring widths and block sizes, considering a 2-way interleaved dual directory and 500 MHz ring links.

Table 3: Snooping rate (nsec.)

block size	ring data width (bits)		
	16	32	64
16 bytes	40	20	10
32 bytes	56	28	14
64 bytes	88	44	22
128 bytes	152	76	38

4.3 Slotted ring vs. split transaction bus

We now use the snooping protocol to compare the performance of the slotted ring with that of a shared split transaction bus. The bus architecture is similar to a split transaction version of the FutureBus+ (IEEE 896.x standard), with a 3-state write-invalidate snooping protocol and physical shared memory partitioned among the processing nodes. Figure 6 compares the performance of 32-bit wide rings, clocked at 250 MHz and 500 MHz, to 64-bit wide buses, clocked at 50 MHz and 100 MHz. The bus parameters were chosen to represent aggressive values considering current technology and the range of system sizes.

The bus clock cycle is constant across system sizes, which is somewhat optimistic because of the electrical limitations of buses mentioned previously. As a result, the pure latency to satisfy a remote miss remains constant for the bus case, whereas it increases roughly linearly with the number of nodes for the ring case. With a 16-byte cache block, the minimum number of bus cycles for a remote miss is six, excluding arbitration delays and the time to fetch the block in the remote memory or cache. The limited bandwidth of the bus makes the actual miss latency values quite sensitive to variations in the processor speed, whereas the latency values for the ring are more stable.

Note that the processor speed is only one of the factors affecting the load on the interconnect. The average miss ratio for shared data and the fraction of shared data references are also good indicators of the load on the interconnect for a given system size. MP3D has a relatively high miss ratio for shared data (see Table 2), and also has a significant fraction of shared data accesses. In the 8 processor MP3D the performance of the 50 MHz bus is comparable to the 250 MHz ring for slower processors ($\leq$ 50 MIPS), but it falls behind for increasingly faster processors due to bus conflicts. For the 16 processor MP3D the performance gap between ring and bus configurations increases as the buses enter saturation while the ring utilization remains under 50% even for 100 MIPS processors. In the 32 processor MP3D both buses are completely saturated, whereas the ring utilization stays under 80%. The behavior of CHOLESKY is very similar to MP3D and is not reported here for lack of space.

The evaluations using WATER show a different behavior. In this case the miss rate values are extremely low, as is the fraction of references to shared data. The load on the interconnect is much lighter than in MP3D. For 8 and 16 processors, the buses only start to saturate for processor speeds higher than 200 MIPS. Even for 32 processors, the two bus systems still show good performance levels for 100 MIPS processors. For the 16 and 32 processor configurations, the pure latencies of the 50 MHz bus and of the 100 MHz bus are shorter than those of the 250 MHz and of the 500 MHz ring (respectively); hence, the bus configurations could outperform the slotted

Figure 6. 32-bit wide slotted ring vs. 64-bit wide split transaction bus

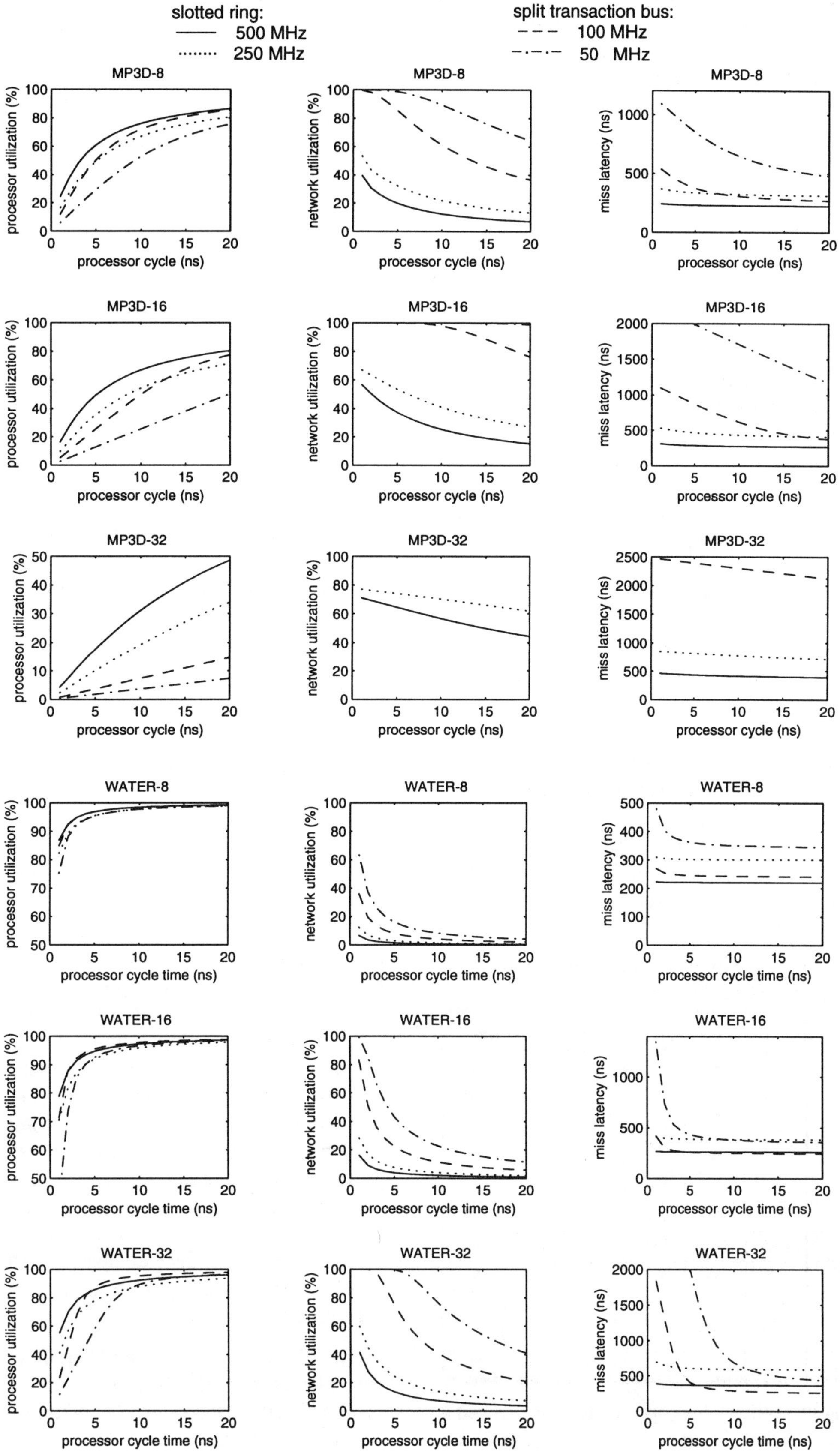

rings for slower processors even if only by a narrow margin. However, in all cases, the slotted ring is less affected by contention delays. Eventually, as the buses reach saturation, the ring configurations show far better performance figures.

For 64 processors the bus systems are completely saturated in all cases. It is also unlikely that buses for 64 processors can be clocked even at 50 MHz, using current bus technology. Therefore, we will not compare buses and rings for 64 processors.

We have applied the hybrid performance model to determine the bus clock cycle required of a 64-bit bus system to reach the same processor utilization (i.e., the same program execution time) as 32-bit slotted ring systems clocked at 250 and 500 MHz, for processor speeds of 100, 200 and 400 MIPS. These results are shown in Table 4. For systems with 8 processors, bus speeds ranging from 80 to 100 MHz are required to match the performance of a 250 MHz ring (with the exception of WATER). It takes bus clock frequencies of 100 to 170 MHz to compete with the 500 MHz ring in systems with 8 processors. For the 16 processor configurations, the range of bus cycles matching the performance of a 500 MHz ring becomes even more challenging, falling between 150 to 300 MHz. For 32 processors, the bus systems to match the ring systems are probably impractical, considering that high-performance buses are more difficult to build for larger number of processors. For all the cases shown in Table 4, the utilization levels of the buses matching ring performance are significantly higher than those of the ring slots. With the exception of WATER8 and WATER16 the bus shows utilization levels above 50%, and is frequently saturated. By contrast, the slotted ring utilizations are seldom above 50%, and never over 75%.

Table 4: Bus clock cycle (nsec.) to match the performance of slotted ring configurations

Benchmarks	250 MHz Ring (MIPS)			500 MHz Ring (MIPS)		
	100	200	400	100	200	400
MP3D 8	12.5	10.3	8.9	7.8	6.6	5.6
WATER 8	19.6	19.1	17.7	10.0	10.0	9.9
CHOLESKY 8	12.8	10.6	9.0	7.6	6.6	5.7
MP3D 16	9.0	7.1	6.2	6.5	4.9	4.0
WATER 16	25.4	21.4	16.5	14.1	12.9	10.9
CHOLESKY 16	6.8	5.4	4.7	4.9	3.7	3.1
MP3D 32	3.8	3.7	3.6	2.4	2.1	2.0
WATER 32	21.4	13.9	9.2	16.2	11.0	7.3
CHOLESKY 32	3.7	3.5	3.4	2.3	2.0	1.9

Considering that today's high speed buses are clocked at 10 to 30 nsec. and that, barring any breakthrough in bus technology, these values are expected to improve rather slowly, it is likely that new bus systems with state-of-the-art microprocessors will be limited to up to 8 processors.

The evaluation results showed here also indicate that the slotted ring could benefit from latency tolerance techniques, such as lockup-free caches, weak ordering schemes [9,11] and multithreaded processors [15] because the large latencies observed for the slotted ring are, in most cases, not caused by heavy contention but by pure delays. In other words, there is latency to be tolerated despite the fact that the network is often underutilized. Since most latency tolerance techniques have the collateral effect of increasing the load on the interconnect because of the overlap of communication and computation, they can be self-defeating in an interconnect working close to saturation. This would probably happen in a split transaction bus using very fast processors. The latencies for the slotted ring however are still relatively stable and the network never saturates in the configurations that we have simulated. This indicates that the ring would be able to accommodate the increase in the load without significantly altering the expected latencies.

5.0 Related work

The performance of unidirectional ring interconnections has been the subject of extensive analysis in the context of Local Area Networks [4]. In the context of distributed systems, Delp et al proposed a token ring distributed shared memory system (Memnet [7]) with cache coherence maintained in hardware by means of a snooping-like coherence protocol. More recently Scott et al [16] have analyzed the performance of the SCI ring, which is an implementation of the register insertion access control strategy. They model the ring as a M/G/1 queue and derive the expected latency of messages with respect to network throughput, assuming an exponentially distributed arrival of messages. The authors point out that the register insertion approach suffers from fairness of access problems and may lead to the starvation of a node. The mechanism proposed by SCI to avoid starvation is shown to impact the effective throughput of the ring. By contrast, starvation of clusters in the slotted ring architecture is easily avoided by preventing a node from reusing a message slot immediately after removing a message from that slot. Our simulations show that this has no significant impact on system performance. Scott also compares a shared bus to the register insertion ring without considering the cache coherence level.

The Hector multiprocessor [19], under development at the University of Toronto, uses a hierarchy of unidirectional slotted rings. Even though the initial Hector architecture did not include hardware support for cache coherence (shared data were marked as uncachable), more recent work by Farkas at al [10] recognizes the need for it and specifies a hierarchical cache protocol based on the broadcasting of requests, as in the snooping protocol used here. Finally, the Kendall Square Research KSR1 [13] is a shared memory multiprocessor commercially available and based on a two-level hierarchy of unidirectional slotted rings with a snooping cache protocol. The implementation of snooping in the KSR1 is not as efficient as the one studied here.

6.0 Conclusion

In this paper we have evaluated a particular architecture for small to medium scale shared memory multiprocessor systems: the unidirectional slotted ring. A comparative analysis of two cache coherence strategies, snooping and directories, for the slotted ring was performed with a hybrid methodology incorporating detailed trace-driven simulations and analytical models. Contrary to common wisdom, the snooping strategy outperforms the directory-based strategy for nearly all system configurations analyzed. The differences in performance between the two protocols can be explained from the particular data sharing patterns of each benchmark.

We have also compared the performance of the slotted ring with that of a split transaction bus under snooping. The results show that, even for systems with as little as 8 processors, the slotted ring can outperform a pipelined split-transaction bus for benchmarks with a significant fraction of remote misses and invalidations. Whereas the speed of bus interconnections is expected to lag further and further behind with respect to microprocessors, we expect the speed of ring interconnections to keep up with future generations of microprocessors.

7.0 References

[1] L. Barroso and M. Dubois, "Cache Coherence on a Slotted Ring", Proceedings of the 1991 International Conf. on Parallel Processing, Vol. I, pp. 230-237, August 1991.

[2] L. Barroso and M. Dubois, "The Performance of Cache-Coherent Ring-based Multiprocessors", University of Southern California, Technical Report No. CENG 92-19, November 1992.

[3] M. Brorsson, F. Dahlgren, H. Nilsson and P. Stenström, "The CacheMire Test Bench - A Flexible and Efficient Approach for Simulation of Multiprocessors", Proceedings of the 26th Annual Simulation Symposium, March 1993.

[4] L. Bhuyan, D. Ghosal, and Q. Yang, "Approximate Analysis of Single and Multiple Ring Networks", IEEE Trans. on Computers, Vol. 38, No. 7, pp. 1027-1040, July 1989.

[5] L. Censier, and P. Feautrier, "A New Solution to Coherence Problems in Multicache Systems", IEEE Trans. on Computers, C-27(12), pp. 1112-1118, December 1978.

[6] D. Chaiken, C. Fields, K. Kurihara and A. Agarwal, "Directory-Based Cache Coherence in Large Scale Multiprocessors", IEEE Computer, Vol. 23, No. 6, pp. 49-59, June 1990.

[7] G. Delp, D. Farber, R. Minnich, J. Smith and M-C. Tam, "Memory as a Network Abstraction", IEEE Network Magazine, pp. 34-41, July 1991.

[8] Digital Equipment Corp., "Alpha Architecture Handbook", DEC, Massachussets, February 1992.

[9] M. Dubois and C. Scheurich, "Memory Access Dependencies in Shared Memory Multiprocessors", IEEE Trans. on Software Eng., 16(6), pp. 660-674, June 1990.

[10] K. Farkas, Z. Vranesic and M. Stumm, "Cache Consistency in Hierarchical Ring-Based Multiprocessors", Proceedings of Supercomputing'92, November 1992.

[11] A. Gupta, J. Hennessy, K. Gharachorloo, T. Mowry and W.D. Weber, "Comparative Evaluation of Latency Reducing and Tolerating Techniques", Proceedings of the 18th Intl. Symp. on Computer Architecture, May 1991.

[12] D. Gustavson, "The Scalable Coherent Interface and Related Standards Projects", IEEE Micro, Vol. 12, No. 1, February 1992.

[13] Kendall Square Research, "Technical Summary", Walthan, Massachusetts, 1992.

[14] D. Menasce, and L. Barroso, "A Methodology for Performance Evaluation of Parallel Applications in Multiprocessors", Journal of Parallel and Distributed Computing, January 1992.

[15] R. Saavedra-Berrera, D. Culler and T. von Eicken, "Analysis of Multithreaded Architecture for Parallel Computing", 2nd Annual ACM Symp. on Parallel Algorithms and Architectures, Greece, July 1990.

[16] S. Scott, J. Goodman and M. Vernon, "Performance of the SCI Ring", Proceedings of the 19th Intl. Symp. on Computer Architecture, June 1985.

[17] H. Schwetman, "CSIM: A C-Based, Process-Oriented Simulation Language", Proceedings of the 1986 Winter Simulation Conference, pp. 387-396, 1986.

[18] J. Singh, W-D. Weber and A. Gupta, "SPLASH: Stanford Parallel Applications for Shared Memory", SIGArch Computer Arch. News, Vol. 20, No. 1, March 1992.

[19] Z. Vranesic, M. Stumm, D. Lewis and R. White, "Hector: A Hierarchically Structured Shared Memory Multiprocessor", IEEE Computer, Vol. 24, No. 1, pp. 72-78, January 1991.

Limitations of Cache Prefetching on a Bus-Based Multiprocessor

Dean M. Tullsen and Susan J. Eggers
Department of Computer Science and Engineering FR-35
University of Washington
Seattle WA 98195

Abstract

Compiler-directed cache prefetching has the potential to hide much of the high memory latency seen by current and future high-performance processors. However, prefetching is not without costs, particularly on a multiprocessor. Prefetching can negatively affect bus utilization, overall cache miss rates, memory latencies and data sharing. We simulated the effects of a particular compiler-directed prefetching algorithm, running on a bus-based multiprocessor. We showed that, despite a high memory latency, this architecture is not very well-suited for prefetching. For several variations on the architecture, speedups for five parallel programs were no greater than 39%, and degradations were as high as 7%, when prefetching was added to the workload. We examined the sources of cache misses, in light of several different prefetching strategies, and pinpointed the causes of the performance changes. Invalidation misses pose a particular problem for current compiler-directed prefetchers. We applied two techniques that reduced their impact: a special prefetching heuristic tailored to write-shared data, and restructuring shared data to reduce false sharing, thus allowing traditional prefetching algorithms to work well.

1 Introduction

Several factors contribute to the increasing need for processors to tolerate high memory latencies, particularly in multiprocessor systems. Certainly the widening gap in speed between CPU's and memory increases memory latencies in uniprocessors and multiprocessors alike[8]. But the discrepancy has an added effect on memory subsystem contention in multiprocessors, lengthening the actual latency seen by CPUs, because of CPU queuing for the interconnect. Second, parallel workloads exhibit more interconnect operations,

caused by data sharing among the processors, resulting in more delays and greater memory subsystem contention. Finally, as processors and memory become more physically distributed, memory latencies necessarily increase.

Software-controlled cache prefetching is a technique that is designed to make processor speeds more tolerant of memory latency. In software-controlled cache prefetching, the CPU executes a special prefetch instruction for data that is to be loaded at some point in the near future. In the best case, the data arrives at the cache before it is needed by the CPU, and the CPU sees its load as a hit. Lockup-free caches[12, 16, 20, 22], which allow the CPU to continue execution during the prefetch, hide the prefetch latency from the CPU.

Although the need to make processors tolerant of high memory latency is much more severe in multiprocessors than in uniprocessors, most studies of cache prefetching have concentrated on uniprocessor architectures[1, 2, 18]. DASH[13] has hardware support for cache prefetching, but to date they have only published the results of micro-benchmark throughput tests. A noteworthy exception is the work by Mowry and Gupta[17], in which simulations were driven by three parallel programs, providing analysis of potential speedups with programmer-directed cache prefetching. However, the multiprocessor architecture they examined (sixteen DASH clusters connected by a high-throughput interconnection network, with only one processor per cluster) avoids the types of contention and interference we wish to study. As a result, they did not include the full effects of contention for a shared bus. We found this effect to be crucial to prefetching performance for the architectures we studied. In addition, we provide more detailed analysis of multiprocessor cache misses, identifying key components that affect performance.

In this paper we address the issue of prefetching in bus-based shared memory multiprocessors. The goal of our work was to gauge its impact on perfor-

This research was supported by ONR Grant No. N00014-92-J-1395 and NSF PYI Award No. MIP-9058-439.

mance and to pinpoint the factors responsible. Our experiments simulated parallel workloads on a bus-based multiprocessor, coupled with a prefetching algorithm that represents the "ideal" for current compiler-directed prefetching technology, in that it has an "oracle" to predict cache misses (apart from misses caused by data sharing). We use this to identify architectures and workloads where prefetching improves performance and where performance degrades. These results give us insight into the particular problems multiprocessors pose to prefetching and allow us to introduce changes to our prefetching algorithm to solve them. Although our studies most closely model a bus-based system, they should extend to other multiprocessor architectures for which memory contention is an issue.

We found that prefetching is a much more complex issue on a shared memory multiprocessor than on a uniprocessor, because of the parallel machine's greater sensitivity to memory subsystem utilization and data sharing effects. In an architecture where memory contention is the primary hindrance to better performance, prefetching often exacerbates the problem rather than relieving it. In addition, there are clear limits to how effective it can be in any shared-memory architecture, if the prefetching algorithm doesn't address problems caused by data sharing. When data sharing effects were not taken into account, we saw maximum speedups that ranged from 1.28 to 1.04 depending on the memory architecture, and a worst-case speedup (slowdown) of .94. A maximum speedup of 1.39 was achieved when special measures were taken to increase prefetching effectiveness on shared data, with a minimum of .95. These results indicate that, for the range of architectures we studied, the potential benefits of prefetching are limited, as compared to results on architectures for which memory contention was not a problem.

The remainder of the paper is organized as follows. Section 2 contains a summary of both documented and hypothesized disadvantages of prefetching on uniprocessors and multiprocessors. Section 3 describes our methodology and justifies our choice of simulation environment. Section 4 presents the results. The conclusions appear in section 5.

2 The Dangers of Prefetching

Although prefetching has been shown to be effective for certain applications and architectures, even on a uniprocessor it can cause a loss in performance if not done carefully[18]. To understand what makes prefetching more challenging on a multiprocessor, we must understand its potential drawbacks, both on uniprocessor and multiprocessor systems and workloads.

Some prefetching costs affect both types of machines. For example, prefetching increases pressure on the cache, since the future working set, i.e., data that is being prefetched, must coexist with the current working set. This will cause the total miss rate[1] to increase if prefetching introduces conflict misses by replacing data that is still in use, or if current accesses cause prefetched data to be replaced before it is loaded. Also, prefetching results in code expansion from both the prefetch instructions and code for techniques, such as loop splitting, that are used to implement many prefetching algorithms. The former can significantly increase execution time[18] and the latter can increase, though likely minimally, the miss rate of instruction or unified caches.

Prefetching has additional costs on shared memory multiprocessors. Prefetching attempts to increase processor utilization by lowering the CPU miss rate, usually a win in a uniprocessor. However, the smaller CPU miss rate is usually achieved at the expense of the total miss rate, i.e., prefetching typically increases memory traffic. A bus-based, shared memory multiprocessor is more sensitive to changes in memory traffic than a uniprocessor. In the extreme, a memory/bus bottlenecked multiprocessor can be completely insensitive to CPU throughput (which varies with CPU hit rates) and completely sensitive to memory throughput (proportional to the total miss rate), resulting in a performance degradation for any prefetching algorithm that increases the total miss rate. To each CPU, this appears as an increase in the access time for CPU misses, due to high memory subsystem contention; to the multiprocessor, it is execution time that increases, in proportion to the increased demand on the memory subsystem.

Second, prefetching of shared data items can increase pressure on the entire coherent cache system. In this case cache misses occur when the future work-

---

[1]Because some terminology becomes ambiguous in the presence of prefetching, we will use the following terms. *Misses* (or *total miss rate*) refer to both prefetch and non-prefetch accesses that do not hit in the cache. *CPU misses* (*CPU miss rate*) are misses on non-prefetch accesses and thus are observed by the CPU. They occur when (1) data is not prefetched and misses in the cache, (2) prefetched data overlays data still being accessed, (3) prefetched data is replaced before it is used and (4) either prefetched or non-prefetched data is invalidated. Misses due to the first three causes, i.e., CPU misses excluding *invalidation misses*, will be referred to as *non-sharing misses*. Finally, *prefetch misses* occur on prefetch accesses only.

ing set for one processor is in conflict with the current working set of other processors. The phenomenon manifests itself in an overall increase in invalidation misses, assuming a write-invalidate coherency protocol. The additional misses occur when a prefetched data item is invalidated by a write in another processor before it is used, or when data is prefetched in an exclusive state, causing invalidation misses in other processors that are still using it. Also, a prefetch instruction can prematurely transition a cache line in another cache from exclusive to shared state, requiring an extra bus operation if that cache line is written.

Last, although not a "danger" of prefetching, we should note the difficulty of predicting invalidation misses. Current compiler-directed prefetching algorithms are becoming more effective at predicting non-sharing misses; however, on many multiprocessor workloads, the majority of cache misses are caused by invalidations of (either true or false) shared cache lines[6]. Predicting invalidation misses so that they can be accurately prefetched will be more difficult than predicting other types of misses, due to the non-deterministic nature of invalidation traffic.

In the next section we discuss the methodology used to isolate and analyze some of these difficulties.

3 Simulation Environment

Our prefetching studies used trace-driven simulation. Traces were generated from real, coarse-grain parallel workloads, and prefetch instructions were inserted into the traces. We simulated several types of bus-based multiprocessors, which differ in the extent to which contention affects memory latency, i.e., we vary bus speeds. Five prefetching strategies were used that differ in when, how and how often prefetching is done. This section details the simulation environment.

3.1 Prefetching Algorithms

Software-directed prefetching schemes either cache prefetch (which brings data into the data cache closest to the processor) or prefetch data into a separate prefetch buffer. Using a prefetch buffer eliminates conflicts with the current working set in the cache. Although they have been shown to be effective in uniprocessors[11], they are less useful in bus-based shared memory machines. Prefetch buffers typically don't snoop on the bus; therefore, no shared data can be prefetched, unless it can be guaranteed not to be written during the interval in which the load might be

executed. For this reason our prefetching algorithms are cache-based.

Our baseline prefetching algorithm contains an optimized prefetcher for nonshared, i.e., "uniprocessor", data misses (those that only depend on the cache configuration). It is able to very accurately predict non-sharing cache hits and misses and never prefetches data that is not used. We emulate this algorithm by adding prefetch instructions to the address traces after they are generated on a shared memory multiprocessor. The candidates for prefetching are identified by running each processor's address stream through a uniprocessor cache filter and marking the data misses. The prefetch instructions are then placed in the instruction stream some distance ahead of the accesses that miss. We will refer to the estimated number of CPU cycles between the prefetch and the actual access as the *prefetch distance*. Since it is an off-line algorithm, the technique represents the "ideal" for current prefetching algorithms, i.e., one that prefetches both scalars and array references, and accurately identifies leading references (first access to a cache line) and capacity and conflict misses. Mowry et al.[18] have shown that compiler algorithms can approximate this ideal very well already; and as existing algorithms improve, they will get closer to this ideal.

To tailor the prefetching algorithm for multiprocessor activity, the optimistic uniprocessor algorithm is augmented in one of our prefetching algorithms to improve the prefetching of write-shared data. Misses to write-shared data can be the result of both cache conflicts and invalidations, so it is reasonable to handle write-shared data differently. A technique which attempts to bring write-shared data into the cache earlier is appropriate when a workload exhibits sequential sharing, but, if the workload exhibits heavy interprocessor contention, it could be harmful. We introduce a scheme that prefetches write-shared data more frequently than other data, using a measure of temporal locality to estimate the likelihood of a shared cache line having been invalidated (see section 4.1).

The overhead associated with each prefetch in our simulations is relatively low, a single instruction and the prefetch access itself, as we continue to assume the existence of effective and efficient prefetching algorithms.

On a multiprocessor with a write-invalidate cache coherency protocol, data can be prefetched in either shared mode (in which case a subsequent write would require an extra invalidating bus operation) or in exclusive mode (which would cause all other cached copies of that cache line to be invalidated). We will refer to the latter as an *exclusive prefetch*. Our simulations support both types of prefetches, as in [17].

3.2 Workload

The address traces were generated with MPTrace[7] on a Sequent Symmetry[14], running the following coarse-grained parallel applications, all written in C (see Table 1). Topopt[3] performs topological optimization on VLSI circuits using a parallel simulated annealing algorithm. Pverify[15] determines whether two boolean circuits are functionally identical. Statistics on the amount of shared data for these programs can be found in [5]. LocusRoute is a commercial quality VLSI standard cell router. Mp3d solves a problem involving particle flow at extremely low density. Water evaluates the forces and potentials in a system of water molecules in liquid state. The latter three are part of the Stanford SPLASH benchmarks[21].

Restricted by the practical limit on trace lengths in multiprocessor trace-driven simulations, a balance must be struck between the desire for large data sets that don't fit in the cache and tracing a reasonable portion of the program. With a very large data structure, one could easily end up tracing only a single loop, which may or not be indicative of the rest of the program. We attempted to solve this by using data sets and local cache sizes that were both about a single order of magnitude smaller than might be expected on current moderately parallel multiprocessors, thus maintaining a realistic ratio of data set to off-chip cache size. This ensured that in most cases neither the critical data structures nor the cache working sets fit into the cache size simulated. The exception is Topopt, which is still interesting because of the high degree of write sharing and the large number of conflict misses it exhibits even with the small shared data set size. We traced approximately 2 million total references per processor for each application.

Program	Data Set	Shared Data	Number of Processes
Topopt	apla.lomim	20 KB	9
Pverify	C880.21.berk1/2	130 KB	12
LocusRoute	Primary1	1.6 MB	12
Mp3d	10,000 molecules	1.9 MB	12
Water	343 molecules	227 KB	12

Table 1: Workload used in experiments

3.3 Multiprocessor Simulations

After the prefetch accesses were added, the traces were run through Charlie[4], a multiprocessor cache simulator, that was modified to handle prefetching and lockup-free caches. Besides modeling the CPU, cache and bus hardware at a low level, Charlie carries out locking and barrier synchronization; therefore, as the interleaving of accesses from the different processors is changed by the behavior of the memory subsystem, Charlie ensures that a legal interleaving is maintained. So, for instance, processors vie for locks and may not acquire them in the same order as the traced run; but they still will acquire each in some legal order, and enter the critical sections one processor at a time.

Since we were interested in studying the effect of prefetching on the bottleneck in low-end shared memory machines, i.e., the bus, we simulated in detail the structure in the cache hierarchy that is adjacent to the bus. We only modeled the data cache, assuming an instruction cache with an insignificantly low miss rate. These caches are direct mapped, copy-back, with one per processor. For all of the simulations presented here they are 32 Kbytes, with a 32 byte block size. Several other configurations were simulated, but those results will not be presented. In many cases, they deviated from the results presented here in relatively predictable ways (e.g. with larger caches, non-sharing misses were reduced, making invalidation miss effects much more dominant; larger block sizes increased false sharing and thus the total number of invalidation misses). Our simulations included both private and shared data, in order to include the effects of interference between the two in the cache.

The cache coherency scheme is the Illinois coherency protocol[19]. Its most important feature for our purposes is that it has a private-clean state for exclusive prefetches. We simulate a 16-deep prefetch instruction buffer, which was sufficiently large to almost always prevent the processor from stalling because the buffer was full. The bus uses a round-robin arbitration scheme that favors blocking loads over prefetches.

We only consider systems with high memory latency. (Prefetching is less useful and possibly harmful if there is little latency to hide.) The processors execute a single cycle per instruction, plus a single cycle per data access, if both accesses are cache hits. This is coupled with a memory subsystem latency of 100 cycles. Given this latency we examine a spectrum of memory architectures from high to low memory utilization. To achieve this, the 100 cycle latency is separated into two components, one in which there is no inter-processor contention and one in which all processors vie for a single resource. Different utilizations of the contended resource are simulated by varying the percentage of the 100 cycles that is attributed to the contended portion. One memory architecture that fits this model well is a split-transaction bus protocol, where the system has enough parallelism in the memory banks/controllers to make the address bus and the memory access relatively conflict free and the data bus transfer the bottleneck. What we vary in this particular application of the model is the percentage of the total memory latency required for the data bus transfer. However, what we are attempting to model is a more generic memory architecture with some central resource that has the potential to saturate. Consequently, we expect that our model will reflect a wider spectrum of memory architectures.

In the simulations in this paper, the "data transfer" portion of the memory latency is varied from 4 to 32 cycles out of the total 100 cycles. In the split transaction bus architecture described above, a data transfer latency of 4 cycles would make the address transmission and memory lookup 96 cycles; if the processor cycle speed was 200 MHz, this would model a memory subsystem with a memory latency of 500 nanoseconds, and a peak throughput of 1.6 GB/second, while the 32 cycle latency corresponds to a memory throughput of 200 MB/second. The 4-cycle latency corresponds to a transfer of 64 bits across the bus every CPU cycle.

4 Results

4.1 Prefetching Strategies

For each memory architecture simulated, we applied the following prefetching strategies to the traces:

- NP (no prefetching) gives us a basis for gauging the effect of each of the prefetching strategies. All execution times are given relative to NP for the same memory architecture and cache configuration.

- PREF is our most basic prefetching algorithm. Data that the filter cache (of the same size as the actual cache) predicts as a miss will be prefetched. All other algorithms differ in only a single characteristic from PREF. The prefetch distance for PREF is 100 cycles.

- EXCL (exclusive prefetch). In EXCL, if the expected miss is a write, the line is brought into the cache in exclusive mode, possibly invalidating copies in other caches. (In PREF, if the

line is held in other caches, it is prefetched in a shared state and invalidations occur with the write.) If the prefetch hits in the cache, no bus operation is initiated, even if the cache line is in the shared state. In sequential sharing, exclusive prefetching saves a bus operation; however, with inter-processor contention, an exclusive prefetch to write-shared data can cause up to twice as many invalidation misses. With the Illinois protocol, all cache reads of data that aren't currently in another cache enter the private state immediately, so there is only a difference between PREF and EXCL when a line is shared among caches. This scheme does not go as far as identifying a read miss followed by a write to the same location, which would be the one instance where exclusive prefetching would actually require fewer bus operations than no prefetching.

- LPD (long prefetch distance). In PREF, the prefetch distance is closely matched to the best-case memory latency of 100 cycles. Contention can cause the real latency to be much higher, however. For this reason, Mowry et al.[18] suggest using a larger prefetch distance to ensure that the prefetched data has time to arrive. We use a prefetch distance of 400 for LPD.

- PWS (prefetch write-shared data more aggressively). Results for PREF will show that it provides good coverage of non-sharing misses, but very poor coverage of invalidation misses, which in most of our workloads represent a large portion of total misses and the vast majority of CPU misses. To improve the coverage of these externally caused and therefore less predictable misses, we introduce some redundant prefetches to cache lines known to be write-shared. They are redundant in the uniprocessor sense, i.e., they are issued for data that would reside in the cache, were it not for invalidations. To emulate a prefetch algorithm that prefetches write-shared data that exhibits poor temporal locality (under the premise that the longer a shared cache line has resided in the cache without being accessed, the more likely it is to have been invalidated), we ran the write-shared data from each trace through a 16-line associative cache filter to get a first-order approximation of temporal locality, selecting the misses for prefetching. These were prefetched in addition to all prefetches identified by PREF. PWS increased the prefetching overhead substantially (by about a factor of 1.5

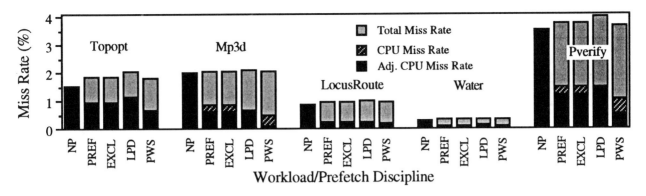

Figure 1: Total and CPU Miss Rates for the Five Workloads

to 2.5), but increased our coverage of invalidation misses.

4.2 Analysis of High Level Metrics

Results for a 32 KB cache with a 32-byte cache line are shown in Figures 1 and 2. The effect of various prefetching strategies on the miss rates is in Figure 1, and on execution time in Figure 2. Because accesses of prefetches still in progress often comprised a large portion of the CPU miss rate, the Adjusted CPU Miss Rate does not include them. The data in Figure 1 is for an 8-cycle data-transfer latency. The only component of the miss rate that varied significantly across memory architectures was the prefetch-in-progress misses (the difference between the CPU miss rate and the adjusted CPU miss rate), which rose as the data bus got slower.

Several observations can be made from these results. First, CPU miss rates fell significantly for all prefetching strategies, for example, 37-71% for PREF (38-77% for adjusted) and 57-80% for PWS (59-94% adjusted) for the results shown in Figure 1. Because we use an oracle prefetcher, one might naively expect even more misses to have been covered. There are three reasons why this didn't happen. First, the prefetch-in-progress misses accounted for a large part of the CPU miss rate in some cases. Second, prefetching actually introduces additional cache conflict misses. Last, and most importantly, data sharing among processors produced invalidation misses, which in most cases are the largest single component of the CPU miss rate, which our oracle prefetcher doesn't predict. (Only PWS attempts to prevent them.) We will discuss these issues in sections 4.3 and 4.4.

Total miss rates increased, as expected, in all simulations with prefetching. Previous studies have focused on CPU miss rates; but for some multiprocessor systems, total miss rate is a more important metric, indicative of the demand at the bottleneck component of the machine.

Program	Pref. Alg.	Data Transfer Latency			
		4 cycles	8 cycles	16 cycles	32 cycles
Topopt	NP	.18	.27	.45	.76
	PREF	.22	.34	.56	.87
	EXCL	.22	.34	.56	.86
	LPD	.23	.35	.59	.90
	PWS	.24	.36	.59	.88
Mp3d	NP	.48	.65	.90	1.00
	PREF	.64	.83	.99	1.00
	EXCL	.64	.83	.99	1.00
	LPD	.64	.84	1.00	1.00
	PWS	.71	.90	1.00	1.00
Locus	NP	.21	.33	.56	.89
	PREF	.27	.42	.70	.97
	EXCL	.27	.42	.70	.96
	LPD	.28	.43	.72	.98
	PWS	.28	.43	.71	.97
Pverify	NP	.42	.63	.92	1.00
	PREF	.57	.81	1.00	1.00
	EXCL	.57	.82	.99	1.00
	LPD	.57	.83	1.00	1.00
	PWS	.65	.91	1.00	1.00
Water	NP	.10	.14	.22	.38
	PREF	.11	.16	.25	.43
	EXCL	.11	.16	.25	.43
	LPD	.11	.16	.26	.45
	PWS	.11	.16	.25	.43

Table 2: Selected bus utilizations

In Table 2 we see how the miss rates affect data-bus utilization as the memory architecture is varied. Bus utilization is the number of cycles the bus was in use divided by the total cycles of the simulation. Bus utilization results can be misleading, if not interpreted correctly. There are two reasons why bus utilization can increase: one is that the same workload produces more bus operations; the second is that the same num-

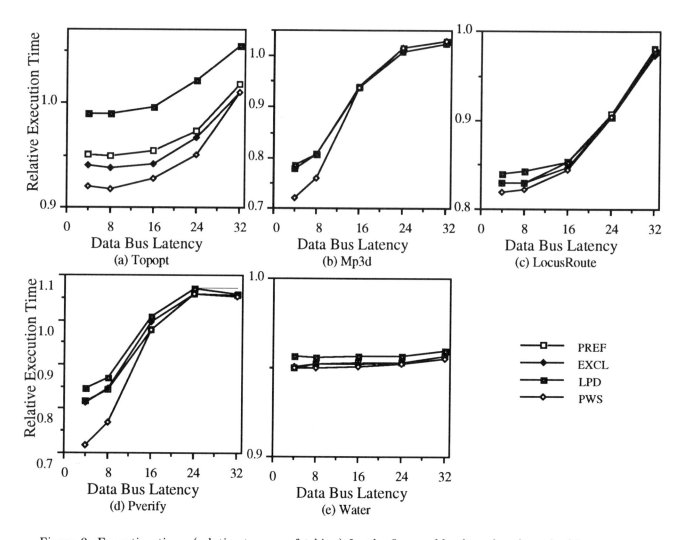

Figure 2: Execution times (relative to no prefetching) for the five workloads and each prefetching strategy.

ber of bus operations occur but over a shorter time period. So, for instance, bus utilization increased with prefetching for the 4-cycle Pverify simulation, both because the total miss rate increased, and because the execution time was reduced. Results in Table 2 indicate that, for all applications and all levels of bus contention, the bus demand increased with prefetching, as expected given the total miss rates from Figure 1.

In Figure 2, we see the effects of prefetching on execution time for the different memory subsystems. As a consequence of the increased memory load from prefetching, execution time increased when the bus was saturated, although not dramatically, because total miss rates rose by small amounts. Execution time typically fell when bus loads were lighter, but again, the performance improvements were not large. There are two reasons for this. First, prefetching causes

an increase in memory latency due to increased contention between processors on the bus. In addition, there is an overhead for prefetching in CPU execution time, although it was relatively small in our experiments (no more than 1% of execution time for PREF, LPD and EXCL and no more than 2% for PWS). In summary, the results indicate that the benefits of prefetching in a bus-based multiprocessor are marginal, except in the case of a very high bandwidth memory subsystem. The largest gain in execution time observed was a 39% speedup and the largest degradation was 7%.

In order to gain insight into how much improvement was actually possible with prefetching, we can look at the processor utilizations (before prefetching). For instance, the average processor utilization for Water was .82 with the fastest bus and .81 with the slowest bus.

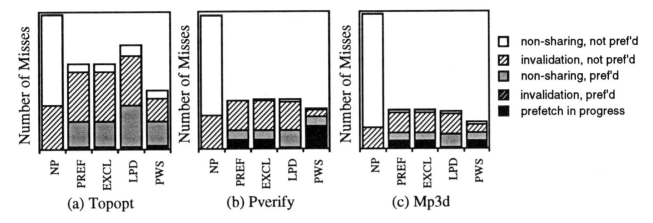

Figure 3: Sources of CPU Misses in Topopt, Pverify and Mp3d

Since the best any memory-latency hiding technique can do is to bring processor utilization to 1, the best speedup that could have been achieved for Water is about 1.2. At the other extreme, the processor utilizations for Mp3d ranged from .39 to .22, so it had room for a speedup of 2.5 with the fast bus and 4.5 with the slow bus, ignoring the overhead of prefetch instructions. So while, Mp3d had the best speedups, it fell far short of the maximum potential speedup possible. For the other workloads, the average processor utilization for Topopt ranged from .65 to .59, Locus-Route ranged from .64 to .54, and Pverify from .41 to .18.

We report much smaller multiprocessor performance improvements than Mowry and Gupta[17], particularly for our lower-throughput memory subsystems. The reasons stem from several differences in our approaches. First, they eliminated bus contention from their model by simulating only one processor per cluster. Second, they began with much higher miss rates due to their choice of simulated caches (for most simulations a 4 KB second-level cache of only shared data). This configuration gave them processor utilizations in the .11 to .19 range before prefetching. Third, they used aggressive program-specific, programmer-directed prefetching techniques, which in some cases are different than the algorithm we emulate.

It should also be noted that predicting the effectiveness of prefetching for a particular workload is difficult, because the same workloads achieve both the largest improvement and the largest degradation, depending upon the memory subsystem architecture. This is because applications that put a heavy load on the memory system will see a larger memory latency and will benefit more from hiding that latency. Those same applications, however, are the first to enter bus saturation and begin degrading with prefetching.

4.3 CPU Miss Component Analysis

We were able to better understand the effects of the different prefetching strategies by analyzing different types of CPU misses. Figure 3 illustrates some of the miss rate component results: Topopt, Pverify, and Mp3d with an 8-cycle data transfer latency.

In this figure, misses fall into the following categories. They are either invalidation misses (the tags match, but the state has been marked invalid) or non-sharing misses (this is a first use or the data has been replaced in the cache). A miss of each type was either prefetched (and disappeared from the cache before use) or not prefetched (the miss was not predicted). The fifth type of miss is *prefetch-in-progress*, which means that the prefetch access was presented to the bus but did not complete by the time the CPU requested the data.

From these results, we observe that for a 32 KB cache there remain a significant proportion of non-sharing misses that are not covered by prefetching, particularly with Topopt. Since our "oracle" prefetcher perfectly predicts non-sharing misses in the absence of prefetches, those that remain are either caused by a prefetch access replacing data that is still being used or a prefetched cache line being replaced before its use. This implies that the degree of conflict between the prefetched data and the current working set can be significant. The magnitude of this conflict, however, would likely be reduced by a victim cache[10] or a set-associative cache. The primary result of a reduction in the number of conflict misses introduced by prefetching would be a reduction in the performance degradations seen in bus saturation.

Increasing the prefetch distance from 100 to 400 (compare PREF to LPD) successfully eliminates the majority of prefetch-in-progress misses, but at the cost of more conflict misses. The earlier the prefetch is begun, the more likely it is to replace something still being used between the prefetch and the subsequent load. Also, the longer the prefetched data sits in the cache before it is used, the more likely it is to be replaced. The numbers for Topopt indicate that the latter is particularly critical. Trading prefetch-in-progress misses for conflict misses is not wise. Prefetch-in-progress misses are the cheapest type of misses, because the processor only has to wait for an access in progress to complete instead of the entire access time. Even with Mp3d, where LPD only adds a small number of conflict misses, there is no gain in execution time. This argues that prefetching algorithms should strive to receive the prefetched data exactly on time. The penalty for being just a few cycles late is small, because the processor must stall less than the time of a full access. The penalty for being a few cycles early is also small, because the chances of losing the data before its use are slight over that period. Our results indicate that increasing the prefetch distance to the point that virtually all prefetches complete does not pay off in performance. Mowry, et al. [18] also studied prefetch distance, noting that only one of their programs degraded with increasing prefetch distance, but they had to restructure four others to eliminate the conflicts that are causing this phenomenon.

Our concern about prefetching exacerbating the sharing problem (extra invalidation misses as a result of each cache trying to hold shared cache lines longer) was for the most part unwarranted. Invalidation misses typically go up slightly with prefetching and somewhat more with exclusive prefetching, but the change is minimal relative to the other effects observed. This invalidation miss behavior confirms that these applications primarily experience sequential sharing.

Although Topopt shows a slight improvement with exclusive prefetching, due to a 2% decline in total bus operations (the result of a 20% decline in invalidate bus operations), for the workloads we considered, exclusive prefetching tracks our base strategy (shared prefetching) extremely closely, both in execution time and in the lower-level metrics. This is because most of the leading references to shared lines are not writes. A compiler might recognize when a read is followed immediately by a write and make more effective use of the exclusive prefetch feature. Mowry and Gupta[17] take advantage of this in their programmer-directed prefetching study.

4.4 Invalidation Misses

The most striking result from Figure 3 is that the limit to effective prefetching (in fact, the limit to performance in general) is invalidation misses on shared data. None of the traditional (uniprocessor-based) prefetching strategies successfully reduces the less predictable invalidation misses, which are the largest component of CPU misses in each of the workloads. Notice that the more effectively we prefetch non-sharing misses, the more invalidation misses become critical to the performance of the application with prefetching.

With PWS, which prefetches write-shared data differently, we have made a first attempt to reduce these misses. Over the range of bus utilizations (data transfer latencies) for which prefetching is already viable, significant improvements in execution time were achieved for some of the workloads, as seen in Figure 2. The fastest bus (4-cycle) results allow us to see the benefit of the improved prefetching of write-shared data most clearly in isolation from the memory contention effects. For that architecture, the speedup of PWS relative to PREF ranged from 0% (Water) to 14% (Pverify, where PREF was 23% faster than no prefetching while PWS achieved a 39% speedup over no prefetching), and CPU miss rates for PWS were 11% to 64% lower than PREF. One reason for the consistent reduction in misses by the write-shared algorithm was that, although PWS increased the number of prefetches, it did not significantly increase the number of CPU conflict misses.

Workload	Total Invalidation Miss Rate	Total False Sharing Miss Rate
Topopt	0.50%	0.36%
Mp3d	0.58%	0.19%
Locus	0.14%	0.08%
Water	0.06%	0.04%
Pverify	0.89%	0.80%

Table 3: Total Invalidation and False Sharing Miss Rates

Table 3 shows that for most of the benchmarks, over half of the invalidation misses could be attributed to false sharing. False sharing occurs when a cache line is shared between two processor caches, but each is accessing different data in it. When one processor modifies a data location, it causes an invalidation in the other's cache, because cache coherency is maintained on a cache block basis. We record a false sharing miss if an invalidation miss is caused by a write from another processor to a word in the local cache line that the local processor has not accessed. Previous results[23, 6] demonstrate that false sharing goes up significantly with larger block sizes. In [9], an algorithm is presented for restructuring shared data to reduce false sharing. While the technique has promise for improving overall performance, for the purpose of this study we are only interested in whether doing so makes prefetching more viable. Tables 4 and 5 show the result of some of the prefetching strategies on restructured Topopt and Pverify. The other programs were not improved significantly by the current restructuring algorithm.

Workload	Prefetch Discipline	CPU MR	Total MR	Total Inval MR	Total FS MR
Topopt	NP	0.60%	0.60%	0.08%	0.05%
	PREF	0.32%	0.77%	0.10%	0.05%
	PWS	0.29%	0.77%	0.09%	0.05%
Pverify	NP	3.23%	3.23%	0.22%	0.16%
	PREF	1.22%	3.40%	0.26%	0.16%
	PWS	1.22%	3.40%	0.26%	0.16%

Table 4: Miss rates for data transfer latency of 8 cycles for restructured programs

The results are dramatic for Topopt. Restructuring eliminated almost all false sharing misses, and also improved data locality to the point that many of the non-sharing misses also disappeared (the invalidation miss rate was cut by a factor of 6, and the non-sharing portion of the miss rate was halved). In Pverify, by contrast, virtually all of the improvement came from the reduction in false sharing misses (in fact, while the invalidation miss rate was reduced by a factor of four, the non-sharing miss rate went up slightly).

Before transformation, Topopt showed little improvement with prefetching due to high bus utilization and cache conflicts caused by the prefetching. After transformation, the cache behavior of Topopt improved to the point that there is little opportunity for further benefits with prefetching. In fact, processor utilization rose to .77-.80 for the restructured Topopt.

With both invalidation misses and load on the bus reduced, Pverify saw a greater benefit from prefetching until the bus again became saturated. The result of the reduction in invalidation misses is that the performance of the simplest prefetching algorithm approached that of the strategy tailored to write-shared

Program	Pref. Algo.	Data Transfer Latency				
		4 cycles	8 cycles	16 cycles	24 cycles	32 cycles
Topopt	PREF	.96	.96	.96	.97	.99
	PWS	.96	.96	.96	.97	.98
Pverify	PREF	.65	.71	.99	1.05	1.05
	PWS	.63	.70	.99	1.05	1.06

Table 5: Relative Execution Times for Restructured Programs

data. In fact, this was true for both applications, despite seeing very different results from restructuring.

5 Summary and Conclusions

The benefits of prefetching are well documented. Results have shown that on several architectures the speedups achieved with prefetching can be quite large. In those cases, the potential costs of prefetching are more than overcome by the benefits. In an architecture that is not so conducive to prefetching, however, the balance of the costs and benefits needs to be more carefully understood.

We have shown that in a multiprocessor system with limited memory bandwidth, prefetching algorithms are not guaranteed to improve performance, even if they successfully reduce the CPU-observed miss rate. Our results indicate that for a variety of applications, simulated on even a fast bus-based multiprocessor, the benefits of prefetching are not large. When an application has good cache behavior (low miss rates), there is little to be gained from prefetching; when it has poor cache behavior, the bus may not have the bandwidth available to make prefetching transparent to the CPU.

Sharing traffic (invalidation misses) represents the biggest challenge to designers and users of parallel machine memories, particularly as caches get larger and invalidation misses dominate parallel performance. We have shown that there is potential that special prefetching algorithms for write-shared data can lessen the impact of invalidation misses. When write-shared data is restructured to reduce false sharing, uniprocessor-oriented prefetching algorithms can also work well, approaching the performance of their write-shared data counterparts.

Acknowledgements

The authors would like to thank Jean-Loup Baer, Ed Felten, Hank Levy, Anoop Gupta and the reviewers, all of whom contributed greatly to the quality of this paper through their reviews. We would also like to thank Tor Jeremiassen for providing the restructured programs.

References

[1] D. Callahan, K. Kennedy, and A. Porterfield. Software prefetching. In *Fourth International Conference on Architectural Support for Programming Languages and Operating Systems*, pages 40–52, April 1991.

[2] W.Y. Chen, S.A. Mahlke, P.P. Chang, and W.W. Hwu. Data access microarchitectures for superscalar processors with compiler-assisted data prefetching. In *Proceedings of 24th International Symposium on Microarchitecture*, 1991.

[3] S. Devadas and A.R. Newton. Topological optimization of multiple level array logic. *IEEE Transactions on Computer-Aided Design*, November 1987.

[4] S.J. Eggers. Simulation analysis of data sharing in shared memory multiprocessors. Technical Report No. UCB/CSD 89/501 (Ph.D. thesis), University of California, Berkeley, March 1989.

[5] S.J. Eggers. Simplicity versus accuracy in a model of cache coherency overhead. *IEEE Transactions on Computers*, 40(8):893–906, August 1991.

[6] S.J. Eggers and T.E. Jeremiassen. Eliminating false sharing. In *International Conference on Parallel Processing*, volume I, pages 377–381, St. Charles IL, August 1991.

[7] S.J. Eggers, D.R. Keppel, E.J. Koldinger, and H.M. Levy. Techniques for inline tracing on a shared-memory multiprocessor. In *Proceedings of the 1990 ACM Sigmetrics*, pages 37–47, Santa Fe NM, May 1990.

[8] J.L. Hennessy and N.P. Jouppi. Computer technology and architecture: An evolving interaction. *IEEE Computer*, 24(9):18–29, September 1991.

[9] T.E. Jeremiassen and S.J. Eggers. Computing per-process summary side-effect information. In *Preliminary Proceedings of the Fifth Workshop on Languages and Compilers for Parallel Computing*, pages 115–122, New Haven CT, August 1992.

[10] N.P. Jouppi. Improving direct-mapped cache performance by the addition of a small fully-associative cache and prefetch buffers. In *17th Annual International Symposium on Computer Architecture*, pages 364–373, May 1990.

[11] A.C. Klaiber and H.M. Levy. An architecture for software-controlled data prefetching. In *18th Annual International Symposium on Computer Architecture*, pages 43–53, May 1991.

[12] D. Kroft. Lockup-free instruction fetch/prefetch cache organization. In *8th Annual International Symposium on Computer Architecture*, pages 81–87, 1981.

[13] D. Lenoski, J. Laudon, T. Joe, D. Nakahira, L. Stevens, A. Gupta, and J. Hennessy. The DASH prototype: Logic overhead and performance. *IEEE Transactions on Parallel and Distributed Systems*. To appear.

[14] R. Lovett and S. Thakkar. The symmetry multiprocessor system. In *International Conference on Parallel Processing*, pages 303–310, University Park PA, August 1988.

[15] H-K. T. Ma, S. Devadas, R. Wei, and A. Sangiovanni-Vincentelli. Logic verification algorithms and their parallel implementation. In *Proceedings of the 24th Design Automation Conference*, pages 283–290, July 1987.

[16] Motorola. *MC88100 RISC Microprocessor User's Manual*. Prentice Hall, 1990.

[17] T.C. Mowry and A. Gupta. Tolerating latency through software-controlled prefetching in shared-memory multiprocessors. *Journal of Parallel and Distributed Computing*, 12(2):87–106, June 1991.

[18] T.C. Mowry, M.S. Lam, and A. Gupta. Design and evaluation of a compiler algorithm for prefetching. In *Fifth International Conference on Architectural Support for Programming Languages and Operating Systems*, pages 62–73, October 1992.

[19] M.S. Papamarcos and J.H. Patel. A low-overhead coherence solution for multiprocessors with private cache memories. In *11th Annual International Symposium on Computer Architecture*, pages 348–354, 1984.

[20] C. Scheurich and M. Dubois. Lockup-free caches in high-performance multiprocessors. *Journal of Parallel and Distributed Computing*, 11(1):25–36, January 1991.

[21] J.P. Singh, W. Weber, and A. Gupta. SPLASH: Stanford parallel applications for shared-memory. Technical Report CSL-TR-91-469, Computer Systems Laboratory, Stanford University, 1991.

[22] G.S. Sohi and M. Franklin. High-bandwidth data memory systems for superscalar processor. In *Fourth International Conference on Architectural Support for Programming Languages and Operating Systems*, pages 53–62, April 1991.

[23] J. Torrellas, M.S. Lam, and J.L. Hennessy. Shared data placement optimizations to reduce multiprocessor cache miss rates. In *International Conference on Parallel Processing*, volume II, pages 266–270, St. Charles IL, August 1990.

Transactional Memory:
Architectural Support for Lock-Free Data Structures

Maurice Herlihy
Digital Equipment Corporation
Cambridge Research Laboratory
Cambridge MA 02139
herlihy@crl.dec.com

J. Eliot B. Moss
Dept. of Computer Science
University of Massachusetts
Amherst, MA 01003
moss@cs.umass.edu

Abstract

A shared data structure is *lock-free* if its operations do not require mutual exclusion. If one process is interrupted in the middle of an operation, other processes will not be prevented from operating on that object. In highly concurrent systems, lock-free data structures avoid common problems associated with conventional locking techniques, including priority inversion, convoying, and difficulty of avoiding deadlock. This paper introduces *transactional memory*, a new multiprocessor architecture intended to make lock-free synchronization as efficient (and easy to use) as conventional techniques based on mutual exclusion. Transactional memory allows programmers to define customized read-modify-write operations that apply to multiple, independently-chosen words of memory. It is implemented by straightforward extensions to any multiprocessor cache-coherence protocol. Simulation results show that transactional memory matches or outperforms the best known locking techniques for simple benchmarks, even in the absence of priority inversion, convoying, and deadlock.

1 Introduction

A shared data structure is *lock-free* if its operations do not require mutual exclusion. If one process is interrupted in the middle of an operation, other processes will not be prevented from operating on that object. Lock-free data structures avoid common problems associated with conventional locking techniques in highly concurrent systems:

- *Priority inversion* occurs when a lower-priority process is preempted while holding a lock needed by higher-priority processes.

- *Convoying* occurs when a process holding a lock is descheduled, perhaps by exhausting its scheduling quantum, by a page fault, or by some other kind of interrupt. When such an interruption occurs, other processes capable of running may be unable to progress.

- *Deadlock* can occur if processes attempt to lock the same set of objects in different orders. Deadlock avoidance can be awkward if processes must lock multiple data objects, particularly if the set of objects is not known in advance.

A number of researchers have investigated techniques for implementing lock-free concurrent data structures using software techniques [2, 4, 19, 25, 26, 32]. Experimental evidence suggests that in the absence of inversion, convoying, or deadlock, software implementations of lock-free data structures often do not perform as well as their locking-based counterparts.

This paper introduces *transactional memory*, a new multiprocessor architecture intended to make lock-free synchronization as efficient (and easy to use) as conventional techniques based on mutual exclusion. Transactional memory allows programmers to define customized read-modify-write operations that apply to multiple, independently-chosen words of memory. It is implemented by straightforward extensions to multiprocessor cache-coherence protocols. Simulation results show that transactional memory is competitive with the best known lock-based techniques for simple benchmarks, even in the absence of priority inversion, convoys, and deadlock.

In Section 2, we describe transactional memory and how to use it. In Section 3 we describe one way to implement transactional memory, and in Section 4 we discuss some alternatives. In Section 5 we present some simulation results, and in Section 6, we give a brief survey of related work.

2 Transactional Memory

A *transaction* is a finite sequence of machine instructions, executed by a single process, satisfying the following properties:

- *Serializability*: Transactions appear to execute serially, meaning that the steps of one transaction never appear to be interleaved with the steps of another. Committed transactions are never observed by different processors to execute in different orders.

- *Atomicity*: Each transaction makes a sequence of tentative changes to shared memory. When the transaction completes, it either *commits*, making its changes visible to other processes (effectively) instantaneously, or it *aborts*, causing its changes to be discarded.

We assume here that a process executes only one transaction at a time. Although the model could be extended to permit overlapping or logically nested transactions, we have seen no examples where they are needed.

2.1 Instructions

Transactional memory provides the following primitive instructions for accessing memory:

- *Load-transactional* (LT) reads the value of a shared memory location into a private register.

- *Load-transactional-exclusive* (LTX) reads the value of a shared memory location into a private register, "hinting" that the location is likely to be updated.

- *Store-transactional* (ST) tentatively writes a value from a private register to a shared memory location. This new value does not become visible to other processors until the transaction successfully commits (see below).

A transaction's *read set* is the set of locations read by LT, and its *write set* is the set of locations accessed by LTX or ST. Its *data set* is the union of the read and write sets.

Transactional memory also provides the following instructions for manipulating transaction state:

- *Commit* (COMMIT) attempts to make the transaction's tentative changes permanent. It *succeeds* only if no

other transaction has updated any location in the transaction's data set, and no other transaction has read any location in this transaction's write set. If it succeeds, the transaction's changes to its write set become visible to other processes. If it *fails*, all changes to the write set are discarded. Either way, COMMIT returns an indication of success or failure.

- *Abort* (ABORT) discards all updates to the write set.

- *Validate* (VALIDATE) tests the current transaction status. A *successful* VALIDATE returns *True*, indicating that the current transaction has not aborted (although it may do so later). An *unsuccessful* VALIDATE returns *False*, indicating that the current transaction has aborted, and discards the transaction's tentative updates.

By combining these primitives, the programmer can define customized read-modify-write operations that operate on arbitrary regions of memory, not just single words. We also support *non-transactional* instructions, such as LOAD and STORE, which do not affect a transaction's read and write sets.

For brevity, we leave undefined how transactional and non-transactional operations interact when applied to the same location.[1] We also leave unspecified the precise circumstances that will cause a transaction to abort. In particular, implementations are free to abort transactions in response to certain interrupts (such as page faults, quantum expiration, etc.), context switches, or to avoid or resolve serialization conflicts.

2.2 Intended Use

Our transactions are intended to replace short critical sections. For example, a lock-free data structure would typically be implemented in the following stylized way (see Section 5 for specific examples). Instead of acquiring a lock, executing the critical section, and releasing the lock, a process would:

1. use LT or LTX to read from a set of locations,

2. use VALIDATE to check that the values read are consistent,

3. use ST to modify a set of locations, and

4. use COMMIT to make the changes permanent. If either the VALIDATE or the COMMIT fails, the process returns to Step (1).

---

[1]One sensible way to define such interactions is to consider a LOAD or STORE as a transaction that always commits, forcing any conflicting transactions to abort.

A more complex transaction, such as one that chains down a linked list (see Figure 3), would alternate LT and VALIDATE instructions. When contention is high, programmers are advised to apply adaptive backoff [3, 28] before retrying.

The VALIDATE instruction is motivated by considerations of software engineering. A set of values in memory is *inconsistent* if it could not have been produced by any serial execution of transactions. An *orphan* is a transaction that continues to execute after it has been aborted (i.e., after another committed transaction has updated its read set). It is impractical to guarantee that every orphan will observe a consistent read set. Although an orphan transaction will never commit, it may be difficult to ensure that an orphan, when confronted with unexpected input, does not store into out-of-range locations, divide by zero, or perform some other illegal action. All values read before a successful VALIDATE are guaranteed to be consistent. Of course, VALIDATE is not always needed, but it simplifies the writing of correct transactions and improves performance by eliminating the need for *ad-hoc* checks.

Our transactions satisfy the same formal serializability and atomicity properties as database-style transactions (viz. [18]), but they are intended to be used very differently. Unlike database transactions, our transactions are short-lived activities that access a relatively small number of memory locations in primary memory. The ideal size and duration of transactions are implementation-dependent, but, roughly speaking, a transaction should be able to run to completion within a single scheduling quantum, and the number of locations accessed should not exceed an architecturally-specified limit.

3   Implementation

In this section, we give an overview of an architecture that supports transactional memory. An associated technical report [20] gives detailed protocols for both bus-based (snoopy cache) and network-based (directory) architectures.

Our design satisfies the following criteria:

- Non-transactional operations use the same caches, cache controller logic, and coherence protocols they would have used in the absence of transactional memory.

- Custom hardware support is restricted to primary caches and the instructions needed to communicate with them.

- Committing or aborting a transaction is an operation local to the cache. It does not require communicating with other processes or writing data back to memory.

Transactional memory is implemented by modifying standard multiprocessor cache coherence protocols. We exploit access rights, which are usually connected with cache residence. In general, access may be non-exclusive (shared) permitting reads, or exclusive, permitting writes. At any time a memory location is either (1) not immediately accessible by any processor (i.e., in memory only), (2) accessible non-exclusively by one or more processors, or (3) accessible exclusively by exactly one processor. Most cache coherence protocols incorporate some form of these access rights.

The basic idea behind our design is simple: any protocol capable of detecting accessibility conflicts can also detect transaction conflict at no extra cost. Before a processor P can load the contents of a location, it must acquire non-exclusive access to that location. Before another processor Q can store to that location, it must acquire exclusive access, and must therefore detect and revoke P's access. If we replace these operations with their transactional counterparts, then it is easy to see that any protocol that detects potential access conflicts also detects the potential transaction conflict between P and Q.

Once a transaction conflict is detected, it can be resolved in a variety of ways. The implementation described here aborts any transaction that tries to revoke access of a transactional entry from another active transaction. This strategy is attractive if one assumes (as we do) that timer (or other) interrupts will abort a stalled transaction after a fixed duration, so there is no danger of a transaction holding resources for too long. Alternative strategies are discussed in [20].

3.1   Example implementation

We describe here how to extend Goodman's "snoopy" protocol for a shared bus [15] to support transactional memory. (See [20] for similar extensions to a directory-based protocol.) We first describe the general implementation strategy, the various cache line states, and possible bus cycles. We then describe the various possible actions of the processor and the bus snooping cache logic.

3.1.1   General approach

To minimize impact on processing non-transactional loads and stores, each processor maintains two caches: a *regular cache* for non-transactional operations, and a *transactional cache* for transactional operations. These caches are exclusive: an entry may reside in one or the other, but not both. Both caches are primary caches (accessed directly by the processor), and secondary caches may exist between them and the memory. In our simulations, the regular cache is a conventional direct-mapped cache. The transactional

Name	Access	Shared?	Modified?
INVALID	none	—	—
VALID	R	Yes	No
DIRTY	R, W	No	Yes
RESERVED	R, W	No	No

Table 1: Cache line states

Name	Meaning
EMPTY	contains no data
NORMAL	contains committed data
XCOMMIT	discard on commit
XABORT	discard on abort

Table 2: Transactional tags

Name	Kind	Meaning	New access
READ	regular	read value	shared
RFO	regular	read value	exclusive
WRITE	both	write back	exclusive
T_READ	trans	read value	shared
T_RFO	trans	read value	exclusive
BUSY	trans	refuse access	unchanged

Table 3: Bus cycles

cache is a small, fully-associative cache with additional logic to facilitate transaction commit and abort. The overall hardware organization is similar to that used by Jouppi for the *victim cache* [22], and indeed one can readily extend the transactional cache to act as a victim cache as well.

The idea is that the transactional cache holds all the tentative writes, *without* propagating them to other processors or to main memory unless the transaction commits. If the transaction aborts, the lines holding tentative writes are dropped (invalidated); if the transaction commits, the lines may then be snooped by other processors, written back to memory upon replacement, etc. We assume that since the transactional cache is small and fully associative it is practical to use parallel logic to handle abort or commit in a single cache cycle.

3.1.2 Cache line states

Following Goodman, each cache line (regular or transactional) has one of the states in Table 1. The possible accesses permitted are reads and/or writes; the "Shared?" column indicates whether sharing is permitted; and the "Modified?" column indicates whether the line may differ from its copy in main memory.

The transactional cache augments these states with separate *transactional tags* shown in Table 2, used as follows. Transactional operations cache two entries: one with transactional tag XCOMMIT and one XABORT. Modifications are made to the XABORT entry. When a transaction commits, it sets the entries marked XCOMMIT to EMPTY, and XABORT to NORMAL. When it aborts, it sets entries marked XABORT to EMPTY, and XCOMMIT to NORMAL.

When the transactional cache needs space for a new entry, it first searches for an EMPTY entry, then for a NORMAL entry, and finally for an XCOMMIT entry. If the XCOMMIT entry is DIRTY, it must be written back. Notice that XCOMMIT entries are used only to enhance performance. When a ST tentatively updates an entry, the old value must be retained in case the transaction aborts. If the old value is resident in the transactional cache and dirty, then it must either be marked XCOMMIT, or it must be written back to memory. Avoiding such write-backs can substantially enhance performance when a processor repeatedly executes transactions that access the same locations. If contention is low, then the transactions will often hit dirty entries in the transactional cache.

3.1.3 Bus cycles

The various kinds of bus cycles are listed in Table 3. The READ (RFO (read-for-ownership)) cycle acquires shared (exclusive) ownership of the cache line. The WRITE cycle updates main memory when the protocol does write through; it is also used when modified items are replaced. Further, memory snoops on the bus so if a modified item is read by another processor, the main memory version is brought up to date. These cycles are all as in Goodman's original protocol. We add three new cycles. The T_READ and T_RFO cycles are analogous to READ and RFO, but request cache lines transactionally. Transactional requests can be *refused* by responding with a BUSY signal. BUSY helps prevent transactions from aborting each other too much. When a transaction receives a BUSY response, it aborts and retries, preventing deadlock or continual mutual aborts. This policy is theoretically subject to starvation, but could be augmented with a queueing mechanism if starvation is a problem in practice.

3.1.4 Processor actions

Each processor maintains two flags: the *transaction active* (TACTIVE) flag indicates whether a transaction is in progress, and if so, the *transaction status* (TSTATUS) flag indicates whether that transaction is active (*True*) or aborted

(*False*). The TACTIVE flag is implicitly set when a transaction executes its first transactional operation. (This implicit approach seems more convenient than providing an explicit *start transaction* instruction.) Non-transactional operations behave exactly as in Goodman's original protocol. Transactional instructions issued by an aborted transaction cause no bus cycles and may return arbitrary values.[2]

We now consider transactional operations issued by an active transaction (TSTATUS is *True*). Suppose the operation is a LT instruction. We probe the transactional cache for an XABORT entry, and return its value if there is one. If there is no XABORT entry, but there is a NORMAL one, we change the NORMAL entry to an XABORT entry, and allocate a second entry with tag XCOMMIT and the same data.[3] If there is no XABORT or NORMAL entry, then we issue a T_READ cycle. If it completes successfully, we set up two transactional cache entries, one tagged XCOMMIT and one XABORT, both with whatever state the Goodman protocol would get on a READ cycle. If we get a BUSY response, we abort the transaction (set TSTATUS to *False*, drop all XABORT entries, and set all XCOMMIT entries to NORMAL) and return arbitrary data.

For LTX we use a T_RFO cycle on a miss rather than a T_READ, and change the cache line state to RESERVED if the T_RFO succeeds. A ST proceeds like a LTX, except it updates the XABORT entry's data. The cache line state is updated as in the Goodman protocol with LT and LTX acting like LOAD and ST acting like STORE.

The VALIDATE instruction returns the TSTATUS flag, and if it is *False*, sets the TACTIVE flag to *False* and the TSTATUS flag to *True*. The ABORT instruction discards cache entries as previously described, and sets TSTATUS to *True* and TACTIVE to *False*. Finally, COMMIT returns TSTATUS, sets TSTATUS to *True* and TACTIVE to *False*, drops all XCOMMIT cache entries, and changes all XABORT tags to NORMAL.

Interrupts and transactional cache overflows abort the current transaction.

3.1.5 Snoopy cache actions

Both the regular cache and the transactional cache snoop on the bus. A cache ignores any bus cycles for lines not in that cache. The regular cache behaves as follows. On a READ or T_READ, if the state is VALID, the cache returns the value. If the state is RESERVED or DIRTY, the cache returns the value and resets the state to VALID. On a RFO or T_RFO, the cache returns the data and invalidates the line.

The transactional cache behaves as follows. If TSTATUS is *False*, or if the cycle is non-transactional (READ and

RFO), the cache acts just like the regular cache, except that it ignores entries with transactional tag other than NORMAL. On T_READ, if the state is VALID, the cache returns the value, and for all other transactional operations it returns BUSY.

Either cache can issue a WRITE request when it needs to replace a cache line. The memory responds only to READ, T_READ, RFO, and T_RFO requests that no cache responds to, and to WRITE requests.

4   Rationale

It would be possible to use a single cache for both transactional and non-transactional data. This approach has two disadvantages: (1) modern caches are usually set associative or direct mapped, and without additional mechanisms to handle set overflows, the set size would determine the maximum transaction size, and (2) the parallel commit/abort logic would have to be provided for a large primary cache, instead of the smaller transactional cache.

For programs to be portable, the instruction set architecture must guarantee a minimum transaction size, thus establishing a lower bound for the transactional cache size. An alternative approach is suggested by the LimitLESS directory-based cache coherence scheme of Chaiken, Kubiatowicz, and Agarwal [6]. This scheme uses a fast, fixed-size hardware implementation for directories. If a directory overflows, the protocol traps into software, and the software emulates a larger directory. A similar approach might be used to respond to transactional cache overflow. Whenever the transactional cache becomes full, it traps into software and emulates a larger transactional cache. This approach has many of the same advantages as the original LimitLESS scheme: the common case is handled in hardware, and the exceptional case in software.

Other transactional operations might be useful. For example, a simple "update-and-commit" operation (like STORE_COND) would be useful for single-word updates. It might also be convenient for a transaction to be able to drop an item from its read or write set. Naturally, such an operation must be used with care.

One could reduce the need for VALIDATE instructions by guaranteeing that an orphan transaction that applies a LT or LTX instruction to a variable always observes some value previously written to that variable. For example, if a shared variable always holds a valid array index, then it would not be necessary to validate that index before using it. Such a change would incur a cost, however, because an orphan transaction might sometimes have to read the variable's value from memory or another processor's cache.

---

[2] As discussed below in Section 4, it is possible to provide stronger guarantees on values read by aborted transactions.

[3] Different variations are possible here. Also, allocating an entry may involve replacing a dirty cache entry, in which case it must be written back, as previously mentioned.

5 Simulations

Transactional memory is intended to make lock-free synchronization as efficient as conventional lock-based techniques. In this section, we present simulation results suggesting that transactional memory is competitive with well-known lock-based techniques on simple benchmarks. Indeed, transactional memory has certain inherent advantages: for any object that spans more than a single word of memory, techniques based on mutual exclusion must employ an explicit lock variable. Because transactional memory has no such locks, it typically requires fewer memory accesses.

We modified a copy of the Proteus simulator [5] to support transactional memory. Proteus is an execution-driven simulator system for multiprocessors developed by Eric Brewer and Chris Dellarocas of MIT. The program to be simulated is written in a superset of C. References to shared memory are transformed into calls to the simulator, which manages the cache and charges for bus or network contention. Other instructions are executed directly, augmented by cycle-counting code inserted by a preprocessor. Proteus does not capture the effects of instruction caches or local caches.

We implemented two versions of transactional memory, one based on Goodman's snoopy protocol for a bus-based architecture, and one based on the Chaiken directory protocol for a (simulated) Alewife machine [1]. Our motive in choosing these particular protocols was simply ease of implementation: the Proteus release includes implementations of both. As noted below, a more complex snoopy protocol could make spin locks more efficient.

Both simulated architectures use 32 processors. The regular cache is a direct-mapped cache with 2048 lines of size 8 bytes, and the transactional cache has 64 8-byte lines. In both architectures, a memory access (without contention) requires 4 cycles. The network architecture uses a two-stage network with wire and switch delays of 1 cycle each.

The ability to commit and abort transactions quickly is critical to the performance of transactional memory. In our simulations, each access to the regular or transactional cache, including transaction commit and abort, is counted as a single cycle. Single-cycle commit requires that the transactional cache provide logic to reset the transactional tag bits in parallel. Moreover, commit must not force newly-committed entries back to memory. Instead, in the implementations simulated here, committed entries are gradually replaced as they are evicted or invalidated by the ongoing cache coherence protocol.

We constructed three simple benchmarks, and compared transactional memory against two software mechanisms and two hardware mechanisms. The software

```
shared int counter;

void process(int work)
{
    int success = 0, backoff = BACKOFF_MIN;
    unsigned wait;

    while (success < work) {
        ST(&counter, LTX(&counter) + 1);
        if (COMMIT()) {
            success++;
            backoff = BACKOFF_MIN;
        }
        else {
            wait = random() % (01 << backoff);
            while (wait--);
            if (backoff < BACKOFF_MAX)
                backoff++;
        }
    }
}
```

Figure 1: Counting Benchmark

```
typedef struct {
    Word deqs;
    Word enqs;
    Word items[QUEUE_SIZE];
} queue;

unsigned queue_deq(queue *q) {
    unsigned head, tail, result;
    unsigned backoff = BACKOFF_MIN
    unsigned wait;
    while (1) {
        result = QUEUE_EMPTY;
        tail = LTX(&q->enqs);
        head = LTX(&q->deqs);
    /* queue not empty? */
        if (head != tail) {
            result =
            LT(&q->items[head % QUEUE_SIZE]);
            /* advance counter */
            ST(&q->deqs, head + 1);
        }
        if (COMMIT()) break;
        /* abort => backoff */
        wait = random() % (01 << backoff);
        while (wait--);
        if (backoff < BACKOFF_MAX)
            backoff++;
    }
    return result;
}
```

Figure 2: Part of Producer/Consumer Benchmark

```
typedef struct list_elem{
  /* next to dequeue */
  struct list_elem *next;
  /* previously enqueued */
  struct list_elem *prev;
  int value;
} entry;

shared entry *Head, *Tail;

void list_enq(entry* new) {

  entry *old_tail;
  unsigned backoff = BACKOFF_MIN;
  unsigned wait;

  new->next = new->prev = NULL;

  while (TRUE) {
    old_tail = (entry*) LTX(&Tail);
    if (VALIDATE()) {
      ST(&new->prev, old_tail);
      if (old_tail == NULL) {
        ST(&Head, new);
      } else {
        ST(&old_tail->next, new);
      }
      ST(&Tail, new);
      if (COMMIT()) return;
    }
    wait = random() % (01 << backoff);
    while (wait--);
    if (backoff < BACKOFF_MAX)
      backoff++;
  }
}
```

Figure 3: Part of Doubly-Linked List Benchmark

mechanisms were (1) test-and-test-and-set (TTS) [30] spin locks with exponential backoff [3, 28], and (2) software queueing [3, 17, 27]. The hardware mechanisms were (1) LOAD_LINKED/STORE_COND (LL/SC) with exponential backoff, and (2) hardware queueing [16]. For a single-word counter benchmark, we ran the LL/SC implementation directly on the shared variable, while on the others we used LL/SC to implement a spin lock. Both software mechanisms perform synchronization in-line, and all schemes that use exponential backoff use the same fixed minimum and maximum backoff durations. We now give a brief review of these techniques.

A *spin lock* is perhaps the simplest way to implement mutual exclusion. Each processor repeatedly applies a *test-and-set* operation until it succeeds in acquiring the lock. As discussed in more detail by Anderson [3], this naïve technique performs poorly because it consumes excessive amounts of processor-to-memory bandwidth. On a cache-coherent architecture, the *test-and-test-and-set* [30] protocol achieves somewhat better performance by repeatedly rereading the cached value of the lock (generating no memory traffic), until it observes the lock is free, and then applying the *test-and-set* operation directly to the lock in memory. Even better performance is achieved by introducing an exponential delay after each unsuccessful attempt to acquire a lock [3, 27]. Because Anderson and Mellor-Crummey et al. have shown that TTS locks with exponential backoff substantially outperform conventional TTS locks on small-scale machines, it is a natural choice for our experiments.

The LL operation copies the value of a shared variable to a local variable. A subsequent SC to that variable will succeed in changing its value only if no other process has modified that variable in the interim. If the operation does not succeed, it leaves the shared variable unchanged. The LL/SC operations are the principal synchronization primitives provided by the MIPS II architecture [29] and Digital's Alpha [31]. On a cache-coherent architecture, these operations are implemented as single-word transactions — a SC succeeds if the processor retains exclusive access to the entry read by the LL.

In *software queuing*, a process that is unable to acquire a lock places itself on a software queue, thus eliminating the need to poll the lock. Variations of queue locks have been proposed by Anderson [3], by Mellor-Crummey and Scott [27], and by Graunke and Thakkar [17]. Our simulations use the algorithm of Mellor-Crummey and Scott. In *hardware queuing*, queue maintenance is incorporated into the cache coherence protocol itself. The queue's head is kept in memory, and unused cache lines are used to hold the queue elements. The directory-based scheme must also keep the queue tail in memory. Our simulations use a queuing scheme roughly based on the QOSB mechanism of Goodman et al. [16].

5.1 Counting Benchmark

In our first benchmark (code in Figure 1), each of n processes increments a shared counter $2^{16}/n$ times, where n ranges from 1 to 32. In this benchmark, transactions and critical sections are very short (two shared memory accesses) and contention is correspondingly high. In Figure 4, the vertical axis shows the number of cycles needed to complete the benchmark, and the horizontal axis shows the number of concurrent processes. With one exception, transactional memory has substantially higher throughput than any of the other mechanisms, at all levels of concurrency, for both bus-based and directory-based architectures. The explanation is simple: transactional memory uses no explicit locks, and therefore requires fewer accesses to shared memory. For example, in the absence of contention, the TTS spin lock makes at least five references for each increment (a read followed by a test-and-set to acquire the lock, the read and write in the critical section, and a write to release the lock). Similar remarks apply to both software and hardware queueing.

By contrast, transactional memory requires only three shared memory accesses (the read and write to the counter, and the commit, which goes to the cache but causes no bus cycles). The only implementation that outperforms transactional memory is one that applies LL/SC directly to the counter, without using a lock variable. Direct LL/SC requires no commit operation, and thus saves a cache reference. In the other benchmarks, however, this advantage is lost because the shared object spans more than one word, and therefore the only way to use LL/SC is as a spin lock.

Several other factors influence performance. Our implementation of hardware queuing suffers somewhat from the need to access memory when adjusting the queue at the beginning and end of each critical section, although this cost might be reduced by a more sophisticated implementation. In the bus architecture, the TTS spin lock suffers because of an artifact of the particular snoopy cache protocol we adapted [15]: the first time a location is modified, it is marked *reserved* and written back. TTS would be more efficient with a cache protocol that leaves the location *dirty* in the cache.

5.2 Producer/Consumer Benchmark

In the *producer/consumer* benchmark (code in Figure 2), n processes share a bounded FIFO buffer, initially empty. Half of the processes produce items, and half consume them. The benchmark finishes when 2^{16} operations have completed. In the bus architecture (Figure 5), all throughputs are essentially flat. Transactional memory has higher throughputs than the others, although the difference is not as dramatic as in the counting benchmark. In the network architecture, all throughputs suffer somewhat as contention increases, although the transactional memory implementations suffers least.

5.3 Doubly-Linked List Benchmark

In the *doubly-linked list* benchmark (code in Figure 3) n processes share a doubly-linked list anchored by *head* and *tail* pointers. Each process dequeues an item by removing the item pointed to by *tail*, and then enqueues it by threading it onto the list at *head*. A process that removes the last item sets both *head* and *tail* to *NULL*, and a process that inserts an item into an empty list sets both *head* and *tail* to point to the new item. The benchmark finishes when 2^{16} operations have completed.

This example is interesting because it has potential concurrency that is difficult to exploit by conventional means. When the queue is non-empty, each transaction modifies *head* or *tail*, but not both, so enqueuers can (in principle) execute without interference from dequeuers, and vice-versa. When the queue is empty, however, transactions must modify both pointers, and enqueuers and dequeuers conflict. This kind of state-dependent concurrency is not realizable (in any simple way) using locks, since an enqueuer does not know if it must lock the *tail* pointer until after it has locked the *head* pointer, and vice-versa for dequeuers. If an enqueuer and dequeuer concurrently find the queue empty, they will deadlock. Consequently, our locking implementations use a single lock. By contrast, the most natural way to implement the queue using transactional memory permits exactly this parallelism. This example also illustrates how VALIDATE is used to check the validity of a pointer before dereferencing it.

The execution times appear in Figure 6. The locking implementations have substantially lower throughput, primarily because they never allow enqueues and dequeues to overlap.

5.4 Limitations

Our implementation relies on the assumption that transactions have short durations and small data sets. The longer a transaction runs, the greater the likelihood it will be aborted by an interrupt or synchronization conflict[4]. The larger the data set, the larger the transactional cache needed, and (perhaps) the more likely a synchronization conflict will occur.

---

[4]The identical concerns apply to current implementations of the LOAD-LINKED and STORE-COND instructions [31, Appendix A].

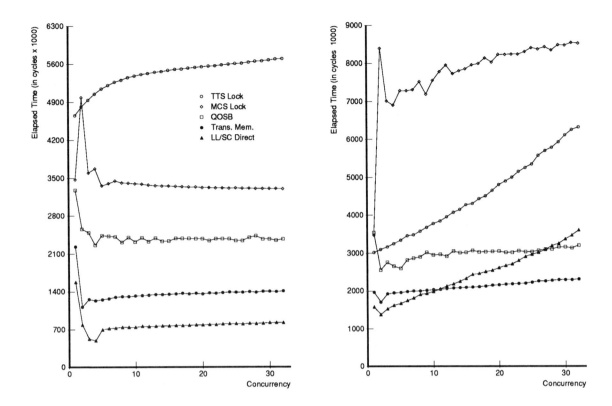

Figure 4: Counting Benchmark: Bus and Network

Such size and length restrictions are reasonable for applications that would otherwise have used short critical sections, but not for applications that would otherwise lock large objects for a long time (such as navigating a B-link tree with a large node size). Support for larger and longer transactions would require more elaborate hardware mechanisms.

The implementation described here does not guarantee forward progress, relying instead on software-level adaptive backoff to reduce the abort rate by spacing out conflicting transactions. Our simulations suggest that adaptive backoff works reasonably well when conflicting transactions have approximately the same duration. If durations differ, however, then longer transactions will be more likely to abort. Some kind of hardware queueing mechanism [16] might alleviate this limitation.

The cache coherence protocols used in our simulations provide a sequentially consistent memory [24]. A number of researchers have proposed weaker notions of correctness that permit more efficient implementations. These alternatives include processor consistency [14], weak consistency [9, 8], release consistency [13], and others[5]. Most of these models guarantee that memory will appear to be

sequentially consistent as long as the programmer executes a *barrier* (or *fence*) instruction at the start and finish of each critical section. The most straightforward way to provide transactional memory semantics on top of a weakly-consistent memory is to have each transactional instruction perform an implicit barrier. Such frequent barriers would limit performance. We believe our implementation can be extended to require barriers only at transaction start, finish, and validate instructions.

6   Related Work

Transactional memory is a direct generalization of the LOAD_LINKED and STORE_COND instructions originally proposed by Jensen et al. [21], and since incorporated into the MIPS II architecture [29] and Digital's Alpha [31]. The LOAD_LINKED instruction is essentially the same as LTX, and STORE_COND is a combination of ST and COMMIT. The LOAD_LINKED/STORE_COND combination can implement any read-modify-write operation, but it is restricted to a single word. Transactional memory has the same flexibility, but can operate on multiple, independently-chosen words.

We are not the first to observe the utility of performing

---

[5]See Gharachorloo et al. [12] for concise descriptions of these models as well as performance comparisons.

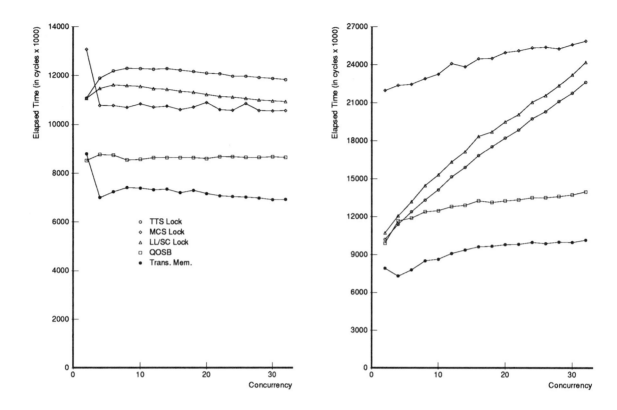

Figure 5: Producer/Consumer Benchmark: Bus and Network

atomic operations on multiple locations. For example, the Motorola 68000 provides a COMPARE&SWAP2 that operates on two independent locations. Massalin and Pu [25] use this instruction for lock-free list manipulation in an operating system kernel. Transactional memory provides more powerful support for this "lock-free" style of programming.

Other work that uses after-the-fact conflict detection to recognize violations of desired correctness conditions include Gharachorloo and Gibbons [11], who propose an implementation of release consistency that exploits an underlying invalidation-based cache protocol to detect violations of sequential consistency, and Franklin and Sohi [10], who propose a hardware architecture that optimistically parallelizes sequential code at runtime.

Other researchers who have investigated architectural support for multi-word synchronization include Knight [23], who suggests using cache coherence protocols to add parallelism to "mostly functional" LISP programs, and the IBM 801 [7], which provides support for database-style locking in hardware. Note that despite superficial similarities in terminology, the synchronization mechanisms provided by transactional memory and by the 801 are intended for entirely different purposes, and use entirely different techniques.

Our approach to performance issues has been heavily influenced by recent work on locking in multiprocessors, including work of Anderson [3], Bershad [4], Graunke and Thakkar [17], and Mellor-Crummey and Scott [27].

7 Conclusions

The primary goal of transactional memory is to make it easier to perform general atomic updates of multiple independent memory words, avoiding the problems of locks (priority inversion, convoying, and deadlock). We sketched how it can be implemented by adding new instructions to the processor, adding a small auxiliary, transactional cache (without disturbing the regular cache), and making straightforward changes to the cache coherence protocol. We investigated transactional memory for its added functionality, but our simulations showed that it outperforms other techniques for atomic updates. This is primarily because transactional memory uses no explicit locks and thus performs fewer shared memory accesses. Since transactional memory offers both improved functionality and better performance, it should be considered in future processor architectures.

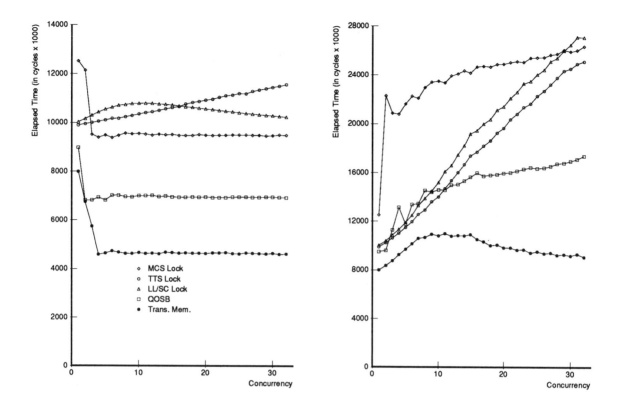

Figure 6: Doubly-Linked List Benchmark: Bus and Network

References

[1] A. Agarwal et al. The MIT Alewife machine: A large-scale distributed-memory multiprocessor. Technical Report TM-454, MIT Lab for Computer Science, 545 Technology Square, Cambridge MA 02139, March 1991. Extended version submitted for publication.

[2] J. Allemany and E.W. Felton. Performance issues in non-blocking synchronization on shared-memory multiprocessors. In *Proceedings of the 11th Annual ACM Symposium on Principles of Distributed Computing*, pages 125–134. ACM, August 1992.

[3] T.E. Anderson. The performance of spin lock alternatives for shared-memory multiprocessors. *IEEE Transactions on Parallel and Distributed Systems*, 1(1):6–16, January 1990.

[4] B.N. Bershad. Practical considerations for lock-free concurrent objects. Technical Report CMU-CS-91-183, Carnegie Mellon University, Pittsburgh, PA, September 1991.

[5] E. A. Brewer, C. N. Dellarocas, A. Colbrook, and W. E. Weihl. PROTEUS: A high-performance parallel architecture simulator. Technical Report MIT/LCS/TR-516, Massachusetts Institute of Technology, September 1991.

[6] D. Chaiken, J. Kubiatowicz, and A. Agarwal. LimitLESS directories: a scalable cache coherence scheme. In *Proceedings of the 4th International Conference on Architectural Support for Programming Langauges and Operating Systems*, pages 224–234. ACM, April 1991.

[7] A. Chang and M.F. Mergen. 801 storage: Architecture and programming. *ACM Transactions on Computer Systems*, 6(1):28–50, February 1988.

[8] Michel Dubois and Christoph Scheurich. Memory access dependencies in shared-memory multiprocessors. *IEEE Transactions on Software Engineering*, 16(6):660–673, June 1990.

[9] Michel Dubois, Christoph Scheurich, and Fayé Briggs. Memory access buffering in multiprocessors. In *Proceedings of the 13th Annual International Symposium on Computer Architecture*, pages 434–442, June 1986.

[10] M. Franklin and G. S. Sohi. The expandable split window paradigm for exploiting fine-grain parallelism. In *Proceedings of the 19th Annual International Symposium on Computer Architecture*, pages 58–67. IEEE, May 1992.

[11] K. Gharachorloo and P. Gibbons. Detecting violations of sequential consistency. In *Proceedings*

of the 2nd Annual Symposium on Parallel Algorithms and Architectures, pages 316–326, July 1991.

[12] Kourosh Gharachorloo, Anoop Gupta, and John Hennessy. Performance evaluation of memory consistency models for shared-memory multiprocessors. In *Fourth International Conference on Architectural Support for Programming Languages and Operating Systems*, pages 245–257, April 1991.

[13] Kourosh Gharachorloo, Dan Lenoski, James Laudon, Phillip Gibbons, Anoop Gupta, and John Hennessy. Memory consistency and event ordering in scalable shared-memory multiprocessors. In *Proceedings of the 17th Annual International Symposium on Computer Architecture*, pages 15–26, June 1990.

[14] James R. Goodman. Cache consistency and sequential consistency. Technical Report 61, SCI Committee, March 1989.

[15] J.R. Goodman. Using cache memory to reduce processor-memory traffic. In *Proceedings of the 12th International Symposium on Computer Architecture*, pages 124–131. IEEE, June 1983.

[16] J.R. Goodman, M.K. Vernon, and P.J. Woest. Efficient synchronization primitives for large-scale cache-coherent multiprocessors. In *Proceedings of the 3rd International Conference on Architectural Support for Programming Languates and Operating Systems*, pages 64–75, April 1989.

[17] G. Graunke and S. Thakkar. Synchronization algorithms for shared-memory multiprocessors. *IEEE Computer*, 23(6):60–70, June 1990.

[18] J.N. Gray. *Notes on Database Operating Systems*, pages 393–481. Springer-Verlag, Berlin, 1978.

[19] M.P. Herlihy. A methodology for implementing highly concurrent data structures. In *Proceedings of the Second ACM SIGPLAN Symposium on Principles and Practice of Parallel Programming*, pages 197–206, March 1990.

[20] M.P. Herlihy and J.E.B. Moss. Transactional memory: Architectural support for lock-free data structures. Technical Report 92/07, Digital Cambridge Research Lab, One Kendall Square, Cambridge MA 02139, December 1992.

[21] E.H. Jensen, G.W. Hagensen, and J.M. Broughton. A new approach to exclusive data access in shared memory multiprocessors. Technical Report UCRL-97663, Lawrence Livermore National Laboratory, November 1987.

[22] N. Jouppi. Improving direct mapped cache performance by the addition of a small fully-associative cache and prefetch buffers. In *17th Annual Internationall Symposium on Computer Architecture*, page 364. ACM SIGARCH, June 1990.

[23] T. Knight. An achitecture for mostly functional languages. In *Conference on Lisp and Functional Programming*, pages 105–112, August 1986.

[24] Leslie Lamport. How to make a multiprocessor computer that correctly executes multiprocess programs. *IEEE Transactions on Computers*, C-28(9):241–248, September 1979.

[25] H. Massalin and C. Pu. A lock-free multiprocessor OS kernel. Technical Report CUCS-005-91, Columbia University Computer Science Dept., 1991.

[26] J.M. Mellor-Crummey. Practical fetch-and-phi algorithms. Technical Report Technical Report 229, Computer Science Dept., University of Rochester, November 1987.

[27] John M. Mellor-Crummey and Michael L. Scott. Algorithms for scalable synchronization on shared-memory multiprocessors. *ACM Transactions on Computer Systems*, 9(1):21–65, February 1991.

[28] R. Metcalfe and D. Boggs. Ethernet: distributed packet switching for local computer networks. *Communications of the ACM*, 19(7):395–404, July 1976.

[29] MIPS Computer Company. The MIPS RISC architecture.

[30] L. Rudolph and Z. Segall. Dynamic decentralized cache schemes for MIMD parallel processors. In *11th Annual International Symposium on Computer Architecture*, pages 340–347, June 1984.

[31] R.L. Sites. *Alpha Architecture Reference Manual*. Digital Press, Maynard, MA, 1992.

[32] J. Wing and C. Gong. Testing and verifying concurrent objects. *Journal of Parallel and Distributed Computing*, 17(2), February 1993.

Evaluation of Mechanisms for Fine-Grained Parallel Programs in the J-Machine and the CM-5

Ellen Spertus[†], Seth Copen Goldstein[‡], Klaus Erik Schauser[‡], Thorsten von Eicken[‡],
David E. Culler[‡], William J. Dally[†]

[†]MIT Artifical Intelligence Laboratory
545 Technology Square
Cambridge, MA 02139
{ellens,billd}@ai.mit.edu

[‡]Computer Science Division — EECS
University of California
Berkeley, CA 94720
tam@cs.berkeley.edu

Abstract

This paper uses an abstract machine approach to compare the mechanisms of two parallel machines: the J-Machine and the CM-5. High-level parallel programs are translated by a single optimizing compiler to a fine-grained abstract parallel machine, TAM. A final compilation step is unique to each machine and optimizes for specifics of the architecture. By determining the cost of the primitives and weighting them by their dynamic frequency in parallel programs, we quantify the effectiveness of the following mechanisms individually and in combination. Efficient processor/network coupling proves valuable. Message dispatch is found to be less valuable without atomic operations that allow the scheduling levels to cooperate. Multiple hardware contexts are of small value when the contexts cooperate and the compiler can partition the register set. Tagged memory provides little gain. Finally, the performance of the overall system is strongly influenced by the performance of the memory system and the frequency of control operations.

Keywords: *Parallel Processing, Performance Analysis, Compilation.*

1 Introduction

Several experimental parallel architectures have been developed in recent years to demonstrate novel hardware mechanisms that may enhance the performance of programs written in emerging parallel languages. For example, Monsoon focuses on Id90, the J-Machine on CST, Alewife on Mul-T, the CM-5 on Fortran90, and Dash and KSR-1 on extensions to C and Fortran. All of these architectures provide a family of mechanisms that collectively support the requirements of the parallel language, are universal enough to support any of the other language paradigms, and are real enough to be constrained by the traditional technology forces. Thus, it would seem that the time has come for parallel architecture research to begin the shift from "big new ideas" to careful quantitative analysis of the effectiveness of various mechanisms. In this paper, we seek to evaluate the set of mechanisms in the MIT J-Machine with respect to the implicitly parallel language Id90 and draw a quantitative comparison with the CM-5.

At the current state of parallel computing, a completely satisfactory quantitative analysis of mechanisms is difficult to achieve because there is no well-established body of machine-independent software reflected in a standard set of benchmarks. There is not even a consensus on the programming languages of choice. Where benchmarks exist, they have been developed specifically for the machine that they are intended to evaluate [14, 9] or specifically avoid emerging languages and the novel mechanisms which could bring them within practical reach [3]. It is also difficult to obtain high-quality compilers for such new languages on more than one machine, yet it is well understood that the architectural support can only be evaluated in the context of sophisticated compilation, rather than direct execution of high-level constructs. Finally, the machines reflect substantially varying engineering budgets and designer capabilities, which should be factored out of the evaluation of the architectural contribution. Simply comparing execution times gives only a crude and noisy calibration, failing to isolate the reasons for the differences.

The method of analysis employed in this paper is as follows. We consider two recent parallel machines: the J-Machine, developed at MIT as a study in universal mechanisms for fine-grained parallelism, and the CM-5, developed at Thinking Machines Corp. as a commercial product supporting data-parallel programs. We take as a basis for comparison a powerful machine-independent parallel language, Id90, which was not the primary target for either architecture, but for which a high-quality compilation system exists. The compiler performs a variety of high-level optimizations in translating the language down to code for a simple abstract machine, TAM [6, 13]. The TAM code is identical for the two machines, controlling for effects of high-level optimizations. The translator from TAM code to machine language, however, employs a variety of machine-specific optimizations reflecting the most advantageous use of the available mechanisms. The performance of isolated mechanisms is reflected in the cost of the individual TAM primitives on the machine. The overall effectiveness of the family of mechanisms is determined by weighting each of the primitives by its frequency in a suite of programs. The J-Machine essentially provides direct hardware support for every aspect of TAM; however, TAM does not use all the mechanisms in the machine. The CM-5 provides a variety of mechanisms for data-parallel programming, which are not useful to TAM. What remains is a very reasonable baseline machine, essentially a collection of workstation-class processors on a dedicated network. Thus, we can compare a sophisticated set of mechanisms against a familiar baseline architecture with respect to the dynamic load presented by Id90 programs compiled to TAM.

Section 2 describes the two architectures under study and explains the salient aspects of TAM. TAM-level dynamic instruction frequencies are produced for a variety of programs to serve as a basis for comparison. Section 3 corrects for a set of architectural and engineering factors that have a significant impact on execution time for the two machines, but for which conventional wisdom (and hindsight) applies. The remaining sections deal with architectural aspects that are unique to parallel computing. Section 4 examines the impact of the processor/network coupling on message-passing cost. Section 5 looks at three mechanisms related to asynchronous message arrival that interact with dynamic scheduling. Section 6 considers the utility of tagged memory words and Section 7 ties together our observations. Two important lessons arise from the study. First, novel mechanisms do not substitute for solid engineering of the processor pipeline and storage hierarchy. Second, mechanisms should not be evaluated in isolation, but in how they work together in the compilation framework for the programming language.

2 Background

2.1 CM-5

The CM-5 [16] is a massively-parallel MIMD computer based on the Sparc processor, interconnected in two identical disjoint "hypertree" networks. Each node consists of a 33 MHz Sparc RISC processor chip-set (including FPU, MMU and 64 KByte cache), 8 MBytes of local DRAM memory and a network interface to the hypertrees and broadcast/scan/prefix control networks. (The node may also contain vector units with additional memory, but we will not address the vector capability.) The network interface consists of a pair of memory-mapped FIFO queues for each of the two data networks. Messages are limited to a maximum of five 32-bit words in length. Message delivery is reliable, but no guarantee is made on ordering. The study uses a 128-node CM-5, although machines of 1024 nodes are currently in the field.

2.2 J-Machine

The J-Machine is a massively-parallel MIMD computer based on the Message-Driven Processor (MDP) interconnected by a 3-D mesh network. The MDP is a single-chip processing node composed of a 16 MHz 32-bit integer unit, a 4K by 36-bit static memory, a closely integrated network interface, a packet router, and an ECC DRAM controller. The on-chip memory is augmented with a 256K by 36-bit off-chip memory. The 36-bit words include 4-bit tags, which indicate data types such as booleans, integers, and user-defined types. Two special tag values *future* and *cfuture* cause a trap when accessed. The MDP has three separate priority levels: background, 0, and 1, each of which has a complete context, consisting of an instruction pointer, four address registers, four general-purpose registers, and other special-purpose registers. A 512-node J-Machine has been built, and a 1024-node machine is planned.

The MDP implements a prioritized scheduler in hardware. When a message arrives at its destination node, it is automatically written into a message queue, consisting of a fixed-size ring buffer in on-chip memory. Background execution is interrupted by priority 0 message reception, which in turn may be interrupted by priority 1 message reception.

2.3 TAM

TAM defines a fine-grained parallel execution model used as a compilation target for Id90. Although it grew out of work on dataflow, it defines a simple model of self-scheduling threads that can be implemented on any machine. The key ways in which TAM differs from "thread packages" are that TAM threads are even lighter weight, the scheduling is integrated with aspects of compilation, such as register allocation, and there is no external scheduler.

A TAM program consists of a collection of *code-blocks*, which typically represent functions or loops in the source program. Each code-block consists of a collection of *threads*, which correspond roughly to basic blocks. Two instructions appear in the same thread only if they can be statically ordered and if no operation whose latency is unbounded occurs between them.

The TAM execution model centers on the *activation frame*, which is the analog of a stack frame for parallel calls. To invoke a code-block, a frame is allocated on a processor and initialized, and arguments are sent to the frame. Initialization consists of setting the values of *synchronization counters* stored within the frame. A thread is allowed to run only when all its antecedents have been executed. To detect the completion of antecedents, a synchronization counter is associated with each thread. The counter is omitted for threads that have only one antecedent, *i.e., unsynchronizing* threads. For each frame, a stack of instruction pointers, called the *continuation vector* (CV), holds the list of threads that are ready to run. The arguments to the code-block, results from subordinate calls, and responses to global heap accesses are received by *inlets*. Inlets are compiler-generated message handlers that copy the arguments into the frame and enable computation dependent on the message. In order to process requests from the network quickly, inlets are small and run at a higher priority than threads.

Maintaining the thread queue in the frames provides a natural two-level scheduling hierarchy. When a frame is scheduled, the *remote* continuation vector (RCV) is copied into the *local* continuation vector (LCV), from which enabled threads are executed until the LCV is empty. The set of threads that run during this time is called a *quantum*. Each processor maintains a queue of *ready* frames with non-empty CVs. A new frame is activated from the queue when a quantum completes.

Global data structures in TAM provide synchronization on a per-element basis to support I-structure and M-structure semantics [10]. In particular, reads of empty elements are deferred until the corresponding write occurs. Accesses to the data structures are split-phase and are performed via special instructions: `ifetch` reads an element by sending a message to the processor containing the data which returns the value to an inlet, `istore` writes a value to an element, resuming any deferred readers, and `ialloc` and `ifree` allocate and deallocate I-structures.

In the current implementation of TAM, instructions are primarily three address, where the operands are constants, registers, or frame locations. TAM registers and frame slots are statically typed into integers, floats, various pointers, and generals. Generals are sufficiently large to contain any TAM type but do not identify the type. Correct compilation ensures that the producer and consumer of a general agree on the type of the contained value. No fixed limit is placed on the number of TAM registers, although the compiler tries to use them as efficiently as possible. The translator from TAM to a target machine is responsible for mapping TAM registers to physical registers or spill areas.

The key issues presented by TAM are the parallel call, dynamic synchronization of computation with asynchronous responses from both remote requests and calls, split-phase remote operations, and the overlap of computation with communication.

2.4 Mapping to the machines

The basic mapping of TAM to the two machines is relatively straightforward. Program code is placed on every processor, but a given code-block invocation takes place on a single processor. Because the compiler may pull loops out into separate code-blocks, these can be spread across the machine to implement parallel loops [7]. The memory on each processor is divided into two areas. One holds small arrays and activation frames. The other holds large arrays, which are spread across all the processors such that logically consecutive elements are on different processors. Memory is managed explicitly through library routines.

The J-Machine implementation of TAM [15] makes direct use of the hardware support for different priority levels. Threads run at the background priority level, allowing them to be quickly interrupted by messages arriving in the priority 0 queue. (Priority 1 is currently not used.) Because each priority level has its own register set, inlets do not interfere with thread execution. An address register is set aside in each register set to hold the frame pointer. Threads use an additional general-purpose register to hold the address of the top of the LCV. Two general-purpose registers are used as temporaries to hold memory operands and to implement complex TAM instructions. The remaining general-purpose register is used to hold one TAM register. All other TAM registers are mapped to the base of on-chip memory, a region that can be addressed easily. Frames are stored in main memory.

A similar approach is followed on the Sparc with inlets using a new register window. However, due to the tight coupling between threads and inlets, it proves to be more efficient to simply partition a single window. The CM-5 implementation [8] uses 32 registers divided into three classes: *global registers* which hold frequently-used values, *TAM registers* which are preserved for the duration of a quantum, and *inlet registers*, used during inlet execution and to pass information from threads to inlets. The CM-5 translator attempts to keep as many TAM variables as possible in the TAM registers and spills the rest into the frame.

2.5 Benchmarks

The empirical basis for comparison is provided by six benchmark programs described below. TAM-level dynamic instruction distributions are collected by running an instrumented version of the program on the CM-5. The translator inserts in-line code to record roughly a hundred specific statistics on each processor, which are combined at the end of the program.[1] These are grouped into the basic

---

[1] The Benchmark programs, raw data, and tools to process the data can be retrieved by anonymous FTP from ftp.cs.berkeley.edu under /ucb/TAM/isca93.tar.Z.

instruction categories in Figure 1. *ALU* includes integer and floating-point arithmetic, *messages* includes instructions executed to handle messages, *heap* includes global I-structure and M-structure accesses, and *control* represents all control-flow instructions including moves to initialize synchronization counters.

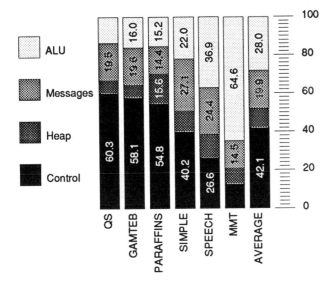

Figure 1: *Dynamic instruction mix statistics for the benchmark programs. The final column shows the arithmetic mean of the distributions.*

Six benchmark programs ranging from 50 to 1,100 lines are used. *QS* is a simple quick-sort using accumulation lists. The input is a list of random numbers. *Gamteb* is a Monte Carlo neutron transport code [4]. It is highly recursive with many conditionals. *Paraffins* [2] enumerates the distinct isomers of paraffins. *Simple* is a hydrodynamics and heat conduction code widely used as an application benchmark, rewritten in Id90 [5, 1]. *Speech* determines cepstral coefficients for speech processing. *MMT* is a simple matrix operation test using 4x4 blocks; two double precision identity matrices are created, multiplied, and subtracted from a third.

The programs toward the left of Figure 1 represent fine-grained parallelism. Notice that they are control intensive and make frequent remote references, as opposed to the blocked matrix multiply which is dominated by arithmetic. We will focus primarily on the two largest programs, Gamteb and Simple.

The Id90 implementations of these programs take about twice as long on a single processor as implementations in standard languages like C or Fortran [6]. Some of this overhead (mostly seen in the amount of control in Figure 1) is recouped in the parallel implementation.

3 Baseline Architectural Issues

By relating the dynamic statistics to the cost of the implementation of each TAM primitive we can obtain an estimate of how time is spent on each machine and isolate the contribution of specific mechanisms. However, there are several significant engineering differences between the study machines including cycle time, pipelining, floating point support, caches, and message size. These differences are determined primarily by circumstances under which the machines were developed and do not reflect significant architectural characteristics. The J-Machine was developed by a small academic team and many tradeoffs were made in favor of reduced design time at the expense of absolute performance. The CM-5 was developed by a relatively small company with significant time-to-market pressures. However, it was able to exploit the sizable investment in the Cypress Sparc chip set. To understand the impact of the novel mechanisms in detail, we first compensate for these differences. In particular we adjust the cycle time, floating point performance, and memory system of the J-Machine to reflect advances in technology and engineering that have occurred since it was implemented.

In this section we develop hypothetical versions of the two machines, called J'-Machine and CM-5', with similar engineering characteristics. The predicted performance breakdown of the two real and two hypothetical machines on our benchmark programs is shown in Figure 2 and explained below. The metric used is cycles per TAM instruction (CPT). The bars show the contribution to the CPT resulting from each class of TAM instruction. Three new segments have been introduced to highlight important implementation issues. The *memory* system segment at the top indicates the penalty introduced due to cache misses. Since the J-Machine manages the movement between SRAM and DRAM explicitly, there is no direct penalty. The *operands* segment reflects the memory access penalty in bringing data into registers for ALU instructions. The *atomicity* segment at the bottom accounts for overhead in ensuring certain operations are atomic. The *heap* bar has been split into three distinct implementation components.

Our main task in the paper is to show how the cost coefficients are determined for each category, and specifically how the novel mechanisms in the J-Machine contribute toward reducing each cost. In this section we address the top two segments, because these have to do with conventional processor efficiency. The remaining sections examine the lower segments, which involve issues that are unique to fine-grained parallelism. The factors that we normalize are the following.

Cycle time and pipelining: The Cypress Sparc processor in the CM-5 has a cycle time of 30 ns and has a four-stage pipeline, while the MDP in the J-Machine has a

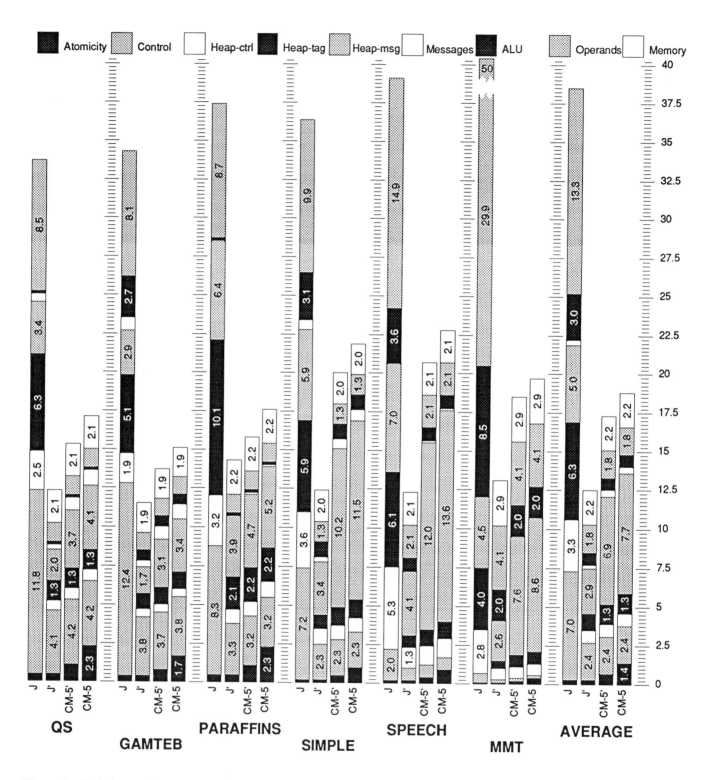

Figure 2: *Relative performance of the J-Machine, the CM-5 and their hypothetical variations on the sample dynamic instruction mix. The variations are used in the study to compensate for differences in engineering which do not offer any new architectural insight. Since the J-Machine does not have a cache, the memory penalty is factored into the other segments.*

cycle time of 62.5 ns and is unpipelined. Since the novel mechanisms of the J-Machine do not fundamentally impact cycle time or pipelining, we ignore these differences. We scale DRAM access time accordingly and measure it in terms of processor cycles. We also assume the MDP has the same control pipeline as the Sparc; in particular, we introduce annulling branches and branch delay slots into the MDP.

Networks and load balancing: In the analysis, we assume the performance characteristics of the network to be identical in the two machines and to affect each processor in a similar way. Similarly, we assume idle time resulting from inadequate parallelism or improper load balancing to affect the two machines equally.

Floating point arithmetic: On the Sparc, floating point operations run on a co-processor and take roughly seven cycles, unless overlapped with integer execution. The MDP has no built-in floating-point hardware, so software routines, typically taking 12–28 cycles, are used. For this analysis, we assume that the J'-Machine has the same floating point support as the Sparc. For all arithmetic-logic operations, operands in the frame must be brought into registers by explicit load instructions (2 cycles for 32-bit operands, 3 cycles for 64-bit), and results must be stored back (3 cycles for 32-bit, 4 cycles for 64-bit).

Storage hierarchy: Both machines have a 3-level memory hierarchy — registers, SRAM, and DRAM. However, the two faster levels differ significantly. The MDP has eight general-purpose or address registers for each of three priority levels. The Sparc has overlapping register windows of 32 registers each. The MDP has on-chip SRAM mapped into the bottom of the address space. One additional cycle is required to read the on-chip SRAM and 6 for off-chip DRAM, which we treat as 2 and 12, respectively, since we have doubled the MDP's clock rate. The Sparc has off-chip SRAM organized as a 64 Kbyte direct-mapped unified data and instruction cache. Cache hits causes a one-cycle processor stall, while refills from DRAM take 20 cycles. We assume that the J'-Machine has as many registers and the same memory system as the Sparc. A cache miss rate of 5% is used.

Message size: The TAM `send` and `receive` instructions do not place a limit on the number of words transferred. Although most messages are small, arguments to a code-block may involve a few tens of data elements. On the J-Machine, these can be delivered in a single message to a single inlet. The CM-5 limits the message size to five 32-bit words; thus, large messages are broken into smaller messages which are each sent to different inlets (to handle possible reordering of the smaller messages), incurring additional overhead. The CM-$5'$ is assumed to be able to send larger packets, 16 words, which is sufficient to hold the biggest message generated in our benchmarks.

Polling: Due to the current implementation of the network interface in the CM-5 the two data networks must be polled separately, which doubles the cost of polls. In the future both data networks will be polled simultaneously, which is what we assume for the CM-$5'$.

Correcting for the memory system and lack of floating point results in a significant improvement of the J'-Machine performance. Observe this improvement affects all the categories in Figure 2. After the correction, the time spent in arithmetic operations and memory access is nearly identical on the two machines. More interestingly, adding a cache and registers results in a more uniform memory system and increases processor state which not only speeds up ALU operations but allows for significant optimizations of all TAM instructions. This is particularly noticeable in how similar the cost of control becomes between the J'-Machine and the CM-$5'$.

The message, control, and heap components are the remaining factors and demonstrate significant differences between the machines. These are examined in detail below to explain precisely how these costs arise.

4 Processor/Network Coupling

This section examines the cost of sending and receiving messages and relates it to architectural features in the two machines. The J-Machine provides extensive message support with an intimate coupling between the processor and network, whereas the CM-5 has a memory-mapped network interface connected to the MBUS on each node.

4.1 TAM requirements

The *messages* segment in Figure 2 reflects the cost of passing arguments and return values for function calls, and of initializing loop constants and forwarding iteration variables for parallel loops. In TAM a message is formed and issued with the `send` instruction, which sends a number of data values to an inlet of a potentially remote frame. The message is received by a `receive` instruction in the destination inlet which extracts the data from the message and stores it into the frame. The adjacent segment of the *heap* segment reflects the cost of the message component of global data structure accesses, represented by `ifetch` and `istore` instructions. Note that a heap fetch requires two messages, a request to the node containing the accessed element and a response with the data.

4.2 Hardware support

On the J-Machine, the SEND instruction appends one or two 32-bit values to the message currently being composed. The first word of the message contains the destination address, and a bit in the SEND instruction indicates the end of the message and completes its injection into the network. Overflow of the output buffer causes a fault. The CM-5 operates similarly with two exceptions: the message data must be stored into the outgoing fixed length FIFO queue of the memory-mapped network interface, and the network interface status register must be checked after each message to verify its successful injection. If the network is backed-up, the CM-5 network interface simply discards additional messages, and the program must retry the SEND until the status register indicates success.

Hardware support for message reception differs substantially on the two machines. The J-Machine implements asynchronous message reception by directly storing messages into an on-chip queue and dispatching to the code indicated by the first word of the message at the head of the queue, i.e., the inlet. The inlet may load the message data one word at a time into registers from there. On the CM-5 message arrival is detected by software polling. When a message has arrived, software loads the first word of the message into a register and dispatches on it. The message data is received through additional loads from the network interface.

While an asynchronous message reception model appears most natural on the J-Machine, an alternate synchronous implementation is also possible: the message dispatch mechanism can be kept generally disabled except for short periods during which the network is essentially polled. This approach maintains the advantage of fast hardware dispatch but lets the compiler control when the computation can be interrupted by inlets. This will be shown to be a useful property in the following section. Similarly, an asynchronous message reception model can be implemented on the CM-5 using interrupts: on message arrival the network interface signals an interrupt, causing the Sparc to trap to the kernel. The kernel forwards the interrupt to the user process by creating a stack frame for the inlet and returning to it.

4.3 Implementation costs

Table 1 shows the cost of sending and receiving a message using synchronous and asynchronous reception on both machines. The start-up cost for sending a message to a remote processor is 3.5 times as high on the CM-5' as on the J'-Machine, mainly due to the status register check. The per-word cost is twice as high on the CM-5', due to the cost of stores across the MBUS. Periodic polling is required in the synchronous reception models. The start-up cost for receiving a message includes the dispatch and the return to the interrupted computation. It is roughly twice as high on the CM-5' with synchronous reception. However, the extremely high receive start-up cost for the asynchronous reception on the CM-5' shows that the user-level interrupt which comes with the hardware dispatch is a

dramatic improvement. The 100 cycles for the kernel trap on the CM-5' is an approximation and assumes that, on average, two to three messages are received back-to-back per interrupt. Notice that the asynchronous model also increases the cost of local messages, in that local messages must be atomic with respect to remote messages. A remote ifetch involves two messages (request and reply), and a remote istore involves a single message.

Given the high message cost on the CM-5', it is advantageous to treat local messages as a special case in software if their frequency is non-negligible, i.e., to exploit send to local frames and ifetch and istore to local structures. The required destination check costs two cycles per message. The rightmost section of Table 1 shows the resulting costs for local messages. This optimization was tried on the J-Machine and found to hurt performance, so the general SEND mechanism is used for all messages. Local messages on the CM-5' are cheaper than on the J'-Machine because the data does not need to be moved in and out of the network interface. The local ifetch and istore entries show that optimizing for local messages can enable further optimizations: the access portion of the ifetch is performed directly in the thread and if the data is present the threads which use it can be enabled cheaply, as discussed in Section 6.

4.4 Discussion

The implementation costs highlight three key points: network access cost is far higher on the CM-5' than on the J'-Machine, receiving is more expensive than sending on both machines, and optimizing for local messages can be valuable. On Simple, where 93% of the messages are remote, the CM-5' spends three times as much time on messages as the J'-Machine. However, on Gamteb where 30% of the messages are local the CM-5' spends only twice as much time.

The high network interface access cost on the CM-5' is due to the node architecture which connects the network interface chip to the MBUS. As a result, all loads and stores take 7 cycles each (8 cycles for double-word loads or stores). Further, checking the status register after every send accounts for 1/3 of the send cost. On the other hand, the J-Machine effectively connects the network interface to the ALU bus. The J-Machine faults if the outgoing send buffers overflow, so, while a fault handler is necessary to retry, the check is free. Asynchronous message reception is prohibitively expensive on the CM-5' due to poor support for user-level interrupts in the Sparc.

Several factors cause message reception to be more expensive than sending. Sending is synchronous to the computation whereas reception is logically asynchronous. Thus values to be sent are typically available in registers, whereas values received must be stored in memory until the waiting

TAM operation	Cycles					
	J'-Machine All Messages		CM-5'			
			Remote Messages		Local Messages	
	sync.	async.	sync.	async.	sync.	async.
Send N-word message	$7+N$	$7+N$	$25+4\lceil\frac{N}{2}\rceil$	$25+4\lceil\frac{N}{2}\rceil$	$2+N$	$4+N$
Receive N-word message	$5+7\lceil\frac{N}{2}\rceil$	$5+7\lceil\frac{N}{2}\rceil$	$13+12\lceil\frac{N}{2}\rceil$	$\approx100+12\lceil\frac{N}{2}\rceil$	$2+4\lceil\frac{N}{2}\rceil$	$4+4\lceil\frac{N}{2}\rceil$
Poll	4	—	9	—	—	—
Ifetch message	24	24	93	≈190	16 or 4†	18 or 4†
Istore message	15	15	60	≈160	2 or 0†	4 or 2†

†: Cost when the element is present for an `ifetch`, or empty for an `istore`.

Table 1: *Local cost for sending and receiving messages.*

computation can be scheduled.[2] Reception involves a dispatch, while sending does not. Finally, stores to the CM-5' network interface can take advantage of the write buffer, while loads see the full latency. On the MDP, the send buffer can be written to at the rate of two words per cycle through the SEND instruction, while reading a word from the message queue takes 3 normalized cycles, the same as any on-chip memory access.

An intimate processor/network coupling reduces the cost of actual message transmission, but we must also account for the cost of dynamic scheduling introduced by messages, since they must be integrated with the rest of the program. Optimizing for local messages raised this issue, which the following sections address in more detail.

5 Dynamic Scheduling and Control Cost

This section examines the cost of control and shows how it is influenced by a combination of hardware mechanisms: prioritized scheduling and dispatch, multiple contexts, and atomic operations. While in a more conventional setting, we would be concerned only with the costs of jumps and branches, in the context of fine-grained parallel programs, the flow of control in the program is closely tied to the asynchronous arrival of messages, so we must also be concerned with the costs of dynamic scheduling and synchronization.

5.1 TAM requirements

The bottom three segments in Figure 2 show the relative cost of control. In TAM control is realized with the fork, switch, post, and swap instructions. Basic control flow is described by the fork instruction, which attempts to enable a thread in the current frame, and switch, which is a conditional fork to one of two threads. If a thread is synchronizing, it has an associated synchronization counter in the frame. Fork will decrement the counter and, if the counter becomes zero, enable the thread. When a fork

---
[2]Moving computation into the inlet, as in a message-driven model, does not help because it replaces memory accesses for storing message data with memory accesses for retrieving local operands.

succeeds then the thread address is pushed onto the LCV, the structure that holds the list of threads that are ready to run for the current frame. At the end of every thread is a stop instruction, which pops the next enabled thread and transfers control to it.

In addition, threads can be enabled from inlets by a post instruction. Whereas fork enables a thread for the currently running frame, post enables a thread for the frame associated with the message, whether it is currently running, idle, or ready. A post of a synchronizing thread requires decrementing the synchronization counter, just as fork does. If the post enables the thread, then it must check the state of the frame. If the frame is idle, it is made ready and placed on the frame queue. Finally, the swap instruction schedules the next frame from the ready queue.

Observe that inlets and threads cooperate in determining the flow of computation, but inlets may preempt threads to handle incoming messages. The two levels of scheduling share the synchronization counters, the continuation vector, and the frame ready queue. Thus, the implementation must guarantee that either thread and frame scheduling operations (*e.g.*, fork, stop, and swap) are atomic with respect to post instructions or that threads and inlets use distinct resources.

5.2 Hardware support

Recall that the J-Machine provides distinct priority levels for threads and inlets with separate register sets, and upon message arrival the hardware dispatches to the inlet, unless interrupts have been explicitly disabled. Since there are no read-modify-write operations on memory, disabling interrupts becomes the primary means of ensuring atomicity. The CM-5 has a single user level, uses a single register set, and, as described in the previous section, uses a synchronous model for receiving messages.

5.3 Implementation

The implementation of the fork, stop, and swap instructions is basically the same on both machines. The translator specializes most forks into fall throughs and branches, which eliminates the corresponding `stop` at the end of the thread. The remaining forks translate into a push onto the LCV. A pointer to the top of the LCV is kept in a register. The top portion of Table 2 shows the cost of the specific code sequences, depending on the position of the `fork` in the thread and whether the destination thread is synchronizing. Taking the dynamic frequencies of these cases into account, the average cost of a `fork` is about 8 cycles on both the CM-5' and J'-Machine. Nonetheless, forks account for roughly half of the cost of control operations. Both machines implement synchronization counters as locations in the frame which must be initialized to the entry count of their associated thread. This incurs the cost of a memory write.

The instruction sequence executed for `post` depends on whether or not the target thread is synchronizing and on the state of the frame. When the frame is idle or ready, the CV pointer is contained in the frame, not a register. Also, if the frame is idle it must be placed on the ready queue. However, if the thread is being posted to the running frame, it can simply be pushed onto the LCV, like a fork. On the J'-Machine, the cost of a `post` to a running frame is higher because the register holding the pointer to the top of the LCV is stored in the low-priority (thread) context, causing a slight penalty for high-priority (inlet) code access. Similarly, determining if the `post` is for the running frame incurs the cost of accessing the other register context.

5.4 CM-5: Compiler-controlled message reception

The CM-5 translator inserts polls into the threads to allow for message reception. The poll incurs a cost of 9 cycles; however, by placing the polls in the appropriate places, it ensures that `fork`, `stop`, and `swap` run atomically relative to `post`. Eliminating the cost of polling by implementing an interrupt-based approach on the CM-5 is impractical for fine-grained parallelism. This is due to the high cost of an interrupt, about the same as 10 polls.

The cost of a `post` is reduced further in inlets that handle an `ifetch` response. If the element being fetched is local and present (see Section 6), the response inlet is inlined into the thread. This eliminates all the inlet overhead and as a result turns the `post` into a `fork`. The result is that the average `post` instruction takes between 9 and 13 cycles depending on the application program.

5.5 J-Machine: Asynchronous message reception

The J-Machine supports two-level scheduling directly, with threads interrupted by the automatic dispatch to an inlet. The challenge with this approach is ensuring that the `fork`, `switch`, and `swap` instructions run atomically.

TAM operation	J'' cycles	J' cycles	CM-5' cycles
Fork a thread			
Fall through	0	0	0
Branch to thread			
unsynchronizing	1	1	1
successful sync.	4	4	4
unsuccessful sync.	13	13	13
Push thread onto CV			
unsynchronizing	5	5	5
successful sync.	10	10	10
unsuccessful sync.	7	7	7
Switch one of two threads	fork+2	fork+2	fork+2
Stop (pop thread from CV)	5	5	5
Poll	0	4	9
Initialize sync. counter	4	4	4
Post a thread from inlet			
Idle frame			
unsynchronizing	19	19	19
successful sync.	24	24	23
unsuccessful sync.	11	7	7
Ready frame			
unsynchronizing	15	15	14
successful sync.	20	20	19
unsuccessful sync.	11	7	7
Running frame			
unsynchronizing	31	10	8
successful sync.	31	15	12
unsuccessful sync.	27	7	7

Table 2: *Cost of TAM synchronization and scheduling instructions. J''-Machine represents the asynchronous J'-Machine, discussed in Section 5.5. For most operations, several different versions reflect the various compiler optimizations or runtime conditions, such as whether a `fork` can be combined with a `stop` into a branch, whether the target thread is synchronizing, and whether the synchronization was successful or not.*

The first approach we adopted was to restrict the use of shared resources, i.e., the synchronization counters and CV pointers. In this approach, each inlet contains code to check whether the inlet frame is the same as the currently-running frame. If so, the synchronization counter and the thread address are pushed onto a special stack which does not interfere with thread execution. When the CV is empty, these posts are processed. Message interrupts are disabled when the special stack is being cleared. Swapping frames is made atomic by explicitly disabling interrupts.

This approach had the advantage of leaving interrupts disabled a minimal amount of time, shortening the waiting time of incoming messages, meaning that requests are serviced more quickly and the queue is less likely to overflow.

However, the cost of a `post` to a running frame (including the subsequent processing) was considered unacceptably high, as shown in Table 2. The cost of an unsuccessful `post` is also higher since the status of the frame must be checked before the synchronization counter is decremented and tested.

By leaving interrupts disabled for a significant proportion of thread execution, the J-Machine can almost be thought of as using polling instead of being fully message-driven. Setting or resetting the interrupt flag on the MDP takes two one-cycle instructions, which makes the J-Machine "poll" instruction 4 cycles.

5.6 Discussion

Control in fine-grained parallel programs involves the integration of asynchronous events with the control flow internal to the computation. In TAM, the two are closely related as the compiler generates the code for both scheduling levels. With this kind of coupling, the compiler can partition the available registers by convention; hardware partitioning into distinct contexts can restrict how registers can be used and can prevent certain optimizations.

The close relationship between the two levels also requires that asynchronous scheduling be complemented by efficient atomic operations on shared resources. Polling for messages avoids this issue and is acceptable for fine-grained parallelism. For instance, in our benchmark programs, polling accounts, on average, for 4% of execution time. It may, however, constitute unnecessary overhead for coarser-grained computation.

In hindsight, it appears that instead of focusing resources on multiple register contexts, it would be more advantageous to provide support for atomicity and fine-grained control operations, like `fork`, which contribute as much as 40% to the cost of running a program.

6 Heap access cost

The I-structure memory model used in TAM requires split-phase access to synchronizing data structures in the global heap. Implementing this memory model has multiple facets: (i) to access a remote heap location involves generating a request message, (ii) to perform synchronization on memory *elements*, each is augmented by a few tag bits which must be checked and updated on every access, and (iii) remote and suspended accesses must be delivered to the computation when they complete. The costs of the first and third parts were described in Sections 4 and 5, respectively. This section focuses on the middle portion and considers whether J-Machine hardware support for tags is beneficial.

6.1 Requirements

In TAM, the heap consists of 64-bit elements, each with a small tag. The tag indicates whether the element is empty, holds data, points to a list of waiting (deferred) readers, or holds a thunk which must be evaluated to yield the data value. The exact state transitions follow Id90 I-structure semantics and permit synchronization on a per-element basis. The discussion in this section focuses on I-structures, but it applies equally to other global heap structures (*e.g.*, M-structures). Three issues arise in implementing I-structure operations: representing the presence bits, checking and updating their state on every access, and maintaining the lists of deferred readers.

6.2 Hardware support

The J-Machine provides tagged memory in hardware to support dynamic typing and dynamic synchronization. Each 32-bit memory word is augmented with 4 tag bits, and instructions may trap on certain tag values. TAM does not require dynamic typing, so it cannot demonstrate the benefit of this use of tags. (A significant component of the high-level compilation process from Id90 to TAM is type inference and resolution of overloading to eliminate the need for dynamic typing.) Tags are used to support the I-structure state transitions, without binding the specific semantics of I-structures in hardware.

6.3 Implementation

On the J-Machine, each I-structure element uses two words and one four-bit tag which will trap on access to futures (empty locations), transferring control to a handler that enqueues deferred reads in a linked list, the head of which is stored in the structure element. Each link in the list holds the node, inlet, and frame information necessary to satisfy the read when a write occurs. When an I-structure is allocated each element's tag must be set to empty, which requires one store per element.

On the CM-5, the tags are stored in a memory area disjoint from the data area. One tag byte is allocated for each 8-byte I-structure element, which allows 8 tags to be cleared at once. All I-structure accesses must explicitly check the tag byte before reading or writing the data. Deferred reads are handled similarly as on the J-Machine.

6.4 Discussion

Table 3 shows the costs of I-structure heap accesses in detail. The simple case of reading a present data element is where hardware tags exhibit some advantage. On the CM-5, the tag check is half of the access cost in this case. With tags, the trap occurs on deferred reads and all stores. Without tags, these cases require only a branch. So the deciding factor is the frequency of the simple case. We find that this differs radically on different programs. On Simple

TAM operation	Cycles	
	J'-Machine	CM-5'
I-fetch		
Data present	6	9
Defer	48	41
I-store		
Cell empty	14	15
Deferred readers	17	22
I-structure allocate (N words)		
Local/remote policy	—	7
Allocate	18	18
Clear tags	$5N$	$.75N$

Table 3: *Access to data structures with synchronization on a per-element basis. The costs shown reflect the memory access including checking and updating the tags. I-structure allocation includes initializing all tags to empty.*

there are more than seven ifetches per istore, and only 3% of the ifetches are deferred. On Gamteb, there are only 1.6 ifetches per istore, and 24% of the ifetches are deferred.

The other difference between the two implementations is the often neglected time to allocate an I-structure, which includes initializing all tags to empty. On the J-Machine, each element must be set separately to the future-tagged value denoting an empty unrequested element. On the CM-5, the tags of eight elements can be initialized using a single store-double instruction.

Returning to the cost breakdown in Figure 2 we see that the cost of actually accessing the heap is only a fraction of the total cost. Once the cost of the message component and the control component are included, it becomes apparent that the primary factor in determining the utility of the hardware mechanisms supporting the global heap is the ratio of local to remote accesses. On remote access, the message handling overhead diminishes the impact of fast tag checking. While treating the local access specially in software reduces both the message and control overhead, it incurs the cost of the tag check. However, when at least 30% of accesses are local, the reduction in control overhead balances the difference in cost of sending messages on the CM-5'.

7   Summary

We have compared the performance of the J-Machine, a recent experimental architecture with several novel mechanisms that support fine-grained parallelism, and the CM-5, a recent commercial architecture using conventional Sparc processors, on fine-grained parallel programs written in Id90. A complete quantitative comparison in this regime is very difficult because there are so many variables that can influence performance and there is little consensus on what constitutes a representative workload. We follow a method of analysis similar to the Abstract Machine Characterization Model used to evaluate a wide range of conventional machines and benchmarks [12]. We normalize for software effects, including programming language, programming style, and high-level compiler optimizations by using a common low-level representation of each program in terms of a Threaded Abstract Machine. Machine-specific optimizations are realized in compiling the TAM code to each machine. Examination of the generated code yields the cost for each TAM primitive. An instrumented version of the program is run to produce roughly a hundred dynamic statistics. These are combined with the machine cost coefficients to obtain the average cycles per TAM instruction.

We look forward to a much broader set of studies following a similar methodology using additional machines and additional language frameworks. Clearly it should be possible to evaluate proposals such as *T [11] in this framework. Although other parallel language implementations may differ from TAM in many ways, the primary ingredients are likely to be similar: message exchange, remote references, synchronization, control flow, and dynamic scheduling. We do anticipate that the granularity of parallelism will have a significant impact on the evaluation. Coarser grained models will not stress the message handling and dynamic scheduling as heavily.

In this comparison we found that traditional architectural issues, such as the average memory access time and the floating point performance had a substantial impact on the performance of the experimental architecture. After correcting for these factors, the fast message send and receive are a clear gain, accounting for as much as a 50% improvement in some programs. Treating local messages as a special case in software compensated for larger message overhead in many programs because it also reduced the control overhead of dynamic scheduling; however, the resulting system is more sensitive to variations in the remote reference frequency. The fast message dispatch mechanism was of modest value in the absence of adequate atomic operations on resources that are shared between the primary computation and the message handlers which operate on its behalf. Multiple disjoint register sets were not of particular value, since code was generated for the different scheduling levels from a single program. The compiler could simply partition the register file, which allows a tight integration of the two levels. The utility of tagged memory was undercut by the high cost of initialization.

Our measurements suggest some directions in the design of parallel computers:

- The network interface should be integrated with the processor register file or cache.

- Fast dispatch to user-level message handlers significantly reduces communication overhead. However, careful attention must be paid to atomicity and sharing between the message handlers and the on-going computation.

- Fine-grained parallel programs are control intensive. When the communication and memory requirements are adequately addressed, this stands out as the primary avenue for further advancement.

- While individual mechanisms need to be efficient in isolation, the interactions among the mechanisms must be carefully considered.

The general observation is that in evaluating novel architectures it is essential to carry the implementation of programming languages to completion, as that is the only way to perceive the completeness and the synergy between the various mechanisms and to determine the relative importance of each component.

Acknowledgments

We are grateful to the anonymous referees for their valuable comments. We would also like to thank Fred Chong, Richard Lethin, and Nate Osgood for their comments on earlier versions of this paper. Computational support at Berkeley was provided by the NSF Infrastructure Grant number CDA-8722788. Funding at MIT was provided in part by the Defense Advanced Research Projects Agency under contracts N00014-87K-0825, F19628-92-C-0045, and N00014-91-J-1698 and in part by a National Science Foundation Presidential Young Investigator Award, Grant MIP-8657531, with matching funds from General Electric Corporation, IBM Corporation, and AT&T. Ellen Spertus is supported by a NSF Graduate Fellowship. Seth Copen Goldstein is supported by an AT&T Graduate Fellowship. Klaus Erik Schauser is supported by an IBM Graduate Fellowship. Thorsten von Eicken is supported by the Semiconductor Research Corporation. David Culler is supported by an NSF Presidential Faculty Fellowship CCR-9253705 and LLNL Grant UCB-ERL-92/172.

References

[1] Arvind and K. Ekanadham. Future Scientific Programming on Parallel Machines. *Journal of Parallel and Distributed Computing*, 5(5):460–493, October 1988.

[2] Arvind, S. K. Heller, and R. S. Nikhil. Programming Generality and Parallel Computers. In *Proc. of the Fourth Int. Symp. on Biological and Artificial Intelligence Systems*, pages 255–286. ESCOM (Leider), Trento, Italy, September 1988.

[3] D. H. Bailey et al. The NAS Parallel Benchmarks — Summary and Preliminary Results. In *Proc. Supercomputing '91*, November 1991.

[4] P. J. Burns, M. Christon, R. Schweitzer, O. M. Lubeck, H. J. Wasserman, M. L. Simmons, and D. V. Pryor. Vectorization of Monte-Carlo Particle Transport: An Architectural Study using the LANL Benchmark "Gamteb". In *Proc. Supercomputing '89*. IEEE Computer Society and ACM SIGARCH, New York, NY, November 1989.

[5] W. P. Crowley, C. P. Hendrickson, and T. E. Rudy. The SIMPLE code. Technical Report UCID 17715, Lawrence Livermore Laboratory, February 1978.

[6] D. Culler, A. Sah, K. Schauser, T. von Eicken, and J. Wawrzynek. Fine-grain Parallelism with Minimal Hardware Support: A Compiler-Controlled Threaded Abstract Machine. In *Proc. of 4th Int. Conf. on Architectural Support for Programming Languages and Operating Systems*, Santa-Clara, CA, April 1991. (Also available as Technical Report UCB/CSD 91/591, CS Div., University of California at Berkeley).

[7] D. E. Culler. Managing Parallelism and Resources in Scientific Dataflow Programs. Technical Report 446, MIT Lab for Comp. Sci., March 1990. (PhD Thesis, Dept. of EECS, MIT).

[8] S. C. Goldstein. Implementation of a Threaded Abstract Machine on Sequential and Multiprocessors. Master's thesis, Computer Science Division — EECS, U.C. Berkeley, 1993. (In preparation, to appear as UCB/CSD Technical Report).

[9] J. Gustafson, G. Montry, and Benner R. Development of Parallel Methods for a 1024-Processor Hypercube. *SIAM Journal on Scientific and Statistical Computing*, 9, 1988.

[10] R. S. Nikhil. ID Language Reference Manual Version 90.1. Technical Report CSG Memo 284-2, MIT Lab for Comp. Sci., 545 Tech. Square, Cambridge, MA, 1991.

[11] R. S. Nikhil, G. M. Papadopoulos, and Arvind. *T: A Killer Micro for A Brave New World. Technical Report CSG Memo 325, MIT Lab for Comp. Sci., 545 Tech. Square, Cambridge, MA, January 1991.

[12] R. H. Saavedra-Barrera and A. J. Smith. Benchmarking and The Abstract Machine Characterization Model. Technical Report UCB/CSD 90/607, U.C. Berkeley, Computer Science Div., November 1990.

[13] K. E. Schauser, D. Culler, and T. von Eicken. Compiler-controlled Multithreading for Lenient Parallel Languages. In *Proceedings of the 1991 Conference on Functional Programming Languages and Computer Architecture*, Cambridge, MA, August 1991. (Also available as Technical Report UCB/CSD 91/640, CS Div., University of California at Berkeley).

[14] J. P. Singh, W.-D. Weber, and A. Gupta. SPLASH: Stanford Parallel Applications for Shared-Memory. Technical Report CSL-TR-91-469, Stanford University, 1991.

[15] E. Spertus. Execution of Dataflow Programs on General-Purpose Hardware. Master's thesis, Department of EECS, Massachusetts Institute of Technology, 545 Tech. Square, Cambridge, MA, August 1992. To be expanded and released as MIT AI Lab Technical Report 1380.

[16] Thinking Machines Corporation, Cambridge, MA. *The Connection Machine CM-5 Technical Summary*, January 1992.

Improving AP1000 Parallel Computer Performance with Message Communication

Takeshi Horie, Kenichi Hayashi, Toshiyuki Shimizu, and Hiroaki Ishihata

Fujitsu Laboratories Ltd.

1015 Kamikodanaka, Nakahara-ku, Kawasaki 211, Japan

Abstract

The performance of message-passing applications depends on cpu speed, communication throughput and latency, and message handling overhead. In this paper we investigate the effect of varying these parameters and applying techniques to reduce message handling overhead on the execution efficiency of ten different applications. Using a message level simulator set up for the architecture of the AP1000, we showed that improving communication performance, especially message handling, improves total performance. If a cpu that is 32 times faster is provided, the total performance increases by less than ten times unless message handling overhead is reduced. Overlapping computation with message reception improves performance significantly. We also discuss how to improve the AP1000 architecture.

1 Introduction

Distributed memory parallel processors (DMPP) based on message passing have offered a cost-effective and feasible approach to supercomputing. The DMPP system is easily scaled up to large systems and many research groups have been studying parallelizing compilers to simplify the programming of DMPPs. Implementations of the DMPP architecture range from experimental prototype systems to commercial systems from Intel [3], NCUBE [1], Ametek [10], and Connection Machine.

Key architecture design issues for DMPPs include the use of high-speed processing elements, low-latency, high-throughput communications in the interconnection network, and message handling mechanism.

This paper presents the quantitative performance evaluation of DMPPs using message level simulation. Ten different applications were selected as benchmarks.

Design Issues for DMPP

One important design issue for DMPP is the balance between cpu and communication performance. In parallel machines the increase of cpu power does not improve performance linearly because of efficiency degradation from communication overhead. It is thus important to investigate quantitatively how cpu power and communication affect DMPP performance.

Communication overhead arises from message handling and the interconnection network. For the interconnection network, there are two performance factors, latency and throughput. In the interconnection network using wormhole routing, the latency is mainly from switching nodes and wire delay, and the throughput is from the channel bit width. For applications in which short messages are frequently transfered, improved latency will become an important factor in achieving high performance. The throughput will become important for applications in which long messages are frequently transfered. We must investigate how performance is affected from the interconnection network performance by using real applications.

We will now investigate message handling overhead in more detail. The message handling mechanism includes message header formatting, message sending to the interconnection network, message searching from the message buffer, a waiting mechanism, and copying to a user area. Message handling consists of two times. One is the fixed overhead time to construct a message and set up the appropriate communication mechanism, and the other is the time proportional to the message length. Several techniques for reducing message handling have been proposed [8, 21, 23, 17]. Fixed overhead time can be reduced by using specialized hardware such as a message formatter and message searcher.

One way to reduce the overhead proportional to the message length is overlapping communication with computation. When sending messages to the interconnection network, this can be done if the sending message area is not accessed by computing. In the same way, when receiving a message, the processor can start computation immediately after the message header arrives unless the receiving message area is accessed soon. In this case, communication can be overlapped with computation while the whole message is transferred into the message buffer or user data area.

Objectives

To design a DMPP, we must consider cpu speed, latency and throughput in the interconnection network, and message handling to achieve good performance. To reduce communication overhead and idle time for synchronization we must apply techniques such as overlapping communication with computation.

The goal of this paper is to quantify the effect that cpu speed, communication latency and throughput, communication overlapping with computation have on DMPP performance and to get ideas on improving the AP1000 architecture.

The results presented in this paper are obtained from message level simulation on ten parallel applications. For our study we developed a message level simulator, called MLSim to simulate and evaluate message-passing architectures. The architecture assumed by MLSim is based on the AP1000 which has interconnection networks for point-to-point and broadcast communications and barrier synchronization, and a low-latency message handling mechanism. MLSim can be used to rapidly investigate the effect of varying communication parameters on the execution efficiency of a wide range of parallel programs. The parallel applications we studied are numerical algorithms which include objects produced from the Dataparallel-C [15] and Oxygen [22] parallelizing compilers.

Related work

Annaratone simulated several numerical and non-numerical algorithms on five DMPPs and quantified the effect that interprocessor communication speed and synchronization overhead have on the performance of the DMPPs [2]. In his paper, however, only communication between neighboring processors was used and messages were not vectorized to reduce communication overhead.

Hsu presented the performance evaluation and trace driven simulation of a hypercube multicomputer running realistic workloads [18]. In his evaluation, overhead for event tracing was included and results were obtained from less than 16 processors. To reflect

current architecture for larger systems and achieve good performance, we must quantify the effect not only of communication latency and throughput, but also communication overlapping with computation.

Johnson presented a framework for modeling the impact of communication locality on system performance and showed this impact using the modeling framework [20]. In his paper, communication transactions are cache coherency transactions and the communication characteristics are quite different from those of message-passing machines.

Outline

After describing the simulation environment used in our study, simulation results of the performance by varying communication and cpu performance and by applying techniques of reducing communication overhead will be presented. Finally we discuss how to improve the AP1000 architecture.

2 Model, Simulation, and Applications

This section presents the architecture and programming models, the simulation environment, and the benchmark applications.

2.1 Architecture and programming models

For our study, we have chosen an architecture that resembles the AP1000 which is a large-scale message-passing machine [19, 24, 16]. The architecture consists of several processing elements connected through a point-to-point interconnection network and special barrier synchronization network. The point-to-point interconnection network also has a broadcast communication feature such as for columns and rows.[1]

The AP1000 supports non-blocking message passing as a basic programming model. The sending processor specifies the destination processor, transmits messages directly to the interconnection network, and waits for completion.[2] The transmitted message is automatically transferred to the message buffer (circular buffer) in the destination processor. The receiving processor accesses the circular buffer directly or copies it to the user area if needed.

---

[1] The third interconnection network of the AP1000, the broadcast network, is not used in this study.

[2] We call this mechanism *line sending* which transfers messages in cache memory directly to the interconnection network.

Figures 1 and 2 show the communication and barrier synchronization model for this study. The delay

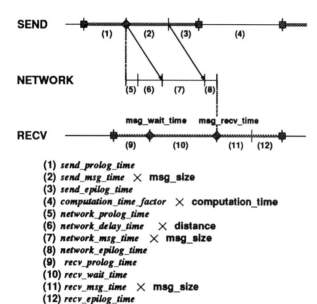

(1) *send_prolog_time*
(2) *send_msg_time* × **msg_size**
(3) *send_epilog_time*
(4) *computation_time_factor* × **computation_time**
(5) *network_prolog_time*
(6) *network_delay_time* × **distance**
(7) *network_msg_time* × **msg_size**
(8) *network_epilog_time*
(9) *recv_prolog_time*
(10) *recv_wait_time*
(11) *recv_msg_time* × **msg_size**
(12) *recv_epilog_time*

Figure 1: Communication model

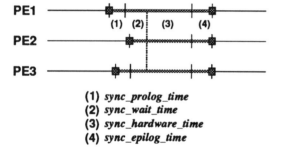

(1) *sync_prolog_time*
(2) *sync_wait_time*
(3) *sync_hardware_time*
(4) *sync_epilog_time*

Figure 2: Barrier synchronization model

of communication and barrier synchronization is as follows:

Sending $send\_prolog\_time$ + $send\_msg\_time$ × msg_size + $send\_epilog\_time$

Receiving without message copying
$recv\_prolog\_time$ + $recv\_wait\_time$ + $recv\_epilog\_time$

Receiving with message copying
$recv\_prolog\_time$ + $recv\_wait\_time$ + $recv\_msg\_time$ × msg_size + $recv\_epilog\_time$

Barrier synchronization
$sync\_prolog\_time$ + $sync\_wait\_time$ + $sync\_hardware\_time$ + $sync\_epilog\_time$

2.2 Simulation

A trace driven simulator for a message-passing parallel computer — Message Level Simulator (MLSim) — has been developed to study communication behavior.

MLSim was implemented on the AP1000 distributed parallel machine. The inputs to MLSim are the execution traces of real applications on the AP1000. The instrumentation was done by inserting probe points in the operating and runtime systems. An event is triggered during application program execution when a probe point is hit. Events are monitored and stored in a trace buffer together with time and message information, as needed. When execution ends, the trace buffer stays in processor memory, without uploading to the host.

We inserted probe points at communication and synchronization library and interrupt service routine entries and exits, at context switching points, and points where the operating and runtime systems communicate in message sending and receiving and barrier synchronization.

MLSim simulates communication behavior by rewriting the timestamp of the trace information. Figure 3 shows the execution of MLSim. MLSim can be

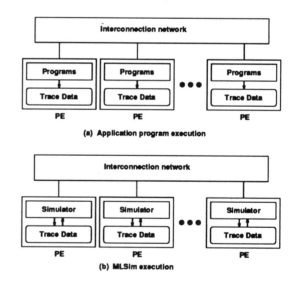

Figure 3: Message Level Simulator

used to rapidly investigate the effect of varying parameters such as communication throughput and latency, message handling overhead, and cpu speed.

There are two reasons for adopting the approach of remaining trace data in the memory on each processor.

- The MLSim performs trace data access and execution in parallel on the AP1000.

- It is impossible for the host computer to store the trace information generated by each processor because the total size of the trace buffer is proportional to the number of processors and is enormous.

The input parameters such as *send_prolog_time* are given for MLSim. MLSim simulates the behavior of communication preserving the order of message communications and barrier synchronization between processors with a delay parameter.

MLSim calculates the time needed for message handling, barrier synchronization, and computation using input parameters. For sending events, a message containing timing information is sent to a target processor. For receiving events, the message received from the source processor is used to calculate the time of message receiving. For barrier synchronization events, the slowest time among processors is calculated to obtain the time when all processors are synchronized. The pure computation time of user programs is derived from the time between the exit point of a communication library and the entry point of the following communication library. This computation time can also be changed by an input parameter.

In addition to the above basic communication simulation, mechanisms such as overlapping communication with computation and multiple contexts, and the overhead for searching for messages in the message buffer can be simulated. Simulation can be performed together with the flit level network simulator developed to investigate the effect of congestion in the interconnection network. However, we do not consider the effect of congestion in this paper because the flit level network simulation is very time-consuming and all applications in our study use regular communication patterns.

MLSim can also calculate statistics such as user time, idle time, and communication overhead time, transferred message size, communication distance, and the number of communication events.

MLSim can be tuned to match the performance of real machines by varying communication parameters. Figure 4 shows the AP1000 communication parameters which are given in microseconds. Using these parameters, we compared the execution time measured on an actual AP1000 with that simulated by MLSim. Table 1 includes the comparison for ten benchmark programs running on the AP1000 with between 64 to 512 processors. Since the errors are within 10%, we are confident of the results of the trace driven studies in this paper.

```
#                          AP1000 model
#
# ---- computation ----        # ---- sync ----
computation_factor   1.0       sync_prolog_time      2.0
#                               sync_hard_time        5.8
# ---- network ----            sync_epilog_time      1.0
network_prolog_time  0.16      # ---- broadcast ----
network_msg_time     0.049     brd_send_prolog_time  6.425
network_delay_time   0.16      brd_send_msg_time     0.049
network_epilog_time  0.0       brd_send_epilog_time  0.0
# ---- point-to-point ----     brd_recv_prolog_time  10.7
send_prolog_time     8.0       brd_recv_msg_time     0.136
send_msg_time        0.049     brd_recv_epilog_time  5.9
send_epilog_time     0.8       brd_sync_time         6.5
recv_prolog_time     8.2       # ---- read message ----
recv_msg_time        0.136     readmsg_prolog_time   6.8
recv_epilog_time     14.0      readmsg_time          0.136
#                               readmsg_epilog_time   0.0
```

Figure 4: AP1000 parameters for MLSim

2.3 Applications

Ten parallel applications were used as benchmarks. The communication workload ranged from high to heavy.

LINPACK solves dense systems of equations by performing block Gaussian elimination. This program was written by Prof. Brent to perform the LINPACK benchmark [5]. The matrix to be solved is 1000×1000.

SCG solves Poisson's differential equation using the scaled conjugate gradient method in which the coefficient matrix is scaled by diagonal elements. The matrix to be solved is 200×200.

MD is a molecular dynamics simulation program [6]. A domain decomposition method is used for 216000 particles.

QCD is a Monte Carlo program for Lattice Quantum Chromo Dynamics (QCD) [13]. The lattice size is $16 \times 16 \times 16 \times 16$.

OCEAN simulates an ocean circulation model. The model used here has one horizontal dimension and two layers. OCEAN is written in Dataparallel-C [15].

SHALLOW solves a set of shallow-water equations using finite difference approximations on a 64×64 grid through 1200 iterations. SHALLOW is written in Dataparallel-C [15].

ORTHES transforms a real square matrix through Householder similarity transformations to an upper Hessenberg matrix. All eigenvectors and eigenvalues are computed for an unsymmetric matrix. ORTHES was produced by the compiler Oxygen [22].

TSDE is used in analyzing the behavior of airfoils in subsonic, transonic, and supersonic regimes by solving a two-dimensional, steady-state transonic small disturbance equation. A finite difference method solves the problem iteratively with a successive over-relaxation scheme. The results refer to 20 iterations of the SOR algorithm. TSDE was produced by the compiler Oxygen [22].

AMBER is a molecular dynamics simulation program which was parallelized by Sato [11]. A particle division method allocates particles randomly to processors. The number of atoms is 2000.

SLALOM is a computer benchmark which solves an optical radiosity in the interior of a box [12]. The number of patches is 500.

In each of these applications only the main execution part is measured. The time required for downloading data and uploading results is not included.

Table 1 lists the application statistics for MLSim.

If this data is obtained directly from the trace information, it would include the overhead for writing trace data and this perturbation would increase the communication time. MLSim offers the correct information without trace overhead.

The size of trace information is significantly large and could not be stored in the host computer file system. In our simulation, this data remains in the memory of each processor. This helps speed up simulation and analysis.

3 Performance Balance of Computation and Communication

Architects of DMPPs need to know whether the significant effort in building the interconnection network and message handling hardware is justified. We evaluated the effect of varying cpu power, communication, latency, and throughput in the interconnection network, and message handling for applications by using MLSim.

3.1 Varying CPU performance

Here we evaluate the effect of varying cpu power without varying communication performance. Cpu power affects both communication and computation performance because most messages in message passing machines are handled by software. We first evaluate the case where only computation performance varies. This is the case that vector processing units

are attached to each processor and the computation code is well vectorized. Figure 5 shows the results of the simulation. The performance for the current AP1000 is assumed as 1.

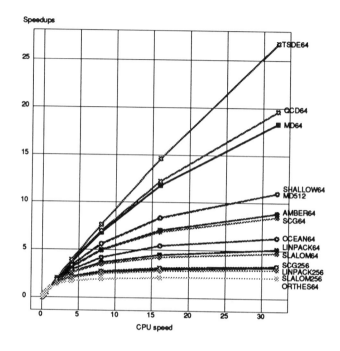

Figure 5: Effect of cpu power

In the second simulation, the message handling overhead is reduced in proportion to the cpu power. Note that only the fixed overhead time in message handling varies. In this case, the current cpu on the AP1000 is replaced with a high speed cpu and the same interconnection network is used. Figure 6 shows the results of the simulation. The performance for the current AP1000 is assumed as 1.

The performance of most applications does not increase much with computation performance increases except computation intensive applications such as MD, TSDE, and QCD. For example, speeding up the cpu by a factor of 32 only improves average performance for all applications by a factor of 10. When the increase of the cpu performance is used to reduce message handling overhead, the performance of OCEAN increases significantly. This is because the average size of messages is small.

3.2 Varying communication performance

To investigate the effect of communication performance on total performance, we simulated ten parallel applications on MLSim and varied the communication

Table 1: Application statistics

Application	PE	Exec. Time on the AP1000	Exec. Time on MLSim	User (%)	Comm. (%)	Idle (%)	Size of Trace(MB)	Size of Msg(B)
LINPACK	64	3.508	3.496 (-0.3)	77.0	10.9	12.0	58.8	368
SCG	64	4.142	4.084 (-1.4)	88.9	8.6	2.5	36.4	804
MD	64	3.885	3.723 (-4.2)	96.4	2.4	1.2	10.1	2201
QCD	64	5.121	5.053 (-1.3)	97.9	2.1	0.1	1.5	19749
OCEAN	64	7.903	8.082 (2.3)	82.4	15.7	2.0	462.0	12
SHALLOW	64	3.929	3.593 (-8.6)	92.3	7.1	0.7	56.9	457
ORTHES	64	1.534	1.691 (10.2)	46.6	41.9	11.5	202.9	8
TSDE	64	1.637	1.629 (-0.5)	93.1	2.1	4.8	3.2	847
AMBER	64	0.989	0.965 (-2.4)	80.8	7.1	12.1	8.0	440
SLALOM	64	2.35	2.366 (0.7)	69.4	10.6	20.0	72.9	207
LINPACK	256	1.403	1.369 (-2.4)	60.3	18.7	21.0	242.6	202
SCG	256	1.255	1.229 (-2.1)	64.1	29.4	6.6	193.2	419
MD	512	0.521	0.500 (-4.0)	89.1	5.9	5.0	39.0	599
ORTHES	256	1.154	1.176 (1.9)	31.4	57.3	11.2	683.7	8
SLALOM	256	1.05	1.100 (4.8)	45.4	16.5	38.1	268.0	112

Application	PE	P-to-P per PE	Brd per PE	GOP per PE	Dist. P-to-P	Send (%)	Recv (%)	Brd (%)	GOP (%)	Sync (%)	Read Msg (%)
LINPACK	64	17	858	1000	1.8	0.0	0.0	20.0	2.8	0.0	0.0
SCG	64	1756	0	893	1.1	2.1	5.5	0.0	3.5	0.0	0.0
MD	64	199	0	10	2.2	0.6	1.0	0.0	0.0	0.0	1.6
QCD	64	28	1	0	1.0	0.5	0.0	0.0	0.0	0.0	1.5
OCEAN	64	41000	0	0	1.1	5.5	12.0	0.0	0.0	0.0	0.0
SHALLOW	64	4800	0	0	1.1	4.4	3.3	0.0	0.0	0.0	0.0
ORTHES	64	0	311	7437	0.0	0.0	0.0	32.5	21.3	0.0	0.0
TSDE	64	167	0	44	3.3	0.5	1.7	0.0	4.5	0.0	0.2
AMBER	64	189	6	75	4.0	0.6	0.4	7.6	10.7	0.0	0.0
SLALOM	64	3450	0	0	2.4	3.0	22.6	0.0	0.0	0.0	5.1
LINPACK	256	29	437	1012	2.3	0.0	0.0	32.9	6.6	0.0	0.0
SCG	256	2666	0	893	1.4	6.7	16.1	0.0	14.5	0.0	0.0
MD	512	199	0	10	3.6	1.6	4.3	0.0	1.5	0.0	3.5
ORTHES	256	0	78	3719	0.0	0.0	0.0	48.8	19.9	0.0	0.0
SLALOM	256	3274	0	0	4.3	4.7	43.4	0.0	0.0	0.0	6.5

- *Exec. Time* is in seconds and data in parentheses is the ratio of execution time compared to the AP1000.
- *User, Comm., Idle, Send, Recv, Brd, GOP, Sync*, and *Read Msg* is the ratio of each time to whole execution time.
- *Idle time* is the time when processor waits for messages and barrier synchronization.
- *Size of trace* is the total amount of trace data in all processors (MBytes).
- *Size of Msg* is an average message length for each sending call which includes both point-to-point and broadcast communications (bytes).
- *P-to-P* is a point-to-point message.
- *Brd* is a broadcast communication.
- *GOP* is a global operation, for example, to get global summation of all processors.
- *Dist. P-to-P* is an average communication distance for each point-to-point communication.
- *Sync* is a barrier synchronization.

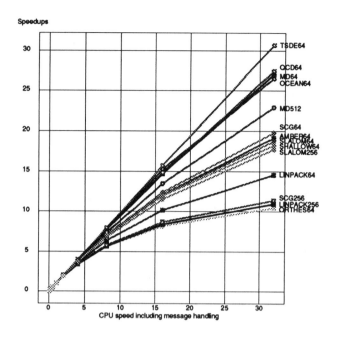

Figure 6: Effect of cpu power including message handling

performance. In this simulation, all communication parameters such as message handling and the interconnection network delay are varied together as a single factor.

Figure 7 shows the results. The communication performance is relative to the current AP1000 (= 1). The total performance is relative to that of no communication overhead. From this figure we can show that not all parallel applications run efficiently on the AP1000.

The performance of SLALOM with 256 processors will be improved by 60% if the communication is 32 times faster. However, speeding up communication by 32 times is not cost effective. A speedup factor of four is the optimal choice for the current cpu power.

3.3 Varying network performance

We evaluated the effect of the interconnection network performance. The delay in the interconnection network using wormhole routing is given as the following equation [7]:

$$T_{delay} = (T_n + T_w)D + (L/W)T_p$$

where T_n is the latency of a node, T_w the latency of a wire, T_p the pipeline period of a node, D the distance hopped by a message, L the message length in bits, and W the width of a channel in bits.

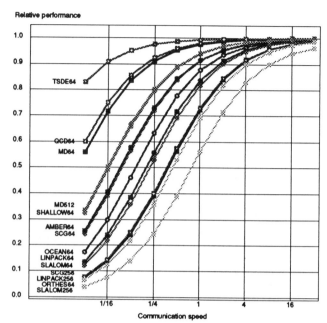

Figure 7: Effect of communication

For short messages the main factor of the communication delay is $(T_n + T_w)D$. For long messages the main factor is $(L/W)T_p$. The first communication factor is called latency and the second one throughput. We evaluated the effect of the interconnection network by varying these factors. Figure 8 shows the effect of network latency.

Figure 9 shows the effect of network throughput.

We found that performance does not increase even when a higher throughput and lower latency interconnection network than that of the current AP1000 is provided. The main factor of communication overhead on the AP1000 is message handling by software.

The performance is more sensitive to throughput performance than latency performance. The performance of TSDE and OCEAN does not vary by the network performance. TSDE requires little communication and in OCEAN, the communication is only between nearest neighbor processors. The message length is also short (12 bytes).

3.4 Varying message handling

Message handling consists of two parts. One is the fixed overhead to construct a message and set up the appropriate communication mechanism. The other is the time proportional to the message length and this is mostly dependent on the interconnection network throughput.

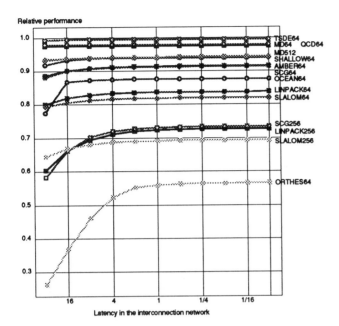

Figure 8: Effect of network latency

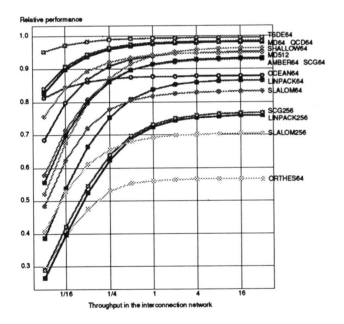

Figure 9: Effect of network throughput

Here we evaluate the effect of only the fixed overhead in message handling to distinguish that from the effect of the interconnection network. Figure 10 shows the results of the simulations. The message handling performance is relative to the current AP1000 (= 1).

In most applications, improvement of message handling increases performance significantly. In compar-

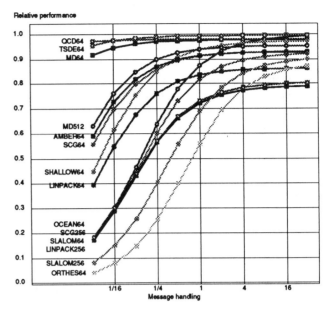

Figure 10: Effect of fixed overhead in message handling

ison with the effect of the interconnection network, the effect of the fixed overhead in message handling is greater. The result in Figure 10 looks similar to that in Figure 7, and shows that the main factor of communication overhead for the AP1000 is software message handling.

4 Overlapping Communication with Computation

We used the following two methods to reduce communication overhead.

- Overlapping computation with sending messages
  Immediately after a processor issues the command for sending messages, it can start computation unless it writes data to the message area. We will evaluate this overlap.

  Another way to overlap computation with sending messages is to copy the message into the message buffer. However, this causes a large overhead of copying and the communication latency becomes high. We thus only consider the case where the processor sends messages directly to the interconnection network.

- Computation overlapping with message receiving
  The processor can start successive computation as

soon as the message header arrives at this processor. This can fully overlap communication with computation while messages are transferred into the user area. This idea can be easily extended to overlapping message copying with computation. This happens when the message request by the receiving processor is later than the arrival of the corresponding message. In this cases, the overhead in message reception is only the idle time while the processor waits for messages.

In the simulations of this section there is no overhead of the fixed message handling and we used a cpu that is four times faster than the AP1000.

4.1 Overlapping computation with sending messages

To overlap computation with sending messages, the sending processor is not allowed to write to the sending area after issuing a sending command which specifies the destination processor ID, message ID, data area to be transferred, and data size. During processor computing, the DMA controller transfers messages to the interconnection network and checks processor access. If the processor writes access to the transferred area, a memory access fault will be caused and the processor will retry the access until the area is available.

The following hardware features are needed to implement this overlapping:

- Register (top and bottom address) and comparator for access checking.
- Direct memory access controller to transfer messages to the network.
- Command queue storing sending information as fifo ordering.

To send messages continuously, multiple comparator-register sets are needed. In this simulation, we evaluate the effect of overlapping computation with sending messages.

Table 2 and Figure 11 show the results of the simulations.

In all applications, the performance gain of sending overlap is very small. A simple explanation for this is the small ratio of the sending overhead time to the total execution time. Another reason is that after processor A sends a message to processor B, processor A later receives a message sent from processor B. Even if sending overhead can be reduced, the sending processor waits for the message because the message arrival time does not change by the overlapping and idle time increases. The idle time of SCG and ORTHES in Figure 11 shows this situation clearly.

Table 2: Effect of communication overlapping with computation

Application	PE	Normal (ms)	Send (%)	Receive (%)
LINPACK	64	1193	1193 (0.0)	753 (36.9)
SCG	64	1178	1142 (3.1)	979 (16.8)
MD	64	991	987 (0.4)	930 (6.2)
QCD	64	1341	1337 (0.3)	1265 (5.6)
OCEAN	64	2189	2171 (0.8)	2183 (0.3)
SHALLOW	64	1081	1002 (7.3)	1071 (0.9)
ORTHES	64	303	303 (0.0)	237 (21.9)
TSDE	64	1353	1352 (0.1)	1333 (1.5)
AMBER	64	285	280 (1.6)	227 (20.1)
SLALOM	64	696	691 (0.7)	540 (22.5)
LINPACK	256	500	500 (0.0)	260 (48.0)
SCG	256	437	408 (6.7)	280 (35.8)
MD	512	141	139 (1.5)	124 (12.3)
ORTHES	256	191	191 (0.0)	132 (30.7)
SLALOM	256	307	300 (2.3)	232 (24.6)

† Data in parentheses is the performance improvement ratio of each case to the normal execution.

4.2 Overlapping computation with message receiving

We consider the architecture for overlapping message reception with computation, and evaluate it using MLSim.

In overlapping computation with message receiving, there is no overhead of transferring messages into memory. The processor cannot proceed with computation until the header of the message arrives. The processor does not need to wait for whole messages. If the message request is earlier than the message arrival, the message is transferred directly into the user area. The processor can start computation after receiving only the header of the message. If the message has already arrived, it is transferred into the message buffer and is then copied to the specified user area. In this case, overlapping can also be performed and the processor can start execution as soon as transfer of the message from the message buffer to the user area starts.

A more aggressive approach is that the processor does not wait for message arrival and only issues a message receiving request. However, this changes the semantics in the message-passing mechanism.

If the processor access address has not arrived yet, an access fault will occur and the processor will retry the access until the area becomes available. The following hardware is needed to implement this overlap-

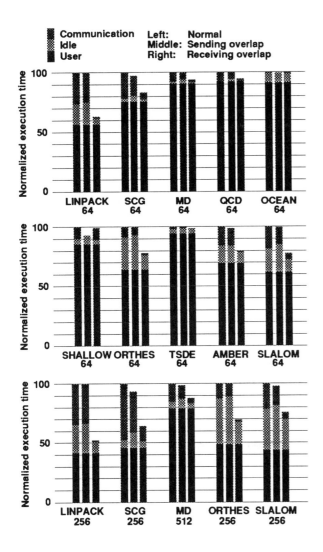

Figure 11: Effect of communication overlapping with computation

ping:

- Two DMA controllers, one for transferring messages from the network to memory (message buffer or user area) and the other for copying messages from the message buffer to the user area.

- A comparator to check access to the user area to which messages are transferred.

Table 2 and Figure 11 show the results of the simulation.

Overlapping computation with receiving messages significantly reduces the communication overhead. The most interesting point of this result is that this overlapping reduces not only communication overhead but also idle time. This situation appears in most applications. Why is the idle time reduced? In most cases, after processor A sends a message to processor B, processor A receives a message sent from processor B later. If the overhead in message reception is reduced and processor B can send the message to processor A earlier, the time of waiting for the message will be reduced. In sending overlaps, even if the sending communication overhead is reduced, the idle time increases and the total execution time does not improve.

5 Conclusion

While several performance evaluations on DMPP have been reported in the past, they did not assume the current DMPP architecture, nor did they consider the effect by overlapping communication with computation. We have investigated the performance of ten parallel applications on message passing parallel machines based on the AP1000 architecture using ML-Sim.

We investigated the effect of varying cpu speed, communication, throughput and latency in the interconnection network, and message handling overhead. We also investigated overlapping computation with message sending and receiving. We will now discuss ways to improve the AP1000 architecture.

CPU CPU power affects both communication and computation performance because messages in most DMPPs are handled by software. Computation power can be easily enhanced by attaching vector processing units to each processor. However, speeding up the cpu by a factor of 32 increases performance by only about 10 times unless message handling overhead is decreased.

Communication Speeding up communications by four times was the optimal choice for the AP1000.

Communication overhead arises from message handling and the interconnection network. In the interconnection network, the throughput performance had a greater effect than the latency. However, the effect of the interconnection network was significantly less than message handling. One reason is that all applications in our study use only regular communication patterns and do not cause congestion in the interconnection network. Another is that the interconnection network uses wormhole routing which provides low-latency communication.

The applications in our study often use broadcast communication feature on the point-to-point interconnection network. This can be seen in Table 1. This feature is also used for global operations[3] and reduces communication overhead significantly.

Message handling includes both fixed overhead time and the time proportional to the message length. The main fixed overhead for message handling is from message formatting in sending and buffer management in receiving. The buffer management is complex because the AP1000 uses a circular buffer and any size of messages can be handled.[4]

The overhead proportional to the message length can be reduced by overlapping communication with computation. The AP1000 uses the line sending and a cpu waits for the completion of message transfer. Thus this method prevents overlapping communication with computation. However from our investigation overlapping computation with sending messages was less effective in reducing overhead. Overlapping computation with message reception improved performance significantly because this reduced message handling overhead and idle time. In LINPACK on 256 processors, the speedup of reception overlapping was almost double.

Barrier synchronization The AP1000 has special hardware for barrier synchronization. However, our applications do not often use this feature. The reason is because in message passing applications, communications such as global operation make all processors synchronize implicitly.

Idle time We found two methods for reducing idle time caused by message synchronization.

One way is to send ready data as soon as possible. This method reduces the length of messages sent. If the data is vectorized to a single message, data cannot be transferred until all the data is ready. This causes the waiting time at the receiving processor to increase. Sending ready data as soon as possible will decrease the idle time. However, this causes a large overhead for message handling because a lot of short messages need to be transferred and application programs must be rewritten to transfer these short messages efficiently.

Another way is to execute another context when one context waits for messages on one processor.

The multiple context reduces idle time without rewriting application programs. This multiple context approach is different from that for hiding the latency of remote data fetch [21, 4, 14]. On message-passing machines, all communications are performed through messages and this method is natural to hide the message waiting time.

We are now investigating the effect of the multiple contexts on DMPP performance.

Programming paradigm Message passing programming paradigms can not avoid message buffering. This is explained by Eicken [9]. The AP1000 does not need buffering for sending messages by applying a line-sending mechanism. However, the overhead of buffer management in receiving remains unsolved.

One way to cope with this problem is to implement complex hardware to manage the message buffer and overlap communication with computation as described in Section 4. Another way is to implement a shared-memory programming paradigm. In this model, the destination memory address is determined by the sender and this avoids message buffering. Overlapping communication with computation and synchronization becomes a programming or compiler issue and this approach would possibly need more communication.[5]

The main point we want to make is that message handling causes a large overhead in message passing applications. Special message handling hardware can reduce this overhead. However, we do not think a message-passing programming paradigm is suitable for data-parallel applications such as those studied in this paper. We are currently searching for a more suitable programming paradigm and its architectural support.

Acknowledgments

We thank Dr. Ishii, Mr. Shiraishi, Mr. Sato and Mr. Ikesaka for their helpful suggestions, Prof. R. Brent at Australian National University for use of the LINPACK program, Dr. R. Ruehl at Swiss Federal Institute of Technology for use of the compiler OXYGEN, Dr. D. Brown at UMIST for use of the MD program, Prof. M. Quinn at Oregon State University

---

[3]In global operation, the data is reduced using a binary tree and the result is then broadcast.

[4]For global operation, the AP1000 uses a special message format that is fixed at 16 bytes.

[5]For example if a processor wants to get data from another processor, synchronization mechanism is needed to know whether the data is ready.

for use of Dataparallel-C, and QCDTARO Collaboration for use of the QCD program. We also thank Dr. N. Suzuki at IBM Japan and the referees for their helpful comments and suggestions.

References

[1] *nCUBE2 Supercomputers Technical Overview*, 1990.

[2] M. Annaratone, C. Pommerell, and Roland Ruhl: "Interprocessor communication speed and performance in distributed-memory parallel processors," In *The 16th Annual International Symposium on Computer Architecture*, pp. 315–324, May 1989.

[3] R. Arlauskas: "iPSC/2 system: a second generation hypercube," In *Third Conference on Hypercube Concurrent Computers and Applications*, pp. 38–42, Jan. 1988.

[4] B. Boothe and A. Ranade: "Improved multithreading techniques for hiding communication latency in multiprocessors," In *The 19th Annual International Symposium on Computer Architecture*, pp. 214–223, May 1992.

[5] R. P. Brent: "The LINPACK benchmark on the AP1000," In *Fourth Symposium on the Frontiers of Massively Parallel Computation*, Oct. 1992.

[6] D. Brown and J. H. R. Clarke: "Parallelization strategies for MD simulations on the AP1000," In *Proceedings of the Second Fujitsu-ANU CAP Workshop*, pp. L–1–10, Nov. 1991.

[7] W. J. Dally: "Performance analysis of k-ary n-cube interconnection networks," *IEEE Transactions on Computers*, 39, 6, pp. 775–785, June 1990.

[8] W. J. Dally, L. Chao, S. Hassoun, W. Horwat, J. Kaplan, P. Song, B. Totty, and S. Wills: "Architecture of a message-driven processor," In *The 14th Annual International Symposium on Computer Architecture*, pp. 189–196, May 1987.

[9] T. Eicken, D. E. Culler, S. C. Goldstein, and K. E. Schauser: "Active messages: a mechanism for integrated communication and computation," In *The 19th Annual International Symposium on Computer Architecture*, pp. 256–266, May 1992.

[10] C. L. Seitz et al.: "The architecture and programming of the Ametek Series 2010 multicomputer," In *Third Conference on Hypercube Concurrent Computers and Applications*, pp. 33–36, Jan. 1988.

[11] H. Sato et al.: "Parallelization of AMBER molecular dynamics program for the AP1000," In *Scalable High Performance Computing Conference 92*, pp. 113–120, April 1992.

[12] J. Gustafson et al.: "Slalom update," *Supercomputing Review*, pp. 56–61, March 1991.

[13] K. Akemi et al.: "QCD on the highly parallel computer AP1000," *Nuclear Physics B*, 26, pp. 644–646, 1992.

[14] A. Gupta, J. Hennessy, K. Gharachorloo, T. Mowry, and W. D. Weber: "Comparative evaluation of latency reducing and tolerating techniques," In *The 18th Annual International Symposium on Computer Architecture*, pp. 254–263, May 1991.

[15] P. J. Hatcher and M. J. Quinn: *Data-Parallel Programming on MIMD Computers*. The MIT Press, 1991.

[16] T. Horie, H. Ishihata, and M. Ikesaka: "Design and implementation of an interconnection network for the AP1000," In *Information Processing 92, Volume I*, pp. 555–561, 1992.

[17] J. M. Hsu and P. Banerjee: "A message passing co-processor for distributed memory multicomputers," In *Supercomputing 90*, pp. 720–729, 1990.

[18] J. M. Hsu and P. Banerjee: "Performance measurement and trace driven simulation of parallel CAD and numerical applications on a hypercube multicomputer," *IEEE Transactions on Parallel and Distributed Systems*, 3, 4, pp. 451–464, July 1992.

[19] H. Ishihata, T. Horie, S. Inano, T. Shimizu, and S. Kato: "An architecture of highly parallel computer AP1000," In *IEEE Pacific Rim Conf. on Communications, Computers and Signal processing*, pp. 13–16, May 1991.

[20] K. L. Johnson: "The impact of communication locality on large-scale multiprocessor performance," In *The 19th Annual International Symposium on Computer Architecture*, pp. 392–402, May 1992.

[21] R. S. Nikhil, G. M. Papadopoulos, and Arvind: "*T: A multithreaded massively parallel architecture," In *The 19th Annual International Symposium on Computer Architecture*, pp. 156–167, May 1992.

[22] R. Ruehl: "Evaluation of compiler generated parallel programs on three multicomputers," In *Proc. of the Sixth International Conference on Supercomputing*, June 1992.

[23] S. Sakai, Y. Yamaguchi, K. Hiraki, and T. Yuba: "An architecture of a dataflow single chip processor," In *The 16th Annual International Symposium on Computer Architecture*, pp. 46–53, May 1989.

[24] T. Shimizu, T. Horie, and H. Ishihata: "Low-latency message communication support for the AP1000," In *The 19th Annual International Symposium on Computer Architecture*, pp. 288–297, May 1992.

SESSION 15:

Memory
Systems and
Interconnection

Performance of Cached DRAM Organizations in Vector Supercomputers

W. -C. Hsu[1]

J. E. Smith

Hewlett-Packard Company
19447 Pruneridge Ave.
Cupertino, CA 95014

Cray Research, Inc.
900 Lowater Rd.
Chippewa Falls, WI 54729

Abstract

DRAMs containing cache memory are studied in the context of vector supercomputers. In particular, we consider systems where processors have no internal data caches and memory reference streams are generated by vector instructions. For this application, we expect that cached DRAMs can provide high bandwidth at relatively low cost.

We study both DRAMs with a single, long cache line and with smaller, multiple cache lines. Memory interleaving schemes that increase data locality are proposed and studied. The interleaving schemes are also shown to lead to non-uniform bank accesses, i.e. hot banks. This suggests there is an important optimization problem involving methods that increase locality to improve performance, but not so much that hot banks diminish performance. We show that for uniprocessor systems, both types of cached DRAMs work well with the proposed interleave methods. For multiprogrammed multiprocessors, the multiple cache line DRAMs work better.

1. Introduction

After years of using simple DRAM organizations that provide data at rates keyed to the performance of internal transistor arrays, chip makers are now in the process of introducing innovative organizations for commodity DRAM parts [Jone92]. They are aimed at reducing the disparity between processor and memory performance in desktop systems, while keeping the costs of such systems low. Consequently, a common characteristic of these new DRAM parts is that they use some form of internal data cacheing.

Vector supercomputers have significantly different characteristics from the desktop systems that are driving the development of new DRAM organizations. Besides the obvious difference in raw processing speeds, vector supercomputers differ from desktop systems in the following ways.

(1) Supercomputers typically do not use data caches for vectors, and sometimes (as in the case of Cray Research systems) they do not cache scalar data, either. There are at least three reasons for this. First, in vector machines memory latencies are amortized over pipelined streams of data references, i.e. vectors. Second, supercomputer-class problems often do not exhibit the locality required to make a data cache effective (although reprogramming and cache blocking compiler algorithms may help in some cases). Third, maintaining cache coherence is perceived to be a difficult problem in vector multiprocessors.

(2) Vector supercomputer systems usually contain multiple processors which either operate in parallel on the same job or independently on different jobs. The new DRAM organizations typically depend on locality that may be significantly reduced in multiprocessor situations [Come92].

(3) The per-processor bandwidth requirements in vector supercomputers are much greater than in PCs and workstations. For example, a vector machine needs sustained bandwidth of several words of data per clock period per processor (6 in the Cray Y-MP C90 [Cray91], for example). This means that highly interleaved memory systems with many banks are necessary.

Despite the significant differences between desktop systems and vector supercomputers, we feel that the new DRAM parts may still yield cost-performance improvements for vector supercomputers, provided the memory system is properly designed. In the supercomputer context, we stress the cost aspect, because current systems often use SRAM for main memory. SRAM provides performance at least equivalent to the best of the new DRAM technologies, but costs much more. As a point of reference, the CRAY Y-MP C90 uses 1024 banks of 15ns SRAM memory. A total of 20,000 SRAM chips are used in the largest size C90 main memory. Consequently, SRAM costs make up a majority of system-wide part costs. Although using traditional DRAM memory can dramatically reduce the cost for the same size memory, the memory bandwidth will also be much lower. For

---

0884-7495/93 $3.00 © 1993 IEEE

instance, if conventional 140ns DRAM memory were used in the C90 instead of 15ns SRAM, many times (8 to 16) more banks would be required to provide comparable memory bandwidth. Any savings in per-chip costs would likely be lost due to the larger number of chips and higher logic and interconnect costs. However, with the new cached DRAM parts it may now be possible to build an affordable memory system with both large size and high memory bandwidth.

In this paper, we look at ways the new cache-oriented DRAM parts and techniques can be adapted for use in high-end vector supercomputers. These methods use the cacheing capabilities of DRAM chips and employ unorthodox interleaving techniques to improve locality, especially in multiprocessor situations. Section 2 provides an overview of the new DRAM organizations. Section 3 proposes memory interleaving methods that are directed toward improving performance. Section 4 describes the system model we are studying, as well as the simulation benchmarks and performance measures we use. Section 5 gives results for our trace-driven simulations. Finally, Section 6 contains conclusions.

2. Cached DRAM Organizations

A wide variety of high performance DRAM parts are possible, but we divide the ones of interest to us into two generic classes.

(1) The first class is a simple outgrowth of static column DRAMs where an entire row of the memory array is latched and may be accessed repeatedly by modifying the column address lines only (as long as consecutive accesses are to addresses within the latched row). In effect, these DRAMs have an internal cache that consists of one large line, i.e. the latched row.

(2) The second class is made up of parts that contain multiple cache lines of conventional length. These on-chip caches can be accessed using direct-mapped or set associative methods, with the tags being held in the off-chip memory controller.

Fig. 1a illustrates the class of single line cached DRAMs, and Fig. 1b illustrates the class of multiple line cached DRAMs. Parts from RAMtron [Bond92] and RAMbus [Farm92] (RAMbus essentially puts two memory banks on a chip) belong to the first class, and DRAMs from Mitsubishi [Hart92] belong to the second class. A common property of both types of cached DRAMs is that the cache-fill bandwidth is very high because the bus connecting the cache and the DRAM memory array is very wide. This feature encourages the use of large line sizes to exploit spatial locality.

For our study, we look at generic versions of these DRAM part types. We want to avoid becoming bogged down in the details (and quirks) of specific implementations and timing. There is currently no standard, *de facto*

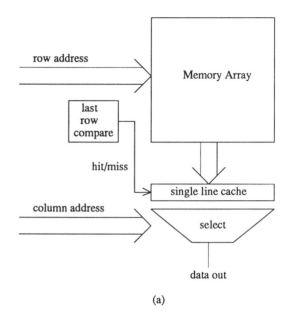

(a)

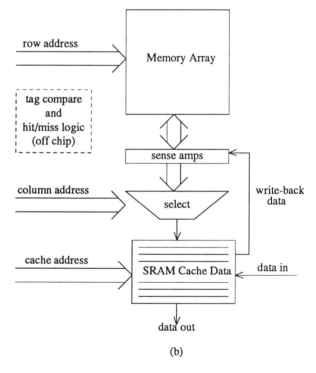

(b)

Fig. 1. Basic DRAM organizations
a) a single line organization,
b) a multi-line organization.

or otherwise, so such details could change, anyway. For both types of RAMs, we assume the internal cache lines are write-back with write-allocate. To make comparisons easier, we simulate parts where the total cache sizes are the same and are of similar size to commercially available parts.

3. Memory Interleaving

To simplify our discussion, we assume word addressing (adjustments for byte addressing are straight-forward). If a memory system has b banks, each containing m words, then there are $\log b$ plus $\log m$ address bits. Traditionally memories are interleaved on low-order address bits. That is, the low order $\log b$ bits are used to select the bank and the high order $\log m$ bits are used to read a word within the bank (see Fig. 2a). This puts all the addresses modulo b in the same bank. Such interleaving is very common in high performance systems, especially when the bank cycle time is slower than the system clock cycle. This interleave scheme has the advantage that each bank will tend to be uniformly referenced (except vector strides that are a multiple of a power-of-two). However, since words at consecutive addresses are placed in different banks, this scheme prevents DRAM caches from effectively exploiting spatial locality. That is, a single cache line held in a DRAM chip contains words that are at logical addresses separated by a large power of two (the number of banks).

An alternative, which increases spatial locality, is to interleave on high order address bits, as shown in Fig. 2b. In this case the high order $\log b$ address bits are used to select the bank. This does increase locality, since consecutive addresses are in the same bank. However, it is also likely to produce highly non-uniform bank references and thus degrade performance for single jobs. For example, consider the vector loop $A(I)=B(I)+C(I)$ with stride one references. While executing this loop, we typically exercise at most three memory banks because there are three reference streams, each with its own spatial locus of reference. Another disadvantage that offsets improvements in spatial locality is that when the cache hit time is slower than the system clock such interleaving can not deliver one word of data per clock period for sequential accesses. Some supercomputers may have clock rates much faster than the hit time of the DRAM cache.

We attempt to blend the two interleaving schemes by distributing the interleave bits in positions other than the highest and lowest order positions. To do this we consider cache line boundaries and/or memory bandwidth capabilities.

One such way of interleaving is to use address bits at the cache line level. If a cache line has p words, then the low order $\log p$ bits and the high order $\log m - \log p$ bits are used to select the word within a bank. The bank address bits are the $\log b$ bits above the low order $\log p$ bits (Fig. 2c). That is, all the words in a cache line are from consecutive memory addresses, then the interleaving moves to the next bank (Fig. 3a). Such a scheme still has significant hot bank problems, as we shall see, especially for DRAMs with a single large line. Also, there is reduced bandwidth for sequential accesses when the cache hit time is slower than the processor cycle time, as explained above.

To overcome these problems we suggest "block" interleaving where the interleave bits are split. For n-way block interleaving, the low order $\log n$ bits are used to address a bank within a bank group, the next $\log p$ bits are used to address the word within the bank, the next $\log b - \log n$ bits are used to select the bank group, and the remaining high order bits are also used to address the word within the bank (Fig. 2d). The addresses placed in each bank are illustrated in Fig. 3b. By this definition, cache line interleaving is also 1-way block interleaving.

4. Simulation Framework

4.1. System Model

Fig. 4 illustrates the systems we simulate. To simplify the simulation model (this is important because of the lengths of the reference streams) the system model assumes a conflict-free interconnection network, with uniform, fixed delays. That is, we apply streams of addresses from the processor(s) directly to memory banks, and then determine if there is a hit or miss within the banks' caches. For simplicity, we assume one cache per bank.

We consider both uniprocessor performance and multi-programmed multiprocessor performance. For

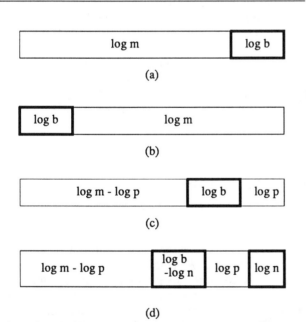

Fig. 2. Different memory interleaving schemes. Assuming there are b banks, m words per bank, and cache line with p words. Bits used for bank address are enclosed in bold lines. a) Low order interleaving, b) high order interleaving, c) cache line interleaving, d) n-way block interleaving.

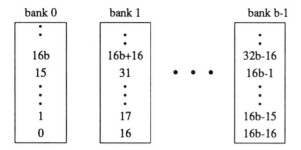

a) Cache Line Interleaving

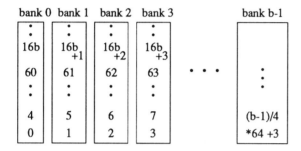

b) 4-way Block Interleaving

Fig. 3. Examples of memory addresses for cache line interleaving and block interleaving. There are b banks, m words per bank, and 16 word cache lines.

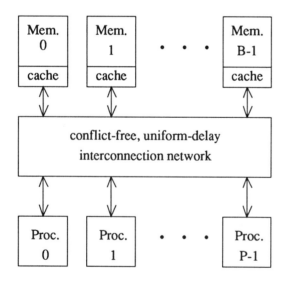

Fig. 4. System model.

uniprocessor performance, a single processor applies its stream of references to the memory system. For multiprogrammed performance, multiple processors apply

independent streams of addresses to the memory banks. In this case, we pick an address from each of the processors in turn, in round-robin fashion. We tried simulations with randomly selected processors and with methods using a small number of consecutive addresses from each processor before moving on. These showed slightly improved performance, but no significant differences from the single reference per processor, round robin method. Therefore, we decided to use the single reference per processor, round robin method throughout our simulations.

Hence, in multiprocessor systems, we simulate a throughput mode of operation, i.e. multiprogramming by interleaving streams from independent jobs into the memory system. While we do not simulate parallel processing, the performance would likely be better because the parallel processing address streams would be likely to exhibit higher locality than independent address streams.

For each of the simulations, we vary the number of memory banks. In an actual well-balanced system, the number of banks would be a loose function of the bank reservation time, processor clock period, and the rate at which the processor can make memory requests. For a simple example, consider the case where the average bank reservation time is eight processor clock periods. Then a system with eight banks would be matched to a processor that makes a memory request every cycle. Sixteen banks would be needed for two such processors, etc. On the other hand, if the bank reservation time is 16 clock periods, then 16 memory banks would be needed for a single processor system. Machines with multiple pipelines can make memory requests at a higher rate, for example, a 4-pipe processor can request four words per cycle with a single vector load instruction. Therefore, a single 4-pipe processor can be considered making memory requests at the same rate as four single-pipe processors. By varying the number of banks in our simulations, we take into account different ratios of total processor request rates and bank cycle times.

4.2. Performance Measures

To measure performance, we primarily use cache miss rates and memory bandwidths. The cache miss rate, the percentage or fraction of references that miss in the DRAM-resident data cache, is a traditional measure of cache performance. We consider that a hit occurs when a reference is contained in the on-chip cache; otherwise there is a miss. Cache miss rates are sometimes considered to be less meaningful measurement of performance in situations where cache miss latency can be overlapped with instruction execution. However, since we are primarily concerned with memory bandwidth, which is determined by bank reservation times instead of access latency, cache miss rates are appropriate.

For simulations of uniprocessors, we average miss rates of the various streams. Using the arithmetic average is an accurate way to determine aggregate miss rate performance. It is as if we normalize by considering the same number of references from each stream, then take the total number of misses divided by the total number of references.

Although miss rate is related to memory bandwidth, we combine miss rate with hit/miss timings and measure bandwidth more directly. We first derive a memory bandwidth measure that indicates an upper-bound bandwidth a particular memory system can provide. We do this by using the measured number of cache hits/misses and corresponding cache/DRAM timing parameters to compute the time it would take to serve all the memory requests. Dividing the total number of memory requests by this time gives us a bandwidth number.

We represent the number of hits in memory bank i as H_i, the number of clean misses in bank i as MC_i, and the number of dirty misses in bank i as MD_i. H, MC, and MD denote the total number of hits, clean misses, and dirty misses summed over all the banks. We represent the hit time as t_h cycles, the clean miss time as t_{mc} cycles, and the dirty miss time as t_{md} cycles. Recall that the number of memory banks is b; then the total time required to service all the requests is:

$$\sum_i (t_h * H_i + t_{mc} * MC_i + t_{md} * MD_i)$$

If we assume that the memory banks receive equal numbers of accesses and equal numbers misses then this sum divided by the number of banks gives the minimum time required to service all the requests. Dividing the total number of requests by this minimum time gives us an upper-bound estimate of memory bandwidth. That is:

potential bandwidth =

$$b * (H + MC + MD) / \sum_i (t_h * H_i + t_{mc} * MC_i + t_{md} * MD_i)$$

We refer to the above bandwidth as "potential" because it assumes all memory banks are always active. If a bank can be idle, then the actual bandwidth is less than the best-case bandwidth calculated with the formula.

As stated above, potential bandwidth also assumes the memory banks are accessed an equal number of times, and that the numbers of hits and misses are equally distributed. That is, there are no "hot" bank(s) that get many more requests than the others (or which have a higher fraction of misses). While we will find that this is generally true for low-order interleaved memory systems, it is not true for the other interleaving schemes where some banks may be much busier than others. To investigate how much impact the hot bank problem has on bandwidth, we define the *effective bandwidth* as follows. First, we keep track of which requests, hits, and misses are handled by each memory bank. Then we can compute the time required by each bank and use the longest bank time as the overall time required. Then the total of all

requests is divided by the longest bank time.

effective bandwidth =

$$(H + MC + MD) / \max_i (t_h * H_i + t_{mc} * MC_i + t_{md} * MD_i)$$

In this case, only the most heavily loaded bank is never idle, and other banks may have some idle time. If the banks are uniformly accessed then the effective bandwidth should equal the potential bandwidth. On the other hand, the difference between potential and effective bandwidth provides a measure of the performance impact of hot banks.

4.3. Benchmarks

To measure performance we use a set of 10 benchmarks shown in Table 1. Among the 10 programs, ARC2D, ARC3D, MDG, MG3D, SPEC77 and TRFD are selected from the optimized Perfect suite [Cybe90]. APPBT, APPLU, MG and FFT are chosen from the NAS parallel benchmark set [Bail91]. Table 1 characterizes the problems according to the number of different words referenced, the total data set size in millions of words, and the trace length (number of memory references). Each trace is generated by simulating a single processor CRAY Y-MP for 40 million instructions (both scalar and vector instructions). Because some applications like APPBT, MG, FFT, and ARC2D have larger vector lengths, their memory traces are longer than others. The trace lengths vary from about 32 million memory references to 652 million references. The first six benchmarks are relatively small (by supercomputer standards) and have problem sizes of about 1 to 7 million words (8 to 56 Mbytes). The last four benchmarks are much larger, and range from 32 to 56 Mwords (256 to 448 Mbytes).

Table 1. Characteristics of benchmark programs.

Programs	Different Words Referenced	Problem Size (MW)	Trace Length (Millions)
ARC2D	4314768	4.9	242.89
ARC3D	798048	1.3	128.64
MDG	1118928	1.4	32.33
MG3D	2085024	7.4	241.41
SPEC77	522112	1.3	147.71
TRFD	218384	3.6	51.79
APPBT	37052912	42.2	652.55
MG	51850160	56.7	319.06
FFT	33893280	42.9	419.46
APPLU	29327760	32.2	232.40

5. Simulation Results

5.1. Single Processor Performance

We begin with uniprocessor simulations. We simulate both a single line cache, and a multiple line cache. To allow us to more easily compare results, we assume exactly the same total cache size in both cases. In particular, we assume a 512 word cache per bank, organized as both a single 512 word line and as 32 lines of 16 words each. In the multi-line case we begin with a direct-mapped cache. We consider four address interleaving methods:

(1) interleave on low order address bits (traditional interleave),

(2) interleave on cache lines,

(3) 2-way block interleaving,

(4) 4-way block interleaving.

Fig. 5 illustrates performance for single jobs. Each of the jobs was run individually, and the miss rates for the ten jobs were then averaged. Overall, we see that miss rates of 10 percent and lower are possible with large single line caches and block or cache line interleaving.

When a single processor is running, the single line cache performs better than the multiple line cache for all cases except where low order bit interleaving is used. Furthermore, with low order interleaving, performance of

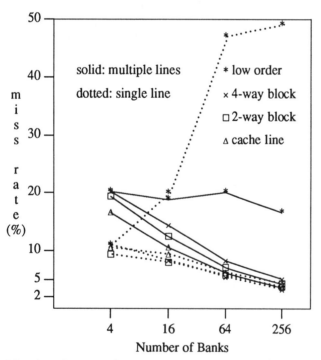

Fig. 5. Miss rates for single processors; average of 10 traces.

the single line cache gets worse as more banks are used. With this type of interleaving, spatial locality is reduced for systems with more memory banks.

For the multiple line cache, more banks provide better opportunities to exploit temporal locality, hence there is generally a lower miss rate with more banks. However, there is still a slight increase in miss rate when going from 16 banks to 64 banks with low order interleaving. In this case, the increase in temporal locality is less than the loss of spatial locality.

For 256 banks spatial locality is almost non-existent with low order bit interleaving; only temporal locality can be exploited. Although the multiple line cache works better than the single line cache, its miss rate is still much higher than non-traditional interleaving methods. This demonstrates that for large scientific jobs such as our benchmark programs, a cached DRAM memory system cannot rely merely on temporal locality to be effective. Non-traditional interleave schemes must be considered.

Interleaving at cache lines intuitively exploits the highest spatial locality of the methods we consider. In Fig. 5, however, for single line caches, 4-way and 2-way block interleaving have lower average miss rates than interleaving at cache lines. This anomaly is due to program ARC2D which has a lot of memory accesses with stride 588 (a multiple of 4). With such strides, spatial locality is reduced for cache line interleaving but is enhanced for the block interleaving.

Fig. 6 and Fig. 7 show the potential and effective bandwidths for single jobs. For generating these graphs, we assume a cache hit takes one cycle, a clean miss takes 14 cycles, and a dirty miss takes 28 cycles. These numbers are consistent with a 10 ns clock period and the Mitsubishi TP-10 CDRAM chip. Fig. 6 shows that single line caches with block interleaving have higher potential bandwidth than multiple line caches. However, due to the hot bank problem, the effective bandwidth of single line caches tends to become lower as the number of banks is increased (Fig. 7). For larger memory systems, the effective bandwidth of a single line cache is reduced by more than a factor of 4 from the potential bandwidth.

This difference between effective and potential bandwidths is an indicator of non-uniform memory bank references. Fig. 8 illustrates the distribution of requests to banks for one of the benchmark programs. This particular benchmark was chosen because it has a particularly obvious hot bank problem; not all the benchmarks are this bad. We see that for cache line interleaving, there is a single hot bank that gets about eight times as many references as any of the others. We also see that for 2-way block interleaving, the hot spot becomes spread over two banks, and for 4-way block interleaving it becomes spread over four banks. This is as one might expect, and it demonstrates the value of using block interleaving for reducing (but, unfortunately, not eliminating) hot bank

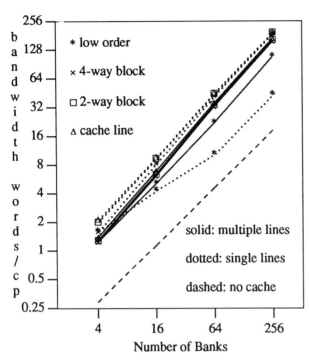

Fig. 6. Potential bandwidth for single processors; average of 10 traces.

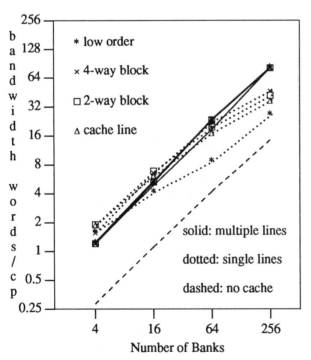

Fig. 7. Effective bandwidth for single processors; average of 10 traces.

problems. However, if two consecutive banks are hot when cache line interleaving is used, 2-way block interleaving may not reduce the problem. For the same reason, 4-way block interleaving may not be an improvement when there are four consecutive banks that are hot. This explains why all three block interleaving schemes (including cache line interleaving) have similar effective bandwidths for multiple line caches as in Fig. 7.

In the ten benchmark programs, we have determined that hot banks occur due to one of the following three cases: (1) there are small active working arrays, (2) vector registers are spilled and reloaded from the run time stack, (3) data blocking algorithms cause intensive data reuse. It seems that some forms of local memory might be able to minimize such redundant memory references, and reduce the hot bank problem associated with cache line interleaving. In other words, systems with processor data caches that are sufficiently large to exploit high temporal locality might not have hot bank problems as severe as the cacheless systems we are considering.

To make sure that our bandwidth results are interpreted correctly, consider ways the bandwidth graphs can be used for designing systems. Recall that our bandwidth graphs are based on the assumption of no idle memory cycles, that is, memory is a saturated resource (either all of memory for potential bandwidth, or at least one

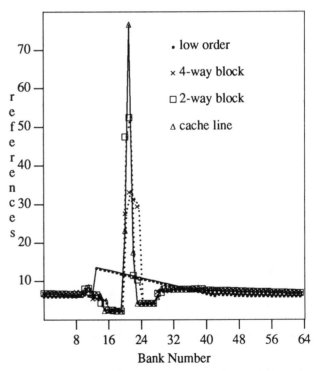

Fig. 8. Hot bank distribution in multiple line caches for program TRFDLG; number of references from a sample of 100K.

memory bank for effective bandwidth). This is a desirable design point when the memory system is the most expensive resource, as is typically the case in vector supercomputers. The saturated memory assumption means that for specific processor configurations, only certain regions of the the bandwidth graphs may be valid. In particular, they are only valid in regions where the processor demand for memory exceeds or equals memory's ability to deliver data. This occurs when the number of processors times the number of memory reference streams per processor is greater than the memory bandwidth.

For example, in Figs. 6 and 7 we are assuming single processors. A processor's memory demand is a function of the number of memory pipelines, and its clock rate. Figs. 6 and 7 assume a system clock period that is the same as the DRAM cache hit time. In this case, a vector uniprocessor operating with eight memory pipelines has a maximum demand of eight references per clock period. A processor with a clock four times as fast and two memory pipelines would have a similar demand. In either case, the memory can be saturated only if it delivers fewer than eight words per cycle. Applying this to Fig. 7, we see that the region of the graph where the bandwidth is eight words per cycle or less is applicable to our example system. Using the applicable region of the graph, it appears that 16 memory banks with a single cache line DRAM and block interleaving is a reasonably good match to the processor demand. On the other hand, if no DRAM cacheing were used, and the memory cycle time were always 14 clock periods, then about 8*14=112 (i.e.128) memory banks would be required to match the potential processor demand. The cost savings of using the cached DRAM organization is very evident.

5.2. Multiple Processor Performance

For multi-program performance, we chose eight of the benchmark programs: APPBT, APPLU, MG, FFT, ARC3D, SPEC77, TRFDLG, and MG3DLG, and ran them on eight different processors with memory requests being made in round-robin fashion. Note that the first four benchmarks are large, and the last four are small (relatively). The eight jobs were placed next to each other in memory, aligned to 2KW boundaries. The miss rate results are in Fig. 9. As might be expected, performance is worse than for a single job. This is because locality tends to be disrupted due to the multiple independent memory streams. However, in systems with larger numbers of memory banks, performance is significantly better; in some cases reaching the same level as a single job.

For single job (uniprocessor) runs, we observed that the single line cache with block interleaving is quite effective in exploiting spatial locality. However, in multi-program runs, the competition from several processes destroy the effectiveness of holding a large

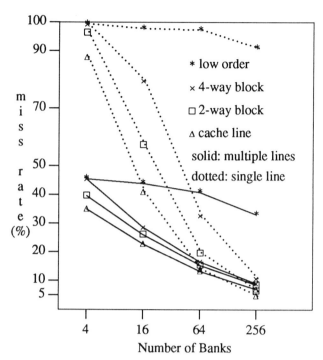

Fig. 9. Miss rate for multi-programmed runs; 8 processes time shared.

cache line. As shown in Fig. 9, the multiple line cache is more robust and more effective than the single line cache unless the number of banks becomes relatively large. We also observe that performance differences in miss rate of non-traditional interleaving for single line caches are significant; for the uniprocessor, the differences were small. This is because several processes are competing for the banks and the cache line in the bank. A higher degree of block interleaving spreads an active line across more banks, increasing the likelihood of conflict and thrashing.

Fig. 10 gives results for the small jobs alone (where one might expect more temporal locality), and Fig. 11 shows performance for the large jobs alone. The miss rates for small jobs are much better. For large jobs, low order interleaving performs poorly: single line caches have nearly a 100% miss rate and multiple line caches have a 45% miss rate even when the number of banks is as high as 256. For large jobs where caches may not exploit a high degree of temporal locality, exploiting spatial locality becomes critical. For instance, block interleaving can bring the miss rate down to near 10% with 256 banks.

Figs. 12 and 13 show potential bandwidth and effective bandwidth, respectively, for multi-programmed jobs. For multiple line caches, cache line interleaving works well for both potential and effective bandwidth. For single line caches, cache line interleaving has the highest potential bandwidth, but the lowest performance

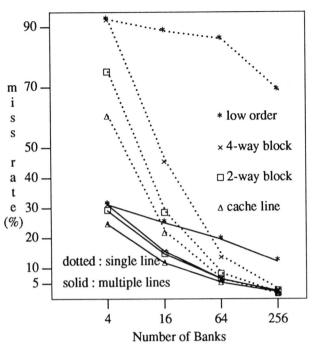

Fig. 10. Miss rate for multi-programmed runs; 4 small processes time shared.

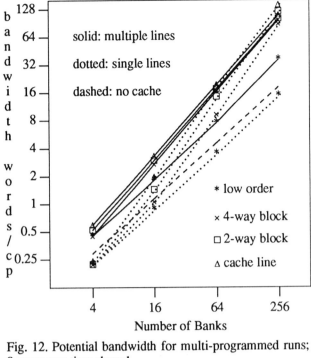

Fig. 12. Potential bandwidth for multi-programmed runs; 8 processes time shared.

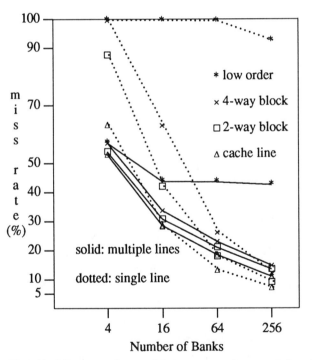

Fig. 11. Miss rate for multi-programmed runs; 4 large processes time shared.

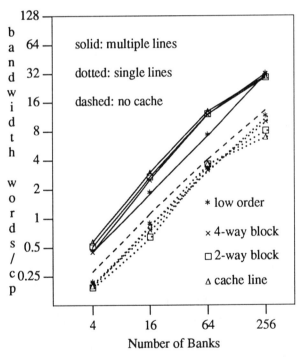

Fig. 13. Effective bandwidth with multi-programming; 8 processes time shared.

in effective bandwidth due to the hot bank problem. Four-way block interleaving has performance close to the better performing one in terms of both potential and effective bandwidth. Fig. 14 illustrates the distribution of requests to banks for multi-program runs with single large line caches. The curve for cache line interleaving has several spikes, and block interleaving smooths out some of the spikes.

6. Conclusions

In this paper we considered the usefulness of new cache-oriented DRAMs for delivering cost-effective bandwidth in vector supercomputers. It is apparent from our simulations that traditional low-order-bit memory interleaving will not take full advantage of the new DRAM parts; spatial locality is reduced too much. We have shown that using other less common interleave schemes, which place successive words in the same DRAM chips, can increase locality and improve performance. Unfortunately, they also tend to produce non-uniform bank usage; the presence of hot banks can reduce overall performance. Consequently, we feel that memory system designs will involve optimizations to increase memory bank locality up to a certain point, but no further.

In uniprocessor environments, cached DRAMs with block interleaving can provide more cost-effective bandwidth. In multiprogramming multiprocessor environments, we have shown that single line cached

DRAMs are unlikely to be effective, consistent with the opinions expressed in [Come92]. On the other hand, we have also shown that multi-line caches with block interleaving schemes can be made to work well.

Single line cached DRAMs are more sensitive to the memory interleaving scheme that is used. We recommend that block interleaving be used. The performance of multi-line caches is less sensitive to interleaving methods, and block interleaving is called for when the cache hit time is slower than processor cycle time.

A disadvantage of non-conventional interleaving schemes that we have not yet discussed is that they lead to systems where the addressing logic external to the chip becomes tuned to internal chip characteristics, i.e. the cache characteristics. If DRAM chips in an optimized system are later replaced with chips having different characteristics, the interleave scheme may no longer be optimal.

Finally, we feel that our results will extend qualitatively to systems other than those we have specifically studied. However, as we observed earlier, the types of program constructs that lead to hot bank problems may have a smaller effect when processors contain data caches that are able to reduce redundant memory traffic significantly. Non-standard interleaving schemes will likely become a key component of memory system design, and the tradeoff between increased spatial locality and hot banks will be an important design issue.

7. References

[Bail91] David H. Bailey et al., "The NAS Parallel Benchmark: Summary and Preliminary Results," IEEE Supercomputing '91, pp 158-165, Nov., 1991

[Bond92] Bondurant D., "Enhanced Dynamic RAM," *IEEE Spectrum*, pp 49, in [Jone92], Oct., 1992

[Come92] Comerford, R. and G. Watson, "Memory catches up," *IEEE Spectrum*, pp 34-35, Oct. 1992.

[Cray92] Cray Research Inc., "CRAY YMP C90 Functional Description Manual," HR-04028, March, 1992.

[Cybe90] Cybenko, G., et al., "Supercomputer Performance Evaluation and the Perfect Benchmarks," *CSRD Report No. 965*, University of Illinois, March, 1990

[Farm92] Farmwald M. and D. Mooring "A Fast Path to One Memory," *IEEE Spectrum*, pp 50-51, Oct. 1992.

[Hart92] Hart C., "Dynamic RAM as Secondary Cache," *IEEE Spectrum*, pp 48, in [Jone92], Oct., 1992

[Jone92] Jones Fred, " A New Era of Fast Dynamic RAMs" *IEEE Spectrum*, pp 43-49, Oct. 1992.

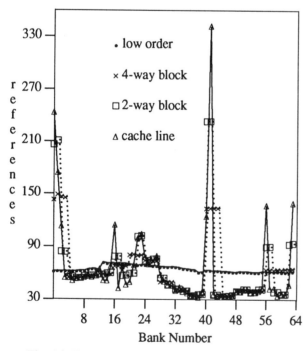

Fig. 14. Hot bank distribution in single line caches; for 8 processes time shared.

The Chinese Remainder Theorem and the Prime Memory System

Q.S. Gao

Chinese Academy of Sciences

Abstract

As we know, the conflict problem is a very important problem in memory system of super computer, there are two kinds of conflict-free memory system approaches: skewing scheme approach and prime memory system approach. Previously published prime memory approaches are complex or wasting 1/p of the memory space for filling the 'holes' [17], where p is the number of memory modules. In this paper, based on Chinese remainder theorem, we present a perfect prime memory system which only need to find the d Mod p without wasting any memory space and without computing the quotient.

I. INTRODUCTION

A fundamental problem in parallel processing is the effective use of parallel memories [1]. Much research work had been done in this topic [1-18]. [2-9] treated the problem of array access and alignment. There are two kinds of conflict-free memory system approaches, one is skewing scheme approach [10-14], another is prime memory system approach. Budnik and Kuck [15] observed that if the number of memory modules is a prime number p, then access to any linear slice of array (n×n) can be achieved without conflict if n is not divisible by p. The first computer with prime memory system is the supercomputer BSP [16], which has 17 memories and 16 processors. Lawrie and Vora [17] describe the prime memory system of BSP in detail, on which the 'holes' be needed for implementation. This means that it wastes one of p memory modules, or increases the complexity

for filling those holes with other data. They also proposed the implementation for some cases such as linear p-vector in detail. Teng [18] propose a simple technique for performing modulus which can be applied to [17]. We [20-21] proposed a high speed multiple-bits division approach, which includes the approach (as a special case) for finding "d Mod p" by parallel "l-bits cycle adder" in one step or by serial "l-bits cycle adder" in $\lceil \frac{log_2 d}{l} \rceil$ steps when $p=2^l - 1$, and similar approach when $p=2^l+1$. Avizienis [19] also proposed an approach for finding "d Mod p" when $p=2^l - 1$ or $p=2^l + 1$. In this paper, we present a perfect prime memory system which only need to find the d Mod p without wasting any memory space and without computing the quotient.

II. THE PRIME MEMORY SYSTEM (PMS)

1. The prime memory system (PMS)

Definition 1: A prime memory system PMS is a memory system which has p memory modules, where p is a prime and larger than 2, (for easy to implement, assume that $p\in \{2^l + 1, 2^l - 1 \| l = 2, 3, ...\}$), each memory module has $m=2^{l'}$ words. The physical address of a word is a pair of integers (u,v), which denote the u-th word in the v-th memory module, where $0 \le u \le m - 1$, $0 \le v \le p - 1$. The logical address of a word is an integer d ($0 \le d \le pm - 1$). The physical address and the logical address of a word must satisfy two conditions as follows:

(1). v=d Mod p.

(2). Every logical address d, d∈ Ω, corresponds to one and only one physical address (u,v), (u,v)∈

Ω', and every physical address (u,v), $(u,v) \in \Omega'$, corresponds to one and only one logical address d, $d \in \Omega$. Where, Ω is a set of integers, Ω' is a set of the pair of integers.

Definition 2: A prime memory system PMS is high efficient if on which $\Omega = \{d \| 0 \leq d \leq pm - 1\}$, and $\Omega' = \{(u,v) \| 0 \leq u \leq m - 1, 0 \leq v \leq p - 1\}$. The relation between d and (u,v) can be represented as an array D[0:m-1,0:p-1], where d=D[u,v] (see Tables 1-3).

2. A prime memory system PMS-1

The prime memory system PMS-1 is an PMS, on which, d=up+v, i.e. $u = \lfloor \frac{d}{p} \rfloor$. The prime memory system PMS-1 is a high efficient PMS, but it need a division $\frac{d}{p}$ for getting the quotient $u = \lfloor \frac{d}{p} \rfloor$ and the remainder v. An example of system PMS-1 is shown in Table 1, where p=3, m=8.

Table 1. An example of the PMS1 with p=3, m=8.

0	1	2
3	4	5
6	7	8
9	10	11
12	13	14
15	16	17
18	19	20
21	22	23

3. The prime memory system (PMS-2) of super computer BSP [16,17]

The prime memory system (PMS-2) proposed by [17] is an PMS, on which $u = \lfloor \frac{d}{p-1} \rfloor$. The prime memory system PMS-2 can be implemented by finding 'd Mod p' without other operation when $p = 2^l + 1$, but only (p-1)/p of d satisfy that $u < m$, this means that it wastes 1/p of memory capacity for setting the 'holes'. Therefore, the prime memory system (PMS-2) proposed by [17] is not high efficient.

An example of PMS-2 is shown in Table 2, where x denotes the hole.

Table 2. An example of the BSP's PMS (PMS-2) with p=3, m=8.

0	1	x
3	x	2
x	4	5
6	7	x
9	x	8
x	10	11
12	13	x
15	x	14

III. The PERFECT PRIME MEMORY SYSTEM PPMS

1. The perfect prime memory system PPMS

The perfect prime memory system is an PSM, on which u=d Mod m, i.e. u is equal to the right l' bits of d, it can be got without any computation and without wasting any memory space. i.e. the perfect prime memory system PPMS can be implemented by finding 'd Mod p' without any other computation and without wasting any memory space.

The perfect prime memory system PPMS is a high efficient PMS which will be proved in section IV. An example of PPMS is show in Table 3.

Table 3. An example of the perfect prime memory system PPMS with p=3, m=8.

0	16	8
9	1	17
18	10	2
3	19	11
12	4	20
21	13	5
6	22	14
15	7	23

2. Theorems

The Chineses remainder theorem: Given two sets of integers $\{a_i \| i = 1, 2, ..., k\}$ and $\{b_i \| i = 1, 2, ..., k\}$, which satisfy the conditions as follows:

a_i, a_j are coprime when $i \neq j$, $i = 1, 2, ..., k$, $j = 1,$

$2, ..., k$:

$$0 \leq b_i < a_i, \quad i = 1, 2, ..., k;$$

$$0 \leq x < \prod_{i=1}^{k} a_i, \quad i = 1, 2, ..., k;$$

and

$$\begin{cases} b_1 = x \, Mod \, a_1, \\ b_2 = x \, Mod \, a_2, \\ \quad ...... \\ b_k = x \, Mod \, a_k; \end{cases}$$

where x is an integer variable. Then x has one and only one solution.

Theorem 1: The memory system PPMS is an PMS and a high efficient PMS. i.e. On PPMS, (1), every one logical address d, $0 \leq d \leq pm - 1$, correspond to one and only one physical address (u,v), $0 \leq u \leq m - 1$, $0 \leq v \leq p - 1$, and (2), every one physical address (u,v), $0 \leq u \leq m - 1$, $0 \leq v \leq p - 1$, correspond to one and only one logical address d, $0 \leq d \leq pm - 1$.

Proof:

(1). Because u=d Mod m, v=d Mod p, therefore, it is obvious, every one logical address d, $0 \leq d \leq pm - 1$, correspond to one and only one physical address (u,v), $0 \leq u \leq m - 1$, $0 \leq v \leq p - 1$.

(2). Because p is a prime and larger than 2, m is a powers of 2, hence p and m are coprime, therefore, according to the Chinese remainder theorem, (where a_1=m, a_2=p, b_1=u, b_2=v and x=d), every one physical address (u,v), $0 \leq u \leq m - 1$, $0 \leq v \leq p - 1$, correspond to one and only one logical address d, $0 \leq d \leq pm - 1$.

Comment:

1. The perfect prime memory system PPMS can be extended to a multiple primes memory system MPPMS. The multiple primes memory system MPPMS has P memory modules, which are divided p_1 1st-groups, every ith-group is divided p_{i+1} (i+1)th-groups, i=1,2,...,k-1, where $p_1, p_2, ..., p_k$ all are primes, $p_i = 2^{l_i} - 1$ or $2^{l_i} + 1$, i=1,2,...,k, P=$p_1 p_2 ... p_k$ and every one of kth-group only has one memory module. The theorems and their proofs in the multiple prime system MPPMS are

similar as in the perfect prime memory system PPMS. But on it the cases of conflict-free accessing is less than the perfect prime memory system's. For example, the condition of conflict-free accessing to any row and column of an n× n array is that n is not divisible by p in PPMS, but it is that n is not divisible by any one of p_i, i=1,2,...,k, in MPPMS. i.e., for example, assume that p=127 in PPMS, p_i=3,5,7 (P=105) in MPPMS, the set $\{n \mid n \text{ is not divisible by } 127\}$ is larger than the set $\{n \mid n \text{ is not divisible by } 3, 5 \text{ and } 7\}$ so much when n less than any large number.

2. d Mod p, p=$2^l - 1$ or p=$2^l + 1$, can be implemented by parallel or serial "cycle adder" [19-21].

References

1. G.H. Barnes, R.M. Brown, M. Kato, D.J. Kuck, D.L. Slotnick and R.A. Stokes, "The ILLIAC IV computer," IEEE T. Computer, Vol. C-28, pp.660-670, Aug. 1979.

2. K.E. Batcher, "The multidimensional access memory in STARAN," IEEE T. Computer, Vol. C-26, pp. 174-177, Feb. 1977.

3. T-Y. Feng, "Data manipulation functions in parallel processors and their implementations," IEEE T. Computer, Vol. C-23, pp.309-318, Mar. 1974.

4. H.S. Stone, "Parallel processing with the perfect shuffle," IEEE T. Computer, Vol. C-20, pp. 153-161, Feb. 1971.

5. R.C. Swanson, "Interconnections for parallel memories to unscramble p-ordered vectors," IEEE T. Computer, Vol. C-23, pp. 1105-1115, Nov. 1974.

6. D.H. Lawrie, "Access and alignment of data in an array processor," IEEE T. Computer, Vol. C-24, pp. 1145-1155, Dec. 1975.

7. T. Lang and H.S. Stone, "A shuffle exchange network with simplified control," IEEE T. Computer, Vol. C-25, pp.55-65, May 1976.

8. T. Lang, "Interconnections between processors and memory modules using the shuffle-exchange

network," IEEE T. Computer, Vol. C-25, pp.496-503, May 1976.

9. S.E. Orcutt, "Implementation of permutation functions in ILLIAC IV-type computers," IEEE T. Computers, Vol. C-25, pp. 929-936, Sept. 1976.

10. A. Deb, "Conflict-free access of arrays–a counter example," IPL Vol. 10, No. 1, pp. 20, 1980.

11. M. Balakrishnan, R. Jain and C.S. Raghavendra, "On array storage for conflict-free access for parallel processors," Proc. 17th International Conference on Parallel Processing, pp. 103-107, 1988.

12. K. Kim and V.K. Kumar, "Perfect Latin square and parallel array access," Proc. 16th Annual International Symposium on Computer Architecture, pp. 372-379, 1989.

13. C.J. Colbourn and K. Heirich, "Conflict-free access to parallel memories," Journal of Parallel and Distributed Computing, Vol. 14, pp. 193-200, 1992.

14. D-L. Lee, "Efficient address generation in a parallel processor," IPL, 1990.

15. P. Budnik and D.J. Kuck, "The organization and use of parallel memories," IEEE T. Computer, Vol. C-20, pp. 1566-1569, Dec. 1971.

16. D.J. Kuck and R. Stokes, "The Burroughs Scientific Processor (BSP)," IEEE T. Computer, Vol. C-31, pp. 363-376, May 1982.

17. D.H. Lawrie and C.R. Vora, "The prime memory system for array access," IEEE T. Computer, Vol. C-31, pp. 435-442, May 1982.

18. M-H. Teng, "Comments on 'The prime memory system for array access'," IEEE T. Computer, Vol. C-32, Nov. 1983.

19. A. Avizienis, "Arithmetic codes: Cost and effectiveness studies for allocation in digital systems design", IEEE T. Computer, Vol. C-20, No. 11, pp. 1322-1331, Nov. 1971.

20. Q.S. Gao, "The Principle of High Speed Multiple-bits division," Technical Report, Computing Technical Institute, Chinese Academy of Sciences, 1959.

21. Q.S. Gao, "Vector Supercomputer Architecture," Scientific Press, 1984.

Odd Memory Systems may be quite interesting*

André Seznec, Jacques Lenfant
IRISA, Campus de Beaulieu
35042 Rennes Cedex, FRANCE
e-mail : seznec@irisa.fr

Abstract

Using a prime number N of memory banks on a vector processor allows a conflict-free access for any slice of N consecutive elements of a vector stored with a stride not multiple of N.

To reject the use of a prime (or odd) number N of memory banks, it is generally advanced that address computation for such a memory system would require systematic Euclidean Division by the number N. We first show that the well known Chinese Remainder Theorem allows to define a very simple mapping of data onto the memory banks for which address computation does not require any Euclidean Division.

Massively parallel SIMD computers may have several thousands of processors. When the memory on such a machine is globally shared, routing vectors from memory to the processors is a major difficulty; the control for the interconnection network cannot be generally computed at execution time. When the number of memory banks and processors is a product of prime numbers, the family of permutations needed for routing vectors from memory to the processors through the interconnection network have very specific properties. The Chinese Remainder Network presented in the paper is able to execute all these permutations in a single path and may be self-routed.

Keywords: *Prime memory systems, vector, SIMD computers, Chinese Remainder Network.*

1 Introduction

As vector parallelism is easiest to detect and to exploit, a large number of vector processors have been built and commercialized since 1965. Vector processors usually resort to the pipeline architecture (e.g., vector register machines as the Cray Series) or to the SIMD architecture where a single sequencing unit controls several identical processing elements (e.g. the Connection Machine).

A vector is an ordered set of words whose addresses form an arithmetic series. In most cases, the bottleneck for performance on vector applications is the parallel (or pipelined) access to vectors on memory: conflicts may arise when accessing vectors. Since 1970, removing this bottleneck has been addressed in a lot of studies [2, 5, 8, 9, 16, 18, 19, 21].

Using a prime number N of memory banks in the memory of a vector processor allows a conflict-free access for any slice of N consecutive elements of a constant-strided vectors which stride is not multiple of N [2]. We shall refer to a memory system with a prime number of memory banks as a prime memory system [11]. By analogy, we shall refer to a memory system built with an odd number of memory banks as an odd memory system.

To reject the use of prime (resp. odd) memory systems, it is generally advanced that address computation requires an Euclidean Division by the prime (resp. odd) number N [11, 19].

In section 2, we present a very simple mapping of data for a prime (or odd) memory system for which address computation does not require any Euclidean Division.

On large *shared memory SIMD computers*, routing at execution time a vector of data from memory to the processors is a major difficulty. In section 3, we consider a SIMD computer where the number of processors and memory banks in a SIMD computer is chosen as the product of distinct prime numbers. The family of permutations needed for routing vectors from memory to processors through the interconnection network on such a SIMD computer is characterized. Then, in section 4, we present a new multistage interconnection network, the Chinese Remainder Network. The Chinese Remainder Network is very easy to control for executing these permutations. Both self-routing control or centralized control are shown to be realistic.

Results presented in this paper may encourage to build large shared memory SIMD computers using a product of prime numbers as the number of memory banks and processors: programming vector applications on such SIMD machines will be easier than programming on the current distributed memory SIMD computers for which performance essentially depends on the data locality in the application.

2 Odd memory system does not require Euclidean division

2.1 Usual data mapping in a parallel memory

In both SIMD machines and vector register processors, several memory banks are used in the design of the memory system.

To obtain a maximum memory throughput on a vector instruction, conflicts on accesses to memory must be avoided.

*This work was partially supported by CNRS (PRC-ANM)

The mapping of word at address A on memory is defined by two functions:

- $m(A)$ the number of the memory bank where word at address A is mapped. We shall refer to m as the bank distribution function.

- $l(A)$ the local address in memory bank $m(A)$. We shall refer to l, as the local displacement funtion.

The mapping of data used in most of the current vector processors is defined by:
let N be the number of memory banks

- $m(A) = A \bmod N$

- $l(A) = A / N$

This mapping is sometimes referred to as low order interleaving.

Figure 1 illustrates this mapping for N=13 and a memory bank size of 16 words.

The following property on distribution of the elements among the memory banks is known since 1971 [2]:

Theorem 2.1 (Distribution Theorem) *When the bank distribution function is defined by $m(A) = A \bmod N$, then for any vector V stored with a stride R:*
$V(i)$ and $V(j)$ are stored in the same memory bank iff $i = j \bmod N/GCD(N, R)$

Then for any vector V stored with a stride R, $N/GCD(N, R)$ consecutive elements of the vector are stored in distinct memory banks. Using a prime number of memory banks ensures a conflict free distribution of any slice of N consecutive elements for all the vectors stored with a stride R not multiple of N.

Moreover, using a prime number induces simple control for memory accesses; only two distributions of elements of a vector slice are possible: conflict free access is possible *or* all the elements lie in the same memory bank.

In statistics on vector applications, members of the Fujitsu VP200 design team [22] mentioned that about 80 % of the vectors are accessed with stride one, and the others are accessed with approximately randomly distributed strides. In order to illustrate the benefit that may be obtained using a prime number instead of a classical power of two as number of memory banks, we consider the average memory throughput on vector accesses of two memory systems : a 257 bank memory system and a 256 bank memory system.

Let us consider a SIMD vector processor consisting in N processors connected to a parallel memory consisting in N memory banks and that a memory request to a vector slice of N consecutive elements may be issued on each cycle.

Let us also consider that each bank is busy for one cycle by a memory request.

When considering the distribution of vector strides previously referred, accessing 100 vector slices of N consecutive elements will require an average of 120 memory cycles (i.e $80 + 20 * (256/257) + 20 * (1/257) * 257)$ on a 257 banks memory system against an average of $180 = 80 + 20 * \Sigma_{i=0,7} 2^i / 2^{i+1} + 20 * (1/256) * 256$ memory cycles on a 256 banks memory system.

A last argument in favor of using a prime memory system is the demand for memory throughput on vector accesses with power-of-two strides in some specific applications [16].

What is wrong with prime memory systems

Unfortunately when using the usual data mapping, address computation for a prime memory system requires arithmetic modulo a fixed prime number:

1. Computing the memory bank number for word at address A requires the computation of $A \bmod N$. Very fast hardware evaluations of such a modulo may be implemented.

2. The computation of the local displacement in the memory bank requires an Euclidean Division by N and this division is quite complex when N is an odd number (in [4], a complex hardware mechanism for fast division by $2^s - 1$ or $2^s + 1$ is presented). This Euclidean Division may lenghten a lot the total address generation.

Therefore, when the usual low-order mapping on memory was used in a vector machine, the number of memory banks was a power of two.

In the next section, we shall see that by only changing the choice of the local displacement function, this Euclidean Division by a prime number can be avoided on prime memory systems.

2.2 Simple is better

A very old arithmetic result known as Chinese Remainder Theorem [1] induces a very elegant way to map elements onto a parallel memory consisting in an odd number N banks of 2^c elements and for which no hardware is needed to compute the local address[2].

Theorem 2.2 (Chinese Remainder Theorem)
Let P_1, P_2, .., P_p be p integers,
let us suppose that each pair (P_i, P_j) is relatively prime (i.e $GCD(P_i, P_j) = 1$) then for each $(X_1, X_2, .., X_p)$ such that :
$\forall 1 \leq i \leq p, 0 \leq X_i < P_i$, there exists one and only one $0 \leq X < \bar{P} = P_1 * P_2 * .. * P_p$ such that :
$\forall 1 \leq i \leq p, X_i \equiv X \bmod P_i$
This bijection is a ring isomorphism from $\mathbf{Z}/\mathbf{P}$ *onto* $\mathbf{Z}/\mathbf{P_1} * \mathbf{Z}/\mathbf{P_2} * \mathbf{Z}/\mathbf{P_p}$.

---

[1] It seems that this result was known more than 2000 years ago by the old Chinese

[2] On the Burroughs Scientific Processor [11], the Euclidean Division was also avoided, but $\frac{1}{17}$ th of the memory was wasted.

Figure 2 illustrates this isomorphism from $\mathbf{Z}/15$ onto $\mathbf{Z}/5 * \mathbf{Z}/3$.

Let us now consider the address mapping defined by:

- $m(A) = A \bmod N$

- $l(A) = A \bmod 2^c$

The Chinese Remainder Theorem ensures that these two functions define is a one-to-one mapping from the address space $\{0, .., N * 2^c - 1\}$ onto the set of memory words of the memory system.

Implementation of local displacement function requires no hardware: the c least significant bits of the address are directly used.

As in the previous section, the bank distribution function is the same as for the usual low order mapping, the Distribution Theorem still holds for this mapping: conflict free access is possible to any slice of N consecutive elements of a vector stored with a stride R not multiple of N.

Then we can state:

"Prime Memory Systems Do Not Require Euclidean Division By a Prime Number"

Odd memory systems

The previous result holds also for odd memory sytems

3 Accessing vectors on large shared memory SIMD machines

In this section, we consider a shared memory SIMD computer built with N processors and N memory banks (figure 4).

First, let us recall that, in a very large shared memory SIMD computer with hundreds or thousands of processors and memory banks, routing vectors from memory to the processors is a major difficulty. Large multistage interconnection networks may be built (e.g Omega network [10] or Benes Network [1] as in the CEDAR project [6] or in the RP3 project [16]. Unfortunately self-routing multistage interconnection network (e.g. Omega-like) are not able to execute all the permutations on its inputs and computing the control for a rearrangeable multistage interconnection network (e.g. a Benes-like network) for an arbitrary permutation is quite unfeasible at execution time [12].

Nevertheless, on a SIMD computer, permutations to be executed on vectors of data flowing out from the memory to the processors are not arbitrary as recalled below.

3.1 Permutations induced by vector accesses on a SIMD computer

On a SIMD computer, the Control Unit initiates the same instruction on all the processors. It particularly initiates the access to the vectors on memory and the computation of the addresses of the elements these vectors.

Let V be a vector stored in memory with stride R and base address $V(0)$. On a SIMD computer, these parameters of a vector may be known by the centralized Control Unit.

Element i of the vector has to be routed back to the processor i. When using the usual bank distribution function of data on memory (see section 2.1), element i of vector V is stored in memory bank $\Lambda_{R,V(0)}^{(N)}(i)$, where $\Lambda_{J,K}^{(N)}$ is defined by :

$$\Lambda_{J,K}^{(N)}: \quad \{0,..,N-1\} \quad \rightarrow \quad \{0,..,N-1\}$$
$$x \quad \rightarrow \quad Jx + K \bmod N$$

To be able to route any slice of N consecutive elements of a vector from memory to the processors, the interconnection network must be able to perform all the connections induced by any function of the family $\{\Lambda_{J,K}^{(N)}\}$.

As the function $\Lambda_{J,K}^{(N)}$ only depends on $J \bmod N$ and $K \bmod N$, the cardinal of the function family $\{\Lambda_{J,K}^{(N)}\}$ is N^2.

The interconnection network will not be a bottleneck for performance, if it is able to execute any function of this family in a minimum number of passes.

Now let us consider some particular values of N.

3.2 N is prime

When N is prime and J is not a multiple of N, $\Lambda_{J,K}^{(N)}$ is a permutation on $\{0, .., N-1\}$. When J is a multiple of N, $\Lambda_{J,K}^{(N)}$ is a constant function.

Then the set of permutations that must be executed through the interconnection network on a SIMD computer with N memory banks and N processors is quite limited (only $N * (N-1)$).

The Benes network $B^{(n)}$ can perform any arbitrary permutation on its 2^n entries. It requires $(2n - 1)$ stages consisting in 2^{n-1} $2 * 2$ switches and then can be pipelined. Unfortunately, algorithms for computing the controls of a Benes-like network at execution time are too space and time consuming for being used at execution time [12].

As we have already mentionned, the parameters of vectors to be accessed may be known in the Control Unit, then the permutation to be executed is characterized by the two parameters J and K. When N is relatively small, a solution may consist in using a Benes network and storing in a ROM memory the control of the network for executing each permutation of the family , but such a solution cannot be used when the number of processors and memory banks exceeds one thousand:

- If $N = 127$ then a memory $127 * 126$ words of $13 * 64$ bits would be needed

- If $N = 4099$ then a memory of $4099 * 4098$ words of $25 * 4096$ bits would be needed : more than one terabit.

3.3 N is a power of two

Considering a SIMD computer with $N = 2^n$ memory banks and processors, Lenfant [14] characterized the family of permutations induced through the interconnection network by routing vectors from the memory to the processors; Seznec [20] gave algorithms to compute a centralized control of the Sigma network, a Benes-like network, for these permutations in $O(n)$ delay. But implementing in hardware such a control unit for a multistage interconnection network would demand some specific hardware development; and there is only one interconnection network control unit per machine!

Using self-routing multistage interconnection network [15] seems more cost-effective. For example, the Omega network may be self routed by all the permutations needed for accessing vectors stored with an odd increment in 2^n memory banks system [14], but the Omega network cannot execute in a single pass the permutations needed for accessing a vector stored with an even stride.

3.4 N is a product of distinct prime numbers

In this section, we study the characteristics of the family $\{\Lambda_{J,K}^{(N)}\}$ when N is the product of n distinct prime numbers $N_1, .., N_n$.

Notation:
As the Chinese Remainder Theorem induces a ring isomorphism from $\mathbf{Z/N}$ onto $\mathbf{Z/N_1} * .. * \mathbf{Z/N_n}$, in this section we shall represent a number $0 \leq x < N$ as the n-uplet $(x_1, x_2, .., x_n)$ such that for all $0 < i \leq n$, $0 \leq x_i < N_i$, $x \equiv x_i \bmod N_i$.

The Chinese Remainder Theorem leads to the following property:

Property 3.1 (Decomposition property)
$\forall\, 0 \leq J = (J_1, .., J_n) < N,$
$\forall\, 0 \leq \overline{K} = (K_1, .., K_n) < N,$
$\forall\, 0 \leq x = (x_1, .., x_n) < N,$
$\Lambda_{J,K}^{(N)}(x) = (\Lambda_{J_1,K_1}^{(N_1)}(x_1), \Lambda_{J_2,K_2}^{(N_2)}(x_2), .., \Lambda_{J_n,K_n}^{(N_n)}(x_n))$

Then function $\Lambda_{J,K}^{(N)}$ may be considered as the composition in any possible order of the n independent functions f_i defined by:

$$f_i : \begin{array}{ccc} \mathbf{Z/N} & \to & \mathbf{Z/N} \\ (x_1,\ x_2,\ ..,x_n) & \to & (y_1,\ y_2,\ ..,\ y_n) \end{array}$$
$$\forall j \neq i,\ y_j = x_j$$
$$y_i = Lambda_{R_i,A_i}^{(P_i)}(x_i)$$

We can note :

$$\Lambda_{J,K}^{(N)} = (\Lambda_{J_1,K_1}^{(N_1)}, \Lambda_{J_2,K_2}^{(N_2)}, .., \Lambda_{J_n,K_n}^{(N_n)}) \qquad (1)$$

This decomposition property suggests to execute $\Lambda_{J,K}^{(N)}$ in n consecutive steps.

As the bijection associated with the Chinese Remainder Theorem is a ring isomorphism, we can characterize the subset of permutations in $\{\Lambda_{J,K}^{(N)}\}$ as follows:

Property 3.2 (Permutation charcteruization)
$\forall\, 0 \leq J = (J_1, .., J_n) < N,\ \forall\, 0 \leq K = (K_1, .., K_n) < N,$

$\Lambda_{J,K}^{(N)}$ is a permutation if and only if $\quad \forall\, 0 < i \leq n$, $J_i \not\equiv 0 \bmod N_i$ i.e $GCD(N,J) = 1$

Notice that this shows that the storage of a slice of N consecutive elements of a vector stored with a stride R is conflict-free if and only if R is not multiple of any of the N_i.

These *permutations* allow to execute all the *functions* $\Lambda_{J,K}^{(N)}$ through an N entries, N exits interconnection network in a minimum number of passes as shown below.

Property 3.3 (Genericity property) *Let us consider a N*N interconnection network able to execute any of the permutations of the family of permutations* $\{\Lambda_{J,K}^{(N)}\}_{GCD(J,N)=1}$ *in a single pass, then this interconnection network is able to execute any of the functions of the family* $\{\Lambda_{J,K}^{(N)}\}$ *in a minimum number of passes.*

Proof:

Let $0 \leq J = (J_1, J_2, .., J_n) < N$, $0 \leq K = (K_1, K_2, .., K_n) < N$
such that $GCD(N,J) \neq 1$.

let us suppose that $J_{i_1} = .. = J_{i_m} = 0$, with $i_1 < .. < i_m$, and that for other index i, $J_i \neq 0$.

For simplicity of notations , we may suppose that $i_1 = 1, .., i_m = m$

Then $\Lambda_{J,K}^{(N)} =$
$(C_{K_1}^{(N_1)}, .., C_{K_m}^{(N_m)}, \Lambda_{J_{m+1},K_{m+1}}^{(N_{m+1})}, .., \Lambda_{J_n,K_n}^{(N_n)})$

where C_H^P is the constant application from $\mathbf{Z/P}$ in itself defined by $C_H^{(P)}(x) = H$

Then each element of $\Lambda_{J,K}^{(N)}(\mathbf{Z/N})$ is the image of $N_1 * .. * N_m$ elements of $\mathbf{Z/N}$.

An exit of an interconnection network can receive data from only one entry in a single pass. Then the minimum number of passes for executing the function $\Lambda_{J,K}^{(N)}(\mathbf{Z/N})$ through a N*N interconnection network is at least $N_1 * .. * N_m$.

Let us consider the partition of $\mathbf{Z/N}$ defined the following subsets $S_{(A_1,..,A_m)}, A_i \in \mathbf{Z/N_i}$, $0 < i \leq m$:

$$S_{(A_1, .., A_m)} = \{X = (X_1, .., X_n) \in \mathbf{Z/N} \, / \, \forall\, 0 < i \leq m, X_i = A_i\}$$

$\Lambda_{J,K}^{(N)}$ may be executed on $S_{(A_1,..,A_m)}$ by executing
$(\Lambda_{1,K_1-A_1}^{(N_1)}, .., \Lambda_{1,K_m-A_m}^{N_m}, \Lambda_{J_{m+1},K_{m+1}}^{(N_{m+1})}, .., \Lambda_{J_n,K_n}^{(N_n)}) =$

$\Lambda^{(N)}_{(1,..,1,J_{m+1},..,J_n),(K_1-A_1,..,K_m-A_m,K_{m+1},..,A_n)}$
through the interconnection network.

Then function $\Lambda^{(N)}_{J,K}$ may be executed in $N_1 * .. * N_m$ (i.e. the minimum possible number) through a N*N interconnection network by executing only permutations of the family $\{\Lambda^{(N)}_{J,K}\}_{GCD(J,N)=1}$. Q.E.D.

4 Chinese Remainder Network

In this section, N is a product of n distinct prime numbers; $N = N_1 * .. * N_n$.

Properties of the function family $\{\Lambda^{(N)}_{J,K}\}$ listed in the previous section have lead us to define a new multistage interconnection network: the Chinese Remainder Network (Figure 5).

Definition 4.1 *In the Chinese Remainder Network, n stages of switches are used .*
Stage i consists in (N/N_i) N_i entries N_i exits switches.
Each of these switches may be labeled with a $(n-1)$-uplet $(x_1, x_2, .., x_{i-1}, x_{i+1}, .., x_p)$; the different stages of the interconnection network are connected as follows:

- *Entry $(x_1, .., x_n)$ of the Chinese Remainder Network is entry x_1 of switch $(x_2, .., x_n)$ of the first stage*

- *Exit x_i of switch $(x_1, x_2, .., x_{i-1}, x_{i+1}, .., x_n)$ in stage i is connected with entry x_{i+1} of switch $(x_1, x_2, .., x_i, x_{i+2}, .., x_n)$ in stage $i+1$.*

- *Exit x_n of switch $(x_1, x_2, .., x_{n-1})$ in stage n is the exit $(x_1, .. , x_n)$ of the Chinese Remainder Network.*

The most interesting property of the Chinese Remainder Network is the following one:

Property 4.2 *If for all $1 \le i \le n$, the switches of stage i of the Chinese Remainder Network are able to execute all the permutations of the family $\{\Lambda^{(N_i)}_{J_i,K_i}\}_{GCD(J_i,N_i)=1}$, then all the permutations of the family $\{\Lambda^{(N)}_{J,K}\}_{GCD(J,N)=1}$ may be executed through the Chinese Remainder Network in a single pass.*

Proof:
let $0 < J = (J_1,.. ,J_n) < N$ such that $GCD(J,N) = 1$,
let $0 \le K = (K_1,.. ,K_n) < N$

In order to execute the permutation $\Lambda^{(N)}_{J,K}$ through the interconnection network, each switch of stage i executes $\Lambda^{(N_i)}_{J_i,K_i}$:

Data coming at entry x_i of the switch $(\Lambda^{(N_1)}_{J_1,K_1}(x_1), .., \Lambda^{(N_{i-1})}_{J_{i-1},K_{i-1}}(x_{i-1}), x_{i+1}, .., x_n)$ is routed to the exit $\Lambda^{(N_i)}_{J_i,K_i}(x_i)$ of the switch.

Then data at entry $x = (x_1, .., x_n)$ of the interconnection network is routed to the exit $(\Lambda^{(N_1)}_{J_1,K_1}(x_1), .., \Lambda^{(N_n)}_{J_n,K_n}(x_n))$ i.e. $\Lambda^{(N)}_{J,K}(x)$.Q.E.D.

From this property and property 3.3 , we can conclude that the Chinese Remainder Network is able to route any slice of N consecutive elements of any vector stored in memory in a minimum number of passes.

4.1 Self-Routing

Let us remark that when crossbar switches are used as basic switches of the Chinese Remainder Network, there is one and one path from each entry to each exit of the interconnection network. Then the Chinese Remainder Network may be easily self-routed:

Destination $(y_1, .., y_n)$ is used to route data coming from entry $(x_1, .., x_n)$ as follows: when the word of data crosses stage i it uses its y_i parcel as exit destination of the stage.

As for Omega-like networks, any permutation that can be executed in a single pass through the Chinese Remainder Network can be self-routed by this mean.

On a SIMD computer built with N memory banks and N processors, there will be no conflict on the interconnection network when accessing a slice of N consecutive element of any vector V stored a stride R prime with N (i.e $GCD(R, N) = 1$).

When accessing a vector stride R is prime with N, using the same low number static priority rule[3] each of the switches of the interconnection will ensure the routing of the slice of N elements of the vector in a minimum number of passes (see proof of Property 3.3).

Such a self-routing facility may be used as follows in a shared memory MIMD machines in order to improve memory throughput:

> When all the processors work on a single vector section, a strong SIMD synchronisation of the processors may be used. This ensures a high memory throughput on this vector section because the use of the Chinese Remainder Network guarantees that no extra conflicts will arise on the interconnection network.

4.2 Self-Routing or centralized control unit

The Chinese Remainder Network may be self-routed for accessing vectors on memory. Nevertheless, implementing this self-routing facility in hardware requires some extra hardware pieces on each processor: n modulos have to be computed. It also requires some control logic in each basic switch of the interconnection network for resolving conflicts.

In this section, we show that, on a true SIMD computer, implementing a centralized control of the Chinese Remainder Network would be more cost-effective.

As recalled in section 3.1, on a SIMD computer the parameters of the vector to be accessed are known in

---

[3]i.e. entry with the lowest number has the prriority

the control unit. The parameters of the permutations to be executed are then also known.

From Property 3.1, we can remark that:

- Controls of the different stages of the Chinese Remainder Network are completely independant.

- Controls for all the switches in stage i are identical; these controls can be directly derived from the stride of the vector and the address of the first element.

A very simple hardware solution may consist in using small memories for storing the·controls of the permutations $\Lambda_{J_i,K_i}^{(N_i)}$ for each N_i. Modulo of the stride number and modulo of the base address will be used for addressing this memories as described in figure 6.

For $N = 4199 = 13*17*19$, three memories of respectively 156 words of 52 bits, 272 words of 85 bits and 342 words of 95 bits would be needed for controlling a Chinese Remainder Network built with crossbar switches as basic switches.

Using a centralized control unit allows to use multistage networks instead of crossbar switches in the Chinese Remainder Network.

For $N = 67*61 = 4087$, we may use 128 entry, 128 exit Benes network and 64 entry, 64 exit Benes network as basic switches, two memories of respectively 4422 words of 832 bits and 3660 words of 352 bits are needed for controlling these switches

Hardware complexity of the processor

It has to be pointed out that using a centralized control of the Chinese Remainder Network eliminates computations of the remainder of the Euclidean Division by N in the basic processor of the SIMD computer:

1. The Euclidean Division has been shown to be unuseful in section 2

2. The computation of modulos are not needed in the processors: these modulos only serve for determining the number of the destination memory bank, addresses of the requests are driven through the interconnection network without explicitally computing this number.

4.3 About conflicts

Let us consider the same stride distribution as in section 2.1. We compare the average memory throughput on a sequence of memory accesses hypothetic shared memory SIMD computers with respectively (when no routing of the interconnection network is considered):

- 4096 memory banks: usual power of two

- 4099 memory banks: 4099 is a prime number

- 4199= 13*17*19 memory banks: the Chinese Remainder Network may be built using basic crossbar switches.

- 4087= 61*67 memory banks: the Chinese Remainder Network may be built using Benes networks as basic switches.

We want to compare the average number T of cycles needed for accessing 100 slices of N consecutive element of vectors:

- N= 4096 : $T = 220 = 80+20*\Sigma_{i=0,11}*2^i/2^{i+1}+ 20*(1/4096)*4096$

- N= 4099 :$T = 120 = 80 + (4098/4099)*20 + (20/4099)*4099$

- N= 4199 : $T = 226$
  T is obtained by
  $T= 80 + 20 *($

$1 * (12 * 16 * 18)/4199$	$\% \, GCD(R, 13 * 17 * 19) = 1$
$+13 * (16 * 18)/4199$	$\% R = 13r, GCD(R, 19 * 17) = 1$
$+17 * (12 * 18)/4199$	$\% R = 17r, GCD(R, 19 * 13) = 1$
$+19 * (12 * 16)/4199$	$\% R = 19r, GCD(R, 13 * 17) = 1$
$+(13 * 17) * 18/4199$	$\% R = 13 * 17r, GCD(R, 19) = 1$
$+(13 * 19) * 16/4199$	$\% R = 13 * 19r, GCD(R, 17) = 1$
$+(17 * 19) * 12/4199$	$\% R = 17 * 19r, GCD(R, 13) = 1$
$+4199 * 1/4199)$	$\% R = 13 * 17 * 19$

- N= 4087 : $T = 159$

As noted in section 2.1, there are less conflicts when the number N of memory banks and processors is prime, but we have noted in section 3.2 that there is no realistic way for controlling an interconnection network for executing the needed permutations.

Using 4096 a power of two as number of memory banks would lead to approximately the same potential memory throughput as using 4199 memory banks : but for accessing vectors on memory, controlling the Chinese Remainder Network is simpler than controlling a classical multistage network.

Using 4087 memory banks would allow to have a better memory throughput; but self-routing on the Chinese Remainder Network would be impossible if Benes network must be used as basic switches.

5 Conclusion

Using a prime memory system for a vector processor allows a conflict-free access for any slice of N consecutive elements of a constant-strided vector which stride is not multiple of N. As shown in section 2.1, this can significantly improve the average memory throughput on vector applications.

It was currently admitted in the computer architecture community that using an odd number N of memory banks induces Euclidean Division by N for computing the local displacement. As very fast Euclidean Division by an odd number is quite difficult to implement in hardware, this has been the major argument advanced for rejecting the use of prime number of memory banks in vector processor memory sytems.

In section 2, we have shown a local displacement function for prime (and odd) memory systems which is immediate to evaluate (the least significant bits of the address are used as local displacement) and allows to use the whole memory.

Massively parallel SIMD computers have become very popular since the introduction of the Connection Machine 1 and 2. On shared memory SIMD computers, routing vectors from memory to the processors through the interconnection network is a the major difficulty: no realistic hardware solution for computing the control for a large multistage interconnection network at execution time had been proposed.

In section 4, we have shown that the family of permutations needed for accessing vectors has very specific properties when the number N of memory banks and processors is a product of n distinct prime numbers $N = N_1 * .. * N_n$. We have presented the Chinese Remainder Network for connecting N memory banks and N processing elements. The Chinese Remainder Network is a self-routing interconnection network for all the permutations induced by vector accesses. In a SIMD computer, the Chinese Remainder Network may also be controlled by a centralized control unit consisting in n small memories. Notice that in this latter case, neither the result of the Euclidean Division by the number of memory banks, nor the remainder of this Euclidean Division has to be computed for addressing the memory.

References

[1] V.E. Benes, "Mathematical Theory of connecting networks and telephone traffic", New York: Academic, 1968

[2] P.Budnick, D.Kuck "The organization and use of parallel memories" IEEE Transaction On Computers, Dec. 1971

[3] B.Chor, C.E. Leiserson, R.L. Rivest, J.B. Shearer "An application of number theory to the organization of raster-graphics memory" Journal of the ACM, Jan. 1986

[4] B. Dupont de Dinechin,"A Ultra Fast Euclidean Division Algorithm for Prime Memory Systems", Supercomputing 91, Nov. 1991

[5] J.M. Frailong, W.Jalby, J.Lenfant "XOR-schemes: a flexible organization in parallel memories" Proceedings of 1985 International Conference on Parallel Processing, Aug. 1985

[6] D. Gajski, D. Kuck, D. Lawrie, A. Sameh "CEDAR a large scale multiprocessor" Proceedings of the International Conference on Parallel Processing, 1985

[7] D.J.Kuck, R.A.Stokes, "The Burroughs Scientific Processor (BSP)" IEEE Transactions on Computers, May 1982.

[8] D.T. Harper, J.R. Jump "Performance evaluation of vector accesses in parallel memories using a skewed storage scheme ", Proceedings of the 13th International Symposium on Computer Architecture, June 1986

[9] D.T. Harper, J.R. Jump "Vector accesses in parallel memories using a skewed storage scheme " IEEE Transactions on Computers, Dec. 1987

[10] D.H. Lawrie "Access and alignment of data in array computer" IEEE Transactions on Computers, Dec. 1975

[11] D.H. Lawrie, C.R. Vora "The prime memory system for array access" IEEE Transactions on Computers, May 1982.

[12] K.Y. Lee, "On the rearrangeability of a (2 log N - 1) stage permutation network" IEEE Transactions on Computers, May 1985.

[13] J.Lenfant, "Parallel permutations of data : A Benes network control algorithm for frequently used permutations" IEEE Transactions on Computers, July 1978.

[14] J.Lenfant, " A versatile mechanism to move data in an array processor" IEEE Transactions on Computers, June 1985

[15] D.Nassimi, S.Sahni "A self-routing Benes network and permutation algorithms" IEEE Transactions on Computers, May 1981.

[16] A.Norton, E.Melton "A class of boolean linear transformations for conflict-free power-of-two stride access", Proceedings of the International Conference on Parallel Processing, 1987

[17] G.F. Pfister & al " The IBM Research Parallel Processor Prototype (RP3): Introduction and Architecture " Proceedings of the International Conference on Parallel Processing, 1985

[18] B.Rau, M.Schlander, D. Yen " The Cydra 5 stride insensitive memory system", Proceedings of the International Conference on Parallel Processing, 1989

[19] B.Rau, "Pseudo-Randomly interleaved memory" Proceedings of the 18th International Symposium on Computer Architecture, 1991

[20] A.Seznec, "A new interconnection network for SIMD computers: the Sigma network $\Sigma^{(n)}$" IEEE Transactions on Computers, July 1987

[21] A.Seznec, J. Lenfant "Interleaved parallel schemes: improving memory throughput on supercomputers" Proceedings of the 19th International Symposium on Computer Architecture, 1992

[22] H.Tamura, Y.Shinkai, F.Isobe "The Supercomputer FACOM VP system" Fujitsu Sc. Tech. J., March 1985

	0	1	2	3	4	5	6	7	8	9	10	11	12
0	0	1	2	3	4	5	6	7	8	9	10	11	12
1	13	14	15	16	17	18	19	20	21	22	23	24	25
2	26	27	28	29	30	31	32	33	34	35	36	37	38
3	39	40	41	42	43	44	45	46	47	48	49	50	51
4	52	53	54	55	56	57	58	59	60	61	62	63	64
5	65	66	67	68	69	70	71	72	73	74	75	76	77
6	78	79	80	81	82	83	84	85	86	87	88	89	90
7	91	92	93	94	95	96	97	98	99	100	101	102	103
8	104	105	106	107	108	109	110	111	112	113	114	115	116
9	117	118	119	120	121	122	123	124	125	126	127	128	129
10	130	131	132	133	134	135	136	137	138	139	140	141	142
11	143	144	145	146	147	148	149	150	151	152	153	154	155
12	156	157	158	159	160	161	162	163	164	165	166	167	168
13	169	170	171	172	173	174	175	176	177	178	179	180	181
14	182	183	184	185	186	187	188	189	190	191	192	193	194
15	195	196	197	198	199	200	201	202	203	204	205	206	207

Figure 1: Usual mapping on a 13 banks parallel memory

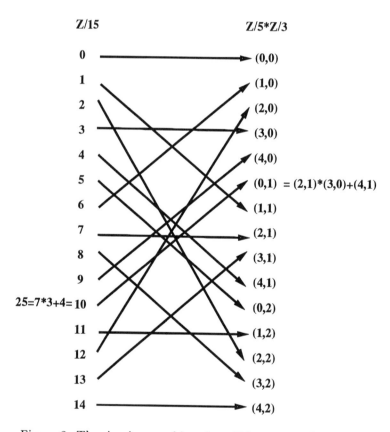

Figure 2: The ring isomorphism from $\mathbf{Z}/15$ onto $\mathbf{Z}/5 * \mathbf{Z}/3$.

	0	1	2	3	4	5	6	7	8	9	10	11	12
0	0	144	80	16	160	96	32	176	112	48	192	128	64
1	65	1	145	81	17	161	97	33	177	113	49	193	129
2	130	66	2	146	82	18	162	98	34	178	114	50	194
3	195	131	67	3	147	83	19	163	99	35	179	115	51
4	52	196	132	68	4	148	84	20	164	100	36	180	116
5	117	53	197	133	69	5	149	85	21	165	101	37	181
6	182	118	54	198	134	70	6	150	86	22	166	102	38
7	39	183	119	55	199	135	71	7	151	87	23	167	103
8	104	40	184	120	56	200	136	72	8	152	88	24	168
9	169	105	41	185	121	57	201	137	73	9	153	89	25
10	26	170	106	42	186	122	58	202	138	74	10	154	90
11	91	27	171	107	43	187	123	59	203	139	75	11	155
12	156	92	28	172	108	44	188	124	60	204	140	76	12
13	13	157	93	29	173	109	45	189	125	61	205	141	77
14	78	14	158	94	30	174	110	46	190	126	62	206	142
15	143	79	15	159	95	31	175	111	47	191	127	63	207

Figure 3: Mapping function induced by Chinese Remainder theorem: N=13

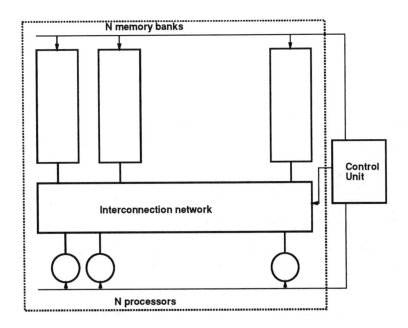

Figure 4: Structure of shared memory SIMD computer

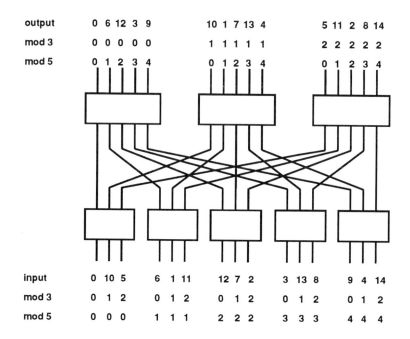

Figure 5: Chinese Remainder Network 15 entries, 15 exits

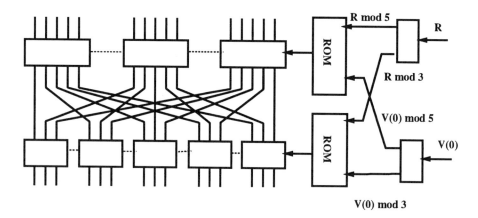

Figure 6: Centralized control for a 15 entry 15 exits Chinese Remainder Network

A Comparison of Adaptive Wormhole Routing Algorithms

Rajendra V. Boppana
Div. of Math. and Computer Science
The Univ. of Texas at San Antonio
San Antonio, TX 78249-0664

Suresh Chalasani
ECE Department
Univ. of Wisconsin-Madison
Madison, WI 53706-1691

Abstract. *Improvement of message latency and network utilization in torus interconnection networks by increasing adaptivity in wormhole routing algorithms is studied. A recently proposed partially adaptive algorithm and four new fully-adaptive routing algorithms are compared with the well-known e-cube algorithm for uniform, hotspot, and local traffic patterns. Our simulations indicate that the partially adaptive north-last algorithm, which causes unbalanced traffic in the network, performs worse than the nonadaptive e-cube routing algorithm for all three traffic patterns. Another result of our study is that the performance does not necessarily improve with full-adaptivity. In particular, a commonly discussed fully-adaptive routing algorithm, which uses 2^n virtual channels per physical channel of a k-ary n-cube, performs worse than e-cube for uniform and hotspot traffic patterns. The other three fully-adaptive algorithms, which give priority to messages based on distances traveled, perform much better than the e-cube and partially-adaptive algorithms for all three traffic patterns. One of the conclusions of this study is that adaptivity, full or partial, is not necessarily a benefit in wormhole routing.*

Keywords: *adaptive routing, deadlocks, multicomputer networks, k-ary n-cubes, message routing, store-and-forward routing, wormhole routing.*

1 Introduction

Point-to-point k-ary n-cube and related networks are being used in many recent experimental and commercial multicomputers and multiprocessors [2, 11, 26, 9, 3]. A k-ary n-cube network has an n-dimensional grid structure with k nodes (processors) in each dimension such that every node is connected to two other nodes in each dimension by direct communication links.

Routing algorithms, which specify how messages can be sent among processors, are crucial for the efficient operation of a parallel computer. For maximum system performance, a routing algorithm should have high throughput and exhibit the following important features [17]: low-latency message delivery, avoidance of *deadlocks*, *livelocks*, and starvation, and ability to work well under various traffic patterns. Since message latencies increase with increase in the number of hops, we consider only *minimal* routing algorithms as per which a message always moves closer to its desti-

nation with each hop taken; another advantage of minimal routing is that livelocks are avoided. The issue of starvation can be avoided by allocating resources such as channels and buffers in FIFO order. Ensuring deadlock-freedom is more difficult and depends heavily on the design of the routing algorithm.

Store-and-forward (SAF) [5] and *wormhole* (WH) [14] are two popular switching techniques for interconnection networks. With SAF technique, the message latency is the product of the number of hops taken and the sum of the average queuing delay and transmission time of the message per hop.

In the WH technique, a message is divided into a sequence of fixed-size units of data, called *flits*. If a communication channel transmits the first flit of a message, it must transmit all the remaining flits of the same message before transmitting flits of another message. At any given time, the flits corresponding to a message occupy contiguous channels in the network. In this method, the message latency is proportional to the sum of the number of cycles spent in waiting for suitable channels to route message flits, number of hops, and message length. To avoid deadlocks, multiple virtual channels are simulated on each physical channel and a pre-defined order is enforced on the allocation of virtual channels to messages.

Minimal fully-adaptive algorithms do not impose any restrictions on the choice of shortest paths to be used in routing messages; in contrast, partially-adaptive minimal algorithms allow only a subset of available minimal paths in routing messages. An adaptive routing algorithm can be either fully- or partially-adaptive. The well-known *e-cube* routing algorithm is an example of non-adaptive routing algorithms, since it has no flexibility in routing messages.

Adaptive routing algorithms have a few disadvantages, however. The complexity of the routing algorithm and, hence, the hardware cost increase with the increase in adaptivity. Furthermore, partially-adaptive routing algorithms that favor some paths more than others can cause highly uneven utilization and early saturation of the network.

Recently, several fully- and partially-adaptive algorithms for deadlock-free wormhole routing [4, 10, 15, 19, 23] have been proposed. The fully-adaptive al-

0884-7495/93 $3.00 © 1993 IEEE

gorithm for k-ary n-cubes by Linder and Harden [23] uses $(n+1)2^{n-1}$ virtual channels per physical channel. The fully-adaptive wormhole algorithm by Berman *et al.* [4] for k-ary n-cubes uses as many as $10(n-1)+6$ virtual channels per physical channel. Felperin *et al.* [16] designed a fully-adaptive WH routing algorithm for tori (k-ary 2-cubes) that uses eight virtual channels per physical channel. Dally [12] proposes augmenting multicomputer networks with express channels to facilitate adaptive routing and reduce the network diameter and message latencies.

In this paper, we present results on the performance of six algorithms for uniform, hotspot, and local traffic patterns on k-ary 2-cubes. We compare a recently proposed partially-adaptive and four fully-adaptive WH routing algorithms with the commonly used *e*-cube algorithm. The north-last algorithm used in this paper is a member of many partially-adaptive algorithms proposed by Glass and Ni [19] based on the elegant *turn* model. One of the four fully-adaptive algorithms used in this study is based on the total number of possible directions that can be taken by a message. It is an improvement (reduces the number of virtual channels used) over the results of Linder and Harden [23] and Felperin *et al.* [16] and a generalization of the result by Dally [11] for mesh networks.

The other three fully-adaptive algorithms are derived from the store-and-forward algorithms [20] based on the the number of hops taken by messages. While routing messages, these algorithms use some form of priority information, in addition to full-adaptivity. One of these algorithms also employs load balancing of virtual channels. The design of these algorithms is based on a recent result on designing deadlock-free WH routing algorithms from SAF routing algorithms [8]. To make the paper self-contained, this method is briefly explained in the next section. For certain cases [8], these algorithms require fewer virtual channels than the previously proposed fully-adaptive algorithms.

The rest of this paper is organized as follows. Section 2 describes the routing algorithms used in our performance study. Section 3 compares the performance of six different WH routing algorithms. Section 4 concludes this paper.

2 Routing Algorithms

In this section, we discuss six different deadlock-free wormhole routing algorithms, used in this study. Out of these six algorithms four are fully-adaptive, one is partially-adaptive, and one is non-adaptive. Three of the four fully-adaptive algorithms are derived from the corresponding SAF routing algorithms, based on our recent results [8] on developing deadlock-free WH

routing algorithms from SAF algorithms.

We first describe these three fully-adaptive routing algorithms, which will be collectively referred to as hop schemes.

2.1 Hop schemes

Notation. In the rest of this paper, we use k^n to denote a k-ary n-cube. Dimensions of k^n are numbered from 0 to $(n - 1)$ and nodes are numbered in each dimension from 0 to $(k - 1)$. Each node is uniquely indexed by an n-tuple using the n numbers it obtained in the n dimensions. We assume the adjacent nodes are connected by two unidirectional communication links. Thus, each node $x = (x_{n-1}, \ldots, x_0)$ has 2 outgoing links from it to nodes $(x_{n-1}, \ldots, x_{i+1}, x_i + 1, x_{i-1}, \ldots, x_0)$ and $(x_{n-1}, \ldots, x_{i+1}, x_i - 1, x_{i-1}, \ldots, x_0)$ in dimension i; the addition and subtraction operations performed here are with respect to modulo k. A node $x = (x_{n-1}, \ldots, x_0)$ in k^n is termed *even* (respectively, *odd*) if $\sum_{i=0}^{i=n-1} x_i$ is even (respectively, odd).

Throughout this paper, a communication channel or a communication link should be taken to mean a physical channel. Every physical channel, virtual channel, and message originating from a node can be given unique number based on the address of the node.

Construction of WH algorithms. Figure 1 illustrates construction of a WH routing algorithm from an SAF algorithm. Figure 1(a) shows the node model used for SAF routing. In SAF routing, buffers in a node are the critical resources. Deadlocks in SAF routing are avoided by partitioning the buffers into several classes — $b_0, b_1, \ldots, b_m$ — and placing constraints on the set of buffer classes a message can occupy in each node. This technique of avoiding SAF deadlocks is known as the *buffer reservation* technique [20].

To derive a WH algorithm from the SAF algorithm, we proceed as follows. First, on each physical channel in the network used for WH routing, we provide virtual channels $c_0, c_1, \ldots, c_m$ and the corresponding flit-buffers (see Figure 1(b)). Next, if a message can occupy a buffer of class b_i at an intermediate node and go through a communication channel in the SAF network (see Figure 1(a)), then in the WH network the message can only reserve virtual channel c_i (see Figure 1(b)). In other words, if the SAF algorithm specifies that a message should occupy buffer of class b_i at a node and can take one channel from the set of physical channels S to complete the next hop, the corresponding WH algorithm specifies that the message at that node should take the next hop using a virtual channel of class c_i on any of the physical channels in the set S.

The above construction allows one to design a WH

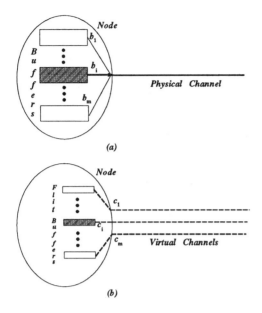

(a)

(b)

Figure 1: Derivation of WH routing from SAF routing.

routing algorithm from any given SAF algorithm with the same degree of adaptivity. However, a WH algorithm derived using the above procedure need not be deadlock-free. The following lemma presents a general condition under which the WH routing algorithm designed from an SAF algorithm is deadlock-free.

Lemma 1 *If the* SAF *routing is deadlock free and the buffers occupied by every message in successive hops have monotonically increasing ranks, then the* WH *routing algorithm derived from the* SAF *algorithm is also deadlock free.*

See [8] for a proof.

A few well-known fully-adaptive SAF schemes based on the number of hops taken [20] satisfy the above lemma, and hence can be used for WH routing.

Positive-hop SAF and WH routing algorithms. In the well-known positive-hop SAF algorithm, the number of buffer classes in each node equals the diameter of the network plus one [20]. A message is placed in a buffer of class 0 in the source node. During routing, a message is placed in buffer of class i in an intermediate node if it completed i hops thus far. Since the maximum number of hops a message can take equals the diameter of the network, the maximum number of buffer classes required in each node for SAF routing equals the diameter of the network plus one; for k^n, this number equals $n\lfloor k/2 \rfloor + 1$.

The corresponding positive-hop (or, PHOP for brevity) WH routing algorithm can be designed by providing $n\lfloor k/2 \rfloor + 1$ virtual channels — $c_0, \ldots, c_{n\lfloor k/2 \rfloor}$ — on each physical link. For example, in 16^2, 17 virtual channels are provided on each physical link. A mes-

sage reserves virtual channel i at an intermediate node to complete hop $i + 1$. As an example, suppose that a message M with source $(4, 4)$ and destination $(2, 2)$ in 6^2 takes the following path:

$$(4, 4) \rightarrow (3, 4) \rightarrow (3, 3) \rightarrow (2, 3) \rightarrow (2, 2)$$

This message M reserves virtual channel c_0 on the link from $(4, 4)$ to $(3, 4)$, c_1 from $(3, 4)$ to $(3, 3)$, c_2 from $(3, 3)$ to $(2, 3)$, and c_3 from $(2, 3)$ to $(2, 2)$.

The PHOP WH scheme is deadlock-free due to the following argument (see [8] for more details). In the SAF scheme, if we assign any buffer of class i a rank of i, it is easy to see that the buffer classes occupied by a message have monotonically increasing ranks. Applying Lemma 1, we conclude that the PHOP WH routing algorithm is deadlock-free.

Negative-hop (NHOP) SAF and WH routing algorithms. In the negative-hop SAF algorithm, the network is partitioned into several subsets, such that no subset contains adjacent nodes (this is the graph coloring problem). Let us assume that these subsets are labeled $1, 2, \ldots, M$ and that each node in a subset with label i is also labeled with i. A hop is a negative hop if it is from a node with a higher label to a node with a lower label; otherwise, it is a positive hop. A message occupies a buffer of class b_i at an intermediate node if and only if the message has taken exactly i negative hops to reach that intermediate node. In the negative-hop SAF scheme, a message that is currently in a buffer of class b_i can only wait for a buffer of either class b_i (if it is waiting for a positive hop) or class b_{i+1} (if it is waiting for a negative hop). Gopal [20] proves that this SAF routing is deadlock free.

For even k, the structure of k^n is a bipartite graph, and its nodes can be partitioned into two subsets (therefore, it can be colored using only two colors). Because adjacent nodes are in distinct partitions, the maximum number of negative hops a message takes is at most half the diameter of k^n, which equals $\lceil n\lfloor k/2 \rfloor / 2 \rceil$. Hence, negative-hop schemes with $\lceil n\lfloor k/2 \rfloor / 2 \rceil + 1$ buffer classes per node can be designed for k^n in a straightforward manner when k is even. For 16^2, for example, 9 buffer classes per node are sufficient with the negative-hop scheme. When k is odd, negative hop schemes that require about the same number of buffer classes per node can be designed [6]; however, the design of such negative-hop schemes for odd k is quite involved and will not be considered any further.

In order to derive the negative-hop WH routing algorithm from the corresponding SAF algorithm, we provide $\lceil n\lfloor k/2 \rfloor / 2 \rceil + 1$ virtual channels on each physical link of k^n. When a message is generated, the total number of negative hops taken is set to zero, current

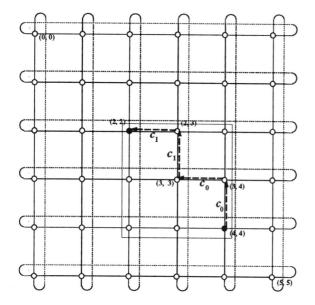

Figure 2: An example to illustrate the negative-hop scheme in 6^2.

host is set to the source node. The following pseudocode describes how a message is routed as per the negative-hop scheme.

while (*current-host* $\neq$ *destination*) **do** {

    1. select the *next-host*.

    2. reserve a virtual channel of class given by
        number-of-negative-hops-taken
        from *current-host* to *next-host*.

    3. if *current-host* is odd, increment
        number-of-negative-hops-taken by one.

    4. *current-host* $\leftarrow$ *next-host*.

}

A message, when it moves from an even node to an odd node, reserves a virtual channel of the same class it reserved in the previous hop; otherwise, it reserves a virtual channel one class higher than what it reserved in the previous hop. Using Lemma 1, it can be shown that the negative-hop WH algorithm is also deadlock-free [8].

An example of the negative hop scheme is shown in Figure 2. In this figure, a message that originates at source node $(4,4)$ is to be routed to destination $(2,2)$ in 6^2. It can be easily shown that, as per the negative-hop scheme, the message can take any of the shortest paths from $(4,4)$ to $(2,2)$ (because of the fully-adaptive nature of the negative-hop algorithm). Suppose that the path taken by the message is

$$(4,4) \rightarrow (3,4) \rightarrow (3,3) \rightarrow (2,3) \rightarrow (2,2).$$

The hop from node $(4,4)$ to node $(3,4)$ is a positive hop and the message reserves virtual channel c_0 in order to complete this hop (recall that in all 4 virtual

channels c_0, c_1, c_2, c_3 need to be multiplexed on each physical channel in order to implement the negative-hop WH scheme in 6^2). At node $(3,4)$, *current-host* is $(3,4)$ and the *number-of-negative-hops-taken* is zero, whereas the value of *next-host* becomes $(3,3)$. The message reserves virtual channel c_0 again while taking the hop from node $(3,4)$ to $(3,3)$ since the *number-of-negative-hops-taken* is still zero. However, the hop from $(3,4)$ to $(3,3)$ is a negative hop; hence, the message reserves virtual channel c_1 from node $(3,3)$ to $(2,3)$. Similarly, the message reserves virtual channel c_1 in its final hop from node $(2,3)$ to node $(2,2)$.

Negative-hop scheme with bonus cards (NBC). The negative hop (also positive hop) scheme described above does not utilize virtual channels evenly: virtual channels with lower numbers are utilized more than virtual channels with higher numbers. For example, all messages use virtual channels numbered c_0, but only messages between diametrically opposite nodes (very few) use virtual channels numbered $c_{\lceil n \lfloor k/2 \rfloor / 2 \rceil}$. Given below is a variation of the negative hop scheme, which attempts to achieve a more uniform utilization of virtual channels.

In the negative-hop with bonus-cards (NBC) scheme, each message is given a few *bonus cards* based on the number of negative hops it can take (which is approximately half the total number of hops it can take) before reaching destination. The number of bonus cards a message M receives at its source node in k^n is given by the following formula.

    Bonus cards =
        Maximum possible negative hops in k^n −
        Negative hops to be taken by M.

A message with no bonus-cards is routed exactly the same as in the case of NHop algorithm. In routing a message with b bonus cards, $b \geq 1$, any of virtual channels numbered $0, 1, \ldots, b$ can be used for the first hop of the message. Thus a message with bonus cards has a wider choice of virtual channels and is likely to choose least congested one for the first hop. The routing of message after the first hop is the same as in the case of NHop scheme. That is, if a message arrives at an intermediate host node via a virtual channel of class c_i, then it uses a virtual channel of class c_{i+1} (if it took a negative hop to reach this node) or c_i (otherwise) to leave the node.

A more flexible version of this NBC scheme is described in [7].

2.2 Fully-adaptive routing based on the enumeration of directions

Another fully-adaptive deadlock-free WH routing scheme for a k-ary n-cube (respectively, mesh) that uses 2^n (respectively, 2^{n-1}) virtual channels per physical channel can be derived based on the recent work of various researchers [11, 16, 23]. We refer to this algorithm as two-power-n (or, 2Pn) algorithm.

Let $s = s_{n-1} \ldots s_0$ and $d = d_{n-1} \ldots d_0$ be the source and destinations of a message being routed. Using s and d an n-bit tag $t = t_{n-1} \ldots t_0$ is created as follows.

$$t_i = \begin{cases} 1 & \text{if } s_i < d_i, \\ 0 & \text{if } s_i > d_i, \\ 0 \text{ or } 1 & \text{if } s_i = t_i. \end{cases} \quad (1)$$

Description of the algorithm. For fully-adaptive deadlock-free routing, we use 2^n virtual channels for each physical channel of the network. Each of these virtual channels is given an n-bit number. For each message to be routed, its tag is computed using (1).

In each hop, a message with tag t chooses the virtual channel with number t on any one of the links of the uncorrected dimensions[1]. □

It can be shown [8] that algorithm two-power-n routes messages free of deadlocks in k-ary n-cubes.

2.3 The North-Last Algorithm

Glass and Ni [19] proposed the north-last algorithm for multi-dimensional meshes and tori. The NLast algorithm works as follows. If destination index is less than source index in dimension 1, then a message must correct dimension 0 first before taking any hops on dimension 1 links; otherwise it is routed fully-adaptively. It prohibits adaptive routing of some messages; for example, in routing a message from node (3,3) to (1,1) in a 10^2 with upper left node being (0,0) and lower right node being (9,9), its path is always through nodes (3,2), (3,1), and (2,1) regardless of the traffic or other conditions in the network. If the four edges of a two-dimensional network are labeled West, East, North, and South, then messages that are going to North do not have adaptivity. Hence the name.

3 Simulation results

To compare the performance of these routing algorithms, we have developed an event-driven simulator. This simulator can be used for k-ary n-cubes (multi-dimensional tori) and multi-dimensional meshes for wormhole routing.

We compare the performances of six deadlock-free wormhole routing algorithms: three fully-adaptive hop schemes (positive-hop, negative-hop, and negative-hop with bonus-cards), partially-adaptive north last algorithm, proposed by Glass and Ni [19], and the well-known non-adaptive e-cube algorithm. We consider only minimal routing of messages.

To limit the search space, we have fixed some important parameters in the following performance comparisons. High-radix, $k \geq 16$, is commonly used for two- and three-dimensional networks [11, 2]. We have conducted our simulations for 16^2 tori. In literature, fixed-length messages with 16, 20, or 24 flits are commonly considered. We have considered 16-flit messages in this study. The message interarrival times are geometrically distributed.

Traffic patterns. We have considered uniform, hotspot, and local traffic patterns. The uniform (or random) traffic pattern could be representative of the traffic generated in massively parallel computations in which array data are distributed among the nodes using hashing techniques. More realistically, the traffic pattern tends to be random coupled with some local or hotspot type traffic [1, 24]. For this reason we have also performed simulations for uniform traffic coupled with a moderate hotspot traffic and completely local traffic.

In the hotspot traffic pattern simulated, a particular node receives some hotspot traffic in addition to the regular uniform traffic. For example, with a hotspot percentage of four, a newly arrived message in 16^2 is directed with 0.0438 probability to the hotspot node and with 0.0038 probability to any other node. That is, the hotspot node receives about 11.5 times more traffic than any other node in the network. In multi-processors, this traffic pattern could be representative of computations in which critical sections (or the corresponding locks) are placed in a single node. When software techniques are used to distribute hotspot traffic, a more representative hotspot traffic is obtained by simulating multiple hotspot nodes each receiving hotspot traffic in addition to the regular uniform traffic. In this paper, we consider hotspot traffic with one hotspot node.

In the local traffic pattern, the traffic generated by node (i, j) in 16^2 is directed with equal probability to any node within the 7×7 mesh consisting of the nodes $\{(x, y) \mid i - 3 \leq x \leq i + 3, j - 3 \leq y \leq j + 3\}$. For a 16×16 torus, this corresponds to a locality factor of 0.4. This local traffic pattern is slightly different from the one considered by Agarwal [1].

Parameters of interest: latency and normalized throughput. We are interested in the average channel utilization, ρ, and average latency, l, of a message. The average latency of a message is

$$w + (m_l + \overline{d} - 1) \times f_t, \quad (2)$$

where $w, m_l, \overline{d}, f_t$ are the average wait time, average length of the message in flits, average number of hops taken by a message, and the time to transfer a flit between neighbors, respectively.

---

[1] The dimensions in which the message needs to take one or more hops in order to reach its destination from the current node.

For uniform traffic, the average number of hops is the average diameter of the network. For a k-ary n-cube, it is approximately $nk/4$; 16^2 has an average diameter of 8.03 for uniform traffic. The number of flits in the message is fixed at 16. It takes one clock cycle to transmit a flit between neighbor nodes. Multiple virtual channels mapped to a physical channel share its bandwidth in time-multiplexed manner; that is, $f_t = 1$.

The average channel utilization refers to the fraction of the physical channel bandwidth utilized in any time interval when the network is in steady state. It is also called the network utilization factor or normalized throughput of the network. The average channel utilization, denoted ρ, is computed as the ratio of network bandwidth utilized to the raw bandwidth available.

$$\rho = \lambda\, m_l\, \overline{d} \times \frac{\text{Number of nodes}}{\text{Number of channels}}, \qquad (3)$$

where $1/\lambda$ is the average message interarrival time. For k^n, this can be simplified to

$$\rho = \frac{\lambda\, m_l\, \overline{d}}{2n}. \qquad (4)$$

The numerator computes the average traffic generated by a node, and the denominator gives the available bandwidth due to the physical channels originating from a node.

Congestion control. If there are no restrictions placed on message injection, the network would be unusable once saturation occurs. Therefore, we have used a simple congestion control based on the one proposed for store-and-forward routing for computer networks [22]. In this method, a node is allowed to inject a message into the network if the number of messages of the same class[2] that are in the node is less than a certain specified limit. With this type of congestion control, it is feasible to simulate the network for traffic rates that would otherwise cause saturation and lead to unbounded delays. Convergence of such simulations need to be checked carefully, however.

Convergence criteria. For better randomness, separate sequences of random numbers are maintained for the distribution of message interarrival time, selection of destination, etc.

For each simulation, sufficient warmup time is provided to allow the network reach steady state. After the warmup time, the network traffic is sampled at periodic intervals. The counters used for statistics gathering are reset at the beginning of each sampling

period. Statistics are gathered during the sampling time and analyzed for convergence. After each sampling period, new streams of random numbers are used for destination selection and message interarrival time, and statistics are not gathered for some period of time. Independent of the convergence criteria, a minimum of three samples and a maximum of 10-15 samples are taken for each simulation. A simulation is terminated if it exceeds the maximum time limit or if the convergence criteria are met.

For the purpose of checking convergence, we partition messages into various classes based on the number hops they require to reach destinations. One convergence check is based on the variance in the latencies reported by messages of each hop-class. This check is based on the population mean (with each hop-class being a stratum of the message population) described in [25]. For each stratum, the average latency and variance are computed. Using proper weights[3] of each stratum in the population, the average message latency, l, and variance of this average latency, $\sigma_l{}^2$, are computed. The 95% confidence interval of the average latency is given by $(l - 2\sigma_l,\, l + 2\sigma_l)$. The value $2\sigma_l$ is the bound on the error of estimation of l.

Another check is based on the variance of the average message latencies for each of the latest three or more samples. For this case also the bound on the error of estimation is computed. If both error bounds are within 5% of the respective averages, the simulation is terminated. For the points before saturation, these criteria are easily satisfied. Longer warmup and sampling times are needed to achieve convergence for points near and beyond saturation.

After the simulation, the average number of messages received in the sampling periods used in the above convergence criteria is computed. The bound on the error of this estimation is almost always less than 1%.

3.1 Simulation of uniform traffic

The average latency and normalized throughput achieved are plotted against offered traffic[4] in Figure 3 for uniform traffic with 16-flit messages. For low traffic load ($\rho \leq 0.25$), all six algorithms have the same latency. The three hop schemes and the other three

---

[2]For the purpose of congestion control, the class of a message is determined as follows. In the case of hop schemes and 2Pn, a message class is based on the virtual channel number it can use. In the case of e-cube and NLast schemes, a message class is based on the particular virtual channel it intends to use.

[3]The weights of each hop-class are based on the frequency with which they appear for the traffic pattern being simulated. For example, for uniform traffic on a 16^2, hop-class 1 has a weight of 0.0157 and hop-class 16 has a weight of 0.0039, since each node has four neighbors but only one diametrically opposite node. In the case of local traffic, the number of hop-classes is six: classes 1 and 6 have weight 0.0833 each, classes 2 and 5 have weight 0.1667 each, and classes 3 and 4 have weight 0.25 each.

[4]Normalized throughputs are considered in performance comparisons.

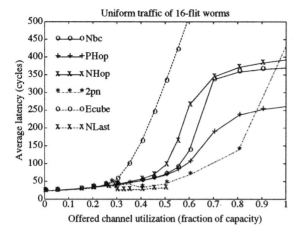

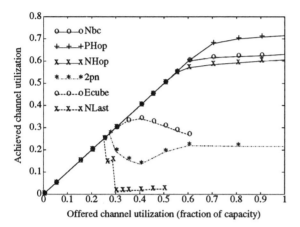

Figure 3: Performance of the routing algorithms for uniform traffic.

algorithms behave differently during and after saturation.

The three algorithms derived from SAF routing have similar throughputs with PHop being slightly better: PHop has better latency and throughput in saturation. In particular, PHop and Nbc begin to saturate after 0.6, and NHop shows signs of saturation at about 0.55. The latencies of all three algorithms rise abruptly at the point of saturation but have bounded values, even for high traffic loads, $\rho \geq 0.75$, due to congestion control. Furthermore, the achieved throughputs of the three algorithms increase steadily. The PHop and Nbc algorithms achieve their peak throughputs of 0.72 and 0.63, respectively, at 100% offered load.

It is not meaningful to compare the saturation latencies of hop schemes with those of the other three algorithms, since the latter ones have lower throughputs. The fully-adaptive 2Pn has lower peak throughput than e-cube and saturates more quickly. The e-cube algorithm has a peak throughput of 0.34, which

occurs at offered traffic of 0.4.[5] Another observation is that e-cube performs better than the partially-adaptive NLast algorithm, which is consistent with the results by Glass and Ni [19] for mesh networks. The effect of congestion control on e-cube in saturation is to limit the rate at which the latency increases and maintain throughput close to the maximum throughput slightly after the point of saturation. The congestion control seems to be less effective for 2Pn and NLast with respect to throughput but keeps message latencies low. Abrupt falls and plateau in the throughput curve of NLast indicate that the congestion control is not effective for certain traffic loads. With a different congestion control, it might be feasible to maintain its peak throughput of 0.25. (Glass and Ni [18] report a peak throughput of approximately 0.23 for this algorithm on a 10×10 mesh.)

3.2 Simulation of hotspot traffic

Performances of the six algorithms for hotspot traffic with 4% hotspot traffic are given in Figure 4. The hotspot node is chosen to be node $(15, 15)$. We have experimented with various different choices for hotspot nodes and found that the NLast yields best results when the hotspot node is $(15, 15)$; performances of the e-cube and hop schemes are unaffected by the choice of the hotspot node.

Compared to uniform traffic, the increase in latencies due to hotspot traffic is negligible when the traffic is low (applied load of 0.2 or less). However, hotspot traffic causes early saturation and latencies in saturation are much higher compared to the uniform traffic case.

Once again, e-cube, NLast, and 2Pn algorithms saturate much earlier than the hop schemes. Of these three, e-cube is the best algorithm yielding a maximum normalized throughput of 0.25. It is consis-

---

[5]To verify the validity of our simulations for e-cube, we compared the peak throughput reported here with those indicated in various previous studies. Song [27] reports peak channel utilizations of 40% for e-cube routing on mesh networks with bidirectional (half-duplex) channels. He also shows that the use of two unidirectional channels to connect adjacent nodes results in lower throughputs. Since we simulate two unidirectional channels for connections between nodes, our results are correspondingly lower. Though torus is slightly different from a two-dimensional mesh, our experiments indicate that e-cube yields similar normalized throughputs on these networks when other parameters such as network size and message length are kept the same. Berman et al. [4] simulate a variant of e-cube (which allows non-minimal routing) and report a peak throughput of 0.2 for message population consisting of a mix of 15- and 31-flit messages on a 31×31 torus. The often reported 50% network utilization obtained by e-cube on mesh networks [26, 13] is based on the bisection bandwidth width arguement, which actually gives a better upper bound on the available bandwidth for meshes with uniform traffic. This value cannot be used to compare channel utilizations, however.

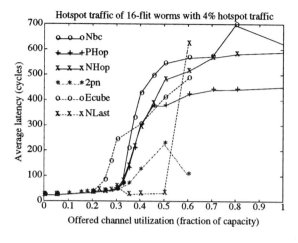

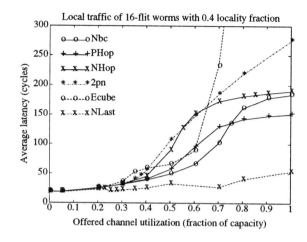

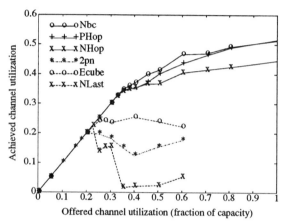

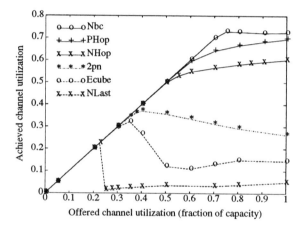

Figure 4: Performance of the routing algorithms for 4% hotspot traffic.

Figure 5: Performance of the routing algorithms for local traffic with 0.4 locality factor.

tently better than 2Pn and NLast algorithms. The peak normalized throughput realized by PHop and Nbc is slightly more than 0.5, while that of NHop is about 0.45. The actual saturation for these algorithms begins at about 0.35. But due to congestion control, the latencies are controlled and normalized throughputs increase steadily.

3.3 Simulation of local traffic

Figure 5 presents the performances of the six algorithms for local traffic with 0.4 locality of fraction. In this case, 2Pn with a peak throughout of 0.37 performs better than *e*-cube, and NLast has the least throughput. Hop schemes have much higher normalized throughput and controlled latencies in saturation region. A noteworthy point is that Nbc with peak throughput of 0.72 performs better than PHop, since it uses more virtual channels (due to bonus cards) in routing messages. It also has the lowest latency among the three hop schemes for up to 0.75 applied traffic load.

3.4 Discussion

The partially-adaptive NLast algorithm does not exhibit better performance than the simpler *e*-cube algorithm. It causes early saturation of the network for the three traffic patterns. It requires complicated routing logic, which could increase the node complexity, node delay per hop, or both. The main problem with the NLast algorithm is that it skews even uniform traffic. However, Glass and Ni [19] report that this class of algorithms perform better than *e*-cube for other types of nonuniform traffic such as matrix transpose.

Our results indicate that the fully-adaptive hop schemes PHop, Nbc, and NHop yield better throughputs for the traffic patterns considered in this study. This could be due to the use of more virtual channels per physical channel [13], balancing the traffic on virtual channels, or both. For example, for uniform traffic, PHop gives better throughput and also uses more virtual channels than any other algorithm. In the case of hotspot traffic, however, Nbc gives better throughput than PHop despite the use of fewer virtual channels. A possible explanation is that the load on virtual channels is balanced in Nbc but not in NHop and PHop algorithms.

The fully-adaptive 2Pn scheme performs worse than the non-adaptive e-cube algorithm for uniform and hotspot traffic. Trying to explain the unexpected low performance of the 2Pn algorithm, we have closely looked at algorithms Nbc and 2Pn. In this light, we have simulated 2Pn and Nbc algorithms for virtual-cut-through routing [21] of 16-flit packets on 16^2 for uniform traffic. The 2Pn algorithm performed as well as Nbc and better than e-cube with respect to both latency and peak throughput.

The 2Pn scheme routes a message at each hop based on the local knowledge available at the current host node. In contrast, Nbc uses local knowledge with some kind of priority information (based on the number of hops taken) to route a message. In the case of packet routing, lack of this information is not a severe handicap to 2Pn, since it employs one-hop lookahead (which is known to yield close to optimal performance for uniform traffic), and the penalty for not choosing the best path is not too severe. In the case of wormhole routing, however, the critical resources (channels) are held for a longer time. Therefore, the penalty for choosing a path that later turns out to be congested is more severe for wormhole routing than for SAF routing. This indicates that the use of priority could be beneficial in wormhole routing.

4 Concluding remarks

In this paper, we have evaluated the effectiveness of several WH routing algorithms with various degrees of adaptivity. We have considered four fully-adaptive (PHop, NHop, Nbc, and 2Pn) algorithms, one partially-adaptive (NLast) algorithm, and the well-known non-adaptive e-cube algorithm. Of the four fully-adaptive algorithms, 2Pn uses the fewest virtual channels, four, for tori.

The remaining three fully-adaptive algorithms, PHop, NHop, and Nbc, are obtained from hop based packet routing algorithms. Algorithm PHop uses as many as 17 virtual channels per physical channel for 16×16 tori. Algorithms NHop and Nbc use nine virtual channels per physical channel. These hop schemes are different from the other three algorithms, since they use some sort of priority information in routing messages. Furthermore, algorithm Nbc tries to balance the load on virtual channels, a feature not given much attention previously. The purpose of our study is to see the improvements in network throughput and message latency with the use of adaptivity and other features. Our observations are summarized as follows.

Fully-adaptive algorithms do not necessarily yield better throughput than non-adaptive algorithms. A case in point is the 2Pn fully-adaptive algorithm. For two-dimensional tori, it looks very attractive, since it provides full-adaptivity with only four virtual channels per physical channel. However, simulation results show that e-cube algorithm outperforms it for uniform and hotspot traffic patterns. On the other hand, the other three fully-adaptive algorithms based on hop schemes, namely, PHop, NHop, and Nbc algorithms, require more virtual channels but improve throughputs substantially. For the traffic patterns used, hop schemes are better than the other three algorithms. A comparison of NHop and Nbc algorithms indicates that balancing traffic on virtual channels yields higher throughput and lower message latency for a given throughput.

Another point of observation is that partially-adaptive algorithms such as NLast [17, 19] do not compare well with e-cube and hop-based algorithms. They have routing logic complexity comparable to that of a fully-adaptive algorithm and performance similar to or worse than that of the non-adaptive e-cube algorithm. This observation does not apply to the planar adaptive routing proposed by Chien and Kim [10], since it is an entirely different type of partially-adaptive algorithm.

We are conducting further simulations of these routing algorithms for multidimensional tori and meshes. In future, we intend to use communication traces obtained from computations on parallel processors to evaluate the performances of routing algorithms. Another issue of interest is evaluation of improvements in throughputs with addition of virtual channels. Dally [13] shows that additional virtual channels improve the performance of e-cube for uniform traffic. Our work here indicates that the use of priority is beneficial in fully-adaptive routing. Further work is needed, for example, to see if the extensive amount of priority information used by PHop is indeed necessary. The issue of balancing load on virtual channels needs to be explored further. Though the number of virtual channels used in hop schemes is a concern, there are ways to reduce this number substantially for NHop based algorithms [6]. We are also studying the implementation aspects of these algorithms.

Acknowledgements

The authors thank Profs. C.S. Raghavendra and D.K. Panda for many discussions and comments on an earlier draft of this paper, Prof. Ram C. Tripathi for discussions on the convergence criteria used in the simulations, and Mr. Francis Ho for help in developing the simulator. The first author's research is supported by NSF Grant CCR-9208784, and the second author's research by a grant from the Graduate School of UW-Madison. Most of the simulations have been performed on the workstations in the CS Lab at UT-San Antonio supported by NSF Grant USE-950407 under ILI program.

References

[1] A. Agarwal. Limits on interconnection network performance. *IEEE Trans. on Parallel and Distributed Systems*, 2(4):398–412, Oct. 1991.

[2] A. Agarwal, *et. al.* The MIT Alewife machine: A large-scale distributed multiprocessor. In *Proc. of Workshop on Scalable Shared Memory Multiprocessors*. Kluwer Academic Publishers, 1991.

[3] R. Alverson, D. Callahan, D. Cummings, B. Koblenz, A. Porterfield, and B. Smith. The Tera computer system. In *Proc. 1990 Int. Conf. on Supercomputing*.

[4] P. E. Berman, L. Gravano, and G. D. Pifarre. Adaptive deadlock- and livelock-free routing with all minimal paths in torus networks. In *Proc. Fourth Symposium on Parallel Algorithms and Architectures*, pages 3–12, 1992.

[5] D. Bertsekas and R. Gallager. *Data Networks*. Prentice-Hall Inc., 1987.

[6] R. V. Boppana and S. Chalasani. Design of hop-based wormhole routing algorithms with reduced virtual channel requirements. In preparation.

[7] R. V. Boppana and S. Chalasani. A comparison of wormhole routing algorithms based on adaptivity. Technical Report UTSA-CS-92-113, University of Texas at San Antonio, Division of Math., Comp. Sci., and Statistics, San Antonio, Texas, Nov. 1992.

[8] R. V. Boppana and S. Chalasani. New wormhole routing algorithms for multicomputers. Technical report, Univ. of Wisconsin-Madison, Dept. of Electrical and Computer Engineering, Madison, WI, 1992. Some of the results will be presented at the 7th Int. Parallel Processing Symposium, 1993.

[9] S. Borkar *et al.* iWarp: An integrated solution to high-speed parallel computing. In *Proc. Supercomputing '88*, pages 330–339.

[10] A. A. Chien and J. H. Kim. Planar-adaptive routing: Low-cost adaptive networks for multiprocessors. In *Proc. 19th Ann. Int. Symp. on Comput. Arch.*, pages 268–277, 1992.

[11] W. J. Dally. Network and processor architecture for message-driven computers. In R. Suaya and G. Birtwislte, editors, *VLSI and Parallel Computation*, chapter 3, pages 140–222. Morgan-Kaufman Publishers, Inc., San Mateo, California, 1990.

[12] W. J. Dally. Express cubes: Improving the performance of k-ary n-cube interconnection networks. *IEEE Trans. on Computers*, 40(9):1016–1023, Sept. 1991.

[13] W. J. Dally. Virtual-channel flow control. *IEEE Trans. on Parallel and Distributed Systems*, 3(2):194–205, Mar. 1992.

[14] W. J. Dally and C. L. Seitz. Deadlock-free message routing in multiprocessor interconnection networks. *IEEE Trans. on Computers*, C-36(5):547–553, 1987.

[15] J. Duato. On the design of deadlock-free adaptive routing algorithms for multicomputers: Theoretical aspects. In *PARLE '91: Parallel Architectures and Languages*, pages 234–243.

[16] S. Felperin, L. Gravano, G. Pifarre, and J. Sanz. Fully-adaptive routing: Packet switching performance and wormhole algorithms. In *Proc. Supercomputing '91*, pages 654–663.

[17] S. A. Felperin, L. Gravano, G. D. Pifarré, and J. L. Sanz. Routing techniques for massively parallel communication. *Proceedings of the IEEE*, 79(4):488–503, 1991.

[18] C. J. Glass and L. M. Ni. Adaptive routing in mesh-connected networks. In *Proc. Int. Confernce on Distributed Computing Systems*, pages 12–19, 1992.

[19] C. J. Glass and L. M. Ni. The turn model for adaptive routing. In *Proc. 19th Ann. Int. Symp. on Comput. Arch.*, pages 278–287, 1992.

[20] I. S. Gopal. Prevention of store-and-forward deadlock in computer networks. *IEEE Trans. on Communications*, COM-33(12):1258–1264, Dec. 1985.

[21] P. Kermani and L. Kleinrock. Virtual Cut-Through: A New Computer Communication Switching Technique. *Computer Networks*, 3:267–286, 1979.

[22] S. S. Lam and M. Reiser. Congestion control of store-and-forward networks by input buffer limits—an analysis. *IEEE Trans. on Communications*, com-27(1):127–133, Jan. 1979.

[23] D. H. Linder and J. C. Harden. An adaptive and fault tolerant wormhole routing strategy for k-ary n-cubes. *IEEE Trans. on Computers*, 40(1):2–12, 1991.

[24] G. F. Pfister and V. A. Norton. Hot spot contention and combining in multistage interconnection networks. *IEEE Trans. on Computers*, c-34(10):943–948, Oct. 1985.

[25] R.L. Scheaffer, et. al. *Elementary Survey Sampling*. Duxbury Press, North Scituate, Mass., 2 edition, 1979.

[26] C. Seitz. Concurrent architectures. In R. Suaya and G. Birtwislte, editors, *VLSI and Parallel Computation*, chapter 1, pages 1–84. Morgan-Kaufman Publishers, Inc., San Mateo, California, 1990.

[27] P. Y. Song. Design of a network for concurrent message passing systems. Master's thesis, Department of Electrical Engineering and Computer Science, MIT, 1988.

Author Index

IEEE Computer Society Press Titles

MONOGRAPHS

Analyzing Computer Architectures
Written by Jerome C. Huck and Michael J. Flynn
(ISBN 0-8186-8857-2); 206 pages

Branch Strategy Taxonomy and Performance Models
Written by Harvey G. Cragon
(ISBN 0-8186-9111-5); 150 pages

Digital Image Warping
Written by George Wolberg
(ISBN 0-8186-8944-7); 340 pages

Implementing Configuration Management:
Hardware, Software, and Firmware
Written by Fletcher J. Buckley
(ISBN 0-7803-0435-7); 256 pages

Information Systems and Decision Processes
Written by Edward A. Stohr and Benn R. Konsynski
(ISBN 0-8186-2802-2); 368 pages

Integrating Design and Test —
CAE Tools for ATE Programming
Written by Kenneth P. Parker
(ISBN 0-8186-8788-6); 160 pages

Optic Flow Computation:
A Unified Perspective
Written by Ajit Singh
(ISBN 0-8186-2602-X); 256 pages

Physical Level Interfaces and Protocols
Written by Uyless Black
(ISBN 0-8186-8824-2); 240 pages

Real-Time Systems Design and Analysis
Written by Phillip A. Laplante
(ISBN 0-7803-0402-0); 360 pages

Software Metrics:
A Practitioner's Guide to
Improved Product Development
Written by Daniel J. Paulish and Karl-Heinrich Möller
(ISBN 0-7803-0444-6); 272 pages

X.25 and Related Protocols
Written by Uyless Black
(ISBN 0-8186-8976-5); 304 pages

TUTORIALS

Advances in ISDN and Broadband ISDN
Edited by William Stallings
(ISBN 0-8186-2797-2); 272 pages

Architectural Alternatives for Exploiting Parallelism
Edited by David J. Lilja
(ISBN 0-8186-2642-9); 464 pages

Artificial Neural Networks —
Concepts and Control Applications
Edited by V. Rao Vemuri
(ISBN 0-8186-9069-0); 520 pages

Artificial Neural Networks —
Concepts and Theory
Edited by Pankaj Mehra and Banjamin Wah
(ISBN 0-8186-8997-8); 680 pages

Autonomous Mobile Robots:
Perception, Mapping and Navigation — Volume 1
Edited by S. S. Iyengar and A. Elfes
(ISBN 0-8186-9018-6); 425 pages

Autonomous Mobile Robots:
Control, Planning, and Architecture — Volume 2
Edited by S. S. Iyengar and A. Elfes
(ISBN 0-8186-9116-6); 425 pages

Broadband Switching:
Architectures, Protocols, Design, and Analysis
Edited by C. Dhas, V. K. Konangi, and M. Sreetharan
(ISBN 0-8186-8926-9); 528 pages

Readings in
Computer-Generated Music
Edited by Denis Baggi
(ISBN 0-8186-2747-6); 232 pages

Computer Arithmetic I
Edited by Earl E. Swartzlander, Jr.
(ISBN 0-8186-8931-5); 398 pages

Computer Arithmetic II
Edited by Earl E. Swartzlander, Jr.
(ISBN 0-8186-8945-5); 412 pages

Computer Communications:
Architectures, Protocols, and Standards
(Third Edition)
Edited by William Stallings
(ISBN 0-8186-2712-3); 360 pages

Computer Graphics Hardware:
Image Generation and Display
Edited by H. K. Reghbati and A. Y. C. Lee
(ISBN 0-8186-0753-X); 384 pages

Computer Graphics: Image Synthesis
Edited by Kenneth Joy, Nelson Max, Charles Grant,
and Lansing Hatfield
(ISBN 0-8186-8854-8); 380 pages

Computer Vision: Principles
Edited by Rangachar Kasturi and Ramesh Jain
(ISBN 0-8186-9102-6); 700 pages

Computer Vision: Advances and Applications
Edited by Rangachar Kasturi and Ramesh Jain
(ISBN 0-8186-9103-4); 720 pages

Current Research in Decision Support Technology
Edited by Robert W. Blanning and David R. King
(ISBN 0-8186-2807-3); 256 pages

Digital Image Processing (Second Edition)
Edited by Rama Chellappa
(ISBN 0-8186-2362-4); 816 pages

Digital Private Branch Exchanges (PBXs)
Edited by Edwin Coover
(ISBN 0-8186-0829-3); 394 pages

Domain Analysis and Software Systems Modeling
Edited by Ruben-Prieto Diaz and Guillermo Arango
(ISBN 0-8186-8996-X); 312 pages

Formal Verification of Hardware Design
Edited by Michael Yoeli
(ISBN 0-8186-9017-8); 340 pages

Groupware: Software for Computer-Supported
Cooperative Work
Edited by David Marca and Geoffrey Bock
(ISBN 0-8186-2637-2); 600 pages

Hard Real-Time Systems
Edited by John A. Stankovic and Krithi Ramamritham
(ISBN 0-8186-0819-6); 624 pages

For further information call toll-free 1-800-CS-BOOKS or write:

IEEE Computer Society Press, 10662 Los Vaqueros Circle, PO Box 3014,
Los Alamitos, California 90720-1264, USA

IEEE Computer Society, 13, avenue de l'Aquilon,
B-1200 Brussels, BELGIUM

IEEE Computer Society, Ooshima Building, 2-19-1 Minami-Aoyama,
Minato-ku, Tokyo 107, JAPAN

Knowledge-Based Systems:
Fundamentals and Tools
Edited by Oscar N. Garcia and Yi-Tzuu Chien
(ISBN 0-8186-1924-4); 512 pages

Local Network Technology (Third Edition)
Edited by William Stallings
(ISBN 0-8186-0825-0); 512 pages

Nearest Neighbor Pattern Classification Techniques
Edited by Belur V. Dasarathy
(ISBN 0-8186-8930-7); 464 pages

Object-Oriented Computing,
Volume 1: Concepts
Edited by Gerald E. Petersen
(ISBN 0-8186-0821-8); 214 pages

Object-Oriented Computing,
Volume 2: Implementations
Edited by Gerald E. Petersen
(ISBN 0-8186-0822-6); 324 pages

Real-Time Systems
Abstractions, Languages, and Design Methodologies
Edited by Krishna M. Kavi
(ISBN 0-8186-3152-X); 550 pages

Reduced Instruction Set Computers (RISC)
(Second Edition)
Edited by William Stallings
(ISBN 0-8186-8943-9); 448 pages

Software Design Techniques (Fourth Edition)
Edited by Peter Freeman and Anthony I. Wasserman
(ISBN 0-8186-0514-6); 730 pages

Software Engineering Project Management
Edited by Richard H. Thayer
(ISBN 0-8186-0751-3); 512 pages

Software Maintenance and Computers
Edited by David H. Longstreet
(ISBN 0-8186-8898-X); 304 pages

Software Management
(Fourth Edition)
Edited by Donald J. Reifer
(ISBN 0-8186-3342-5); 656 pages

Software Reengineering
Edited by Robert S. Arnold
(ISBN 0-8186-3272-0); 688 pages

Software Reuse — Emerging Technology
Edited by Will Tracz
(ISBN 0-8186-0846-3); 400 pages

Software Risk Management
Edited by Barry W. Boehm
(ISBN 0-8186-8906-4); 508 pages

Standards, Guidelines and Examples on System
and Software Requirements Engineering
Edited by Merlin Dorfman and Richard H. Thayer
(ISBN 0-8186-8922-6); 626 pages

System and Software Requirements Engineering
Edited by Richard H. Thayer and Merlin Dorfman
(ISBN 0-8186-8921-8); 740 pages

Systems Network Architecture
Edited by Edwin R. Coover
(ISBN 0-8186-9131-X); 464 pages

Test Access Port and Boundary-Scan Architecture
Edited by Colin M. Maunder and Rodham E. Tulloss
(ISBN 0-8186-9070-4); 400 pages

Visual Programming Environments: Paradigms and Systems
Edited by Ephraim Glinert
(ISBN 0-8186-8973-0); 680 pages

Visual Programming Environments: Applications and Issues
Edited by Ephraim Glinert
(ISBN 0-8186-8974-9); 704 pages

Visualization in Scientific Computing
Edited by G. M. Nielson, B. Shriver, and L. Rosenblum
(ISBN 0-8186-8979-X); 304 pages

Volume Visualization
Edited by Arie Kaufman
(ISBN 0-8186-9020-8); 494 pages

REPRINT COLLECTIONS

Distributed Computing Systems:
Concepts and Structures
Edited by A. L. Ananda and B. Srinivasan
(ISBN 0-8186-8975-0); 416 pages

Expert Systems:
A Software Methodology for Modern Applications
Edited by Peter G. Raeth
(ISBN 0-8186-8904-8); 476 pages

Milestones in Software Evolution
Edited by Paul W. Oman and Ted G. Lewis
(ISBN 0-8186-9033-X); 332 pages

Object-Oriented Databases
Edited by Ez Nahouraii and Fred Petry
(ISBN 0-8186-8929-3); 256 pages

Validating and Verifying Knowledge-Based Systems
Edited by Uma G. Gupta
(ISBN 0-8186-8995-1); 400 pages

ARTIFICIAL NEURAL NETWORKS TECHNOLOGY SERIES

Artificial Neural Networks —
Concept Learning
Edited by Joachim Diederich
(ISBN 0-8186-2015-3); 160 pages

Artificial Neural Networks —
Electronic Implementation
Edited by Nelson Morgan
(ISBN 0-8186-2029-3); 144 pages

Artificial Neural Networks —
Theoretical Concepts
Edited by V. Rao Vemuri
(ISBN 0-8186-0855-2); 160 pages

SOFTWARE TECHNOLOGY SERIES

Bridging Faults and IDDQ Testing
Edited by Yashwant K. Malaiya and Rochit Rajsuman
(ISBN 0-8186-3215-1); 128 pages

Computer-Aided Software Engineering (CASE)
(2nd Edition)
Edited by Elliot Chikofsky
(ISBN 0-8186-3590-8); 184 pages

Fault-Tolerant Software Systems:
Techniques and Applications
Edited by Hoang Pham
(ISBN 0-8186-3210-0); 128 pages

Software Reliability Models:
Theoretical Development, Evaluation, and Applications
Edited by Yashwant K. Malaiya and Pradip K. Srimani
(ISBN 0-8186-2110-9); 136 pages

MATHEMATICS TECHNOLOGY SERIES

Computer Algorithms
Edited by Jun-ichi Aoe
(ISBN 0-8186-2123-0); 154 pages

Distributed Mutual Exclusion Algorithms
Edited by Pradip K. Srimani and Sunil R. Das
(ISBN 0-8186-3380-8); 168 pages

Genetic Algorithms
Edited by Bill P. Buckles and Frederick E. Petry
(ISBN 0-81862935-5); 120 pages

Multiple-Valued Logic in VLSI Design
Edited by Jon T. Butler
(ISBN 0-8186-2127-3); 128 pages